A 45 R P aMble
On A Flat Foot

By Steven Elliott

A 45 R P aMble On A Flat Foot
Steven Elliott

Memoir
Music History
Modern Music

Celticfrog Publishing, Clearwater BC

CELTICFROG PUBLISHING

Observations
of popular music in
the 1970s & 1980s
through lists of
45 RPM record song titles
in his personal collection

By Steven Elliott,
audiophile, musician
& record collector

In Memory of

John Kollar

1959 - 2007

PART A
CHAPTERS

PART B
APPENDICES

1. Albums
2. B Sides
3. Book Lore
4. Brands
5. Chart Lore
6. Concerts
7. Early Ramble
8. Highlights & Ideas
9. Internet
10. Lists by Chapter
11. Muzik Lists I - The Singles
12. Muzik Lists II - The Rest
13. Names
14. Sa Flatt Ft Group Medleys
15. Stores
16. Terms
17. Title Notes I - The Singles
18. Title Notes II - The Rest
19. Singles I - The Overlap
20. Singles II - The Rest
21. Singles III - B [A]
22. Singles IV - By Artist
23. All Roads Lead To Yes

INTRODUCTION

What follows is a story about my own 7 inch 45 rpm record collection. Much of the story is lists of those records, based on different themes. There are detailed lists in the addendum/appendix as well. In writing this piece, I take no prisoners, pull no punches, I just tell it like it is. If it seems biased, disjointed, incoherent, or preachy, that's probably because it is. So just take it for what it is, albeit a few hundred pages, a ramble. Fact or fiction? It's mostly fact but some fiction to tie up the bits I can't remember so well.

This story started back in 2006 and was less than a page long. I used to write to paper first, then computer, now first a memo app then the *45 R P aMble [gem]*. Gem is used in this book to indicate an original idea. The book started as a short collection of ideas about the 45 rpm record, grew into a ramble, and is now an amble, a *45 R P aMble*.

For the most part, I have stayed away from names, referring only to "friends" who have influenced me in my musical journey. I know who they are and they know who they are and that's all that matters. No offence ladies but most of those people are men.

The ramble has evolved a great deal to this point. I am constantly thinking of items to add to the story. There's a little something in here for everyone. It's easy to read in bits and pieces. You don't have to read it from cover to cover, without putting it down. Things are discussed in the chapters where they are most applicable.

It's not so much about the musicians and their lives as it is about their music, mostly groups, rather than soloists, mostly from the seventies and eighties, often British artists, artists with a keyboard influence, and the records, singles much more than albums.

When I started this story way back in 2006, I thought that only the music from the seventies was old. Now that all that time has passed, I now admit that the music from the eighties is now also old.

There are lots of hard facts about who made the records, when they were made, and how the records charted. The beauty of the charts is that a particular song even charted at all, not whether it made number one. The sum of the songs as a collective is greater and much more important than the individual songs themselves. I've tried several times recreating a list of top songs, mentioned most often in this story, but that quickly loses its appeal and momentum.

There are many things discussed in the story, some of them in depth, but many of them just bits and pieces, examples and samples. The focus on singles also means there aren't all kinds of details in the story that would come from an album collection and all the liner notes and stories that go with it.

There are many lists of records in this story. My 2001 file *Mzk01 [gem appendices 11 & 12]* was a huge source of input and inspiration for these lists. The lists of songs are not all inclusive, with most of them based on my own singles collection. The lists are focused on one of four things: audible or sound attributes; visual aspects of sleeves or labels on the records themselves; places they were bought; or when they were bought. The visual aspects of the records are shared across the three singles as visual art chapters. The story doesn't include lists of songs based solely on the song title because that requires little musical knowledge or skill or talent. I should qualify that by saying I do have one list, where I have listed songs that have the same title but are actually very different tunes.

There are more than two-hundred lists, that's at least a list every page. Songs are listed in alphabetical order, excluding articles like a, an & the. I sang with mom and dad at church, where we kept track of our music in folders, usually alphabetically. Dad took that a step further and filed his music with a, an & the as first words. What this meant was that he had three subsets of music instead of one. Sorry dad, one set of music was good enough for me.

While I have not listed A and B titles for every record, I have listed B titles in several cases and noted them in brackets with a single slash *(/b)* ; where both A and B titles are hits, they are noted with a double slash ; where A titles are the same but B titles are different ; where the B title for one record is actually the A title for another record ; where the B title had radio airplay ; where the B title did not appear originally on a vinyl album and where the B side is mentioned in this story because it is a really good song. In most cases, the listing of singles in the appendices does not include B sides for songs for which I only have one record.

I like color a lot, that's why I talk about picture sleeves, the official sleeves in the chapter about singles as art and the homemade ones in the chapter about my collection. I've essentially book ended the story by talking about picture sleeves.

Each list is numbered by chapter and then by the list in that chapter, i.e.. 1.1. I have also noted the origin of the list, whether it is from the *45 R P aMble* itself, from the 1984 *Singles Inventory [gem, see also si84 in appendices 19 & 20]*, the terms of the 2009 discography *Th45zz [gem, see also th45zz in appendices 19 & 20]*, or the music lists of 2001, *Mzk01*. *Th45zz* discography did actually originate back in 2002 but did not include the more detailed terms of the 2009 version. There are a few references to the 2002 version but not many. The Inspiration for names of files and lists comes largely from my work experience with inventories and database management and the detailed documentation that went with it.

Tapes are a big part of this story as well, fifty years' worth. Recording vinyl to analog tape was the original way of backing up your music collection, years ahead of modern-day digital backups.

What I like about this story is the history behind it. For a subject that I didn't care much about in high school in Ottawa and Toronto, I now like history a lot. It is full of stories and this one is no different. But remember, the basis for much of the music listed here is single, not album, oriented. 1973 is now the benchmark for when I started collecting 45 RPM records. Okay I admit it. I'm a 45 RPM Fanatic/Geek/Maniac, a 45RPMManiac!

Ramble On[1]

---

[1] *Ramble On*, Led Zeppelin, *Led Zeppelin II*, Atlantic Records, 1969.

PART A

CHAPTERS

ONE

JUST SINGLES

"Whatever happened to the 45 RPM record?"

45 RPM records, or "singles", were considered a poor man's version of the LP record, meaning you couldn't afford the LP. Singles were what you heard on top forty AM radio, not the traditionally "less commercial" FM radio. They were poor (shorter) versions of album tracks. Initially, the 45 was created in spite of the album, equaling the difference between 33 and 78. Louis Rastelli discounted this idea when he commented in the article about "60th Anniversary of the LP record".[2] Solos were shorter or nonexistent. Otherwise, the singles just ended early.

Singles were poorly made. If they were punched off centre, you could tell, like you were listening on a boat. Singles by themselves were inconvenient, but not when played and taped in succession. By the way, audio cassette tapes were originally called compact cassettes. See chapter 29, *Home Recording II - Making Tapes.* That made them sound more like albums, by more than one artist if you wished.

Singles were the symbol of AM radio, songs going up and down the charts. However, FM radio would not be what it is today without the DJs like John Majhor, 1953-2007, 1050 CHUM 1975-1986, who spun the singles on AM radio.

What better than to have two of your favourite songs on one disc, the double hit singles. Even if it is overlap or overkill, it's still nice to collect and have.

Some singles started out as A and B sides and grew into double hits. Led Zeppelin had many of these that I will talk about in chapter fifteen, entitled *Zeppelin Singles Morphology [gem 5.8, 8.2 & 15.1].* There are at least six singles that were not issued as double hits but morphed into double hits. Except For *We Are The Champions*, all the titles listed in the other eight double hits here were at one time or another their own A sides. Alan Parsons' *Don't Let It Show* and *Lucifer* were released as A sides from completely

---

[2] *60th Anniversary Of The LP Record*, Louis Rastelli, Globe & Mail, July 24, 2009,
https://www.theglobeandmail.com/opinion/revolutionary-thinking/article4213508/

different albums back in the seventies. Queens' *We Will Rock You & We Are The Champions* were back-to-back tracks on *News Of The World*.

I should clarify that the one exception in this list is the first entry by the Doobie Brothers. As Andy Cowan mentions in his book *B Side,*[3] *Black Water* received much airplay initially, even as the B side to *Another Park Another Sunday*. To take this a step further, the response to the song was so good that *Black Water* was rereleased as its own A side, one of the few B side songs to ever do this.

Years after appearing as a B side on several different singles including *Heart Of Gold, Sugar Mountain* was released as its' own A side, in conjunction with the release of the 1977 compilation album *Decade*. In Andy Cowans' book, *B Side, Sugar Mountain* shows as the B side to *The Loner*, rather than *Heart Of Gold*, in this list. For Yes, *Don't Kill The Whale* was released as an A side in the UK, while it was released as a B side in the US.[4] Others like *Space Oddity, Stand By Me, Take Me Home Country Roads & Thank God I'm A Country Boy* started out as A and B sides and morphed into double hits.

1.1 ~ Morph I - Various

1. *Another Park Another Sunday \\ Black Water* - **The Doobie Brothers**
2. *Damned If I Do \\ You Lie Down With Dogs, Don't Answer Me \\ Don't Let It Show, You Don't Believe \\ Lucifer, You Lie Down With Dogs \\ Lucifer & You're Gonna Get Your Fingers Burned \\ Psychobabble* - **The Alan Parsons Project**
3. *Every Breath You Take \\ Murder By Numbers* - **The Police**
4. *Heart Of Gold \\ Sugar Mountain* - **Neil Young**
5. *Release Release \\ Don't Kill The Whale* - **Yes**
6. *Space Oddity \\ The Man Who Sold The World* - **David Bowie**
7. *Stand By Me \\ Yakety Yak* - **Ben E. King**
8. *Take Me Home Country Roads / Poems, Prayers & Promises, Sunshine On My Shoulder & Thank God I'm A Country Boy* - **John Denver**
9. *That's All \\ Taking It All Too Hard* - **Genesis**
10. *Tonight She Comes \\ Just What I Needed* - **The Cars**
11. *We Are The Champions \\ We Will Rock You* - **Queen**
12. *Wildflower \\ The Writing's On The Wall* - **Skylark**

A number of singles released originally as A and B sides morphed into double hits on the Golden Treasures (Quality Records) label, whether they were really double hits or not…

1.2 ~ Morph II - Golden Treasures

1. *Candy Man, The \\ I Want To Be Happy* - **Sammy Davis Jr.**
2. *Do I Love You \\ So Long City* - **Paul Anka**
3. *Falling In Love \\ So Good At Lovin' You* - **Hamilton, Joe Frank & Reynolds**
4. *Funny Face \\ How Close You Came (To Being Gone)* - **Donna Fargo**
5. *Hot Rod Lincoln \\ My Home In My Hand* - **Commander Cody & His Lost Planet Airmen**
6. *Hustle, The \\ Hey Girl, Come & Get It* - **Van McCoy & The Soul City Symphony**
7. *I'd Love You To Want Me \\ Am I True To Myself* - **Lobo**
8. *I'm Stoned In Love With You \\ Make It Last* - **The Stylistics**

[3] *B Side*, Andy Cowan, Headpress, 2023, p.50 & p.320
[4] *Yesyears*, Yes, Atlantic, 1991

9. *Moonlight Feels Right* - **Starbuck**
10. *More More More (original / instrumental)* - **The Andrea True Connection**
11. *Popcorn* - **Hot Butter**
12. *Rock & Roll Part 1 \\ Rock & Roll Part 2* - **Gary Glitter**
13. *So You Are A Star \\ Ma Ma Ma Baby* - **The Hudson Brothers**
14. *Summer In The City \\ Nashville Cats* - **Lovin' Spoonful**
15. *Sweet City Woman \\ Gator Road* - **The Stampeders**
16. *Tie A Yellow Ribbon Round The Ole Oak Tree \\ I Can't Believe How Much I Love You* - **Dawn**
17. *Wipeout \\ Surfer Joe* - **Surfaris**

American Woman / No Sugar Tonight by The Guess Who and *Junior's Farm / Sally G* by Paul McCartney & Wings were originally released with sides A & B both receiving radio airplay.

There were also double hit reissued singles by Eric Records. The neat thing about this group of records is that there were many issued with one artist on side A and another on side B.

1.3 ~ Eric Records
1. *Don't Let The Sun Catch You Crying // Girl On A Swing* - **Gerry & The Pacemakers**
2. *Green Tambourine* - **Lemon Peppers** // *Yummy Yummy Yummy* - **Ohio Express**
3. *How Long* - **Ace** // *In A Broken Dream* - **Python Lee Jackson**
4. *La Bamba // Donna* - **Ritchie Valens**
5. *Layla* - **Derek & The Dominos** // *Montego Bay* - **Bobby Bloom**
6. *Louie Louie* - **The Kingsmen** // *Twist & Shout* - **The Isley Brothers**
7. *Rock & Roll Hoochie Koo* - **Rick Derringer** // *Time Of The Season* - **The Zombies**

This story contains more than ninety double hit singles. Promotional copies of 45s were made by such companies as A&M, Arista, Atlantic and CBS records. While some had a different song on each side, others had the same song, stereo on one side and mono on the other. That was back in the day when AM music stations existed and did not broadcast in stereo.

Collecting singles is *not* just to have them but to *play* them also. If you tape them or burn them to CD, they will live a long and happy life. The silver linings of singles are the B-sides that did not always make their way on to an album. They are treasures, only to appear later if at all on boxed sets, compilations, or repackaged albums.

If you take geography into account, there were two different places and times where music was very different. The first was top forty radio in the early seventies in Ottawa versus Toronto. The second was top forty radio in the early eighties in Brampton versus Toronto.

I remember playing "Toss the Ball at the Plates to Win a Prize" with a friend at the CNE in Toronto in 1979 and won the Styx single *Blue Collar Man.* I was surprised years later to see a similar game called "Toss the Ball at the 45 RPM Record to win a different sort of prize" game. I found it hard to watch.

The Eighties meant the explosion of the 12 inch single. They were very popular, especially for dance music. Many were remixed versions of the original song. *Dream Rain Time [gem 12.5]* is my nod to Simple Minds and the 12 inch remixed single. You could also get three or four or five songs on a record instead of the traditional two with the 7 inch single. The sound is great, in most cases better than the smaller traditional singles.

UK singles have always been excellent in their sound quality, with the convenience of small album style centres. Collecting singles into the nineties remained possible by UK and US makers, while Canadian makers were quick to phase out vinyl in favor of the CD. I have noted in chapters about Genesis, (Alan) Parsons, U2 & Yes, that a large portion of the singles collected of those groups was due to the US pressings of many catalogue titles. This is the first list to introduce the mention of records from another country. Besides the UK [UK] & the US [US], there is Belgium [BEL], Germany [DEU], Japan [JAP] & the former Yugoslavia [YUG]. Across the rest of the book, these countries include France [FRA], Italy [ITA] & The Netherlands [NDR].

In some cases, singles are just hard to find. Note that the Babe Ruth B side *Theme From "For A Few Dollars More"* was what charted on Ottawa's CFGO Top 30. When the *Top 400 Of All Time* appeared the same summer in 1974,[5] the full length version of the song, *The Mexican*, was what showed up on that list, ranked #14 and was the highest charting song for that year. It didn't show up at all on the 1974 Year-end Top 100. Very strange!

Brain Salad Surgery has a cover that opens like a window. *C'est La Vie* and *Sole Survivor* have both long and short versions. Tears For Fears, Simple Minds, U2 & Ultravox feature gatefold covers. Led Zeppelin, Supertramp & Tears For Fears all include non-album B sides. *Listen To The Music* and *Nights In White Satin* are much shorter versions. *Run Through The Light* is restructured from it's original version. Labels for Elton John and Queen feature album specific artwork.

This list shows a sample of what I refer to as rare finds …

1.4 ~ Rare

1. *Ain't Nobody But Me / Sister Moonshine, Breakfast In America / Gone Hollywood* [UK], *Dreamer / Bloody Well Right* [US] & *Lady / You Started Laughing* - **Supertramp**
2. *Black Dog \\ Misty Mountain Hop* [JPN], *Immigrant Song / Hey Hey What Can I Do* & *Stairway to Heaven // Whole Lotta Love* [UK] - **Led Zeppelin**
3. *Brain Salad Surgery* [UK] - **Emerson, Lake & Palmer**
4. *C'est La Vie (long / short)* [US] & *I Believe In Father Christmas* - **Greg Lake**
5. *Cover Of A Rolling Stone* - **Dr. Hook**
6. *Dancing With Tears In My Eyes* [UK] - **Ultravox**
7. *Desire* - **U2**
8. *Entangled / Ripples, Follow You Follow Me // A Trick Of The Tail* [UK], *I Know What I Like (In Your Wardrobe) // Counting Out Time* [UK], *I Know What I Like (In Your Wardrobe) // Lamb Lies Down On Broadway* [US] & *Your Own Special Way / It's Yourself* - **Genesis**
9. *Everybody Wants To Rule The World / Pharoahs, Head Over Heels / When In Love With A Blind Man & I Believe* [UK] - **Tears For Fears**
10. *Into The Lens (I Am A Camera) / Does It Really Happen?* [UK & US], *It Can Happen* [DEU], *Run Through The Light / Man In A White Car* [US] & *Soon* [US] - **Yes**
11. *It's All I Can Do / Candy - O* [UK] & *My Best Friend's Girl / Moving In Stereo* [UK] - **The Cars**
12. *Just You'n Me* [YUG] - **Chicago**
13. *Listen To The Music (short) / Toulouse Street* - **The Doobie Brothers**
14. *Nights In White Satin (short) / Cities* [US] - **The Moody Blues**

---

[5] *Top 300 Of All Time*, CFGO 1440 AM, Ottawa, 1974.

15. *Sanctify Yourself* [UK] & *Someone Somewhere In Summertime* [UK] - **Simple Minds**
16. *Sole Survivor (long / short)* [US] - **Asia**
17. *Someone Saved My Life Tonight* [UK] - **Elton John**
18. *Turn Of A Friendly Card / Snake Eyes / Games People Play* [DEU] - **The Alan Parsons Project**
19. *Watching The Wheels* [BEL] - **John Lennon**
20. *We Are The Champions / We Will Rock You* [UK] - **Queen**
21. *Wells Fargo / Theme From "For A Few Dollars More"* - **Babe Ruth**

Next up are groups of similar songs. First is a collection of songs covered by artists other than the originals (noted in parentheses). For most of these tunes, I have only the cover, not the original…

1.5 ~ Cover Versions I - 60s & 70s - America

1. *Bad Side Of The Moon* - **April Wine** [Canada] **(Elton John)**
2. *Black Magic Woman* - **Santana (Fleetwood Mac)**
3. *Bongo Rock* - **The Incredible Bongo Band (Preston Epps)**
4. *Brother Louie* - **The Stories (Hot Chocolate)**
5. *Danny's Song* - **Anne Murray** [Canada] **(Loggins & Messina)**
6. *Dream A Little Dream Of Me* - **Cass Elliot (Ozzie Nelson)**
7. *Drift Away* - **Dobie Gray (Mentor Williams / John Henry Kurtz)**
8. *Mama Told Me (Not To Come)* - **Three Dog Night (Randy Newman)** & *Show Must Go On* - **Three Dog Night (Leo Sayer)**
9. *First Cut Is The Deepest* - **Keith Hampshire (Cat Stevens)**
10. *Freedom For The Stallion* - **Edward Bear** [Canada] **(Three Dog Night)**
11. *Get Ready & I Know I'm Losing You* - **Rare Earth (The Temptations)**
12. *Hello It's Me* - **Todd Rundgren (Nazz)**
13. *Hit The Road Jack* - **The Stampeders** [Canada] **(Ray Charles)**
14. *I Believe In Music* - **Gallery (Mac Davis)**
15. *I Can Dance (Long Tall Glasses) & Train* - **Shooter** [Canada] **(Leo Sayer)**
16. *Indian Reservation* - **The Raiders (Don Fardon)**
17. *Leaving On A Jet Plane* - **Peter. Paul & Mary (John Denver)**
18. *Locomotion, The* **(Little Eva)** & *Some Kinda Wonderful* **(Soul Brothers Six)** - **Grand Funk**
19. *Louie Louie* - **The Kingsmen** // *Twist & Shout* - **The Isley Brothers (Bert Russell)**
20. *Mandy* - **Barry Manilow** (*Brandy* - **Scott English**)
21. *Only Sixteen* - **Dr. Hook (Sam Cooke)**
22. *Reach Out (I'll Be There)* - **Gloria Gaynor (The Four Tops)**
23. *Rockin' Pneumonia* [US] - **Johnny Rivers (Huey Piano Smith)**
24. *Rocky Mountain Way* - **Triumph** [Canada] **(Joe Walsh)**
25. *Soul Man* - **The Blues Brothers (Sam & Dave)**
26. *Take Me In Your Arms (Rock Me)* - **The Doobie Brothers & Charity Brown (Kim Weston)**
27. *There's A Kind Of Hush (All Over The World)* - **The Carpenters (Herman's Hermits)**
28. *Ticket To Ride* - **Carpenters (The Beatles)**

29. *Turn Turn Turn* - **The Byrds (Pete Seeger)**

30. *You're No Good* - **Linda Ronstadt (Betty Everett / Dee Dee Warwick)**

1.6 ~ Cover Versions II - 60s & 70s - UK

1. *Another Saturday Night* - **Cat Stevens (Sam Cooke)**

2. *Blinded By The Light* - **Manfred Mann** [South Africa] **(Bruce Springsteen)**

3. *Cocaine* **(JJ Cale)** & *I Shot The Sheriff* **(Bob Marley)** - **Eric Clapton**

4. *First Cut Is The Deepest* - **Rod Stewart (Cat Stevens)**

5. *Honky Tonk Train Blues* - **Keith Emerson (Meade Lux Lewis)**

6. *Hooked On A Feeling* - **Blue Suede** [Sweden] **(B. J. Thomas)**

7. *Letter (Live)* - **Joe Cocker (Box Tops)**

8. *Love Hurts* - **Nazareth (Roy Orbison)**

9. *Lucy In The Sky With Diamonds* - **Elton John (The Beatles)**

10. *Never My Love* - **Blue Suede** [Sweden] **(The Association)**

11. *Only You* - **Ringo Starr (The Platters)**

12. *Pinball Wizard* - **Elton John (The Who)**

13. *Stand By Me* - **John Lennon (Ben E King)**

14. *Whole Lotta Love* - **Led Zeppelin** (*You Need Love* - **Willie Dixon**)

15. *Wild Thing* - **Fancy (The Troggs)**

16. *You're Sixteen* - **Ringo Starr (Johnny Burnette)**

1.7 ~ Cover Versions III - 80s & 90s

1. *Always Something There To Remind Me* - **Naked Eyes (Sandie Shaw)**

2. *Angel Of The Morning* - **Juice Newton (Merilee Rush)**

3. *California Dreaming* - **The Beach Boys (The Mamas & The Papas)**

4. *Cat's In The Cradle* - **Ugly Kid Joe (Harry Chapin)**

5. *Dancing In The Street* - **David Bowie & Mick Jagger (Martha & The Vandellas)**

6. *Girls Just Wanna Have Fun* - **Cyndi Lauper (Robert Hazard)**

7. *If You Don't Know Me By Now* - **Simply Red (Harold Melvin & The Bluenotes Featuring Teddy Pendergrass)**

8. *Putting On The Ritz* - **Taco (Harry Richman / Irving Berlin)**

9. *Revolution* - **The Thompson Twins (The Beatles)**

10. *Sea Of Love* - **The Honeydrippers (Phil Phillips)**

11. *Tainted Love* - **Soft Cell (Gloria Jones)**

12. *Unchained Melody* - **U2 (Jimmy Young)**

13. *Under My Thumb* - **Streetheart (The Rolling Stones)**

14. *Under The Boardwalk* - **John Mellencamp (Drifters)**

15. *Venus* - **Bananarama (Shocking Blue)**

16. *You Can't Hurry Love* - **Phil Collins & The Stray Cats (The Supremes)**

Other tunes are their own tunes but might have classical tunes included, say in the chorus. Many thanks to Graham Betts for his book *Infographic Guide To Music* and page 110, classics go pop, in compiling this list.[6] Some of the tunes are also noted in the folk tune chapter twenty-one, *Sa Flatt Ft [gem 21.3 - 21.15]*. Notice that many of the covers are by Emerson, Lake & Palmer...

---

[6] *Infographic Guide To Music*, Graham Betts, Octopus Books, an Hachette UK Company, 2014, p.110

1.8 ~ A Classical Borrow

1. *All By Myself* - **Eric Carmen** (*Piano Concerto #2 In C Minor* - **Rachmaninoff**)
2. *Also Sprach Zarathustra (2001)* - **Deodato (Strauss)**
3. *Could It Be Magic* - **Barry Manilow** (*Prelude In C Minor* - **Chopin**)
4. *Fanfare For The Common Man* - **Emerson, Lake & Palmer (Copeland)**
5. *Fifth Of Beethoven* - **Walter Murphy** (*5ᵗʰ Symphony* - **Beethoven**)
6. *Great Gates Of Kiev* - **Emerson Lake & Palmer** (*Pictures At An Exhibition* - **Mussorgsky**)
7. *I Believe In Father Christmas* - **Greg Lake** (*Troika, Lieutenant Kije* - **Prokofiev**)
8. *Jerusalem* - **Emerson, Lake & Palmer (Parry)**
9. *Nutrocker* - **Emerson, Lake & Palmer (B Bumble & The Stingers**, *March Of The Toy Soldiers, The Nutcracker* - **Tchaikovsky)**
10. *Russians* - **Sting** (*Romance, Lieutenant Kije* - **Prokofiev**)
11. *Whiter Shade Of Pale* - **Procal Harum** (*Orchestral Suite #3, Air* - **J S Bach**)

This collection of songs have the same name but the tunes are very different. For all of these, I do have at least one of the songs mentioned on a 45. Most entries have two songs but four of them have three, *Better Days, Lady, Magic & Power Of Love.* The list features The Cars, The Alan Parsons Project, Pink Floyd, Supertramp & U2. Brackets denotes an album track and (/b) denotes a B side.

1.9 ~ Different Tune

1. *Better Days* - **(Emerson, Lake & Palmer), Ozark Mountain Daredevils** (/b) & **Supertramp**
2. *Call On Me* - **Bread** (/b) & **Chicago**
3. *Crazy* - **Men At Work** (/b)**, Seal & Supertramp**
4. *Day After Day* - **Badfinger & The Alan Parsons Project**
5. *Don't Leave Me Now* - **Pink Floyd & (Supertramp)**
6. *Dreaming* - **Blondie & Orchestral Manoeuvres In The Dark**
7. *Entertainer* - **Marvin Hamlisch & Billy Joel**
8. *Free As A Bird* - **The Beatles & Supertramp**
9. *Games People Play* - **The Alan Parsons Project & The Spinners**
10. *Gloria* - **Laura Branigan & U2**
11. *Hey You* - **Bachman - Turner Overdrive & (Pink Floyd)**
12. *Hold On* - **Ian Thomas, Triumph** (/b) **& (Yes)**
13. *I Need You* - **America & Foreigner** (/b)
14. *Lady* - **The Commodores, Styx & Supertramp**
15. *Let's Go* - **The Cars & Wang Chung**
16. *Limelight* - **The Alan Parsons Project & Rush**
17. *Locomotion* - **Grand Funk & Orchestral Manoeuvres In The Dark**
18. *Magic* - **The Cars, Olivia Newton - John & Pilot**
19. *Once In A Lifetime* - **Chicago** (/b) **& The Talking Heads**
20. *Only You* - **Ringo Starr & Yaz**
21. *Peace Of Mind* - **Boston & Loggins & Messina** (/b)
22. *Power Of Love* - **Celine Dion, Frankie Goes To Hollywood & Huey Lewis & The News**

23. *Time* - **The Alan Parsons Project & (Pink Floyd)**
24. *The Voice* - **The Moody Blues & (The Alan Parsons Project)**
25. *Touch & Go* - **The Cars & Emerson, Lake & Powell**
26. *Walk On* - **(U2) & Neil Young**
27. *Without You* - **The Doobie Brothers (/b) & Harry Nilsson**

While there were many maxi 12" singles, with three and four and five songs on them, there were very few maxi 7" singles. These each have three songs, one on the first side and two on the second, not to be confused with the three track albums like Monty Pythons' *Matching Tie & Handkerchief*[7]. Side one had one groove, while side two had two grooves so it depended on which groove you dropped the needle in which song you heard. Nine of these include …

1.10 ~ Three Songs
1. *Feels Like The First Time / Cold As Ice / Long Long Way From Home* [UK]- **Foreigner**
2. *I Still Haven't Found What I'm Looking For / Spanish Eyes / Deep in The Heart, In God's Country / Bullet The Blue Sky / Running To Stand Still, Where The Streets Have No Name / Silver & Gold / Sweetest Thing & With or Without You / Hold On To Love / Walk To The Water* - **U2**
3. *I'd Like To Teach The World To Sing* - **Coke Commercial / Laurie Bauer Singers / Dr. Music**
4. *Ring Out Solstice Bells / A Christmas Song / Another Christmas Song / Magic Bells (Ring Out Solstice Bells)* [UK] - **Jethro Tull**
5. *Spot The Pigeon EP - Match Of The Day / Pigeons / Inside & Out* [UK] - **Genesis**
6. *Turn Of A Friendly Card / Snake Eyes / Games People Play* [DEU] - **The Alan Parsons Project**

The four singles by U2 were 45 rpm on side 1 where the hit song was and 33 & 1/3 rpm on side 2 where the two other songs were. The *I'd Like* single featured the original Coke commercial as one of the three songs on the record. The Foreigner single *Feels* looked just like the album cover. The Alan Parsons single *Turn* looked just like the album cover and was a green record, as mentioned here.

---

[7] *Matching Tie & Handkerchief*, Monty Pythons Flying Circus, Arista, 1973

TWO

SINGLES AS VISUAL ART
I - LABELS

This chapter is the first of three that talks about singles as visual art, not how we normally think of music which is a full on audible medium. The difference between a label and a sleeve is as follows: the label is what is actually printed on the middle portion of the physical record, while the sleeve is what houses and protects that physical record. This chapter focuses on the label, while the next chapter focuses on the picture sleeve.

The year a song was recorded and produced was not stamped on vinyl records and specifically singles, until the early 1970s, around 1972. There were picture sleeves in the 1970s; just not as popular or prolific as they were in the eighties. Apple & Capital Records had the most picture sleeves for 45 rpm records in the 1970s. I will describe these in The Seventies Canadian Corner and Chicago & Beatles chapters.

In 1975, *Sister Golden Hair* (America) was the only single to appear on both of the final personal copies of the CHUM and CFRA charts, even though they were both issued several months apart. In chapter twenty-five about seventies radio & charts, I include *The Sister Golden Hair Charts [gem 25.6 & 25.7]. Sister* featured one of my favourite record labels of all time, the mid seventies version of Warner Bros. Records (est. 1958), featuring a tree lined street of Burbank California and the words in capital letters "BURBANK, HOME OF WARNER BROS. RECORDS".

The timeframe of the Burbank version of the record label was the same time that I was a teenager in Ottawa. During that time, I probably collected more Burbank singles by the Doobie Brothers than any other group. Including both America and the Doobie Brothers, here's the list...

2.1 ~ Warner I - Burbank Trees

1. *Another Park Another Sunday / Black Water, Black Water / Song To See You Through, China Grove, Long Train Running / Without You, Long Train Running // Listen To The Music, Take Me In Your Arms (Rock Me) & Takin' It To The Streets* - **The Doobie Brothers**
2. *Blinded By The Light / Spirit In The Night* - **Manfred Mann**
3. *Daisy Jane, Lonely People, Rainbow Song, Sister Golden Hair / Midnight, Tin Man // Don't Cross The River, Tin Man / In The Country & Today's The Day* - **America**
4. *December 1963 (Oh What A Night)* - **Frankie Valli & The Four Seasons**
5. *Diamond Girl & Get Closer* - **Seals & Crofts**
6. *Don't Stop, Dreams & You Make Loving Fun* - **Fleetwood Mac**
7. *Dream Weaver / Let It Out, Love Is Alive / Much Higher & Light Of Smiles* - **Gary Wright**
8. *First Cut Is The Deepest & You're In My Heart* - **Rod Stewart**
9. *I Never Cry / Go To Hell , School's Out / Gutter Cat & You & Me / It's Hot Tonight* - **Alice Cooper**
10. *Let Your Love Flow* - **The Bellamy Brothers**
11. *Long Tall Glasses, When I Need You & You Make Me Feel like Dancing* - **Leo Sayer**
12. *Paloma Blanca* - **The George Baker Selection**
13. *Smoke On The Water (original & Live)* - **Deep Purple**
14. *Windy* - **The Association**
15. *You Light Up My Life* - **Debbie Boone**

Earlier versions of the Warner label were green. *Hello Hurray, Summer Breeze & Ventura Highway* (the latter two bought as a pair in the fall of 1973) were all examples. Still earlier there was an orange version with black lettering that included *Classical Gas.* That orange was very similar to early versions of Columbia

Singles weren't always recorded in stereo. In fact, many of the sixties singles were recorded in mono. Stereo singles came on strong in the late sixties. However, this did not make mono singles poorer sounding just different. Some mono singles have better sound quality than stereo singles. Many of these included artists who were distributed originally by Kinney Music.

2.2 ~ Kinney

1. *Beautiful* - **Gordon Lightfoot** - Reprise
2. *Doctor My Eyes* - **Jackson Browne** - Asylum
3. *Everything I Own / I Don't Love You & Let Your Love Go / Too Much Love* - **Bread** - Elektra
4. *First Time Ever I Saw Your Face / Trade Winds* - **Roberta Flack** - Atlantic
5. *Heart Of Gold / Sugar Mountain & Old Man / The Needle Gone & The Damage Done* - **Neil Young** - Reprise
6. *Horse With No Name & I Need You* - **America** - Warner Brothers
7. *Riders On The Storm* - **The Doors** - Elektra
8. *Roundabout / Long Distance Runaround* - **Yes** - Atlantic
9. *Take It Easy / Get You In The Mood* - **The Eagles** - Asylum
10. *Taxi / Empty* - **Harry Chapin** - Elektra

As an interesting little side story, a family friend once commented that the only difference between mono and stereo was that mono sound was coming out of one speaker and stereo out of two. Uh, sorry, no. Mono is the same sound coming out of both speakers. Stereo is unique sound coming out of each speaker.

Kinney became WEA Music in 1970 and could have been called WEAR Music, if you included all the different record labels, Asylum, Atco, Atlantic, Elektra, Reprise and of course, The Rolling Stones. See their list at the end of this chapter. WEA created its own label in the eighties for artists like Alphaville, Howard Jones & Peter Schilling.

A close favourite to the Burbank label was the Mercury Label (est. 1945) with trees and skyscrapers. Bachman - Turner Overdrive had several of these singles in the mid-seventies, a later generation of labels to the red ones *Let It Ride & Taking Care Of Business*. Alongside Canadians Bachman - Turner Overdrive, note the US pressings of Rush songs (The Canadian pressings of other Rush songs were on Anthem Records). The singles include …

2.3 ~ Mercury

1. *Hey You, Looking Out For Number One, Roll On Down The Highway & You Ain't Seen Nothin' Yet* - **Bachman - Turner Overdrive**
2. *I Don't Like Mondays* - **The Boomtown Rats**
3. *I'm Not In Love* - **10 CC**
4. *New World Man & Spirit Of Radio* - **Rush**
5. *(The) Night Chicago Died* - **Paper Lace**
6. *Sultans Of Swing* - **Dire Straits**

The middle building on the label is the *IBM Plaza Building* in Chicago, similar to the *Seagram's Building*[8] in New York City and the *Toronto Dominion Centre*[9] towers, designed by architect Mies Van Der Rohe.[10] I reference Mies and his iconic black buildings in chapter seven. The New York building was used in films like *Scrooged* with Bill Murray[11] and *Family Man* with Nicholas Cage.[12]

The next label was the two stage Elektra label (est. 1950), first the caterpillar *(/c)*, from the early to mid-seventies, then the butterfly *(/b)*, from the mid to late seventies, both holding on to a stylized letter E on a background that was a combination of blue, green, grey & purple.

Bread had at least seven different songs with the caterpillar. Most of the songs with the Butterfly were by Queen, before the days of the plain red label. The combined Elektra list looks like this (all are caterpillar unless noted with bf for butterfly) …

2.4 ~ Elektra I - Caterpillar & Butterfly I

1. *All I Can Do / Got A Lot On My Head (bf), It's All I Can Do / Candy-O & My Best Friend's Girl / Moving In Stereo* - **The Cars**
2. *Aubrey, Baby I'm A Want You / Truckin', Diary, Everything I Own / I Don't Love You, The Guitar Man, If / Take Comfort, Let Your Love Go / Too Much Love, Lost Without Your Love (bf) & Sweet Surrender* - **Bread**

---

[8] Seagram's Building, New York City, Mies Van Der Rohe, Architect, 1958
[9] Toronto Dominion Centre, Toronto, Ontario, Mies Van Der Rohe, Architect, 1966
[10] Mies Van Der Rohe, German American Architect, 1886-1969
[11] *Scrooged*, Film, Bill Murray, Paramount, 1988
[12] *Family Man*, Film, Nicholas Cage, Universal, 2000

3. *Bohemian Rhapsody, Killer Queen, Tie Your Mother Down & You're My Best Friend -* **Queen (bf)**
4. *Cat's In The Cradle, I Wanna Learn A Love Song & Taxi / Empty -* **Harry Chapin**
5. *I'd Like To Teach The World To Sing -* **The New Seekers**
6. *Just The Two Of Us -* **Grover Washington**
7. *Love Her Madly & Riders On The Storm -* **The Doors**
8. *Nobody Does It Better (bf) & You're So Vain / His Friends Are More Than Fond Of Robin -* **Carly Simon**
9. *Save Me -* **Atomic Rooster**

In the seventies, before changing to the Atco and Atlantic labels, Genesis had a very unique looking label, Famous Charisma, the fourth favourite. Originally, the label had wonderfully detailed coloured artwork from the Lewis Carroll[13] story *Alice's Adventures in Wonderland.*[14] It featured the Mad Hatter as the central figure along with the White Rabbit & The Cheshire Cat (*I Know What I Like, Twilight Alehouse & Turn It On Again*). *Turn It On Again* only made the top 40 in the UK. Genesis changed from Famous Charisma to Atco to Atlantic, while Yes changed the other way from Atlantic to Atco.

Then there was a blue background with the Mad Hatter and Charisma in white letters (*Your Own Special Way / It's Yourself*). *Games Without Frontiers & I Don't Remember* by Peter Gabriel were the opposite with a white background and the Mad Hatter and Charisma in Teal letters. Finally, there were just the words Famous label in black lettering on a silver background (*Spot The Pigeon EP - Match Of The Day / Pigeons / Inside & Out & Duchess*).

The MCA (est. 1942)[15] singles with a rainbow on a black background were a staple for seventies collectors. Elton John singles were a big part of this. *Crocodile Rock* appeared on a plain black background with white lettering, the only MCA single I have ever seen like it. Early US versions of ABC Dunhill had a similar colour look to MCA label with the rainbow, the ABC Dunhill logos in colour on a black background. Further still, Decca (D) (est. 1929)[16] & Liberty (L) labels were black with colour trim and Spotlight (S) labels were black with a multi coloured car. For *The Dark Side Of The Label [gem, see also 2.11]*, the ABC, Decca, Liberty, MCA & Spotlight list looks like this (only non MCA labels are indicated, ABC, D, L & S)...

2.5 ~ The Dark Side Of The Label [gem]
I - ABC/Dunhill Decca Liberty MCA Spotlight

1. *Bennie & The Jets, The Bitch is Back, Crocodile Rock, Daniel, Don't Let The Sun Go Down On Me, Goodbye Yellow Brick Road, Grow Some Funk Of Your Own, Island Girl, Lucy In The Sky With Diamonds, Philadelphia Freedom, Rocket Man, Saturday Night's Alright For Fighting & Someone Saved My Life Tonight -* **Elton John**
2. *Black & White, Eli's Coming, Mama Told Me & The Show Must Go On -* **Three Dog Night (ABC - US)**
3. *Blueberry Hill -* **Fats Domino**
4. *Doo Wah Diddy Diddy -* **Manfred Mann (S)**
5. *Garden Party -* **Rick Nelson (D)**
6. *Gimmie Some Lovin' -* **The Spencer Davis Group (S)**

---

[13] Lewis Carroll, British Author, 1832-1898
[14] *Alices Adventures In Wonderland*, Lewis Carroll, 1865
[15] *Infographic Guide To Music*, Graham Betts, Cassell, 2014, p.15
[16] *Infographic Guide To Music*, Graham Betts, Cassell, 2014, p.14

7. *Going Up The Country* - **Canned Heat (L)**
8. *Green Eyed Lady* - **Sugarloaf (L) & (S)**
9. *Gypsies, Tramps & Thieves & Half Breed* - **Cher**
10. *Hawaii Five-O* - **The Ventures (L)**
11. *If You Love Me Let Me Know* - **Olivia Newton - John**
12. *I'll Have To Say I Love You In A Song, It Doesn't Have To Be That Way & Time In A Bottle* - **Jim Croce (ABC - US)**
13. *Pinball Wizard / Dogs Pt. 2 & Squeeze Box* - **The Who**
14. *Raise A Little Hell & We're Here For A Good Time* - **Trooper**
15. *Silent Night Holy Night* - **Bing Crosby (D)**
16. *Sweet Caroline* - **Neil Diamond**

The MCA look of the rainbow on the black background is not unlike the colour scheme for Pink Floyds' *Dark Side Of The Moon*, with the prism on a black background. So, I refer to this list as *The Dark Side Of The Label I.* The later version of the label would still have the rainbow but on a light blue background.

Another favourite was Atlantic Records. Turkish born Ahmet Ertegun[17] was the founder and initially singed many R&B artists to his label like Ray Charles, The Drifters, Aretha Franklin, Wilson Pickett & Percy Sledge.

The impact of Atlantic records on my collection has been big and includes Abba, Average White Band, Laura Branigan, Collective Soul, Phil Collins, Alice Cooper, Crosby, Stills & Nash, Dr. John, Emerson, Lake & Palmer, Roberta Flack, Foreigner, Genesis, INXS, Led Zeppelin, Bette Midler, Otis Redding, The Spinners & Yes.

Some artists had their logos or monographs printed on their record labels … Abba, America, Bread, The Carpenters, Chicago, Culture Club, Dexy's Midnight Runners, Electric Light Orchestra, Foreigner, Gowan, Heart, Human League, Icicle Works, Jon & Vangelis, Platinum Blonde, Styx, The Thompson Twins & Yazoo.

Into the late seventies, Warner adopted a very different look from the tree lined boulevard. At first, I thought the artwork was forgettable, a white background with a small version of the Warner logo. However, when you look more closely at the logo, the colours are awesome, varying shades of red, pink, orange, blue, green & grey. The background was plain but had a pin stripe pattern running through it, horizontally. Some of the artists are carryovers from the tree lined street list - Here is the list…

2.6 ~ Warner II - Colour Logo & Pinstripes I
1. *Along Comes A Woman, Hard Habit To Break / Remember The Feeling, Will You Still Love Me / 26 Or 6 To 4 86 & You're The Inspiration / Once In A Lifetime* - **Chicago**
2. *Arthur's Theme / Minstrel Gigolo, Arthur's Theme // Say You'll Be Mine, Ride Like The Wind / Minstrel Gigolo, Sailing // Ride Like The Wind & Say You'll Be Mine / Spinning* - **Christopher Cross**
3. *Athena* - **The Who**
4. *Batdance* - **Prince**
5. *Big Love, Everywhere, Little Lies & Tusk* - **Fleetwood Mac**
6. *Calling Elvis* - **Dire Straits**

---

[17] Ahmet Ertegun, 1923-2006, Owner & Founder of Atlantic Records, Rockefeller Plaza, New York, 1947

7. *Centerfield* - **John Fogerty**
8. *Classical Gas // Baroque-A-Nova* - **Mason Williams**
9. *Do Ya Think I'm Sexy & First Cut Is The Deepest* - **Rod Stewart**
10. *Dream Weaver // Love Is Alive* - **Gary Wright**
11. *Everybody Hurts & Losing My Religion* - **REM**
12. *Jump 7 & 12 & Panama* - **Van Halen**
13. *La Bamba* - **Los Lobos**
14. *Legs / Bad Girl, Legs // Sharp Dressed Man, Sharp Dressed Man / I Got The 6 & TV Dinners* - **ZZ Top**
15. *Life In A Northern Town* - **The Dream Academy**
16. *Lotta Love* - **Nicolette Larson**
17. *Moondance // Domino* - **Van Morrison**
18. *Rock Lobster* - **B 52s**
19. *Schools Out // I'm Eighteen* - **Alice Cooper**
20. *Smoke On The Water // Woman From Tokyo* - **Deep Purple**
21. *Take On Me* - **A-Ha**
22. *Minute By Minute / Sweet Feelin', What A Fool Believes / Don't Stop To Watch The Wheels & What A Fool Believes // It Keeps You Running & What A Fool Believes // Minute By Minute* - **The Doobie Brothers**
23. *You Can Call Me Al* - **Paul Simon**

In the late seventies and early eighties, Island (est. 1959)[18] had two neat labels. The American label was a combination of green, orange, yellow & purple, while The Canadian label was a combination of the green, orange, yellow & blue…

2.7 ~ Island
1. *New Year's Day / Treasure & Two Hearts Beat As One / Endless Deep* - **U2**
2. *Still In The Game, Valerie & While You See A Chance* - **Steve Winwood**
3. *Video Killed The Radio Star* - **The Buggles**

Also, in the late seventies and early eighties, Chrysalis introduced many new artists to its' lineup, (Jethro Tull had signed with the label in the seventies, recording the likes of *Bungle In The Jungle*) rolling the Elektra caterpillar then butterfly insignias in to one, presenting their version in blue and white. All seven Blondie Songs appear in the top ten of the "fifteen songs you must know" from *The Story Of Blondie*[19]…

2.8 ~ Butterfly II - Chrysalis
1. *Atomic, Call Me, Dreaming, Heart Of Glass, One Way Or Another, Rapture, & The Tide Is High* - **Blondie**
2. *Dancing With Tears In My Eyes & One Small Day* - **Ultravox & Midge Ure**
3. *Eyes Without A Face, Flesh For Fantasy & White Wedding* - **Billy Idol**
4. *Gold & True* - **Spandau Ballet**

---

[18] *Infographic Guide To Music*, Graham Betts, Cassell, 2014, p.15
[19] *The Story of Blondie*, 360Media, 2024

5. *Heart & Soul, Heart Of Rock & Roll, I Want A New Drug, The Power Of Love & Stuck With You* - **Huey Lewis & The News**
6. *Heartbreaker, Love Is A Battlefield, Shattered, We Belong, We Live For Love & You Better Run* - **Pat Benatar**
7. *Here Comes The Night & Hot Time in The City* - **Nick Gilder**
8. *Only You Can Rock Me* - **UFO**

In 1980, Geffen records appeared. The style of the label very closely resembled the Warner colour label with the pinstripes running horizontally across the label in the background. The logo itself was a globe with an imbedded letter G. The second generation featured a black background, giving it a very different look. Here is the first generation list…

2.9 ~ Pinstripes II - Geffen
1. *All She Wants To Do Is Dance & Boys Of Summer* - **Don Henley**
2. *Crazy For You* - **Madonna**
3. *Dance Hall Days* - **Wang Chung**
4. *Don't Cry, Only Time Will Tell, The Smile Has Left Your Eyes & Sole Survivor (long / short)* - **Asia**
5. *Empty Garden & I Guess That's Why They Call It The Blues* - **Elton John**
6. *(Just Like) Starting Over, Watching The Wheels & Woman* - **John Lennon**
7. *Our House* - **Madness**
8. *Shock The Monkey / Soft Dog* - **Peter Gabriel**

In the eighties, EMI America (est. 1931)[20] probably introduced more artists to its lineup than the other labels mentioned here. It had a classic look, a rainbow of colours spelling out the name, EMI on the top line and America on the second line, on a grey background, lots of David Bowie here…

2.10 ~ EMI
1. *Always Something There To Remind Me & Promises Promises* - **The Naked Eyes**
2. *Bette Davis Eyes / Miss You Tonight & Invitation To Dance* - **Kim Carnes**
3. *Centerfold & Freeze Frame* - **J. Geils Band**
4. *China Girl, Let's Dance & Modern Love* - **David Bowie**
5. *Dancing In The Street* - **David Bowie & Mick Jagger**
6. *For Your Eyes Only, Morning Train & Strut* - **Sheena Easton**
7. *Hearts / Freeway* - **Marty Balin**
8. *It's A Sin & West End Girls* - **The Pet Shop Boys**
9. *It's My Life* - **Talk Talk**
10. *Missing You* - **John Waite**
11. *Rock This Town* - **The Stray Cats**
12. *This Is Not America* - **David Bowie & Pat Metheny**

---

[20] *Infographic Guide To Music*, Graham Betts, Cassell, 2014, p.14

Through the seventies and eighties, **Capitol** (est. 1942)[21] had a classic looking black label with a rainbow of other colours circling the outside, similar to the colours of the MCA and ABC labels listed earlier, this on entitles *The Dark Side Of The Label II [gem see also 2.5]*...

2.11 ~ The Dark Side Of The Label [gem] II - Capitol

1. *Angel Of The Morning* - **Juice Newton**
2. *Boy Inside The Man* - **Tom Cochrane & Red Rider**
3. *California Dreaming* - **The Beach Boys**
4. *Diamond Sun, Don't Forget Me (When I'm Gone) & Someday* - **Glass Tiger**
5. *Don't Dream It's Over* - **Crowded House**
6. *Edge Of A Dream* - **Joe Cocker**
7. *Europa & The Pirate Twins, Hyperactive, I Scare Myself & May The Cube Be With You* - **Thomas Dolby**
8. *Let It Go* - **Luba**
9. *Like A Rock & Old Time Rock & Roll* - **Bob Segar**
10. *My Sharona* - **The Knack**
11. *My Sweet Lord // Isn't It A Pity* - **George Harrison**
12. *Opportunities* - **The Pet Shop Boys**
13. *New Moon On Monday, The Reflex, Save A Prayer & Wild Boys* - **Duran Duran**
14. *Radio Ga Ga* - **Queen**
15. *Spies Like Us / My Carnival* - **Paul McCartney**
16. *Suddenly Last Summer / Some Things Never Change* - **The Motels**
17. *These Dreams* - **Heart**
18. *Tonight I Celebrate / Born To Love* - **Roberta Flack & Peabo Bryson**

In the late 1980s, **Elektra** and **Asylum** (a) revamped the look of their forty-fives, remarkably similar to the look of the classic red and black **Atlantic** label and the gold and black **Atlantic Gold Standard** label.

2.12 ~ Elektra II & Asylum Late 80s

1. *Drive & Tonight She Comes // Just What I Needed* - **The Cars**
2. *Easier Said Than Done* - **Jon Anderson**
3. *Holding Back The Years, If You Don't Know Me By Now, Money's Too Tight To Mention & The Right Thing* - **Simply Red**
4. *Please Come Home For Christmas (a)* - **The Eagles**

Going a step further, some seventies & eighties singles had custom labels. Seven of the following entries are from the seventies, Grand Funk, Elton John, Klaatu, Pink Floyd, Queen, Ringo Starr & Wings. The rest are all from the eighties. Paul McCartney & Wings had the most for the seventies, while Simple Minds had the most for the eighties.

[21] *Infographic Guide To Music*, Graham Betts, Cassell, 2014, p.15

2.13 ~ Custom Labels I - Domestic

1. *A View To A Kill & Union of The Snake* - **Duran Duran**
2. *All Those Years Ago, Got My Mind Set On You, This Is Love & When We Was Fab* - **George Harrison**
3. *Another Brick In The Wall Part 2* - **Pink Floyd**
4. *Another Day In Paradise / Heat On The Street, I Wish It Would Rain Down & In The Air Tonight / The Roof Is Leaking* - **Phil Collins**
5. *Arias & Symphonies, Romantic Traffic & Smiling In Winter* - **The Spoons**
6. *Bad Time, Some Kinda Wonderful / Wild & We're An American Band / Creepin'* - **Grand Funk**
7. *Black Cars* - **Gino Vanelli**
8. *Break It Up & Waiting For A Girl Like You* - **Foreigner**
9. *Cannonball / Ever Open Door* - **Supertramp**
10. *Christmas Time / Reggae Christmas* - **Bryan Adams**
11. *Church Of The Poison Mind & Time (Clock Of The Heart)* - **Culture Club**
12. *Electricity* - **Orchestral Manoeuvres In The Dark**
13. *Flashdance (What A Feeling)* - **Irene Cara**
14. *Hello Again* - **Neil Diamond**
15. *Hi Hi Hi, Let 'Em In, Letting Go, Listen To What The Man Said, Maybe I'm Amazed (Live), My Love / The Mess (Live), Silly Love Songs, Venus & Mars Rock Show & With A Little Luck* - **Paul McCartney & Wings**
16. *Let's Go Crazy, Purple Rain & When Doves Cry* - **Prince**
17. *Magic* - **Olivia Newton - John**
18. *Mixed Emotions* - **The Rolling Stones**
19. *No No Song, Only You, Photograph* [Apple] *& You're Sixteen* - **Ringo Starr**
20. *Pale Shelter* - **Tears For Fears**
21. *Power Of Love & Two Tribes* - **Frankie Goes To Hollywood**
22. *Sitting At The Wheel* - **The Moody Blues**
23. *Twisting By The Pool* - **Dire Straits**
24. *We're Off Ya Know* - **Klaatu**

2.14 ~ Custom Labels II - Import

1. *Abacab / Another Record* [UK], *Illegal Alien / Turn It On Again (Live)* [UK], *Mama / It's Gonna Get Better* [US] *& That's All / Taking It All Too Hard* [UK] - **Genesis**
2. *Big Log* [US] - **Robert Plant**
3. *De Do Do Do De Da Da Da / Sermon* [UK] *& Don't Stand So Close To Me / Friends* [ITA] - **The Police**
4. *Discotheque & Staring At The Sun* [US] - **U2**
5. *Hey Big Brother & Ma* [US] - **Rare Earth**
6. *I Missed Again / I'm Not Moving* [US] - **Phil Collins**
7. *Lebanon & Life On Your Own* [UK] - **The Human League**
8. *Love Song, Sanctify Yourself, Someone Somewhere In Summertime, Up On The Catwalk, Waterfront & Waterfront 89* [UK] - **Simple Minds**
9. *Never Turn Away* [UK] - **Orchestral Manoeuvres In The Dark**

10. *Someone Saved My Life Tonight* [UK] - **Elton John**
11. *Turn Of A Friendly Card / Snake Eyes / Games People Play* [DEU] - **The Alan Parsons Project**
12. *We Are The Champions // We Will Rock You* [UK] - **Queen**

Of all of the custom labels just mentioned, several are very impressive. The first, *Someone Saved My Life Tonight* is like a mini version of the album cover, *Captain Fantastic & The Brown Dirt Cowboy*. The second, *We Are The Champions // We Will Rock You*, features the logo from the group's album *A Night At The Opera*. The Third, *Turn Of A Friendly Card*, is a mini version of the album by the same name. The fourth, *Abacab*, the artwork is just like that on the album of the same name. The fifth, *Another Brick In The Wall Part 2*, features artwork similar to what is on the album labels.

Thanks again to Graham Betts and his *Infographic Guide To Music* for the dates that record companies were established (page 16 in his book). For the record (see what I did there?), I have set up a list for the records mentioned earlier in this chapter, with the Rolling Stones own label.

2.15 ~ *The Rolling Stones Own Label*
Angie, Beast Of Burden, Brown Sugar, Doo Doo Doo Doo Doo Heartbreaker, Emotional Rescue, It's Only Rock & Roll, Miss You, Mixed Emotions, She's So Cold & Start Me Up

THREE

SINGLES AS VISUAL ART
II - PICTURE SLEEVES

This is the second of three chapters about singles as visual art. Collecting singles with picture sleeve covers (mostly from the 1980s) meant different things. There were many single picture sleeve singles that were very similar to the albums they were taken from…

3.1 ~ Sleeve Cover Like Album I - US Artists

1. *Against The Wind [AGAINST THE WIND]* - **Bob Seger**
2. *Crumblin' Down [UH HUH], Paper In Fire* [US] *[THE LONESOME JUBILEE] & Small Town [SMALLTOWN]* - **John Cougar Mellencamp**
3. *Diamond Sun & I'm Still Searching [DIAMOND SUN] & Don't Forget Me When I'm Gone [THIN RED LINE]* - **Glass Tiger** [CAN]
4. *I'll Be Good To Ya [LOOK OUT FOR #1]* - **The Brothers Johnson**
5. *It's Too Late [TAPESTRY] & Jazzman* [US] *[WRAP AROUND JOY]* - **Carole King**
6. *Jackie Blue* [US] *[IT'LL SHINE WHEN IT SHINES]* - **Ozark Mountain Daredevils**
7. *(The) Locomotion [SHININ' ON] & We're An American Band / Creepin' [WE'RE AN AMERICAN BAND]* - **Grand Funk**
8. *Oh Sherrie / Don't Tell Me Why You're Leaving [STREET TALK]* - **Steve Perry**
9. *Run To You [RECKLESS]* - **Bryan Adams** [CAN]
10. *Soul Man* [US] *[THE BLUES BROTHERS]* - **The Blues Brothers**
11. *We Don't Need Another Hero [MAD MAX BEYOND THUNDERDOME] & What's Love Got To Do With It? [PRIVATE DANCER]* - **Tina Turner**

3.2 ~ Sleeve Cover Like Album II - UK Artists

1. *(The) Riddle [THE RIDDLE]* - **Nik Kershaw**
2. *Abacab* [UK] *[ABACAB]* - **Genesis**
3. *Adventures In Modern Recording* [UK] *[ADVENTURES IN MODERN RECORDING]* - **The Buggles**
4. *Another Brick In The Wall Pt. 2 [THE WALL]* - **Pink Floyd**
5. *Black Dog \\ Misty Mountain Hop* [JAP] *[LED ZEPPELIN IV]* - **Led Zeppelin**
6. *Brain Salad Surgery* [UK] *[BRAIN SALAD SURGERY]* - **Emerson, Lake & Palmer**
7. *Can't Get it Out Of My Head* [US] *[ELDORADO]* - **The Electric Light Orchestra**
8. *Conquistador [LIVE IN CONCERT WITH THE EDMONTON SYMPHONY ORCHESTRA]* - **Procal Harum**
9. *Don't Answer Me [AMMONIA AVENUE], Eye In The Sky [EYE IN THE SKY], Let's Talk About Me [VULTURE CULTURE], Lucifer / I'd Rather Be A Man* [UK] *[EVE] & Stereotomy* [DEU & UK] *[STEREOTOMY]* - **The Alan Parsons Project**
10. *Don't Cry [ALPHA]* - **Asia**
11. *Don't Stop [RUMOURS]* - **Fleetwood Mac**
12. *Double Vision [DOUBLE VISION] & Feels Like The First Time / Cold As Ice / Long Long Way From Home* [UK] *[FOREIGNER]* - **Foreigner**
13. *Crazy* [NDR] *[FAMOUS LAST WORDS], Dreamer / From Now On [CRIME OF THE CENTURY] & Dreamer (Live)* [FRA & ITA] *[PARIS]* - **Supertramp**
14. *Invisible Sun* [UK] *[GHOST IN THE MACHINE]* - **The Police**
15. *Killer Queen* [DEU] *[QUEEN II] & We Are The Champions // We Will Rock You* [UK] *[NEWS OF THE WORLD]* - **Queen**
16. *Less Cities, More Moving People [PHANTOMS] & Saved By Zero* [US] *[REACH THE BEACH]* - **The Fixx**
17. *Let's Dance [LET'S DANCE]* - **David Bowie**
18. *Mirror Man [KEEP FEELING FASCINATION]* - **The Human League**
19. *Once Upon A Long Ago [ALL THE BEST]* - **Paul McCartney**
20. *Only You [GOODNITE VIENNA]* - **Ringo Starr**
21. *Only You Can Rock Me [OBSESSION]* - **UFO**
22. *Promised You A Miracle (Live) [LIVE IN THE CITY OF LIGHT]* - **Simple Minds**
23. *Show Me The Way [FRAMPTON COMES ALIVE]* - **Peter Frampton**
24. *Touch & Go [EMERSON, LAKE & POWELL]* - **Emerson, Lake & Powell**
25. *Two Hearts Beat As One* [US] *[WAR]* - **U2**
26. *Windpower* [UK] *[BLINDED BY SCIENCE / THE GOLDEN AGE OF WIRELESS]* - **Thomas Dolby**

    Going a step further, there are some albums that spawned entire groups of picture sleeve singles that were similar to both the album they were taken from and to each other (Many of these are discussed in the group chapters ten through eighteen in this story).

3.3 ~ Sleeve Covers Like Album
III - Several From The Same Album

1. *Alive & Kicking, All The Things She Said, Ghostdancing & Sanctify Yourself [ONCE UPON A TIME]* - **Simple Minds**
2. *All I Want Is You* [US], *Angel Of Harlem, Desire & When Love Comes To Town [RATTLE & HUM], I Still Haven't Found What I'm Looking For, In God's Country, Where The Streets Have No Name & With Or Without You [THE JOSHUA TREE]* - **U2**
3. *Back In The High Life, Finer Things, Higher Love & Valerie '87 [BACK IN THE HIGH LIFE]* - **Steve Winwood**
4. *Break It Up, Juke Box Hero, Urgent & Waiting For A Girl Like You [4], I Want To Know What Love Is & That Was Yesterday [AGENT PROVOCATUER]* - **Foreigner**
5. *Breakfast In America* [UK], *Goodbye Stranger* [ITA], *Take The Long Way Home* [FRA] *& The Logical Song* [ITA] *[BREAKFAST IN AMERICA]* - **Supertramp**
6. *Don't You Want Me & Open Your Heart [DARE]* - **The Human League**
7. *Duchess* [UK] *& Misunderstanding* [UK & US] *[DUKE]* - **Genesis**
8. *Every Breath You Take & King Of Pain [SYNCHRONICITY]* - **The Police**
9. *Everybody Wants To Rule The World, Head Over Heels, I Believe* [UK] *& Shout [SONGS FROM THE BIG CHAIR]* - **Tears For Fears**
10. *(The) Gold Bug / Snake Eyes* [NDR] *& Turn Of A Friendly Card / Snake Eyes / Games People Play* [DEU] *[THE TURN OF A FRIENDLY CARD]* - **The Alan Parsons Project**
11. *Heat Of The Moment, Only Time Will Tell & Sole Survivor* [UK] *[ASIA]* - **Asia**
12. *It Can Happen, Leave It & Owner Of A Lonely Heart [90125]* - **Yes**
13. *(Just Like) Starting Over & Watching The Wheels* [BEL] *[DOUBLE FANTASY]* - **John Lennon**
14. *(The) Lebanon & Life On Your Own* [UK] *[HYSTERIA]* - **The Human League**
15. *One More Night & Sussudio [NO JACKET REQUIRED]* - **Phil Collins**
16. *Union Of The Snake & The Wild Boys [ARENA]* - **Duran Duran**

While Grand Funk's *We're An American Band & The Loco Motion* weren't from the same album, the sleeves were very similar. Some picture sleeves even came in gatefold format, similar to many album jackets …

3.4 ~ Gatefold

1. *Brain Salad Surgery* [UK] - **Emerson, Lake & Palmer**
2. *Dancing With Tears in My Eyes* [UK] - **Ultravox**
3. *Desire* - **U2**
4. *Fields Of Fire* - **Big Country**
5. *Head Over Heels & I Believe* [UK] - **Tears For Fears**
6. *In The Air Tonight* - **Phil Collins**
7. *Never Surrender* - **Corey Hart**
8. *Sanctify Yourself* [UK] - **Simple Minds**

Desire had a single disk, *Sanctify Yourself* and *I Believe* each had two disks. *Dancing & In The Air Tonight* each had a booklet. *Head Over Heels, Fields Of Fire & Never Surrender* each folded out into a poster.

Colour Discs popped up from time to time as well but for the most part were very rare and hard to find. They were so bright and colourful and really stood out on the turntable, especially spinning on a black platter, when most records just blended right in…

3.5 ~ Colour Vinyl

1. *Brain Salad Surgery* - **Emerson, Lake & Palmer** - clear
2. *Christmas Time / Reggae Christmas* - **Bryan Adams** - green
3. *Only You Can Rock Me* - **UFO** - red
4. *Purple Rain* - **Prince** - purple
5. *Rudolph The Red Nosed Reindeer* - **Corey Hart** - red.
6. *She's A River* [UK] - **Simple Minds** - blue
7. *Turn Of A Friendly Card / Snake Eyes / Games People Play* [DEU]
   - **The Alan Parsons Project** - green
8. *Up On The Catwalk* [UK] - **Simple Minds** - white
9. *We're An American Band* - **Grand Funk** - gold.

UK singles have always been excellent in their sound quality and the convenience of small album style centres. Collecting singles into the nineties remained possible by UK and US makers, while Canadian makers were quick to phase out vinyl in favor of the CD.

For all the picture sleeves that are out there, there aren't very many that have lyrics on the back side of the sleeve. Here is a sample of those that did…

3.6 ~ Lyrics

1. *Advice For The Young At Heart, Sowing The Seeds Of Love & Woman In Chains*
   [SOWING THE SEEDS OF LOVE] - **Tears for Fears**,
2. *Born In The USA, Dancing In The Dark, Glory Days, Hungry Heart, I'm On Fire & My*
   Hometown - **Bruce Springsteen**
3. *Christmas Time* - **Bryan Adams**
4. *Don't Answer Me & Prime Time [AMMONIA AVENUE]* - **The Alan Parsons Project**
5. *Ebony & Ivory* - **Paul McCartney & Stevie Wonder**
6. *Englishman In New York, We'll Be Together [NOTHING LIKE THE SUN] &Russians*
   [DREAM OF THE BLUE TURTLE] - **Sting**
7. *I Believe In Father Christmas* - **Greg Lake**
8. *I Go Crazy* - **Flesh For Lulu**
9. *Illegal Alien & Spot The Pigeon (Match Of The Day / Pigeons / Inside & Out)* [UK] -
   Genesis
10. *Last Song & Walking On Back* - **Edward Bear**
11. *Moonlight Desires* - **Gowan**

FOUR

SINGLES & ALBUMS

Listening (and recording) is divided into two categories, passive and active. Listening to albums or tapes is passive (you start the record or the tape and then you leave it alone for the next twenty minutes). Listening to singles is active (every three or four minutes you change the record for another).

Singles are pretty simple. I like that. You put the needle on side A or B and you get the song you want, every time. Albums are more complicated, especially when songs don't have clean breaks between them and you have to find just the right spot for the one you want. Some Albums, like *Pictures At An Exhibition* by Emerson, Lake & Palmer, you can't even see the breaks between the grooves.

"Album notes were like cereal boxes." Regardless of how boring the cereal box was, you still liked it in front of you while you were eating the cereal. Having the album and sleeve in front of you while you listen enhances the listening experience.

Remixed versions of songs actually recorded years later but paled in comparison to the originals include...

4.1 ~ Remix By Year
1. *25 Or 6 To 4 86* - **Chicago**
2. *Don't Stand So Close To Me 86* - **The Police**
3. *Drift Away 79* - **Dobie Gray**
4. *Valerie 87* - **Steve Winwood**
5. *Waterfront 89* - **Simple Minds**

The single sound was different as well. It's not a poor cousin or relative of the album. In fact, it may be stronger than the album sound, clearer vocals, less tinny guitar and heavier bass. After all, the record is tracking faster through the grooves so there is less room for deviation or error. Going a step further, vinyl singles may sound even better when you tape them. You can adjust the levels of the songs, just the way you like.

Examples of those singles that sound better than the same album cuts include ...

4.2 ~ Sounds Better Than Album [gem]
1. *Don't Kill The Whale / Abeline* [UK] & *Run Through The Light* [US] - **Yes**
2. *Dream On* - **Aerosmith**
3. *I Believe In Father Christmas* - **Greg Lake**
4. *Just A Smile (/b) [Magic]* - **Pilot**
5. *Mothers Talk* - **Tears For Fears**
6. *See The Lights* [UK] - **Simple Minds**
7. *Sweetest Thing [Where The Streets Have No Name & Silver & Gold]* - **U2**
8. *Time* [US] - **The Alan Parsons Project**

The guitars in both *Don't Kill The Whale* and *Dream On* have lots of echo and a fuller sound. *Don't Kill The Whale* on the UK pressing is also much better sounding than the US pressing as the B side of *Release Release*. *I Believe In Father Christmas* has the choral and orchestral accompaniment. *Just A Smile, Mothers Talk, Run Through The Light* and *See The Lights* all have a richer remixed sound. The vocals on *Time* are much cleaner and clearer. As mentioned elsewhere, *Run Through The Light* is a restructured version of the original. While *Pharoahs* and *When In Love With A Blind Man* are considered their own tunes, they are really remixed versions of *Everybody Wants To Rule The World* & *The Working Hour*, respectively. Roland Orzabal clarified on *Saturnine Martial & Lunatic* (an album full of B sides, remixes and other original material) that he actually wrote *When In Love With A Blind Man* before he wrote *The Working Hour*.

Various artists' albums by Ronco and K-tel, as advertised on TV in the early seventies, were a quick way to gather a decent collection of tunes. While some tunes were familiar, others were not, like Eric Clapton's *Let It Rain*. There were way too many tunes on there to have the full versions, two and three minutes most of the time. The vinyl sandwich dictated how many tunes you could safely get on to one record.

Even with the short versions, the overall song selections were good. Case in point, *Believe In Music* was the first K-tel album I ever bought. Some of the cuts include...

4.3 ~ K-TEL
1. *Brandy (You're A Fine Girl)* - **Looking Glass**
2. *Sunny Days* - **Lighthouse**
3. *Long Cool Woman In A Black Dress* - **The Hollies**
4. *Backstabbers* - **The O'Jays**
5. *Hold Your Head Up* - **Argent**
6. *Let it Rain* - **Eric Clapton**
7. *I Believe In Music* - **Gallery**

Geffen records pushed the vinyl sandwich rule to the max. Their artists added more tracks to their albums and the sound suffered; it wasn't as good. The A&M Audiophile series seemed impressive at first but in the end were no better than the regular pressings, especially Supertramp's *Crime Of The Century*.

Japanese pressings were good if you had $40 to spend on an album. The modern day 180 gram pressings of vinyl albums can cost as much.

Often it was reissued greatest hits albums where the versions of the songs weren't as good as the originals. Examples of this include ...

4.4 ~ Greatest I - Reissues
1. *The John Lennon Collection* (Geffen as noted above)
2. *Eric Clapton's Greatest Hits*
3. **Chicago**'s' *If You Leave Me Now* (another best of / greatest hits collection).

First time greatest hits albums were often better like *Chicago IX* and John Lennon's *Shaved Fish*. Most of all, the first greatest hits albums by a group were the best. Many of the greatest hits started appearing in the mid-seventies. They were exciting, fun and neat because it was your favourite groups' songs on one record. Besides Lennon - *Shaved Fish* and Chicago - *9 Greatest Hits*, there were...

4.5 ~ Greatest II - Originals
1. **Eagles, The** - *Their Greatest Hits*
2. **Electric Light Orchestra, The** - *OLE ELO*
3. **Doobie Brothers, The** - *The Best Of...*
4. **Elton John** - *Greatest Hits*
5. **Three Dog Night** - *Golden Biscuits*

My brother Richard bought me a special 180 gram copy of *Chicago 9* in 2020. The songs were the same but the artwork for the back cover was also used for the front cover, so no members of the band on the scaffolding painting the group logo and the album title *Greatest Hits* was altered to include *1969 to 1974*.

By the time they got to a greatest hits volume 2 or a best of (the difference is discussed ahead of list 4.8), neither the idea nor the collection of songs themselves was nearly as fresh. I passed on many of the greatest hits collections as I had enough of the singles to make my own greatest hits tapes (see chapter twenty-nine on recording - tapes), Chicago, the Doobie Brothers, The Fixx, Foreigner, Human League, the Moody Blues, Orchestral Manoeuvres In The Dark, the Police and Styx.

A *Wrap Around Album [gem 4.6 & 4.7]* is not a physical description like a gatefold. It is a temporal description of an album that enters the charts at the back end of one year and continues into the next.

Each of the following examples charted as a top album at the end of one year in the seventies and continued into the next ...

4.6 ~ Wrap I - 70s
1. *Band On The Run* (73/74) - **Paul McCartney & Wings**
2. *Dark Side Of The Moon* (73/74) & *The Wall* (79/80) - **Pink Floyd**
3. *Fly Like An Eagle* (76/77) - **The Steve Miller Band**
4. *Foreigner* (77/78) & *Double Vision* (78/79) - **Foreigner**
5. *Goodbye Yellow Brick Road* (73/74) & *Greatest Hits* (74/75) - **Elton John**
6. *News Of The World* (77/78) - **Queen**
7. *One Of These Nights* (75/76), *Their Greatest Hits* (75/76), *Hotel California* (77/78) & *The Long Run* (79/80) - **The Eagles**
8. *Stranger, The* (77/78) & *52nd Street* (78/79) - **Billy Joel**

9. *Zoso* (71/72), *Houses Of The Holy* (74/75) & *In Through The Out Door* (79/80) - **Led Zeppelin**

Pink Floyd, The Eagles and Led Zeppelin had three albums on that list that actually wrapped around two decades, with *The Wall, The Long Run & In Through The Out Door*. Each of the following examples charted their way into the list of top albums in the eighties two years in a row ...

4.7 ~ Wrap II - 80s

1. *90125* (83/84) - **Yes**
2. *Abacab* (81/82), *Genesis* (83/84) & *Invisible Touch* (86/87) - **Genesis**
3. *Back In The High Life* (86/87) & *Roll With It* (88/89) - **Steve Winwood**
4. *Famous Last Words* (82/83) - **Supertramp**
5. *Once Upon A Time* (85/86) - **Simple Minds**
6. *Sowing The Seeds Of Love* (89/90) - **Tears For Fears**
7. *Turn Of A Friendly Card* (80/81) & *Stereotomy* (86/87) - **The Alan Parsons Project**
8. *Unforgettable Fire, The* (84/85), *The Joshua Tree* (87/88) & *Rattle & Hum* (88/89) - **U2**
9. *Zenyatta Mondatta* (80/81) - **The Police**

If Albums give you a fuller picture of what a group is about, then collecting singles from across a catalogue takes you a good part of the way there. It's when the singles are whittled down to the popular ones from the popular albums that you miss a groups' musical journey and the good, even great, music that went along with it. That is where many radio stations spend most of their time. What happened to the "Deeper Cuts"?

Don't confuse great songs with great albums. Great albums are usually full of great songs while great songs appear on albums whether those albums are great or not. In fact, there are many great songs that stand out on albums because the albums are not great. You can't dismiss all the songs on an album just because the album isn't considered great. Especially songs when a group is starting out or in the twilight time of their career.

There used to be a marked difference between who was on the singles charts and the album charts. Some artists were just on the singles chart, some were on the album charts, while some were on both. Nowadays many artists are on both. Kind of like how actors used to do movies or television but not both. Now there is much crossover between the two.

If you collected singles instead of albums, you got a different sense for what an artist's music was about. The same goes for collecting compilations instead of original albums (like Beatles' *1962-1966* instead of *Rubber Soul*). As one friend put it, if you collected just compilations, you didn't get the full picture. Going further, compilations included two categories, greatest hits (singles oriented like Joel Whitburn's T*op 40 Hits*[22]) and best of (includes album tracks like Joel Whitburn's S*ongs and Artists*[23]).

One thing I have never understood about facts and statistics for the recording industry is measuring record sales in terms of dollars. Wouldn't it be a much more accurate measure if you used the number of units sold, rather than the dollar amount that those units translate into?

Through the seventies and the eighties there have been numerous hit songs that never made it to any greatest hits or best of albums, except for later releases of CDs. Sample tunes include:

[22] *Top 40 Hits*, Joel Whitburn, Record Research, 1993
[23] *Songs & Artists*, Joel Whitburn, Record Research, 2006.

4.8 ~ Not On Greatest

1. *Another Park Another Sunday* - **The Doobie Brothers**
2. *Don't Kill The Whale [Release Release & Abeline (/b)]* - **Yes**
3. *Glittering Prize* - **Simple Minds**
4. *Helen Wheels* - **Paul McCartney & Wings**
5. *In God's Country* - **U2**
6. *Telegraph* - **Orchestral Manoeuvres In The Dark**.

Until my longtime friend Michael visited me in Ottawa and encouraged me to listen to the B sides of my then very small 45 collection in 1974, I never gave them a second thought. There have been many B side treasures or diamonds in the rough. For the most part they were singles previously unreleased on albums. These include…

4.9 ~ B Side Treasures I - 70s

1. *Abeline [Don't Kill The Whale]* [UK] - **Yes**
2. *Hey Hey What Can I Do [Immigrant Song]* - **Led Zeppelin**
3. *Inside & Out [Follow You Follow Me & Spot The Pigeons]* [UK] - **Genesis**
4. *Theme From "For A Few Dollars More" [Wells Fargo]* - **Babe Ruth**
5. *You Started Laughing [Lady]* - **Supertramp**

4.10 ~ B Side Treasures II - 80s

1. *Crazy [Down Under]* - **Men At Work**
2. *Deeper & Deeper [Are We Ourselves?]* - **The Fixx**
3. *Luminous Times & Hold On To Love [With Or Without You], Silver & Gold & The Sweetest Thing [Where The Streets Have No Name] & Spanish Eyes & Deep In The Heart [I Still Haven't Found What I'm Looking For]* - **U2**
4. *Pharoahs [Everybody Wants To Rule The World] & When In Love With A Blind Man [Head Over Heels]* - **Tears For Fears**
5. *Ride Easy [Heat Of The Moment]* - **Asia**
6. *Someone To Talk To [Wrapped Around Your Finger]* - **The Police**

For some groups there are several B side treasures. These have all been included in their own appendix Two. Some groups even took to making different versions of the covers of the same record. Appendix twenty includes the titles from lists 4.9 & 4.10, appendix two, as well as all the other B sides mentioned in the story.

Collecting singles, in the long run, was harder than collecting albums. Albums were available longer in stores than their single counterparts. If an album featured several singles, it would stay on the charts for longer, even crossing from one year into another, while each of the singles would come and go. Even reissued double sided singles would only stay in the store for a shorter time.

Collecting singles is even harder now. Where records are sold, new or used, there are always albums but there are very few places now that sell singles. And of those places that do sell singles, most offer a much smaller selection than that of albums.

FIVE

THE GEOGRAPHY
OF SINGLES

I studied geography in university so I thought I would include a chapter from that point of view. For songs that were played on the radio, there were marked differences in both time and place, depending on where you were. American and British radio and charts were very different. Canadian radio and charts were more of a cross between the two. Also, it often took longer for British music to make it to Canadian Radio. Notice that most of these entries are from the seventies. By the time the eighties arrived, time and place had become much less of a factor or difference in release dates.

*Monster Mash (*Bobby Boris Pickett) first charted in 1962, then again in 1973. There are a couple of instances where the difference between single and album spans years. *Nights in White Satin* (Moody Blues) appeared on *Days Of Future Passed* in 1967 but was not released as a single for five years (1972). *Space Oddity* (David Bowie) appeared on the album *Space Oddity* in 1969 but was not released for four years after that (1973). *Beginnings, I'm A Man & Questions 67 & 68* all appeared on the debut album *Chicago Transit Authority* in 1969 but didn't appear as singles until 1971. Babe Ruth released *First Base* in 1972 but didn't release *The Mexican (Theme From "For A Few Dollars More")* until 1974. *Make Me Do (Anything You Want)* (A Foot In Cold Water) charted again in 1975 on CFGO in Ottawa. *Dream On* (Aerosmith) was re-released in 1976 and *West End Girls* (Pet Shop Boys) was re-released in 1986. Chicago, Queen & The Sweet lead the way here.

5.1 ~ Delay From UK, Albums Then Singles & Re-Releases
1. *Monster Mash* - **Bobby Boris Pickett** (62 & 73)
2. *Nights In White Satin* - **The Moody Blues** (67 & 72)
3. *Beginnings, I'm A Man & Questions 67 & 68* - **Chicago** (69 Album & 71)
4. *Space Oddity* - **David Bowie** (69 Album & 73)

5. *Make Me Do (Anything You Want)* - **A Foot In Cold Water** (Jul 72 & Jan 75 CFGO)
6. *Theme From "For A Few Dollars More"* - **Babe Ruth** (Sept 72 Album & 74 CFGO)
7. *Dream On* - **Aerosmith** (Billboard 73 & 76)
8. *Daniel* - **Elton John** (Jan 73 UK & Jun 73 CAN)
9. *Rock On* - **David Essex** (Sept 73 UK & Mar 74 CAN)
10. *Ballroom Blitz* - **The Sweet** (Oct 73 UK & 75 CAN)
11. *Radar Love* - **Golden Earring** (Jan 74 UK & Aug 74 CAN)
12. *Emma* - **Hot Chocolate** (Mar 74 UK & May 75 CAN)
13. *Killer Queen* - **Queen** (Nov 74 UK & May 75 CFGO)
14. *Magic* - **Pilot** (Nov 74 UK & Jul 75 CAN)
15. *How Long* - **Ace** (Dec 74 UK & May 75 CAN)
16. *Fox On The Run* - **The Sweet** (April 75 UK & Jan 76 CAN)
17. *Paloma Blanca* - **The George Baker Selection** (Oct 75 UK & Feb 76 CAN)
18. *Bohemian Rhapsody* - **Queen** (Nov 75 UK & Apr 76 CAN)
19. *Blinded By The Light* - **Manfred Mann** (Sept 76 UK & Feb 77 CAN)
20. *Dancing Queen* - **Abba** (Sept 76 UK & Feb 77 CAN)
21. *West End Girls* - **Pet Shop Boys** (85 CFNY & 86)

Where singles were made showed a definite geography. Similar to singles that had more than one picture sleeve, are those singles that had more than one B side, each made in a different country. This only includes original singles, not reissued double hit singles. The singles here are from Genesis, The Police & Supertramp...

5.2 ~ Same A Different B
1. *Better Days* - **Supertramp** - *Brother Where You Bound* [FRA] & *No In Between* [CAN]
2. *Don't Stand So Close To Me* - **The Police** - *Friends* [ITA] & *A Sermon* [CAN]
3. *Dreamer* - **Supertramp** - *Bloody Well Right* [US] & *From Now On* [CAN]
4. *Dreamer (Live)* - **Supertramp** - *From Now On* [US] & *You Started Laughing* [FRA & ITA]
5. *Follow You Follow Me* - **Genesis** - *Ballad Of Big* [CAN] & *Inside & Out* [US]
6. *Spirits In The Material World* - **The Police** - *Hungry For You* [US] & *Low Life* [UK]
7. *Walking On The Moon* - **The Police** - *Bring On The Night* [UK] & *Visions Of The Night* [CAN]
8. *Your Own Special Way* - **Genesis** - *In That Quiet Earth* [CAN] & *It's Yourself* [UK]

Collecting can mean completely different covers from other countries. Some of these other countries include France, Germany, Italy, The Netherlands, The United Kingdom and The United States. For all of these singles, there were very different picture sleeves for the same singles ...

5.3 ~ Different Sleeves
1. *Arthur's Theme* [CAN & UK] - **Christopher Cross**
2. *Better Days* [CAN & FRA], *Dreamer (Live)* [FRA, ITA & US], *Goodbye Stranger* [ITA & US], *The Logical Song* [ITA & US], *My Kind Of Lady* [ITA & UK] & *Take The Long Way Home* [CAN & FRA] - **Supertramp**
3. *Dancing With Tears In My Eyes* [CAN & UK] - **Ultravox**

4. *Don't Stand So Close To Me* [CAN & ITA] *& Spirits In The Material World* [UK & US]
   - **The Police**
5. *Killer Queen* [DEU & NDR] - **Queen**
6. *Old & Wise & Stereotomy* [DEU & UK] - **The Alan Parsons Project**
7. *Roll With It* [CAN & DEU] - **Steve Winwood**
8. *Sole Survivor* [CAN & UK] - **Asia**

Many of the Canadian and American covers of the Supertramp singles listed above, including *Better Days, Goodbye Stranger, My Kind Of Lady & Take The Long Way Home* paled in comparison with their UK and European counterparts.

US Singles have always made up a large part of my collection. Over the years Atlantic Records in the US has released a series called Atlantic Oldies…

5.4 ~ Atlantic Oldies - US

1. *Against All Odds // I Cannot Believe It's True, Another Day In Paradise // Who Said I Would & Something Happened On The Way To Heaven // Hang In Long Enough* - **Phil Collins**
2. *Chiquitita // The Winner Takes It All, Fernando // Dancing Queen, The Name Of The Game // Take A Chance On Me & SOS // Ring Ring* - **Abba**
3. *Follow You Follow Me // Illegal Alien, I Know What I Like (In Your Wardrobe) // The Lamb Lies Down On Broadway, Invisible Touch // Throwing it All Away, Land Of Confusion // Tonight Tonight Tonight, Mama // In Too Deep, Man On The Corner // Paperlate & Your Own Special Way // Go West Young Man* - **Genesis**
4. *Gloria // Solitaire* - **Laura Branigan**
5. *If I Were A Carpenter // Dream Lover* - **Bobby Darin**
6. *Killing Me Softly With His Song // Trade Winds* - **Roberta Flack**
7. *Sitting On The Dock Of The Bay // My Lover's Prayer* - **Otis Redding**
8. *Teach Your Children // Woodstock* - **Crosby, Stills, Nash & Young**
9. *Urgent // Waiting For A Girl Like You* - **Foreigner**
10. *When A Man Loves A Woman // Take Time To Know Her* - **Percy Sledge**

Genesis singles from the album *We Can't Dance* feature the same branding logo on the label but in purple, rather than the traditional red colour. I'm tagging Collective Soul on to the end of this list too cause their records have the same purple colours…

5.5 ~ Genesis We Can't Dance - US

1. *Hold On My Heart / Way Of The World, I Can't Dance / On The Shoreline & No Son Of Mine / Living Forever*
2. *Shine, (The) World I Know* - **Collective Soul**

Many of the singles from The Alan Parsons Project catalogue are US pressings and many (but not all) of those are from earlier albums…

5.6 ~ Parsons - US

1. *Psychobabble [EYE IN THE SKY]*
2. *Day After Day & I Wouldn't Want To Be Like You [I ROBOT]*
3. *Raven & System Of Dr. Tarr & Professor Feather [TALES OF MYSTERY & IMAGINATION]*
4. *Snake Eyes & Time [TURN OF A FRIENDLY CARD]*
5. *What Goes Up [PYROMANIA]*

It's very interesting to me that for my favourite group, Yes, except for UK pressings of *Don't Kill The Whale & Going For The One*, all the other singles I have from 1972 through 1980 are US pressings. Two of those pressings share Canadian and American versions, *America & And You & I. Into The Lens* shares UK & US pressings.

5.7 ~ Yes - US

1. *America / Total Mass Retain & And You & I [CLOSE TO THE EDGE]*
2. *Soon / Sound Chaser [RELAYER]*
3. *Wonderous Stories / Awaken [GOING FOR THE ONE]*
4. *Release Release / Don't Kill The Whale [TORMATO]*
5. *Into The Lens (I Am A Camera) / Does It Really Happen? & Run Thru The Light / Man In A White Car [DRAMA]*

Over many years, mostly in the eighties, I frequently travelled to Buffalo and visited the Record Theatre (mostly) and came away with the following…

5.8 ~ Bought I - Buffalo

1. *All I Want Is You* - **U2**
2. *Another Day In Paradise // Who Said I Would & I Missed Again / I'm Not Moving* - **Phil Collins**
3. *Black Dog // Misty Mountain Hop, Communication Breakdown // Good Times Bad Times, D'Yer Ma'Ker // The Crunge, Over The Hills & Far Away // Dancing Days & Rock & Roll // Four Sticks* - **Led Zeppelin**
4. *Fragile* - **Sting**
5. *Free Bird (Live) & Sweet Home Alabama* - **Lynyrd Skynyrd**
6. *Just The Way You Are // Anthony's Song (Movin' Out)* - **Billy Joel**
7. *MacArthur's Park* - **Richard Harris**
8. *Mr. Roboto* - **Styx**
9. *No Son Of Mine* - **Genesis**
10. *Rikki Don't Lose That Number* - **Steely Dan**
11. *Run Like Hell // Comfortably Numb & Money* - **Pink Floyd**
12. *Tubular Bells* - **Mike Oldfield**
13. *Where Evil Grows // Seasons In The Sun* - **Terry Jacks & The Poppy Family**

In 2017 and 2018, I noticed a newer label in the 45 collector bins, entitled Collectables, US pressings of double hits singles, in Narberth, PA.. Titles on this label include …

5.9 ~ Collectables Back To Back Hits - US

1. *Bad Moon Rising // Lodi, Have You Ever Seen The Rain // Hey Tonight & Proud Mary // Born On The Bayou* - **Creedence Clearwater Revival**
2. *Bette Davis Eyes // Goldfinger* - **Kim Carnes**
3. *Born To Wander // I Just Want To Celebrate* - **Rare Earth**
4. *Cry* - **Godley & Creme** // *Cry* - **Waterfront**
5. *Danny's Song // You Needed Me* - **Anne Murray**
6. *Goodbye Yellow Brick Road // Bite Your Lip & Nikita // Take Me To The Pilot* - **Elton John**
7. *I Heard It Through The Grapevine // You* - **Marvin Gaye**
8. *If I Ever Lose My Faith In You // Shape Of My Heart* - **Sting**
9. *Joker, The // Swingtown* - **The Steve Miller Band**
10. *Letter, The // Sweet Cream Ladies* - **The Box Tops**
11. *Piano Man // The Entertainer* - **Billy Joel**
12. *Reach Out I'll Be There // Standing In The Shadows Of Love* - **The Four Tops**
13. *Suddenly Last Summer // Only The Lonely* - **The Motels**
14. *Sunny* - **Bobby Bloom** // *Rockford Files* - **Mike Post**
15. *Take The Long Way Home // It's Raining Again* - **Supertramp**
16. *Tonight I Celebrate My Love* - **Peabo Bryson & Roberta Flack** // *For Your Love* - **Ed Townsend**
17. *Up On Cripple Creek // The Weight* - **The Band**
18. *We're An American Band // Some Kinda Wonderful* - **Grand Funk**
19. *You Little Trustmaker // Miss Grace* - **The Tymes**
20. *You've Lost That Lovin' Feeling // Unchained Melody* - **The Righteous Brothers**

Over the years, I have collected records in many different places, Toronto; Ottawa; throughout Ontario and BC; Stateside in Buffalo (Record Theatre), California, Clearwater, Florida (*Hotel California* - Eagles), East Hampton and Vermont ; and as far away as England and France. Here are some of the records I have bought Stateside…

5.10 ~ Bought II - US

1. *Dreamer* - **Supertramp** & *Jackie Blue* - The **Ozark Mountain Daredevils** - Hardwick, Vermont, 1976
2. *Hold Your Head Up* - **Argent** & *Lady* - **Styx** - Reno, Nevada, 1983
3. *Into The Lens / Does It Really Happen?* - **Yes** - Boo Boo Records, San Luis Obispo, California, 1983
4. *America // Your Move* - **Yes** - Nickelodeon Records & Tapes, Century City, California, 1983
5. *Drift Away 79* - **Dobie Gray** - Hollywood, California, 1983
6. *Iris & One Step Ahead* - **Split Enz** - East Hampton, Long Island, New York, 1983
7. *Hotel California & Life In The Fast Lane* - **The Eagles** - Dunn's Vinyl Museum, Clearwater, Florida, 1991,
8. *Turn Of A Friendly Card / Snake Eyes / Games People Play* [DEU] - **The Alan Parsons Project** - Atlantic Sounds, Daytona Beach, Florida, 2016
9. *Hearts* - **Marty Balin** // *What's Forever For?* - **Michael Murphy**

I Can Dream About You - **Dan Hartman** // *Rocky Topp* - **Terri Gibbs**
- Gallery Of Sound, Dickson City, Pennsylvania, 2024

In the spring of 1984, I travelled to England with my family. I remember going to the HMV flagship store on Oxford Street near Hyde Park in London and hearing the Cyndi Lauper hit *Time After Time.* As I travelled, I collected more than thirty singles from record stores across the country, during a two week stay.

The first single in the list I bought was *Breakfast In America,* at the Heron Square open air market in Richmond - Upon - Thames, England, a southwest suburb of London. I remember the day well. After touring Kew Gardens and Hampton Court in the rain, the sun was shining by the time I happened upon the market.

5.11 ~ Bought III - UK

1. *Breakfast In America, Dreamer (Live) & Take The Long Way Home (Live)* - **Supertramp**
2. *De Do Do Do De Da Da Da / The Sermon, Wrapped Around Your Finger / Someone To Talk To & Synchronicity II / Once Upon A Daydream* - **The Police**
3. *Duchess, Follow You Follow Me // A Trick Of The Tail, I Know What I Like (In Your Wardrobe) // Counting Out Time, Illegal Alien / Turn It On Again (Live), That's All // Taking It All Too Hard & Your Own Special Way / It's Yourself* - **Genesis**
4. *Genetic Engineering* - **Orchestral Manoeuvres In The Dark**
5. *Girl's School / Mull Of Kintyre, Live & Let Die & With A Little Luck* - **Wings**
6. *Going For The One & Wonderous Stories* - **Yes**
7. *Honky Tonk Train Blues* - **Keith Emerson**
8. *I Got The Message* - **Men Without Hats**
9. *Jerusalem & Peter Gunn (Live)* - **Emerson, Lake & Palmer**
10. *Let My Love Open The Door* - **Pete Townsend**
11. *Lucifer & Old & Wise* - T**he Alan Parsons Project**
12. *Sole Survivor* - **Asia**

The Scottish group Simple Minds make up the largest collection of UK pressings, twelve of them listed here...

5.12 ~ Simple Minds - UK

1. *Love Song [SONS & FASCINATION]*
2. *Someone Somewhere In Summertime [NEW GOLD DREAM]*
3. *Up On The Catwalk & Waterfront [SPARKLE IN THE RAIN]*
4. *Sanctify Yourself [ONCE UPON A TIME]*
5. *This Is Your Land & Waterfront 89 [STREET FIGHTING YEARS]*
6. *See The Lights [REAL LIFE]*
7. *Hypnotized & She's A River [GOOD NEWS FROM THE NEXT WORLD]*

Next up, I present a collection of U2 double hit singles released in the late 1980s by Island Records in the US. They were titled *Revival Of The Fittest.* The black sleeves with gold writing looked very similar to the artwork for both *The Joshua Tree* album and singles and *The Unforgettable Fire* Mini LP.

5.13 ~ U2 - *Revival Of The Fittest* - US

1. *Gloria (Live) // Sunday Bloody Sunday*
2. *I Will Follow (Live) // Pride (In The Name Of Love)*
3. *New Year's Day // Two Hearts Beat As One*
4. *I Still Haven't Found What I'm Looking For // Where The Streets Have No Name*
5. *With Or Without You // In God's Country*

The US also released the singles of *Stay (Faraway So Close)* from *Zooropa* And *Discotheque* and *Staring At The Sun* From *Pop*. Very similar to Revival are the double hit singles entitled Spun Gold (also made in the US) featuring both Elektra and Asylum artists.

5.14 ~ *Spun Gold - Elektra & Asylum* - US

1. *Already Gone // Tequila Sunrise & Take It Easy // Witchy Woman* - **The Eagles**
2. *Help Me // Free Man In Paris* - **Joni Mitchell**
3. *If You Don't Know Me By Now // You've Got It* - **Simply Red**
4. *Just What I Needed // Good Times Roll* - **The Cars**
5. *Kokomo* - **The Beach Boys** *// Tutti Frutti* - **Little Richard**
6. *L. A. Woman // Roadhouse Blues, Light My Fire // Love Me Two Times & Touch Me // Hello I Love You* - **The Doors**
7. *Taxi // Wold* - **Harry Chapin**
8. *Thank You For Being A Friend // Lonely Boy* - **Andrew Gold**

This group is something of a repeat. They are Warner Back To Back Hits, already noted in chapter two as *Warner 1 The Burbank Trees (wb), Warner 2 The Coloured Logo (wc) and The Green Label (wg)*.

5.15 ~ *Warner Back To Back Hits* - US

1. *Black Water // Take Me In Your Arms (Rock Me) (wc)* - **The Doobie Brothers**
2. *Classical Gas // Baroque - A - Nova (wc)* - **Mason Williams**
3. *Legs // Sharped Dressed Man (wc)* - **ZZ Top**
4. *Listen To The Music // Long Train Running (wb)* - **The Doobie Brothers**
5. *Moondance // Domino (wc)* - **Van Morrison**
6. *Tin Man // Don't Cross The River (wb)* - **America**
7. *Windy // Never My Love (wb)* - **The Association**
8. *You've Got A Friend // Steamroller (wg)* - **James Taylor**

And now for the Columbia double hit singles from the States.

5.16 ~ *CBS Silver Back To Back Hits* - US

1. *America // For Emily, Whenever I May Find Her & Mrs. Robinson // Old Friends & Book Ends* - **Simon & Garfunkel**
2. *Colour My World // I'm A Man, Make Me Smile // 25 Or 6 To 4 & Old Days // Brand New Love Affair* - **Chicago**
3. *Hold Your Head Up // God Gave Rock & Roll To You* - **Argent**
4. *Just The Way You Are // Moving Out (Anthony's Song)* - **Billy Joel**

5. *Mr. Tambourine Man // All I Really Want To Do* - **The Byrds**
6. *Oh Sherrie // Foolish Heart* - **Steve Perry**
7. *Peace Of Mind // Don't Look Back* - **Boston**
8. *Your Mama Don't Dance // Peace Of Mind* - **Loggins & Messina**

On a visit to Broke'n Records and TJ's CDs in Port Charlotte, Florida in the spring of 2023, I picked up no fewer than five back to back hit singles by Creedence Clearwater Revival on their Fantasy label. Medley USA itself includes four of the songs in this list...

5.17 ~ Creedence Fantasy Back To Back Hits
1. *Commotion // Green River*
2. *Fortunate Son // Down On The Corner*
3. *Medley USA (Travellin' Band / The Midnight Special / Born On The Bayou / Proud Mary / Lookin' Out My Back Door / Green River) // Bad Moon Rising*
4. *Proud Mary // Born On The Bayou*
5. *Travellin' Band // Who'll Stop The Rain?*

US pressings of records have always been an important part of my collection, right back to the very first two singles I bought in Hardwick, Vermont in 1976, *Dreamer / Bloody Well Right* by Supertramp and *Jackie Blue* by The Ozark Mountain Daredevils. My US collection includes more than three-hundred titles in this story. UK pressings are a distant second at less than one-hundred.

SIX

VINYL & CD

Records are much more visual than CDs. When you put a record on a turntable you can see where the song starts and where it finishes. Titles for singles are printed even larger than the same tracks on albums. You can almost read them as they go around and around the table. CDs for the most part are out of sight when they spin and only the track number and minute and second indicators tell you where you are.

While CDs and MP3s may be more convenient than vinyl, the sound has suffered. I'll take a vinyl skip over a digital skip, any day. The pops and scratches are gone but the digital sound has been flattened. Highs, lows and loud sections are diminished, while midranges and soft sections are exaggerated. There's not enough Oomph! The grass isn't greener on the other side! The warmth and contrast that is music is missing.

My obsession with good music, most notably vinyl versus CD is very similar to a landline phone versus a cell phone or a voice over IP (VOIP) network. While the landline costs more than the cell or VOIP, it excels in quality. If power goes down, you lose cell and VOIP but you still have land lines. What good is the cell or VOIP if the two people talking can't understand each other?

Put your CD into your computer and play it on windows media player and watch the sound bars go up and down. The bars are much livelier on homemade CDs converted from vinyl than they are on the store bought ones.

Some vinyl is easier to find than others. Some titles were not released to CD, either in their original format or at all. Like Jack Black said in *High Fidelity*[24] ... "It's almost impossible to find, especially on CD, yet another cruel trick played on all those dummies that got rid of their turntables." What separates those who grew up with vinyl and later cassettes and those who didn't is that music albums used to have sides to them, one and two and maybe even three and four and five and six. Younger generations now ask the

---

[24] *High Fidelity*, Film starring John Cusack & Jack Black, Touchstone, 2000

question "What does he mean when he says side two?" Even the way you listen to an album changes when you do (not) have sides.

iPods may give you thousands of songs at your fingertips but they don't sound as good. Remixed or remastered CD versions of albums that first appeared on vinyl are recognizable but clearly aren't the originals that we have come to know and love. Peter Weller remarked in *The New Age*[25] that DVD looks better than VHS but vinyl still sounds better than CD. In turn, CD sounds better than MP3s and other downloadable versions of music files.

The sound disparity applies more to popular music than it does classical music. The CD lends itself better to the normally cleaner and larger orchestral sound than it does to the often muddier and noisier sound of popular groups which are smaller. Most new popular music does not have a vinyl tradition so the CD sound becomes the benchmark.

Remember, music, specifically good music, never goes out of style. Music is something you listen to, not something you watch. So, listen to music separate from TVs and computers. Don't confuse music videos or DVDs with music in its pure form. Just like reading, listening enables you to create your own experiences and images, not someone else's'.

Start out with music that sounds as good as it can be. Don't settle for second best. What's cheap or a bargain (sound quality and price) may not turn out that way in the end. Remember, when you're older and you don't hear as well (pardon me?) then the better your music was to start with the better it's going to sound in the end. The difference between Vinyl and CD is difficult to explain and really only realized when you listen to it. If you can't tell the difference, just go with the CD sound. Like Supertramp said "*If Everyone Was listening...*"

I have offered the gift of music, vinyl records converted to CD, to many people. Some have accepted, while others have declined in favour of downloading their own music. But the CD sound of digital music is only a glimpse of what your music could really sound like. While Bluetooth technology makes music available more easily than ever before, the sound is absolutely forgettable, a distant relative of what it really should be.

Records, tapes, mix tapes, CDs, yellow 45 rpm adapters, Discwasher brushes are artifacts only for those who only think they are obsolete and not useful anymore. I prefer artifacts over quickly, neatly and conveniently but poorly recreated technical versions of what only resembles real music. No throwing away what is still useful. I have four Discwashers, my own and one from each of my dad, my father in-law and my friend Ian. Not all of what Anna Jane Grossman talks about in her book is *Obsolete.*[26]

How about finding a specific part of a song you want. The issue of dropping the needle down on a record and in the middle of a song aside, you can actually get to a specific part of a song faster on a record than you can on a CD, it's like telling the time on an analogue clock versus a digital one, you can see the time right away versus having to translate what the digital image looks like in analogue form. Also, the anticipation of the start of a song after the *Needle Drop [gem ch.6, ch.8 & 29.1]* is what vinyl is all about, not the instant start when you choose a CD track.

You can get to the start of a track faster on a CD but there's something missing where you had taped a record album and you had to wait to get to the song you wanted. Patience my friends. There is something neat about a record album, taking the inner sleeve out of the album jacket, taking the record out of the inner sleeve, putting the record on the turntable, starting the turntable spinning, cleaning the record, then dropping the needle, then the magic happens.

---

[25] *The New Age*, Film starring Peter Weller & Judy Davis, Warner, 1994
[26] *Obsolete*, Anna Jane Grossman, Harry N Abrahams, 2009

The *Needle Drop* is an awesome sound, so long as the volume isn't up too high. It is the sure fire sign that the song is about to begin. You can even hear the *Needle Drop* in songs like *Earache My Eye* (Cheech & Chong) and *Calling Occupants of Interplanetary Craft* (Klaatu)

Absolutely nothing compares with vinyl; sound like there never has been before and never will be again. Searching for your favourite singles or albums was hard work. But once you found what you were looking for, it was real and tangible. You could touch and hold on to your favourite singles and/or albums. It wasn't just an entry in a long list of songs on a hard drive. Once you bought your vinyl, then you couldn't wait to get home to open it and play it.

SEVEN

THE MUSICAL
EXPERIENCE / JOURNEY

Our musical experiences and journeys are all different. There are many kinds of music to choose from, classical, opera, popular, country, soul, rap, rock, folk, celtic…. It comes in many forms, vinyl, albums, singles, cassettes, eight tracks, reel to reel, CD, DVD, burned and downloaded. What is similar is that we all collect it, crave it, desire it and wish for it. Music is very soothing and therapeutic, especially when you are tired or not feeling well. It's like an alternate drug or medicine to get you through.

The experience of listening to different types of music is important. You start your listening in one area; it grows and morphs to include other areas or genres or types of music. It is important to balance things out by leaving your comfort zone for other types of music. Then you can get back to where you started and appreciate it. Songs sound especially good when you haven't listened to them for a while. Even listening to your favourite music, you often alternate between groups (albums) and compilations (radio or various tapes & CDs).

We all listen differently, firsthand on the radio, someone else plays it for you, or you buy the music unheard. Some music holds its appeal, some fades and some grows and improves with age. When you hear songs, to you they're either new or old. Even an old song can be new, hearing it for the first time. When you hear the songs, you think of people, places and events that happened years ago but so vivid it's like they just happened yesterday.

Sometimes we romanticize about the good old days that certain pieces of music will take us back there. But I prefer to think of it as a more familiar time to the present where you are now. Sure, parts of it may have been good but like in all stages of life there were difficult parts as well. So, in reality, the music takes you to familiar places, temporally and spatially, some good and others not so good.

It's amazing that whenever you heard a song when it was on the chart that you never really knew or even began to know at that moment just how great it was or would become. Only after it left the charts, months or even years later did you know. Sometimes it's like you couldn't or didn't know the greatness of a song because it was too close. Also, consider the staying power of songs that originally only charted for a few weeks but now live on in popularity all these years later.

Music is the ultimate nonprescription drug. Whether we are playing an instrument or listening to music, it has tremendous therapeutic and healing power, especially when we are sick and/or tired, to get us through the darker times in our lives and get us back to the lighter ones.

Times change, people change, moods change. Often you will focus on particular types of music for particular moments in time. Then you move on to other types of music again. There is nothing quite like listening to a piece of music that you haven't heard for a while. Moving between different types of music allows you to go back to certain genres and pieces, when you want to.

Many describe one decade or type of music so much better than another. Remember that you need all those differences to put them into context. Some may not have liked the music of the eighties. However, you can't take that in isolation. The music experience of the eighties put the experience of the seventies into context and paved the way for the music of the nineties and the 00s.

The same song will sound quite different depending on the context it's played in. The usual context is the album so you know which songs come before and after. However, songs in compilations or on radio sound quite different because you don't know which songs are going to come before and after that.

Songs by themselves have their own context. There may be parts of songs that you like better than others. However, what makes them better is that you experience the entire song and hear those parts along the way. Those parts have much less impact when just played by themselves.

Songs live on while the artists that created them are constantly changing. Groups don't stay the same. Membership changes so some stay while others go to other groups. Great groups don't exist in isolation. Some groups would never have existed if it weren't for groups that broke up before they came along.

Bubble gum music, pop music played mostly on the old AM radio, if you want to call it that, is just bubble gum. Music is like books and movies, sometimes you want something you can sink your teeth into and think about on a deeper level and other times you just want something simple so you can sit back and enjoy it and be entertained.

Musicians, especially those who play and record, talk about the moments when they achieve a certain "place", a chord or note or goal or plateau. And in doing so, sometimes the tape machine is *not* always running. It is in some of those moments that the same feeling or experience is never attained or experienced or visited quite the same way again.

The musical experience has changed greatly over the years. More than ever, it has changed from a listening experience to a visual one. People spend their money on big screen televisions and computers. They spend little money on stereo "Sound Systems". Listening to music has become a lost art. There are stories of teenagers playing music so loud on their iPods that they have permanent hearing loss. Also, watch out for those teens listening to their iPods while they rollerblade all over the place.

The music that we like/love does not always translate into the recording artists that we like/love. The rhetoric about groups and their music comes and goes. The online commentary is OK but how much do we need to know about whether the members of our favourite groups got along? It's the music not the rhetoric that lives on and matters most. It's amazing that it's been three decades now, the nineties, the 00s and the teens, that kids have not listened to new music on vinyl. Some have never even listened to music on CDS, only downloaded music.

The stereo has evolved over time. Consoles were big in the sixties. Components took over in the seventies. Components continued in the eighties but the look went from silver and metal to black. I call this

Components & The Mies Van Der Rohe Effect [gem]. Mies Van Der Rohe was a German American Architect. He designed black buildings like the IBM tower in Chicago and the components took on a similar look. The components also evolved into mini systems; components designed as a complete unit.

Stereo also went in a portable direction, first a bigger direction and second a smaller compact direction. The "BOOM BOXES" were big and heavy and "in your face loud". Then there was The SONY WALKMAN[27], a handheld portable audio cassette player that became all the rage. The SONY DISCMAN[28] (a CD WALKMAN) soon followed and into the 2000s came even smaller iPods and MP3 players. As the size of the unit decreased, the capacity for storage increased but the quality of the sound did not.

The next generation sometimes warms to the music of their parents / aunts / uncles. This way, the music is reborn, if you will, to that next generation, along with the album and concert sales. Music is also rediscovered when used in film / motion pictures / movies.

Some of us listen to music; others play it, still others both. Some are trained to read and play, like taking formal lessons. Some listen to others and imitate them (playing by ear), like sitting around the kitchen after dinner listening to your uncle play his guitar. It's kind of like the difference between the written and oral traditions of storytelling. No one is better than the other and good musicians are skilled and accomplished, regardless of how they learned their trade. If you've got it, you've got it, whatever you call it, the feel, the gift, the groove, the knack, the rhythm, the skill and the talent.

Some music makes us feel happy and other music makes us sad. Some winds us up, some calms us down. John Cusack said in *High Fidelity*,[29] "What came first, the music or the misery? Did I listen to pop music because I was miserable? Or was I miserable because I listened to pop music?"

Listening to many types of music from many different eras is important. It makes you a better, more appreciative listener. Some types you will listen to more than others but try to listen to as many as you can to make your musical experience and knowledge more complete. We need it all (good and not so good) to appreciate the other and enrich and experience our lives. What ties us together is that music grips us and moves us like nothing else. A day camp director once said a requirement for youth camp was you had to be able to play a musical instrument, not just sing. It was one way they could connect with the kids.

The universality of music is in the voices of those who sing it. The speaking voice is very different from the singing one. The result is that you cannot tell where somebody is from by their singing. They may speak a different language or English with a different accent. That doesn't matter. What does matter is how good the singing sounds and how much you enjoy listening to it. The musical journey is ultimately just that. Larry Mullen Jr. of U2 described *Rattle & Hum* that way.

Music, as a form of entertainment is one of the cheapest that there is, from the price it costs at the store, to the savings you get by playing music that isn't video related. There is much more energy spent in creating the visual image than the sound that goes with it. Sting said it best that you don't have to have an audience to play your own musical instrument or sing your own song.

You can see what has happened to radio. At one time, top 30/40 radio was a catch all for everything. You could turn on CHUM or CFRA and hear music from across the spectrum, country, soul, pop, rock, etc. It didn't matter if artists were more albums or single focused or more popular, when it came to the top 30/40, every song on the chart was unique and a separate piece that made up the chart "puzzle". Except for chart position, all songs were on an equal footing, no one more important than the next.

What we ended up doing was creating many different specialized stations so that you had to change the station if you wanted to hear a different type of music. The ultimate example of this is satellite radio

---

[27] Sony Walkman, 1979
[28] Sony Discman, 1984
[29] John Cusack quote from film *High Fidelity*, Touchstone, 2000

where there are separate stations for single artists like The Beatles, Elvis Presley, Bruce Springsteen and The Grateful Dead. It's basically listening to music that is stored in separate silos. You can't appreciate different kinds of music when you don't hear them back to back anymore, unless you have downloaded a wide variety of songs into the same mix.

EIGHT

THE ART OF RECORDING

This chapter is the first of three that talk about recording. Besides putting together a collection of your favourite songs, singles or otherwise, it was a way of putting them all together at your fingertips. Let's face it, recording your vinyl to analogue tape is the best way to back up your music and give your vinyl extended life.

The best scenario for taping is from turntable to tape deck. Belt and direct drive turntables are the best but the main thing is that you have one. I take it back; it does make a difference how good a turntable you have. The better the turntable, specifically the stylus (needle), the better the vinyl record will sound. In fact, you can almost tell by the "needle drop" just how good your vinyl is going to sound. It's the duo of art and science, the better the system (science) the better the song (art) sounds.

If you had a record player on a stereo that wasn't that good then the record itself wouldn't sound that good. Listening to the CD sound for the first time might have been much better than the poor sounding stereo that you used to listen to your records on. So, for many, the vinyl sound would have been inferior not superior to the CD sound they listen to now.

Every step of the way impacts the quality of the sound. You need good equipment all along the way, the turntable, the needle, the tone arm weight, the amp, the cables connecting the components to the amp, the loudness, the bass, the treble, the speakers, the wire from amp to speakers, the headphones, the tape deck, the tape brand, the tape bias, the recording level, Dolby on to tape, Dolby off to play back, the CD player.

One weak link in the process can change good sound back to normal or regular sound. Speakers aren't supposed to be on the floor, are they? Forget it, they sound better on the floor than they do anywhere else. Your stereo setup does become your very own. Every step of the way, as mentioned above makes your setup very unique. Both the make and style of components you have and where they are gives you a unique sound. Better equipment can give two results. Your better quality records will sound better while your poorer quality records will sound poorer.

When dubbing tape, use separate decks to control record levels and enhance sound. Record at normal speed or in real time. How can something recorded at high speed sound as good? Also, remember that when you are recording from vinyl you are doing so in real time. You can't do it any faster so just relax and enjoy the process because the results are awesome.

To be an audiophile and be conscious of high fidelity, you don't have to spend a fortune. My home stereo system is not that expensive but still puts out a good sound. My components include a turntable with a good needle/stylus, a 5 CD platter player, an amplifier, two double tape decks and a turntable to CD converter, a CD music burner and good speakers. Relatively speaking, I have not had to spend the fortune that is mentioned in articles to get good quality sound.

For Audio Tape, use high bias chrome, not normal bias and have Dolby noise reduction on when you record and off when you playback *[gem]*. Metal tapes are even better but are harder to find. The difference between chrome and metal is harder to tell than between regular and chrome.

At one time, Maxell made a UD XL chrome tape that sounded even better than the XL tape. In later years, they only made the XL tape. Maxell fans will remember the iconic television commercial with the butler playing the usual favourite of the man sitting on the chair, the classical music *The Ride Of The Valkyries*, by Richard Wagner and Giscard Rasquin. The man has to catch his glass of wine from falling as it travels the full distance from the front side to the back side of the sound speaker, as the music plays on. That commercial also confirmed the figure of the man in the chair as a legendary logo for Maxell.

TDK was similar in that they made an SA-X tape that sounded better than the SA but only made the SA version in later years. As late as 1988, Sony was still making four types of chrome tapes, UX, UX-S, UX-ES & UX Pro. Short tapes are the strongest if you can find them. Give your poor quality store bought pre-recorded tapes new life. Take the tape out of the old, pre-recorded shell and put it into a new blank shell *[gem]*.

There are many ways you can record with each of those giving you a slightly different result, vinyl to tape or CD, tape to tape or CD and CD to tape or CD. And every time you rerecord something you get the next generation of that same recording. When you tape from CD to CD you need to crank up the sound, or rather, the recording level. The reason for this is the original CD seems to be understated in many cases. Cranking up the sound only when you are playing it back doesn't compare with recording it loud enough to begin with.

The CD machine does not render the tape deck useless. Nothing could be further from the truth. While you may not record as much on the tape deck, you will continue to use it for playback for quite some time. When you make "Various" type tapes, not just albums to tapes, it takes much time and effort to do so. Wait until the tapes wear out, then you can recreate them on CD.

Remember also that once you put a collection of various songs together, just go with it. There are only so many hours in the day. Whether the recording is as good as you wanted it to be or not, you have the songs together so don't spend time reinventing the wheel. Wait until the tape/CD goes by the bye, then you can do a better job of it the next time you recreate it.

So, the same is true for CDs, Recreating your "Various" tapes, on to CD (either from vinyl or existing tapes) will also take much time and effort to do. For those with large tape collections of their vinyl, consider recording to CD only what you haven't already recorded to tape. You will need to be active in the recording of singles or marking the breaks between album tracks you record. In the end, vinyl to chrome audio tape (not CD) is still the best sound.

For years now, I have always taken it for granted that people with music collections taped them as well as listen to them but that's not so. Many have listened to their records, especially albums, over and over without taping them. It strikes me also that there is a difference between recording music versus downloading it. It seems the traditional recording of music is more of an art, whereas the downloading of music is more of a technical skill.

Records are the easiest sources to record from. You can see the start and finish for singles and the start and finish and breaks between the songs for albums. Just be sure to have enough light so you can see the breaks when it is an album that you are not so familiar with.

Lion and Atco Records had a label that was very similar to Atlantic Records. Yes, Atco was a subgroup of Atlantic Records. The visual image of these labels was classic and very simple, two distinctive halves, blue and yellow for Lion, yellow and white for Atco and black & red, black & gold (both Gold Standard in Canada and Oldies Series in the US) and black & purple for Atlantic. It was easy to find the start of the song after you lowered the needle and watched the record spin on the table.

I have created four Halves lists. First is a various list where five of the six are half labels, while Daffodil is almost a half label. Second are the black and gold version records of the Atlantic artists, (G) Gold Standard [Canada] & (O) Oldies Series [US]. The list for the black and red version of Atlantic would just be too big. Third are the almost halves of Motown and fourth are the almost halves of Arista Flashback.

First are the various, featuring Atco (A), Daffodil (DF), Deram (DR), Elektra (E), Famous Charisma (F), Lion (L) & Reprise (R).

8.1 ~ Label Halves I - Various

1. *Control Of Me & Cry Your Eyes Out* - **Les Emmerson** (L)
2. *Entangled / Ripples & Your Own Special Way* - **Genesis** (A)
3. *Hello I Love You* - **The Doors** (E)
4. *How Can You Mend A Broken Heart?* [US]*, I Started A Joke* [US] *& I've Gotta Get A Message To You* [US] - **The Bee Gees** (A)
5. *I Know What I Like (In Your Wardrobe) / Twilight Alehouse* [UK] *& Turn It On Again / Behind The Lines* [UK] - **Genesis** (F)
6. *I'm A Stranger Here* - **The Five Man Electrical Band** (L)
7. *It Don't Matter To Me / Call On Me* - **Bread** (E)
8. *Juicy Lucy & Knee Deep In Love* - **Klaatu** (DF)
9. *Love Is The Drug* - **Roxy Music** (A)
10. *Nights In White Satin & Tuesday Afternoon* - **The Moody Blues** (DR)
11. *Sideshow* - **Blue Magic** (A)
12. *Sunshine Of Your Love* [US] *& White Room* [US] - **Cream** (A)
13. *You Really Got Me* - **The Kinks** (R)

Second are the Atlantic Gold Standard (CAN) & Oldies Series (US)…

8.2 ~ Label Halves II - Atlantic Gold & Oldies

1. *Abacab // No Reply At All (G), Follow You Follow Me // Misunderstanding (G), I Know What I Like (In Your Wardrobe) // The Lamb Lies Down On Broadway (O) & Your Own Special Way // Go West Young Man (O)* - **Genesis**
2. *Against All Odds // I Cannot Believe It's True & In the Air Tonight // I Missed Again* - **Phil Collins** (G)
3. *America // Your Move (O), Owner Of A Lonely Heart // Leave It (G) & Roundabout // Your Move (G)* - **Yes**

4. *Black Dog // Misty Mountain Hop (G), D'Yer Ma'Ker // The Crunge (G), Fool In The Rain // Hot Dog (G), Immigrant Song // Hey Hey What Can I Do (G), Over The Hills & Far Away // Dancing Days (G), Rock & Roll // Four Sticks (G) & Whole Lotta Love // Living Loving Maid (G)* - **Led Zeppelin**

5. *Chiquitita // Winner Takes It All & The Name Of The Game // Take A Chance On Me* - **Abba** (O)

6. *Cold As Ice // Feels Like The First Time & Head Games // Dirty White Boy* - **Foreigner** (G)

7. *Gloria // Solitaire* - **Laura Branigan** (G) & (O)

8. *If I were A Carpenter // Dream Lover* - **Bobby Darin** (O)

9. *Killing Me Softly With His Song // Feel Like Making Love & Where Is The Love // First Time Ever I Saw Your Face* - **Roberta Flack** (G)

10. *Lucky Man // From The Beginning* - **Emerson, Lake & Palmer** (G)

11. *Only Women Bleed* - **Alice Cooper** (G)

12. *Save The Last Dance For Me // When My Little Girl Is Smiling & Under The Boardwalk // Ruby Baby* - **The Drifters** (O)

13. *Teach Your Children // Woodstock* - **Crosby, Stills, Nash & Young** (O)

14. *When A Man Loves A Woman // Take Time To Know Her* - **Percy Sledge** (G) & (O)

Fool In The Rain / Hot Dog was originally released on the swan song label but appeared in this list as a Gold Standard issue

Third are the almost halves of Motown…

8.3 ~ *Label Almost Halves I - Motown*

1. *ABC & I'll Be There* - **The Jackson 5**

2. *Ain't No Mountain High Enough* - **Diana Ross**

3. *All Night Long, Dancing On The Ceiling, Hello, Say You Say Me, Truly & You Are The One* - **Lionel Ritchie**

4. *Easy, Lady (You Bring Me Up), Nightshift, Oh No, Sail On, Still & Three Times A Lady* - **The Commodores**

5. *I Just Called To Say I Love You, I Wish & You Are The Sunshine Of My Life / Tuesday Heartbreak* - **Stevie Wonder**

6. *On The One For Fun* - **The Dazz Band**

7. *You Can't Hurry Love* - **The Supremes**

Fourth are the almost halves of Arista Flashback

8.4 ~ *Label Almost Halves II - Arista Flashback*

1. *All By Myself // Never Gonna Fall In Love Again* - **Eric Carmen**

2. *Eye In The Sky // Psychobabble & Time // Games People Play* - **The Alan Parsons Project**

3. *I'm A Believer // Pleasant Valley Sunday* - **The Monkees**

4. *Could It Be Magic // I Write The Songs & Mandy // It's A Miracle* - **Barry Manilow**

5. *Precious & Few* - **Climax**

There is another group of labels that have an interesting look but also are missing an important piece of information. The UK versions of Arista, Famous Charisma, Mercury & Virgin are included here. The labels are described as debossed or injection molded, black detail including words were grooved right into either a silver or blue *(/bl)* background. Alan Parsons had a couple of singles with both silver and blue versions *(Arista /sl & /bl)*. However, all other singles are assumed to be silver unless noted. Except for *This Is Your Land* by Simple Minds (Virgin), none of these singles have a time stamp on them. In the world of recording, this can be problematic, unless of course you know all the time stamps of your records by heart. Here they are…

8.5 ~ Label UK No Time

1. *Don't Mess With Doctor Dream, Hold Me Now & Revolution* - **The Thompson Twins** - Arista *(/bl)*
2. *Duchess, Misunderstanding, Spot The Pigeon & Tell Me Why* - **Genesis** - Famous Charisma
3. *Eye In The Sky (/sl & /bl), Lucifer, Old & Wise (/s & /b), Prime Time & Stereotomy* - **The Alan Parsons Project** - Arista
4. *Groovy Kind Of Love* - **Phil Collins** - Virgin
5. *Head Over Heels (/bl), I Believe & Mad World* - **Tears For Fears** - Mercury
6. *See The Lights & This Is Your Land* - **Simple Minds** - Virgin
7. *You Sexy Thing* - **Hot Chocolate** - EMI

With tapes and CDs as sources you need to be listening and have a good idea of where the breaks in the songs are. Recording takes patience. You have to combine the hard skills of doing the recording itself (managing the turntable tone arm and the tape deck controls and constantly looking and listening) with the soft skills of choosing the songs that will go together to make the play list. Recording is an ongoing skill that has to be done on a regular basis in order to achieve a skill level of any kind. The sound itself is like life, some parts of it are smooth and other parts are rough. Famous quotes over the years include "I didn't know there was a difference between mono and stereo or type 1 and type 2 audio tapes."

Chrome or otherwise, you will know right away the quality of both the tape you are using and the job you do recording on to it when you are taping acoustic rather than electric instruments, especially guitar and piano. The acoustic sound on tape or CD is either really good or just ordinary, nothing in the middle. Poorer quality or damaged tape will not pass the `acoustic test`.

Audio Tape has now survived for a long time and is still a force to be reckoned with when it comes to modern culture. The 2010 movie *Leap Year*[30] is a testament to this. When unruly car passenger Anna (Amy Adams[31]) takes Declan's' (Matthew Goode[32]) audio tape out of the tape machine and tosses it out of the car window, Declan screams "No one touches the music" and slams on the car brakes. His car is too old to have a CD player, just an audio tape deck. Also, modern day police forces conducting interviews still prefer audio tape recordings over those recorded to CD.

I am impressed by copies of store bought cassettes that I have made on to chrome tapes. While I have played the copies time and time again, leaving the original for a rainy day, the copies still stand up and sound better.

---

[30] *Leap Year*, Film, Universal, Spyglass, 2010
[31] Amy Adams, American Actress, 1974
[32] Matthew Goode, British Actor, 1978

Recording or making a compilation tape is a complicated process. John Cusack noted in *High Fidelity*, "The making of a compilation tape … is hard to do and takes ages longer than it might seem. " Recording, specifically from vinyl, is an addiction, especially the compilation or mix format. Once you get the itch to record (the most basic form of backing up your vinyl) you're hooked. It's always there. It may speed up at times, slow down at other times but it never goes away.

Recording, especially the compilation tapes and CDs, is messy. It's all part of the artistic/creative process. First, who is the tape for and what's the theme? What songs do you want and which order do they go in? Second, is the List. It starts out neat and ends up a mess! Third, are the sources (vinyl / cassette / CD). Take them out of their sleeves / jackets / cases and the recording session soon resembles a war zone. Fourth, every song is different and so are the recording levels.

The Classic Vinyl rock station on Sirius XM satellite radio plays the first generation of classic rock songs. The Classic Rewind rock station on Sirius XM satellite radio plays the next generation of classic rock songs. I started taping my records less than a year after I started collecting them so while Sirius makes the distinction between vinyl and rewind over different periods of time, there has never been a separation for me between collecting records and taping them.

The creation and logging of song lists becomes something by itself. It starts out in one direction and heads off somewhere else. Ultimately it's the list that becomes the "Thing" or the moment in history. It' becomes a unique collection or selection of songs, captured so it can be relived later, over and over, especially in the case of a compilation CD or tape that dies. The remedy / solution is "Just make another one".

The list, the moment in history is something that you create. You put the songs together in the order that you want, no one else. So, in the end, the result is yours. It's something you have created, something you have accomplished. It doesn't matter how many times you hear a particular song or group of songs, hearing them in a different order or context gives the songs a new sound.

The various or mixed tapes became works of art. First was the sound which may or may not have been well recorded, both good and poor segues between songs, some too loud, some too quiet, etc. Second was the visual or art part which may or may not have been well designed and or put together. Some may have been carefully designed complete with song lists while some may have been thrown together with songs scribbled down as the recorder went through the process.

When you first put the songs together you don't think that you'll keep the tape that you might change it around and make it better but you don't get back to it so those songs stay together and become a fixture over a longer and longer period of time. In creating tapes for someone else, you are putting together something that sounds a certain way to you but a different way to the receiver. You can search forever for the best group of songs but remember that perfection slows down the process of ever making the tape.

There are three things to remember when you are making a compilation tape, backup, backup and backup. You never know when you might want to send the same compilation tape to someone else. It's easier to go to tape first then to CD. Also, tapes that take you hours, days, weeks, even months to make, can literally be unraveled by little hands in a matter of seconds or minutes. Albums are different, just go from album to CD.

Going back to the previous section, I took it for granted that everyone taped their records. I also took it for granted that they did compilation tapes. However, what often stands in the way is the time it takes to organize the songs that make up the compilation. Along with that is the space you need to keep track of all of those different records.

As time goes by, people have less space to store their music and less time to record it. That's where downloading comes in because you can store everything on your computer and you don't have to do it in real time. You can actually do it much faster than that. However, remember that you are left with poorer sound and give/sell/throw away, most of the time, people sell or throw away, rather than give away. Also, more time and thought and effort goes into a compilation tape/CD than downloading a boatload of songs.

Going back to the music being therapeutic, there is much to do to gather and record what goes into a compilation tape but that's the beauty of it, you can pull it out and listen to it whenever you want, to help you while you are at home or at work or again even when you are not feeling well to get you into a better place and frame of mind.

When you go from vinyl to digital you have different choices. The truest sound is going from a music machine to a CD. No computer. This way you actually feel like you are listening to your original vinyl but on a CD instead. You can also convert from vinyl to CD using a computer to make files of each song. Remember that you need enough space for your computer as well as your turntable to do this.

However, forget about the software that cleans up the sound, all those pops and scratches (let's call them the noise). When you take away the noise, you take away the imperfections that bring fullness and richness and warmth to the sound. You take the sound farther and farther away from what it was originally. What you end up with is sound so clean it's sterile and noticeably different but not as good as the original. I would rather listen to a handful of songs with pops and scratches than a boatload of cleaned versions of songs. Don't confuse a cleaner sound with a better sound. Music is not always neat and tidy so why clean it up?

In this day and age of lighting fast technology, the CD making machine and process are a throwback to the old days. Forget about downloading what you want when you want and having it somewhere on your hard drive or your iPod, this is about skill and craftsmanship, about setting different levels for each song you record, about taking time and care in creating a work of art that you can hold on to when you are done.

The best thing about recording is the feeling of accomplishment, that after an hour or so of recording, you made something and it's something tangible that you can be proud of and feel good about. Sometimes it's good, sometimes it's not so good but it's still yours and no one can take that away from you. I've been recording so long; I feel like I could do it in my sleep. However, there are still times when it takes much attention and concentration.

The other thing that makes recording pleasing is the adrenaline rush you get. Something about the live aspect of recording that isn't like anything else. It's the choreography of playing the records and recording them just the way you want. Regardless of how many times you record something, even the exact same song from the exact same record, it's not quite the same each time. The recording level, the needle weight, how soon you start and finish the recording is slightly different each time.

Burning / Dubbing / Recording / Taping popular music is straightforward because the levels within one piece are pretty comparable. Taping classical music is more complicated. There is much variance in tempo and volume there. Progressive Rock Music is often varied as well. This means knowing and/or learning the music ahead of time so you can set the levels properly.

Taping itself is a very selfish time consuming process. Some may say you need to look after the important things in your life like other people before indulging in things like recording. However, making tapes and having them to listen to helps you push your way through life to get to the important things.

NINE

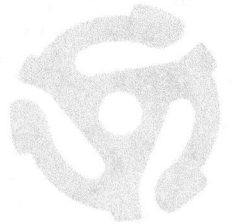

THE ART OF
COLLECTING

Collecting (acquiring, gathering, labeling, locating, managing, organizing, sorting, storing) is not for the faint of heart. It's time consuming but most of all it's a passion and a labour of love, one that can only be explained and understood by other collectors who have lived the experience. Collecting is like making order out of chaos, making sense of the mess. It's something you can do yourself and that you ultimately have control of. Collections start out looking one way and evolve into something quite different.

Collecting music, especially vinyl, is something that has to be experienced, it can't be explained. The journey to find the music can be as thrilling as having it in the end. Acquiring and collecting music does not always follow political correctness. In fact, if collecting music was a reflection of artists we approved of as persons; collections would be a lot different and a lot smaller, maybe even non-existent.

One of the best things about having a collection is that it's yours and it's something that you see and touch. Looking through your collection for titles to listen to and/or to tape is a very therapeutic process. If things are stressful, you can go and "visit" with your record collection. Sorting it different ways keeps you thinking and gives your collection a new look each time. For the most part, I sort my collection alphabetically by artist.

The type of collecting you do makes all the difference. Singles are the most tactile of all, they have only paper sleeves and you can slide the record out to look at them. Albums are next, the basic size is the same, but some are thinner and some are thicker. Some have shrink wrapped covers; others still have an extra outer plastic sleeve. Cassettes and CDs are a distant third and fourth, both come in solid plastic type boxes with shrink wrap and there is little difference from one to the next, similar in style and makeup to a carton of cigarettes.

Labels for singles were usually the record company name with the song title and artist stamped on to it. 1050 CHUM charts even had the record labels listed for every song on the CHUM 30. On occasion, singles like Ringo's' *Photograph* would have their own special labels. Special labels were more common with LPS than with singles, also probably because the hole in the middle of an album was a lot smaller than the hole in the middle of a single. The larger singles hole would distort a custom label more than with an album.

Collecting is ultimately a way of (not) dealing with what's going on around you. It's a way of coping. But it's also a way of running away because you can't always cope or deal with all the babble, gibberish, malarkey, rhetoric, rubbish, shenanigans, stories and whatever else that life often has to offer.

Immersing yourself in music can also be viewed as a very self-indulgent activity. Is it a poor alternative to actually dealing with something or escapism? Maybe. But at the same time, it all helps in getting us back to where we need to be, in a better place. Collecting and /or getting rid of records is very far from "the green thing to do".

Collecting is something that occurs over a long period of time and is continuous. It never really stops. The artists you collect changes over time as well. Sometimes, collecting is current. You collect records when they are current because they were current, you wanted them right then and you could afford them. You didn't collect either what you didn't like or couldn't afford at the time. Collecting is the ultimate in excess, collecting both what you do and don't want in the end. There is very little about collecting that resembles rational.

Other times and in most cases, for most people, collecting is more latent in nature. Long periods of time and the availability of money make it possible for you to collect more music and specifically older music. Either you liked it at the time but couldn't afford it or you didn't like it at the time so you didn't collect it. Now, you still like it and have the money or you didn't like it before but now you do and you have the money.

Another part of collecting was the visual aspect of albums. They were large in size so the artwork was created, in most cases, to fill that space. *ALBUM COVER ALBUM*[33] was published in several volumes celebrating the album cover. The same album covers in CD size just aren't the same. This same sentiment has been lamented by many. You know they are the same records but visually just don't come close.

Make sure that when you loan out your records that the borrowers know how to look after them. Record cleaning fluid is ok when used in moderation. If you use too much you can mark and even damage the records enough that they can't be played anymore. Then you will need to go searching for those titles again. In a recent documentary about collecting vinyl, some do not feel they are focused collectors just people who enjoy music and accumulate vinyl at the same time.

What's next? How can collectors be eco-friendlier and greener? What is the "Green Thing to do?" Long live the turntable, the tape deck and the 45 RPM record. Think of the passion that goes into collecting and think about whether you need to keep collecting and who is it benefiting.

7 inch vinyl is viewed by many as a waste of vinyl. If you're going to make a record, why not make an LP, it doesn't take that much more vinyl to make an LP than it does a single. Well, maybe but then you wouldn't have the stronger single sound, the multiple copies (convenient when you are playing and taping a song numerous times) or different versions of the song and/or the sleeve.

The best way is to reduce / reuse / recycle. If you have an old turntable and/or tape deck that works, hold on to it and/or give it to someone that would love to use it. The same with your 45zz. Hold on to them or pass them on to someone who can use them. Share the love (*I Believe In Music* ... "music is love and love is music if you know what I mean" - Gallery).

---

[33] Album Cover Album, Hipgnosis, 1977

A close second to that piece would be *The Last Resort* (Eagles). Using America as the backdrop, people have immigrated to the United States for years. Many of them travelled west. But once they reached the Pacific there was nowhere else to go. "There is no more new frontier, we have got to make it here, we satisfy our endless needs to justify our bloody deeds."

As Sir Ken Robinson, with a PHD in education and a proponent for creativity and innovation in education,[34] described the learning process as "Organic" not "Linear" (*Technology Education Design [TED] Conference 2006*[35] & *2010*[36]), the process of collecting can be described in much the same, way. When you start out collecting you might have a definite idea of where you want your collection to go, a "Linear destination". However, once the collection starts growing it takes on an organic quality and often times ends up somewhere completely different.

---

[34] Sir Ken Robinson, British Education Innovator, 1950-2020
[35] TED Conference 2006, Monterey, California
[36] TED Conference 2010, Long Beach, California

TEN

THE
CANADIAN CORNER

This chapter is the first of ten that focus on groups. In the summer of 1973, when I was still buying just singles, 7UP did a promotion they called *Rock Caps.*[37] Under the cap of each 7UP product you bought was the face of a musician in one of five well known Canadian bands at the time. The bands included April Wine, Crowbar, Edward Bear, The Guess Who & Lighthouse.

A short time later, Columbia and 7UP teamed up to make the album *Together*, featuring the music of four of the five groups listed above, April Wine (*Bad Side Of The Moon*), Crowbar, Edward Bear (*Fly Across The Sea, Masquerade & You, Me & Mexico*) & Lighthouse *(Sunny Days & You Girl)*.

Lady Run Lady Hide was the very first single that I ever bought by April Wine, on the Aquarius label, back in the days when the label was a combination of light blue and green, with the figure of Aquarius right in the artwork. In July of 1977, I saw them perform at the Ottawa Civic Centre. Kim Mitchell of Max Webster and Q107 fame used to refer to April Wine as Myles Goodwin & The Whiners.

As he collected albums, Michael (audiophile, bandmate, classmate, teammate, record store owner and musician extraordinaire) sent me singles to Ottawa, the ones he felt he didn't need anymore. Two of those were double hit US singles with blue labels by Bachman - Turner Overdrive, *Blue Collar/Let It Ride* and *Takin' Care Of Business/You Ain't Seen Nothin' Yet.* Michael also created for me a replica of the *BTO Greatest Hits* album cover.

Last Song (Edward Bear) and *You're So Vain* (Carly Simon) were the very first two 45 RPM records that I ever bought and I still own them both. It's interesting that *Last Song* was sold in a Picture Sleeve format, something that only became much more popular in the 1980s. As mentioned earlier, Edward Bear

---

[37] 7UP Rock Caps, Canadian promotion, 1973.

also released picture sleeves for *Fly Across The Sea, Last Song, Masquerade & Walking On Back*. *Last Song & Walking on Back* had lyrics printed on the back of their picture sleeves (3.6).

In 1986, a family friend took a music course at Carleton University.[38] This was the first time a rock music course had ever been offered at a university. It was a course about the history and the roots of rock and roll music. She even shared some printouts of required readings from the course.

She also went to school with Les Emmerson, of The Five Man Electrical Band and remarked how he was more of a mischief maker than he was a student. Longtime friend, audiophile, bandmate, classmate & teammate Ian got to know Les years later and he said that if it weren't for Les meeting his wife to be and getting married to her that he wouldn't be alive today. Dean Hagopian, a past member of The Five Man Electrical Band (early on known as the Staccatos), was also a DJ for CFGO radio in Ottawa in the mid-1970s.

If there was one Green Rock Anthem for the ages that you would pick, what would it be? Well for me it would have to be, without a doubt, the 1973 song *I'm A Stranger Here* (The Five Man Electrical Band). It's a picture painted by aliens visiting earth, commenting even then that we had gone a long way in screwing up what was once a Paradise of a place.

I never saw The Guess Who perform live but did see Randy Bachman perform live in Stratford in 2010. His performance was part of the 2010 Hockey Day In Canada celebrations. He played a concert full of both Bachman - Turner Overdrive songs (*Let It Ride, Takin' Care Of Business & You Ain't Seen Nothing Yet*), as well as Guess Who songs (*No Time & Undun*).

I started collecting records on the Nimbus 9 label, featuring grapes on a beige background, after Randy Bachman had left the band to form Bachman - Turner Overdrive. The first record I collected records on that label was *Follow Your Daughter Home*.

Burton Cummings said it best on touring into the 90s and the 00s. "I look out into the audience and see all these teenagers singing our songs. They weren't even alive when these songs were recorded and they know the words better than we do."

The Canadian group Lighthouse modelled themselves after Chicago, featuring a horn section and violins. In late 1973, I purchased my first single by the group, *Pretty Lady*, on the GRT label, the first with Skip Prokop singing the lead vocals. Other artists to record on that label were Ian Thomas (*Painted Ladies and Long Long Way*), Shooter (*I Can Dance* and *Train*) and James Leroy (*Touch Of Magic* and *Make It All Worthwhile*).

In 1974, Lighthouse released *Good Day* on the GRT label, featuring the title track by the same name and *Got A Feeling*. Both songs charted on the CFGO Top 30 but did not chart in Toronto. In the summer of 1975 at Britannia Park in Ottawa,[39] I watched former Lighthouse member Bob McBride perform a concert with his own band. The concert was just a few minutes away from Crystal Bay where my dad worked at Bell Northern Research,[40] in the days long before Northern Telecom.

In the summer of 2018, I purchased a previously owned copy of the US version of the album *Good Day*. While the music on the album is identical to the Canadian album, the artwork of the US album is very different. The US album features a rural setting but the Canadian album features a picture of Skip Prokop, amid flashy looking graphics.

Based On The 7UP promotion in 1973, here's a summary of songs that I have just talked about…

[38] Rock Music, Course 30.227, Carleton University, 1986, Dr. John Shepherd, Course Co-ordinator.
[39] Britannia Park, City Of Ottawa, Ontario, 1975.
[40] Bell Northen Research, Carling Avenue, Ottawa, Ontario, 1973.

10.1 ~ The 7UP Canadian Corner

1. *Bad Side Of The Moon, Cum Hear The Band, I Wouldn't Want To Lose Your Love &
   Lady Run Lady Hide* - **April Wine** - Blue & Green Aquarius label
2. *Clap For The Wolfman, Dancing Fool, Follow Your Daughter Home, Glamour Boy,
   Orly, Running Back To Saskatoon & Star Baby* - **The Guess Who** - Purple & Beige
   Nimbus 9 label
3. *Fly Across The Sea, Last Song, Masquerade & Walking On Back* - **Edward Bear** -
   Capitol Picture Sleeves
4. *Hat's Off To The Stranger, Pretty Lady, Sunny Days & You Girl* - **Lighthouse** - Red
   White & Black GRT label
5. *Oh What A Feeling* - **Crowbar**

In the 1990s, I spent much time recording music videos from Much Music and Much More Music on to VHS tapes. In chapter 14, I will detail the video compilation for U2. Here, I put together an intended list of videos by Bryan Adams but never actually compiled them. Here is that list...

10.2 ~ Bryan Adams Music Videos

All For Love (/w **Sting & Rod Stewart**), *Cuts Like A Knife, Reggae Christmas, Run To You, Somebody, Summer Of '69 & This Time*

Finally, a nod to those Canadian artists that were not so well known outside of Canada and if they were, these hits were not so well known outside of Canada.

10.3 ~ Canadiana - The Lesser Knowns I - The 70s

1. *Armageddon & Night To Remember* - **Prism**
2. *Blue Collar* - **Bachman - Turner Overdrive**
3. *California Jam, Juicy Lucy, Knee Deep In Love & We're Off Ya Know* - **Klaatu**
4. *Can You Give It All To Me & Hold On Lovers* - **Myles & Lenny**
5. *Carry Me, Devil You, Minstrel Gypsy, Oh My Lady & Wild Eyes* - **The Stampeders**
6. *Control Of Me, Cry Your Eyes Out & Watching The World Go By* - **Les Emmerson**
7. *Dance A Little Step* - **Mashmakhan**
8. *Daytime Nighttime & First Cut Is The Deepest* - **Keith Hampshire**
9. *Diamonds Diamonds, Let Go The Line & A Million Vacations* - **Max Webster**
10. *Do It Right & Pretty City Lady* - **Bob McBride**
11. *Finally (With You)* - **The Cooper Brothers**
12. *(A) Good Song* - **Valdy**
13. *Goodbye Superdad* - **Bill King**
14. *Hold On & Long Long Way* - **The Ian Thomas Band**
15. *I Can Dance (Long Tall Glasses) & Train* - **Shooter**
16. *I Just Want To Make Music* - **Ken Tobias**
17. *I'm A Stranger Here & Werewolf* - **The Five Man Electrical Band**
18. *I'm Running After You* - **Major Hoople's Boarding House**
19. *It Wouldn't Have Made Any Difference & One Night Lovers* - **Tom Middleton**
20. *Make Me Do (Anything You Want)* - **A Foot In Cold Water**

21. *Molly* - **Bearfoot**
22. *Raise A Little Hell, Two For The Show & We're Here For A Good Time* - **Trooper**
23. *Sitting On A Poor Man's Throne & You're Still The One* - **Copper Penny**
24. *(A) Touch Of Magic* - **James Leroy**
25. *What The Hell I Got* - **Pagliaro**
26. *Wildflower* - **Skylark**
27. *You Can't Dance* - **Jackson Hawke**

10.4 ~ Canadiana - The Lesser Knowns II - The 80s

1. *Arias & Symphonies, Romantic Traffic & Smiling In Winter* - **The Spoons**
2. *At The Feet Of The Moon & Rise Up* - **The Parachute Club**
3. *Black Cars* - **Gino Vanelli**
4. *Black Stations, White Stations* - **M&M**
5. *Boy Inside The Man* - **Tom Cochrane & Red Rider**
6. *Cinderella Man, Limelight, Spirit Of Radio, Subdivisions & Tom Sawyer* - **Rush**
7. *Crying Over You, Doesn't Really Matter & Standing In The Dark* - **Platinum Blonde**
8. *Echo Beach* - **Martha & The Muffins**
9. *Eyes Of A Stranger* - **The Payolas**
10. *(The) Flyer, Scratching The Surface & What Do I Know* - **Saga**
11. *Go For A Soda & Patio Lanterns* - **Kim Mitchell**
12. *I Got The Message & I Like* - **Men Without Hats**
13. *Kid Is Hot Tonight, Turn Me Loose & Working For The Weekend* - **Loverboy**
14. *Kiss You (When It's Dangerous)* - **Eight Seconds**
15. *Let It Go* - **Luba**
16. *Listen To The Radio* - **The Pukkah Orchestra**
17. *Lovers In A Dangerous Time* - **Bruce Cockburn**
18. *Runaway (With My Love) 12* - **Tapps**
19. *Showdown At Big Sky & Somewhere Down The Lazy River* - **Robbie Robertson**
20. *Stay In The Light* - **Honeymoon Suite**
21. *Under My Thumb* - **Streetheart**
22. *Young & Restless* - **Prism**

Cycling back to the 7UP groups, here are their lesser known tunes...

10.5 ~ Canadiana - The Lesser Knowns III - The 7UP Groups

1. *Bad Side Of The Moon, Cum Hear The Band, I Wouldn't Want To Lose Your Love & Lady Run Lady Hide* - **April Wine**
2. *Fly Across The Sea, Masquerade & Walking On Back* - **Edward Bear**
3. *Follow Your Daughter Home, Glamour Boy, Orly & Running Back To Saskatoon* - **The Guess Who**
4. *Hat's Off To The Stranger, Pretty Lady & You Girl* - **Lighthouse**

ELEVEN

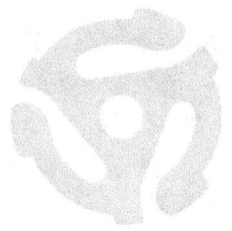

CHICAGO &
THE BEATLES

James Pankow, trombone player for Chicago, wrote most of Chicago's horn arrangements. In June of 1974, CFRA featured Chicago for their very first *special of the month.* The special featured most of the group's hits through their first six albums.

11.1 ~ 1ST CFRA Special Of The Month - Chicago
Beginnings, Does Anybody Really Know What Time It Is?, I'm A Man, Questions
67 & 68, 25 Or 6 To 4, Colour My World, Make Me Smile, Free, Lowdown, Dialogue,
Saturday In The Park, Feeling Stronger Everyday & Just You'n Me.

That same month, *(I've Been) Searchin' So Long* was at the top of the charts. It served as a watermark, highlighting the vocalists, the emergence of Peter Cetera and the fading of Terry Kath.

Early in 1975, I bought *Chicago's Greatest Hits*, my first current album by that group. It's interesting that for a greatest hits album, two of the songs were album versions, *25 Or 6 To 4* and *Beginnings.* Then I created my very first singles compilation tape by Chicago, *(I've Been) Searchin' So Long, 25 or 6 to 4, Feeling Stronger Everyday, Just You'n Me, Saturday In The Park & Where Do We Go From Here*

Later that year I also bought *Chicago Gold*, a piano/guitar/vocals collection of Chicago songs. It included more groups of songs than those found on *Chicago's Greatest Hits (IX).* In the spring of 1975, classmate and longtime friend John Kollar (John K, not to be confused with John Kay of Steppenwolf) and I went on a school band trip to KCI in Kitchener, [41] where many of us witnessed the excitement and skill of

---

[41]Kitchener Collegiate Institute, Kitchener, Ontario, 1855

Collage.[42] In early 1976 our high school stage band in Ottawa played music by Chicago entitled *Chicago Ork.*[43]

In 1975 Chicago released *Anthology One* piano music,[44] including all the songs from albums one through four. Years later, I bought that same book. There were facsimiles of each of the album covers inside. From those pages I made five of my own picture sleeves *Make Me Smile // 25 Or 6 To 4 (Chicago II), Does Anybody Really Know What Time It Is? // Free & Lowdown (Chicago III) and 25 Or 6 To 4 (Chicago IV).*

In the summer of 1977, I watched a *Chicago live special* on TV at the Caribou Ranch where they had recorded several of their albums.[45] That same summer I gave away many of my Chicago singles to a friend (the same five mentioned earlier). After buying *the Transit Authority*, *#8* and *#9 (Greatest Hits)*, I did not feel the need to keep most of those singles. It would be another ten years before I would collect many of those same singles that I gave away.

I have the New York Times advertisement for Chicago appearing at the Aqueduct Raceway in July of 1979.[46] It was originally scheduled for Belmont Park Raceway but there were so many fans who wanted to see the concert that it had to be relocated.

In the summer of 1980, I collected many double hit singles released in the seventies, entitled CBS Hall Of Fame *Beginnings // Questions 67 & 68, Brand New Love Affair // Old Days, Colour My World // I'm A Man, Does Anybody Really Know What Time It Is? // Free and (I've Been) Searchin' So Long // Call On Me.*

For most of the Hall Of Fame singles, the month and year the song was charted was noted on the record itself. Most were on a dark red background, while others were on a light blue background.

I saw Chicago live three times, at the CNE in 1983 and 1987 and 2015 at the Molson Amphitheatre (Budweiser Stage). In 2015, they played with Earth, Wind & Fire, in one of the best concerts I have ever seen. Earth, Wind & Fire played the first set, Chicago played the second set and both bands played together for a six number encore, including tunes like *25 or 6 to 4, Does Anybody Really Know What Time It Is?, September & Shining Star.*

I saw Chicago and Earth Wind & Fire again in 2024 at the Budweiser Stage. Some of the Earth, Wind & Fire setlist included *After The Love Has Gone, Boogie Wonderland, Got To Get You into My Life, Let's Groove, Shining Star, Sing A Song & That's The Way Of The World.* The Chicago setlist included no fewer than seventeen songs. Once again the highlight of the show was both bands together playing six encore *(en)* numbers. The final number was a rocking version of 25 Or 6 To 4. Here is that list…

11.2 ~ *Earth, Wind & Fire & Chicago - 2024 Toronto*
Introduction, Dialogue, Call On Me, If You Leave Me Now, Ballet For A Girl In Buchannon (Make Me Smile & Colour My World), Old Days, Hard Habit To Break, You're The Inspiration, Beginnings, I'm A Man, Just You'n Me, Hard To Say I'm Sorry, Saturday In The Park, Feeling Stronger Everyday, Free (en), Does Anybody Really Know What Time It Is? (en) & 25 Or 6 To 4 (en).

My collection of Beatles records was latent or an afterthought if you will. I never listened to the Beatles while they were together and most of the albums I bought were double album compilations, *Red*

---

[42] Collage, Jazz Band, Kitchener Collegiate Institute, 1975
[43] Chicago Ork, High School Jazz Band Music, 1976
[44] *Chicago Anthology One*, piano, vocals, chords, Hal Leonard, 1975
[45] *Chicago Live At The Caribou Ranch*, 1977
[46] *Chicago Live At The Aqueduct Raceway*, 1979

1962-1966, Blue 1967-1970, Rock'n Roll Music, Love Songs and *Live At The BBC (cassette)*. If this story is much about singles, rather than albums, then why is my Beatles singles collection so small? Well, the size of the catalogue was daunting at first, especially when I was younger and didn't have all that money to spend on it. As the years went by, I just never got around to collecting any more.

I still have the original *Red* and *Blue* stickers listing all the songs on both of *1962-1966* and *1967-1970* albums. It's impressive that the *Blue* and *Red* albums rank second and third for highest selling Beatles albums behind *The White Album*. I bought *1967-1970* in *1973* and *1962-1966 in 1974*. Only one of my Beatles albums, *Magical Mystery Tour*, was an original. I only ever collected a handful of singles.

In 1974, there were two different Beatles weekends on Ottawa radio stations. The first was in June on CFGO.[47] I remember this because my family and I drove from Ottawa to Montreal to watch the Montreal Expos play a Saturday game against the Chicago Cubs.[48] The cubs beat the expos 2 - 1 and I remember that we had car trouble part way home on the way back to Ottawa. While stopped at an OPP station somewhere just inside the Ontario border, we discussed what to do next. We had a second car back home in Ottawa but didn't easily know how to get back to get it. Then along came two young fellows from New Brunswick. They just happened to be on their way to Ottawa to visit their aunt. So, mom and I rode back to Ottawa with them, to get the second car, listening to Beatles and they seemed to know the words to all the songs. By the way, their aunt lived only a few minutes from where we lived.

The second Beatles weekend was in September on CFRA[49]. I remember because that's the weekend I was recovering from having my lower impacted wisdom teeth removed. Lots of drugs for the first week, as well as Beatles music and all the chocolate milk I could drink that first weekend. To celebrate further, my aunt bought me the Beatles Red Album, *1962-1966*.

Michael made his own personal album discography of The Beatles[50] for me, a nice keepsake. I also have *The Beatles Illustrated Lyrics*[51] and *The Beatles As Musicians, The Quarrymen Through Rubber Soul.*[52] As for piano music, I have only *Wings Over America,*[53] including some Beatles tunes. I bought both the *Chicago Gold*[54] and *Wings Over America* piano/vocal/chord books at the Billings Bridge[55] location of the Ottawa record store chain Treble Clef. To accommodate being able to play the music, without holding the book with one hand and playing with the other, I cut all the bindings off and three hole punched each page and put them into binders. In recent years, I have gone a step further and trimmed the pages and put them into plastic sleeves, for ease of playing and to extend the life of the pages, many ripped and torn where the three holes were.

Paul, John & Ringo were only a handful of seventies artists who released their singles with picture sleeves, Paul on Capital and John & Ringo on Apple, *Listen To What The Man Said, Mind Games, Photograph, You're Sixteen & Only You.*

In the seventies, Paul & Ringo had custom labels printed right on the singles themselves (mentioned previously in Singles as Art chapter). These were *Hi Hi Hi, Let 'Em In, Letting Go, Listen To What The Man Said, My Love, Silly Love Songs, Maybe I'm Amazed, Venus & Mars Rock Show, With & Little Luck, Photograph & You're 16.*

---

[47] *Beatles Weekend*, CFGO, Ottawa, Chart #92, June 24, 1974

[48] Montreal Expos 1 vs Chicago Cubs 2, Jarry Park, Montreal, Saturday, June 29, 1974

[49] *Beatles Weekend*, CFRA, Ottawa, September 1974

[50] The Beatles Discography, Michael, Toronto, 1974

[51] *The Beatles Illustrated Lyrics*, Alan Aldridge, Dalacorte Press, 1969

[52] *The Beatles As Musicians, The Quarrymen Through Rubber Soul*, Walter Everett, Oxford University Press, 2001

[53] *Wings Over America*, piano, vocals, chords, Mpl Communications, 1977

[54] *Chicago Gold*, piano, vocals ,chords, Screen Gems Columbia, 1975

[55] Billings Bridge Shopping Centre, Ottawa, 1954

Through the seventies, Paul McCartney & Wings released many standalone singles, not included on albums. These songs included *Another Day, Goodnight Tonight, Hi Hi Hi, Junior's Farm / Sally G, Live & Let Die & Mull Of Kintyre.*

McCartney recorded some songs that were like <u>Mini Suites</u>, which I will mention again later. These included *Band On The Run, Hi Hi Hi, Listen To What The Man Said & Uncle Albert / Admiral Halsey.*

In 1975, I bought my very first Paul McCartney & Wings picture sleeve single, *Listen To What The Man Said.* In 1977, Wings had much success, especially in the UK, with their hit *Mull Of Kintyre.* It was actually the B side of the single *Girls' School.* In the late seventies I watched the Beatles tribute band Liverpool perform at my North York high school, Earl Haig Secondary School.

In 1984, *Pipes Of Peace* reached #1 in UK but didn't reach the top 40 in North America. Much Music host VJ Diego Fuentes commented on what a great Christmas video this was, circa Christmas Day during World War I.

The 1984 film/album *Give My Regards To Broadstreet* sprang Sir Paul yet another top ten hit in *No More Lonely Nights.* While the new version of *Silly Love Songs* was a pale imitation of the 1976 original, it was the clever reworking of six Beatles tunes that made the film/record memorable, *Good Day Sunshine, Yesterday, Here, There & Everywhere, For No One, Eleanor Rigby & The Long & Winding Road.*

Remember the hype in the late eighties when they started rereleasing The Beatles album collection on CD? Remember in the 2000s when they started repackaging CDs in general in gatefold jackets to make them even look like the original albums?

In 1987, Sir Paul wrote the fluffy, dreamy, candy pop song *Once Upon A Long Ago.* Not his greatest work but when you've got talent and a voice like that, it doesn't matter. The song only made it to the top 40 in the UK and was included on the UK/Canadian version of *All The Best,* along with *Mull Of Kintyre* and *Pipes Of Peace.* None of the three were included on the US version, a reflection of their no showings in the US top 40. *All The Best* was a next generation version of *Wings Greatest Hits.* The *Once* picture sleeve was almost identical to the *All The Best* album cover.

The closest I ever got to a Beatles concert was Paul McCartney *Flowers In The Dirt* tour[56] in 1989, at the Skydome, now The Rogers Centre[57]. Beatles tunes outnumbered McCartney tunes about thirteen to eight. Two of them were current hits, *My Brave Face & This One.* That left only six older McCartney tunes, *Band On The Run, Jet, Live & Let Die, Maybe I'm Amazed, Coming Up & Ebony & Ivory.* Being there was nice and listening was even better. It was the visual part that was not so great. With the roof closed, it sounds like you're in a barn and the large TV screens in the outfield showed just how far out of sync the visual was with the sound.

In 2009, Sir Ken Robinson[58] published a book entitled *The Element*[59]. In the book he details how people have ended up doing what they do. He interviewed Sir Paul (Sir Ken and George were also from Liverpool) who explained that he learned nothing from his music teacher and that no one felt that either he or George had any musical talent at all.

In 2014, Rolling Stone Published Paul's Top 40 Songs and here is my part of that collection[60]...

---

[56] *Flowers In The Dirt Tour*, Paul McCartney, Skydome, Toronto, 1989
[57] Skydome, 1989, now The Rogers Centre
[58] Sir Ken Robinson, British Education Expert, 1950-2020
[59] *The Element*, Sir Ken Robinson, Penguin Books, 2009
[60] Paul McCartney, 40 Years, Rolling Stone, 2014, p.84

11.3~ McCartney - Top 40 Songs

1.*Maybe I'm Amazed*, 2.*Band On The Run*, 3.*Too Many People (/b)*, 4.*Live & Let Die*, 5.*Uncle Albert / Admiral Halsey*, 6.*Jet*, 8.*Hi Hi Hi*, 9.*Another Day*, 10.*Venus & Mars / Rock Show*, 12.*Let Me Roll It (/b)*, 15.*Silly Love Songs*, 16.*Nineteen Hundred & Eighty Five (/b)*, 17.*Junior's Farm*, 18.*Coming Up*, 19.*With A Little Luck*, 23.*Listen To What The Man Said*, 29.*Goodnight Tonight*, 31.*Say Say Say*, 37.*Mull Of Kintyre (/b)* & 40.*C Moon (/b)*

It's interesting to note that of the twenty songs listed here, seven were issued as non-album singles, proof of the power of the 45, back in the day. McCartney and the other Beatles released some singles for which neither the A nor the B side were from an album. Six of these records were mentioned previously in the McCartney 40 songs…

11.4 ~ (Ex) Beatles - A & B Side Non Album Singles

1. *Another Day / Oh Woman Oh Why & Spies Like Us / My Carnival* - **Paul**
2. *Back Off Bugaloo / Blindman & It Don't Come Easy / Early 1970* - **Ringo**
3. *Ballad Of John & Yoko / Old Brown Shoe & Hey Jude / Revolution* - **Beatles**
4. *Girl's School / Mull Of Kintyre, Goodnight Tonight / Daytime Nighttime Suffering, Hi Hi Hi / C Moon & Live & Let Die / I Lie Around* - **Wings**
5. *Junior's Farm / Sally G* - **Paul & Wings**

In 2017, I bought new pressings of both *Rubber Soul & Sergeant Pepper's Lonely Hearts Club Band.* Back in the seventies, I had borrowed the *Rubber Soul* album from the library and had quite enjoyed it. I had also borrowed *Magic Christian Music* by Badfinger featuring the single *Come & Get It*, on the Apple label with a very strong Beatles influence. Paul McCartney wrote the song.

It's hard to believe that the Beatles only toured internationally as a super group for about four or five years. As Ringo described it in a recent interview, he didn't mind that they stopped touring because whenever they did play live, they could barely hear themselves with all the fans yelling and screaming all the way through their shows. The audio monitors were useless so they had to continually look at each other to know where they were in each song.

TWELVE

NeWavEighties

This chapter is the first of two about music of the nineteen-eighties. The Eighties misunderstood classic rock. While some seventies groups reinvented themselves, others emerged for the first time. Of these, bands like Simple Minds (similar to U2 on *Sparkle In The Rain* and *Once Upon A Time*, care of Steve Lillywhite), Split Enz, Tears For Fears (Like Yes and *90125* and *Big Generator*, four years was too long from *Songs From The Big Chair* to *Sowing The Seeds Of Love*), The Cars, The Police, The Fixx and Thomas Dolby were passed over as "Classic". It's interesting that of the groups listed in the title of this chapter, I never saw any of them play live.

For Thomas Dolby's *Golden Age Of Wireless*, I created an extended version of it, using all five tracks from the EP *Blinded By Science, The Golden Age Of Wireless / Blinded By Science.* They were all extended versions of tracks found on *Golden…* Of those, *One Of Our Submarines* is one of the greatest techno pop tunes of all time. *Golden* singles included *Europa & The Pirate Twins, She Blinded Me With Science & Windpower.*

It's interesting to note that the EP *Blinded By Science* started out as the title on the CHUM FM album chart, while it was later replaced with *Golden Age Of Wireless.*

Only *She Blinded Me* would make the top 40. The follow-up album *Flat Earth* had a definite jazz feel to it. Trombones were featured on the lounge song *I Scare Myself* and the up tempo number *Hyperactive. Dissidents* rounded out the group of three picture sleeve singles.

The 1985 Grammy Award show featured four well known keyboardists, Howard Jones, Thomas Dolby, Herbie Hancock and Stevie Wonder (see soul paragraph above).[61] You could swear there was an orchestra playing. For many years, Dolby was the music director for the Technology Education Design (TED) conferences in California. [62] Actress Daphne Zuniga created, directed and produced the only full

---

[61] The 1985 Grammy Awards, Thomas Dolby, Herbie Hancock, Howard Jones, Stevie Wonder
[62] TED, Technology Education & Design

length film of the annual event, entitled *The Future We Will Create (2007)*.[63] Sir Ken Robinson was a repeat speaker at TED (see the section on collecting).[64] Dolby played a smart reworked version of *One Of Our Submarines* at one of the TED conferences.

The Fixx appeared from England in the early eighties but strangely enough none of their singles ever made the UK top 40. Only *Stand Or Fall* from *Shuttered Rooms* made the Canadian top 40 and only *Sign Of Fire* from *Reach The Beach* made the US top 40. *One Thing Leads To Another* & *Saved By Zero* joined *Sign* to make three picture sleeves from the album, *Reach The Beach. Phantoms*, 1984, had picture sleeves for *Are We Ourselves, I Will (12), Less Cities More Moving People and Sunshine In The Shade*. Only *Are* made the UK top 40. The single *Deeper And Deeper* (the B side of *Are We Ourselves*) was featured in the movie *Streets Of Fire*. I visited Universal Studios in 1983 when they were filming it on the back lot and we couldn't see much of the main street because of that film. The bass guitar sound and style of Dan Brown with all its' energy and bounce was very similar to the way Sting played bass guitar for The Police in spots.

In 1982, John K and I took our girlfriends to a discotheque in Hull where I heard for the first time *Enola Gay* by Orchestral Manoeuvres In The Dark (OMD). That got me started on a collection of records by that group. Fast forward to 1988, the year that OMD released the album *The Best Of*. Years later I would buy the piano music for that album. Of all the piano books I have, it's the only one that I ever bought that had facsimiles of 45 picture sleeves for every song on the album. By then, I had picture sleeves for six songs on the album. For five more, I made my own picture sleeves from that piano book.

12.1 ~ O M D - I - Commercial Picture Sleeves
Dreaming, Electricity, Forever (Live & Die), Locomotion, Messages & So In Love.

12.2 ~ O M D - II - Homemade Picture Sleeves
Enola Gay, Joan Of Arc, Secret, Souvenir & Tesla Girl.

My copy of *Genetic Engineering* actually has the label on it for the single *Telegraph*, not *Genetic Engineering*.

The late Trevor Key designed the cover for the last single noted here, *Tesla Girls*, as well as *Genetic Engineering*. He designed covers for other artists like Midge Ure (*If I Was*) and Phil Collins (*I Don't Care Anymore, I Wish It Would Rain Down, In The Air Tonight, One More Night, Sussudio* & *You Can't Hurry Love*).

For both songs *Can't Stand Losing You* from *Outlandos D'Amour* and *Walking On The Moon* from *Regatta De Blanc*, the Police singles only made the UK top 40. Two years in a row, they charted two albums on the CHUM FM Top Album List - In 1980, they charted *Regatta De Blanc* with *Zenyatta Mondatta* and in 1981 they charted *Zenyatta Mondatta* with *Ghost In The Machine*. For their album *Ghost*, they had several picture sleeve singles, *Every Little Thing She Does Is Magic, Invisible Sun* & *Spirits In The Material World. Invisible Sun* only made the UK top 40. As mentioned earlier, both *Don't Stand So Close To Me* from *Zenyatta* and *Spirits* from *Ghost* each had two distinctly different picture sleeves.

They packaged up more picture sleeve singles for their album, *Synchronicity, Every Breath You Take* (my first Police picture sleeve single), *King Of Pain, Synchronicity II* & *Wrapped Around Your Finger. Synchronicity* would be the last studio album for the group, before Sting would go on to make a solo career for himself. His solo singles *Englishman In New York, Russians* & *We'll Be Together* all featured picture

---

[63] *The Future We Will Create*, TED, Daphne Zuniga, 2007
[64] Sir Ken Robinson, 1950-2020, TED Speaker, 2006 & 2010

sleeves with lyrics on the back side (3.6). While living and working in London in the summer of 1984, my brother Richard met the tall lanky American drummer Stewart Copeland at a party.

In 2023, 360 Media published *Sting, The Stories Behind His Greatest Songs*, both with The Police and as a solo artist. I have all of the Police songs and a handful of the solo songs…

12.3 ~ Sting Greatest Songs I - The Police
De Do Do Do De Da Da Da, Don't Stand So Close To Me (Original & 86), Every Breath You Take, Every Little Thing She Does Is Magic, King Of Pain, Roxanne, Spirits In The Material World, Synchronicity II & Wrapped Around Your Finger.

12.4 ~ Sting Greatest Songs II - Solo
All For Love (with **Bryan Adams & Rod Stewart**), *All This Time, If I Ever Lose My Faith In You, If You Love Somebody, Set Them Free, Russians & We'll Be Together.*

In 1982, I bought my first ever Simple Minds single, a picture sleeve of *Glittering Prize*. While Mel Gaynor played drums for just some of the tracks on *New Gold Dream*, he started playing drums full time on *Sparkle In The Rain*. His signature sound for simple minds was loud drums, we're talking Bob Siebenberg (Supertramp) loud or even John Bonham (Led Zeppelin) loud.

Simple Minds were quick to introduce picture sleeves into their catalogue. However, none of the singles from *New Gold Dream* (*Someone Somewhere In Summertime, Promised You A Miracle* and *Glittering Prize*, mentioned above) or *Sparkle In The Rain* (*Up On The Catwalk, Speed Your Love To Me* and *Waterfront*) even made the top 40.

In 1985, after their most successful US single ever, *Don't You Forget About Me*, one that they didn't even write themselves, Simple Minds also put together several picture sleeve singles for their album *Once Upon A Time; Alive & Kicking, All The Things She Said, Ghostdancing* and *Sanctify Yourself. All The Things* made the top 40 but only in the UK. The album appeared on the CHUM FM album list in both 1985 and 1986.

I made an extended version of songs from *New Gold Dream (New), Sparkle In The Rain (Sparkle) and Once Upon A Time (Once)* called *Dream Rain Time [gem]. Someone Somewhere* has a 16 bar guitar intro by Charlie Burchill on the 12" remix, one of the best parts of the entire song and is often the way they perform it live. In the book Desert Island Discs, Bono says "You feel some early U2 in this song and we learned from them".[65] The piano at the start of the *Waterfront* 12" remix is some of the best Simple Minds piano I have ever heard.

12.5 ~ Simple Minds - Dream Rain Time [gem]
1. *Someone Somewhere In Summertime & Promised You A Miracle [NEW GOLD DREAM]*
2. *Up On The Catwalk, Speed Your Love To Me & Waterfront [SPARKLE IN THE RAIN]*
3. *Sanctify Yourself & All The Things She Said [ONCE UPON A TIME]*

1989 Simple Minds recorded *Belfast Child*, their only #1 UK hit ever. Adapted from the traditional Irish folk tune *She Moved Through The Fair,* it's a real old fashioned drinking song with a total Celtic vibe. Yes alumnus member and producer Trevor Horn produced *Ballad Of The Streets* and *Street Fighting Years. Belfast Child* was on both.

---

[65] *Desert Island Discs*, Ian Gittens, Penguin, 2022, p.451

See The Lights, an early 90s single from *Real Life* is gone but not forgotten, beautiful artistry by Guitarist Charlie Burchill. The acoustic album from 2016 seems like unsimple minds. There are no electric guitars or loud drums. The single only made the top 40 in Canada.

I visited Bath England with my family in the spring of 1984. That is where Tears For Fears were based. *Mad World* only made the top 40 in the UK. They began recording *Songs From The Big Chair* later that summer and packaged a handful of picture sleeve singles for the album, *Everybody Wants To Rule The World, Head Over Heels, I Believe, Mothers Talk* and *Shout* (my first Tears picture sleeve single). *Songs* was not their last album but their most successful ever. The single version of *Mother's Talk* had a louder, more echoey, stadium sound than the original. *When In Love With A Blind Man*, The B side to *Head Over Heels*, is a remix of *The Working Hour. Pharoahs*, The B side to *Everybody Wants To Rule The World*, is an elegant, graceful and lovely reworking of *Everybody*. It's not just a great B side or Tears For Fears song, It's a great song. Period. I added all three to what I called the *Songs From The Pharoahs & A Blind Man* version of *Songs From The Big Chair. Everybody* is also the only single by any group, not just Tears For Fears, for which I have 7", 10" and 12" formats.

There was a four year gap before the recording of *Sowing The Seeds Of Love,* in 1989, much like the four year gap for Yes when *Big Generator* appeared in 1987. By that time, they had lost the momentum of the success of *Songs From The Big Chair.* However, having said that the album *Sowing* did do well enough along with picture sleeves of *Advice For The Young At Heart, Sowing The Seeds Of Love & Woman In Chains*, to appear on both CHUM FM top album lists in 1989 & 1990. See the chapter *Sounds And Feels Like A Toe Tappin' Folk Tune, Sa Flatt Ft*, for more details about the title track, *Sowing The Seeds Of Love.*

It is neat that the logo artwork for Simple Minds *Promised You A Miracle Live* was very similar to Tears For Fears (*Shout, Everybody Wants To Rule The World, Mothers Talk, I Believe & Head Over Heels*) three lines of words arranged vertically to describe and name the group.

When The Thompson Twins (all three of them) recorded their breakout album *Into The Gap* in 1983, they released no fewer than three singles, each featuring a picture sleeve, *Doctor Doctor, Hold Me Now & You Take Me Up.* They also remixed some of those versions and put them together in an album they called *Out Of The Gap.* Their follow-up album, *Here's To Future Days* featured more picture sleeve singles, *Don't Mess With Doctor Dream, King For A Day, Lay Your Hands On Me & Revolution.* Neither *Don't Mess* or *Revolution* made the top 40.

In the summer of 1984, my brother Richard lived in London and attended a mega concert at Wembley stadium including Elton John, Big Country, Kool & The Gang, Nik Kershaw & Wang Chung. [66] He worked that summer at a pizza restaurant near Victoria Station. He said that the members of The Thompson Twins were regular customers. [67]

In 2010, I attended a Randy Bachman concert. He's been through the wars but is still a good showman and storyteller. In the late 1970s, many Gretsch guitars were stolen from his home. He then saw Tom Bailey of The Thompson Twins playing one of them in a rock video in the early 1980s. Somehow Tom and gotten a hold of it. Randy met him at a concert and asked him for the guitar back. Tom said oh yes I know the one but I never take it on tour with me. So, I asked Randy after the 2010 show at the meet and greet if he ever got his guitar back from Tom Bailey. He said, "no and I probably never will."[68] The Thompson Twins recorded *Nothing In Common* for the movie of the same name. While the song did not

---

[66] Elton John Concert, Wembley Stadium, June 30, 1984, also featured Big Country, Kool & The Gang, Nik Kershaw & Wang Chung, https://www.concertarchives.org/concerts/elton-john-big-country-kool-the-gang-nik-kershaw-wang-chung-067daa98-cc24-499a-82d9-ec2d1637e726.

[67] Thompson Twins were regular customers at pizza restaurant where my brother Richard worked in the summer of 1984.

[68] Randy Bachman Meet & Greet, Stratford Festival Theatre, Wednesday, January 27, 2010.

make the top 40, Tom Hanks starred with two famous actors, Eva Marie Saint and Jackie Gleason. It would be one of Jackies' last movies.

In chapter ten, I indicated some Bryan Adams songs, amidst many other artists, that I had recorded on VHS tape from Much Music and Much More Music but never compiled together just the Bryan Adams songs. Here, I have listed out the same thing for some Madonna songs...

12.6 ~ Madonna Music Videos
Borderline, Crazy For You, Holiday, Like A Prayer, Like A Virgin, Live To Tell, Material Girl, Oh Father, Papa Don't Preach & Vogue

THIRTEEN

NOT NeWavEighties

This is the second of two chapters that talk about groups from the nineteen-eighties. Like The Police, Foreigner had a mix of UK and US personnel in their band. They had recorded several successful albums in the late seventies, including *Foreigner* with hits like *Cold As Ice & Feels Like The First Time and Double Vision*, with hits like *Double Vision & Hot Blooded*.

They continued that success with the 1980 album *4* that featured sleeves for four singles that all looked like the numbers from a movie screen countdown, 4, *Break It Up*, 3, *Juke Box Hero*, 2, *Waiting For A Girl Like You* & 1, *Urgent*.

The Follow-up album *Agent Provocateur* meant three more picture sleeve singles, *I Want To Know What Love Is, Reaction To Action and That Was Yesterday*. With *I Want To Know* they finally had a number one hit. The song had a gospel feel to it that played out in the video. It was very similar in style and substance to **U2**s' live version of *I Still Haven't Found What I'm Looking For* that would be recorded for the album *Rattle & Hum*.

It seems that U2 was one of the few Classic rock acts to outlast these others and make it out of the eighties. The 1983 album *War* was produced by Steve Lilywhite and sounds a lot like the 1984 Simple Minds album *Sparkle in The Rain*, which he also produced. *New Year's Day* (from the *War* album) only made the top 40 in the UK.

U2 charted both *Under A Blood Red Sky* and *The Unforgettable Fire* on both the CHUM FM and Q107 Top Albums list for 1984. *The Unforgettable Fire* would chart again in 1985.

After the *Unforgettable Fire* album and mini album and the mini album *Wide Awake In America*, U2 released a promotional cassette in Canada. It included a selection of songs across most of their albums to that point. As far as I know, it was never released on vinyl.

13.1 ~ U2 Sampler

A - *I Will Follow, Gloria, Sunday Bloody Sunday, Two Hearts Beat As One, 40, Eleven O'clock Tick Tock (Live) & New Years Day (Live)*

B - *A Sort Of Homecoming, Unforgettable Fire, 4th Of July, Three Sunrises, Bad (Live) & Pride (In The Name Of Love)*

Whether it is deliberate or not, there is a striking resemblance in graphics for **U2**'s *Unforgettable Fire Mini Album* and *the Joshua Tree*. I already had many of the B Side songs on the extended version of the *Best Of 1980 - 1990*. I put the original *Joshua* tracks together with 6 different single B Sides (in BOLD letters) …

13.2 ~ Joshua B Sides

1. *With or Without You / Hold On To Love / Walk To The Water*
2. *I Still Haven't Found What I'm Looking For / Spanish Eyes / Deep In The Heart*
3. *Where The Streets Have No Name / Silver & Gold / Sweetest Thing*

The singles all had one A side single that played at 45 rpm and two B side singles that played at 33 rpm. *In God's Country*, was the fourth single from the album, one of U2's best ever, not just from the *Joshua Tree*. The American versions only had a single song at 45 rpm on side B, like *Bullet The Blue Sky* with *In God's Country*, *Spanish Eyes* with *I Still Haven't Found What I'm Looking For* and *Silver & Gold* with *Where The Streets Have No Name*. They were all black labels, as opposed to the white Canadian labels. I then added the three *Unforgettable Fire Mini LP* bonus tracks, *The Three Sunrises, Love Comes Tumbling & Bass Trap*, calling it *The Joshua Tree Extended Version*.

The 1987 version of *Sweetest Thing*, released as a B side song to *Where The Streets Have No Name* was a much better sounding and stronger version than the one released in the 90s for the best of 1990 - 2000 album.

I also created a specialized tape of U2 videos, entitled, *U2 The Much Videos* ...

13.3 ~ U2 The Much Videos

1. *New Year's Day & Two Hearts Beat As One [WAR]*
2. *I Will Follow (Live), Sunday Bloody Sunday (Live) & New Year's Day (Live) [UNDER A BLOOD RED SKY]*
3. *Where The Streets Have No Name & With Or Without You [THE JOSHUA TREE]*
4. *Desire, Angel Of Harlem & All I Want Is You [RATTLE & HUM]*
5. *Even Better Than The Real Thing, One, Who's Gonna Ride Your Wild Horses, The Fly & Mysterious Ways [ACHTUNG BABY]*
6. *Stay (Faraway, So Close!) [ZOOROPA]*
7. *Miss Sarajevo [PASSENGERS]*
8. *Discotheque [POP]*
9. *Pride (In The Name Of Love) [UNFORGETTABLE FIRE]*
10. *The Sweetest Thing [SINGLES 80 - 90]*

A handful of the songs at the front end of the tape included songs from the live album *Under A Blood Red Sky*. For a couple of the live songs, I have collected double hit US singles, *Gloria (Live) / Sunday*

Bloody Sunday and *I Will Follow (Live)* / *Pride (In The Name Of Love)*. The Original *Pride (In The Name Of love)* single was my first U2 picture sleeve.

I missed my chance to get the boxed set of *Joshua Tree* picture sleeve when I saw it, complete with *Where The Streets Have No Name, I Still Haven't Found What I'm Looking For, With Or Without You & In God's Country*, which only made the UK top 40. *One Tree Hill* is what I would call the fifth single from the album *The Joshua Tree*. The song was released only in Australia and New Zealand, borrowing the identical picture sleeve cover with Bono on it from *In God's Country*. The song is an ode to Greg Carroll who was Maori (indigenous) from New Zealand. He was killed riding a motorcycle while in Ireland with U2, running an errand for the band. Greg was a U2 roadie, personal assistant and close friend to Bono. One Tree Hill is a volcanic formation native to New Zealand. Greg took Bono there shortly after they met in 1984. It was one of Greg's favourite places and that inspired Bono to write a song about that place and the connection that Greg had with it.[69]

I never saw them in concert but did see the 1988 rockumentary *Rattle & Hum*. Four singles were released from that album, *All I Want Is You, Angel Of Harlem, Desire* and *When Love Comes Town,* which only made the UK top 40. I think my favourite is *All I Want Is You.* It only made the top 40 in the UK. As far as I know, none of the *Rattle* singles were ever rereleased as double hits like those from *The Joshua Tree.*

The four singles for both *The Joshua Tree* and *Rattle & Hum* were similar in that each picture sleeve featured a different member of the band.

There was a version of *Bad* in the movie. While it was excluded from the album, The *Wide Awake In America* mini album featured a great live version, not unlike the *Rattle and Hum* film version. *The Joshua Tree* appeared on both CHUM FM album lists for 1987 & 1988, while *Rattle & Hum* appeared on both CHUM FM album lists for 1988 & 1989.

U2 were at their creative peak with the next album, *Achtung Baby*, certainly better than *Rattle* and right on par with *Joshua.* Even though there were no less than five singles released on *Achtung*, it was the first time that **U2** singles were very difficult to find. To date, I have no vinyl singles from the album, only the cassette singles…

13.4 ~ *Achtung Baby* Cassette Singles
1. *Even Better Than The Real Thing* / *Salome* / *Where Did It All Go Wrong?*
2. *(The) Fly* / *Alex Descends Into Hell For A Bottle Of Milk* / *The Lounge Fly Mix*
3. *Mysterious Ways* / *Mysterious Ways (Solar Plexus Magic Hour Remix)*
4. *One* / *Lady With The Spinning Head* / *Satellite Of Love*
5. *Who's Gonna Ride Your Wild Horses? (The Temple Bar Edit)* / *Paint It Black* / *Fortunate Son*

I bought three different nineties albums on vinyl, *Achtung, All That You Can't Leave Behind* and *The Best of 1990 - 2000*. From the nineties, The albums *Zooropa* and *Pop* were difficult to find on vinyl so I have them on cassette only. What I did buy were three singles, all US pressings, between the two albums, *Stay (Faraway, So Close!), Staring At The Sun & Discotheque. The Best Of 1990 - 2000* was not as good a collection of songs as *1980 - 1990* but there were some songs like *Hold Me Thrill Me* and *Miss Sarajevo* that I did not have on vinyl already. *Hold Me* was an *Achtung Baby* leftover, featured on the *Batman Forever* soundtrack. *Miss Sarajevo* was performed by U2 as The Passengers, along with Luciano Pavarotti.

---

[69] *25 Albums That Rocked The World*, Chris Charlesworth, Omnibus Press, 2008 & *U2, The Stories Behind Every U2 Song*, Niall Stokes, Carlton Books, 2009.

In 2006, U2 released the *U2 Piano Collection*. From the twenty songs in the collection, I have ten of the singles and of those five of them were from *The Joshua Tree*, The other five were from four other albums.

13.5 ~ U2 Piano Collection
1.All I Want Is You, 4.I Still Haven't Found What I'm Looking For, 8.New Year's Day, 11.Pride (In The Name Of Love), 12.Running To Stand Still (/b), 14. Stay (Faraway, So Close!), 16.Sunday Bloody Sunday, 17.The Sweetest Thing (/b), 19.Where The Streets Have No Name & 20.With Or Without You

In 2008, U2 recorded a cover version of Greg Lakes' *I Believe In Father Christmas*. In 2011, the TV special *From the Sky Down* celebrated the twentieth Anniversary of *Achtung*, the album that almost didn't happen and whose divisive Berlin recording sessions almost marked the end of one the world's greatest rock bands. There are several pricy boxed sets of *Achtung* to mark the anniversary. Between the vinyl version of the LP and cassette singles with B sides, the anniversary packages don't seem that appealing. I would still like to get my hands on the five singles. That's my inner voice, the 45 RPManiac talking. Except for *All That You Can't Leave Behind*, U2 has not made much noise since *Achtung*. What's most impressive about U2 is that other than the Beatles (and they were together less than ten years) U2 membership has not changed since it began more than forty-five years ago.

I liked the variety in the Island singles, for The Buggles, U2 & Steve Winwood. First there was red, yellow, blue & green in Canada and purple & green stateside. Then, there was a trimmed Canadian version with the four colours just around the edge. Then there were the US versions, single hits with a blue and yellow logo on a black background and double hits with a black logo on a gold background.

In the 1960s, a teenager named Steve Winwood stormed his way on to the music scene with The Spencer Davis Group. The double hit record *Gimmie Some Lovin' / Keep On Runnin'* showcased his talent, especially with the unforgettable organ part on *Gimmie Some Lovin'*. There is a Chicago connection. Chicago covered the Steve Winwood song *I'm A Man* on their debut album *Chicago Transit Authority*. Years later he was part of Traffic. I remember seeing the album *Shootout At The Fantasy Factory* on the album list of the weekly CHUM charts in the spring of 1973. I have never actually heard the album but probably should listen to it.

In the early 1980s, Steve Winwood set off on a successful solo career, first with *Arc Of A Diver* (*While You See A Chance & Night Train*) in 1981 and then *Talking Back To The Night (Still In The Game & Valerie)* in 1982. Then in 1986, Steve recorded his blockbuster album *Back In The High Life*, which charted two years in a row, on the CHUM FM top album list for both 1986 & 1987. Picture sleeves from this album included *Back In The High Life, Finer Things, Higher Love & Valerie 87*. The follow-up *Roll With It* also did well enough to chart two years in a row on the CHUM FM top album list, in 1988 and 1989. It featured picture sleeves of *Don't You Know What The Night Can Do?* and *Holding On* and two different picture sleeves of *Roll With It*.

FOURTEEN

KING CRIMSON
MOODY BLUES, ELP & GENESIS

In March of 1978, I bought the album *In The Court Of The Crimson King* (King Crimson). Greg Lake was the lead singer. This album was released in 1969 and was true prog rock but way ahead of its time. Greg Lake played with King Crimson before ELP. I shared this album with Longtime friend Alex at his house just days after I bought it. As Lake describes in the *Royal Albert Hall* video, he was originally a guitarist. Robert Fripp told him he was welcome to join King Crimson but as a bassist. The rest, as they say, is history.

In April of 1978, I bought *A Trick Of The Tail* by Genesis and *Trilogy* by Emerson, Lake & Palmer. Both of these albums had mellotron connections. *In The Court Of The Crimson King* featured a mellotron. The second track of *A Trick* Of The Tail was *Entangled* and featured Steve Hackett, Mike Rutherford and Tony Banks all playing acoustic guitar, and Tony Banks playing the aforementioned mellotron. The song is very different from others on the album, written in triple time but with no drums.

The Beatles were probably the first to use a mellotron. It was a keyboard that used prerecorded tapes right inside the keyboard case, instead of hammers or pipes. The Moody Blues had used a mellotron starting with *Days Of Future Passed* in 1967. The mellotron was a good substitute for a full orchestra and much cheaper.

While the Moody Blues faded in the mid-seventies. John Lodge & Justin Hayward did record *Blue Jays* together. They reinvented themselves at the start of the eighties with *Long Distance Voyageur*. That meant three top thirty/forty hits, with ex-Yes keyboardist Patrick Moraz from Switzerland, *Gemini Dream, Talking Out Of Turn & The Voice* (not to be confused with the song of the same name by The Alan Parsons Project). *Talking Out Of Turn* only made the top 40 in Canada, as did *Tuesday Afternoon* in 1967 and as would *I Know You're Out There Somewhere* in 1988.

The Moody Blues and Emerson, Lake & Palmer (ELP) were part of the *Isle Of Wight Festival* in 1970. The Moody Blues were the well-established prog rockers, while ELP were just getting started.

Greg Lake spent most of his ELP time on electric bass to match Emerson on keyboards and Palmer on drums. Lake spent less time on acoustic guitar, the dichotomy and juxtaposition I describe as *The Tale Of Two Lakes [gem]*. Lakes' powerful folk rock ballads like *Lucky Man, From The Beginning, I Believe In Father Christmas, C'est La Vie, Watching Over You* and *Footprints In The Snow*, feature awesome acoustic guitar skill and talent that few have matched.

The 1973 Emerson, Lake & Palmer album *Brain Salad Surgery* featured a jacket cover that opened like two doors swinging open, one to the left and the other to the right. Reissued versions of the album had the same picture but opened only like a normal album jacket. *Karn Evil 9 1st Impression Part 2* has been a huge part in concerts, not to mention the 1974 live album they named after those unforgettable words, "Welcome Back My Friends To The Show That Never Ends".

Actually, *Karn Evil 9 1st Impression Part 1* is an even better piece of music, highlighted by the elaborate organ intro. However, both parts of *Karn Evil 9* together make up one of my favourite ELP pieces. In this piece Lake plays a lot of electric guitar to counter Emerson and his Hammond organ and it would be an understatement to say the organ was loud, like The Who or Led Zeppelin loud.

Brain Salad Surgery was chock a block full of take no prisoners lyrics. *Benny The Bouncer* is a throwback to the old days. During the middle part of the song, you can picture a knock 'em down drag 'em out saloon fight as the honkytonk piano rolls along. You could also tell that ELP was actually having fun when they played this one.

The song of the same title appeared later on *Works Volume 2*. It was actually recorded as the title track for the album *Brain Salad Surgery* but was never included. *Chiquitita* by Abba also used a honky Tonk piano in the latter part of that song. I also remember Dr. John talking about brain salad surgery in his song *Right Place Wrong Time*, recorded before the album *Brian Salad Surgery* was recorded.

I Believe In Father Christmas reached #2 on the UK charts in 1975. It would have reached number one if it hadn't been for some guy named Freddie Mercury writing a little ditty called *Bohemian Rhapsody*. *Father Christmas* never even cracked the top 40 in Canada or the US. Once you've heard the original 1975 single version with choral and orchestral accompaniment, the studio version from *Works 2* in 1978 pales in comparison. Before the Atlantic Label, several early ELP singles were on the Cotillion label and included titles like *From The Beginning, Lucky Man, The Nutrocker & Stones Of Years*. Several other later import singles were on the Manticore label, including *Jerusalem, Brain Salad Surgery & Honky Tonk Train Blues*.

In June of 1977, friends bought me *Works Volume 1*, my first current album by that group. It was an ambitious album, complete with orchestra. Emerson wrote his own Piano Concerto. Palmer had his own side of a disc. His featured a smart reworking of Tank from their first album, but not as good as the original and without the solo in the middle. Lake tunes included *C'est La Vie, Nobody Loves You & Closer To Believing*.

Someone once commented that *C'est La Vie* was nothing more than a reworking of the *Brain Salad Surgery* song *Still You Turn Me On*. While the lyrics may be similar in theme, *Still You Turn Me On* doesn't begin to compare musically with *C'est La Vie*.

The group side showcased *Fanfare For The Common Man* which was a huge hit in the UK but didn't make the jump to North America and the epic *Pirates*. Physically, it resembled *Yessongs* and *Going For The One*, in that it opened into three panels instead of two. The Orchestra proved problematic on tour. It was dropped for the Toronto concert but picked up again for the Montreal concert. According to Emerson, Lake wrote *C'est La Vie* in Paris in 1975, two years ahead of the release of *Works Volume 1*.

In 1978 I bought the first of two compilation songbooks by ELP, entitled just *Emerson Lake & Palmer*. Dad knew much of the music by ELP. They often reworked existing music. Aaron Copeland was a favourite, pieces like *Hoedown* and *Fanfare For The Common Man* (huge in the UK but small and misunderstood in North America). Emerson also reworked hymns like *Jerusalem. I Believe In Father Christmas* (especially the single version) was not just a great Christmas rock song but a great rock song.

In 1992, John K and I saw ELP play at the Kingswood Music Theatre at Canada's Wonderland. [70] It was a great show for a band that had all but disappeared in the 1980s. The tour was to promote the *Black Moon* album, something of a comeback at the time. Affairs Of The Heart was a ballad that Greg Lake wrote with Buggles and Yes keyboardist Geoff Downes. The opening track of the concert, *Tarkus Eruption*, featured Emerson playing two different keyboards, while talking with one of the sound technicians. They played a rocking version of *Fanfare For The Common Man*, complete with Emerson tossing his Hammond organ around the stage, just like back in the old days. The songs from my catalogue included *Fanfare For The Common Man, From The Beginning, Knife Edge (/b), Lucky Man & Stones Of Years*

It's no coincidence there is a connection to Canada's Wonderland where ELP performed their 1992 *Black Moon* concert in Maple Concert, *Black Moon & Canada's Wonderland, The Two Carousels [gem]*. The front and back covers of the album feature an antique carousel, that looks just like the one at Canada's Wonderland, originally built in Philadelphia in 1928, it was relocated to the park for its' opening in 1981, only steps away from the Kingswood Theatre.[71] It only took me twenty five years to make that connection. The Album cover is a throwback to the days when album cover art was important and if an antique carousel doesn't say retro, I don't know what does.

Dad found a write-up on the concert, written by Alan Niester who was to be covering a Metallica concert that was cancelled. Thanks to Setlist.fm, here are the songs from that concert. Encore number is noted with *(en)*…

14.1 ~ ELP @ Kingswood Music Theatre, Maple, 1992
2.*Tarkus (Stones Of Years /b)* 3.*Knife Edge (/b)*, 8.*From The Beginning*, 11.*Lucky Man*, 13.*Pictures At An Exhibition (Great Gates Of Kiev /b)* & 14.*Fanfare For The Common Man (en)*.

Live at the Royal Albert Hall (both CD & VHS) captured the magic of the *Black Moon* tour as well as many stories from years of recording and touring. John K & I saw ELP again at Kingswood in 1996 with Jethro Tull but they were not as impressive as they were in 1992, as Keith Emerson was recovering from a hand injury at the time.

Watching the 1993 Video of *Live At The Royal Albert Hall*, Greg Lake told an amusing story. They toured Verona, Italy but when they got there, nothing was setup. "They got the day wrong." So, they set up a wooden frame at the back of the stage, complete with fireworks for the show. When the show started, the fireworks were so heavy that the frame fell over and the fireworks started shooting out into the audience. Greg Lake also explained that the carpet he used for years was not an ego thing but very necessary to keep him from getting shocked when he stood too close to the microphone.

In 1999, I bought the second of two ELP Compilation songbooks, this one entitled, *Greatest Hits*, from 1996**.** Along with *Jeremy Bender* from the first songbook, There were four others from the second songbook, in my collection, *C'est La Vie, From The Beginning, I Believe In Father Christmas & Lucky Man*.

Keyboardist Keith Emerson passed in March of 2016, while bassists Greg Lake and John Wetton passed in December 2016 and January of 2017 respectively. In the summer of 2017, I bought a 25th anniversary remastered vinyl version of *Black Moon*. Reissued on the Manticore label rather than the

---

[70] *Black Moon Tour*, ELP, Kingswood Music Theatre, Canada's Wonderland, Maple, Ontario, August 1992
[71] Antique Carousel, Canada's Wonderland, Maple, Ontario, originally built in Philadelphia in 1928

Victory label it originally appeared on, it was made at only 140 grams, instead of the newer 180 gram records. As Lake described it, the heavier weight doesn't translate into better sound, in fact it's not as good. Even if you weren't a fan of ELP, you have to admit that their logo was pretty cool.

I recently bought the promotional single for the album *Brain Salad Surgery*. The single includes the song of the same name, along with a medley of songs from the album *Brain Salad Surgery*. The neat thing about the single is that it has a jacket designed exactly like the original album cover. Yes, like two doors, one opening to the left and the other to the right.

In 1975, I taped Genesis Live on CKCU FM Radio Carleton[72], though poor in quality. Songs from that post *Lamb* concert included *Watcher Of The Skies, Lillywhite Lilith, The Waiting Room, Anyway, It, Musical Box, Happy The Man & Twilight Alehouse*

In the late seventies, Michael made a Genesis booklet for me, detailing all the groups' albums up to and including *Wind & Wuthering,* another great keepsake. He also created and gave me discographies for The Beatles, Led Zeppelin and Rush. Years later, I remember a friend and I going to the York University listening library. I was supposed to be listening to classical music for a music appreciation course but instead we listened to the tape I had made of the *genesis CKCU 93.live concert.*

As I mentioned earlier, I bought *A Trick Of The Tail* alongside ELP's *Trilogy* in April of 1978. *A Trick Of The Tail* (1976) was described in the Genesis pages of allmusic as being much similar to *Selling England By The Pound,* than the previous *Lamb Lies Down On Broadway.* [73] *A Trick Of The Tail,* I believe, was their best album ever. The drum track on *Squonk,* following *Entangled* (mentioned earlier), was described by Phil Collins as their tribute to the Led Zeppelin classic *Kashmir.* Like I comment on the Supertramp song *Gone Hollywood* in chapter sixteen, *Squonk* has lots and lots of cymbals.

Collins was described as sounding even more like Peter Gabriel than Gabriel himself. Gabriel wished his band mates success but begrudged the successful sales of *Trick* surpassing all the previous Genesis albums combined. Longtime friend Chris commented that he really liked the song *Ripples.* Alex also liked it enough to have me include the song on his mix tape, *29.1 Alex*. The song ranks ninth of their top 40 prog songs.[74] It starts with a gorgeous combination of acoustic guitar and piano. It is actually two pieces stitched together, along with some Ringo-like drum fills.[75] I refer to the song as *Reeples [gem]*, because that's how it sounds when Phil sings the chorus the second time around.

The departure of guitarist Hackett was to spell the end of Genesis after *Wind & Wuthering.* For a close friend, they were never the same again. He was right. While they did create lots more great music, it was different.

Mike Rutherford was a good guitarist but didn't have the magical touch of Steve Hackett, especially on acoustic guitar. *Inside and Out* was not released on *Wind & Wuthering* but appeared on the B Side of the *Spot The Pigeon* single, a memorable exit song from Hackett, a throwback to the *Wind* album and my first ever Genesis picture sleeve single.

My brother Richard bought the piano music book that featured all the music for both *A Trick Of The Tail* and *Wind & Wuthering.* A lot of the music I couldn't play but I did have fun trying.

The departure of Steve Hackett had just the opposite effect. *And Then There Were Three* in 1978 gave Genesis its' first hit single ever, *Follow You Follow Me.* Alan Neister described Genesis as masters of themes, even when it came to solos.

---

[72] *Genesis Live*, CKCU 93.Live, 1975
[73] *Classic Rock*, Allmusic Guide, Backbeat Books, 2007, p.79
[74] *Genesis, Their 40 Greatest Songs*, Prog, 2019. p.47
[75] *Genesis, The Ultimate Music Guide*, Uncut, 2019, p.53

At the time of the 1982 *Abacab* tour, which I was able to see, Genesis was a major pop music success. The album cover had several versions, all the same design but with different colour combinations. That album was my first current album by that group. The album charted on the CHUM FM top albums list in 1981 & 1982. Thanks to Setlist.fm, here are the songs including encores...

14.2 ~ Genesis @ CNE Stadium August 1982
2.Behind The Lines (/b), 3.Follow You, Follow Me, 4.Dodo (/b), 5.Abacab, 7.Misunderstanding, 12.Turn It On Again, 15.The Lamb Lies Down On Broadway (en) & 17.I Know What I Like (In Your Wardrobe) (en).

When the *Genesis* album came along in 1983, Genesis was grooving with several videos for the MTV / Much Music audience. Phil Collins said in a video interview that the laughing in *Mama* was influenced by the laughing in *The Message* by Grandmaster Flash & The Furious Five. *Mama* was used for the tour name as the album was called just *Genesis*. The album charted on the CHUM FM top album list in both 1983 & 1984.

In 1984, I visited a WH Smith Book Store in England, the first I had ever seen that sold records, including singles. Two of the records I bought were by Genesis, *Follow You Follow Me / A Trick Of The Tail* and *I Know What I Like (In Your Wardrobe) / Counting Out Time*. Both were part of the Old Gold Collection, which I had not seen previously and have only seen one of since. That was *Do It Again / Rikki Don't Lose That Number* by Steely Dan. The design of the record label and sleeve were brown and yellow, very similar to the cover of the album *A Trick Of The Tail*, in the case of the *Follow You Follow Me / A Trick Of The Tail* single.

I also bought the single *That's All [gem 21.11]*, a central part of the folk tune chapter twenty-one, in between chapter twenty, about structure and chapter twenty-two, about sound. The UK single had *Taking It All Too Hard* as the B side, compared with *Second Home By The Sea* as the B side in Canada. *Second Home By The Sea,* track four side one of *Genesis,* is one of the best and longest Genesis songs ever to showcase Tony on keyboards, especially the synthesizer, supported by Mike's rhythm style guitar and Phil's driving drum beat.

In 1985, Phil Collins released his third and most successful album to that point, *No Jacket Required*. It potted three picture sleeve singles in the form of *One More Night, Sussudio & Take Me Home*. Phil once commented that *Take Me Home* was not about getting home to relax but about taking home someone who had dementia. The radio slogan for his *No Jacket* tour was "Rub a dub dub, hot tub in a pub, it's the Phil Collins club, so rub a dub dub".

With *Invisible Touch* in 1986, Genesis had fine-tuned their hit writing skills, with no fewer than five singles released on that album, *In Too Deep, Invisible Touch, Land Of Confusion, Throwing It All Away* and *Tonight Tonight Tonight*. The album charted on the CHUM FM top album list in both 1986 & 1987. Mike Rutherford formed his own group in the late 1980s with former Ace frontman Paul Carrack (*How Long*). The group was called Mike & The Mechanics and featured the songs *Silent Running & The Living Years*.

We Can't Dance in 1991 saw no fewer than five singles released, all of them US pressings, with purple rather than the traditional red labels, *No Son Of Mine, Jesus He Knows Me, I Can't Dance, Tell Me Why & Hold On My Heart*. *We Can't Dance* also featured Phil writing a song, something he had not done much of before. That song was *Driving The Last Spike*, an epic one in both sound and story. One fan described *Fading Lights* as "the last great prog rock song ever recorded". It's hard to believe that song is more than thirty years old. *Hold On My Heart* always sounded more like a Phil Collins song than a Genesis song.

Tony Banks said in an interview (*Genesis on We Can't Dance*, YouTube), about *Fading Lights*, you don't know it's your last song (save *Calling All Stations*) at the time that you record it. You don't know how close you are to something / someone / somewhere in space and time, until you move away from it. Like the song says, "Another chance hello, another goodbye and so many things we'll never see again, days of life that seemed so unimportant, they seem to matter and to count much later on".

The Genesis tour that followed *We Can't Dance* was entitled; *Live The Way We Walk*. Phil Collins explained about live song endings in the video documentary of *Live The Way We Walk*. Some songs that didn't have endings on the albums had endings live in concert. *Mama* is an example of this. Groups do this a fair bit, that's inventing endings for songs that never had endings so they can play them live.

I created an extended track CD, entitled *Genesis Selling A Trick Dance [gem]*, with seven songs from four different albums …

14.3 ~ Genesis Selling A Trick Dance [gem]
1. *Dancing With The Moonlit Night & Firth Of Fifth [SELLING ENGLAND BY THE POUND]*
2. *Entangled & Ripples [A TRICK OF THE TAIL]*
3. *Home By The Sea & Second Home By The Sea [GENESIS]*
4. *Driving The Last Spike & Fading Lights [WE CAN'T DANCE]*

Ray Wilson, who replaced Phil Collins as lead singer only on *Calling All Stations*, has recreated a revival of sorts of live Genesis music entitled *Genesis Klassik*. It features a unique version of the *Trick Of The Tail* song *Ripples*. The Overlap Singles Appendix is filled with far more Genesis singles than by any other group.

In July of 2019, Prog subscribers cast their votes for the top 40 Genesis tunes of all time. Here is my part of that collection…

14.4 ~ Genesis Top 40 Songs
9.*Ripples (/b)*, 11.*I Know What I Like (In Your Wardrobe)*, 12.*The Lamb Lies Down On Broadway*, 14.*Home By The Sea & Second Home By The Sea (/b)*, 16.*Entangled*, 17.*Follow You, Follow Me*, 20.*Mama*, 27.*Abacab*, 28.*A Trick Of The Tail* & 36.*Duchess*

There were only eight of the forty songs from the eighties and only three of them singles, *Abacab, Duchess & Mama*. It's interesting that many of those fans are stuck in the seventies, a lot like fans of Yes.

In October of 2019, I bought Genesis' *We Can't Dance*. While the album was not originally a double album, it was pressed on two vinyl discs to maintain better sound, as discussed along with the Geffen effect way back in chapter four, Singles & Albums.

FIFTEEN

LED ZEPPELIN
ALAN PARSONS & PINK FLOYD

On the last day of school, grade 10, June 1976, I bought Led Zeppelin *IV* (ZOSO) and *Dark Side Of The Moon.* The single *Money* would only make the top 40 in the US. At the time, I was sixteen and Jimmy Page was thirty-two, twice my age. I still have the original sticker for *Led Zeppelin IV*, which features the track listing in black lettering on a white background. Now, the reissued sticker has white lettering on a black background. *Houses of the holy* had a similar sticker with the track listing in black lettering on a white background.

The two albums have been noted in *25 Albums That Rocked The World* by **Chris Charlesworth.**[76] A friend also bought these two albums together. For all the Atlantic singles I have, I have never seen this scenario with any other group. Golden Treasures by Quality Records did reissue traditional A and B sides as double hits but that was usually just for one or two singles, not the handful like Zeppelin. Led Zeppelin had at least seven singles that started out as regular red label Atlantic singles and were later reissued as double hit Atlantic Gold…

15.1 ~ Zeppelin Singles I - Morphology
1. *Black Dog // Misty Mountain Hop*
2. *Communication Breakdown // Good Times Bad Times*
3. *D'Yer Ma'Ker // The Crunge*
4. *Immigrant Song // Hey Hey What Can I Do*
5. *Over The Hills & Far Away // Dancing Days*
6. *Rock & Roll // Four Sticks*

---

[76] *25 Albums That Rocked The World*, Chris Charlesworth, Omnibus Press, 2008, p.95 & p.124

7. *Whole Lotta Love // Living Loving Maid*

Michael gave me the single *Immigrant Song / Hey Hey What Can I Do*, after he bought *Led Zeppelin III*, except that *Hey Hey* was not on the album. This legendary B side has become a rock classic. In the late seventies, he made a Zeppelin booklet for me, detailing all of the groups' albums up to and including *Presence*, including some impressive artwork from Albums *II & Zoso*.

Stairway was never released as a charted single even though stations like CJCS FM play it as part of their greatest hits format. The *Stairway / Whole Lotta Love* double hit single was released originally only as a not for sale promotional single for radio station airplay. Over time, it, along with others, started to appear in circulation in retail record stores. My dad used to kid me that when I played *Whole Lotta Love* that it sounded like the record was skipping, especially the guitar part at the beginning of the song.

The neatest cover version I have ever heard of *Stairway To Heaven* was by The Idols at Café De La Terrasse at Glendon College, in 1981[77] All the verses except for the last one were done in a punk rock style. The last verse was done in a Reggae style. I have a postcard of the concerts in Oakland, the last that Zeppelin ever performed on a North American Tour. Scottish comedian Billy Connelly once interviewed drummer John Bonham about his drumming. Bonham was very modest about both himself and his abilities. [78]

In early 1979, a high school friend then studying at York University, invited me to sit in on his radio show at Radio York and do my own play list (the station started in 1969[79]). The only song I remember from that playlist was *(I've Been) Searchin' So Long* by Chicago. [80] Later that spring, I was part of a high school jam session. I sat in front of the drum kit to keep it from moving, while the group hammered out tunes like *Rock and Roll* (Led Zeppelin) and *Tie Your Mother Down* (Queen).

In late 1979, Zeppelin released the album *In Through The Out Door*. Both the front and back covers were hidden by a pseudo kraft paper wrapper with the album name stamped in the corner, to make it look like a package you would unwrap. Once open, there were different pictures of the same bar/tavern on the front and the back. In fact, there were about six different pictures that were all interchanged between the front and the back, depending on which version of the album you bought. From that album, *All My Love* only made the top 40 in Canada.

In March of 2022, Rolling Stone released their list of the Zeppelin Top 40[81]. Here is my collection from that list…

15.2 ~ Zeppelin Singles II - Rolling Stone Top 40 Songs
> 1.*Whole Lotta Love*, 2.*Stairway To Heaven*, 3.*Black Dog*, 6.*Good Times Bad Times*, 7.*Immigrant Song*, 9.*Rock & Roll*, 10.*Misty Mountain Hop*, 12.*Communication Breakdown*, 16.*Over The Hills & Far Away*, 20.*D'Yer Ma'Ker*, 21.*Dancing Days*, 24.*Fool In The Rain*, 33.*Living Loving Maid* & 37.*Four Sticks*.

In the late 1970s, I bought a deleted album entitled *Pilot*. The first two tracks were big hits, *Just A Smile* (in the UK) and *Magic* (internationally). *January* was a bigger hit than either of those, making it to the top 40 but only in the UK. Several of the members Pilot went on to become part of The Alan Parsons Project.

[77] *Stairway To Heaven*, The Idols, Café De La Terrasse, Glendon College, York University, 1981
[78] *From The Archive : Billy Connolly And John Bonham*, https://www.youtube.com/watch?v=PzCetFD-rrE
[79] *Spin Doctors*, York U Magazine, Fall 2013
[80] Radio York, York University, 1979
[81] *Led Zeppelin, Inside Their Music & Legend*, Rolling Stone. March 2022, p.68

The group of band mates from Ottawa visited me in Toronto in 1977 and brought *I Robot* by The Alan Parsons Project. I had never heard of the group before and don't remember any of the music from the album at the time. I remember traveling to France in 1986 and walking through the Charles De Gaul airport. Riding the escalators, I recognized it as the cover for that same *I Robot* album. [82] The song *The Voice* (yes, long before the TV show by the same name), featured an instrumental section that sounded very much like the Temptation song *Papa Was A Rolling Stone*. It also sounded similar to *The Theme From SHAFT* by Isaac Hayes. Hayes was a recurring guest star on the television show *Rockford Files* and he used to call James Garner (Rockford) Rockfish.

In 1980, Parsons released the single *Damned If I Do*, the first Parsons song on a CHUM chart, the first Parsons song to break the Billboard top 40 and the first Parsons song I ever remember hearing on the radio. In 1982, I bought the single, along with *Blinded By The Light*, the Manfred Mann version of the Bruce Springsteen song by the same name. The artwork on the *Damned If I Do* label featured a 3D A for Arista. The full list with the 3D A is here…

15.3 ~ Alan **Parsons Singles With 3D A For Arista**
1. *Damned If I Do / If I Could Change Your Mind, Damned If I Do / You Lie Down With Dogs, You Lie Down With Dogs \\ Lucifer & You Won't Be There [EVE]*
2. *Psychobabble & You're Gonna Get Your Fingers Burned [EYE IN THE SKY]*
3. *Games People Play, Snake Eyes & Time [TURN OF A FRIENDLY CARD]*

That same year, I remember buying *Turn Of A Friendly Card*. (The Alan Parsons Project - APP) The record sounded good except there was a skip in the second last song on side two. I took the record back to the store and had them play it. Then they found another copy but it had the same skip. The master must have been messed up on a batch of them so I bought it at another store, no skip on that one. That album charted in both 1980 & 1981 on the CHUM FM top album list.

Still in 1982, I bought the album *Eye in the Sky. You're Gonna Get Your Fingers Burned* only made the top 40 in Canada. Several years later I would buy the title track single, one that would go on to become the highest charting single by the group, number 3 on the Billboard charts. *Old & Wise* was available with two very different picture sleeves. Longtime friend Jeff described *Old & Wise* as one of his favourite pop songs, not just one of his favourite Parsons songs. On the album, the song *Eye In The Sky* is preceded by the instrumental *Sirius*. The Chicago Bulls Championship Teams of the 1980s, with the likes of Michael Jordan, Scottie Pippen & Dennis Rodman, used to play *Sirius* on the public address system at the old Chicago Stadium, when they were introducing the players at the start of the game, a way of winding up the fans. [83] Parsons played the song in 1998, along with *Games People Play*, when they toured with Yes.

In 1984, Parsons released *Ammonia Avenue*, featuring the song *Don't Answer Me*, a picture sleeve identical to the album cover and one of the best rock videos of the 1980s, alongside *Take On Me* by A-Ha and the fifth Parsons song to crack the Billboard top 30. I bought *Scratching The Surface* by Saga, at the same time. In 1986, Parsons recorded *Stereotomy*, which would chart on both the 1986 & 1987 CHUM FM top album list. It featured a picture sleeve for the single *Limelight* and two very different picture sleeves for the single of the title track, *Stereotomy*. In 1991, Parsons played in Belgium at *The Night At The Proms*. They played a stirring rendition of *Old & Wise*, featuring Pilot Alumnus and Parsons bass player David Paton on lead vocals[84].

---

[82] *I Robot*, 1977, album cover art, 1977, Charle De Gaulle's Airport, 1986
[83] *Sirius*, Eye In The Sky, Alan Parsons Project, 1982
[84] *Old & Wise - The Alan Parsons Project - David Paton*, https://www.youtube.com/watch?v=BT2U76Fbea0

In the mid-eighties, I missed an opportunity to pick up a 4 album vinyl set of *I Robot, Pyramid, Eve & Turn Of A Friendly Card.* The artwork was all done in the style of *Turn Of A Friendly Card*, all with different face cards.

In 1998 The Alan Parsons Project opened for Yes at the Molson Amphitheater. Thanks to Setlist.fm, here are the songs…

15.4 ~ *Alan Parsons (& Yes) In Concert, 1998, Toronto*
1.The System Of Dr. Tarr & Professor Feather, 2.I Wouldn't Want To Be Like You, 5.Prime Time, 8.Standing On Higher Ground, 10.The Gold Bug, 11.Eye In The Sky, 12.Don't Answer Me & 13.Games People Play.

In March of 2016, In a Daytona Beach Florida record store, I bought a twenty-fifth anniversary Alan Parsons single that included *Turn Of A Friendly Card, Snake Eyes & Games People Play.* The cover was basically a replica of the album, *Turn Of A Friendly Card.*

Parsons was and is a great musician. He has worked with the likes of The Beatles, Pink Floyd, Pilot, Al Stewart and the Hollies and has recruited many musicians (like the Zombies Colin Blunstone) for many of the APP studio albums. In 1983, I bought the single *Hold Your Head Up*, by Argent, yes the former Zombies member and piano/keyboard player, Rod Argent. Years later, I recorded the video of a GAP commercial that had the same sound and feel as The Zombies song *She's Not There. She's Not There* was one of the first pop songs to use a minor third rather than a major third in its' melody. Along with *Hold Your Head Up*, I also bought *Lady*, the first hit song by the group Styx.

Back in 1967, Parsons entered the music industry, around the time of The Beatles *Sergeant Pepper's Lonely Hearts Club Band.* He couldn't get over all the different sounds he was hearing. That album alone was a great inspiration for him.[85]

Dark Side Of The Moon first appeared in April of 1973 on the CHUM chart list of top 10 albums and was still in the top 10 when I moved to Ottawa in August of 1973. It was on the CFRA top 10 in September as well. Okay, let's face the facts. You're not a true Pink Floyd fan unless you still have the original red and green posters (and maybe even the day and night pyramid stickers) that came with your *Dark Side Of The Moon* vinyl album. But don't kid yourself, the posters and stickers weren't a gimmick to get you to buy the album, it was a masterpiece of sound and engineering all by itself. I still marvel at the work Parsons did to pull it all together, especially all those wonderful sound effects.

In 1975, Floyd recorded *Wish You Were Here*, in part, a tribute to the late band member Syd Barrett. In his 1997 book *Rocking The Classics*, it's quite impressive that the author Edward Macan compares the suite *Shine On You Crazy Diamond Part One* with three other epic prog tunes, ELP & *Tarkus*, Genesis & *Firth Of Fifth* and Yes & *Close To The Edge.* While very different than the other three, it still stands up quite nicely.

In 1977, they released *Animals*, alongside other prog rock albums *Quietist Moments, Going For The One* and *Works.* The album cover was highlighted by a picture of the Battersea power station in London. I Remember friends were going to see the concert at Olympic stadium in Montreal and they bragged about how they were going to bring back the giant inflatable pig.

In 1979, they released *The Wall*, in part, an autobiography by Roger Waters. It was highlighted by tunes such as *Another Brick In The Wall Pt. 2, Comfortably Numb* and *Hey You.* Who can forget the words "if you don't eat your meat, you can't have any pudding! how can you have any pudding if you don't eat your meat?" That same album was also made into a movie.

LaserFloyd in 1984 seemed to be a logical step for a band that started out way back there in the psychedelic years of the late 60s. I watched it at the Planetarium beside The ROM. The music selections were

---

[85] *The Best Of The Alan Parsons Project* (Piano, Vocal & Chords), Columbia Pictures Publications, 1983

from five Floyd albums, including *Money* from *Dark Side Of The Moon* and *Another Brick In The Wall Pt 2*, *Comfortably Numb* and *Run Like Hell*, all from *The Wall*. A friend remarked that *Welcome To The Machine* from the album *Wish You Were Here* reminded him of his automotive mechanic job. I did not get to see *Laser Zeppelin*.

In the early 2000s, Roger Waters brought his *Wall* show tour to the Rogers Centre. The single *Run Like Hell* only made the top 40 in Canada. The CBC Meteorologist in the early 2000s was Claire Martin from England. Her connection to Roger Waters was that she was one of the kids in the original video of *Another Brick In The Wall*. [86]

A big part of what ties these three groups together is their album artwork, much of it designed by Hipgnosis…

15.5 ~ Hipgnosis Albums
1. *Houses Of The Holy & In Through The Out Door* - **Led Zeppelin**
2. *Tales Of Mystery & Imagination, I Robot, Pyramid, Eve, Eye In The Sky, Ammonia Avenue, Vulture Culture & Stereotomy.* - **The Alan Parsons Project**
3. *Dark Side Of The Moon & Wish You Were Here.* - **Pink Floyd**

Finally, here is a bridge to the next chapter. Groups in the 1970s, pre videos, had a better shot at anonymity. Specifically, it was two groups that fell into this category, Pink Floyd and Supertramp. They were able to wander about in public without being noticed. Imagine that. Fame and fortune and anonymity.

---

[86] Claire Martin, CBC Meteorologist & kid in *Another Brick In The Wall Part 2* video, 1979 // *The Wall*, Roger Waters, Rogers Centre, July 14, 2007

SIXTEEN

SUPERTRAMP

I remember seeing *Crime Of The Century* at a party in late 1975 but I had no idea what it was about or that *Dreamer* was one of the tracks. At the same party I remember seeing an album cover with the red shoes from *The Wizard Of Oz*, it was the album *Eldorado* by The Electric Light Orchestra. In March break, 1976, Alex and I were shopping at Sam The Record Man on Yonge Street in Toronto. Another shopper, in his late teens / early twenties paid us a couple of bucks to buy concert tickets for a group called Supertramp, on their *Crisis? What Crisis?* tour.[87] Tickets per single buyers were limited. *You Started Laughing*, the B side to *Lady*, did not appear on the Crisis album but was a haunting studio version of the same track recorded live on *Paris*.

On vacation in Hardwick, Vermont, in the summer of 1976, I found a record store and bought *Jackie Blue* (Ozark Mountain Daredevils) and *Dreamer* (Supertramp). This was the original issue of the single with the *Bloody Well Right* B side, not *From Now On* and my first time buying records stateside. *Bloody Well Right* was Supertramp's first US hit, reaching #35 on the Billboard chart.[88] In the early 80s, I would buy the *Dreamer* single with *From Now On*, my first ever Supertramp picture sleeve single.

In June of 1977, I recorded Supertramp's' *Quietist Moments* from either CKCU or CHEZ, I can't remember. The tape did not last long. In July, I saw them for the very first time at the Ottawa Civic Centre, a smaller sized arena that made for a very intimate setting, on their *Quietist Moments* tour. I remember Roger Hodgson, blowing smoke up into the air, in between the verses of *Asylum*. The price for the concert was only $6 and the warm-up band was Irishman Chris de Burgh. His band sang backup on *From Now On*. In August, some Ottawa friends visited me in Toronto and bought me the album and I retaped it.

I purchased a DVD many years ago now, entitled *Supertramp, Gateway To New Horizons*. It was recorded at Queen Mary's College in London, England, 1977, not long after Quietist Moments was released.

---

87 Tickets, Supertramp Concert, *Crisis What Crisis Tour*, March 1976, Sam The Record Man, 333 Yonge Street, Toronto.
88 *Music That Rocked The World*, Peter Murray, Rockus, 2008

It's not nearly as well-known as Paris but has an early rawness to it. The songs included *Another Man's Woman, Babaji, Bloody Well Right, Dreamer, From Now On, Give A Little Bit, Lady & Poor Boy*.

In December of 1977, I bought *Crime Of The Century*, along with the Genesis album *Wind & Wuthering*. I remember Q107 DJ Alex Hindmarch, a transplanted Englishman, commenting that what was missing from *Quietist* moments were the electric pianos that were so much a part of the *Crime* and *Crisis* sound. [99] Supertramp had great live sound, back in the day, compared with other groups that we're touring. I remember John Helliwell talking about putting the money they made directly into improving their sound system.

The Supertramp laser light show in the summer of 1978 at the MacMillan Space Centre (Planetarium) in Vancouver BC,[89] followed closely on the heels of the *Laserock* Show in March at the McLaughlin Planetarium of the Royal Ontario Museum. The show featured much of the music from the albums *Crime, Crisis?* and *Quietist Moments*.

While *Quietist Moments* featured older songs, *Breakfast In America* featured brand new tunes. In 1978, Ritchie Yorke, the host of a weekly program on Q107, wrote two articles about *Breakfast In America*.[90] The album was originally known as *Working Title* and featured two new songs by Roger Hodgson, *The Logical Song* and Take *The Long Way Home* and a hard driving song by Rick Davies entitled *Heartbreaker* (later renamed *Gone Hollywood*). Both *Goodbye Stranger* and *The Logical* Song were each released with two very different picture sleeves. I first listened to *Breakfast In America* at Alex's house.

The original newspaper ad from the June 1979 Toronto Star, promoting a third Supertramp show on their *Breakfast in Canada* tour in July, shows just how much wider the newspaper page width used to be back then. I attended the third show (120,000 fans across 3 days, a record at the time), when they played *Rudy*. It was then that I viewed an early rock video with two friends. During the middle portion of the song, they showed a film of a train leaving the train station, speeding up as the song did and travelling at high speed, then slowing down and returning to the station, as the song slowed down again. Hodgson and Helliwell also played a memorable duet version of *Even In The Quietist Moments*.

Here is my collection from setlist.fm…

16.1 ~ *Supertramp, Breakfast In Canada, Exhibition Stadium, July 1979*
2.From Now On (/b), 3.Gone Hollywood (/b), 4.Bloody Well Right (/b), 5.Breakfast In America, 6.Goodbye Stranger, 7.Sister Moonshine (/b), 11.Even In The Quietist Moments (/b), 12.The Logical Song, 14.Give A Little Bit, 15.Dreamer, 16.Rudy (/b) & 17.Take The Long Way Home.

Alan Niester described the Toronto shows that would go down in history.[91] *Fool's Overture* was awesome performed live. For the *Breakfast In Canada* tour, Supertramp added three minor chords to the ending, giving it a more finished sound. Throughout the show, the rhythm of Bassist Dougie Thomson and drummer Bob Benberg was relentless, John Helliwell was a great showman and Davies and Hodgson dazzled us with white keyboards, illuminated with coloured lights from underneath.

One of the best drummers ever (including John Bonham), Davies had commented at one of their first jam sessions that he had never heard a louder drummer than Benberg, mostly just symbols.[92] The song *Gone Hollywood* (the b side to *Breakfast In America*) brings this to mind, right from where Rick starts to sing

[89] *Supertramp Laser Light Show*, MacMillan Space Centre, Planetarium, Vancouver, BC, 1978
[90] 2 Supertramp articles about upcoming *Working Title* (*Breakfast In America*) album by Ritchie Yorke, 1978.
[91] *Breakfast In Canada*, concert review, Alan Neister, July 1979
[92] *The Supertramp Book*, Martin Melhuish, Omnibee Press, 1986, p.55.

,"you're not what I'm looking for, ain't nothing new, in my life today", continuing for the rest of the song, lots and lots of symbols. Besides the drums, I would say three of the loudest Supertramp songs are *Ain't Nobody But Me, Bloody Well Right* and *Goodbye Stranger*. For these pieces, Davies plays the main piano part, while Hodgson plays very loud electric guitar in a supporting role.

For all you oatmeal lovers, Supertramp's' Scottish bass guitarist Dougie Thompson was a fan of *Scott's Porridge*. That was most appropriate back when the album *Breakfast In America* was on the charts. When I attended University, I played Supertramp on the piano for Orientation in 1979 (*If Everyone Was listening*) and 1982 (*Downstream & Lord Is It Mine*). *Downstream* was a solo piano piece by Rick Davies.

Martin Melhuish, who would write the *Supertramp Book* biography, published in 1985, also wrote an article about the upcoming *Breakfast In America* Album in October of 1978.[93] The interesting part about the article was what he had to say about the title track. Roger said in fact that the song was not a new song but it was written way back in 1972, even before *Crime Of The Century*. Chris Roberts wrote in the Take A Bow section of The Prog Magazine *Top 100 Icons* issue in 2019 that Roger had written the song in 1969, at the age of 19.[94] That's three years ahead of the 1972 that Martin Melhuish talked about. Imagine that. *Breakfast America* was written in the sixties.

I find it interesting that after all these years, the Supertramp song *Breakfast* gets lots of airplay on AM & FM air waves. It has nothing to do with how good a song it is. The thing is this. *The Logical Song, Goodbye Stranger* and *Take The Long Way Home* were the only three singles released from the album *Breakfast* into the North American market. The *Logical* and *Goodbye* sleeve covers similar to the *BIA* album cover with the waitress were the best. *Breakfast*, the title track from *Breakfast* was only released in the UK. The only chart I have that shows the title track from *Breakfast In America* (position #334) is the Q107 *Top 500 Rock Songs Of The Century*.[95].

The *Dreamer (Live) / You Started Laughing (Live)* single showed a cover that was basically identical to the *Paris* album. *The Dreamer (Live) / From Now On (Live)* sleeve showed a close up of the arc de triomphe, miles better than the *Paris* lookalike. The back panel showed the group heading backstage to begin their show. *Take The Long Way Home (Live) / From Now On (Live)* used that same photo as it's front panel. I have the *Breakfast In America (Live) / You Started Laughing (Live)* single but without a picture sleeve.

In 1984, after *Famous Last Words* and before *Brother Where You Bound*, I bought a German pressing of a Supertramp greatest hits album entitled *Dies Sons Einer Supergruppe*. The special thing about this record was that all the songs on side one were sung by Roger Hodgson and all the songs on side two by Rick Davies.

In 2004, Hodgson performed with a symphony orchestra in Paris, the evening was entitled *Night At The Proms*.[96] The symphony performed *Fool's Overture* with Hodgson on Piano/Keyboard. This is a fantastic version. The strings, saxophone, horns, drums, flute, singers and Hodgson are all awesome. Everyone talks about how great Hodgson was but Davies was great too. Originally a drummer, Davies brought a solid and unique sense of rhythm to his keyboard playing. His singing was the perfect complement to Hodgsons' and included an impressive body of work.

Yes, Hodgson tunes may be more popular and recognizable, but the five musicians in the studio and on stage together is what made Supertramp great. The Hodgson concert footage I have seen pales in comparison with the *Quietist* and *Breakfast* concerts I did see. The rhythm and jazz based keyboards by the

---

[93] *Breakfast In America With Supertramp*, Martin Melhuish, The New Music, October 1978.

[94] *100 Icons*, Prog Magazine, Take A Bow Section, August 2019, p.124.

[95] *Top 500 Rock Songs Of The Century*, Q107, Jan. 7, 2000.

[96] *A Night At The Proms With Roger Hodgeson*, Paris, 2004, https://www. youtube. com/watch?v=6aWDxuhD0FI

cynic Davies was the perfect contrast to the pop based keyboards of the dreamer and optimist Hodgson. Davies started his music career as a drummer and his keyboard playing always had a very percussive edge and style to it.

The title of the groups' final album featuring Hodgson was Ominous. *Famous Last Words* would be his last as a Tramp and the final song *Don't Leave Me Now* was autobiographical in scope and haunting in sound. It is perhaps one of Bob Siebenberg's loudest drum tracks ever, not just for that album. The harmonica makes the ending very similar to the title track from *Crime*. *Crazy* was only a top forty hit in Canada, while *My Kind Of Lady* only a top forty in the US. *My Kind Of Lady* also had two distinctly different picture sleeves. The album charted on the CHUM FM top album list in both 1982 & 1983.

A friend told me he was a Supertramp fan but that he was disappointed with *Famous*, especially *It's Raining Again*, I disagree and think that it was and still is a good pop song. Henry Mietkiewicz wrote in the Star about the *Famous Last Words* Tour, "*It's Raining Again* captured the essence of Hodgeson's pop sensibilities with near falsetto singing and a bright delivery that sounded like a 1980s version of the Cowsills".[97] Chris Roberts also wrote in the Take A Bow section of The Prog Magazine *Top 100 Icons* issue, that *It's Raining Again* had attained legendary status when Roger played it alongside *Give A Little Bit* as an encore number at the Royal Albert Hall in 2019.[98]

In 2016, I bought the DVD of the *Paris tour*, a memento of the album. The B side *You Started Laughing* was immortalized with a live version on that album. The artwork for the groups' name on the cover was taken from the inner sleeve of *Breakfast In America* and appeared also on several singles including the title track. The live version of *Fools Overture* had a great ending, with three additional chords to the original studio version.

Across the collection there are no fewer than ten titles featuring the A side that appear twice (in some cases more)…

[97] *Supertramp returns to loyal fans, Henry Mietkiewicz, Toronto Star, 1983.*
[98] *100 Icons*, Prog Magazine, Take A Bow Section, August 2019, p. 124.

SEVENTEEN

YES I - SEVENTIES

This chapter is the first of two chapters about the rock group Yes. In the summer of 1972, I attended a camp near Kingston Ontario with Alex and heard the single *Roundabout [gem]* by Yes, care of Rock Radio in Watertown New York. I refer to it as Rock Radio because I have yet to figure out which actual station it was. [99] I refer to this moment as *The Watertown Roundabout [gem, see also 25.1]*.[100]

I listened to a live version of *Roundabout* from *Yessongs* at a youth group Easter service celebration lunch, in April of 1975. I did recognize the song but knew that it was different from the original. After hearing the original single again in August of 1975, at Alex's cottage, I began my search for it.

When I couldn't find it, I started collecting Yes albums (the first was *Fragile* with *Roundabout* and then *Close To The Edge*), around the same time as my FM Radio Phase. In just a two year period, from 1975 to 1977, I collected seven out of their ten albums to that point

For a song that I couldn't stand when I first heard it, *And You & I* is now one of my favourites and one of their greatest ever. The rest is history, 23 singles and all but a couple of albums later. I dare say that if I had found the single almost right away that I might not have bothered to collect the albums.

The Single *Roundabout* bears out this dichotomy of all my record collecting. The collecting started out with singles and was complimented part way along with albums. Still, it was this single by a prog rock band, clocking in at about three and a half minutes that started the whole collection, with the album version at over eight minutes and live versions reaching almost ten minutes in length. The *Fragile* album jacket came in a couple of different gatefold styles, one where the record slid into the outside edge of the jacket and the other where the record slid into the inside edge of the jacket. There were also two different endings to the album. First, *Heart of The Sunrise* finished by itself. Second, it finished with a reprise of the earlier track *We Have Heaven*.

---

[99] *Watertown Rock Radio*, Watertown, New York, July 1972
[100] *The Watertown Roundabout*, Watertown, New York, 1972

The visual aspect of collecting (earlier on in this ramble) was due to Roger Dean and his artwork. Much of it was done for Yes. He designed an early logo (for *Close To The Edge* in 1972) that is still recognized by Yes fans today. He introduced a next generation Yes Logo for the *Yesyears* boxed set, a full record size cover, even if it only came in CD & Cassette. The artwork was wonderful, masterful and beautiful, captured in two different books, *Views* in 1975[101] and *Magnetic Storm* in 1984.[102] The art was from a faraway place and reminds us of much of the artwork that has appeared in fantasy type movies and games and videos.

Roger Dean designed many of the Yes Tour stage sets, based on his drawings for *Topographic Oceans, Relayer* & *Drama*. He created artwork for other groups besides Yes, including Uriah Heep (*Demons & Wizards, The Magician's Birthday).*

Yes recorded *Relayer* in 1974 without Keyboardist Rick Wakeman (Wakeman had been a session musician, prior to his days with The Strawbs and Yes, playing for artists like Elton John, David Bowie and Cat Stevens). Instead, they went with Swiss keyboardist Patrick Moraz. Jon Anderson had wanted Greek keyboardist Vangelis (don't make me say his first name) but that didn't work out (see Wikipedia).[103] They did collaborate in the early eighties. Imagine Yes with Vangelis, different than with either Wakeman or Tony Kaye. It's hard to believe that Jon and Vangelis recorded their debut album in 1981. *Gates Of Delirium*, from *Relayer*, clocks in as the longest Yes song ever. This is the first time I ever remember hearing Jon Anderson's voice with a real edge to it. The live version from *Yesshows* highlights an even edgier voice than on the album.

In the summer of 1977, Ottawa high school band mates bought me two different albums. The first was *Going For The One* by Yes, their first in three years and the first in six that had more than three tracks. It was the first current Yes album that I had acquired, since starting my collection of Yes albums in 1975. For this story, I have remarked how *All Five Going Songs Have Endings [gem]*. While many recorded songs fade away, all five of the songs on this album have endings. Of special note is the instrumentation. It was listed for each song, not just the album as a whole. *Parallels* and *Awaken* featured Rick Wakeman playing a church organ several miles away from the studio connected by a phone line to where the rest of the band were playing.[104]

Awaken was the signature long song of the album, a masterpiece that has stood up very well over time. One thing I must say though is that none of the numerous live performances or recorded live versions can match the original. Of special note is the break in the middle that marks the soft point of the church organ that then builds into a grand sound, nothing short of magnificent. The magic of the original was in how Wakemans' up and down and before and after keyboard patterns and sequences seemed to fit together just right. The overwhelming feeling listening to the live versions is that he was trying to get back to the original patterns and sequences but never quite did.

The album opened out into three panels, just like the three LP live album *Yessongs* from 1973. *Wonderous Stories* was the only single from the album to make the top forty and only in the UK. This was a going away present ahead of my move from Ottawa to Toronto. The same group of friends visited me in Toronto after my move and gave me *Even In The Quietist Moments* by Supertramp, my first current album by that group. *Going* is perhaps one of the best and balanced Yes albums ever.

[101] *Views*, Roger Dean, 1975
[102] *Magnetic Storm*, Martin Dean, 1984
[103] Jon Anderson on Vangelis, *Yes The Authorized Biography,* Dan Hedges, Sidgewick & Jackson, 1981, p.95
[104] Rick Wakeman on the recording Of Awaken, *Yes The Ultimate Music Guide,* Uncut, 2018, p.69

Jon remarked years later in the *Yesyears* video that groups that learned their trade in playing and performing in the seventies meant they did not have to depend on the video medium to maintain their success in the eighties.[105]

In May of 1979 and a year later in 1980, I watched Yes at Maple Leaf Gardens, both times with the same friend. For Toronto Maple Leaf Fans, we were sitting in the grays in 1979, about as far away as you can get from the floor and the Greens in 1980, not quite as far away. Both times they played "In The Round" on a circular revolving stage, in the very middle of the arena. This must have been a challenge for the musicians, hanging microphones and all. This was great for the fans in that you had a good view of the stage regardless of your seat.

The 1979 show was highlighted by a suite that included *Long Distance Runaround / The Fish (Fragile) / The Gates Of Delirium / Soon (Relayer)*. The *Gates Of Delirium* part was great, the instrumental ahead of the ending *Soon*. It was a bar of four four time followed by a bar of seven four time, showcasing each of the group members' talent, Howe's spacey slide guitar, Wakeman's elegant keyboards, Squire's relentless bass and White's killer drums. The instrumental was a good follow-up to *The Fish* which was written in seven four time. I have since put the suite together on a two track CD. I call the tracks *Long/Fish & Gates/Soon*.

I recorded a CHUM FM broadcast (The King Biscuit Flower Hour) of Yes performing live in Los Angeles in early 1979 on their *Tormato* tour[106]...

17.1 ~ Yes Live In Los Angeles 1979
1.*Opening from Close Encounters*, 2.*Siberian Khatru*, 3.*Heart Of The Sunrise*,
4.*Circus Of Heaven*, 5.*Don't Kill The Whale*, 6.*The Clap*, 7.*Starship Trooper*, 8.*Madrigal*,
9.*On The Silent Wings Of Freedom*, 10.*I've Seen All Good People* & 11.*Roundabout*

The concert was performed at the Fabulous Forum in Inglewood, California, a suburb of Los Angeles and the former home of the Kings & the Lakers, long before the days of the Staples Center.

I noticed in some of the souvenir programs in years after the *Tormato* tour that *Tormato* was not included in the discography in the back of the program. Sure, *Tormato* was not the best Yes album but it still had some great tunes on it, especially *On The Silent Wings Of Freedom*, never played again after that tour, except for bits and pieces of it in *Whitefish* duets played by Squire and White.

The opening guitar part on the single version of *Don't Kill The Whale*, the first Yes single I ever bought and the only one in my collection that has a picture sleeve with Roger Dean artwork on it (the yes logo with the song title), is much better that the album version. The synthesizer solo by Rick Wakeman stands up very well next to the guitar solos by Steve Howe. Finally, the live version on the 2002 Classic tour featured an awesome drum back beat from Alan White.

In 1995 the tribute *album Tales From Yesterday - A View From The South Side Of The Sky* was released. It featured two very original and refreshing versions of *Don't Kill The Whale* by Magellan and *Release Release* by Shadow Gallery. In 1996, *Keys To Ascension* was recorded at the Fremont Theatre in San Luis Obispo, California. It featured a really neat version of *Onward* with an extended acoustic guitar introduction.

For the two albums *Going For The One* and *Tormato* (and the single *Don't Kill The Whale*), the classic Yes logo was incorporated right in with the album and single song titles, to create three unique logos. Both album covers were designed by Hipgnosis, rather than Roger Dean. *Tormato* was to have been named

---

[105] Jon Anderson on performing in the 1980s, *Yesyears* video, 1991.
[106] *Yes Live In Los Angeles*, 1979, The King Biscuit Flower Hour, Chum FM.

Yes Tor after the nearby hilltop formation in Devon England, however the artwork went in a different direction. Having studied Geography in college, I did enjoy the map look that the group kept for the inner sleeve.

Most British bands, including Yes, Supertramp, Pink Floyd, Genesis and Emerson, Lake & Palmer, among others, all enjoyed more initial success in Canada than they did in the United States.

EIGHTEEN

YES II
EIGHTIES & LATER

This chapter is the second of two about Yes and the last about groups. The 1980 *Drama* concert was a different show without Anderson or Wakeman but still great. Fans panned this version of Yes because Trevor Horn did not have the vocal range of Anderson. Toronto was the very first date on the *Drama* tour, only eleven days after the album's release. I did not know the music, as did many others. It was neat that the souvenir program laid out a single page for each of the six songs, complete with lyrics and graphics. I remember Geoff Downes' keyboard setup because he had a computer screen. The stage was in the round, like the year before but was improved to include ramps instead of steps and was a much darker colour than the original.

In Dan Hedges' *Yes, An Authorized Biography,* Chris Squire described Downes as "the best keyboard player Yes has ever had. He listens better".[107] The cover artwork was taken from the live album *Yesshows. Drama* rocked hard (*All Music Classic Rock Required Listening Guide*),[108] even harder than *Relayer.* One critic (*Listal.com*) remarked "it was the closest Yes ever got to heavy metal music". The classic yes logo even had a steely look to it on the *Drama* cover.

As far as I can remember, the Yes *Drama* concert program was the only one I ever bought that had words to the songs, including *White Car*, referred to in the program as *Man In A White Car,* written by Downes and reportedly inspired by Gary Numan.[109] The single remix of *Run Through The Light* was even better than the original, with Alan White hammering out two very loud triplets in the middle of the song. Trevor played bass on that song. After *Drama* and before *Asia,* Geoff Downes & Trevor Horn regrouped as The Buggles and remixed *Into The Lens* as *I Am A Camera.*

---

[107] Dan Hedges on Geoff Downes, *Yes An Authorized Biography*, Dan Hedges, Sidgewick & Jackson, 1981, p.136
[108] *Drama* review, Allmusic Guide, 1980, p.247
[109] *Yes, The Ultimate Guide*, Uncut, 2018, p.77

Roger Dean continued with his artwork for Yes into the eighties and forward including *Drama* (1980), *Yesshows* (1980), *Classic Yes* (1981), *Anderson, Bruford, Wakeman & Howe* (1989), *Yesyears* (1991), *Keys To Ascension I & II* (1996), *The Ladder* (1998) & *Fly From Here* (2011). He also created covers for Asia (*Asia*, 1982, *Alpha*, 1983 & *Astra, 1985*). His artwork has been captured in calendars as well, *Roger Dean 1994 Calendar & Surrealscapes 2011 by Roger Dean.*[110] The 1994 calendar of Roger Dean's artwork and a dinosaur calendar created for the same year with a cover he designed were both published by the UK company Pomegranate.[111]

Downes and Howe went on to join Asia and write some good tunes, including *Heat Of The Moment, Only Time Will Tell, Sole Survivor & The Smile Has Left Your Eyes*. Downes played some of the loudest piano chords I have ever heard on *Sole Survivor*. A friend with whom I jammed and recorded *Nights In White Satin*, a long time seventies Yes fan, remarked that *Drama* was the best Yes album he had heard in years. A cousin even recognized the music from *Drama* when I was playing it (not very well) on the piano.

In the winter of 1982, seven years after its release, six years after I bought it and five years after I had raved about it to a close friend, he finally agreed that *Relayer* was a great album. Anderson used Tolstoy's *War and Peace*[112] as the inspiration for *The Gates Of Delirium*, the first part about War and the final part, *Soon*, about peace. That format was similar to *The Ritual*, from the previous album *Tales From Topographic Oceans*, with the lengthy first part of the song and then a ballad ending, entitled *Nous Sommes Du Soleil*. Years later, in the early 2000s, I finally found the single, *Soon*. Roger Dean noted about his artwork on *Relayer* that it was very different. Most were watercolours, while this was done with pencil, one of his favourites, with a very gothic look to it. Also in 1982, Chris Squire and Alan White teamed up to record the Christmas tune *Run With The Fox*. It never made it to the top forty.

In the spring of 1983, I travelled to California. I stopped in a San Luis Obispo record store and bought *Into The Lens (I Am A Camera) / Does It Really Happen?* from *Drama* in 1980. Flash forward to 1996, when Yes played several evenings of music at the Fremont theatre, in San Luis Obispo. That music was recorded as *Keys To Ascension*. The lineup was termed "Classic Yes" (see my explanation up ahead). *Keys to Ascension* was very reminiscent to *Yes Live In LA 79* that I recorded, during the *Tormato* tour, with *Siberian Khatru* as the first song in the set list.

In August of 1984, my wife and I saw Yes on their *90125* tour at Exhibition Stadium, later captured on the album *9012live*. The opening two tracks may be the best I have ever heard from them, *Cinema* (instrumental) and *Leave It* (all five band members singing acapella to start the song). Back in 1979, as noted earlier, I had also seen Supertramp at Exhibition Stadium on their *Breakfast In Canada* Tour. I have the ticket stubs from both concerts, the seats were just one apart.

The title *90125* represents the middle five numbers of the album's seven catalogue number. The album appeared on the CHUM FM top album list in both 1983 & 1984. The album spawned three picture sleeve singles, *Owner of A Lonely Heart, Leave It & It Can Happen. It Can Happen* was a European single and listed June and July concert dates and locations on the back side. Trevor Horn produced the album. The three singles, the *1984 world tour program* cover and the identical live solos album were all variations of the *90125* cover. They all had a very directional, nautical look to them. Trevor Horn also produced *Cry* by Godley & Creme in 1984

Trevor Rabin brought waves of new fans into the Yes fold with his songwriting on *90125, Big Generator, Union* and *Talk*. He had a much rougher sounding edge to his guitar playing than Steve. Trevor's' vocals were strong, like Jon and Chris. This was showcased when they opened the concert with

[110] *Roger Dean* Calendar, 1994 & *Surrealscapes* Calendar, 2011
[111] *Dinosaur* Calendar, Roger Dean, Pomegranate, 1994
[112] *War & Peace*, Tolstoy, 1867

Cinema and then all five singing acapella on *Leave It,* one of the best multi vocal performances I had ever seen. Roger Hodgson sang with Yes on *Walls* from *Talk.* Jon Anderson asked him to join Yes around the time of *Talk.* Roger thanked him but explained that it wasn't the right time or the right fit.[113]

If I look back to the Trevor Rabin years, the eighties and nineties, the music grew a lot. He was taking Yes into a new direction of uncharted territory and waters. It was still Yes but different than the seventies Yes. Again, Trevor brought many more fans into the Yes fold with his unique style, not better or worse than Steve, just different. It's too bad that there is often too much "Holding On" to Yes' seventies music. Trevor wrote numerous feature film scores after he left Yes and recently recorded the album *Jacaranda,* a wonderful showcasing of his musical talent.

In 1985, Jon released a Christmas album entitled *Three Ships*, highlighted by the single *Easier Said Than Done.* In 1987, Jon teamed up with Larry Gowan to perform the backing vocals on the Gowan single *Moonlight Desires.*

Just call me Mr. Yes Fanatic. From Maple Leaf Gardens in 1979 to the Molson Amphitheatre in 2002, I saw Yes a total of ten (yes 10) times, including the 1991 *Union* tour with eight musicians in the lineup. I distinctly remember the song *Lift Me Up*, with all eight musicians playing at once, including Alan White on the drum kit and Bill Bruford standing up playing electronic drums.

When the soundtrack for *Batman Forever* was released in 1995, Trevor Horn played bass for Seal on *Kiss From A Rose* and produced *Nobody Lives Without Love* for Scottish singer Eddi Reader.

The very first time I saw Yes in 1979 was the Classic lineup of Jon Anderson, Steve Howe, Chris Squire, Rick Wakeman & Alan White. The very last time I saw Yes in 2002 was only the second time I saw the Classic lineup and was the first time the Classic lineup had been together since San Luis Obispo in 1996. So, I guess you could say that I bookended all ten concerts I saw with the Classic lineup.

The term "Classic Yes" is very misleading. It was used at San Louis Obispo in 1996 and on the 2002 tour. It refers to the lineup with Anderson, Squire, Howe, Wakeman and White. The three "Classic" albums were *The Yes Album* (1971), *Fragile* (1971) and *Close* (1972). Bill Bruford appeared on all three, not White, and Kaye played on *The Yes Album*, not Wakeman. It was three later albums that had the "Classic" lineup: *Tales From Topographic Oceans* (1973), *Going* (1977) and *Tormato* (1978), all non-existent on modern day radio.

As I mentioned back in chapter 14, in 1998 The Alan Parsons Project opened for Yes at the Molson Amphitheatre. Setlist.fm prepared a setlist and here are the songs: *1.The System Of Dr. Tarr & Professor Feather, 2.I Wouldn't Want To Be Like You, 5.Prime Time, 8.Standing On Higher Ground, 10.The Gold Bug, 11.Eye In The Sky, 12.Don't Answer Me & 13.Games People Play.*

In 2002, John K and I had second row seats so you could almost reach out and shake their hands. Show highlights included *Don't Kill The Whale* from *Tormato* and *South Side Of The Sky* from *Fragile.* Rick Wakeman made two comments on the *Yesyears* video in 1992. First, he was the first rock keyboard player ever to stack his keyboards while playing on stage and often thinks of this when he goes to see bar bands play.[114] Second, he said that with all the changes in the Yes lineup over the years, whoever was in the band at a certain time had the privilege of playing the Yes music and carrying on the Yes tradition.

I created a map back around 2000, entitled *All Roads Lead to YES [gem appendix 22].* It was loosely based on the yes family tree taken from the insert found in the *Yesyears* boxed set.[115] *All Roads* took the Yes family tree quite a bit further. It was partially inspired by the Parsons / Yes tour of 1998. John K and I also went to that concert. Parsons is the other group besides Yes that is central to the map. This was six degrees of

---

[113] ***Roger Hodgson collaboration represents road not taken for Yes: 'One of those things that fizzled out'***, Something Else, Dec 25, 2014, https://somethingelsereviews.com/2014/12/25/roger-hodgson-yes-trevor-rabin/
[114] Rick Wakeman on stacking keyboards, *Yesyears*, 1991
[115] Yes Family Tree, *Yesyears*, boxed Audio Set (Cassette & CD), 1991

separation for all other groups and individuals as they related to either Yes or Parsons. While it is very difficult to read when you look at it, you get the idea about how many groups link back to Yes in some way. Oh yes. For anyone who is paying attention, I have included the group Badfinger twice.

In 2004, Trevor Horn and Geoff Downes and Bruce Willey and the rest of The Buggles, performed *Video Killed The Radio Star* at *The Princes Trust Concert*, the first time they had played the song live in twenty-five years.[116]

I created an extended track CD, entitled *Close Revealing Gates Awaken [gem]*, with four different songs from four different albums…

18.1 ~ Close Revealing Gates Awaken [gem]
1. *Close, Close to The Edge [CLOSE TO THE EDGE]*
2. *Revealing, The Revealing Science Of God [TALES FROM TOPOGRAPHIC OCEANS]*
3. *Gates, The Gates Of Delirium (Soon) [RELAYER]*
4. *Awaken, Awaken [GOING FOR THE ONE]*

Early in the summer of 2011 Yes released *Fly From Here*, their first studio album in ten years. The Buggles, Downes (keyboards) and Horn (producer & backing vocals), were back. The title track/suite was a *Drama* leftover. The album was the best since *90125* (including *The Ladder* and *Talk*). It was quite simply the follow-up to *Drama,* just thirty-one years later. Let's call it *Drama II.* I have listened to *Drama* steadily over the years, one of my favourite albums ever (not just by Yes). I had paired it with *Asia* on the same 90 minute tape.

While Anderson and the Wakeman had to leave the group for health reasons, the music on *Fly From Here (Drama II)* was remarkably good. Benoit David replaced Anderson. He sounded a lot like Horn but with better strength and range. Downes' keyboards were less about virtuosity (Wakeman) and more choppy but absolutely dreamy. David also sang several of the songs from *Drama*, while he toured with the group. Anderson chose not to sing any of those tunes when he toured. With the former Buggles on the *Fly* album, note how I discuss in "What is Classic?" that technopop is a distant cousin to classical/progressive rock.

Anderson himself used the analogy of a bus travelling along a road in describing the group. Every so often the bus stops, some people get on, some stay on, others get off. While the membership may change, the vision of the group continues and soldiers on.

In February of 2012, Benoit (like Anderson) had to leave Yes because of his ailing voice, perhaps too much strain over three years as Anderson's replacement. Then, Jon Davison, of Glass Hammer, replaced David and began touring with Yes in 2012.[117] Brilliant moments come and go in life and David's' departure after only one studio album is a case in point. A shadow of its former self? Maybe. However, Yes soldiers on, for all of us who just can't get enough of this stuff.

Late in 2012, Yes announced that it would tour in 2013, playing three albums, *The Yes Album, Close To The Edge & Going For The One* in their entirety. I initially thought this was exciting. However, to be a true Yes fan, you need to embrace all the other versions of the band that recorded and toured through the 80s, 90s, 00s & 10s. That way, you grow your experience and appreciation of Yes and you don't get "Stuck In The Seventies".

In 2013, Yes lost its first ever alumni, guitar player Peter Banks. In 2015, Yes lost its co-founding and longest standing member, bassist Chris Squire. He arguably made more of an impact as a bassist than either Greg Lake or John Wetton. Billy Sherwood stepped up as the new Yes bassist. Later that same year, I revisited Boo Boo Records in San Luis Obispo, where I had first visited in 1983 and where Yes had recorded their *Keys*

---

[116] *Video Killed The Radio Star*, The Buggles (Trevor Horn, Geoff Downes, Bruce Wooley & The Camera Club & others), The Princes Trust, 2004, https://youtu. be/Zm0QQDMoRPU.
[117] Jon Davison (of Glass Hammer) joins Yes and replaces Benoit David.

To Ascension albums back in 1996. The book *Record Store Days* celebrates stores like Boo Boo Records, including that store as well.

In 2016, Jon Anderson, Trevor Rabin and Rick Wakeman began touring, to promote their album *ARW* and to perform long time Yes music, as well. Noted here is the revival of eighties and nineties Yes music, when Trevor was a major part of the band. In 2017, Yes was inducted into the Rock & Roll Hall Of Fame and *Drama* finally got the respect it deserved via the release of the live album *Topographic Drama*. In 2018, Yes celebrated fifty years as a rock band.

In early 2022, Classic Rock Platinum Series Magazine published the top 40 songs by Yes. Here is my part of the list…

18.2 ~ Top 40 Songs

1.*Close to The Edge (Total Mass Retain /b)*, 2.*And You & I*, 4.*Roundabout*, 6.*Awaken (/b)*, 8.*Gates Of Delirium (Soon)*, 9.*I've Seen All Good People (Your Move)*, 11.*Long Distance Runaround (/b)*, 13.*Owner Of A Lonely Heart*, 14.*Wonderous Stories*, 16.*Going For The One*, 20.*Sound Chaser (/b)*, 21.*America*, 26.*Parallels (/b)*, 28.*It Can Happen*, 31.*Don't Kill The Whale*, 32.*Love Will Find A Way* & 33.*Leave It*.

For a band that was known mostly for its albums, Yes released quite a few singles, nineteen in this collection. Only Chicago, Genesis, Paul McCartney & The Alan Parsons Project have more.

In May of 2022, Yes lost drummer Alan White, second in Yes longevity only to the late Chris Squire. While it may have looked like White had more longevity than Squire it wasn't all fulltime. He had been sharing the drumming duties with Jay Schellen since about 2016. Apart from White's incredible drumming skills, I always loved the piano part he wrote at the conclusion of *Ritual (Nous Sommes De Soleil)* on *Topographic Oceans*[118]. Rick Wakeman described White as a gentle soul, except for when he was sitting behind his drum kit. White joined Yes way back there in the summer of 1972, when I first heard the single *Roundabout*, launching me into my long time interest in popular music. White now passes the torch on to Schellen.

In June of 2024, Yes released a vintage version of the 1971 album *Fragile*. I purchased it just two days after it was released at the Gallery Of Sound in Dickson City, Pennsylvania. With an LP of the original album as part of the package, *Heart Of The Sunrise* features the *We Have Heaven Reprise* at it's conclusion. The first version I ever bought of *Fragile* in September of 1975, featured the same *We Have Heaven Reprise*.

---

[118] *The Complete Story Yes*, Classic Rock Platinum Series, 2021, p.42

NINETEEN

WHAT IS CLASSIC
& WHAT IS CRAZY HIPPIE
ORGAN MUSIC?

These next four chapters are the meat and potatoes of the story, the structure and sound of music. This chapter is about both the structure and sound of *Classical Rock*. *Classical Rock*, or progressive rock, as I usually call it began way back there in the late 1960s and early 1970s. It came from what started as psychedelic rock. First up was …

19.1 ~ Psychedelic Rock
1. *Sgt. Pepper's Lonely Hearts Club Band* - **The Beatles,** 1967
2. *Days Of Future Passed* - **The Moody Blues,** 1967
3. *Tommy* - **The Who,** 1969
4. *Jesus Christ Superstar* - **Andrew Lloyd Webber & Tim Rice,** 1971
5. *Live With The Edmonton Symphony Orchestra* - **Procal Harum,** 1972

For each of these aforementioned pieces, large orchestras performed with the bands, bridging the gap between classical and rock music. ELP (*Works Volume 1,* 1977) and Yes, (*Classic Yes Tour*, 2002) continued this trend when they toured with Orchestras. There were other "Concept Albums" along the way, including …

19.2 ~ Concept Albums
1. *Tarkus* - **Emerson Lake & Palmer,** 1971
2. *Close To The Edge* - **Yes,** 1972
3. *Crime Of The Century* - **Supertramp,** 1974

4. *Lamb Lies Down On Broadway, The* - **Genesis,** 1975
5. *Wall, The* - **Pink Floyd,** 1979

Annie Lennox of the Eurythmics said *Whiter Shade Of Pale* was the first single she ever bought. The tradition of playing with orchestras has continued, especially the *Night At The Proms*, including Alan Parsons, Alphaville, Deep Purple, Foreigner, Orchestral Manoeuvres In The Dark, Roger Hodgson, Simple Minds, Styx, Tears For Fears and many others.[119] In the next chapter, *Structure*, I talk about "Suites" which have their origins in classical music. The Buggles played in the 2004 *Prince's Trust Concert*, similar to the *Night At The Proms*.

Classic Rock is usually referred to as album oriented rock from the time period starting in the 1960s and ending in the 1980s. This follows closely the phasing out of vinyl and phasing in of CDs. My experience has been with CILQ107 FM in Toronto, CHEZ106 in Ottawa and CKDK103.9 in Woodstock,[120] now a country station, formerly "The Greatest Hits" and before that Classic Rock 103.9 "The Hawk" (sister station to CILQ107 in Toronto).

In 2011 CKDK changed again from greatest hits to an adult format. All the Classic is gone and as Jim Stafford would say "All good things got to come to an end (it's the same with the *Wildwood Weed*)". Classic Rock, in an antique sense, could just be any rock music that's at least twenty-five years old.

I do have the *Classic Rock All Music Guide,*[121] same reviews of albums that can be found on the Allmusic website. On a side note, classic rock often means talented guitarists, bassists, or drummers but that's not all. Keyboardists are talented too, classically influenced and trained "art" and "progressive" rockers.

The following is a big part of this entire story. While it is easy for most of us to think of lots of guitar and piano tunes, it's not so easy to think of organ tunes. Most of us can remember the sound of an organ as kids from going to church or even the circus. How's that for two extremes? What follows are samples of impressive rock organ tunes, tunes in which the organ is very prominent.

Many of the tunes are from the period 1965-1975, the same period Andy Frost uses for *Psychedelic Psunday* on Q107.[122] I must admit that the idea comes from the late seventies, when high school / university friend Eric commented about a fellow Trent University classmate. The student was from either Grimsby or Beamsville and referred to progressive rock music with organ as *Crazy Hippie Organ Music [gem 19.7]*[123] Then there was a weekend full of Organ inspired music on Q107 in the early 2000s, *The Big Organ Weekend.*[124] Organ crosses many genres of music, classical, country, jazz, pop, rock & techno.

There are entries by over forty groups in this category, the largest in the collection along with homemade picture sleeves. At first, I broke the list in two. The Andy Frost list was first and then the songs that were released in 1976 and after. Then I changed it to Before Ottawa (pre summer 1973), Ottawa (summer 1973 - summer 1977) & After Ottawa (post summer 1977), highlighting my increased interest in popular music in Ottawa in the mid-seventies. In fact, many of the pre Ottawa tunes were played in abundance while I lived in Ottawa …

---

[119] Night At The Proms Concert Series
[120] Classic Rock The Hawk, CKDK103.9, Woodstock, ON
[121] *Classic Rock Allmusic Guide,* Backbeat Books, 2007
[122] *Psychedelic Psunday*, Andy Frost, Q107, CILQ FM, Toronto
[123] *Crazy Hippie Organ Music*, Trent University, 1979
[124] *Big Organ Weekend*, Q107, CILQ FM, Toronto, early 2000s.

19.3 ~ Organ I - Toronto To 1973

1. *As The Years Go By* - **Mashmakhan**
2. *Baby I Love You* - **Andy Kim**
3. *Black Magic Woman* - **Santana**
4. *Born to Be Wild & Magic Carpet Ride* - **Steppenwolf**
5. *Dance To The Music* - **Sly & The Family Stone**
6. *Doo Wah Diddy Diddy* - **Manfred Mann**
7. *Eli's Coming, Family Of Man, Liar, One Man Band & Shambala* - **Three Dog Night**
8. *Fly Across The Sea, Last Song & Masquerade* - **Edward Bear**
9. *Gimmie Some Lovin'* - **The Spencer Davis Group**
10. *Green Eyed Lady* - **Sugarloaf**
11. *Hello I Love You, Light My Fire & Touch Me* - **The Doors**
12. *Hitchin' A Ride* - **Vanity Fare**
13. *Hocus Pocus* - **Focus**
14. *Joy* - **Apollo 100**
15. *Love The One You're With* - **Stephen Stills**
16. *Lowdown* - **Chicago**
17. *Right Place Wrong Time* - **Dr. John**
18. *Tie A Yellow Ribbon Round The Ole Oak Tree* - **Dawn**
19. *Time Of The Season* - **The Zombies**
20. *Up On Cripple Creek* - **The Band**
21. *When A Man Loves A Woman* - **Percy Sledge**
22. *Why Can't We Live Together* - **Timmy Thomas**
23. *You're Still The One* - **Copper Penny**
24. *You've Made Me So Very Happy* - **Blood, Sweat & Tears**

19.4 ~ Organ II - Ottawa 1973 to 1977

1. *Another Saturday Night* - **Cat Stevens**
2. *Blinded by The Light* - **Manfred Mann**
3. *Born To Run* - **Bruce Springsteen**
4. *Cold As Ice* - **Foreigner**
5. *Dance A Little Step* - **Mashmakhan**
6. *Don't Call Us We'll Call You* - **Sugarloaf**
7. *Don't Fear The Reaper* - **Blue Oyster Cult**
8. *Emma* - **Hot Chocolate**
9. *Fly Like An Eagle* - **The Steve Miller Band**
10. *Foreplay (/b) & Longtime* - **Boston**
11. *Holding On To Yesterday* - **Ambrosia**
12. *I Can Help* - **Billy Swan**
13. *Some Kinda Wonderful & We're An American Band* - **Grand Funk**
14. *Walking On Back* - **Edward Bear**

19.5 ~ Organ III - Toronto From 1977

1. *Advice For The Young At Heart & Shout* - **Tears For Fears**
2. *All This Time & If I Ever Lose My Faith In You* - **Sting**
3. *Centerfield* - **John Fogerty**
4. *Cuts Like A Knife, Reggae Christmas (/b) & Straight From The Heart* - **Bryan Adams**
5. *Dirty Laundry* - **Don Henley**
6. *Don't Dream It's Over* - **Crowded House**
7. *Echo Beach* - **Martha & The Muffins**
8. *Everyday Is A Winding Road* - **Sheryl Crow**
9. *Everybody Hurts* - **REM**
10. *Forever (Live & Die)* - **Orchestral Manoeuvres In The Dark**
11. *Freeze Frame* - **The J Geils Band**
12. *Girls Just Wanna Have Fun* - **Lauper, Cindy**
13. *Glory Days & Merry Christmas Baby* - **Bruce Springsteen**
14. *Heart Of Glass & One Way Or Another* - **Blondie**
15. *How Much I Feel (/b)* - **Ambrosia**
16. *Hurts So Good & Jack & Diane* - **John Cougar Mellencamp**
17. *I Got You & One Step Ahead* - **Split Enz**
18. *I Want A New Drug* - **Huey Lewis & The News**
19. *Let My Love Open The Door* - **Pete Townsend**
20. *Life's Been Good* - **Joe Walsh**
21. *New Song* - **Howard Jones**
22. *Rock Lobster* - **B 52s**
23. *Roll With It & While You See A Chance* - **Steve Winwood**
24. *Tainted Love* - **Soft Cell**
25. *Take On Me* - **A-Ha**
26. *Wake Me Up Before You Go* - **Wham**
27. *Walk Of Life* - **Dire Straits**

The next list spans across all three time periods and is an elite list of tunes with organ and piano. Prog tunes that fit this criterion are listed here, rather than the next list. While most are regular piano, I have especially noted the electric piano *(/e)*. Three Dog Night leads the way here…

19.6 ~ Organ IV - & A Piano

1. *Ain't Nobody But Me, The Logical Song & Take The Long Way Home* - **Supertramp**
2. *Awaken (/b) & Into The Lens* - **Yes**
3. *Bennie & The Jets & Crocodile Rock* - **Elton John**
4. *Black & White, Let Me Serenade You, Never Been To Spain, An Old Fashioned Love Song & The Show Must Go On* - **Three Dog Night**
5. *Carry On Wayward Son* - **Kansas**
6. *Close Your Eyes (/e)* - **Edward Bear**
7. *Don't Let It Show* - **The Alan Parsons Project**
8. *Hello It's Me* - **Todd Rundgren**
9. *I Shot The Sheriff* - **Eric Clapton**

10. *Just A Smile (/e)* - **Pilot**
11. *Lady* - **Styx**
12. *Love Her Madly* - **The Doors**
13. *Maybe I'm Amazed & Maybe I'm Amazed (Live)* - **Paul McCartney & Wings**
14. *New Kid In Town (/e) & The Last Resort (/b)* - **The Eagles**
15. *Pioneer & Six Months In A Leaky Boat* - **Split Enz**
16. *Ramblin' Man* - **The Allman Brothers Band**
17. *Run Baby Run (/b)* - **Sheryl Crow**
18. *Sole Survivor* - **Asia**
19. *Sowing The Seeds Of Love (/e)* - **Tears For Fears**
20. *That's All* - **Genesis**
21. *The Things We Do For Love* - **10 CC**
22. *Total Eclipse Of The Heart* - **Bonnie Tyler**
23. *Up On The Catwalk* - **Simple Minds**
24. *Will It Go Round In Circles* - **Billy Preston**

This next list covers the three periods of organ music, *19.3 Toronto, 19.4 Ottawa & 19.5 Toronto* and while it does not include songs and groups with organ & piano *(19.6)*, it focuses on the prog tunes with just organ, or the *Crazy Hippie Organ Music [gem].*

19.7 ~ Organ V - Crazy Hippie Organ Music [gem]
1. *Abacab, Follow You Follow Me, I Know What I Like (In Your Wardrobe), Mama & No Son Of Mine* - **Genesis**
2. *America, And You & I Pt. 1, Does It Really Happen? (/b), Love Will Find A Way, Parallels (/b), Release Release, Roundabout & Your Move* - **Yes**
3. *Blue Collar Man, Mademoiselle & Mr. Roboto* - **Styx**
4. *Conquistador & White Shade Of Pale* - **Procal Harum**
5. *Do It Again* - **Steely Dan**
6. *Fanfare For The Common Man, Jerusalem & Stones Of Years* - **Emerson, Lake & Palmer**
7. *Free As A Bird, Just Another Nervous Wreck (/b) & Sister Moonshine (/b)* - **Supertramp**
8. *Hi Hi Hi & Letting Go* - **Paul McCartney & Wings**
9. *Hold Your Head Up* - **Argent**
10. *Hush, Smoke On The Water & Smoke on The Water (Live)* - **Deep Purple**

Prog Magazine celebrated ten years in 2020. It featured the top 100 progressive rock albums of all time.[125] I have put a different spin on it and listed out all the albums I have in that list for which I also have singles. It's a great synergy of two major parts of my record collecting, top 40 singles & progressive rock music. Here's what it looks like…

---

[125] 100 Most Influential Progressive Rock Albums Of All Time, 2020

19.8 ~ Prog Top Albums & Singles

1. 1. *[CLOSE TO THE EDGE] And You & I Pt. 1 & 2* - **Yes**
2. 3. *[SELLING ENGLAND BY THE POUND] I Know What I Like (In Your Wardrobe)* - **Genesis**
3. 4. *[DARK SIDE OF THE MOON] Money / Any Colour You Like* - **Pink Floyd**
4. 8. *[THE LAMB LIES DOWN ON BROADWAY] Counting Out Time & The Lamb Lies Down On Broadway* - **Genesis**
5. 10. *[FRAGILE] Roundabout / Long Distance Runaround* - **Yes**
6. 11. *[BRAIN SALAD SURGERY] Excerpts From Brain Salad Surgery & Jerusalem* - **Emerson, Lake & Palmer**
7. 13. *[MOVING PICTURES] Limelight / YYZ & Tom Sawyer / Witch Hunt* - **Rush**
8. 16. *[THE WALL] Another Brick In The Wall Part Two / One Of My Turns, Run Like Hell // Comfortably Numb & Run Like Hell / Don't Leave Me Now* - **Pink Floyd**
9. 19. *[RELAYER] Soon / Sound Chaser* - **Yes**
10. 21. *[A TRICK OF THE TAIL] Entangled / Ripples & A Trick Of The Tail* - **Genesis**
11. 26. *[GOING FOR THE ONE] Going For The One / Parallels & Wonderous Stories / Awaken* - **Yes**
12. 28. *[TARKUS] Stones Of Years / Time & A Place* - **Emerson, Lake & Palmer**
13. 32. *[THE YES ALBUM] Your Move / The Clap* - **Yes**
14. 42. *[TRILOGY] From The Beginning / Living Sin* - **Emerson, Lake & Palmer**
15. 44. *[WIND & WUTHERING] Your Own Special Way / In That Quiet Earth* - **Genesis**
16. 53. *[FAREWELL TO KINGS] Cinderella Man / A Farewell To Kings* - **Rush**
17. 60. *[TUBULAR BELLS] Tubular Bells* - **Mike Oldfield**
18. 69. *[PERMANENT WAVES] Spirit Of Radio / Circumstances* - **Rush**
19. 77. *[CRIME OF THE CENTURY] Dreamer / Bloody Well Right* - **Supertramp**
20. 79. *[EMERSON, LAKE & PALMER] Knife Edge & Lucky Man* - **Emerson, Lake & Palmer**
21. 81. *[LEFTOVERTURE] Carry On Wayward Son / Questions Of My Childhood* - **Kansas**
22. 100. *[DRAMA] Into The Lens / Does It Really Happen? & Run Thru The Light / Man In A White Car* - **Yes**

Drama brought together a third major part of my record collecting, new wave & techno pop, alongside top 40 singles and progressive rock. Keep an eye out shortly for the discussion about prog rock and classical rock having two distant cousins, one of them new wave.

The decline of progressive rock is a lot like watching Television. Sometimes, people want to watch something they can really learn something from, like listening to *Classical Rock*. Other times, they just want to watch something that will entertain them, like listening to the old AM bubble gum music or the more mainstream straight ahead rock'n roll sound. The all-time rock and roll lists you see highlight the fact that there is very little in the way of progressive rock.

Next up is another spin on a prog list. In 2019. Prog celebrated issue #100 by highlighting one-hundred personalities who changed the progressive rock landscape. Prog musicians talk about other prog musicians and mention songs that make them think of those musicians. The songs by those musicians form the basis of this list. The musicians who are writing about their favourite musicians are also noted.

19.9 ~ Prog Top Icons & Singles

1. *Awaken* - **Rick Wakeman (Yes)** - Sean Timms (Southern Empire), p.68
2. *Breakfast In America & Take The Long Way Home* - **Roger Hodgson (Supertramp)** - Damian Wilson (Headspace, Wilson & Wakeman), p.49
3. *Come Sail Away* - **Dennis DeYoung (Styx)** - Jeff Scott Soto (Sons Of Apollo), p.43
4. *Counting Out Time, Mama & Ripples* - **Mike Rutherford (Genesis)** - Greg Spawton (Big Big Train), p.60
5. *Fanfare for The Common Man* - **Keith Emerson (Emerson, Lake & Palmer)** - Geoff Downes (Asia, Buggles & Yes), p.67
6. *Going For The One & Owner Of a Lonely Heart* - **Jon Anderson (Yes)** - Steve Hogarth (Marillion), p.92
7. *Live & Let Die & Maybe I'm Amazed* - **Paul McCartney** - Pete Trowavas (Marillion), p.70
8. *Long Distance Runaround & Roundabout* - **Bill Bruford (Yes)** - Rick Wakeman (Yes), p.84
9. *Love Will Find A Way* - **Trevor Rabin (Yes)** - John Mitchell (Frost, Kino, Lonely Robot), p.67
10. *Roundabout* - **Steve Howe (Yes)** - Mike Keneally, p.85
11. *Sledgehammer* - **Tony Levin (Peter Gabriel)** - Guy Pratt (Nick Mason's Saucerful Of Secrets), p.88
12. *Tubular Bells* - **Mike Oldfield** - Bob Reed (Magenta), p.77
13. *Whiter Shade Of Pale* - **Gary Brooker (Procol Harum)** - Roine Stolt, p.45

Classical Rock had "Two Distant Cousins". The first was soul music, i.e. The Chi-Lites, Earth, Wind & Fire, Roberta Flack, The O'Jays, The Spinners, The Stylistics, The Three Degrees, War and Bill Withers. This music type was predominantly American. What tied them together was the instrumentation, orchestral sound, horns, woodwinds and strings, specifically violins. While synthesizers replaced strings in later types of music, including soul, there was no mistaking the real string sound.

John K gave me an interesting book about the history of popular music, *Off The Record: An Oral History Of Popular Music* by Joe Smith & Mitchell Fink. Not knowing how important the book was at the time, I gave it away. Many of the groups mentioned here, from the Philadelphia music scene, were mentioned in that book. My *Sweet Soul* mix goes like this ...

19.10 ~ Mix I - Sweet Soul

1. *Betcha By Golly Wow* - **The Stylistics**
2. *Billie Jean* - **Michael Jackson**
3. *Cisko Kid* - **War**
4. *Could It Be I'm Falling In Love* - **The Spinners**
5. *Drift Away* - **Dobie Gray**
6. *Everybody Plays The Fool* - **The Main Ingredient**
7. *Feel Like Making Love* - **Roberta Flack**
8. *If You Don't Know Me By Now* - **Harold Melvin & The Blue Notes with Teddy Pendergrass**
9. *Lean On Me* - **Bill Withers**
10. *Love Train* - **The O'Jays**

11. *Me & Mrs. Jones* - **Billy Paul**
12. *My Cherie Amour* - **Stevie Wonder**
13. *Oh Girl* - **The Chi-Lites**
14. *Sideshow* - **Blue Magic**
15. *That's The Way Of The World* - **Earth, Wind & Fire**
16. *Walking In Rhythm* - **The Blackbyrds**
17. *When Will I See You Again* - **The Three Degrees**

The second was electronic / new wave / synth pop / techno pop music, starting with Hot Butter, Kraftwerk, Nash The Slash, 10 CC, Tangerine Dream, Vangelis, Gary Wright and continuing with Orchestral Manoeuvres In The Dark, The Human League, The Buggles, Thomas Dolby, Howard Jones, Nik Kershaw, Gary Numan and many others. This music type was predominantly British with some German and others.

The electronic/new wave (electropop / synthpop / technopop) sound featured a very tuneful sound but has been much maligned, especially by their use of keyboards. The link was a "synthesized" Symphony/Orchestra sound. I bought *The Encyclopedia Of New Wave*[126] and *Is It Live, The Story Of Much Music,*[127] both valuable and insightful resources and ample proof that music from the eighties did not "suck". My *NeWavEighties [gem]* highlights many of the artists mentioned above …

19.11 ~ Mix II - NeWavEighties
1. *99 Red Balloons* - **Nena**
2. *Always Something There To Remind Me* - **The Naked Eyes**
3. *Dance Hall Days* - **Wang Chung**
4. *Dancing With Tears In My Eyes* - **Ultravox**
5. *Don't You Want Me* - **The Human League**
6. *Enola Gay* - **Orchestral Manoeuvres In The Dark**
7. *Friends Of Mr. Cairo* - **Jon & Vangelis**
8. *Hold Me Now* - **The Thompson Twins**
9. *I Got You* - **Split Enz**
10. *It's My Life* - **Talk Talk**
11. *Major Tom* - **Peter Schilling**
12. *New Song* - **Howard Jones**
13. *One Night In Bangkok* - **Murray Head**
14. *One Thing Leads To Another* - **The Fixx**
15. *Pale Shelter* - **Tears For Fears**
16. *She Blinded Me With Science* - **Thomas Dolby**
17. *Take On Me* - **A-Ha**
18. *West End Girls* - **The Pet Shop Boys**
19. *Wishing (If I Had A Photograph Of You)* - **A Flock Of Seagulls**

Yes has bridged the techno/prog gap on several occasions. Geoff Downes and Trevor Horn of The Buggles added their techno sound to the Yes Prog Rock sound on *Drama* in 1980. One of their loudest albums ever, *Drama* was arguably the closest Yes ever got to a heavy metal sound. Jon Anderson recorded

[126] *Encyclopedia Of New Wave*, Daniel Bukszpan, Sterling, New York, 2012
[127] *Is It Live, The Story Of Much Music*, Christopher Ward, Random House Canada, 2016

The *Friends Of Mr. Cairo* with Vangelis in 1981, after failing to land Vangelis as the keyboardist for *Relayer* (1974) and settled for Patrick Moraz instead. Rick Wakeman even got into the techno sound when he released the single *I'm So Straight I'm A Weirdo*.

Examples of winds & horns over top of electronics are saxophones on Vangelis' *Love Theme* from *Blade Runner*, Floyds' *Shine On You Crazy Diamond Part One*, Supertramp's' *Fool's Overture* and trombone on Dolby's *I Scare Myself* and *Hyperactive*. Parts of the *Blade Runner* soundtrack sound like an orchestra.

Blade Runner itself (The Film) brings another classic recording element to this *R P aMble*. The climactic scene with Roy Batty delivering his *Tears In Rain* soliloquy is preceded by Deckard running away from Batty and jumping from the rooftop of one building to the next. As Batty emerges from the building onto the first rooftop, you can see a huge TDK sign in the background.

In 2019, the year in which the story of *Blade Runner* was set, I bought the 180 gram vinyl version of *Blade Runner* by Vangelis. Vangelis didn't release the full version of the original *Blade Runner* soundtrack until twelve years after the movies' release, in 1994. I didn't think the vinyl version of what is basically electronic music could be any better than the CD. I was pleasantly mistaken.

The last list in this chapter is a nod to musicians making contributions to songs by other musicians, mostly producing and one composing (c).

19.12 ~ Musicians Contributing To Songs By Other Musicians

1. **Alan Parsons** - *Any Colour You Like & Money* - **Pink Floyd,** *January, Just A Smile, Just Let Me Be & Magic* - **Pilot** & *On The Border, Time Passages & Year Of The Cat* - **Al Stewart**
2. **Jeff Lynn** - *Got My Mind Set On You, This Is Love & When We Was Fab* - **George Harrison**
3. **Les Emmerson** - *Finally (With You)* - **The Cooper Brothers**
4. **Paul McCartney** (c) - *Come & Get It* - **Badfinger**
5. **Randy Bachman** - *Raise A Little Hell, Two For The Show & We're Here For A Good Time* - **Trooper**
6. **Rick Derringer** - *Frankenstein* - **The Edgar Winter Group**
7. **Todd Rundgren** - *The Loco Motion & We're An American Band / Creepin'* - **Grand Funk Railroad** & *Bat Out Of Hell // Heaven Can Wait & Two Out Of Three Ain't Bad* - **Meatloaf**
8. **Trevor Horn** - *Cry* - **Godley & Creme** & *Kiss From A Rose* - **Seal**

TWENTY

STRUCTURE - THE BLUES,
SUITES, SWING & WALTZES

This chapter is the second of four chapters on structure and sound and will focus on structure, specifically suites, long and short versions, chord changes and waltzes. Suites or extended pieces of music are a big part of rock music, specifically, classical, or progressive rock. John K bought me a great book, *Rocking The Classics.*[128] Part of it is an in depth study of four pieces of progressive rock music …

20.1 ~ Rocking The Classics
1. *Close To The Edge* - **Yes**
2. *Firth Of Fifth* - **Genesis**
3. *Tarkus* - **ELP**
4. *Shine On You Crazy Diamond Part One* - **Pink Floyd.**

It's a good read for both fans and musicians alike. This truly is Classic Rock. Here are other examples of suites…

20.2 ~ Suites I - Regular
1. **Boston** - *[BOSTON] Foreplay / Long Time*
2. **Cars, The** - *[THE CARS] (from side two) You're All I've Got Tonight / Bye Bye Love / Moving In Stereo / All Mixed Up*
3. **Chicago** - *[CHICAGO II] Ballet For A Girl In Buchanan (Colour My World & Make Me Smile)*

---

[128] *Rocking The Classics*, Edward Macan, Oxford University Press, 1997, p.85

4. **Genesis** - *Live The Way We Walk Tour 1993 - Firth Of Fifth, Follow You Follow Me, I Know What I Like (In Your Wardrobe) & That's All*
5. **McCartney, Paul** - *[GIVE MY REGARDS TO BROAD STREET] Yesterday / Here There & Everywhere / Wanderlust*
6. **Parsons Project, The Alan** - *[TURN OF A FRIENDLY CARD] Turn Of A Friendly Card*
7. **U2** - *[ACHTUNG BABY] So Cruel, Mysterious Ways & Throwing Your Arms Around The World*
8. **Yes** - *Tormato Tour 1979 - Long Distance Runaround / The Fish / The Gates Of Delirium / Soon*

Going further there are single pieces we can call *Mini Suites.* This is a combination of songs that have tempo changes over different sections, while others maintain the same tempo but add in themes beyond their initial verses and choruses. Many of these entries were originally part of the list of songs over five minutes in length, they are now just in this list. Those that are part waltzes (some also originally part of the songs over five minutes) are in their own list, 20.16. Examples of Mini Suites from various artists might include …

20.3 ~ Suites II - Mini
1. *(I've Been} Searchin' So Long & Feeling Stronger Everyday* - **Chicago**
2. *And You & I Pt. 1, Awaken Pt. 1(/b), Does It Really Happen? (/b) & Soon* - **Yes**
3. *Aquarius & Let The Sunshine* - **The Fifth Dimension**
4. *Band On The Run, Hi Hi Hi, Live & Let Die, Listen To What The Man Said, Pipes Of Peace, Uncle Albert & Admiral Halsey & Venus & Mars Rock Show* - **Paul McCartney & Wings**
5. *Crazy On You* - **Heart**
6. *Don't Let It Show* - **The Alan Parsons Project**
7. *Freedom* - **George Michael**
8. *Inside & Out (/b)* - **Genesis**
9. *Layla* - **Derek & The Dominoes**
10. *Let It Rain* - **Eric Clapton**
11. *One Night In Bangkok* - **Murray Head**
12. *Pioneer & Six Months In A Leaky Boat* - **Split Enz**
13. *Question* - **The Moody Blues**
14. *Rudy (/b)* - **Supertramp**
15. *Sowing The Seeds Of Love* - **Tears For Fears**
16. *Stairway To Heaven* - **Led Zeppelin**

I remember John Scholls saying the *Art Rock Weekend* (2006) [26.2] was a chance to hear the long songs that you didn't hear as often.[129] Taking this into context, it makes the next two lists all that much more impressive. I call it the *five minute club.* These were the songs that were longer than five minutes that were played back in the days of AM top forty radio in the seventies and eighties and nineties. In those days, it was always a case of shorter is better…

---

[129] Art Rock Weekend, Q107, CILQ FM, Toronto, November 10 & 11, 2006

20.4 ~ The Five Minute Club I - Lone

1. *Also Sprach Zarathustra (2001)* - **Deodato**
2. *Cuts Like A Knife* - **Bryan Adams**
3. *Damn I Wish I Was Your Lover* - **Sophie B Hawkins**
4. *Discotheque* - **U2**
5. *Earache My Eye* - **Cheech & Chong**
6. *Freedom* - **George Michael**
7. *Hey Jude* - **The Beatles**
8. *Hold Your Head Up* - **Argent**
9. *Isn't Life Strange* - **The Moody Blues**
10. *L. A. Woman* - **The Doors**
11. *Layla* - **Derek & The Dominoes**
12. *Leaving Las Vegas (/b)* - **Sheryl Crow**
13. *Let It Rain* - **Eric Clapton**
14. *Knife Edge (/b)* - **Emerson, Lake & Palmer**
15. *Magic Man* - **Heart**
16. *Make Me Do (Anything You Want)* - **A Foot In Cold Water**
17. *My Sweet Lord // Isn't It A Pity* - **George Harrison**
18. *Only Women Bleed* - **Alice Cooper**
19. *Pioneer & Six Months In A Leaky Boat* - **Split Enz**
20. *Power Of Love* - **Frankie Goes To Hollywood**
21. *Radar Love* - **Golden Earring**
22. *She Blinded Me With Science* - **Thomas Dolby**
23. *Sole Survivor* - **Asia**
24. *Space Oddity* - **David Bowie**
25. *Sweet Home Alabama* - **Lynyrd Skynyrd**
26. *Taxi* - **Harry Chapin**
27. *Who Are You* - **The Who**
28. *Vultures In The City (/b)* - **Anderson Bruford Wakeman & Howe**
29. *Wreck Of The Edmund Fitzgerald* - **Gordon Lightfoot**

Genesis, Supertramp and Yes each have an impressive list, thanks to a healthy number of B side entries.

20.5 ~ The Five Minute Club II - Several

1. *Alive & Kicking, Don't You (Forget About Me) (Live), Hypnotized & This Is Your Land* - **Simple Minds**
2. *And You & I, Awaken (/b), City Of Love (Live) (/b), Does It Really Happen? (/b), It Can Happen (Live) (/b), Lift Me Up, Parallels (/b), Release Release & Roundabout (Live) // I've Seen All Good People (Live)* - **Yes**
3. *Band On The Run, Let 'Em In, Maybe I'm Amazed (Live), Silly Love Songs & With A Little Luck* - **Paul McCartney & Wings**
4. *Bennie & The Jets, Honky Cat, Lucy In The Sky With Diamonds, Philadelphia Freedom & Someone Saved My Life Tonight* - **Elton John**
5. *Bohemian Rhapsody & We Are The Champions // We Will Rock You* - **Queen**

6. *Bonnie (/b), Brother Where You Bound (/b), Even In The Quietist Moments (/b), Gone Hollywood (/b), Goodbye Stranger, Rudy (/b) & Take The Long Way Home -* **Supertramp**
7. *Calling Elvis & The Sultans Of Swing -* **Dire Straits**
8. *Dirty Laundry & End Of The Innocence -* **Don Henley**
9. *Dodo (/b), Inside & Out (/b), It's Gonna Get Better (/b), The Last Domino (/b), Mama, No Son Of Mine, Second Home By The Sea (/b) & Way Of The World (/b) -* **Genesis**
10. *Fool In the Rain, Stairway To Heaven & Whole Lotta Love (You Need Love -* **Willie Dixon***) -* **Led Zeppelin**
11. *Hotel California, The Last Resort (/b) & New Kid In Town -* **The Eagles**
12. *I Robot (/b) & Urbania (/b) -* **The Alan Parsons Project**
13. *I Wish It Would Rain Down & In The Air Tonight -* **Phil Collins**
14. *In Your Eyes & Red Rain -* **Peter Gabriel**
15. *Like A Prayer & Vogue -* **Madonna**
16. *Sowing The Seeds Of Love & Woman In Chains -* **Tears For Fears**
17. *Synchronicity II & Wrapped Around Your Finger -* **The Police**

But bigger (/longer/) is not always better. Some songs have good long versions, while others just drone on way too long. Singles came in different versions, album, edited, or remixed. One song could have several versions.

Back in chapter four, singles & albums, I talked about singles that were better sounding versions than the album versions they had been created from. One of those songs, *Run Through The Light,* leads into this next list. The list is a group of songs that were restructured, where sections of the songs were put in different places. Here they are…

20.6 ~ Restructured Versions
1. *Abacab -* **Genesis**
2. *Another Brick In The Wall Pt. II -* **Pink Floyd**
3. *Beginnings & Make Me Smile -* **Chicago**
4. *Dreamboat Annie -* **Heart**
5. *I Am The Walrus (/b) -* **The Beatles**
6. *New Year's Day -* **U2**
7. *Run Through The Light (/b) & Total Mass Retain -* **Yes**
8. *Waterfront -* **Simple Minds**

Another Brick In the Wall Pt II and *Waterfront* have specially created intros. The ending of *Abacab* is a repeat of the introduction, where the album had a guitar solo. The single version of *Dreamboat Annie,* the long version, where it was its own A side, not the B side of *Crazy On You,* features the guitar solo from the front end of *Crazy On You. New Years Day* ends with a return to the chorus, not a return to a verse like on the album. *Beginnings* also ends by going back to the chorus of whoa whoa whoa etc.. *I Am The Walrus* features an extra bar before the Yellow matter custard verse. Finally, *Run Through The Light,* while it doesn't have a section that changed places, features an ending. The album version just fades out. *Total Mass Retain* borrows the keyboard intro from *Solid Time Of Change*

The American blues follows a basic one-four-five chord change. A selection of songs with this progression might go something like this…

20.7 ~ 1-4-5 Chord Change

1. *(I Can't Get No) Satisfaction* - **The Rolling Stones**
2. *Angel Of Harlem, Desire & When Love Comes To Town* - **U2**
3. *Bongo Rock* - **Incredible Bongo Band (Preston Epps)**
4. *Boogie Woogie Bugle Boy* - **Bette Midler**
5. *Clap For The Wolfman* - **The Guess Who**
6. *Devil You, Hit The Road Jack & Wild Eyes* - **The Stampeders**
7. *Don't Bring Me Down & Roll Over Beethoven* - T**he Electric Light Orchestra**
8. *Dueling Banjos* - **Eric Weisberg**
9. *Going For The One* - **Yes**
10. *Going Up The Country* - **Canned Heat**
11. *Heart Of Rock & Roll & I Want A New Drug* - **Huey Lewis**
12. *Honky Tonk Train Blues* - **Keith Emerson (Meade Lux Lewis)**
13. *Hot Dog & Rock & Roll* - **Led Zeppelin**
14. *I Can Dance (Long Tall Glasses)* - **Shooter (Leo Sayer)**
15. *I'm Down* - T**he Beatles**
16. *Johnny B Goode (/b)* - **Chuck Berry**
17. *Long Cool Woman In A Black Dress* - **The Hollies**
18. *Long Tall Glasses* - **Leo Sayer**
19. *Old Time Rock & Roll* - **Bob Segar**
20. *Ramblin' Man* - **The Allman Brothers Band**
21. *Rockin' At Midnight* - **The Honeydrippers**
22. *Rockin' Pneumonia* - **Johnny Rivers**
23. *Rodeo Song* - **Garry Lee**
24. *Sharp Dressed Man* - **ZZ Top**
25. *Straight Shootin' Woman* - **Steppenwolf**
26. *Streak, The* - **Ray Stevens**
27. *Stuck In The Middle* - **Stealers Wheel**
28. *Sweet Transvestite* - **Rocky Horror Show**
29. *This Flight Tonight* - **Nazareth**
30. *Wipeout* - **Surfaris**

There are some tunes that are very similar but instead of a one four five one chord change you get a major one, relative minor, four, five, chord change.

20.8 ~ 1-Minor-4-5 Chord Change

1. *Crocodile Rock* - **Elton John**
2. *D'Yer Ma'Ker* - **Led Zeppelin**
3. *Enola Gay* - **Orchestral Manoeuvres In The Dark**
4. *Monster Mash* - **Bobby Boris Pickett**
5. *Stand By Me* - **Ben E. King** (original) & **John Lennon** (cover)
6. *True Blue* - **Madonna**

Popular music written in triple time like a waltz is often hard to find and very unique. Most of all because most popular music is based on a back beat and songs in triple time don't have a back beat. Many of these tunes, like the *Classical Rock 22* and *Sweet Soul* mixes, have an orchestral sound to them. Some tunes have three basic beats on top with three faster beats underneath, like a ¾ or 6/8 time, while other tunes have four basic beats on top with three faster beats underneath, like a 12/8 time. I have broken the list into five parts, pop, rock, partly, 145 & formerly waltzes.

There are many basic pop waltzes, in either ¾ or 6/8 time. I first heard **Sheryl Crow**'s *Strong Enough* on the teen drama *Beverly Hills 90210*.

20.9 ~ Basic Waltzes I - UK & International

1. *Ain't Nobody But Me* - **Supertramp**
2. *Day After Day* - **The Alan Parsons Project**
3. *Entangled* - **Genesis**
4. *House Of The Rising Sun* - **The Animals**
5. *Kiss From A Rose* - **Seal**
6. *Let Me Roll It (/b) & Mull Of Kintyre* - **Paul McCartney & Wings**
7. *Lucky Man* - **Emerson, Lake & Palmer**
8. *Morning Has Broken* - **Cat Stevens**
9. *Never Tear Us Apart* - **INXS** (Australia)
10. *Nights In White Satin* - **The Moody Blues**
11. *Somebody To Love & We Are The Champions* - **Queen**
12. *When I Need You* - **Leo Sayer**

20.10 ~ Basic Waltzes II - US & Canada

1. *America & Scarborough Fair* - **Simon & Garfunkel**
2. *Annie's Song* - **John Denver**
3. *Chipmunks Song* - **The Chipmunks**
4. *Colour My World* - **Chicago**
5. *Everybody Hurts* - **REM**
6. *Funny Face* - **Donna Fargo**
7. *I've Been Down This Road Before (/b)* - **B J Thomas**
8. *If You Don't Know Me By Now* - **Harold Melvin & The Blue Notes Featuring Teddy Pendergrass & Simply Red**
9. *Me & Mrs. Jones* - **Billy Paul**
10. *Only Love Can Break Your Heart* - **Neil Young** [CAN]
11. *Piano Man & She's Always A Woman To Me* - **Billy Joel**
12. *Please Come Home For Christmas, Pretty Maids All In A Row (/b) & Take It To The Limit* - **The Eagles**
13. *Run Baby Run (/b) & Strong Enough* - **Sheryl Crow**
14. *Theme From A Summer Place* - **Percy Faith**
15. *Time In A Bottle* - **Jim Croce**
16. *When A Man Loves A Woman* - **Percy Sledge**
17. *Wreck Of The Edmund Fitzgerald* - **Gordon Lightfoot** [CAN]
18. *You Light Up My Life* - **Debbie Boone**

There are many slower and/or quieter waltzlike songs, in complex 12/8 triple time, or four basic beats and each of those has three beats. I refer to these as triplet tunes. If you join the first two beats of the triplet together, so you have a long note and then a short note, that is your basic swing beat. This list is more pop than rock …

20.11 ~ Triplet / Swing Tunes I - Pop Soloists UK & International

1. *Clair* - **Gilbert O'Sullivan**
2. *Downstream* - **Rick Davies**
3. *Hallowed Be Thy Name (/b)* - **Greg Lake**
4. *I Guess That's Why They Call It The Blues* - **Elton John**
5. *Moondance* - **Van Morrison**
6. *Morning Train* - **Sheena Easton**
7. *Patricia The Stripper* - **Chris De Burgh**
8. *Rock'n Roll* - **Gary Glitter**
9. *Sea Of Love* - **Honeydrippers & Phil Phillips**
10. *Windpower* - **Thomas Dolby**
11. *You're In My Heart* - **Rod Stewart**

20.12 ~ Triplet / Swing Tunes II - Pop Soloists US & Canada

1. *Back Home Again* - **John Denver**
2. *Behind Closed Doors* - **Charlie Rich**
3. *Doctor My Eyes* - **Jackson Browne**
4. *Dream A Little Dream Of Me* - **Mama Cass**
5. *Holly Jolly Christmas* - **Burl Ives**
6. *Leave Me Alone* - **Helen Reddy**
7. *Lido Shuffle* - **Boz Scaggs**
8. *Long Time Blues (/b)* - **Mason Williams**
9. *Loves Me Like A Rock* - **Paul Simon**
10. *Needle Gone & The Damage Done* - **Neil Young** [CAN]
11. *Never Gonna Fall In Love Again* - **Eric Carmen**
12. *Oh Babe What Would You Say* - **Hurricane Smith**
13. *OK Blue Jays* - **Lenz, Kosinec & Hampshire**
14. *Raindrops Keep Falling On My Head* - **B J Thomas**
15. *Song Sung Blue* - **Neil Diamond**
16. *Theme From New York New York* - **Frank Sinatra**
17. *This Guys In Love With You* - **Herp Albert**
18. *True Blue* - **Madonna**
19. *Twelfth Of Never* - **Donny Osmond**
20. *Welcome Back* - **John Sebastien**
21. *You Don't Mess Around With Jim* - **Jim Croce**

20.13 ~ Triplet / Swing Tunes III - Pop Groups

1. *Beach Baby* - **First Class**
2. *Close To You* - **The Carpenters**
3. *Diamond Girl* - **Seals & Crofts**

4. *Happy Together* - **The Turtles**
5. *Horse With No Name* - **America**
6. *How Can You Mend A Broken Heart?* - **The Bee Gees**
7. *I'd Like To Teach The World To Sing* - **Coke (The Hilltop Singers) & The New Seekers**
8. *I'm Running After You* - **Major Hoople's Boarding House**
9. *I've Got You Under My Skin* - **Frank Sinatra & Bono**
10. *Indian Reservation* - **The Raiders**
11. *Leaving On A Jet Plane* - **Peter. Paul & Mary**
12. *Let Your Love Go (/b)* - **Bread**
13. *Minute By Minute* - **The Doobie Brothers**
14. *Only Sixteen* - **Dr. Hook**
15. *Rockin' At Midnight* - **The Honeydrippers**
16. *Still The One* - **Orleans**

Here are the faster and/or louder waltzlike tunes 12/8 triple time, this list is more rock than pop …

20.14 ~ Triplet / Swing Tunes IV - Rock

1. *America* - **Yes**
2. *Albert Flasher & The Rain Dance* - **The Guess Who**
3. *Call Me* - **Blondie**
4. *Can't Get Enough* - **Bad Company**
5. *Cold As Ice* - **Foreigner**
6. *Does Anybody Really Know What Time It Is?* - **Chicago**
7. *Don't Forget Me (When I'm Gone)* - **Glass Tiger**
8. *Don't Stop* - **Fleetwood Mac**
9. *Fanfare For The Common Man* - **Emerson, Lake & Palmer**
10. *Foreplay (/b)* - **Boston**
11. *Higher Ground* - **Stevie Wonder**
12. *Hold The Line* - **Toto**
13. *Joy* - **Apollo 100**
14. *Let Me Serenade You* - **Three Dog Night**
15. *Reeling In The Years* - **Steely Dan**
16. *Rocky Mountain Way* - **Triumph**
17. *Roxy Roller* - **Sweeney Todd**
18. *School's Out* - **Alice Cooper**
19. *Some Kinda Wonderful* - **Grand Funk**
20. *Straight Shootin' Woman* - **Steppenwolf**
21. *The Things We Do For Love* - **10 C. C.**
22. *Turn To Stone* - **The Electric Light Orchestra**
23. *Walking On The Moon* - **The Police**
24. *Waterfront* - **Simple Minds**
25. *White Hot* - **Red Rider**
26. *You Better Run* - **Pat Benatar**
27. *You Girl* - **Lighthouse**

20.15 ~ Triplet / Swing Tunes V - Several

1. *Everybody Wants To Rule The World, I Believe, I Believe (Live) & Pharoahs (/b)* - **Tears For Fears**
2. *Gold Bug (/b) & I'd Rather Be A Man (/b)* - **The Alan Parsons Project**
3. *Helen Wheels, Hi Hi Hi & I Lie Around (/b)* - **Paul McCartney & Wings**
4. *I Do I Do I Do I Do & Waterloo* - **Abba**
5. *If This Is It & Stuck With You* - **Huey Lewis & The News**
6. *It's Still Rock'n Roll To Me & Vienna (/b)* - **Billy Joel**
7. *(Just Like) Starting Over & Nobody Told Me* - **John Lennon**
8. *Killer Queen, Tie Your Mother Down & You're My Best Friend* - **Queen**
9. *Light Up (/b) & Mademoiselle* - **Styx**
10. *Last Song & Walking On Back* - **Edward Bear**
11. *Misunderstanding, Way Of The World (/b) & A Trick Of The Tail* - **Genesis**
12. *My Kind Of Lady, Take The Long Way Home (Original & Live) & You Started Laughing (Original & Live) (/b)* - **Supertramp**
13. *Old Brown Shoe (/b) & Revolution* - **The Beatles**
14. *Love Me Two Times, People Are Strange & Roadhouse Blues* - **The Doors**

From that list there are some tunes where only part of the song has the waltz tempo happening, sometimes in the introduction, in the middle, or at the end. In Many ways, this makes them like the mini suites I described earlier in this chapter. There are several more pieces that, while they are not waltzes, are based on tunes that were originally waltzes *(/o)*. Here is that list…

20.16 ~ Original Waltzes, Part Waltzes & Part Triplet / Swing Tunes

1. *Ace Of Swords (/b)* - **The Alan Parsons Project**
2. *All By Myself* - **Eric Carmen**
3. *America* - **Simon & Garfunkel**
4. *And You & I, Awaken (/b) & Soon* - **Yes**
5. *Bohemian Rhapsody* - **Queen**
6. *Brand New Love Affair & Saturday In The Park* - **Chicago**
7. *Brother Where You Bound (/b)* - **Supertramp**
8. *C'est La Vie, From The Beginning & Jerusalem (/o)* - **Emerson, Lake & Palmer**
9. *Come On Eileen* - **Dexy's Midnight Runners**
10. *Fool In The Rain* - **Led Zeppelin**
11. *Frankenstein* - **The Edgar Winter Group**
12. *Greensleeves (What Child Is This?) (/o)* - **Mason Williams**
13. *Looking Out For #1* - **Bachman - Turner Overdrive**
14. *Lucy In The Sky With Diamonds* - **Elton John**
15. *Run With The Fox (The Sussex Carol)(/o)* - **Chris Squire & Alan White**
16. *Tuesday Afternoon* - **The Moody Blues**
17. *Where The Streets Have No Name* - **U2**
18. *Your Own Special Way* - **Genesis**

It is very interesting to me that there are many fast waltzes or triple time pieces that also share a basic one four five chord change...

20.17 ~ Triplet / Swing Tunes VI - 1-4-5 Chord Change

1. *Anyway You Want* - **Chicago**
2. *Bad Bad Leroy Brown* - **Jim Croce**
3. *Blueberry Hill* - **Fats Domino**
4. *Boogie Man Gonna Get Ya* - **Catfish Hodge**
5. *Crazy Little Thing Called Love* - **Queen**
6. *Framed* - **Cheech & Chong**
7. *Heartache Tonight* - **The Eagles**
8. *I Can Help* - **Billy Swan**
9. *I've Seen All Good People* - **Yes**
10. *Rock This Town* - **The Stray Cats**
11. *Spirit In The Sky* - **Norman Greenbaum**
12. *Tiger In A Spotlight (Live)* - **Emerson, Lake & Palmer**
13. *Tush* - **ZZ Top**
14. *Tutti Frutti (/b)* - **Little Richard**
15. *You're Sixteen* - **Ringo Starr**
16. *Your Mama Don't Dance* - **Loggins & Messina**

TWENTY - ONE

SOUNDS AND FEELS LIKE
A TOE TAPPIN' FOLK TUNE
SA FLATT FT
(AKA) IT'S A FLAT FOOT (SONG)

This chapter is the third that talks about structure and sound. It is the story of The Toe Tappin' Folk Tune. I used to think that the only way you could be good at music was if you were formally trained, that somehow classical music was the benchmark for other kinds of music and that country and folk music were second rate at best. However, after all these years, I have changed my tune and now, nothing could be further from the truth.

Cousin Ian White is a perfect example of what has helped me to change my mind about this kind of music. He has entertained his fans with his acoustic guitar playing for years at a café in downtown Toronto, as well as making a cassette and a cd along the way.

I remember *Hootenanny*, a country style piece that I played in my High School Senior Band, along with John K,[130] in Ottawa in the seventies. It was arranged by Harold Watkins for concert band and was a suite of pieces that included both *Michael Rowed The Boat Ashore* and *The Arkansas Traveler*. It was a lot of fun to play. The *Hootenanny* medley or suite of tunes rooted itself in what I call historical folk tunes. Much of the tradition for these came from the skill of finger picking guitar playing. Other folk tunes, especially Christmas songs and nursery rhymes, are not included in the list…

---

[130] John Kollar & high school in Ottawa, 1976

21.1 ~ Historical Folk Tunes

1. *Arkansas Traveler* - **Col. Sanford C Faulkner**
2. *Baby Elephant Walk* - **Henry Mancini**
3. *Ballad Of Jed Clampett (Theme From The Beverly Hillbillies)* - **Paul Henning / Lester Flatt / Earl Scruggs**
4. *Buffalo Gals* - **John Hodges**
5. *Celebrated Ethiopian Song / Camptown Races* - **Stephen Foster**
6. *Circus Theme* - **Alexander Nakarada**
7. *Down By The Bay* - Unknown
8. *Green Acres Theme* - **Vic Mizzy**
9. *Hello Mother Hello Father* - **Alan Sherman**
10. *Hoedown* - **Aaron Copeland (ELP / Mad Pudding)**
11. *Johnny Appleseed* - Unknown
12. *Merry Go Round Broke Down (Looney Tunes Theme)* - **Cliff Friend**
13. *Michael Rowed The Boat Ashore* - **Tony Saleton**
14. *Peter & The Wolf* - **Sergey Prokofiev**
15. *Peter Gunn* - **Henry Mancini (ELP)**
16. *Tradition (Fiddler On The Roof)* - **Jerry Bock**
17. *When The Chariot Comes / She'll Be Coming Round The Mountain* - Unknown
18. *When The Saints Go Marching In* - Unknown
19. *When The World's On Fire* - **The Carter Family,** *You Are My Sunshine* - **Jim Davis & Charlie Mitchell** & *This Land Is Your Land* - **Woody Guthrie**
20. *Yankee Doodle* - Unknown

I created *Southern Country Folk 14 [gem]* in 2014 to celebrate forty years of making cassette tapes from recordings at home. This compilation was inspired in large part by *Hootenanny*.[131] I never thought I even had enough records to make a various country collection, but in the end, I think it turned out pretty nicely.

Whatever (rock) you call it; Americana, country, folk, heartland, southern, southern fried, or swamp, just listen to the banjos, cow bells, fiddles, howlin' harmonicas, honky tonk pianos, twangy guitars and whacky wood blocks and it all goes together nicely, all on one tape (CD). Most of the tunes are from the seventies, back in the days of top forty radio, when you could hear the full range of music types, including country, on the same station. Y'all enjoy this hootenanny now! Ya hear! The list of songs is as follows:

21.2 ~ Mix - Southern Country Folk 14 [gem]

1. *Intro* - 1050 CHUM
2. *Black Water* - **The Doobie Brothers**
3. *Cherry Bomb* - **John Mellencamp**
4. *Dead Skunk* - **Loudon Wainwright III**
5. *Desire* - **U2**
6. *Heart Of Gold* - **Neil Young**
7. *Hot Dog* - **Led Zeppelin**
8. *I Can Help* - **Billy Swan**
9. *If You Wanna Get To Heaven* - **The Ozark Mountain Daredevils**

---

[131] *Hootenanny*, Concert Band Piece, Harold Walters, Rubank Inc, 1973

10. *(The) Joker* - **The Steve Miller Band**
11. *Night Moves* - **Bob Segar**
12. *Ramblin' Man* - **The Allman Brothers Band**
13. *Sally G (/b)* - **Paul McCartney & Wings**
14. *Strong Enough* - **Sheryl Crowe**
15. *Stuck In The Middle With You* - **Stealers Wheel**
16. *Sweet Home Alabama* - **Lynyrd Skynyrd**
17. *Try & Love Again* - **The Eagles**
18. *When Will I Be Loved* - **Linda Ronstadt**
19. *Wildfire* - **Michael Murphy**
20. *Wildwood Weed* - **Jim Stafford**

Many of the tunes have a toe tappin' sound, *Black Water, Desire, Hot Dog, Ramblin' Man, Sally G, Sweet Home Alabama & Wildwood Weed.* Again, I revisit what I wrote way back in chapter seven…

Some of us listen to music; others play it, still others both. Some are trained to read and play, like taking formal lessons. Some listen to others and imitate them (playing by ear), like sitting around the kitchen after dinner listening to your uncle play his guitar. It's kind of like the difference between the written and oral traditions of storytelling. No one is better than the other and good musicians are skilled and accomplished, regardless of how they learned their trade. If you've got it, you've got it, whatever you call it, the feel, the gift, the groove, the knack, the rhythm, the skill and the talent.

Let's take the folk tune a step further. During the Genesis interview about the making of the album *Genesis*, entitled *Genesis On Genesis,*[132] Phil Collins, Mike Rutherford and Tony Banks talked about the song *That's All*, a catchy song written at a walking pace (andante) with a steady "one and two and three and four" beat. Tony Banks said the Beatles song *Rocky Racoon* inspired his piano part. Mike Rutherford referred to it as sounding like a Beatle-y "chug song" (For me, THE Beatle-y "chug song" is *I Am The Walrus. Free As A Bird,* released almost thirty years later in 1995, is very similar to *The Walrus,* just slower moving). *That's All* featured a McCartney style melody and a basic Ringo drum beat / feel / groove / shuffle.[133] It was the first Genesis single to make the top ten in the US. Right there alongside *That's All* is *I Know What I Like* (ranked #11 prog song back in chapter 14), a Beatle-like cousin, ten years its senior and the group's first UK hit.[134] Phil played a "Beatle-ish groove" and joined Peter at the chorus in what made for a great duet.[135] The B side to the Canadian version of *That's All, Second Home by The Sea,* also fits the bill as a chug song.

During the *Live The Way We Walk* tour, **Genesis** put together a medley of old songs. The back end of the medley featured *I Know What I Like (In Your Wardrobe), That's All* and *Follow You Follow Me,* all three with an identical drumbeat. I included this as a suite in the previous chapter along with *A Firth Of Fifth.*

I remember my brother Richard, a graduate of the University Of Toronto, commenting on how the video for *Head Over Heels* had been filmed at the Emmanuel College Library. Questlove wrote in *Music Is History* that *Head Over Heels* had a "superhero sounding piano intro".[136] *Heels* is another chug song, although with a definitely heavier back beat. My brother went on to say that when it was first released that

---

[132] *Genesis on Genesis*, video, 1991, https://youtube. com/watch?v=snqKZ9_rATg
[133] *Genesis The Ultimate Music Guide*, Uncut, January 2019, p.106
[134] *Genesis The Ultimate Music Guide*, Uncut, January 2019, p.29
[135] *Not Dead Yet*, Phil Collins, Crown Archetype, New York, 2016, p.107
[136] *Music Is History*, Questlove, Abrams Image, New York, 2021, p.192

the sound, lyrics and video of *Sowing The Seeds Of Love* by Tears For Fears was heavily influenced by The Beatles, something echoed in the 30th anniversary issue of the music magazine *Classic Pop*.[137] Roland Orzabal explained that *I Am The Walrus* was a big influence on *Sowing*. From *Music Is History*, by Questlove, Michael Azzerad wrote that *Sowing* has all the bells and whistles from the *Magical Mystery Tour* Era.[138] Questlove himself described *Sowing* as a lot like *The Walrus* but with a funkier chord progression. *Sowing* reached number one after 10 weeks on the CFNY top 30 in October of 1989.

    When In Love With A Blind Man was what I thought was a remix of *The Working Hour* as I stated in chapter twelve. However, on the 2023 album, *Saturnine Martial & Lunatic*, a collection of non-album B sides and other treasures, Roland notes that *When In Love* predated *The Working Hour*. Head, *Sowing* and *When* make up what I call the "Tears trio of flat foot chug songs".

    Instead of guitar, John Lennon played the electric piano for *The Walrus*, drawing inspiration from indulging in some recreational drugs and reading Lewis Carroll's *The Walrus & The Carpenter* and admitted that his lyrics were mostly just nonsense.[139] *The Walrus* clocked in as the longest song of *The Mystery Tour* and while it was relegated to the B side of *Hello Goodbye*, *The Walrus* has held up much better over time. From the book *Here There & Everywhere, The 100 Best Beatles Songs*, Stephen Spignesi and Michael Lewis ranked *The Walrus* at #11.[140] Stephen said that from a Playboy Interview, John remarked that "much of what the Electric Light Orchestra was doing in the 1970s was a continuation of what I started with *The Walrus*" (i.e.. *Can't Get It Out Of My Head* & *Strange Magic*). Each time that Michael listened to *The Walrus*, he was impressed with its relentless marching sound. *For No One* on *Revolver* and *Sgt. Pepper* both served as "chug songs" ahead of *The Walrus*, while *Hey Bulldog* followed afterward. Fans of Q107 voted *The Walrus* in at #348 on the 1992 All Time *Classic 500*,[141] while raising it to the lofty heights of #76 on the *Top 500 Rock Songs Of The Century*[142] list in 2000.

    Back to Ringo and *That's All*. So I started thinking about how the Ringo beat / feel / groove / shuffle could fit together with the historical folk tunes that I just listed on the previous page. (Ringo keeps the beat / feel / groove / shuffle alive with songs like *Only You* and George Harrison's *When We Was Fab.*) Next up was creating lists of songs of different genres but all linked with the same basic tempo and catchy beat / feel / groove / shuffle underneath, most with a definite backbeat. It has both a car turn signal and clock tick tock sound and feel to it, the latter like the sound affect used in the Genesis song *No Son Of Mine*.

    The catalogue of songs that follows includes eleven different genres of music. Many of the songs are a bit rough around the edges and unpolished but don't confuse that with sloppy. There are also many that sound a bit offbeat, with syncopated parts and drum shuffles. The lists were extremely difficult to assemble as I kept changing my mind about what songs would be included. For all of these lists, compared with the rest of the 45 R P aMble story, I have only included a single song per artist (except for the very last list of chug songs).

    Searching beats per minute on sites like jog.fm, getsongbpm and songsbpm helped me to fine tune the lists in this chapter. Cousin and triathlete Paul used to put song playlists together on cassettes for bike training back in the nineties, long before those internet bpm sites. To this day he still has many cassettes that he plays on a cassette machine that he has in his car.

---

[137] Classic Pop, November / December 2020, p.26

[138] *Music Is History*, Questlove, Abrams Image, New York, 2021, p.193

[139] *The Beatles 100 Greatest Songs*, Rolling Stone, 2013.

[140] *Here There & Everywhere, The 100 Best Beatles Songs*, Stephen Spignesi & Michael Lewis, Black Dog & Leventhal Publishing, New York, 2004.

[141] *Classic 500*, Q107, 1992

[142] *Top 500 Rock Songs Of The Century*, Q107, January 2000

Back to the story. I call the lists <u>S</u>ounds <u>A</u>nd <u>F</u>eels <u>L</u>ike <u>A</u> <u>T</u>oe <u>T</u>appin' <u>F</u>olk <u>T</u>une, aka *SA FLATT FT [gem 21.3 - 21.15]* or "it's a flat foot (song)". Hence the book title *A 45 R P aMble On A Flat Foot*. The term flat foot is also code for my total lack of skill and style when it comes to dancing. The songs are mostly those that you can tap your feet to but they aren't really fast enough to dance to. The different genres are essentially their own top thirties, going by the number of tunes in each list. There are no mini suites, no tunes in waltz time and no tunes using a one four five chord change or its cousin the one minor four five chord change.

Even progressive rock groups Emerson, Lake & Palmer and Yes waded into country music territory with tunes like *Hoedown, Take A Pebble, The Clap & Starship Trooper Disillusion.* Yes, *Hoedown* was the piece written by the famous American composer Aaron Copeland and was also performed by the Vancouver celtic music group Mad Pudding in the 1990s.

First up are the country tunes. Seven of them appeared in the preceding mix entitled *Southern Country Folk 14.* This first list features four b sides, more than any other list. There is one each from Beatles Ringo and Paul, with John playing acoustic guitar for Ringo. ELP gives us a piano that sounds like the wild west. The banjo alone gets Steve Miller on this list. Finally, Otis Redding sings a song that could actually be considered country.

21.3 ~ <u>S</u>ounds <u>A</u>nd <u>F</u>eels <u>L</u>ike <u>A</u> <u>T</u>oe <u>T</u>appin' <u>F</u>olk <u>T</u>une - AKA Sa Flatt Ft - AKA It's A Flat Foot (Song) - Country

1. *'39 (/b)* - **Queen**
2. *50 Ways To Leave Your Lover* - **Paul Simon**
3. *Alone Again (Naturally)* - **Gilbert O'Sullivan**
4. *Bad Moon Rising* - **Creedence Clearwater Revival**
5. *Black Water* - **The Doobie Brothers**
6. *Dead Skunk* - **Loudon Wainwright III**
7. *I Shot The Sheriff* - **Eric Clapton (Bob Marley)**
8. *Jack & Diane* - **John Cougar Mellencamp**
9. *Jeremy Bender(/b)* - **Emerson, Lake & Palmer**
10. *Joker* - **The Steve Miller Band**
11. *Leaving Las Vegas (/b)* - **Sheryl Crowe**
12. *Life's Been Good* - **Joe Walsh**
13. *Long Run* - **The Eagles**
14. *Never Going Back Again (/b)* - **Fleetwood Mac**
15. *Only You* - **Ringo Starr (The Platters)**
16. *Ramblin' Man* - **The Allman Brothers Band**
17. *Sally G (/b)* - **Paul McCartney & Wings**
18. *Sitting On The Dock Of The Bay* - **Otis Redding**
19. *Southern Nights* - **Glen Campbell**
20. *Sweet Home Alabama* - **Lynyrd Skynyrd**
21. *Teach Your Children* - **Crosby Stills Nash & Young**
22. *Thank God I'm A Country Boy* - **John Denver**
23. *Tin Man* - **America**
24. *Touch Of Magic* - **James Leroy**
25. *Wildfire* - **Michael Murphy**
26. *You Are What I Am* - **Gordon Lightfoot**

This next list is folk, after all we are talking about folk tunes. While not all the songs are actual folk tunes, they quite easily could be, taking into account the lyric, melody and sound. A David Crosby acoustic guitar is the key to a Phil Collins folk sound. Bobby Darin departs from his normal pop sound and Gallery does their version of an early ELP synthesizer solo. Both David Gates (Bread) & Al Stewart have absolutely dreamy voices. Supertramp trade in their polished prog sound for a lighter touch.

21.4 ~ Sa Flatt Ft - Folk

1. *Another Day In Paradise* - **Phil Collins**
2. *Can You Give It All To Me* - **Myles & Lenny**
3. *Dance With Me* - **Orleans**
4. *Do You Really Want To Hurt Me?* - **Culture Club**
5. *Eight Miles High* - **The Byrds**
6. *A Good Song* - **Valdy**
7. *I Believe In Music* - **Gallery**
8. *I Got A Name* - **Jim Croce**
9. *I'd Love You To Want Me* - **Lobo**
10. *If I Were A Carpenter* - **Bobby Darin**
11. *Indiana Wants Me* - **R Dean Taylor**
12. *Make It With You* - **Bread**
13. *Old Fashioned Love Song* - **Three Dog Night**
14. *On The Border* - **Al Stewart**
15. *Sister Moonshine (/b)* - **Supertramp**
16. *Summer Breeze* - **Seals & Crofts**
17. *You've Got A Friend* - **James Taylor**

While not all the entries in the funk, R&B and soul list may fall directly into one of those categories or genres, they all have a very funky and soulful sound to them, It's interesting that this list is very different from the *Sweet Soul* mix back in chapter 19. The intro drumbeat by The BT Express is very similar to the mid-song drum beat by Andrea True. Bryan Adams, The Average White Band, The Bee Gees, EWF, The O'Jays & Wild Cherry really bring the groove here. The Stylistics share their true soul.

21.5 ~ Sa Flatt Ft - Funk, R&B & Soul

1. *ABC* - **The Jackson 5**
2. *Born To Wander* - **Rare Earth**
3. *Come And Get Your Love* - **Redbone**
4. *Couldn't Get It Right* - **The Climax Blues Band**
5. *Crazy* - **Seal**
6. *Do It ('Til You're Satisfied)* - **B T Express**
7. *Everybody Plays The Fool* - **The Main Ingredient**
8. *For The Love Of The Money* - **The O'Jays**
9. *I'll Be Good To Ya* - **The Brothers Johnson**
10. *I'm Stoned In love With You* - **The Stylistics**
11. *Just The Two Of Us* - **Grover Washington**
12. *Kung Fu Fighting* - **Carl Douglas**
13. *Love The One You're With* - **Stephen Stills**

14. *Pick Up The Pieces* - **The Average White Band**

15. *Play That Funky Music* - **Wild Cherry**

16. *Reggae Christmas (/b)* - **Bryan Adams**

17. *Rock Your Baby* - **George McRae**

18. *Sexual Healing* - **Marvin Gaye**

19. *Shining Star* - **Earth Wind & Fire**

20. *Stayin' Alive* - **The Bee Gees**

21. *Tell Me Something Good* - **Rufus**

22. *Thank You* - **Sly & The Family Stone**

23. *Why Can't We Live Together* - **Timmy Thomas**

The jazz tunes are not specifically jazz tunes but many do have a jazz sound and style, highlighted by drums, electric piano, electric guitar, horns, organ & piano. Babe Ruth gives us a great pairing of electric guitar and electric piano. Mashmakhan, Billy Preston & Sugarloaf really rock the organ here. Chicago dazzles with the organ and guitar. Keith Hampshire shows us what big band music used to sound like.

21.6 ~ Sa Flatt Ft - Jazz

1. *Africa* - **Toto**

2. *Chameleon* - **Herbie Hancock**

3. *Dance A Little Step* - **Mashmakhan**

4. *Daytime Nighttime* - **Keith Hampshire**

5. *December 63 (Oh What A Night)* - **Frankie Valli & The Four Seasons**

6. *Don't Call Us We'll Call You* - **Sugarloaf**

7. *Down Under* - **Men At Work**

8. *Forever (Live and Die)* - **Orchestral Manoeuvres In The Dark**

9. *Hello It's Me* - **Todd Rundgren (Nazz)**

10. *Holding Back The Years* - **Simply Red**

11. *Honky Cat* - **Elton John**

12. *Life Is A Carnival* - **The Band**

13. *Lowdown* - **Chicago**

14. *Puttin' On The Ritz* - **Taco**

15. *Reminiscing* - **The Little River Band**

16. *Riders On The Storm* - **The Doors**

17. *Sitting On A Poor Man's Throne* - **Copper Penny**

18. *Spinning Wheel* - **Blood, Sweat & Tears**

19. *Superstition* - **Stevie Wonder**

20. *Theme From "For A Few Dollars More" (The Mexican) (/b)* - **Babe Ruth**

21. *Things Can Only Get Better* - **Howard Jones**

22. *True* - **Spandau Ballet**

23. *Why Can't We Be Friends?* - **War**

24. *Why Me?* - **Styx**

25. *Will It Go Round In Circles* - **Billy Preston**

There are many new wave tunes, all closely resembling the folk tune format. Many of them feature real drums, not just machine or robot drums and while keyboards are a given, many have outstanding guitar and bass parts. This list is also very different from the *NeWavEighties* mix back in chapter 19. Kraftwerk gives us an early look at new wave from back in the seventies. Nik Kershaw offers up clever military drums. Synthesized drums give pop stars Billy Idol & Mr. Mister a new wave sound.

21.7 ~ Sa Flatt Ft - New Wave Electro Pop
1. *Autobahn* - **Kraftwerk**
2. *Broken Wings* - **Mr. Mister**
3. *Burning Down The House* - **The Talking Heads**
4. *Cry* - **Godley & Creme**
5. *Dance Hall Days* - **Wang Chung**
6. *Eyes Without A Face* - **Billy Idol**
7. *Human* - **The Human League**
8. *I Can't Wait* - **Nu Shooz**
9. *Kiss You (When It's Dangerous)* - **8 Seconds**
10. *Lady In Red* - **Chris De Burgh**
11. *On TV* - **The Buggles**
12. *Only You (12)* - **Yaz**
13. *(The) Riddle* - **Nik Kershaw**
14. *Rock Me Amadeus* - **Falco**
15. *Something About You* - **Level 42**
16. *You Take Me Up* - **The Thompson Twins**

There's not much difference between the Pop tunes and the Rock tunes, except to say that the Pop tunes are lighter, in structure and in sound. There are many tunes that could fit into either category. The drum intros by The Fine Young Cannibals and INXS are almost identical. Starship & Glass Tiger share very similar styles. Outstanding piano comes from Pilot. Max Webster surprises us with a more mellow approach than usual. I remember hearing the song on Chris' car radio and I couldn't believe him when he told me it was Max.

21.8 ~ Sa Flatt Ft - Pop
1. *Back In The High Life* - **Steve Winwood**
2. *Boy Inside The Man* - **Tom Cochrane & Red Rider**
3. *Don't Dream It's Over* - **Crowded House**
4. *Fly Across The Sea* - **Edward Bear**
5. *Jackie Blue* - **Ozark Mountain Daredevils**
6. *Let Go The Line* - **Max Webster**
7. *Magic* - **Pilot**
8. *Missing You* - **John Waite**
9. *Need You Tonight* - **INXS**
10. *Never Surrender* - **Corey Hart**
11. *Sara* - **Starship**
12. *Scratching The Surface* - **Saga**
13. *Seasons In The Sun* - **Terry Jacks**
14. *She Drives Me Crazy* - **The Fine Young Cannibals**
15. *Someday* - **Glass Tiger**

16. *Summer In The City* - **The Lovin Spoonful**
17. *Stand By Me* - **John Lennon**
18. *Vultures In The City (/b)* - **Anderson Bruford Wakeman & Howe**

For many songs, the louder guitar and vocal parts mean they're on the rock list, not the pop list. Canadians April Wine, Bachman - Turner Overdrive & Lighthouse put in a strong showing here. Argent & Deep Purple organ brings life to the carnival. Rick Derringer & Steve Perry both bring us loud guitars and vocals.

21.9 ~ Sa Flatt Ft - Rock

1. *Another Brick In The Wall Pt. 2* - **Pink Floyd**
2. *Bad Side Of The Moon* - **April Wine**
3. *Big Log* - **Robert Plant**
4. *Criminal Mind* - **Gowan**
5. *Earache My Eye* - **Cheech & Chong & Alice Bowie**
6. *Hats Off To The Stranger* - **Lighthouse**
7. *Hold Your Head Up* - **Argent**
8. *Hush* - **Deep Purple**
9. *Let It Ride* - **Bachman - Turner Overdrive**
10. *Love Hurts* - **Nazareth (Roy Orbison)**
11. *Oh Sherrie* - **Steve Perry**
12. *Right Place Wrong Time* - **Dr John**
13. *Rock & Roll Hoochie Koo* - **Rick Derringer**
14. *Running With The Devil (12)* - **Van Halen**
15. *Stay (Faraway So Close)* - **U2**
16. *TV Dinners* - **ZZ Top**

For the next list are the twice as fast tunes, across many different genres. You're just doubling the "one and two and three and four and" count. Two piano pieces that dad played for years fit exactly into this category. One was in a major key and the other in a minor key. Note the drum parts (what I call a stutter step) by the Dutch bands Focus and Golden Earring are very similar, with the Sweet not too far behind.

21.10 ~ Sa Flatt Ft - Twice As Fast

1. *Absolutely Right* - **The Five Man Electrical Band**
2. *Ballroom Blitz* - **The Sweet**
3. *Boys Of Summer* - **Don Henley**
4. *Get It Right The First Time (/b)* - **Billy Joel**
5. *Hocus Pocus* - **Focus**
6. *Hyperactive* - **Thomas Dolby**
7. *I'm On Fire* - **Bruce Springsteen**
8. *Let My Love Open The Door* - **Pete Townsend**
9. *Long Distance Runaround (/b)* - **Yes**
10. *Magic Carpet Ride* - **Steppenwolf**
11. *(The) Night Chicago Died* - **Paper Lace**
12. *Radar Love* - **Golden Earring**

13. *Rock Lobster* - **B 52s**
14. *Rockford Files* - **Mike Post**
15. *Stay In The Light* -**Honeymoon Suite**
16. *Steppin' Out* - **Joe Jackson**
17. *Tie A Yellow Ribbon Round The Ole Oak Tree* - **Dawn**
18. *Time Warp* - **The Rocky Horror Picture Show**
19. *Tubthumping* - **Chumbawumba**
20. *Walk Of Life* - **Dire Straits**
21. *Who Are You* - **The Who**
22. *You Can't Dance* - **Jackson Hawke**

And now for a list of tunes that have something going on somewhere that gives them an orchestral sound, choir, drums, horns, organ, strings, synthesizer. A-Ha, The Fixx, Peter Schilling and The Spoons could all just as easily be in the fast list or the new wave list. Deodato is all jazz, bass, bongos, drum kit, electric guitar, horns, electric piano & strings. It's the keyboards not the drums that get Rick Wakeman on to this list.

21.11 ~ Sa Flatt Ft - Orchestral

1. *Also Sprach Zarathustra (2001)* - **Deodato**
2. *Arias & Symphonies* - **The Spoons**
3. *Breakdown (/b)* - **The Alan Parsons Project**
4. *Brother Louie* - **The Stories (Hot Chocolate)**
5. *Bungle In The Jungle* - **Jethro Tull**
6. *Could It be I'm Falling in Love* - **The Spinners**
7. *Cry Your Eyes Out* - **Les Emmerson**
8. *Glittering Prize* - **Simple Minds**
9. *Greensleeves* - **Mason Williams (Richard Jones)**
10. *I Want To Know What Love Is* - **Foreigner**
11. *I'm So Straight I'm A Weirdo* - **Rick Wakeman**
12. *Less Cities More Moving People* - **The Fixx**
13. *Listen To The Radio* - **The Pukkah Orchestra**
14. *Living Years* - **Mike & The Mechanics**
15. *Madame Butterfly* - **Malcolm McLaren**
16. *Major Tom* - **Peter Schilling**
17. *Night To Remember* - **Prism**
18. *Precious & Few* - **Climax**
19. *Ruby Tuesday* - **The Rolling Stones**
20. *Sadeness* - **Enigma**
21. *Sounds Of Silence* - **Simon & Garfunkel**
22. *Summer (The First Time)* - **Bobby Goldsboro**
23. *Take On Me* - **A-Ha**
24. *These Eyes* - **The Guess Who**

Finally, I have created a summary list of the chug songs, starting with the discussion earlier in the chapter, after the Southern Country Folk 14 Mix. What really makes a chug song? It's the slow and steady, straight ahead count of one and two and three and four and the combination of bass, drums, and lots of chord support from both keyboards and guitars. The Beatles, ELO, George Harrison and Tears For Fears anchor the list with their chug songs. ELO has two and Tears has three. Progressive rock group Genesis has THE Flat Foot song in this list, *That's All,* as well as three others..

21.12 ~ Sa Flatt Ft - Chug Songs
1. *The Air That I Breathe* - **The Hollies**
2. *Can't Get It Out Of My Head & Strange Magic* - **The Electric Light Orchestra**
3. *Come & Get It* - **Badfinger**
4. *Dr. Marvello (/b)* - **Klaatu**
5. *Emma* - **Hot Chocolate**
6. *Fame* - **David Bowie**
7. *Follow You, Follow Me, I Know What I Like (In Your Wardrobe), Second Home By The Sea (/b) & That's All* - **Genesis**
8. *Freedom* - **George Michael**
9. *Good Times Roll* - **The Cars**
10. *Head Over Heels, Sowing The Seeds Of love & When In Love With A Blind Man (/b)* - **Tears For Fears**
11. *Heart Of Gold* - **Neil Young**
12. *Hello Hurray* - **Alice Cooper**
13. *I Am The Walrus (/b)* - **The Beatles**
14. *If I Ever Lose My Faith In You* - **Sting**
15. *In Your Eyes* - **Peter Gabriel**
16. *Love Is Alive* - **Gary Wright**
17. *Minstrel Gypsy* - **The Stampeders**
18. *One Step Ahead* - **Split Enz**
19. *Sweet Emotion* - **Aerosmith**
20. *Tom Sawyer* - **Rush**
21. *When We Was Fab* - **George Harrison**
22. *Whole Lotta Love* - **Led Zeppelin**
23. *Wild Thing* - **(Chip Taylor & The Wild Ones) The Troggs**

The following list is a last minute addition to the chapter that I call Girl Power. I created the category back in the 2009 version of my collection, *th45zz,* but never really did anything with it. So while these titles were spread across many categories, I thought putting them together would be a neat way to recognize that unused category from 2009.

21.13 ~ Sa Flatt Ft - Girl Power
1. *99 Red Balloons* - **Nena**
2. *Chiquitita* - **Abba**
3. *Damn I Wish I Was Your Lover* - **Sophie B Hawkins**
4. *Echo Beach* - **Martha & The Muffins**
5. *Feel Like Making Love* - **Roberta Flack**
6. *Fly Robin Fly* - **The Silver Convention**
7. *Free Man In Paris* - **Joni Mitchell**

8. *Gypsies Tramps & Thieves* - **Cher**
9. *It's Too Late* - **Carole King**
10. *La Isla Bonita* - **Madonna**
11. *Love Is A Battlefield* - **Pat Benatar**
12. *Magic* - **Olivia Newton - John**
13. *Magic Man* - **Heart**
14. *Middle Of The Road* - **The Pretenders**
15. *Midnight At The Oasis* - **Maria Muldaur**
16. *More More More* - **The Andrea True Connection**
17. *Tide Is High* - **Blondie**
18. *Top Of The World* - **The Carpenters**
19. *Walk Like An Egyptian* - **The Bangles**
20. *We Don't Need Another Hero* - **Tina Turner**
21. *You're No Good* - **Linda Ronstadt**
22. *You're So Vain* - **Carly Simon**

    The summer 2023 edition of the CAA magazine featured a road trip playlist from Edwin, the singer for I Mother Earth. Four of his ten songs appear in lists in this chapter: *Crazy, In Your Eyes, Superstition & Tom Sawyer [FLAT]*.

    Earlier, I talked about how difficult it was to come up with just one song per artist. As I went along, there were many different songs that were in the chapter at one point (some were swapped in and out several times) but ultimately did not make the final cut. What I have taken away from that is a list of medleys by more than a dozen different groups. These are listed separately as appendix Fourteen. The only entries that are not part of the collection are those for the Beatles.

    To Sum up this part of the story, I heard a song on the radio recently that links together my high school hootenanny experience and the Genesis song *That's All*. The song I am referring to is the country version of *That's All* by Doc Walker, recorded back in 2008.

TWENTY - TWO

SOUND

    This chapter is the fourth and final that talks about structure and sound. This one will focus on sound: instrumentals, sound effects, voice, winds, strings & drums. While I dearly love the sounds of an orchestra, listings in this chapter do not specifically include all those songs that have a full orchestra or part of an orchestra.

    Instrumental songs reminded me of all my music training in piano and trombone. Instrumental songs also highlighted the variety that was common on top forty radio in the seventies and the eighties. The variety crossed many musical genres, all the way from easy listening and soft rock to hard rock.

22.1 ~ Instrumental Only I

1. *Also Sprach Zarathustra* - **Deodato**
2. *Axel F* - **Harold Faltermeyer**
3. *Bongo Rock* - **The Incredible Bongo Band**
4. *Chameleon* - **Herbie Hancock**
5. *Chariots Of Fire* - **Vangelis**
6. *Classical Gas & Greensleeves* - **Mason Williams**
7. *Dueling Banjos* - **Eric Weissberg**
8. *Entertainer* - **Marvin Hamlisch**
9. *Fanfare For The Common Man, Honky Tonk Train Blues* (**Keith Emerson**), *The Nutrocker & Peter Gunn* - **Emerson, Lake & Palmer**
10. *Feels So Good* - **Chuck Mangione**
11. *Foreplay (/b)* - **Boston**
12. *Frankenstein* - **The Edgar Winter Group**
13. *Homecoming* - **Hagood Hardy**
14. *Joy* - **Apollo 100**

15. *Love Theme From St Elmo's Fire* - **David Foster**
16. *Lucifer* - **The Alan Parsons Project**
17. *Paloma Blanca* - **The George Baker Selection**
18. *Popcorn* - **Hot Butter**
19. *Rockford Files, The* - **Mike Post**
20. *Scorpio* - **Dennis Coffey**
21. *Slat Key Soquel Rag (/b)* - **The Doobie Brothers**
22. *Songbird* - **Kenny G**
23. *Star Wars Theme / Cantina Band* - **Meco**
24. *Theme From A Summer Place* - **Percy Faith**
25. *Theme From SWAT* - **THP Orchestra**
26. *Tubular Bells* - **Mike Oldfield**

This next list includes b sides *(/b)* and limited vocals or singing *(/v)*. Alan Parsons has many entries in this category.

22.2 ~ Instrumental Only II - B Sides & Limited Vocals
1. *The Ace Of Swords (/b), The Gold Bug (/b), Hawkeye (/b), I Robot (/b), Lucifer & Nucleus (/b)* - **The Alan Parsons Project**
2. *Any Colour You Like (/b)* - **Pink Floyd**
3. *Baroque - A - Nova (/v)* - **Mason Williams**
4. *Clap, The (/b)* - **Steve Howe**
5. *Endless Deep(/b)* - **U2**
6. *Hocus Pocus (/v)* - **Focus**
7. *Humbug (/b)* - **Greg Lake**
8. *Overture From Tommy (/b)* - **The Who**
9. *Pharoahs (/b)* - **Tears For Fears**
10. *Pick Up The Pieces (/v)* - **The Average White Band**
11. *Second Home By The Sea (/b/v)* - **Genesis**
12. *Song To See You Through (/b)* - **The Doobie Brothers**
13. *TSOP- The Sound Of Philadelphia (/v)* - **MFSB - Mother Father Sister Brother**
14. *Theme From "For A Few Dollars More" (/b)* - **Babe Ruth**

Not too different from instrumental numbers are those songs that have sound effects in them. There is quite a range of effects too. Chicago, Heart & Otis Redding all feature waves.

22.3 ~ Sound Effects But No Voices
1. Airplane - *Sowing The Seeds Of Love* - **Tears For Fears**
2. Birds - *Even In the Quietist Moments (/b)* - **Supertramp** & *Free As A Bird* - **The Beatles**
3. Birds & waves - *Salty Dog* - **Procol Harum** & *Summer (The First Time)* - **Bobby Goldsboro**
4. Camera shutter - *Freeze Frame* - **J Geils Band**
5. Cars - *Run Like Hell* - **Pink Floyd**
6. Cars & Motorcycles - *Urbania (/b)* - **The Alan Parsons Project**
7. Cash registers - *Snake Eyes* - **The Alan Parsons Project**

8. Clocks - *No Son Of Mine* - **Genesis**
9. Creaky doors & bubbling water - *Monster Mash* - **Bobby Boris Pickett**
10. Cutlery & dishes - *I Know What I Like (In Your Wardrobe)* - **Genesis**
11. Dial tones - *Don't Call Us, We'll Call You* - **Sugarloaf** & *Telephone Line* - **The Electric Light Orchestra**
12. Doorbells - *Let 'Em In* - **Wings**
13. Horses - *Abeline (/b)* - **Yes**
14. Howling - *Hush* - **Deep Purple**
15. Lions & tigers - *Bungle In The Jungle* - **Jethro Tull**
16. Motorcycles - *Anthony's Song (Moving Out)* - **Billy Joel**
17. Sirens - *Juicy Lucy* - **Klaatu**
18. Springs - *I Can't Dance* - **Genesis**
19. Switches - *Genetic Engineering* - **Orchestral Manoeuvres In The Dark**
20. Traffic & audio tape - *Illegal Alien* - **Genesis**
21. Trains - *Damn I Wish I Was Your Lover* - **Sophie B Hawkins**
22. Waves - *Sitting On The Dock Of The Bay* - **Otis Redding**, *Dreamboat Annie* - **Heart** & *Wishing You Were Here* - **Chicago**
23. Whistles - *Allentown* - **Billy Joel** & *The Logical Song* - **Supertramp**

Voices make up the largest part of this chapter with no fewer than seven different categories. First up are voices, speaking, including crowds and giggling, in combination with other sounds. Crowds are popular with the Buggles, Elton John, Klaatu & Yes.

22.4 ~ Voice I - With Other Sound Effects
1. Cars - *Autobahn* - **Kraftwerk**
2. Cash registers - *Money* - **Pink Floyd**
3. Clocks - *Russians* - **Sting**
4. Crowds - *Adventures In Modern Recording* - **The Buggles**, *Bennie & The Jets* - **Elton John**, *California Jam* - **Klaatu** & *Release Release* - **Yes**
5. Giggling - *Clair* - **Gilbert O'Sullivan**
6. Gunfire & cars skidding - *Friends Of Mr. Cairo* - **Jon & Vangelis**
7. Helicopters - *Pharoahs (/b)* - **Tears for Fears**
8. Radio & Sonar - *Windpower* - **Thomas Dolby**
9. Sirens - *Indiana Wants Me* - **R Dean Taylor**
10. Traffic & people walking - *West End Girls* - **The Pet Shop Boys**
11. Trains - *Rudy (/b)* - **Supertramp**

Next up are voices by themselves, that's speaking, not singing. *Earache My Eye* is basically a comedy sketch book ended with music.

22.5 ~ Voice II - Voices Only
1. *Better Days* - **Supertramp**
2. *Clap For The Wolfman* - **The Guess Who**
3. *Earache My Eye* - **Cheech & Chong** (featuring Alice Bowie)
4. *Hyperactive & She Blinded Me With Science* - **Thomas Dolby**

5. *I Am The Walrus (/b)* - **The Beatles**
6. *I'm Not In Love* - **10 CC**
7. *Industrial Disease* - **Dire Straits**
8. *Let's Talk About Me* - **The Alan Parsons Project**
9. *Love Is A Battlefield* - **Pat Benatar**
10. *Only You* - **Ringo Starr**
11. *Spill The Wine* - **Eric Burden & War**
12. *Streak, The* - **Ray Stevens**
13. *Twilight Zone* - **Golden Earing**
14. *Uncle Albert & Admiral Halsey* - **Paul McCartney**

A number of songs feature group members counting down to the start of the song. *Turn It On Again* features two versions, one with the countdown and one without. Also, *Turn It On Again* is also one of the few pieces on which Tony Banks plays an electric piano.

22.6 ~ Voice III - With A Countdown
1. *Boogie Man Gonna Get Ya* - **Catfish Hodge**
2. *Cisko Kid* - **War**
3. *Coming Up (Live)* - **Paul McCartney**
4. *Don't Bring Me Down* - **The Electric Light Orchestra**
5. *Gloria (Live)* - **U2**
6. *Hot Dog (/b)* - **Led Zeppelin**
7. *I Just Want To Celebrate* - **Rare Earth**
8. *Invisible Sun* - **The Police**
9. *Jeremy Bender (/b)* - **Emerson, Lake & Palmer**
10. *Nobody Told Me* - **John Lennon**
11. *Reggae Christmas (/b)* - **Bryan Adams**
12. *Sweet Home Alabama* - **Lynyrd Skynyrd**
13. *Take The Long Way Home (Live)* - **Supertramp**
14. *Turn It On Again* - **Genesis**
15. *Waterfront* - **Simple Minds**
16. *When We Was Fab* - **George Harrison**

Speaking of voices, here is a collection of songs by well-known groups but the singing is not by the regular lead singer, many of them are the bass players. The first two on the list that I remember were *Roll On Down The Highway* and *Oowatanite*, in 1975.

22.7 ~ Voice IV - Different Lead Singer
1. *Drive & Moving In Stereo (/b)* - **The Cars - Benjamin Orr (Ric Ocasik)**
2. *Ooowatanite* - **April Wine - Jimmy Clench (Myles Goodwin)**
3. *Pretty Maids All In A Row (/b)* - **The Eagles - Joe Walsh (Don Henley)**
4. *Roll On Down The Highway* - **Bachman - Turner Overdrive - Fred Turner (Randy Bachman)**
5. *Someone To Talk To (/b)* - **The Police - Andy Somers (Sting)**
6. *Take It To The Limit* - **The Eagles - Randy Meisner (Don Henley)**

In the fall of 1980, I joined the church choir and stayed on for about eight years. These last three voice lists were inspired by the time spent there. The first is a list of songs with choirs in them. Supertramp has strong endings here. *It's Raining Again* features a children's chorus and *From Now On* featured the voices of the Chris De Burgh band, when I saw them tour with Supertramp on their *Quietist Moments* tour in Ottawa in 1977.

22.8 ~ Voice V - Choir

1. *After The Goldrush* - **Prelude**
2. *Another Brick In The Wall Part 2* - **Pink Floyd**
3. *Breakdown (/b) & I Robot (/b)* - **The Alan Parsons Project**
4. *C'est La Vie & I Believe In Father Christmas* - **Greg Lake**
5. *From Now On (/b) & It's Raining Again* - **Supertramp**
6. *I Want To Know What Love Is* - **Foreigner**
7. *Like A Prayer* - **Madonna**
8. *Living Years* - **Mike & The Mechanics**
9. *Run With The Fox* - **Chris Squire & Alan White**
10. *Sadeness* - **Enigma**
11. *School's Out* - **Alice Cooper**
12. *Sing* - **The Carpenters**
13. *Somebody To Love* - **Queen**

The second is a list of songs with acapella sections, however long or short. The introduction to *Leave It* includes all five members of Yes. As always, Queen is strong vocally.

22.9 ~ Voice VI - Acapella

1. *After The Goldrush* - **Prelude**
2. *Another Day, No More Lonely Nights & Uncle Albert & Admiral Halsey* - **Paul McCartney**
3. *At The Feet Of The Moon* - **The Parachute Club**
4. *Black Dog, Stairway To Heaven & Whole Lotta Love* - **Led Zeppelin**
5. *Black Water* - **The Doobie Brothers**
6. *Bohemian Rhapsody & Somebody To Love* - **Queen**
7. *Carry On Wayward Son* - **Kansas**
8. *Dialogue* - **Chicago**
9. *Don't Worry Be Happy* - **Bobby McFerrin**
10. *Hooked On A Feeling* - **Blue Suede**
11. *Killing Me Softly With His Song* - **Roberta Flack**
12. *Kiss From A Rose* - **Seal**
13. *Leave It & Your Move* - **Yes**
14. *Oh Sherrie* - **Steve Perry**
15. *Sadeness* - **Enigma**
16. *Shining Star* - **Earth, Wind & Fire**
17. *Take A Chance On Me* - **Abba**

The third is a list of songs with whistling. It's too bad that in the edited version of *Goodbye Stranger* the whistling is not even included.

22.10 ~ Voice VII - Whistling

1. *Centerfold* - **The J Geils Band**
2. *Clair* - **Gilbert O'Sullivan**
3. *Cry Your Eyes Out* - **Les Emmerson**
4. *Games Without Frontiers* - **Peter Gabriel**
5. *Goodbye Stranger* - **Supertramp**
6. *Hocus Pocus* - **Focus**
7. *Love Is A Battlefield* - **Pat Benatar**
8. *Riddle, The* - **Nik Kershaw**
9. *Sitting On The Dock Of The Bay* - **Otis Redding**
10. *Spill The Wine* - **Eric Burden & War**
11. *Walk Like An Egyptian* - **The Bangles**

Music attracts us for many different reasons. Some of us like particular musicians and groups regardless of the song. Some of us like some music by a group and not the rest. Some songs attract us for their loud and/or grandiose parts, Other songs attract us for their various instruments. These instruments could include (among others) clarinet, flute, harmonica, trombone and trumpet.

First are the winds; most are the flute but others include the clarinet (/c), oboe (/o), piccolo (/p), and recorder (/r). The musicians include the likes of Burton Cummings (The Guess Who), Ian Anderson (Jethro Tull), Ray Thomas (The Moody Blues), Peter Gabriel (Genesis) & Walter Parazaider (Chicago) all on flute, John Paul Jones (Led Zeppelin) on recorder and John Helliwell (Supertramp) on clarinet and piccolo. *Ace Of Swords* and *Betcha By Golly Wow* have beautiful oboe parts.

22.11 ~ Winds I - Clarinet & Flute

1. *Ace Of Swords (/b /o)* - **The Alan Parsons Project**
2. *Bad Side Of The Moon* - **April Wine**
3. *Betcha By Golly Wow (/o)* - **The Stylistics**
4. *Better Days, Breakfast In America (/c), Even In The Quietist Moments (/b /c), Sister Moonshine (/b, /p) & Take The Long Way Home (/c)* - **Supertramp**
5. *Born To Wander* - **Rare Earth**
6. *Bungle In The Jungle & Living In The Past* - **Jethro Tull**
7. *California Dreamin'* - **The Mamas & The Papas**
8. *Colour My World & Harry Truman (/c)* - **Chicago**
9. *Dance A Little Step* - **Mashmakhan**
10. *Down Under* - **Men At Work**
11. *Echo Beach* - **Martha & The Muffins**
12. *Follow Your Daughter Home & Undun (/b)* - **The Guess Who**
13. *Get It Right The First Time (/b)* - **Billy Joel**
14. *Going Up The Country* - **Canned Heat**
15. *Hocus Pocus* - **Focus**
16. *Hyperactive & Windpower* - **Thomas Dolby**
17. *I Just Want To Make Music* - **Tobias**

18. *I Know What I Like (In Your Wardrobe)* - **Genesis**
19. *Kung Fu Fighting* - **Karl Douglas**
20. *Listen To What The Man Said (/c)* - **Wings**
21. *Lotta Love* - **Nicolette Larson**
22. *Nights In White Satin & Tuesday Afternoon* - **The Moody Blues**
23. *One Night In Bangkok* - **Murray Head**
24. *Ruby Tuesday* - **The Rolling Stones**
25. *Rudolph The Red Nosed Reindeer* - **Corey Hart**
26. *Solisbury Hill* - **Peter Gabriel**
27. *Spill The Wine* - **Eric Burden & War**
28. *Stairway To Heaven (/r)* - **Led Zeppelin**
29. *Walking In Rhythm* - **The Blackbyrds**

Second are the harmonicas. The *howlin harmonicas* of *Southern Country Folk 14* from the last chapter lead the way here; *Desire, Heart Of Gold & If You Wanna Get To Heaven.*

22.12 ~ Winds II - Harmonica
1. *Boogie On Reggae Woman* - **Stevie Wonder**
2. *Church Of The Poison Mind & Karma Chameleon* - **Culture Club**
3. *Desire* - **U2**
4. *Europa & The Pirate Twins* - **Thomas Dolby**
5. *He Ain't Heavy He's My Brother* - **The Hollies**
6. *Heart Of Gold* - **Neil Young**
7. *Heart Of Rock & Roll* - **Huey Lewis**
8. *I Saw Mommy Kissing Santa Claus* - **John Mellencamp**
9. *If I Ever Lose My Faith In You* - **Sting**
10. *If You Wanna Get To Heaven* - **The Ozark Mountain Daredevils**
11. *Long Train Running* - **The Doobie Brothers**
12. *Love Will Find A Way* - **Yes**
13. *Miss You* - **The Rolling Stones**
14. *Piano Man* - **Billy Joel**
15. *Oh Girl* - **The Chi-Lites**
16. *Oh My Lady* - **The Stampeders**
17. *Rockford Files* - **Mike Post**
18. *Running To Stand Still (/b)* - **U2**
19. *Sara* - **Starship**
20. *Sister Moonshine (/b) & Take The Long Way Home* - **Supertramp**
21. *Suicide Blonde* - **INXS**
22. *Tie A Yellow Ribbon Round The Ole Oak Tree* - **Dawn**
23. *Will It Go Round In Circles* - **Billy Preston**
24. *You Take Me Up* - **The Thompson Twins**

Third, are the brass. I played the trombone in high school, very much inspired by Chicago's James Pankow. Thomas Dolby gives us both trombone & trumpet in *I Scare Myself*. However, the jewels of this list have to be the french horn parts in the Hollies' *Air That I Breathe* and the Whos' *Overture From Tommy.*

22.13 ~ Horns - Trombone & Trumpet (& French Horn)

1. *Air That I Breathe (/fh)* - **The Hollies**
2. *Beginnings (/tu & /to) & Does Anybody Really Know What Time It Is? (/tu & /to)* - **Chicago**
3. *Boogie Woogie Bugle Boy (/tu)* - **Bette Midler**
4. *Conquistador (/tu)* - **Procal Harum**
5. *Dr. Marvello (/tu /b)* - **Klaatu**
6. *Hello It's Me (/to)* - **Todd Rundgren**
7. *Holding Back The Years (/tu)* - **Simply Red**
8. *Hyperactive (/to) & I Scare Myself* (/tu & /to) - **Thomas Dolby**
9. *Last Song (/tu)* - **Edward Bear**
10. *Let 'Em In* (/to) - **Wings**
11. *Overture From Tommy (/fh)* - **The Who**
12. *Raindrops Keep Falling On My Head* (/tu) - **B J Thomas**
13. *Sun Goes By* (/tu) - **Dr. Music**
14. *These Eyes* (/tu) - **The Guess Who**
15. *This Guys In Love With You* (/tu) - **Herp Albert**
16. *Touch Of Magic* (/tu) - **James Leroy**
17. *Tub Thumping* (/tu) - **Chumbawumba**
18. *Uncle Albert / Admiral Halsey* (/tu) - **Paul McCartney**

Next up are the strings. First are the violins (aka fiddles if it's country music). Most (not all) of these pieces highlight solo violins, rather than entire string sections with many violins.

22.14 ~ Strings I - Violin

1. *Black Water* - **The Doobie Brothers**
2. *Bungle In The Jungle* - **Jethro Tull**
3. *Can You Give It All To Me* - **Myles & Lenny**
4. *Check It Out & I Saw Mommy Kissing Santa Clause* - **John Mellencamp**
5. *Come On Eileen* - **Dexy's Midnight Runners**
6. *Dead Skunk* - **Loudon Wainright III**
7. *Dust In The Wind* - **Kansas**
8. *Livin' Thing & Roll Over Beethoven* - **The Electric Light Orchestra**
9. *Love Will Find A Way (33)* - **Yes**
10. *Orly* - **The Guess Who**
11. *Sunday Bloody Sunday* - **U2**
12. *Year Of The Cat* - **Al Stewart**

The second string list includes both guitar and piano. Many of these songs attract us for their subtleties. They are all very effective and powerful. Thomas Dolby's' *I Scare Myself* does double duty again, this time with both guitar and piano.

142

22.15 ~ Strings II - Bits Of Guitar & Piano

1. *Another Day In Paradise (/g), I Wish It Would Rain Down (/g) & In The Air Tonight (/g)* - **Phil Collins**
2. *Baker Street (/p)* - **Gerry Rafferty**
3. *Betcha By Golly Wow (/p)* - **The Stylistics**
4. *Blinded By The Light (/g)* - **Manfred Mann**
5. *Broken Wings* - **Mr. Mister**
6. *Calling Elvis (/g/p) & Sultans Of Swing (/g)* - **Dire Straits**
7. *Dancing In The Moonlight (/g)* - **King Harvest**
8. *Diamond Girl (/g)* - **Seals & Crofts**
9. *Do It Again (/g)* - **Steely Dan**
10. *Drift Away (/g)* - **Dobie Gray**
11. *I Scare Myself (/g/p) & She Blinded Me With Science* (/g) - **Thomas Dolby**
12. *I'm Not In Love (/p)* - **10 CC**
13. *Let Go The Line (/g)* - **Max Webster**
14. *Long Tall Glasses (/g/p)* - **Leo Sayer**
15. *Midnight At The Oasis (/g)* - **Maria Muldaur**
16. *Money (/p)* - **Pink Floyd**
17. *Moonlight Desires (/g)* - **Gowan**
18. *My Life (/p)* - **Billy Joel**
19. *Oh Sherrie (/g)* - **Steve Perry**
20. *Only You (/g)* - **Ringo Starr**
21. *Overkill (/g)* - **Men At Work**
22. *Pharoahs (/b) (/g/p) & When In Love With A Blind Man (/b) (/p)* - **Tears For Fears**
23. *Sitting On A Poor Man's Throne (/g/p)* - **Copper Penny**
24. *Way Of The World (/b) (/p)* - **Genesis**
25. *We Don't Need Another Hero (/g)* - **Tina Turner**
26. *Wreck Of The Edmund Fitzgerald (/g)* - **Gordon Lightfoot**

The last section is about drums or no drums at all. The military sound and style is like a throwback to a different era.

22.16 ~ Military Drums

1. *50 Ways To Leave Your Lover* - **Paul Simon**
2. *Ace Of Swords (/b) & Don't Answer Me* - **The Alan Parsons Project**
3. *All This Time* - **Sting**
4. *Billy Don't Be A Hero* - **Bo Donaldson & The Heywoods**
5. *Brass Band In African Chimes (/b)* - **Simple Minds**
6. *Fernando* - **Abba**
7. *Dr. Marvello (/b)* - **Klaatu**
8. *I Am The Walrus (/b)* - **The Beatles**
9. *Let 'Em In & Pipes Of Peace* - **Paul McCartney & Wings**
10. *Lift Me Up & Man In A White Car* - **Yes**
11. *One Tin Soldier* - **The Original Cast**
12. *Pharoahs & When In Love With A Blind Man* - **Tears For Fears**

13. *(The) Riddle* - **Nik Kershaw**
14. *(A) Salty Dog (/b)* - **Procal Harum**
15. *Sunday Bloody Sunday* - **U2**
16. *Tusk* - **Fleetwood Mac**

It's very rare when a piece of popular music doesn't have drums or percussion of any kind. The song here, as already mentioned in chapter 14, is *Entangled*, by Genesis, with three of the four musicians in the group playing acoustic guitar, Steve Hackett, Mike Rutherford & Tony Banks. The folk fraternity has a strong showing here, Bread, Cat Stevens, Gordon Lightfoot, Greg Lake, Jim Croce, John Denver, Neil Young & Peter, Paul & Mary.

22.17 ~ No Drums

1. *Annie's Song, Sunshine On My Shoulder & Thank God I'm A Country Boy* - **John Denver**
2. *Beautiful & If You Could Read My Mind* - **Gordon Lightfoot**
3. *C'est La Vie & Watching Over You* - **Greg Lake (Emerson, Lake & Palmer)**
4. *(The) Clap (/b)* - **Steve Howe (Yes)**
5. *Dueling Banjos* - **Eric Weisberg**
6. *Downstream (/b)* - **Rick Davies (Supertramp)**
7. *Dust In The Wind* - **Kansas**
8. *Entangled* - **Genesis**
9. *I'm Not In Love* - **10 CC**
10. *If* - **Bread**
11. *Wonderous Stories* - **Yes**
12. *Leaving On A Jet Plane* - **Peter. Paul & Mary**
13. *Morning Has Broken* - **Cat Stevens**
14. *(The) Needle Gone & The Damage Done & Sugar Mountain* - **Neil Young**
15. *Russians* - **Sting**
16. *She's Always A Woman To Me* - **Billy Joel**
17. *Slat Key Soquel Rag (/b)* - **The Doobie Brothers**
18. *Time In A Bottle* - **Jim Croce**
19. *Tubular Bells* - **Mike Oldfield**
20. *We Will Rock You* - **Queen**
21. *Yesterday* - **The Beatles**
22. *You Are So Beautiful* - **Joe Cocker**

Cycling back to the instrumental categories I started with, here is a list of songs that have instrumental duos in them. They are not real duets but they are close to it. Sometimes the instruments are playing together. Other times they are alternating. Included here are accordion (ac), acoustic guitar (ag), acoustic piano (ap), banjo (b), clarinet (cl), drums (d), electric guitar (eg), electric piano (ep), flute (f), harmonica (h), organ (o), saxophone (sx), synthesizer (sy) and violin (v). The focus is on two different instruments so it doesn't include duets with two guitars like *Hotel California* or *Layla* or *Owner Of A Lonely Heart*.

22.18 ~ Instrumental Duos

1. *Abacab (eg/sy) & Second Home By The Sea (eg/sy)* - **Genesis**
2. *Any Colour You Like (/b) (eg/o)* - **Pink Floyd**
3. *Black Water (ag/v)* - **The Doobie Brothers**
4. *C'est La Vie (ac/ag)* - **Greg Lake**
5. *Don't Kill The Whale (eg/sy), Going For The One (ap/eg), Long Distance Runaround (eg/ep) & Release Release (d/eg)* - **Yes**
6. *Dueling Banjos (ag/b)* - **Eric Weissberg**
7. *Frankenstein (eg/sx)* - **The Edgar Winter Group**
8. *Hot Dog (ag/ap)* - **Led Zeppelin**
9. *If You Wanna Get To Heaven (eg/h)* - **The Ozark Mountain Daredevils**
10. *(The) Mexican (eg/ep)* - **Babe Ruth**
11. *New Year's Day (ap/eg)* - **U2**
12. *Only Time Will Tell (eg/sy) & Sole Survivor (eg/o)* - **Asia**
13. *Take The Long Way Home (cl/h) & You Started Laughing (ep/sx)* - **Supertramp**
14. *Why Me? (eg/sx)* - **Styx**

TWENTY - THREE

FAMILY & FRIENDS

My godfather was an accomplished musician and audiophile. He had the right idea. When you went to his house to listen to music you did it in the basement where the shelves were full of vinyl and the music was so loud that if you could hear each other talking it was a bonus.

My parents taught me from an earlier age that music and television were in fact quite different. To mark that difference, music was played on the stereo in the living room and television was watched in the family room. I have carried this tradition forward. My brother Richard commented in the early seventies, that he had a teacher who had a stereo set up in his classroom. The teacher would go on to say that "If you could not hear the music, then the music was too loud!". Years later, into the 2010s, I bought a new amplifier and I will never forget the salesman's words of advice, You don't appreciate the quality of a stereo system, when you play music loudly, only when you play it softly.

In the spring of 1973, my dad remarked, when this collection began that in a few months I wouldn't be listening to the handful of singles I had collected to that point. I took them with me to an overnight fundraising wake-athon at the local church. The handful included …

23.1 ~ Bought Spring 1973
1. *Also Sprach Zarathustra (2001)* - **Deodato**
2. *Control Of Me* - **Les Emmerson**
3. *Crocodile Rock & Daniel* - **Elton John**
4. *Dead Skunk / Needless To Say* - **Loudon Wainwright III**
5. *Dueling Banjos* - **Eric Weisberg**
6. *Follow Your Daughter Home* - **The Guess Who**
7. *Frankenstein* - **The Edgar Winter Group**
8. *Heart Of Gold / Sugar Mountain* - **Neil Young**
9. *Horse With No Name* - **America**

10. *I'm A Stranger Here* - **The Five Man Electrical Band**
11. *Lady Run Lady Hide* - **April Wine**
12. *Last Song / Best Friend* - **Edward Bear**
13. *My Love / The Mess (Live)* - **Paul McCartney**
14. *Stuck In The Middle With You* - **Stealers Wheel**
15. *Tie A Yellow Ribbon Round The Ole Oak Tree* - **Dawn**
16. *You Are The Sunshine Of My Life* - **Stevie Wonder**
17. *You're So Vain / His Friends Are More Than Fond Of Robin* - **Carly Simon**

Well, the much-listened-to handful now numbers more than 1800. Many years later Dad would transport several baskets full of my 45s in his car on one of our moving days.

By the fall of 1973, I was listening to CFRA and CFGO radio in Ottawa. In the fall of 1974, a Classmate commented early in high school that most of what was played on top forty radio was bubble gum. So, about a year later, I started listening to FM Rock Radio and buying albums, rather than just singles. However, the FM only idea lasted maybe six months and then I went back to my AM roots. I decided then that both the FM (albums) and AM (singles) streams were important to stay in touch with popular music. If AM music was bubble gum, then I have spent years and years blowing awesome bubbles.

In the spring of 1976, the High School Concert Band went on a year-end trip to Toronto. My host played *In A Glass House* (Gentle Giant) as wake-up music for me, the sound of breaking glass, a prog rock band with counterpoint thrown into the mix. Theirs' was my first rock concert ever, alongside Starcastle. *In A Glass House* was never released domestically on vinyl. I played the original into the ground. Replacement pressings have never been as good.

Christmas 1977 I remember making a blunderous foot in mouth comment to my Aunt who was gracious enough to give me some audio cassette tapes for Christmas. As I thanked her I commented that really I liked the type II Chrome tapes rather than the type I regular low noise tapes.

Summer 1978 was a great music moment for me, out on the back deck; my dad was visiting with my godfather and me when my high school music teacher paid us a visit. That was lots of music talent all in the same place. Reel to Reel tape recording was the ultimate in recording. Both my godfather and my high school teacher had them and used them extensively. A band mate also had one and his use of recording different tracks was awesome. I even knew someone in the early 80s that used VHS tape to record music.

Dad used to joke around sometimes with the music I listened to. His favourite was the repetition in Led Zeppelins' song *Whole Lotta Love* and he used to say to me, "Steve, I think your record is skipping again".

In the mid-seventies, while I was living in Ottawa, Michael gifted me a handful of singles that he had replaced with albums…

23.2 ~ From Michael
1. *Let It Ride \\ Blue Collar & Taking Care Of Business // You Ain't Seen Nothin' Yet -* **Bachman - Turner Overdrive**
2. *D'yer Ma'ker \ The Crunge* - **Led Zeppelin**
3. *Only Women* - **Alice Cooper**
4. *Shout It Out Loud* - **Kiss**

By the time I had moved back to Toronto, Michael had made four different group booklets for me, three I have already mentioned, Beatles, Genesis & Zeppelin. The fourth was about Rush. I knew very little about Rush and decided to give the booklet to my bandmate, classmate, schoolmate, John K, as big a fan of Rush as Michael.

In the late seventies, another friend borrowed a handful of singles from me. When he returned them to me, they were in rough shape. What I realized was that he had doused them all with record fluid before playing them. When the fluid dried it left marks and made gross sounds when I played the records again. I even called him up at home after midnight to tell him how upset I was.

In the spring & summer of 1979, I clearly remember two different high school jams, the first with five other high school colleagues/friends. There was a guitarist, pianist, bassist, drummer and two horn players. The first three entries were from that jam. The last two were from sitting in front of a drum kit, to keep it from moving, while several others played the tunes. Here are all five together…

23.3 ~ High School Jam
1. *25 Or 6 To 4 & Anyway You Want* - **Chicago**
2. *Framed* - **Cheech & Chong** and
3. *Nights In White Satin* - **The Moody Blues**

4. *Rock & Roll* - **Led Zeppelin** and
5. *Tie Your Mother Down* - **Queen**

We recorded *Nights In White Satin* and then played the tape in the car while we cruised the neighbourhood. In the early eighties, I tried my hand at being DJ for the local youth group. I was good, not great, but mostly, I had a lot of fun doing it. My warm-up music for many of those dances was *Drama* by Yes. Note that three of these tunes, *Anyway You Want, Framed & Tie Your Mother Down* are triplet tunes that I talked about in chapter twenty on structure.

In the mid-eighties, a colleague said he did not need an album / CD / record collection because the music they played on CHUM FM was all the music that he needed to hear, current tunes plus older ones, just enough to give him the mix he needed. Maybe I missed something but just listening to the radio has never done it for me. Playing music that I wanted to hear at a particular moment was always important, not just waiting for a radio station DJ to play it. The radio was a good starting point in getting to know the songs.

A colleague I worked with during a labour strike in 1988 told me that in his younger days back in the 1960s, he and his high school aged friends would get together and DJ dances, complete with current 45 RPM records of the day.

In 1994, John K and his girlfriend and my wife and I attended one of the last concerts ever at Exhibition Stadium in Toronto. Hell had frozen over and The Eagles were back on tour. The stage was in the east end zone, instead of in front of the north grandstand. Oh, I forgot. Henley said to *Get Over It* (see below). They played a great show featuring The Eagles as well as solo pieces, from Don Henley (DH), Joe Walsh (JW) and Glenn Frey (GF). Part of the setlist included …

23.4 ~ Eagles Hell Freezes Over Exhibition Stadium
All She Wants To Do Is Dance, Already Gone, Boys Of Summer, Dirty Laundry, Heartache Tonight, Hotel California, I Can't Tell You Why, Life In The Fast Lane, Life's Been Good, Lyin' Eyes, New Kid In Town, One Of These Nights, Pretty Maids All In A Row, Take It Easy, Tequila Sunrise & You Belong To The City

In January 2022, Rolling Stone released their Top 40 Eagles Songs[143]. Here is my collection from that list…

23.5 ~ Eagles Rolling Stone Top 40 Songs

1.Hotel California, 2.Take It Easy, 5.New Kid In Town, 6.Already Gone, 7.Lyin' Eyes, 8.Life In The Fast Lane, 9.One Of These Nights, 10.Heartache Tonight, 11.I Can't Tell You Why, 13.Tequila Sunrise, 14.Best Of My Love, 15.Take It To The Limit, 17.Witchy Woman, 27.The Last Resort, 30.Victim Of Love, 38.Pretty Maids All In A Row & 39.Please Come Home For Christmas

Like the Eagles, many artists in the late eighties and early nineties recorded acoustic unplugged versions of songs they had recorded in earlier years. One of these artists was Eric Clapton. He recorded an acoustic version of *Layla.* The version was nice enough but paled in comparison to the original that featured Duane Allmans' slide guitar.

In the 1990s, my brother Andrew gifted me a handful of singles. Some were by artists already in my collection but many more were not, a way of adding different music to my collection. The most noticeable was an instant mini catalogue by The Commodores. The titles included the following …

23.6 ~ From Andrew 1990s

1. *After The Love Has Gone // Boogie Wonderland* - **Earth, Wind & Fire**
2. *Armageddon* - **Prism**
3. *Bat Out Of Hell // Heaven Can Wait* - **Meatloaf**
4. *Big Shot // Honesty* - **Billy Joel**
5. *Easy, Lady, Oh No, Sail On & Still* - **The Commodores**
6. *Girls Just Wanna Have Fun* - **Cyndi Lauper**
7. *Morning Has Broken* - **Cat Stevens**
8. *On The One For Fun* - **The Dazz Band**
9. *Purple Rain* - **Prince & The Revolution**
10. *Sexual Healing* - **Marvin Gaye**
11. *TV Dinners* - **ZZ Top**
12. *Uprock* - **The Rock Steady Crew**
13. *Wake Up & Live* - **Bob Marley**
14. *Wherever I Lay My Hat (That's My Home)* - **Paul Young**
15. *Yah Mo B There* - **James Ingram**

Sometime after that, longtime friend Douglas gifted me a handful of his records as well. Most were of the pop genre, rather than rock, but still good tunes...

23.7 ~ From Douglas 1990s

1. *Billy Don't Be A Hero* - **Bo Donaldson & The Heywoods**
2. *Candyman, The* - **Sammy David Jr.**
3. *Cracklin' Rosie* - **Neil Diamond**

---

[143] *Eagles The Ultimate Guide*, Rolling Stone, January 2022, p.82

4. *Dead Skunk // Bell Bottom Pants & Dead Skunk / Needless To Say* - **Loudon Wainwright III**
5. *Disco Duck* - **Rick Dees**
6. *Hitchin' A Ride // Early In The Morning & Hitchin' A Ride / Man Child* - **Vanity Fare**
7. *Lion Sleeps Tonight, The* - **The Tokens**
8. *Love Grows* - **Edison Lighthouse**
9. *Love Is Blue* - **Paul Mauriat**
10. *Love Me Love Me Love & Poor Little Fool* - **Frank Mills**
11. *Raise A Little Hell* - **Trooper**
12. *Streak, The* - **Ray Stevens**
13. *Say Has Anybody Seen My Sweety Gypsy Rose & Tie A Yellow Ribbon Round The Ole Oak Tree* - **Dawn**
14. *That's The Way I Like It* - **K. C. & The Sunshine Band**

During a garage sale that I hosted in the early 00s, a buyer told me a neat story. He lived in a sprawling ranch style bungalow in the Guildwood neighborhood of Toronto. He had a large rectangular shaped room in his basement with a billiard table in the middle of the room, a doorway in one corner, a chair in the second corner, billiard equipment in the third corner, and a stereo system in the last corner. On every wall, the shelves were full of vinyl from floor to ceiling. This was a wonderful way to teach his teenage kids and their friends how to play billiards and listen to vinyl and how to care for both.

In the fall of 2016, I joined the Revival Vinyl Society.[144] I didn't know what it was at first, maybe a place to go to buy and sell records. No, not at all. It is a chance to get together once a month with other audiophiles in a restaurant setting (The Revival House Belfry Bar[145]) and listen to vinyl records. It's a throwback to the old days when you listened to vinyl records in the wood paneled recreation room in your basement. Restaurant Owner is Rob Wigan and DJ is Mista D. Each member of the society brings a couple of their records, noting the song or songs they want to hear, and that becomes the DJ play list - My playlist at each gathering across the years looks like this, including notations for two songs (& after the artist) and album cuts (33), in chronological order, first from 2016 & 2017…

23.8 ~ Revival Vinyl Society I - The Album Cuts
1. *Going For The One [GOING FOR THE ONE]* **Yes, 2016**
2. *The Meaning [CRISIS? WHAT CRISIS?]* **Supertramp**
3. *Mysterious Ways [ACHTUNG BABY]* **U2, 2017**
4. *Cutting It Fine [ASIA]* **Asia**
5. *One Of Our Submarines [GOLDEN AGE OF WIRELESS]* **Thomas Dolby**
6. *Burning Bridges [BLACK MOON]* **ELP**
7. *The Voice [I ROBOT]* **The Alan Parsons Project**
8. *Good Day [GOOD DAY]* **Lighthouse, 2018**
9. *Blade Runner End Titles [BLADE RUNNER]* **Vangelis, 2019**
10. *Nobody Lives Without Love [BATMAN FOREVER]* **Eddi Reader**
11. *25 Or 6 To 4 [CHICAGO II]* **Chicago**
12. *Driving The Last Spike [WE CAN'T DANCE]* **Genesis, 2020**
13. *Freedom For My People [RATTLE & HUM]* **Adam & Satan, 2021**

---

[144] Revival Vinyl Society at the Revival House Restaurant, Est. 2016
[145] Belfry Bar, Revival House Restaurant

14. *Tarkus Eruption [TARKUS]* **Emerson, Lake & Palmer, 2022**
15. *Cinema [90125]* **Yes, 2023**
16. *Love Comes Tumbling [UNFORGETTABLE FIRE MINI LP]* **U2**
17. *Narnia -* **Steve Walsh & Steve Hackett** *& How Can I ? -* **Richie Havens & Steve Hackett -** *[PLEASE DON'T TOUCH]*
18. *Just The Same [FREE HAND]* **Gentle Giant**
19. *Fairy Tale Of New York [IF I SHOULD FALL FROM GRACE WITH GOD]* **The Pogues**
20. *Vermillion Sands [ADVENTURES IN MODERN RECORDING]* **The Buggles**
21. *When In Love With & Blind Man & Pharoahs [SATURNINE MARTIAL & LUNATIC]* **Tears For Fears, 2024**

In the spirit of the chapter about the flat foot song, I have indicated here all those tunes which fall in to that category.

23.9 ~ Revival Vinyl Society II - The Singles

1. *Dance A Little Step* [FLAT] - **Mashmakhan, 2016**
2. *The Nutrocker -* **Emerson, Lake & Palmer** *& I Believe In Father Christmas -* **Greg Lake**
3. *See The Lights* [UK] - **Simple Minds, 2017**
4. *Year Of The Cat -* **Al Stewart**
5. *Everyday Is A Winding Road* [US] - **Sheryl Crow** *& Wildwood Weed -* **Jim Stafford**
6. *Pioneer & Six Months In A Leaky Boat -* **Split Enz** *& Roundabout -* **Yes**
7. *Belfast Child (12) -* **Simple Minds**
8. *I'd Like To Teach The World To Sing -* **The Hilltop Singers**
9. *Crazy* [FLAT] - **Seal, 2018**
10. *Pharoahs* -* **Tears For Fears**
11. *Reggae Christmas* [FLAT] - **Bryan Adams**
12. *Lift Me Up* [FLAT] - **Yes, 2019**
13. *Lowdown* [FLAT] [US] - **Chicago**
14. *Rodeo Song* [US] - **Garry Lee** *& Hyperactive* [FLAT] - **Thomas Dolby**
15. *Enola Gay -* **Orchestral Manoeuvres In The Dark** *& Crocodile Rock -* **Elton John**
16. *I'm A Stranger Here -* **The Five Man Electrical Band**
17. *Greensleeves* [FLAT] - **Mason Williams** *& Run With The Fox -* **Chris Squire & Alan White**
18. *I Am The Walrus* [FLAT] - **The Beatles** *& I Know What I Like (In Your Wardrobe)* [FLAT] [UK] - **Genesis, 2022**
19. *Sound Chaser* [US] - **Yes, 2023**
20. *Sister Golden Hair* [US] - **America**
21. *Jeremy Bender* [FLAT] - **Emerson, Lake & Palmer** *& I Believe In Music* [FLAT] - **Gallery**
22. *Ain't Nobody But Me -* **Supertramp**
23. *Cry Your Eyes Out* [FLAT] - **Les Emmerson, 2024**
24. *When In Love With A Blind Man* [FLAT] *& Pharoahs* -* **Tears For Fears**
25. *Nights In White Satin (short version)* [US] - **The Moody Blues**

As I have been part of these vinyl society meetings since 2016, I have offered up background did you know information as well as trivia to make the song selections a little more interesting and give them some meaning.

Speaking of *The Meaning* by Supertramp, it is one of just a few written in triple or waltz time, with Roger Hodgson playing the complex waltz part underneath on the acoustic guitar. *Burning Bridges* by Emerson Lake & Palmer draws together the symbolism of the carousel on the album cover and the carousel that was just around the corner from the Kingswood Music Theatre at Canada's Wonderland. For The Voice, I asked people what other songs it reminded them of, hoping someone would say *Papa Was A Rolling Stone* by The Temptations. Someone did mention that tune but someone else mentioned *Theme from Shaft* by Isaac Hayes.

Crazy by Seal is not to be confused with *Crazy* by Patsy Cline, one of the greatest country songs of all time by one of the greatest country singers of all time. The Patsy Cline version is featured in *Field Of Dreams*[146] in the feed store scene when Kevin Costner (Ray) asks another farmer if he has ever heard voices. The next thing you know they are saying that Ray is hearing voices. At that moment, the Patsy Cline song is playing in the background, a great movie moment.

When I shared *Pharoahs* by Tears For Fears, I asked what song it reminded them of, hoping someone would say *Everybody Wants To Rule The World*. DJ Mista D had to help the group to come up with that song. When I offered up Bryan Adams *Reggae Christmas* for the play list at the 2018 Christmas get together, DJ Mista D explained I couldn't put it on the list because he already had. For the entire song *Enola Gay* and part of the song *Crocodile Rock*, the chord progression is identical, major, relative minor, fourth & fifth. So, at one of the Revival nights, after a few bars of *Enola Gay, I* sang the chorus to *Crocodile Rock* at the same time. At the 2019 Christmas gathering, two fellow Revival Society members remarked on the great the classical guitar playing by Mason Williams on *Greensleeves*. Mista D commented at the Revival Society 2022 Halloween Party that while he wasn't a Beatles fan, he was a fan of *I Am The Walrus.*

As a nod to the late Yes drummer Alan White, I shared a writeup about the two tunes *Sound Chaser & Cinema*, highlighting his unending skills. *Love Comes Tumbling* is an *Unforgettable Fire* Mini EP tune that followed instead of coming before *The Unforgettable Fire*, and featured artwork that was more like *The Joshua Tree*. Finally, I asked fellow society members to identify the only song to appear on both final personal copies of the CHUM and CFRA charts. It was *Sister Golden Hair* by America. *Jeremy Bender* and *I Believe In Music* were shared as examples of Flat Foot Songs. *Ain't Nobody But Me* was shared as a basic waltz. *When In Love With A Blind Man* and *Pharoahs* were shared as reworked versions of other Tears For Fears songs. *Nights In White Satin* was shared as a rare short version of that song.

23.10 ~ Revival Vinyl Society III - Did You Know?
1. *The Meaning (33) [CRISIS? WHAT CRISIS?]* **Supertramp** (The Waltz)
2. *Burning Bridges (33) [BLACK MOON]* **ELP** (Canada's Wonderland)
3. *The Voice (33) [I ROBOT]* **The Alan Parsons Project**
4. *Crazy* - **Seal**
5. *Pharoahs* - **Tears For Fears** (Everybody Wants)
6. *Reggae Christmas* - **Bryan Adams**
7. *Enola Gay* - **Orchestral Manoeuvres In The Dark** & *Crocodile Rock* - **Elton John** (1 Minor 4 5 Chord Change)
8. *Greensleeves* - **Mason Williams**

---

[146] *Crazy*, Patsy Kline, 1961, *Field Of Dreams*, Universal, 1988

9. *I Am The Walrus* - **The Beatles** (extra bar)
10. *Sound Chaser* [US] & *Cinema (33) [90125]* **Yes**
11. *Love Comes Tumbling (33) [UNFORGETTABLE FIRE MINI LP]* **U2**
12. *Sister Golden Hair* [US] - **America** (*The Sister Golden Hair Chart*)
13. *Just The Same (33) [FREE HAND]* **Gentle Giant** (Top 10 Album)
14. *Jeremy Bender* - **Emerson, Lake & Palmer** & *I Believe In Music* - **Gallery** (*The Flat Foot Song*)
15. *Ain't Nobody But Me* - **Supertramp** (The Waltz)
16. *When In Love With A Blind Man & Pharoahs* - **Tears For Fears** (*The Working Hour & Everybody Wants To Rule The World*)
17. *Nights In White Satin* [US]- **The Moody Blues** (*short version*)

The influence of friends was a strong one for sure. Some reminded me of groups, like whole albums or a handful of singles by a particular group. Others reminded me of single songs.

John K passed away in 2007 and left behind him many memories, The Alan Parsons Project concert with Yes in 1998, Blue Jay Baseball Games, The Eagles concert at the CNE in 1994, Emerson, Lake & Palmer concerts at Canada's Wonderland in 1992 & 1996, playing trombone together at JS Woodsworth High School in Ottawa from 1975 to 1977, listening to Gary Wright's *Dream Weaver & Love Is Alive* at a high volume at his Ottawa home in the summer of 1976, and Yes concerts in 1994, 1998, 1999, 2001 & 2002. After he passed, his mother gifted me most of his CD collection. This had been one of his final requests.

Most notably are those people (too numerous to mention and if I miss someone I get in trouble) with whom I attended various and assorted rock concerts. The first large scale rock concert was, as previously mentioned, Gentle Giant in Ottawa at the Civic Centre in 1976. The last large scale rock concert was Chicago & Earth Wind & Fire in Toronto at the Molson Amphitheatre in 2015. That was about forty years' worth of rock concerts, attended with many different friends.

Both Maple Leaf Gardens and CNE Stadium were home to many music concerts, in addition to the sports events of the Maple Leafs, Argonauts, and Blue Jays. CNE Stadium has been torn down and Maple Leaf Gardens has been rebuilt, giving it a totally different look. They are both now part of the history of the City Of Toronto. I only ever saw three music concerts at Maple Leaf Gardens, and all three were by the rock group Yes, *Tormato* (1979), *Drama* (1980) and *Big Generator* (1987).

In contrast, I saw eight different concerts by eight different groups at the CNE …

23.11 ~ CNE Concerts
1. 1979 - **Supertramp** - *Breakfast in America*
2. 1980 - **The Cars** - *Panorama*
3. 1982 - **Genesis** - *Abacab*
4. 1984 - **Yes** - *90125*
5. 1985 - **Tina Turner** - *Private Dancer*
6. 1986 - **Elton John** - *Leather Jackets*
7. 1987 - **Chicago** - *Chicago 18*
8. 1994 - **The Eagles** - *Hell Freezes Over*

Finally, for all my love of eighties music, as discussed in chapters twelve and thirteen, I never attended any concerts by any groups from the eighties.

TWENTY - FOUR

MY JOURNEY

Many of the albums I first started buying/collecting were progressive rock. Ah yes, progressive rock, you say? Yes, I say, and I can't help it. Whatever you call it, art, classical, extended, extravagant, grandiose, orchestral, overdone, pompous, pretentious, progressive, snob, symphonic rock, it forms the second of two basic parts to the collection, the first being the singles. Also note the contrast or dichotomy of progressive songs with long drawn out album versions and edited single versions.

In the fall if 1972, I started buying hockey biographies about Roger Crozier,[147] Gordie Howe,[148] Derek Sanderson,[149] and Bobby Orr.[150] I bought them at a small neighborhood store called The Book Note.[151] The store also sold records but I didn't notice them until I started buying records in the spring of 1973.

When I first moved to Ottawa in the Fall of 1973, I assembled a small collection of 45s, just from Miracle Mart[152] alone, including many new artists compared to the Toronto collection from the spring of 1973…

24.1 ~ Bought Ottawa 1973 Miracle Mart
1. *Angie* - **The Rolling Stones**
2. *Bongo Rock* - **The Incredible Bongo Band**
3. *Cry Your Eyes Out* - **Les Emmerson**
4. *Helen Wheels* - **Paul McCartney & Wings**

---

[147] *Daredevil Goalie Roger Crozier*, Tom Cohen, Rutledge books, 1967
[148] *Gordie Howe*, Stan Fischler, Grossett & Dunlap, 1967
[149] *Derek Sanderson, I've Got To Be Me*, Stan Fischler, Dell Publishing, 1972
[150] *Bobby Orr & The Big Bad Bruins*, Stan Fischler, Dell Publishing, 1970
[151] The Book Note, Victoria Van Horne Plaza, North York, 1972 & 1973
[152] Miracle Mart, Pascal/Miracle Mart/Steinberg plaza. Merivale Rd, Nepean, 1973

5. *Hello It's Me* - **Todd Rundgren**
6. *Just You'n Me* - **Chicago**
7. *Mind Games* - **John Lennon**
8. *Morning After, The* - **Maureen McGovern**
9. *Painted Ladies* - **Ian Thomas**
10. *Photograph* - **Ringo Starr**
11. *Pretty Lady* - **Lighthouse**

In the spring of 1974, I was part of an Easter service with the youth group of Dominion Chalmers church[153] in downtown Ottawa. I remember that we didn't say The Lord's Prayer but instead played a recording of the song *The Lord's Prayer* sung by the Australian nun, Sister Janet Mead.

Here is a side note on the buying of records. I can remember from time to time picking out a record I wanted and then realized in between the record rack and the cashier line up that I did not have any money to pay for it (remember this was the 1970s before bank machines and debit cards) and this record was the last one. I would then, horrors horrors, take the record and stash it somewhere else in the store, go and get some money, come back, and retrieve it.

What I really liked were the record stores when they wrote the names of the groups and singles and albums using black marking pen on to white and yellow card stock. Printing with Dymo guns or Letraset or whatever lettering they were using at the time just wasn't the same.

In the late seventies, I saw a full page advertisement from *the New York Times*, promoting a Billy Joel concert in New York City.[154] This was back in the days when you could not order your concert tickets online, you had to go to a ticket kiosk somewhere to buy them. Featured across the two pages were what must have been a couple of hundred record stores in the New York City area where you could buy concert tickets, impressive.

As a consolation to not having the New York Times advertisement, I have a Toronto Star advertisement showing the Billy Joel *Live From Long Island*[155] concert VHS tape on sale at all 83 Ontario locations of the Video Station stores that were listed. I had several of the Billy Joel light blue Hall Of Fame 45s, *Piano Man / The Entertainer*, *Just The Way You Are / She's Always A Woman* and *Big Shot / Honesty*.

At one point in the late seventies, I had taken many of my LP records out of their jackets and then tacked the album jackets on the wall in the form of an album cover quilt.

High school / university friend Eric had started his vinyl collection in the late seventies, punk mostly. I remember he had a brand new turntable with a Discwasher brush though I can't remember the make of the table. He went off to a small Ontario university in the fall. He commented that a classmate of his who also liked punk music referred to and described progressive rock music as *Crazy Hippie Organ Music*.

In 1978, I saw Harry Chapin in concert at the Ontario Place Forum[156] with Alex. Chapin was a great singer, songwriter and entertainer. It was an enjoyable show, even in the pouring rain.

By the time of the late 1970s, I had a routine where I would walk along Yonge Street (usually from Bloor Street down to Queen Street) in downtown Toronto and check out every store that I passed. Many of these included A&A Records, Cheapies, Circle Of Sound, Discus, Dunn's Vinyl Museum, Flipside, Incredible Record Store, Kops & Vintage Sounds (Queen), Mister Sound, Music World, Record Peddler,

---

[153] Dominion Chalmers United Church, Cooper Street, Ottawa
[154] Billy Joel Concert advertisement, New York Times, late 1970s
[155] Billy Joel Live From Long Island, video tape for sale at Video Station, 1983
[156] Harry Chapin, Ontario Place Forum, Toronto, 1978

Record World, Records On Wheels, Sam The Record Man & Vortex. Other neighborhoods included the Danforth (Blue Note) and Queen Street (Discovery, Driftwood & Kops & Vintage Sounds).

Delete bins had good stuff in them and you could always tell the delete jacket because it had a cut in from the edge or a hole punched through it, either way near the corner. I spent so much time in record stores (not music stores as they are now known) that other store customers would mistake me for a record store clerk. You can always tell audiophiles, guys looking through racks of albums and they can pass over album jacks with the touch of a single finger. There's no time to stop and look and each album jacket when you've got hundreds to look at.

Back in the day, Sam The Record Man locations each had their own bags, with their locations printed on them. I frequented many of them…Barrie Downtown, Bayview Village, Danforth Avenue, Fairview Mall, Hamilton Downtown, Scarborough Town Centre, Yonge & Eglinton, Yonge Street Downtown & Yorkdale. At one point Cheapies records bags sported the logo/monograph/wording of the radio station 104.5 CHUM FM.

In the summer of 1980, I shopped at record stores throughout Scarborough and North York, on my bike rides home from work, including Music World at Fairview Mall, A&A Records at Bridlewood Mall and Scarborough Town Centre and Sam The Record Man at Bayview Village, Eglinton Square and Fairview Mall, more micro geography, and where I collected many of my first double hit singles…

24.2 ~ Bought Summer 1980 I - Double Hits
1. *(I've Been) Searchin' So Long // Call On Me* - **Chicago**
2. *Air That I Breathe // Jennifer Eccles, He Ain't Heavy, He's My Brother // Carrie Ann & Long Cool Woman In A Black Dress // Long Dark Road* - **The Hollies**
3. *All By Myself // Never Gonna Fall In Love Again* - **Eric Carmen**
4. *Baby I'm A Want You // Everything I Own, If // Let Your Love Go & Make It With You // It Don't Matter To Me* - **Bread**
5. *Barracuda // Treat Me Well* - **Heart**
6. *Dream On // Sweet Emotion* - **Aerosmith**
7. *Dream Weaver // Love Is Alive* - **Gary Wright**
8. *Just The Way You Are // She's Always A Woman To Me* - **Billy Joel**
9. *Mandy // It's A Miracle* - **Barry Manilow**
10. *My Cherie Amour // Don't Know Why I Love You* - **Stevie Wonder**
11. *Night Moves // Main Street* - **Bob Segar**
12. *Sailing // Ride Like The Wind* - **Christopher Cross**
13. *Shining Star // That's The Way Of The World* - **Earth, Wind & Fire**
14. *Wildfire // Mansion On The Hill* - **Michael Murphy**
15. *Your Mama Don't Dance // Peace Of Mind* - **Loggins & Messina**

While many of them were double hits, many were not but they were still significant in establishing my collection in those early days. They include…

24.3 ~ Bought Summer 1980 II - Single Hits
1. *Dancing Queen / That's Me & Knowing Me Knowing You* - **Abba**
2. *I'm So Straight I'm A Weirdo* - **Rick Wakeman**
3. *Lotta Love* - **Nicolette Larson**
4. *Miracles* - **Jefferson Starship**

5. *My Sharona* - **The Knack**
6. *One Way Or Another* - **Blondie**
7. *Song Sung Blue* - **Neil Diamond**
8. *Sultans Of Swing* - **Dire Straits**
9. *Summer (The First Time)* - **Bobby Goldsboro**
10. *Sun Goes By* - **Dr. Music**
11. *Video Killed The Radio Star* - **The Buggles**
12. *Wreck Of The Edmund Fitzgerald* - **Gordon Lightfoot**

1980 also meant my own personal stereo system and two major markers. I remember bringing the stereo home. I think it was 2 in the morning before I had it all set up. First, the albums I had listened to on my dad's stereo now sounded better. Second, and more importantly, the singles I had played on my dad's standalone mono record player sounded amazing, like they had new life, like they had never sounded before.

One thing I have always wondered about my turntable. The stop / interrupt button that lifts the tone arm from the record is right underneath the tone arm, not at the centre or the left. Even a tall guy like me needs to be at a certain height to lift the tone arm or you are going to hit the stop / interrupt button by mistake before you even get started.

1980 also meant a return to my record buying roots, 1973. That was riding my bicycle to the record store. Well, the eleven mile trip home from my summer job at parks often meant a detour through Scarborough and parts of North York, frequenting records stores, on my way home. This was the first time in many years where my focus shifted from buying albums back to buying singles. Scarborough was home to A&A Records on Warden Avenue and WEA Music on Birchmount Road, while North York was home to CBS Records on Leslie Street.

My brain cramped in early 1981. The single *Photograph* (Ringo Starr) which I had played for years had developed a bump or a scratch and the result was the record kept skipping. Well, I tried and tried to get it not to skip, even putting extra weight on the needle. I was so upset I took the record off the turntable and fired it across the room, broke it and threw it and the original picture sleeve in the garbage. It took me years to find another copy with the picture sleeve.

In the early 80s, I frequented both Sam The Record Man and Dunn's Vinyl Museum downtown on Yonge Street. Based on the number of clear sleeves I have from the vinyl museum, I collected close to three hundred records from that franchise of stores. While there were many trips to Dunn's that resulted in forty-fives at a bargain price, the same can't be said for Sam's Downtown. However, in 1983, on one particular July afternoon at Sam's Downtown, I picked up all of these singles, highlighted by a pair for each of Cheech & Chong, Copper Penny & Supertramp …

24.4 ~ Bought Sam The Record Man Bargains 1983
1. *Ain't Nobody But Me & Lady* - **Supertramp**
2. *Billie Jean* - **Michael Jackson**
3. *Boogie Man Gonna Get Ya* - **Catfish Hodge**
4. *Earache My Eye & Framed* - **Cheech & Chong**
5. *Goodbye Superdad* - **Bill King**
6. *Jazzman* - **Carole King**
7. *Light Of Smiles* - **Gary Wright**
8. *Sitting On A Poor Man's Throne & You're Still The One* - **Copper Penny**
9. *Walking In Rhythm* - **The Blackbyrds**

10. *You're No Good* - **Linda Ronstadt**

It's hard to believe but my first real written record of my vinyl collection, both single and album was not done until July of 1983. This collection was organized by artist. The next written record was the spring of 1984. That was for singles and it was organized by title, not artist. In 1990, my brother Andrew updated my inventory as *The SDE Discography* and in 2008, I updated my inventory as *Th45zz*.

In the winter of 1984 - 1985, I lived in Brantford and worked in Ancaster. While working in Ancaster, I frequented many a record store in Hamilton and gathered many of what were current new wave hits, care of Thomas Dolby, The Human League and A Flock of Seagulls, among others.

24.5 ~ Bought In Hamilton 1984 & 1985

1. *Boys Of Summer, The* - **Don Henley**
2. *Change* - **Tears For Fears**
3. *Hyperactive & I Scare Myself* - **Thomas Dolby**
4. *Less Cities, More Moving People* - **The Fixx**
5. *Let's Talk About Me* - **The Alan Parsons Project**
6. *Life On Your Own* - **The Human League**
7. *More You Live The More You Love, The & Never Again (The Dancer)* - **A Flock Of Seagulls**
8. *One Night In Bangkok* - **Murray Head**
9. *One Small Day* - **Midge Ure**
10. *Tesla Girl* - **Orchestral Manoeuvres In The Dark**

In the summer of 1986, my 45 RPM collection suffered a setback. Having acquired many albums for which I had singles from those same albums, I viewed the singles as expendable, not necessary, overkill. I used the singles as prizes at a church games day. It was only years later, after I had recollected all but two of the songs, *Cover of Rolling Stone* (Dr. Hook) and *Theme From "For A Few Dollars More"* (Babe Ruth), the edited version of *The Mexican*, that I realized how very valuable and meaningful those singles were to begin with. I have recently reacquired both of those singles.

Here is the original list of items I put up on the auction block …

24.6 ~ Ping Pong Pitch [gem]

1. *Carry on Wayward Son / Questions Of My Childhood* - **Kansas**
2. *Cover Of Rolling Stone* - **Dr. Hook**
3. *Crazy / Dreamboat Annie* - **Heart**
4. *Dancing Queen / That's Me* - **Abba**
5. *Dream On // Sweet Emotion & Walk This Way* - **Aerosmith**
6. *Frankenstein / Undercover Man* - **The Edgar Winter Group**
7. *Goodbye Yellow Brick Road / Young Man's Blues* - **Elton John**
8. *Hold Your Head Up / Closer To Heaven* - **Argent**
9. *I Shot The Sheriff* - **Eric Clapton**
10. *Let Me Serenade You, Old Fashioned Love Song & Shambala* - **Three Dog Night**
11. *Listen To The Music / Toulouse Street & Long Train Running / Without You* - **The Doobie Brothers**
12. *Long Cool Woman In A Black Dress / Look What We've Got & Sandy* - **The Hollies**

13. *Spot The Pigeon EP - Match Of The Day / Pigeons / Inside & Out* - **Genesis**
14. *No Time & These Eyes* - **The Guess Who**
15. *On TV / I Am A Camera & Video Killed The Radio Star* - **The Buggles**
16. *Peter Gunn / Tiger In A Spotlight (Live)* - **Emerson, Lake & Palmer**
17. *Roll Over Beethoven & Telephone Line* - **The Electric Light Orchestra**
18. *Roundabout / Long Distance Runaround & Your Move / The Clap* - **Yes**
19. *Wells Fargo / Theme From "For A Few Dollars More"* - **Babe Ruth**

Dad commented on going to Sam The Record Man, downtown on Yonge Street, and he turned to see Sam Sniderman but didn't know if it was him or a cutout. He looked back a couple of times and, sure enough, it was Sam himself. After I got married, mom commented on how dad had remarked that he knew I wasn't living there anymore because he couldn't hear my stereo playing music.

While the focus of this ramble has been not to list out the top songs of the day or the year or the decade or whatever, the focus has been to list many of my favourite groups. By way of mentioning tapes and concerts and listing out the song tallies between the ramble and the index you can see who my favourites are. For a long time, I was and still am partial to the music group rather than the solo artist, though often those who start out as members of a group branch out and become solo artists in their own right.

In 1976, I vacationed in Vermont and bought my first two singles ever stateside, *Dreamer / Bloody Well Right* by Supertramp and *Jackie Blue* by The Ozark Mountain Daredevils. In the early nineties, I visited the Clearwater Florida location of *Dunn's Vinyl Museum* (a well-known downtown Toronto record store) and picked up *Hotel California / Pretty Maids All In A Row* by The Eagles. The Yonge Street store was the original, along with the Bloor street store. Later on, there was a store on Lakeshore Blvd west, just east of Royal York, then it moved further west on Lakeshore near Islington, In New Toronto.

Some singles that I have bought in pairs over the years are included here…

24.7 ~ Pairs
1. *Last Song / Best Friend* - **Edward Bear** & *You're So Vain / His Friends Are More Than Fond Of Robin* - **Carly Simon**, 1973
2. *Heart Of Gold / Sugar Mountain* - **Neil Young** & *Horse With No Name* - **America**
3. *Summer Breez* - **Seals & Crofts** & *Ventura Highway / Saturn Nights* - **America**
4. *Dreamer / Bloody Well Right* - **Supertramp** & *Jackie Blue* - **The Ozark Mountain Daredevils**, 1976
5. *Dreamer / From Now On* - **Supertramp** & *Into The Lens (I Am A Camera)* - **Yes**, 1981
6. *Blinded By The Light // Spirit In The Night* - **Manfred Mann** & *Damned If I Do* - **The Alan Parsons Project**, 1982
7. *Hold Your Head Up / Closer To Heaven* - **Argent** & *Lady* - **Styx**, 1983
8. *Don't Answer Me* - **The Alan Parsons Project** & *Scratching The Surface* - **Saga**, 1984
9. *Forever Young* - **Alphaville** & *So In Love* - **Orchestral Manoeuvres In The Dark**, 1985

In the mid-nineties, I knew that I was losing touch with popular music. For example, I was so excited to hear the newest album at the time by INXS, entitled *Elegantly Wasted*. There was a particular song on it that I liked so I bought the album. I listened to the whole thing and it was good but I realized the song I liked wasn't on there. The song was *Precious Declaration* by the Georgia rock band Collective Soul.

The late eighties and early to mid-nineties was a bit of a lost period of collecting for me. There was very little to buy on vinyl. Cassette singles had neat looking sleeves and the sound was OK but not as good as vinyl singles. I even used some sleeves to make homemade picture sleeves for the same titles on vinyl. The tape itself didn't look any different than an album cassette tape. The shells were exactly the same size, not like the mini cassettes used for phone messages or handheld Dictaphones. I swapped shells for tapes that were in poor condition. Some did sound better after the switch.

Some titles started out as cassette singles, indicated by *(/c)* then later as vinyl singles. The other titles are those that I bought as vinyl single right away. While these singles are not iconic in and of themselves, they are iconic as a group only because there weren't as many made in the nineties as had been in the eighties. Many of the singles are made stateside and labels have bar codes on them, which was not the case in the eighties.

24.8 ~ 90s Singles

1. *All For Love (/c)* - **Bryan Adams, Rod Stewart & Sting**
2. *All I Wanna Do, Can't Cry Anymore, Everyday Is A Winding Road (/c) & Strong Enough* - **Sheryl Crow**
3. *All This Time (/c) & If I Ever Lose My Faith In You (/c)* - **Sting**
4. *Calling Elvis (/c)* - **Dire Straits**
5. *Cats In The Cradle* - **Ugly Kid Joe**
6. *Crazy & Kiss From A Rose* - **Seal**
7. *Damn I Wish I Was Your Lover (/c)* - **Sophie B. Hawkins**
8. *Discotheque (/c), Staring At The Sun (/c) & Stay (Faraway, So Close!) (/c)* [US] - **U2**
9. *Everybody Hurts, Losing My Religion & One I Love, The* - **REM**
10. *Freedom* - George Michael
11. *Hold On My Heart, I Can't Dance (/c), No Son Of Mine & Tell Me Why* - **Genesis**
12. *Hypnotized, See The Lights (/c) & She's A River* [UK] - **Simple Minds**
13. *Lift Me Up* - **Yes**
14. *Power Of Love (/c)* - **Celine Dion**
15. *Sadeness (/c)* - **Enigma**
16. *Shine & The World I Know* - **Collective Soul**
17. *Vogue* - **Madonna**

I've looked at many different top dance songs for the nineties and none include either *Crazy* by Seal or *Damn I Wish I Was Your Lover* by Sophie B. Hawkins. Both play at a fairly slow pace so maybe that's why they aren't considered legitimate dance numbers.

In the late 1990s my mom gave me my dads' old **Aiwa** handheld tape player, complete with an equalizer, something similar to the one advertised in Rolling Stone magazine in September of 1988. I was too hard on it so it didn't last long but did enjoy it while it was still working. I was not buying CDs yet so I resorted to buying both albums and singles on cassette tape. I currently have a CD I made of music from that period and for which I still do not have vinyl copies of those songs. The later 00s have meant a reawakening for me. My stereo went into hiding in the early 00s, when my boys were young. I remember my older son dismantling a mixed cassette tape that had taken me hours to make, in a matter of minutes. Only in the later 00s was I able to bring my stereo out again and resume listening and taping on a full sized stereo in a convenient location.

Back in the early 00s, I created a desktop picture, entitled *The Quilt*. There are about 24 pictures in total that make up *The Quilt*. Among them are six with baseball parks and eight with album cover artwork. The rest of the artwork is taken from science fiction movies and shoe advertisements.

In the 2010s, I visited Old Navy and bought a selection of T-Shirts with different musical themes. These themes included cassette tapes & players, headphones, records & players and stereo components.

I don't worry about what the critics say about a particular group or artist. After all, their job is to be critical. Look at the groups that had strained relationships with the media, Zeppelin & The Eagles, and they succeeded in spite of that. I learned early on that articles about albums and concerts (and sporting events) often don't resemble the event itself, like getting a different version of the same car accident, depending on who you speak to. I have often asked myself if the critics/writers were at the same event that I was.

I also don't worry about whether a group is deemed to have reinvented itself or sold out to make some more money. Whether a group or single artist survives or not, it's the music that matters the most. Let's not spend our energy on the what ifs of Hendrix or Morrison or Joplin. Jack Black said in *High Fidelity*, "is it better for an artist to burn out quickly or to fade away gradually?". Carl Palmer put it perfectly when he said, in the *Live At The Royal Albert Hall* video, "At the end of the day, people appreciate good music".

What I miss the most, as time goes by, is when the music is missing or is not there. I notice this right away when I go to visit other family and friends. Because I place such a high value on music, I can't understand why others don't feel the same way. Music isn't just something that plays or is played in the background nor should it be the last thing you do in the day, only when you have time. You need to make time for it. You do it as you go along, to get you through your day. If I am away from it long enough, I become agitated and uncomfortable. I can only spend so long being quiet before I need music again.

Early in the 2010s, I had to have my cousin Ian White explain something to me. While I pride myself on being an audiophile, I never understood while double albums paired sides 1 with 4 and 2 with 3. For some old phonographs there was a catch arm above the turntable where you could cue up additional albums to the one you were playing. This way you could play sides 1 and 2 or three and four. I can't believe someone had to explain that to me.

If you want to buy brand new vinyl you can but there are only a few places to do this, now that HMV is no longer in business. One of those is Sunrise Records whose locations have a fair sized vinyl record selection. I have bought three albums at Sunrise that I call the Sunrise B's because, you guessed it, they all start with B…

24.9 ~ Sunrise Bs

1. *Batman Forever* - **Various Artists**
2. *Black Moon* - **Emerson, Lake & Palmer**
3. *Blade Runner* - **Vangelis**

Batman Forever, like Genesis' *We Can't Dance* was not originally a double album but was pressed on two vinyl discs to maintain better sound, as discussed way back in chapter four, Singles & Albums. Trevor Horn played Bass for the Seal song *Kiss From A Rose* and produced *Nobody Lives Without Love* for Eddie Reader.

Michael comments that while there is a vinyl resurgence, not all those enthusiasts still have a decent stereo nor they have invested in a new system of good quality. The two go very much hand in hand.

In 2016, Emily Gatlin missed the boat with her *101 Greatest American Rock Songs.*[157] The songs were good but not the greatest. What about all the groups she missed (never mind their songs)? : Bob Segar, Boston, The Byrds, The Cars, Chicago, Sheryl Crowe, The Doobie Brothers, Journey, Steely Dan, Steve

---

[157] *101 Greatest American Rock Songs*, Emily Gatlin, 2016

Miller, Styx, Sugarloaf, Three Dog Night & Edgar Winter. There was a definite preference to single artists or lead singers over groups.

In 2016, I put more singles on the auction block but I now miss all of the double hit singles that are listed here …

24.10 ~ Double Hits Missing

1. *Follow You Follow Me // Misunderstanding* - **Genesis**
2. *The Joker // Rock'n Me* - **The Steve Miller Band**
3. *Logical Song // Goodbye Stranger* - **Supertramp**
4. *Love Will Find A Way // Rhythm Of Love* - **Yes**
5. *Time // Games People Play* - **The Alan Parsons Project**

In July of 2021 I found the double hit single *Dreamer & Give A Little Bit* which was on this list. The weird thing about this copy is while it doesn't look like the standard Memories version of the double hit records, white with numerous memories logos splashed across the label, it looks more like a regular side a/b version of an early eighties single, red with black trim.

In late 2019, I bought the album *Jagged Little Pill* by Alanis Morrisette. The best thing about a large vinyl record collection is that the focus isn't all in one place. You can browse through and listen to just what you want to hear at any particular time, like country, easy listening, instrumental, orchestral, popular, progressive rock, rock, soul, techno pop, etc.

Another lesson to be learned is in the form of backing up your originals, vinyl, cassettes or even CDs.

In September of 2022, my wife and I saw Elton John on his *Farewell Yellow Brick Road* tour. He played for over two hours and cranked out about two dozen songs. His vocals have faded over the years but he can still pound out the keys. Not bad for a seventy-five year old. We saw him on September the 8th, the same day that Queen Elizabeth passed away. He paid a great tribute to her, spoke dearly of her, of hard she worked, and of how much he will miss her. Songs that I have included …

24.11~ Elton John - Farewell Yellow Brick Road

1.Bennie & The Jets, 2.Philadelphia Freedom, 3.I Guess That's Why They Call It The Blues, 7.Rocket Man, 9.Someone Saved My Life Tonight, 14.Sad Songs, 16.Don't Let The Sun Go Down On Me, 17.(The) Bitch Is Back, 19.Crocodile Rock, 20.Saturday Night's Alright For Fighting, 22.Your Song (en) & 23.Goodbye Yellow Brick Road (en)

While I have never seen Billy Joel live, my wife and I did watch the ABC special, celebrating his ten year residency at Madison Square Garden. The collector's edition magazine *Billy Joel Live At Madison Square Garden*, highlights that residency and lists out fifteen essential tracks. Here are a dozen of those…

24.12~ Billy Joel - Live At Madison Square Garden - Essential Tracks

1.Piano Man, 4.My Life, 5.Moving Out (Anthony's Song), 6.It's Still Rock And Roll To Me, 7.She's Always A Woman To Me, 8.The Entertainer, 9.Just The Way You Are, 10.Uptown Girl, 12.Allentown, 13.You May Be Right, 14.She's Got A Way & 15.We Didn't Start The Fire

The flip side of better sounding new technology is that the original feel and mood of the song is lost. There was a reason that a song was written, sung, performed, and recorded a certain way. Most often, you can't make a song any better than the original.

My Passion for music, collecting it, listening to it, performing it, and recording it is hard to describe. What I do know is that what began back in 1973 continues to grip me and comfort me today and inspires me and drives me to wherever it is that I am headed.

My worst fear is to have sound like the commercial in which Sergio Del Zio and his friend who are having a party and one says "crank up the tape machine" and the other says "it is cranked".

Here is my music motto. Remember, music is life. It makes the world go round. Everything else is just details. Long live the turntable, the tape deck, and the 45 rpm record.

TWENTY - FIVE

RADIO & CHARTS I
SEVENTIES

This is the first of two chapters that talk about radio and charts, this chapter the seventies. In the summer of 1972, at summer camp I attended with Alex near Kingston, Ontario, and we listened to *Rock Radio*[158] from Watertown, New York, combining music and comedy. I have yet to determine which Watertown radio station that was. This was long before stations like Q107 had "Comedy Breaks". I especially remember some of the early Cheech & Chong sketches *Officer Stadanko*. That's when I heard *Roundabout* (Yes). It profoundly impacted my interest in popular music. Again, like I said in chapter seventeen, *Yes I - Seventies*, I refer to this moment as *The Watertown Roundabout [gem]*.[159]

On that same Rock Radio station from Watertown New York, I also heard the single *Day By Day*, from the musical *Godspell*.[160] I would later buy the album and watch the musical in the winter of 1972-1973. Many of the cast would go on to popular TV shows like SCTV (Martin Short, Andrea Martin, Dave Thomas & Eugene Levy) and Saturday Night Live (Gilda Radner). My son played the drum for *Day by Day*, in a summer camp production of *Godspell* in 2014.

A list of those Watertown tunes that charted that summer included…

25.1 ~ Watertown
1. *Alone Again (Naturally)* - **Gilbert O'Sullivan**
2. *Brandy (You're A Fine Girl)* - **Looking Glass**
3. *Conquistador* - **Procal Harum**
4. *Day By Day* - **Godspell**

---

[158] Rock Radio (Station Unknown), Watertown, New York, 1972
[159] *The Watertown Roundabout*, Watertown, New York, 1972
[160] *Godspell*, Bayview Playhouse, Toronto, Ontario, 1972

5. *Layla* - **Derek & The Dominos**
6. *Lean On Me* - **Bill Withers**
7. *Long Cool Woman (In A Black Dress)* - **The Hollies**
8. *Outa Space* - **Billy Preston**
9. *Rocket Man* - **Elton John**
10. *Take It Easy* - **The Eagles**

Radio showed their geography by the songs they played and included on their charts. The CFRA Top 100 for 1973 was almost identical to the 1050 CHUM Top 100 for 1973, even though the week to week charts were totally different. The weekly and yearly charts for both CFRA and CHUM also used a Cooper font.

Things are not always as they appear, or in the case of radio, things are not always as they sound. In my early days of listing out songs that I liked but didn't have on record, it was often a challenge to get the title right. I'd be telling a friend about a particular song and I would give it a particular title and they would quickly correct me saying oh no such and such is the real title of that one.

In the fall of 1972, I started listening regularly to Toronto Maple Leaf hockey broadcasts on CKFH. The radio was a transistor, a Christmas present from my grandparents. After the broadcasts, they would continue with their top thirty/forty music selections. This was a continuation of the listening to popular music that began earlier that summer in Parham, Ontario.

Back in the days when there were personal copies of charts available, the weekly charts looked physically like this: CHUM charts opened up like a book; CFGO Ottawa, CKOC Hamilton and CKLW Windsor charts opened up to the top, like a flip chart; and CFRA charts were single pages that didn't need opening. Yearly charts were different sizes. Some from the Toronto Sun and Now Magazine fit on one page. Others including the Globe and Mail Fanfare section fit on two pages. Others still from the wider newspapers of the 1970s, The Toronto Star and The Ottawa Citizen opened out on to four pages. Many of the all-time lists, came in a poster format, rolled up to start with.

By the spring of 1973, I had settled into listening to 1050 CHUM on a regular basis, collecting the charts every week and listening to all the regular radio personalities including Dave Charles, Duke Roberts, Jay Nelson, Jim Van Horne, Mark Edwards, Pat St John, Roger Ashby, Scott Carpenter, Terry Steele & Tom Rivers. Nevin Grant, program director of Hamilton's CKOC for many years, includes Charles, Nelson, Carpenter and Rivers in his book, *Growing Up With The Hits.*[161]

It's always been interesting to me that song titles, like book titles or film titles appear in mixed case, meaning the first letter of every word in the title is capitalized. This is quite different from sentence case, if you were writing a document, an essay, a paper, a story, or a thesis.

As my wife reminds me, radio channel surfing was a well-practiced art, long before television channel surfing. We all did it for one reason or another, you got tired of the song you were listening to, you like the song you were listening to but wanted to hear it again on another station, or you wanted to be the first one to guess the name and the artist of a particular song. That was time consuming because you had to listen for the name of the song and the artist. Digital Days would provide all that information for you on a display or a screen somewhere.

The CHUM chart note went like this … the listing of records here in is the opinion of CHUM based on its survey of record sales listener requests and CHUM's judgement of the records appeal.

---

[161] *Growing Up With The Hits*, Nevin Grant, Manor House, 2015, p.184 & p.185

Over the May long weekend in 1973, 1050 CHUM played the *CHUM 500*.[162] This was not an all-time list but a list of each of the top 100s from 1968 through 1972. I had heard many of these songs in the short time that I had listened to the radio, since the summer camp in 1972 but I had never heard them, all laid out like this before. This would be in the heart of what later would become the *Psychedelic Pseventies*[163] Show on Q107 with Andy Frost. In that same spring of 1973, I began the ritual of visiting record stores on a regular basis.

My 1973 move to Ottawa was the start of a two year supply of CHUM Charts from Michael. It also meant getting used to two new radio stations CFRA and CFGO and their personalities. Michael also compiled a combination of CFGO CFRA & CHUM charts for more than two years, entitled CHFGO. He would also send me detailed discographies of the likes of the Beatles, Genesis, Led Zeppelin & Rush.

CFGO was established in Ottawa in 1972. The first and second years of the station were celebrated with the *Top 300* (1973)[164] and *Top 400* (1974) *Songs Of All Time*.[165] One year into its existence, **CFGO** printed the Top 10 from its inaugural chart in September of 1972.[166] Six of the ten songs included …

25.2 ~ CFGO 1972

1. *Black & White* - **Three Dog Night**
2. *Go All The Way* - **The Raspberries**
3. *Guitar Man* - **Bread**
4. *Long Cool Woman In A Black Dress* - **The Hollies**
5. *Rock & Roll Part 2* - **Gary Glitter**
6. *Saturday in The Park* - **Chicago**

CFGO[167] and CFRA both played music you couldn't hear on Toronto stations like 1050 CHUM. Truth be told, CFGO worked harder at recruiting listeners, publishing *All Time Top 300*[168] and *400* lists in 1973 and 1974 and featuring a *Live Concert Weekend in 1976*, making it sound more like FM radio. Over half of the entries on the following list had airplay on CFGO only, not CFRA. CFRA seemed to spend most of its time coasting, thanks to the likes of Shelley Emmond, Ken "The General" Grant, Lowell Green & Trevor Kidd. I got to know the micro geography of the Ottawa record stores, both Sam The Record Man (Bayshore, Carlingwood, Lincoln Fields, Merivale Mall and The Sparks Street Mall) and Treble Clef (Billings Bridge, Merivale Road & Rideau Street).

While eight of these titles are not in the singles collection *(/no)*, the list includes …

25.3 ~ Ottawa CFGO & CFRA

1. *#9 Dream & Stand By Me* - **John Lennon**
2. *After The Goldrush* - **Prelude**
3. *American Tune* - **Paul Simon** *(/no)*
4. *Another Park Another Sunday* - **The Doobie Brothers**
5. *Bongo Rock & Let There Be Drums (/no)*- **The Incredible Bongo Band**
6. *Dance A Little Step* - **Mashmakhan**

---

[162] *The CHUM 500*, 1050 CHUM, Victoria Day Weekend, May 1973
[163] *The Psychedelic Pseventies*, Andy Frost, Q107, CILQ FM, Toronto, ON
[164] *Top 300 Songs Of All Time*, CFGO, 1973
[165] *Top 400 Songs Of All Time*, CFGO, August 1974
[166] Reprinted in CFGO Top 30, Issue 52, September 3, 1973.
[167] CFGO AM 1440, Ottawa, Ontario, 1973.
[168] All Time Top 300, CFGO AM 1440, Ottawa, Ontario, 1973.

7. *Dirty Work* - **Songbird** *(/no)*
8. *Earache My Eye & Framed* - **Cheech & Chong**
9. *Finally (With You)* - **The Cooper Brothers**
10. *Good Day & Got A Feeling (/no)* - **Lighthouse**
11. *Harry Truman* - **Chicago**
12. *Make It All Worthwhile* - **James Leroy & Denim** *(/no)*
13. *My Music* - **Loggins & Messina**
14. *Rebel Rebel* - **David Bowie** *(/no)*
15. *Saturday Night's Alright For Fighting* - **Elton John**
16. *So You Are A Star* - **The Hudson Brothers**
17. *Space Race* - **Billy Preston** *(/no)*
18. *Summertime* - **Copper Penny** *(/no)*
19. *Theme from "For A Few Dollars More"* - **Babe Ruth**
20. *Walk On* - **Neil Young**
21. *Walking On Back* - **Edward Bear.**

The Radio personalities on CFRA included Al Dubois, Bill Drake, Dave Watts, Jim Keith, Ken "The General" Grant, Ric Johnson, Shelley Emmond, Steve Emery, Steve Young, Stu Hillgrove, Terry Morgan, Tom Jeffries & Trevor Kidd.

These listings give a slightly different take on the top songs versus Toronto stations. CFGO charts had a description of the listing of songs identical to the 1050 CHUM charts; The listing of records herein is the opinion of CFGO based on its survey of record sales, listener requests and CFGO's judgement of record's appeal.

Some of the CFGO DJs included Art Stevens, Casey Fox, Charlie O'Brien, Dan Ferguson, Dean Hagopian, Frank Sassin, Gary Michaels, Joe Evans, John L'Heuri, Mike Kooper (Cooper), Mike Paris, Ric Allen, Richard Money, Rick Shannon, Scottie Lomax, Steve Derringer & Tom Lucas.

It's funny how you remember songs or groups of songs from a particular point in time. At two different points in time, I remember three songs together on the charts. I call them chart buddies.

First in November of 1973, I remember three songs that started with the letter P. Second, in February of 1975, I remember three songs that started with the letter B.

25.4 ~ Chart Buddies
1. *Painted Ladies* - **Ian Thomas**
2. *Photograph* - **Ringo Starr**
3. *Pretty Lady* - **Lighthouse**

4. *Best Of My Love* - **The Eagles**
5. *Black Water* - **The Doobie Brothers**
6. *Bungle In The Jungle* - **Jethro Tull**

Also, it's interesting to note that CFGO published several different all time lists, while CFRA never did, nor at least in the mid-seventies, when I lived there from 1973 through 1977.

On May 13, 1974, **CFGO** weekly chart # 86[169] was printed in a different better wider font but they went back to the regular font the next week. Did anyone notice that it was better? Maybe it was too expensive. Or as Pink Floyd would Say "Is There Anybody In There?" By the way, *The Streak* by Ray Stevens was #1 that week. Those were the days when I collected many singles just from the current top 30, more than half of the thirty songs on that chart. Here are many of the songs that appeared on that chart...

25.5 ~ CFGO Century Gothic Font 1974 [gem]

1. 1. *Streak, The* - **Ray Stevens**
2. 3. *Locomotion, The* - **Grand Funk**
3. 4. *Midnight At The Oasis* - **Maria Muldaur**
4. 5. *TSOP* - **MFSB**
5. 6. *Tubular Bells* - **Mike Oldfield**
6. 7. *Show Must Go On, The* - **Three Dog Night**
7. 8. *(I've Been) Searchin' So Long* - **Chicago**
8. 11. *Band On The Run* - **Paul McCartney & Wings**
9. 12. *Let It Ride* - **Bachman - Turner Overdrive**
10. 13. *Billy Don't Be A Hero* - **Bo Donaldson & The Heywoods**
11. 15. *Piano Man* - **Billy Joel**
12. 16. *Hooked On A Feeling* - **Blue Suede**
13. 22. *For The Love Of The Money* - **The O'Jays**
14. 23. *Werewolf* - **The Five Man Electrical Band**
15. 25. *Chameleon* - **Herbie Hancock**
16. 27. *Oh Very Young* - **Cat Stevens**
17. 29. *Another Park Another Sunday* - **The Doobie Brothers**

In 1974, Mike Cooper, DJ at CFGO 1440 radio in Ottawa pulled up stakes and moved to Toronto, joining the team of DJs at 1050 CHUM, along with Chuck Morgan and Dude Walker. Years later, Mike would move to CHFI and would also be involved in the iconic Christmas time radio special, showcasing his talent with the spoken word. Michael also supplied me with year-end CHUM Top 100 charts for 1974, 1975 & 1976. 1975 marked the beginning of the end for the 45 rpm single, the final personal copies of top thirty charts for both CHUM Toronto in April and CFRA Ottawa in July.

In the 1990s, I punched holes in the edges of the Top 100s and put them into binders, often using the old style sheet protectors where the holes were part of the letter page. In the 2000s, I bought the new style sheet protector where the holes were separate from the letter page and were closed at the bottom. Many of the Top 100s fit into the new protectors. In 2017, for the Top 100s that were two big, I used two old style sheet protectors for each but put them in a folder rather than in a binder.

1975 marked the end of personal copies of the weekly top thirty charts for CHUM radio in Toronto and CFRA radio in Ottawa. The charts continued to appear as weekly newspaper versions but for collectors like me it just wasn't the same. Maybe it was just my imagination, but it seemed to be harder to follow the songs going up and down the chart after that because you had to be watching for the chart in the newspaper.

The final personal charts for CHUM in Toronto and CFRA in Ottawa appeared on April 26[170] & July 14, 1975[171], respectively. What tied them together, as mentioned way back in chapter one, was the

---

[169] Different Font, CFGO Chart # 86, May 13, 1974
[170] Final Personal Top 30 Chart, 1050 CHUM, Toronto, April 26, 1975
[171] Final Personal Top 30 Chart, CFRA 58, Ottawa, July 14, 1975

appearance of *Sister Golden Hair* by America. It was the only song to appear on both of those charts. I call them the *Sister Golden Hair Charts [gem]*. Elton John appeared on both charts but with different entries. Here are songs from the CHUM chart in April…

25.6 ~ Sister Golden Hair Charts [gem] I - CHUM Toronto

1. 1. *It's A Miracle* - **Barry Manilow**
2. 3. *Philadelphia Freedom* - **Elton John**
3. 6. *Jackie Blue* - **The Ozark Mountain Daredevils**
4. 7. *Pinball Wizard* - **Elton John**
5. 8. *How Long* - **Ace**
6. 9. *Don't Call Us We'll Call You* - **Sugarloaf**
7. 10. *Lady Marmalade* - **LaBelle**
8. 11. *Emma* - **Hot Chocolate**
9. 16. *Sister Golden Hair* - **America**
10. 17. *Walking In Rhythm* - **The Blackbyrds**
11. 18. *Autobahn* - **Kraftwerk**
12. 19. *No No Song* - **Ringo Starr**
13. 20. *Old Days* - **Chicago**
14. 27. *Shining Star* - **Earth, Wind & Fire**

Here are songs from the CFRA chart in July…

25.7 ~ Sister Golden Hair Charts [gem] II - CFRA Ottawa

1. 1. *Magic* - **Pilot**
2. 2. *Love Will Keep Us Together* - **The Captain & Tenille**
3. 5. *Listen To What The Main Said* - **Wings**
4. 10. *I'm Not In Love* - **10.CC**
5. 12. *Hey You* - **Bachman - Turner Overdrive**
6. 13. *Someone Saved My Life Tonight* - **Elton John**
7. 14. *Wildfire* - **Michael Murphy**
8. 16. *Only Women* - **Alice Cooper**
9. 17. *Take Me In Your Arms (Rock Me)* - **The Doobie Brothers**
10. 19. *One Of These Nights* - **The Eagles**
11. 21. *Hit The Road Jack* - **The Stampeders**
12. 29. *The Rockford Files* - **Mike Post**
13. 30. *Sister Golden Hair* - **America**

1975 also marked the growing popularity of disco music. While it flourished, its earlier cousin, soul, disappeared. Stars like The Chi-Lites, Earth, Wind & Fire, Roberta Flack, The O'Jays, The Spinners, The Stylistics, The Three Degrees, War and Bill Withers, faded away. Only the likes of Michael Jackson and Stevie Wonder soldiered on. Years later rap and hip hop music would appear but it would never come close to the style and grace of the "Soul Sound".

Ottawa's first FM rock radio station was CKCU, broadcast part-time from the Carleton University School of Journalism. It was November of 1975 and Steve Colwill was the first on air DJ (CHEZ FM, later known as Classic Rock CHEZ 106, became the first full time FM rock radio station in Ottawa in March of

1977[172]). The newspaper ran an anniversary ad in the Ottawa Citizen, on November 13, 1976[173], celebrating one year. Colwill was a part of CHEZ as well.

In March of 1976, CFTR Toronto introduced its top 30 chart alongside CHUM. Chart # 1 included the following tracks…

25.8 ~ CFTR 1976

1. 2. *Theme From S. W. A. T.* - **T. H. P. Orchestra**
2. 3. *All By Myself* - **Eric Carmen**
3. 4. *Dream Weaver* - **Gary Wright**
4. 5. *December 1963* - **The Four Seasons**
5. 7. *Love Hurts* - **Nazareth**
6. 10. *Love Is The Drug* - **Roxy Music**
7. 14. *Dream On* - **Aerosmith**
8. 17. *Crazy On You* - **Heart**
9. 18. *Bohemian Rhapsody* - **Queen**
10. 20. *Grow Some Funk Of Your Own* - **Elton John**
11. 24. *Only Sixteen* - **Dr. Hook**
12. 28. *Show Me The Way* - **Peter Frampton**
13. 30. *Lorelei* - **Styx**
14. *(-). Shout It Out Loud* - **Kiss**

In the summer of 1976, my namesake, Steve Elliott, hosted the overnight show for 1050 CHUM. In Ottawa Ontario, in the early seventies, there was a DJ at CFRA 58 named Terry Morgan. In 1976, Terry moved to 1050 CHUM in Toronto and changed his name to Steve Elliott[174]. He hosted the overnight show, from midnight to 5 am. Sound waves do strange things at night, so I was able to record his show all the way from Ottawa. I especially like the hourly announcement, i.e. "it's 1.30 in the superstar summer, this is Steve Elliott doin' it for you". I have created a sound bite of it, what I now consider to be an iconic radio moment. In the mid-2000s, Jack FM, adopted the same background music that 1050 CHUM had used in 1976 when my namesake announced the time between songs.

I recorded parts of several of his shows over that summer, all the way from Ottawa …

25.9 ~ CHUM 1976 Steve Elliott [gem]

1. *(I've Been) Searchin' So Long & Make Me Smile* - **Chicago**
2. *Do It ('Til You're Satisfied)* - **B T Express**
3. *Magic* - **Pilot**
4. *More More More* - **The Andrea True Connection**
5. *Rock & Roll Music* - **The Beach Boys**
6. *Rock On* - **David Essex**
7. *Takin' It To The Streets* - **The Doobie Brothers**
8. *Wildfire* - **Michael Murphy**
9. *You're My Best Friend* - **Queen**

---

[172] *ON Air Tonight*, CHEZ 106 FM, March 1977
[173] *CKCU. 1 Year Later*, November 1976
[174] Terry Morgan, CFRA 58, Ottawa, Steve Elliott, 1050 CHUM, Toronto, 1976

It seems the nighttime airwaves did crazy things, crazy enough to hear a Toronto station clearly way over in Ottawa. Next up, I also created my own ZAP top twenty charts. The charts started with music from 1973 and ended with music in 1976. They didn't make it out of the seventies either but it was fun making them.

One weekend in the summer of 1976, CFGO 1440 Top thirty/forty radio in Ottawa ("The GO 14") made a major departure from its normal playlist format. They played an entire weekend of live music, a fantasy live concert if you will with many bands attending, *CFGO Live Weekend Sounded Like FM [gem].* Introducing the songs was an announcer that sounded just like Rod Serling, long time host of the science fiction TV classics *The Twilight Zone* and *The Night Gallery.* Some of the music I had heard before, especially Yes music from *Yessongs.* But for the most part, these were album type cuts saved for Fm radio but being played on top thirty/forty AM radio. It sounded amazing.

Here are almost two dozen groups with live singles (many of the titles are B sides) …

25.10 ~ Live

1. *Baby I Love Your Way, Do You Feel Like I Do & Show Me The Way [FRAMPTON COMES ALIVE]* - **Peter Frampton** -
2. *Bennie & The Jets* - **Elton John**
3. *Book Of Brilliant Things (/b), Don't You Forget About Me (/b), Love Song (/b), Promised You A Miracle [LIVE IN THE CITY OF LIGHT] & Street Hassle* - **Simple Minds**
4. *Breakfast In America, Dreamer, From Now On (/b), Take The Long Way Home & You Started Laughing (/b) [PARIS]* - **Supertramp**
5. *City Of Love (/b), It Can Happen (/b) & I've Seen All Good People & Roundabout* - **Yes**
6. *Closer To The Heart & Tom Sawyer (/b)* - **Rush**
7. *Coming Up, Maybe I'm Amazed & The Mess (/b)* - **Paul McCartney & Wings**
8. *Conquistador* - **Procal Harum**
9. *Dreaming While You Sleep (/b) & Turn It On Again (/b)* - **Genesis**
10. *Eastbound Train (/b)* - **Dire Straits**
11. *Free Bird* - **Lynyrd Skynyrd**
12. *Head Games (/b)* - **Foreigner**
13. *Heaven (/b)* - **Bryan Adams**
14. *I Believe* - **Tears For Fears**
15. *I Never Cry // You & Me* - **Alice Cooper**
16. *I Ran (So Far Away) (/b)* - **A Flock Of Seagulls**
17. *Gloria & I Will Follow [UNDER A BLOOD RED SKY]* - **U2**
18. *Letter* - **Joe Cocker**
19. *Merry Christmas Baby & Santa Claus Is Coming To Town (/b)* - **Bruce Springsteen**
20. *Peter Gunn/Knife Edge & Tiger In A Spotlight (/b)* - **Emerson, Lake & Palmer**
21. *Rudolph The Red Nosed Reindeer* - **Corey Hart**
22. *Running Back To Saskatoon* - **The Guess Who**
23. *Smoke On The Water (/b)* - **Deep Purple**

In the seventies, in Ottawa, Ontario, you could pick up radio stations from far away at nighttime. 1050 CHUM Toronto was one you could pick up but there were others, much further away. The first was WABC New York. The second was WCFL Chicago. Come morning, these stations would fade but the nighttime was a smorgasbord for listening to far away stations.

Radio stations have often played both longer and shorter versions of singles (radio is discussed in more detail in chapters twenty-five & twenty-six of this story). CFGO and CFRA both played short versions of several seventies tunes. *Band On The Run* started with the guitar intro before "If We Ever Get Out Of Here". *Give A Little Bit* went straight into the first verse after "Alright". *Just You'n Me* didn't even have the saxophone solo.

25.11 ~ Short Versions 70s
1. *Band On The Run* - **Paul McCartney & Wings**
2. *Give A Little Bit* - **Supertramp**
3. *Just You'n Me* - **Chicago**

In March of 1977, **Ottawa** went fulltime FM rock radio with CHEZ 106, as highlighted by the same day ad in the Ottawa Citizen, on Friday, the 25th. By August the 1st, I had only collected four of the songs on the CFGO top 30. Quite a change from having collected more than half of the singles from the CFGO top 30 in May of 1974. But by this time, I was buying more albums …

25.12 ~ Albums 1977 I - Current
1. *Even In The Quietist Moments* - **Supertramp**
2. *Going For The One* - **Yes**
3. *Hotel California* - **The Eagles**
4. *Works Volume One* - **Emerson, Lake & Palmer**

Both *Going For The One* and *Even In The Quietist Moments* were gifted to me by long time band mates and friends from Ottawa, in July and August respectively. Years later I would collect other albums from the summer of 1977 like …

25.13 ~ Albums 1977 II - Later
1. *3.47 E. S. T.* - **Klaatu**
2. *I Robot* - **The Alan Parsons Project**
3. *Rumours* - **Fleetwood Mac**

In August, I moved back to Toronto and I remember seeing the bus and subway ads for a new station called Q107, *On Air June 1*. I started collecting weekly charts, as soon as they started publishing them. One of my favourite all time charts was the Q107 *Top 107 Of The Seventies*[175], published in January of 1980 in the *Fanfare* section of *The Globe & Mail*. This had many great songs on it and served as a benchmark/watershed for the move/transition from the seventies to the eighties. The move to the eighties didn't register right away since my music listening had always been in the seventies and suddenly it was the eighties. The list was like a summary of my two seventies music interests, top 30 and progressive rock. I have noted those songs that appeared on the list that are also in my collection.

---

[175] Q107 Top 107 Of The Seventies, Q107, CILQ FM, Toronto, January 1980

TWENTY - SIX

RADIO & CHARTS II
EIGHTIES FORWARD

This is the second of two chapters that talk about radio and charts, this one the eighties. The early eighties meant listening to new wave / techno pop / alternative music played on newer stations like CFNY 102.1 The edge, *The Spirit Of Radio, Music Of The 80s*. In the late seventies and early eighties, led by CHUM Alumnus Dave Marsden, CFNY brought to Toronto what I call the British New Wave Invasion. I specifically remember him playing an extended version of *Major Tom* by Peter Schilling. The seven inch single features the English version on one side and the German version on the other. Many of the groups would be played on 1050 CHUM and CFTR in the mid-eighties but CFNY brought them to us first. This time frame directly mirrored the time that I spent in college. These titles include …

26.1 ~ CFNY New Wave
1. *Arias & Symphonies & Smiling In Winter* - **The Spoons**
2. *Back On The Chain Gang* - **The Pretenders**
3. *Roxanne, I Can't Stand Losing You & Walking On The Moon* - **The Police**
4. *Don't' Go & Situation* - **Yaz (featuring Alison Moyet)**
5. *Europa & The Pirate Twins & I Scare Myself* - **Thomas Dolby**
6. *Fields Of Fire* - **Big Country**
7. *Genetic Engineering* [UK] , *Messages* [UK] & *Souvenir* - **Orchestral Manoeuvres In The Dark**
8. *Glittering Prize* [NDR], *Speed Your Love To Me, Up On The Catwalk* [UK] & *Waterfront* [UK] - **Simple Minds**
9. *Living In The Plastic Age* - **The Buggles**
10. *Mad World* - **Tears For Fears**

11. *Never Again The Dancer & The More You Live The More You Love* - **A Flock Of Seagulls**
12. *One Small Day* - **Midge Ure**
13. *Open Your Heart* - **The Human League**
14. *Red Skies & I Will* - **The Fixx**
15. *The Flyer & What Do I Know* - **Saga**
16. *West End Girls* (original release 1984, rerelease 1985) - **The Pet Shop Boys**

CFNY charts up to and including 1984 were printed in NOW magazine, as *The Spirit Of Radio*. The 1985 chart was still the Spirit Of Radio but was printed in the Toronto Star. By 1988, the list was printed in the Toronto Sun, with the new slogan Modern Rock.

CFNY published a regular page entitled *Music Of The Eighties* in the entertainment publication Now Magazine.[176] Pages included notes about current songs and albums, as well as top songs of the year. A friend worked at Radio Glendon and helped to shape the culture of music there, much of it new wave, as seen on the charts, *Into The 80s* back then.[177] I also collected weekly charts for FM 96 in London in the early eighties, where my wife went to school.

In the winter of 1983/1984, I worked in a warehouse and we used to listen to Q107. I specifically remember the morning show with Scruff Connors & Gene Valaitis. Part way through 1984, I decided that I would slow down my popular music collection in favour of classical music. Well, that lasted a few months until I was back at the popular collection stronger than ever.

In the spring of 1984, my brother Richard found me a jewel of a record chart book, while he was working in London, England. To that point and since then, all chart books I had seen had listed songs like my collections above, either by song title or artist. This book, *Top Twenty*, by Tony Jasper,[178] was an actual listing of the week by week charts from the fifties to the eighties, from number one down to roughly number twenty. In the winter of 1984/1985, I worked in an office where we listened to CNFY. The two radio personalities I remember the most were James Scott & Ted (Walker) Woloshyn.

James Scott used to play the original version of *West End Girls* on his afternoon show, long before it was rereleased in 1986. Dave Marsden played the extended 12" UK version of *Major Tom* one night. It sounded most impressive and I bought it soon after that. I know with the 7" 45, the UK version is on side A while the German version is on side B.

I had seen Ted on the cover of a CKCO chart years earlier as Ted Walker. I was at a dinner in the early 1990s in Toronto and heard Ted speak. He had just taken over the morning spot on CFRB that had been held forever by the legendary Wally Crouter. I remember him saying at the start of his talk, "I know what you're going to say, I don't look anything like I sound".

The mid-eighties were celebrated by CKSL in London with Top *300 Songs Of All Time* listings in both 1984[179] and 1985.[180] These listings were different again from either the Toronto or the Ottawa charts. On October the 5th, 1985, The Toronto Blue Jays won the American League East championship for the first time in their nine year history. As the music played on in between innings, I remember clearly hearing the Alphaville song, *Forever Young*. It is profound to think the words of the song applied to both the Blue Jays

---

[176] *Music Of The Eighties*, CFNY FM, The Spirit Of Radio, 1982
[177] *Into The Eighties*, Glendon College Radio, York University, 1980
[178] *Top Twenty*, Top Of The Pops & BBC 1, Tony Jasper, 1984
[179] *Top 300 Songs Of All Time*, CKSL, London, 1984
[180] *Top 300 Songs Of All Time*, CKSL, London, 1985

and me. I had bought the single earlier that summer along with *So In Love* by Orchestral Manoeuvres In The Dark.

1985 was the last year for 1050 CHUM top songs of the year. The last weekly chart was printed in The Toronto Sun in June of 1986 so there were no top songs for that year. CFNY started printing their top albums of the year for 1985 in The Toronto Star, still as *The Spirit Of Radio*, after having printed them previously in Now Magazine.

In 1990, CFNY published their *Top 102 songs of the eighties.*[181] This list ranks up there as a classic alongside the Q107 *Top 107 of the seventies.* While the seventies lists included both my favourite top forty songs and prog rock songs, the eighties lists included much of the new wave music of the eighties that I came to know and love.

Close to the same time, I bought the CHUM Chart book.[182] That edition included all songs charted on CHUM from 1957 up until 1983. Fast forward to 2011 and I picked up a very similar book, *The Top Twenty Hit Singles Charts,*[183] by Dave McAleer. While the Jasper book had the UK weekly charts listed, McAleer's book has both the UK and US weekly charts listed side by side. Going a step further, Ted Yates wrote about the hits of the 60s and the 70s. In The 70s book, he uses UK, US and Canadian sources to compile his top lists. For Canadian fans this gives a better picture of what we listened to.

Something that struck me funny was the development of AM Stereo in the late eighties and early nineties. At the time there were many music format radio stations on the AM dial so it seemed to make sense except that you had to have a radio with stereo capability to hear the difference. After that, there were some radio stations, like CBC Radio One in Toronto that left the AM dial for the FM dial. Then you had CBC Radio One and CBC Radio Two both on the FM dial.

Still further to that, the AM music stations went the way of the dodo bird, Most FM radio was underground in the seventies but became more mainstream in the eighties. So FM formats of the early eighties sounded like top forty stations from the seventies. 1050 CHUM was an example of this. Originally it was a top forty station that changed to an oldies format. Then the oldies format gave way to THE TEAM, a sports format station, to give the FAN 590 a run for its money. When THE TEAM failed miserably in the ratings, 1050 CHUM the top thirty station had a revival of its music format for a time.

However, in the end, it disappeared for a second time, giving way this time to the radio version of CP24. A big disappointment for me was the quashing of the 1050 CHUM charts on the 1050 CHUM website. That website gave way to 1050 CHUM CP24 all-news radio but now there is a CHUM tribute site which has a listing of all the CHUM charts ever issued. http://chumtribute. ca/topics/chum-charts/

Besides that former CHUM Chart website, there are a few other sites which feature charts or "surveys" on them. There are very few charts on these sites, basically showing samples of charts, like CFRA & CFGO from Ottawa, not the detailed weekly collection on the former CHUM site.

CILQ FM 107 put on what I think was one of their greatest theme weekends of all time. Remembrance Day Weekend 2006 was also known as *The Art Rock Weekend.*[184] Yes, this was a paradise / smorgasbord for all those prog rock fans out there like me. I remember specifically *Fools' Overture* for the Sunday morning Remembrance Day portion of the weekend. While the Sunday music had mostly album cuts, the Saturday music had many single cuts...

---

[181] *Top 102 Songs Of The Eighties*, CFNY, Spirit Of Radio, Modern Rock, January 1990
[182] *CHUM Chart Book* to 1983, Stardust Productions, 1984
[183] *The Top Twenty Hit Singles Charts*, Dave McAleer, Carlton Books, 1994
[184] The Art Rock Weekend, Q107, CILQ FM, Toronto, November 10 & 11, 2006

26.2 ~ Q107 2006 Art Rock Weekend November 10 & 11

1. *And You & I Pt. 1, The Clap, Roundabout & Your Move* - **Yes**
2. *Black Dog & Hey Hey What Can I Do* - **Led Zeppelin**
3. *Black Water* - **The Doobie Brothers**
4. *Bohemian Rhapsody* - **Queen**
5. *Bungle In The Jungle* - **Jethro Tull**
6. *Cuts Like A Knife* - **Bryan Adams**
7. *Fanfare For The Common Man & Lucky Man* - **Emerson, Lake & Palmer**
8. *Free Ride* - **The Edgar Winter Group**
9. *Hello It's Me* - **Todd Rundgren**
10. *I Know What I Like (In Your Wardrobe)* - **Genesis**
11. *I'm A Stranger Here* - **The Five Man Electrical Band**
12. *Message In A Bottle* - **The Police**
13. *Money* - **Pink Floyd**
14. *Nights In White Satin* - **The Moody Blues**
15. *One Tin Soldier* - **The Original Cast**
16. *Ramblin' Man* - **The Allman Brothers Band**
17. *Running Back To Saskatoon* - **The Guess Who**
18. *Sugar Mountain* - **Neil Young**
19. *Sweet Home Alabama* - **Lynyrd Skynyrd**
20. *Where The Streets Have No Name* - **U2**
21. *You Could Have Been A Lady* - **April Wine**

I was thrilled to meet Q107 radio personality Andy Frost in April of 2007, just outside the Hard Rock Café studio, in downtown Toronto, during a break in the middle of one of his shows. I remarked how I had lived in Toronto for many years and had listened to him on *Psychedelic Psunday* for years and thoroughly enjoyed it. I also commented that it was great to meet someone so knowledgeable and who was a real audiophile.

I shared some of my early top 100 charts with him and he said that he had included those with his already massive collection of other charts and books that he took with him to the studio and other places. One of those charts was the CHUM 500, featuring the top 100s from 1968 through 1972. Those were the middle five years of *Psychedelic Psunday*.

Now for CKDK, The Hawk, in Woodstock. After a couple of format changes, from sister station to Q107 to "The Greatest Hits Of All Time", I've come full circle, back to radio with a strong singles Influence - Most recently, I have noted all the singles in this collection that appeared on the Hawk's *Top 1039 Of All Time*,[185] in January of 2008.

I like some of the comments on radio these days. One of my favourites is from 102.3 JACK FM in London.[186] "He's been looking for a needle for his MP3 player since Christmas (it's now July)." A couple more are from 1039 FM in Woodstock & London. "If your record collection is bigger than your CD collection then you've found your radio station. In your basement there's a box of records, and in that box of

---

[185] *Top 1039 Of All Time*, CKDK The Hawk, Woodstock, ON, Jan 2008
[186] 102.3 JACK FM, London, Ontario

records there's a bunch of 45s, and in some of those 45s you've even got some of those old yellow centerpieces that you had to put in the middle of the record to hear this…"

Few if any radio stations play a cross section of top thirty/forty music anymore. There are some exceptions. One, At Chrisman time, the same radio stations will play a wide genre of songs, thus giving us *Christmas Time Sounds Like Good Old Top 40 Radio [gem]*. That's instead of satellite or silo radio where there's a different station for every kind of music.

I remember it was play as many songs as you could in an hour with more commercials so the shorter the songs the better. WCFL Chicago even played their records faster so as the hours went by, they could actually get more songs on to their playlists. The instant media of the internet has now pretty much closed this gap between time and space.

Charts are closely connected with music radio and have played a huge part in the growth of my collection. Radio stations from across Ontario like Hamilton (CKOC), London (CFPL FM 96, CJBK and CKSL), Ottawa (CFGO, CFRA), Toronto (CFTR, CILQ107, CHUM AM & FM), Windsor (CKLW) & Woodstock (CKDK FM 103.9); have cranked out charts on a weekly, yearly, and all time basis.

Canadian Music Publication RPM and Sam The Record Man had their weekly charts. Colleges like Glendon at York and radio stations like CFNY have given us a different view of what music is and isn't important. I have created weekly, yearly, all time charts, and lists, as have several friends. Other authors have published chart books, many with songs by title and artist, while a few have put together chart books with the weekly listings by ranking, not by title or artist.

I recently sent CKCU a scan of a November 1976 program listing from the Ottawa Citizen and sent CHEZ 106 a scan of the newspaper ad that appeared the first day the radio station was launched in March of 1977. The ranking of songs on the charts has never been as important as the collection of songs. Being part of the top thirty or forty was always the key, not what position it reached or how long it stayed on the chart.

CJCS Radio in Stratford changed from 1240 AM to 107.1 JUICE FM in 2017.[187] The format was still hits from the 60s, 70s, 80s and 90s but with a new FM sound. It was like the old days of top forty radio but with FM quality. Many of the voice spots were done by well-known Canadian TV & Radio voice specialist David Kaye.[188] His voice is a very familiar one. He used to do voice spots for Q107 (also 107.1) in Toronto, CHEZ 106 in Ottawa and CKDK 103.9 The Hawk in Woodstock. The only downside is that you can't go east to Kitchener without JUICE getting knocked off the air by Q107. In May of 2018, history was made when both Andy Frost and *Psycheledic Psundays* made their exit from Q107. In the summer of 2022, JUICE was renamed to CJCS Classic Hits.

Like CFRA & CFGO in the seventies, CJCS often plays short versions of late seventies and eighties tunes. The ending of *Does It Really Happen?* just starts without a fade in. The chorus of *Goodbye Stranger* starts right away without the sixteen bar intro. Neither *Take The Long Way Home* nor *Where The Streets Have no Name* have a fade in. *In Your Eyes* only has an eight bar intro, instead of sixteen. *Shout* doesn't repeat "Shout shout let it all out…" before going into "in violent times…".

26.3 ~ Short Versions Late 70s & 80s
1. *Does It Really Happen? (/b)* - **Yes**
2. *Goodbye Stranger & Take The Long Way Home* - **Supertramp**
3. *In Your Eyes* - **Peter Gabriel**
4. *Nova Heart* - **The Spoons**

---

[187] 1240 AM CJCS, 107.1 Juice FM, CJCS FM, Stratford, Ontario
[188] David Kaye, Radio Voice Personality, Q107, Toronto, Ontario, CKDK, Woodstock, Ontario, Juice FM, Stratford, Ontario

5. *Shout* - **Tears For Fears**
6. *Where The Streets Have No Name* - **U2**
7. *Who Are You* - **The Who**

Billy Joel always lamented the short AM versions of songs like his own *Piano Man*. Many longer versions are not part of this collection but are noted here as versions played by CJCS hit radio, even though back in the day the long versions were not the hits…

26.4 ~ Long Versions
1. *25 Or 6 To 4* - **Chicago**
2. *Another Brick On The Wall Pt. 2, Comfortably Numb & Money* - **Pink Floyd**
3. *Another Day In Paradise* - **Phil Collins**
4. *Baker Street* - **Gerry Rafferty**
5. *Blinded By The Light* - **Manfred Mann**
6. *Can't Get Enough* - **Bad Company**
7. *Carry On Wayward Son* - **Kansas**
8. *Come On Eileen* - **Dexy's Midnight Runners**
9. *Dream On & Sweet Emotion* - **Aerosmith**
10. *Jackie Blue* - **The Ozark Mountain Daredevils**
11. *Let Go The Line* - **Max Webster**
12. *Magic Man* - **Heart**
13. *Major Tom* - **Peter Schilling**
14. *Message In A Bottle* - The **Police**
15. *My Girl (Gone Gone Gone)* - **Chilliwack**
16. *New Year's Day* - **U2**
17. *Night Moves* - **Bob Segar**
18. *Only Women Bleed* - **Alice Cooper**
19. *Pretty Lady* - **Lighthouse**
20. *Scratching The Surface* - **Saga**
21. *Signs* - **The Five Man Electrical Band**
22. *Twilight Zone* - **Golden Earring**
23. *Urgent* - **Foreigner**
24. *Wouldn't It Be Good* - **Nik Kershaw**

Single versions of *Autobahn* and *Tubular Bells* seemed enjoyable compared to the entire side versions on the album. Further still, There are many singles for which there are both short and long versions. About half of these were singles reissued as double hits. The list includes…

26.5 ~ Long & Short Versions L & S
1. *Alive & Kicking* - **Simple Minds**
2. *C'est La Vie & From The Beginning* - **Greg Lake**
3. *Crazy On You, Dreamboat Annie & Magic Man* - **Heart**
4. *Do It Again* - **Steely Dan**
5. *Dream Weaver & Love Is Alive* - **Gary Wright**
6. *Feels Like The First Time* - **Foreigner**

7. *Follow You Follow Me, I Know What I Like (In Your Wardrobe) & Your Own Special Way* - **Genesis**
8. *Green Eyed Lady* - **Sugarloaf**
9. *Hold Your Head Up* - **Argent**
10. *In The Air Tonight* - **Phil Collins**
11. *Leave It & Owner Of A Lonely Heart* - **Yes**
12. *Listen To The Music* - **The Doobie Brothers**
13. *Nights In White Satin* - **The Moody Blues**
14. *Only Women Bleed* - **Alice Cooper**
15. *Piano Man* - **Billy Joel**
16. *Smoke On The Water* - **Deep Purple**
17. *Sole Survivor* - **Asia**
18. *Take The Long Way Home* - **Supertramp**
19. *Turn Me Loose* - **Loverboy**

I have two promotional singles from the US, one for *C'est La Vie*, with short and long versions of that song on either side, and the other for *Sole Survivor*, with short and long versions of that song on either side. For Heart songs *Crazy On You* and *Dreamboat Annie* the only difference between the short and long versions was the acoustic intro from *Crazy On You*, used on both songs. I have shorter versions of both *Listen To The Music* and *Nights In White Satin*. For *Listen*, there are only four bars in the intro instead of eight. For *Nights,* Justin starts singing almost right away, sings only half of each of the second and third verses and then the song fades out before it's regular ending.

Jamie Cottle, announcer for CJCS in Stratford describes how the station is now considered a classic hits FM music station rather than an oldies FM music station, cycling through a top 40 type play list. It's interesting to note that they often play many tracks that weren't played originally on top 40 radio. While it never charted as a top 40 single, *Stairway To Heaven* appeared twice on the *CKSL AM Top 300 Of All Time*, two years in a row, #2 in 1984 & #1 in 1985.

26.6 ~ Not AM Top 40
1. *Bloody Well Right* [US] *& Breakfast In America* [UK] - **Supertramp**
2. *Comfortably Numb* [US] *& Money* - **Pink Floyd**
3. *Dreamboat Annie* [US] - **Heart**
4. *New Year's Day & Sunday Bloody Sunday* [US] - **U2**
5. *Stairway To Heaven* [UK] - **Led Zeppelin**
6. *Sweet Emotion* - **Aerosmith**

Other singles sounded better than their poorer CD remix cousins that now get radio play. These include …

26.7 ~ Poorer Than Single
1. *Baker Street* - **Gerry Rafferty**
2. *C'est La Vie* - **Emerson, Lake & Palmer**
3. *Carry On Wayward Son* - **Kansas**
4. *Money* - **Pink Floyd**
5. *Sweetest Thing, The* - **U2**

6. *Wildfire* - **Michael Murphy**

I always enjoyed collecting, first personal charts, second newspaper charts, and later, chart books. I always found them like a piece of history. The collection of songs was the important thing, not which ones were number one or which ones stayed on the chart the longest.

Jamie Cottle can speak from experience about short and long and poor and better versions of songs.

TWENTY - SEVEN

TELEVISION & FILM

Television and film have also been a powerful source of inspiration when it comes to music. In 1971, my parents acquired a copy of *I'd Like To Teach The World To Sing*,[189] the inspirational song from the Coke commercial, from a family friend who worked at Coke.

In late 1971 or early 1972, in grade 6, I remember watching the 1940 animated Disney movie *Fantasia*.[190] I remember it for several reasons. First, there were at least six classes all located in one giant room, on the lower floor of one of the first open concept public schools, not just in Toronto, but in all of Canada. If one class was watching a film, then we we're all watching a film, if you get my meaning. So we were all watching the movie. Second, I especially liked the dinosaur sequence, being a dinosaur geek from age five and I am still one. The music for that was *Rite Of Spring* by Igor Stravinsky.[191] Third, my father said my grandmother took him to watch it and he was terrified by the scene in the cemetery. The music was *Night On Bald Mountain*, by the Russian composer Modest Mussorgsky.[192]

When City TV first went on the air in the early seventies, they used the song *Sweet City Woman* by The Stampeders quite a bit. In late 1974, I watched *CBOT rock concert*[175]. It featured music by four major acts …

27.1 ~ CBOT Rock Concert
1. *Father of Night* - **Manfred Mann**
2. *It's Only Rock & Roll* - **The Rolling Stones**
3. *New World Rising* - **The Electric Light Orchestra**

---

[189] *I'd Like To Teach The World To Sing*, Coca Cola, 1971
[190] *Fantasia*, Walt Disney Film, 1940
[191] *Rite Of Spring*, Igor Stravinsky, *Fantasia*, Walt Disney Film, 1940
[192] *Night On Bald Mountain*, Modest Mussorgsky, *Fantasia*, Walt Disney Film, 1940

4. *Tubular Bells* - **Mike Oldfield**

What I first thought was just one of a regular series of concerts was not. Through the seventies, especially before there was Saturday Night Live, there were several music concert shows that showcased the talent that you heard on the radio. Burt Sugarman's *Midnight Special*, Don Kirschner's *Rock Concert* and Don Cornelius' *Soul Train* were three of the biggest shows going on in this category.

In the spring of 1975, Michael & I went to the theatre to watch *Tommy The Movie*[176], starring Elton John, Eric Clapton, Keith Moon, John Entwistle, Pete Townsend, Roger Daltry & Tina Turner, before hearing the original that fall. I have both The Who and Elton John versions of *Pinball Wizard*. Oh yes, and for all you Toronto Maple Leaf Fans, don't you think Borje Salming and Roger Daltrey looked a lot alike?

One of the youth group members in Ottawa explained, as we played basketball at Algonquin College one winter evening in 1976 that he spent time as DJ in the booth just next to the gym. His favourite thing to do was to put on a long piece of music, like something from *Close To The Edge* (Yes). Then he could shoot hoops for a while and not have to worry about running back to the booth to change records. After the game, we enjoyed pizza and watched The Rolling Stones film *Gimmie Shelter*[177], including the concert at Altamont with the Hell's Angels and people getting stabbed.

In 1978, Ian and I viewed what I believe to be a precursor to the rock video. It was *Laserock*[193] at the McLaughlin Planetarium of the Royal Ontario Museum. It was basically a Laser Light show, updated from the original *Laserium* shows that had featured classical music. This show featured rock music, a good portion of it that I would term progressive rock. Titles not in my singles collection are noted with (/no). The complete set list looked like this …

27.2 ~ Laserock

1. *Automation Horrorscope* - **Nektar** *(/no)*
2. *Nucleus/Day After Day* - **The Alan Parsons Project**
3. *Roundabout* - **Yes**
4. *Rocky Mountain Way* - **Joe Walsh** *(/no)*
5. *Oxygene Part 2* - **Jean Michel Jarre** *(/no)*
6. *Listen To The Music* - **The Doobie Brothers**
7. *Shining Star* - **Earth, Wind & Fire**
8. *Song To The Sun* - **Jefferson Starship** *(/no)*
9. *Overture/Communion With The Sun* - **Utopia** *(/no)*
10. *Rhiannon* - **Fleetwood Mac** *(/no)*
11. *Day At The Dog Races* - **Little Feat** *(/no)*
12. *New Orleans* - **Emerson, Lake & Palmer** *(/no)*
13. *Dance On A Volcano* - **Genesis** *(/no)*
14. *Frankenstein* - **The Edgar Winter Group**

In the late seventies, *WKRP In Cincinnati*[194] made its way to television. It was a crazy and zany sitcom about a radio station and all that goes with it. What was most important was that you felt like you were listening to top forty radio but you were watching it.

While most music videos appeared in the eighties, There were a number that appeared in the seventies or were recreated later…

---

[193] *Laserock*, Mclaughlin Planetarium, Royal Ontario Museum, March 1978
[194] *WKRP In Cincinnati*, MTM CBS, 1978-1982

27.3 ~ 70s Videos

1. *Angie & It's Only Rock & Roll* - **The Rolling Stones**
2. *Bohemian Rhapsody* - **Queen**
3. *Born To Run* - **Bruce Springsteen**
4. *Comfortably Numb* - **Pink Floyd**
5. *Dancing Queen* - **Abba**
6. *Dreaming & Heart Of Glass* - **Blondie**
7. *Goodbye Stranger* - **Supertramp**
8. *Imagine* - **John Lennon**
9. *Let's Go* - **The Cars**
10. *(The) Long Run* - **The Eagles**
11. *Night Moves & Old Time Rock & Roll* - **Bob Segar**
12. *Sweet Emotion* - **Aerosmith**
13. *Video Killed The Radio Star* - **The Buggles**

There were great music TV moments in the early eighties. The first was Marvin Gaye singing the *Star Spangled Banner* at an NBA All Star Game.[195] The next was The New Music. This was the beginning of Much Music. Hosts on the show included: JD Roberts, Jeannie Beker, Laurie Brown, Denise Donlan & Kim Clarke Champniss. After that was my brother Andrew and me watching *City Limits* on City TV with Christopher Ward. That was five hours of music videos beginning at midnight and going until 5 AM Sundays.

That was before Much Music was launched as its own separate TV station. *Is This Live?*,[196] written by Christopher Ward himself, is a book celebrating the Much Music experience. The early Much VJs included: Bill Welychka, Diego Fuentes, Erica Ehm, Master T, Mike Williams, Monica Deohl, Natalie Richard, Rick Campanelli, Sook Yin Lee, Steve Anthony, Terry David Mulligan & Ziggy Lorenc.

There are many Much moments that stand out. Diego Fuentes introduced Paul McCartneys' *Pipes Of Peace* and explained how it fit into Christmas. Christopher Ward interviewed Supertramp on the release of their album *Brother Where You Bound.* Rick Davies described *Cannonball* as Discotramp. Terry David Mulligan spoke on two different Christmas episodes of *Much West.* In the first one, he sat on the beach in Stanley Park in Vancouver and talked about grounded planes messing up family Christmases. In the second one, he rode the Grouse Mountain Skyride with other skiers and talked about how great the Pogue's *Fairy Tale Of New York* video was. Bill Welychka played rugby catch in the studio with Jim Kerr of Simple Minds. George Strombolopoulos interviewed U2. Annie Lennox talked about *A Whiter Shade Of Pale*[197] by Procal Harum as the first 45 rpm record she ever bought, on an episode of *The New Music.*[198]

During the eighties, there were several pop songs that were released at the same time as movies. Huey Lewis recorded *The Power Of Love* for *Back To The Future.*[199] I remember visiting Universal Studios in 1983 and seeing the famous town square with the city hall and the famous clock tower. However, that part of the back lot with the city square and clock tower was damaged by fire and is no longer there as I can tell you from having visited Universal again in 2015.

[195] *Star Spangled Banner*, Marvin Gaye, 1982 NBA All-Star Game
[196] *Is This Live?, The Story Of Much Music*, Christopher Ward, Randon House Canada, 2016
[197] *A Whiter Shade Of Pale*, Procal Harum, 1967
[198] *Medusa*, Annie Lennox Interview, The New Music, 1995
[199] *The Power Of Love*, Huey Lewis, *Back To The Future*, Universal Pictures, 1985

After their initial success in the late sixties and early seventies, The Bee Gees reinvented themselves once for their main course album and then again for the blockbuster movie *Saturday Night Fever* in 1977.[200] They had no fewer than three songs featured in the movie, *How Deep Is Your Love, Night Fever & Stayin' Alive.*

Phil Collins wrote the book on movie songs in the 1980s. First he recorded the title track for *Against All Odds.*[201] Second, he recorded *Separate Lives* for *White Nights.*[202] Both were released with picture sleeves. Third, he wrote the songs *Groovy Kind Of Love & Two Hearts* for *Buster.*[203] U2 filmed an entire movie for their 1988 album *Rattle & Hum*, including *All I Want Is You, Angel Of Harlem, Desire & When Love Comes To Town.*[204]

27.4 ~ Movies I - 60s & 70s

1. *Dueling Banjos [Deliverance]* - **Eric Weisberg**
2. *Entertainer [The Sting]* - **Marvin Hamlisch**
3. *Live & Let Die [Live & Let Die]* - **Wings**
4. *(The) Morning After [Poseidon Adventure]* - **Maureen McGovern**
5. *Mrs. Robinson [The Graduate]* - **Simon & Garfunkel**
6. *Nobody Does It Better [The Spy Who Loved Me]* - **Carly Simon**
7. *Pinball Wizard [Tommy]* - **Elton John**
8. *Raindrops Keep Falling On My Head [Butch Cassidy & The Sundance Kid]* - **B J Thomas**
9. *Theme From Shaft [Shaft]* - **Isaac Hayes**

27.5 ~ Movies II - 80s & 90s

1. *Arthur's Theme [Arthur]* - **Christopher Cross**
2. *Call Me [American Gigolo]* - **Blondie**
3. *Chariots Of Fire [Chariots Of Fire]* - **Vangelis**
4. *Crazy For You [Vision Quest]* - **Madonna**
5. *Deeper & Deeper [Streets Of Fire]* - **The Fixx**
6. *Don't You (Forget About Me) [The Breakfast Club]* - **Simple Minds**
7. *I Go Crazy [Some Kind Of Wonderful]* - **Flesh For Lulu**
8. *I Just Called To Say I Love You [Woman In Red]* - **Stevie Wonder**
9. *Kiss From A Rose [Batman Forever]* - **U2**
10. *Let The River Run [Working Girl]* - **Carly Simon**
11. *Love Theme [St. Elmo's Fire]* - **David Foster**
12. *Magic [Xanadu]* - **Olivia Newton - John**
13. *Nothing In Common [Nothing In Common]* - **The Thompson Twins**
14. *Power Of Love [Back To The Future]* - **Huey Lewis**
15. *Purple Rain & When Doves Cry [Purple Rain]* - **Prince**
16. *Sweet Freedom [Running Scared]* - **Michael McDonald**
17. *Take My Breath Away [Top Gun]* - **Berlin**

---

[200] *Saturday Night Fever* Film, Paramount Pictures, 1977, *Saturday Night Fever* Soundtrack, RSO Records, 1977, *How Deep Is Your Love?*, *Night Fever, Stayin' Alive*, Bee Gees
[201] *Against All Odds,* Columbia Pictures, 1984
[202] *White Nights,* Columbia Pictures, 1985
[203] *Buster,* Vestron Pictures, 1988
[204] *Rattle & Hum, All I Want Is You, Angel Of Harlem, Desire & When Love Comes To Town*, U2, Paramount (film), Island (soundtrack), 1988

18. *This Is Not America [The Falcon & The Snowman]* - **David Bowie & Pat Metheny**
19. *Up Where We Belong [An Officer & A Gentleman]* - **Joe Cocker & Jennifer Warnes**
20. *View To A Kill [View To A Kill]* - **Duran Duran**
21. *We Don't Need Another Hero [Mad Max Beyond Thunderdome]* - **Tina Turner**
22. *What A Feeling [Flashdance]* - **Irene Cara**
23. *Who's That Girl [Who's That Girl]* - **Madonna**

I also assembled over twenty different video tapes, each with at least 25 dubbed songs on each. That's a second generation recording of over 500 songs, one at a time. The quality is not that good but the collection is. While there are many videos that I do not have on vinyl there is a crossover of at least 150. Most of the Much VJs mentioned above are on the tapes somewhere.

I remember watching the short open air microphone video booth *Speakers Corner* on *Much Music* in the nineties. Two guys were singing a song together but each guy was taking a turn singing every other note. For sure that was a lot harder than it sounded.

In 1995, Trevor Horn played bass for Seal in the *Batman Forever*[205] movie song *Kiss From a Rose.*[206] He also produced the song *Nobody Lives Without Love*, by Eddie Reader, from that same *Batman* film.[207] Through the nineties, there was another musical Influence - The show *Heartbeat*[208] aired on TV Ontario beginning in about 1992. The timeframe was the 1960s. There was a lot of good music here. I now have no fewer than four different *Heartbeat* music discs, three of them double discs. It was a rediscovery of sixties music…

27.6 ~ Singles 60S - Heartbeat
1. *Don't Let The Sun Catch You Crying & How Do You Do It?* - **Gerry & The Pacemakers**
2. *Mr. Tambourine Man* - **The Byrds**
3. *Scarborough Fair* - **Simon & Garfunkel**
4. *Keep On Running* - **The Spencer Davis Group**
5. *House Of The Rising Sun* - **The Animals**
6. *If I Were A Carpenter* - **Bobby Darin**
7. *Lay Lady Lay* - **Bob Dylan**
8. *Letter* - **Box Tops**
9. *She's Not There* - **The Zombies**
10. *Silence Is Golden* - **The Tremeloes**
11. *Sitting On The Dock Of The Bay* - **Otis Redding**
12. *Whiter Shade Of Pale, A* - **Procal Harum**
13. *World Without Love* - **Peter & Gordon**
14. *You Really Got Me* - **The Kinks**

The opening credits for Heartbeat in later years showed a 45 rpm record spinning on a turntable. I liked the episode in which Constable Mike Bradley played DJ and even had his own wooden box full of, you

---

[205] *Batman Forever*, Warner Bros, 1995
[206] *Kiss From A Rose*, Seal, 1995
[207] *Nobody Lives Without Love*, Eddi Reader, 1995
[208] *Heartbeat*, TV Ontario

guessed it, 45 RPM records. Many of the groups featured played a "Beat" style of music, including Gerry & The Pacemakers, Herman's Hermits, The (early) Hollies, The Searchers & The Zombies, among others.

If you want to get technical, there was some music played on the show that was from the seventies, not the sixties. Case in point is The Hollies, just mentioned above. *He Ain't Heavy He's My Brother* (1970) was used in season four episode fifteen. *The Air That I Breathe* (1974) was used in Nick and Jo's wedding episode. Sixties Hollies for me would be *Bus Stop* (1966), of course.

Why is it, in movie trailers, that you hear particular music playing? Then a funny thing happens when you go to see the movie. It's not that the music doesn't match with the scene(s) that you saw in the trailer, either it only appears at the end of the movie or sometimes doesn't play in the movie at all. *One* (U2) plays in the trailer for *Family Man*[209] but never plays in the movie itself.

---

[209] *Family Man*, 2000, *One, Achtung Baby*, U2, 1991

TWENTY - EIGHT

HOME RECORDING I
BENCHMARKS (MK)

This is the second of three chapters that talk about recording, the first of two chapters that talk about home recording. For Christmas of 1971, I was given a transistor radio, MK1. In the spring of 1973, I bought my first 45 RPM records. Dad let me use his portable record player, MK2. In the winter of 1974, mom helped me buy a tape recorder, only mono, not stereo capability, MK3 *[gem]*, the first in a series of "backing up my vinyl collection", "saving the wear and tear on my records for a rainy day". The way of changing the mode the recorder was in was controlled by a large shifter like button that was more like a car gear shift than it was like a selection of touch keys or buttons. If for no other reason, it was just as important to have the tape machine because I did not have my own stereo at the time. So If I wanted to listen to the music I had on record, more often than playing the record, the next best thing to do was make a tape. At the same time, I started using dad's console to make my tapes, call it MK4.

While I can't remember the exact model number, possibly the Dual 1009, dad's stereo did have a Dual turntable. The book Revolution, refers to the Dual 1019 turntable as its "iconic model in the marketplace".[210]

When I first started recording, I did not know that you could re-record to a cassette for which you had already knocked out the notches at either end of the top of the tape, MK5. It took me months to figure out that if you recovered the notch holes with scotch tape that you could re-record again. I bought my first pair of headphones MK6 (in 1975) and then again (in 1980) when the first pair wore out. Headphones come and go and they do get better over time but somewhere along the way there is something special that you don't forget. Sure, headphones now are better but these are special, good, great, actually. Some things just

---

[210] *Revolution, The History Of Turntable Design*, Gideon Schwartz, Phaidon. com, 2022, p.102

feel more like home. Dad had a booming voice and it was even louder when he had headphones on and he was telling you about the music he was listening to.

Most of my records would not be playable today if I had not started recording them all those years ago. Mom helped me pick this one out. I remember telling my aunt the blank tapes she was buying me weren't the best quality (type I instead of type II). A foot in mouth moment, yes, but even then, I knew the difference.

The poor quality of CD sound is like a flashback to my first combination stereo radio & cassette player in 1978, MK7. Dad helped me pick this one out. Recording from the radio to cassette on that machine resulted in much the same exaggeration of sounds (my recording of *Yes Live in LA*, early 1979, from the King Biscuit Flower Hour on CHUM FM … I saw them that spring at Maple Leaf Gardens. I thought for sure we would have come further than that in almost forty-five years.

A side note to the recording of Yes *Live in Los Angeles* in 1979. I remember thinking that some of the songs sounded different. But it wasn't the live sound versus the studio sound that was different, it was something else. Then I figured it out. It was the live song endings that Genesis talked about earlier.

Also in the late seventies, I remember making a voice tape recording with Alex. We bought the cheapest compact cassette we could find at Canadian Tire. The quality was so bad there were parts of the voice recording that weren't even audible. I also discovered that if you had trouble with one tape you could open up the shell for that tape, open up the shell of a new tape, take the new tape out of the new shell and put the old tape in the new shell, MK8. It didn't always work but sometimes it did.

In 1979, I built five different shelving units, two corner shelves, and three lower two shelf units. Rather than cut in half, the corner shelves had the front portion cut away. This left just enough room for the components at the front and lots of room to hide stuff behind. The lower shelves stored books on the top, complete with my original bookshelf speakers, and record albums on the bottom.

Storage for the records was an issue for some time. There were boxes and baskets and, yes, the wire racks (oh man what a disaster even though they looked like a good idea at the time) for singles and albums, whatever your preference. Then I found clear Rubbermaid bins that were a perfect fit for the 7 inch single.

MK9 was my first real stereo, an amplifier, turntable & speakers. My turntable was the Technics SL D2. Again, I refer to *Revolution, The History Of Turntable Design*.[211] The book commented that "no other brand of turntable can convincingly compete for creating the mise-en-scene of analogue culture from the 1970s to the 1990s". MK10 was a tape deck. I could control the input levels.

MK11 was several years later and not an equipment marker but an important step in how you do your recording. Playing back with or without Dolby allows you to control the high sounds in the output. Recording with Dolby on gives you even better output, whether you listen with Dolby on or not. I knew then that recording was fun but serious stuff. I could now have music that sounded better than dad's stereo from the sixties and I could record it too.

MK12 was the Sony Walkman I in the late eighties. MK13 was the Sony Discman that I got in the early nineties. MK14 was a dual tape deck. I could make duplicates of "time intensive original" various tapes.

MK15 was a second dual tape deck. I had the ability to control tape levels, going from one deck to another. The only way to get around this would have been to buy a cassette deck, so expensive and better part of 1K in price, where you control the dub levels from cassette A to cassette B.

MK16 was a platter CD player that could house five at once. MK17 was a music burner machine to make CDs. I can go straight from phono or tape or CD to CD, without a computer (to clean up the sound)

---

[211] *Revolution, The History Of Turntable Design*, Gideon Schwartz, Phaidon. com, 2022, p.185

and get results more like vinyl than store bought CDs. The sound really is awesome, that's old school awesome, not the current day watered down version. Creating CDs (especially various) versus tapes changes the way you organize your play/song lists, now in 80 minute groups instead of 60 (2 x30) or 90 (2 x 45).

It seems to me that creating a play list for cassette or CD takes a great deal of time and skill. The reason for this is you have to put together a group of songs that will end after thirty (half a 60 minute tape), thirty-seven (half a 74 minute tape), forty five (half a 90 minute tape), or 80 minutes (the most you can put on a CD). It's really weird that the move from record to tape to CD means there are no more sides one and two or A and B.

There is an underlying time factor involved in listening to the tapes / CDs after they are made. Whichever the format, tape or CD, there are a certain number of songs that can fill that time and space. Even if you aren't paying attention to all of the music as it's playing, you do know that a certain amount of time has passed once you get to the end of the tape / CD. At the same time, if you are paying attention to the music and know the order of the songs, you can tell how much of the tape or CD playlist has elapsed just by what song is playing currently.

Putting together a compilation isn't just talking about tallying up the times for a bunch of songs and throwing them together. There needs to be something that ties them together, an artist or mood or theme or type or year(s). There needs to be some flow to the songs or it makes it a lot harder to listen to. All you do with an iPod is load up an endless collection of songs. Yes there is a start and a finish but it's much harder to tell where that is when there are hundreds of songs versus a dozen or so.

From the earliest days of listening to my vinyl records on my dad's console stereo to the modern day technical challenges of my recording tower and all its components, I have been forever in search of "not perfect" but "great sound". As the aforementioned benchmarks of my recording experience bear out, in terms of that "great sound", U2 put it best when they said *I Still Haven't Found What I'm Looking For.*

After struggling with recording for years, I bought myself a new amplifier so now I can get down to business again. While the amplifier is stronger and will give you a bigger and louder sound, the hidden beauty of a better amp is how much better the music sounds when you play it quietly. Remember that the baseline for all CD production is audio tape especially if the selection of songs is taken from across various sources rather than just a single album.

The thing I miss about the old amp are the window gauges with the analogue needles that wave back and forth depending on the volume of the music.

I joked with Coke in July about its "Move to the Beat" campaign. On the 12 can cartons and 2L bottles, the image of the turntable shows the tone arm on the wrong side, the left side. Either they did this on purpose just so guys like me could talk about it or the designer is someone who has never ever seen a real turntable before in his entire life. By the time the small bottles and cans with the turntable came along, they had put the tone arm on the correct side, the right side.

MK18 was upgraded stereo cables running between various stereo components. The sound is great, awesome, and magical, like I've never heard before. I have seen the light, or in this case, I have heard the sound, I have found a happy place. I may now be able to put the *I Still Haven't Found* cliché to rest. Recording is something that takes years to get good at. It's not just a case of waking up one day and deciding that you are going to be good at recording music. It doesn't happen like that.

MK19 is the current setup for recording, a large four shelf open tower, AKA "The Recording Tower" where components are stacked with extra space between them for good ventilation. Those spaces are created using items like plastic pop bottle caps or empty plastic tape spools *[gem].*

I remember recently thinking my amplifier might be a little flakey so I went to the store and bought another one. I brought it home and took the stereo apart, replacing the old amplifier with the new amplifier.

Once I powered it up it didn't sound nearly as good. I kept adjusting the levels but it didn't ever get any better. Sometimes you just don't realize how good the equipment you already have is.

More recently, I finally replaced the amplifier, MK20. At first it didn't sound so good but it just needed to warm up. Once it was warmed up it sounded great. Recording even sounds better with the newer more powerful amplifier. I had a friend comment recently that he didn't like the vinyl to CD machines because you couldn't adjust the base and the treble. I think I missed something because I have been making good sounding tapes for years and have only ever been able to adjust the volume levels not the bass or the treble.

Sleeves for records have always been important. For vinyl single sleeves that got beaten up pretty badly in the early years, I bought replacement sleeves in bulk from A&A records, close to one hundred in total. For albums, I favoured the "Angel Sleeve" style, that's paper sleeve on the outside with a plastic sleeve on the inside. For singles, they were plain paper sleeves with centre cutouts to view the titles. This goes a long way to prolonging the life of vinyl records.

Headphones come and go and they do get better over time but somewhere along the way there is something special that you don't forget. In my case it's the first (1975) and second time around (1980) that I bought my Yamaha HP 1 headphones. They finally fell apart earlier this year so I replaced them with a pair from SONY. One earpiece falling off wasn't the problem. Not being able to hear out of it was.

Sure, headphones now are better but these are special, good, great, actually. Some things just feel more like home. iPod and MP3 earplugs are not as good as Walkman and Discman earphones, if only that they are much shorter. I guess maybe it's because I have an iPod MK21 and I find the shorter earplugs just plain frustrating.

In the 1990s, I spent much time recording and rerecording hundreds of music videos, thinking that this might be part of the evolution of my record collection. However, the quality, neither the sound nor the visual, on VHS, was nearly the same as the vinyl collection going on to cassette tape. One of the big challenges is the (in) accuracy of the VHS tape position when you are stopping and starting.

To make a long story short, the benchmarks of recording are as follows. The best result you can get is going from vinyl to chrome audio tape, better than vinyl to CD. However, if you had time, the conversion from vinyl to chrome tape and then to CD would give you the best result of all. Small detail here, this is time consuming, meaning that you are doing the recording process twice. As you get older you realize that you don't have this luxury.

Much of my experience in recording has been setting the recording levels way up from the recommended flat levels that manufacturers suggest. This way you get a stronger sound but beware of the fine line between stronger sound and distortion. Sometimes the auto record level is a nice feature to use to keep away from those distorted outputs and results.

Most recently, tapes are being phased out, specifically those type II chrome tapes, much better quality than the type I low noise tapes. This is too bad because some of the best sound is from vinyl to tape with Dolby and then tape without Dolby to CD. Also, the fade in/out feature of the CD machine is much rougher than the tape deck(s).

There is much that affects the sound of what you are listening to: the cartridge and stylus; the angle the stylus fits in the vinyl groove; the weight on the tone arm; the type of turntable, i.e. Belt or direct drive; the amplifier that you are using; the speakers you are using; and the wire that connects those same speakers to the amplifier. By the way, good speakers don't improve the sound if the other parts of the system aren't up to snuff.

Recording singles was much easier in two different cases. First, for labels like Atlantic, Columbia and Lion by Polydor, the top of the label was one colour and the bottom was another. Even the Famous

Charisma Label had a very similar look. This made it easy to follow the record label as it circled the table before the music started. Second, sometimes you could hear the start of the song ghosting ever so quietly, one revolution ahead of the real sound.

What's next? What I want to do mostly is convert people's vinyl records to CD. My goal is to bring people's favourite music back to them, music that maybe they haven't listened to for a long time. I want the music to sound as good as it did when they first listened to it. This would be like re-awakening music inside of them.

I have been recording now since 1974 and have recently decided on a designation for my tape recording skills. I am an HMTRP, a home music tape recording professional. This includes recording to CD but for the sake of the title stays as HMTRP. This has been a self-taught process, trial and error, you know, good judgment comes from experience and experience comes from bad judgment. I have made some great tapes along the way, as well as some forgettable ones.

In July of 2011, Popular Mechanics published the 101 gadgets that changed the world. Entry #8 included many of the benchmarks already listed in this chapter, Phonograph (#8) MK2, Transistor Radio (#16) MK1, Cassette Tape (#50) MK3, Walkman (#45) MK12, Discman (#30) MK13 & MP3 Player (#42) MK21.[212]

In 2014 Graham Betts published his book *Infographic Guide To Music*. Page 60 about How We Listened, also featured many of the same items, the Portable Record Player (1952) MK2, Transistor Radio (1954) MK1, Cassette Tape (1963) MK3, Sony Walkman (1979) MK12, Discman (1984) MK13 & MP3 Player (1998) MK21.[213]

[212] *101 Gadgets That Changed The World*, Popular Mechanics, July 2011.
[213] *Infographic Guide To Music*, Graham Betts, Octopus Books, an Hachette UK Company, 2014, p.60

TWENTY - NINE

HOME RECORDING II
MAKING TAPES

This is the second chapter that talks about home recording and the last chapter that talks about recording in general. I should start out by saying the attraction to cassette tapes was at first a necessity because I did not have a stereo of my own but secondly a way of backing up my record collection. The use of tapes has in no way been a way of replacing the records themselves. Think of it as a way of extending the life of my records by playing tapes of them instead.

Blank tape packaging in the early seventies was different than it is today. Back then, the cover art for the tape was actually one side of the index card. Now the cover art is usually just in plastic wrap, while the index card is two sided. When I first made tapes and filled out the index, I often still left the index facing inward instead of outward. It took a friend to show me it made more sense to have the song lists showing so you didn't have to open the case to see them. I have a stockpile of index cards and labels from the beginning of time.

My various tapes had their origin in early 1974, taping songs from the radio, whole sections of the weekly top thirty. Unfortunately, these tapes did not make it out of the seventies.

Putting into practice my recording of records, specifically singles, using my new stereo, I created more singles compilation tapes in 1980, like the Chicago tape (75), sometimes with one group, sometimes several but under the same record label. Many of the various tapes that I have made have been singles (not album) driven, partly due to the origins of my collection also being singles (not album) driven. Tapes of singles are harder to recreate than tapes of albums.

In April of 1981, I recorded the church Cantata *Olivet To Calvary*[174], using my BENCHMARK TWO stereo cassette machine. At the time, I didn't think much of it and thought the sound was OK. Looking back on it, the sound was reasonably good. When my wife went to school at Western in the fall of 1981, I recorded a case full of mix tapes and albums for her. All of those tapes still exist today, in the same case.

Over the years, several friends even made me mix tapes. One friend, in particular, made me three tapes, a great keepsake, to this day. Fast forward to 2008. I sang in a church choir and requested a copy of a Christmas concert that we did. However, making a copy of the tape that someone else recorded, playing the tape as loud as I could, I could only salvage one song from a two-hour concert. What the heck happened there?

This reinforces my belief that recording is not just a technical skill but also a listening skill, knowing what it is that you want to record before you start touching any buttons or switches. I recall others who have done church recording and sound system work in the past and marvel at the job they did to get the best sound possible, taking into consideration all of the factors involved.

I have created several different types of singles audio tapes from this collection. The first is various; some follow a very rough chronology, where songs within a few years are put on the same tape. Others are just various tunes selected at random. The second I call *Singles* by a particular group, like a commercial best of or greatest hits but instead are homemade versions of the same. The third is song titles that are recorded in alphabetical order. The fourth is to start with a slow song and record consecutive songs that get faster and faster in their tempo.

I have created them mostly where there are few or no albums by those groups. I have noted them as /Tape and then the length, either _60, _45 or _½_45. The singles tapes include Bachman-Turner Overdrive; Chicago; The Doobie Brothers; Edward Bear; The Ex-Beatles (Harrison, Lennon, McCartney, Starr); The Five Man Electrical Band; The Fixx; Foreigner; The Human League; Lighthouse; The Moody Blues; Orchestral Manoeuvres In The Dark; Styx; & Steve Winwood.

Different friends have selected a playlist of songs from my collection for me to tape. Here's the *Alex Mix…*

29.1 ~ Mix I - Alex

1. *Groovy Kind Of Love & I Wish It Would Rain Down* - **Phil Collins**
2. *Jerusalem* - **Emerson, Lake & Palmer**
3. *Love Theme From St Elmos's Fire* - **David Foster**
4. *No Son Of Mine* - **Genesis**
5. *Criminal Mind* - **Gowan**
6. *It's Still Rock'n Roll To Me* - **Billy Joel**
7. *Nobody Told Me* - **John Lennon**
8. *Living Years, The* - **Mike & The Mechanics**
9. *Can You Give It All To Me* - **Myles & Lenny**
10. *Rikki Don't Lose That Number* - **Steely Dan**
11. *It's Raining Again & Free As A Bird* - **Supertramp**
12. *Africa* - **Toto**
13. *Venus & Mars Rock Show & Listen To What The Man Said* - **Wings**
14. *Power Of Love* - **Huey Lewis & The News**
15. *West End Girls* - **The Pet Shop Boys**
16. *Someday* - **Glass Tiger**
17. *Ripples* - **Genesis**

I have also made from time to time, copies of various audio cassette tapes that people have made for me. I have given these copies to the same people, family and friends, who gave me the tapes as gifts and presents to begin with. Several friends have made their own tapes over the years and played them at parties, work, and church. I have a binder full of dozens and dozens of mixed playlists that I have written down but never actually recorded.

I have created a couple of different CDs with music from the late 80s and 90s. One is for those songs that I have on vinyl. The other is for songs that I have on cassette but not vinyl. I am still searching for those same titles on vinyl and hope to put them on CD someday as well.

The quality of tapes is hard to figure out. Safe to say that many commercial audio tapes are/were not very well made. I have made copies of commercial tapes and played them over and over and they have lasted longer and sound as good or better than the originals that they were made from.

The idea of *The Needle Drop* came to me originally, recording the above mentioned song *Power Of Love* by Huey Lewis, in the *Alex* mix when I didn't wait for the needle drop before pressing record. I have since incorporated it into the beginnings of many of my tapes. In 2009, I made a *School Carnival Mix*, which looked like this …

29.2 ~ Mix II - School Carnival

1. *Boogie Woogie Bugle Boy* - **Bette Midler**
2. *Clap For The Wolfman* - **The Guess Who**
3. *Crazy Little Thing Called Love* - **Queen**
4. *Fool In The Rain* - **Led Zeppelin**
5. *Let 'Em In* - **Wings**
6. *Long Tall Glasses* - **Leo Sayer**
7. *Magic* - **Pilot**
8. *Rockin' Pneumonia* - **Johnny Rivers**
9. *The Sheriff* - **Emerson, Lake & Palmer**
10. *The Show Must Go On* - **Three Dog Night**
11. *Stuck In The Middle* - **Stealers Wheel**
12. *Will It Go Round In Circles* - **Billy Preston**
13. *Angel Of Harlem* - **U2**
14. *Come On Eileen* - **Dexy's Midnight Runners**
15. *Everyday Is A Winding Road* - **Sheryl Crow**
16. *I Can't Dance* - **Genesis**
17. *Leave It* - **Yes**
18. *My Kind Of Lady* - **Supertramp**
19. *Power Of Love* - **Huey Lewis & The News**
20. *Putting On The Ritz* - **Taco**
21. *Pioneer & Six Months In A Leaky Boat* - **Split Enz**

I finished creating the CD *Merry Christmas Rock [gem]* in December of 2010. It started out as two different cassette mixes, Merry Christmas Rock from the late 1980s and More Christmas Rock from the early nineties. The CD starts with the More Christmas Rock mix, then features a three song bridge (8, 9 & 10) to the Merry Christmas Rock mix…

29.3 ~ Mix III - Merry Christmas Rock [gem]

1. *Peace On Earth / Little Drummer Boy* - **David Bowie & Bing Crosby**
2. *Christmas Song* - **Natalie Cole**
3. *Rudolph The Red Nosed Reindeer* - **The California Raisins**
4. *Merry Christmas Baby* - **Bruce Springsteen**
5. *I Saw Mommy Kissing Santa Claus* - **John Mellencamp**
6. *Wonderful Christmas Time* - **Paul McCartney**
7. *Holly Jolly Christmas* - **Burl Ives**
8. *Easier Said Than Done* - **Jon Anderson**
9. *Put A Little Love In Your Heart* - **Annie Lennox & Al Green**
10. *Please Come Home For Christmas* - **The Eagles**
11. *I Believe In Father Christmas (LP)* - **Greg Lake**
12. *Happy Christmas (War Is Over)* - **John Lennon**
13. *Santa Claus Is Coming To Town* - **Bruce Springsteen**
14. *Power Of Love* - **Frankie Goes To Hollywood**
15. *Do They Know It's Christmas* - **Band Aid**
16. *Run With The Fox* - **Chris Squire & Alan White**
17. *I Believe In Father Christmas (45)* - **Greg Lake**

This followed on the heels of *Merry Christmas Rock I* in 2008. That was created from *Merry Christmas Rock* in the late 80s and *More Christmas Rock*, in the early nineties. Those were rituals or traditions if you will and now the CDs pick up where the tapes left off.

I am forever creating new lists of various compilations that I might like or that I think other people may like. In many cases these lists stay as lists and either take a long time making it to tape/CD or not even at all. I have also saved many indexes of old compilation / mix tapes that no longer exist so I can recreate them when I want to. It's like having several generations of mix tapes at my disposal.

I recently purchased fifty blank type II chrome audio cassettes which you can't really buy anywhere else anymore except maybe online. Tapes are good for creating various originals before recording to CD. Also, as I record more and more to CD, this frees up a boatload of chrome tape backups. Ah yes, you are not supposed to record over and over on cassette tapes but within reason the results are just fine, especially if the chrome tapes are hard to find any more.

I also have found a large stash of normal bias tapes with a heavier bass sound, very comparable to the chrome tapes I was just speaking of. Regardless of how critical I am of my own recording, different results each time depending on the sources and the outputs, the results are still better than the commercially created CDs.

I first began frequenting the garage sale circuit back in the 1980s. I have recently purchased many flea market chrome tapes that people have already recorded on. Besides the fact that the ultimate tape is one that you only record on once, most have been recorded on very few times at the most. This still makes them a valuable item, in the scheme of things. As they say, one man's garbage is another man's gold or one man's trash is another man's treasure.

The chrome tapes used to be in abundance in many different places, including A&A Records, Cheapies, Ed Mirvish, Everything For A Dollar Store, Music World, Sam The Record Man and Yonge Street Electronics Stores, just to name a few.

Tape storage has always been a challenge, as they accumulate faster than I can store them. The first unit was a carousel but you had to take the tapes out of their cases, if they had them, to put them into the carousel. Then there was the case that opened at the top, not at the side, and when you carried it would open whenever it wanted dumping all your tapes out on the ground.

Then there were brief case style carry cases that made much more sense, except that you still had to lift and move them to open them. Next was stacking shallow clear bins without the lids. You still had to lift them but it was faster than having to open the briefcases. Then came the cases with three drawers, the best yet. Similar to that were the single drawer library card files.

After that were custom made wall units with slots for single tapes. After that were units with shelves with spaces for several tapes at a time. Finally, the ultimate storage for cassette tapes would be an old library card file cabinet but you need lots of space to do that.

2014 marked forty years of taping for me so I created two different tapes to mark the anniversary. First, I mentioned earlier, Southern Country Folk in the Great American Folk Tune. First is the story of *Classical Rock 22 [gem]*. Second is Classical Rock is not to be confused with Classic Rock. While people are impressed with albums, singles, not so much. So, I wanted to put together a singles collection (only one is an album track). The pieces range in time from the late sixties to the early eighties, with most from the mid-seventies.

There are four connections to classical music. One, many are progressive rock songs. Two is the instrumentation (including acoustic guitar, acoustic piano, choir, horns, orchestra, organ and strings). Three, many of the artists are from the UK and have had some classical music training. Four, structurally, many pieces are made up of different sections, like a suite.

For a collection of popular songs, they are all awesome examples of the differences and dynamics that make music so special, including loud, soft, slow & fast. The original version of this CD was created as a gift. The 2014 version had five more pieces, *Also Sprach Zarathustra, C'est La Vie, Can't Get It Out Of My Head, Cats In The Cradle* and *Year Of The Cat* but did not include *Wasted Time. Soapbox Opera* was chosen over *Fool's Overture* and the compilation celebrated my forty years of making audio tapes from singles & albums (1974). The 2022 version has *I Am The Walrus* instead of *A Day In The Life* and each of *C'est La Vie, Entangled* and *Tuesday Afternoon* revert back to their single versions. The Intro is by a DJ, my namesake, who worked at 1050 CHUM in the mid-seventies. For *White Car*, I refer to it as *Man In A White Car*, as per the way it was printed in the original *Drama* Tour Concert Program. Greg Lake, Paul McCartney, Alan Parsons and Yes all do extra time in this compilation. It's surprising that there are only three repeats from the Crazy Hippie Organ lists here, Procal Harum, Emerson, Lake & Palmer & Split Enz. The list of the songs is as follows:

29.4 ~ Mix IV - Classical Rock 22 [gem]
1. *Introduction* [76]
2. *(I've Been) Searchin' So Long* - **Chicago** [74]
3. *Ace Of Swords, The (/b)* - **The Alan Parsons Project** [80]
4. *Air That I Breathe, The* - **The Hollies** [74]
5. *Also Sprach Zarathustra* - **Deodato** [73]
6. *C'est La Vie* - **Greg Lake** [77]
7. *Can't Get It Out Of My Head* - **The Electric Light Orchestra** [74]
8. *Cat's In The Cradle* - **Harry Chapin** [74]
9. *Classical Gas* - **Mason Williams** [68]
10. *Conquistador* - **Procal Harum** [72]
11. *I Am The Walrus* - **The Beatles** [67]
12. *Entangled* - **Genesis** [76]

13. *Jerusalem* - **Emerson, Lake & Palmer** [73]
14. *Live & Let Die* - **Paul McCartney & Wings** [73]
15. *Man In A White Car (/b)* - **Yes** [80]
16. *Pioneer & Six Months In A Leaky Boat* - **Split Enz** [82]
17. *Soapbox Opera* (33) - **Supertramp** [75]
18. *Tuesday Afternoon* - **The Moody Blues** [67]
19. *Wonderous Stories* - **Yes** [77]
20. *Year Of The Cat* - **Al Stewart** [77]

Three of the tracks were chosen originally as album tracks over the singles. The album version of *C'est La Vie* has the fuller solo in the middle. The album version of *Entangled* includes the instrumental conclusion but sounds so much better. The album version of *Tuesday Afternoon* is the full version with orchestra. Like *Entangled*, Emerson Lake and Palmer released a single of *The Nutrocker* which also suffered from very poor sound quality. On the other hand, the single version of *Jerusalem* was a good recording, in fact the volume actually increases at the start of the second verse. Similar to *Jerusalem*, Supertramp's' opening song from *Breakfast In America*, *Gone Hollywood*, also increases in volume part way through the song.

Going back to Classical Rock for a moment and then taking a step back, a collection of classical pop tunes might look/sound like this…

29.5 ~ Mix V - Classical Pop
1. *#9 Dream* - **John Lennon**
2. *Alone Again (Naturally)* - **Gilbert O'Sullivan**
3. *Bohemian Rhapsody* - **Queen**
4. *Bungle In The Jungle* - **Jethro Tull**
5. *Can You Give It All To Me* - **Myles & Lenny**
6. *Comfortably Numb* - **Pink Floyd**
7. *I'm Not In Love* - **10 CC**
8. *Long Long Way* - **Ian Thomas**
9. *Lucy In The Sky With Diamonds* - **Elton John**
10. *Never Gonna Fall In Love Again* - **Eric Carmen**
11. *Only Women* - **Alice Cooper**
12. *Photograph* - **Ringo Starr**
13. *Russians* - **Sting**
14. *Song Sung Blue* - **Neil Diamond**
15. *Space Oddity* - **David Bowie**
16. *Take It To The Limit* - **The Eagles**
17. *Vienna (/b)* - **Billy Joel**

Over the years I have recorded albums and added bonus tracks that didn't appear on the albums originally but were somehow connected, like B sides, edited versions, extended versions, live versions, remixed, or restructured versions.

29.6 ~ Album Bonus Tracks

1. *Abacab, [ABACAB]* **Genesis**

2. *Bad & A Sort Of Homecoming [RATTLE & HUM]* **U2**

3. *Bass Trap, Love Comes Tumbling & Three Sunrises [UNFORGETTABLE FIRE]* **U2**

4. *City Of Love (Live) & It Can Happen (Live) [9012LIVE]* **Yes**

5. *Deep In The Heart, Hold On To Love, Silver & Gold, Spanish Eyes, Sweetest Thing & Walk To The Water [THE JOSHUA TREE]* **U2**

6. *Flying North, One Of Our Submarines & Windpower [BLINDED BY SCIENCE / THE GOLDEN AGE OF WIRELESS]* **Thomas Dolby**

7. *Hold Me Thrill Me, Kiss Me Kill Me [ACHTUNG BABY]* **U2**

8. *Inside & Out* [US & UK] *[WIND & WUTHERING]* **Genesis**

9. *Into The Lens* [US & UK] *& Run Through The Light* [US] *[DRAMA]* **Yes**

10. *New Year's Day [WAR]* **U2**

11. *Pharoahs & When In Love With A Blind Man [SONGS FROM THE BIG CHAIR]* **Tears For Fears**

12. *Soon* [US] *[RELAYER]* **Yes**

13. *You Started Laughing [CRISIS? WHAT CRISIS?]* **Supertramp**

THIRTY

SINGLES AS VISUAL ART III
HOMEMADE PICTURE SLEEVES

This is the third and final chapter that talks about singles as visual art. For singles in my collection that didn't have picture sleeves, I made my own. This was like arts and crafts all over again, measuring, cutting (on a real mat), gluing, taping, marking & labeling. The best materials were covers from albums (OAC), cassettes (OCAC, OCSC), concert programs (CPC), piano music (PVCC) and postcards (POST). These were all original items, not copies or facsimiles, and not taken from books about album covers or live concerts with many artists.

The four groups of homemade sleeves *[gem]* that follow make up one a category of singles, the largest category in size in the entire story, along with the songs with organ category back in the *What is classic?* chapter.

The Old Album Cover materials means I have acquired at least one other copy of an album along the way, paving way for me to use the first album covers for the homemade picture sleeves. These albums were albums I liked and played so much that I had to buy replacements. Good news bad news here, I was able to use the covers to make single covers but I had to buy another copy of the album in the process.

Here is the first group, the homemade picture sleeves from old album covers…

30.1 ~ Homemade I - Album Covers
1. *America // Your Move & America / Total Mass Retain [YESTERDAYS], Going For The One & Wonderous Stories (UK & US) [GOING FOR THE ONE] & Roundabout / Long Distance Runaround [FRAGILE]* **Yes**
2. *Another Day & Uncle Albert & Admiral Halsey [WINGS GREATEST HITS] & Letting Go & Venus & Mars Rock Show [VENUS & MARS]* **Paul McCartney & Wings**
3. *California Jam, [3.47 E. S. T.] & We're Off Ya Know [HOPE]* **Klaatu**

4. *Call On Me / Prelude To Aire & Feeling Stronger Everyday [CHICAGO IX, GREATEST HITS]* **Chicago**
5. *Crazy [FAMOUS LAST WORDS], Dreamer / Bloody Well Right [CRIME OF THE CENTURY] & Logical Song // Goodbye Stranger [BREAKFAST IN AMERICA]* **Supertramp**
6. *Fanfare For The Common Man [WORKS VOL. 1], Honky Tonk Train Blues & I Believe in Father Christmas [WORKS VOL. 2] & Jerusalem [BRAIN SALAD SURGERY]* **Emerson, Lake & Palmer**
7. *Follow You, Follow Me / Ballad Of Big [AND THEN THERE WERE THREE], Follow You, Follow Me // A Trick Of The Tail [A TRICK OF THE TAIL], Taking It All Too Hard / Silver Rainbow [GENESIS] & Your Own Special Way / It's Yourself [WIND & WUTHERING]* **Genesis**
8. *Games People Play / Ace Of Swords, Snake Eyes / I Don't Wanna Go Home & Time / The Gold Bug [TURN OF A FRIENDLY CARD] & Psychobabble / Children Of The Moon & You're Gonna Get Your Fingers Burned / Psychobabble [EYE IN THE SKY]* **The Alan Parsons Project**
9. *I Got You [TRUE COLOURS] & Pioneer & Six Months In A Leaky Boat [TIME & TIDE]* **Split Enz**

The second group covers full paged art like album covers, Books (B), Calendars (CA), Concert Programs (CO) and Piano Music (PI).

30.2 ~ *Homemade II - Book Covers*

1. *Abacab // No Reply At All & No Reply At All / Dodo [ABACAB_CO], Mama // In Too Deep [MAMA_CO] & No Son Of Mine [DELUXE ANTHOLOGY_PI]* **Genesis**
2. *Ain't Nobody But Me [CRISIS? WHAT CRISIS?_PI], Give A Little Bit // Dreamer [EVEN IN THE QUIETIST MOMENTS_PI / CRIME OF THE CENTURY_PI] & Take The Long Way Home // It's Raining Again [BREAKFAST IN AMERICA_PI]* **Supertramp**
3. *And You & I Pt. 1 & Lift Me Up [UNION_CO], Into The Lens (I Am A Camera) / Does It Really Happen? [DRAMA_CO], Owner Of A Lonely Heart // Leave It [90125_CO], Release Release / Don't Kill The Whale [TORMATO_CO], Roundabout // Your Move [FRAGILE_PI], Run Through The Light [YES COMPLETE PIANO] & Your Move / The Clap [THE YES ALBUM_PI]* **Yes**
4. *Beginnings // Questions 67 & 68 & Colour My World // I'm A Man [CHICAGO GOLD_PI]* **Chicago**
5. *C'est La Vie, Lucky Man // From The Beginning & Peter Gunn / Tiger In A Spotlight (Live) [ELP PIANO]* **Emerson Lake & Palmer**
6. *Hi Hi Hi, Live & Let Die & Maybe I'm Amazed* live *[WINGS OVER AMERICA_PI]* **Wings**
7. *I Still Haven't Found What I'm Looking For / Spanish Eyes & Where The Streets Have No Name / Silver & Gold [THE JOSHUA TREE_B], I Still Haven't Found What I'm Looking For // Where The Streets Have No Name & With Or Without You // In God's Country [THE JOSHUA TREE_PI] & New Year's Day / Treasure [THE PIANO COLLECTION]* **U2**
8. *If You Leave [BEST OF OMD_PI]* **Orchestral Manoeuvres In The Dark**
9. *Imagine, (CA)* **John Lennon**
10. *Money [DARK SIDE OF THE MOON_PI]* **Pink Floyd**

11. *Still In The Game & Valerie [TALKING BACK TO THE NIGHT_PI]* **Steve Winwood**
12. *You Don't Believe [BEST OF THE ALAN PARSONS PROJECT_PI]* **The Alan Parsons Project**

The third group includes Cassette Albums (CA), Cassette Singles (CS), Decals (DC), Newspaper Colour Photos (NPCP) & Postcards (PC)

30.3 ~ Homemade III - Various
1. *Big Time, In Your Eyes, Red Rain & Sledgehammer, [SO_PC]* **Peter Gabriel**
2. *Black Dog // Misty Mountain Hop, Immigrant Song // Hey Hey What Can I Do, Stairway To Heaven // Whole Lotta Love & Whole Lotta Love // Living Loving Maid, (DC), Communication Breakdown // Good Times Bad Times, [LED ZEPPELIN I_PC] & Rock & Roll // Four Sticks [IV ZOSO_DC]* **Led Zeppelin**
3. *Calling Elvis [ON EVERY STREET_CA] & Industrial Disease, (NPCP)* - **Dire Straits**
4. *Cinderella Man / A Farewell To Kings (NPCP)* **Rush**
5. *Don't You (Forget About Me) // Alive & Kicking [ONCE UPON A TIME_PC]* **Simple Minds**
6. *Everyday Is A Winding Road (CS)* **Sheryl Crowe**
7. *Gloria // Sunday Bloody Sunday [UNDER A BLOOD RED SKY_PC], I Will Follow (Live) // Pride (In The Name Of Love) [THE UNFORGETTABLE FIRE_PC] & New Year's Day // Two Hearts Beat As One, (PC)* **U2**
8. *If I Ever Lose My Faith In You [THE SUMMONERS TALE_PC] & If You Love Somebody, Set Them Free, (NPCP)* **Sting**
9. *Land Of Confusion // Tonight Tonight Tonight & Land Of Confusion / Feeding The Fire, (PC)* **Genesis**
10. *Let Go The Line (NPCP)* **Max Webster**
11. *Rhythm Of Love / City Of Love (Live) [BIG GENERATOR_DC] & Soon, (PC)* **Yes**
12. *These Eyes (PC)* **The Guess Who**

The fourth and final group is full paged art using interior pages of Piano Books (PII) and Record Sleeves (SL),

30.4 ~ Homemade IV - Interiors
1. *25 Or 6 To 4 / Where Do We Go From Here, Does Anybody Really Know What Time It Is? // Free & Lowdown / Loneliness Is Just A Word & Make Me Smile // 25 Or 6 To 4, [CHICAGO ANTHOLOGY 1_PII], Gone Long Gone, [HOT STREETS_SL], Hard Habit To Break // You're The Inspiration, [CHICAGO XVII_SL], Old Days / Hideaway [CHICAGO VIII_SL] & Wishing You Were Here [CHICAGO IX GREATEST HITS_SL]* **Chicago**
2. *Enola Gay, Joan Of Arc, Secret, Souvenir & Tesla Girl [BEST OF OMD_PII]* **Orchestral Manoeuvres in The Dark**
3. *Entangled / Ripples [A TRICK OF THE TAIL_SL] & Man On The Corner / Submarine [ABACAB_SL]* **Genesis**
4. *Fool In The Rain [IN THROUGH THE OUT DOOR_SL]* **Led Zeppelin**
5. *Hotel California / Pretty Maids All In A Row [HOTEL CALIFORNIA_SL]* **The Eagles**
6. *Just The Way You Are // She's Always A Woman To Me [THE STRANGER_SL]* **Billy Joel**

I started the homemade picture sleeves in college, in the early 1980s. I carefully chose covers from albums, concert programs, decals, piano music, postcards and tapes so there were no disconnects, meaning the right album(s) for the right song(s) inside the sleeve. None of the artwork covers are copies. They are all originals. I also created cassette covers, using many of the same sources that I had used for my singles. It's interesting that for a record collection so focused on the sounds of each song, I was also very focused on the visual aspect.

THIRTY - ONE

45 R P AMBLE ROUNDUP
THE BUILDING
BLOCKS

One was **music performance**, there were piano lessons, mom playing music on the radio and dad playing records on the stereo, me playing in the high school concert and stage bands and singing with mom and dad in the church choir when I was in university.

Two was **top forty radio**, Yes *Roundabout* from Watertown New York in 1972, 1430 CKFH (1972) after Maple Leaf hockey games and 1050 CHUM (1973) in Toronto, CFRA 58 and CFGO 1440 in Ottawa (1973) and CFTR 680 in Toronto.

Three was the look and the sound of **collecting 7" 45 rpm singles**, quite different from albums because they usually weren't sealed. There were coloured disks, double hits, gatefold & foldout styles, sleeves with pictures and lyrics, and different versions (short, long & remixed). There were many genres like blues, celtic, country, dance, folk, gospel, new wave, pop, rock & soul.

Four was a subgroup of **Three, the 7" single B sides**. Sure, people may refer to vinyl albums as having a side one and a side two but anyone who is anyone refers to singles as having an A side and a B side. The B sides were where all the treasures were, especially live versions of the A side or other songs altogether. Best of all were the B sides that were originals, never released on the original vinyl albums.

Five was the world of **charts**, starting in 1973 with weekly and annual CHUM charts and then all-time CFGO charts. Later there were chart books, many chart books.

Six was **equipment** starting with a mono tape recorder in 1974, the beginning of my vinyl backups, and continuing with an amplifier, turntable, tape decks, CD platters and CD music burners, along with bottle caps, tape shells & tape spools.

Seven was **recording** on audio tape from both record and radio, deciding which songs would go together and later, in the era of City Lights and Much Music, recording on video tape, with lots and lots of dubbing.

Eight was **Yes** *Roundabout* in 1972 and again in 1975 and **progressive rock albums** by Yes, Supertramp, Genesis, ELP, Alan Parsons and Pink Floyd. The focus here was on groups rather than solo artists.

Nine was **FM Radio**, including CKCU in 1975, CHEZ in 1977, CHUM FM, Q107 in 1977 and CFNY in the early 80s.

Ten as **attending live concerts** and collecting concert programs, starting with Gentle Giant, Starcastle in 1976 and Supertramp & April Wine in 1977.

Eleven was **Piano music** like *Chicago Gold* in 1976 and *Wings Over America* in 1977

Twelve was the **geography of collecting singles**. They were made all over the place, Canada, America, Britain, Germany, France, Holland & Italy. And they were bought all over the place too. The collection is basically seventies in nature, outnumbering eighties titles by about two to one.

Thirteen was **New Wave music** in the early eighties, *NeWavEighties*, fueled by stations like CFNY, *The Spirit Of Radio*, long before it was *Modern Rock.*

Fourteen was a **record inventory** in 1983, a **singles inventory** in 1984, a singles update by brother Andrew in 1990, *Mzk01* lists in 2001, and then my singles update in 2009 as *th45zz*. I also created terms to describe them.

Fifteen was **making 7" single picture sleeves** starting in 1982 and later cassette covers with Crayola & Sharpie markers.

Sixteen was a **chance to meet celebrities**, like Andy Frost from Q107 in 2007 and Randy Bachman of The Guess Who and BTO in 2010.

For this list only, I have made references in the singles appendices for a number of these entries down to the specific number, like 31.1.25 for *Sister Golden Hair Charts.*

31.1 ~ Seventeen, All Those Hidden Gems…

1. *1050 CHUM's Steve Elliott* \ '76, *25.9*
2. *A 45 R P aMble* \ '06, *Intro*
3. *All Five Going Songs Have Endings* \ '77, *ch.17*
4. *All Roads Lead To Yes* \ '00, *app.22*
5. *Benchmarks* \ '20, *ch.28, MK 1-21*
6. *Black Moon & Canada's Wonderland, The Two Carousels* \ '92, *ch.14*
7. *(The) CFGO Century Gothic Chart* \ '74, *ch.25*
8. *CFGO Live Weekend Sounded Like FM* \ '76, *ch.25*
9. *Christmas Time Sounds Like Good Old Top 40 Radio* \ '15, *ch.26*
10. *Classical Rock* \ '14 \ '22, *29.4*
11. *Close Revealing Gates Awaken* \ '14, *18.1*
12. *Components & The Mies Van Der Rohe Effect* \ '90s, *ch.7*
13. *Crazy Hippie Organ Music* \ '79, *19.7*
14. *(The) Dark Side Of The Label* \ '23, *2.5 & 2.11*
15. *Dream Rain Time* \ '90s, *12.5*
16. *Genesis Selling A Trick Dance* \ '14, *14.2*
17. *Homemade Picture Sleeves* \ '82, *30.1-30.4*
18. *Merry Christmas Rock* \ '93, *29.3*
19. *Mzk01* \ '01, *Intro*
20. *(The) Needle Drop &The Power Of Love* \ '07, *ch.6, ch.8 & 29.1*
21. *(The) NeWavEighties* \ '15, *12.1-12.5, 19.11*
22. *Record Dolby on playback Dolby off* \ '84, *ch.8*

PART B

APPENDICIES

ONE

ALBUMS

1. **Beatles, The** - *Revolver, Rubber Soul, Sgt. Pepper's Lonely Hearts Club Band, Magical Mystery Tour, 1962 - 1966, 1967 - 1970, Rock & Roll Music (Volumes 1 & 2) & Love Songs*
2. **Buggles, The** - *Adventures In Modern Recording*
3. **Chicago** - *IX Greatest Hits & If You Leave Me Now*
4. **Clapton, Eric** - *Greatest Hits*
5. **Crow, Sheryl** - *Tuesday Night Music Club*
6. **Dolby, Thomas** - *Blinded By Science, The Golden Age Of Wireless & The Flat Earth*
7. **Doobie Brothers, The** - *Best Of*
8. **Eagles, The** - *Their Greatest Hits*
9. **Electric Light Orchestra, The** - *OLE ELO & Greatest Hits*
10. **Emerson, Lake & Palmer** - *Tarkus, Brain Salad Surgery, Works Volume I, Works Volume II & Black Moon*
11. **Fixx, The** - *Shuttered Room, Reach The Beach & Phantoms*
12. **Foreigner** - *Foreigner, Double Vision, 4 & Agent Provocateur*
13. **Genesis** - *Selling England By The Pound, The Lamb Lies Down On Broadway, A Trick Of The Tail, Wind & Wuthering, And Then There Were Three, Duke, Abacab, Genesis, Invisible Touch & We Can't Dance*
14. **John, Elton** - *Greatest Hits*
15. **Kansas** - *Leftoverture*
16. **Led Zeppelin** - *Zoso (IV) & In Through The Out Door*
17. **Lennon, John** - *Shaved Fish & John Lennon Collection*
18. **Lighthouse** - *Good Day*
19. **McCartney, Paul** - *Wings Greatest, Give My Regards To Broad Street & All The Best*
20. **Moody Blues, The** - *Days Of Future Passed & Long Distance Voyageur*
21. **Morisette, Alanis** - *Jagged Little Pill*
22. **Parsons Project, The Alan** - *I Robot, Turn Of A Friendly Card, Eye In The Sky, Ammonia Avenue & Stereotomy*
23. **Pink Floyd** - *Dark Side Of The Moon, Wish You Were Here, Animals & (The) Wall*
24. **Pogues, The** - *If I Should Fall From Grace With God*
25. **Police, The** - *Outlandos D'Amour, Regatta De Blanc, Zenyatta Mondatta, Ghost In The Machine & Synchronicity*
26. **Procal Harum** - *Live With The Edmonton Symphony Orchestra*
27. **Simple Minds** - *New Gold Dream, Sparkle In The Rain, Once Upon A Time, Street Fighting Years & Real Life*
28. **Supertramp** - *Crime Of The Century, Crisis? What Crisis?, Even In The Quietist Moments, Breakfast, In America, Paris, Famous Last Words & Brother Where You Bound*
29. **Tears For Fears** - *The Hurting, Saturnine Martial & Lunatic, Songs From The Big Chair &*

Sowing The Seeds Of Love

30. **Thompson Twins** - *Into The Gap & Out Of The Gap*
31. **Three Dog Night** - *Golden Biscuits & Joy To The World*
32. **U2** - *War, Under A Blood Red Sky, The Unforgettable Fire, The Joshua Tree, Rattle & Hum, The Best of 1980-1990, Achtung Baby, All That You Can't Leave Behind & The Best of 1990-2000, Songs Of Surrender*
33. **Vangelis** - *Blade Runner*
34. **Various Soundtrack** - *Batman Forever*
35. **Webber, Andrew Lloyd & Tim Rice** - *J C Superstar*
36. **Who, The** - *Tommy*
37. **Winwood, Steve** - *Arc Of A Diver, Talking Back To The Night, Back In The High Life, Roll With It*
38. **Yes** - *Fragile, Close To The Edge, Yessongs, Tales From Topographic Oceans, Relayer, Going For The One, Tormato, Drama, Yesshows, Classic Yes, 90125, Union, Talk, The Ladder & Fly From Here*

TWO

B SIDES

These lists are extensions of the B Side lists 4.9, 4.10 & 11.4.

Beatles Family
1. *The Mess (My Love)* - **Paul & Wings**
2. *Mull Of Kintyre (Girls' School)* - **Wings**

Genesis Family
1. *Evidence Of Autumn (Misunderstanding)* - ***Duke***
2. *Inside & Out (Spot The Pigeon)*
3. *Twilight Alehouse (Your Own Special Way)* - ***Wind & Wuthering***

The Police
1. *Low Life (Spirits In The Material World - UK)* - ***Ghost In The Machine***
2. *Murder By Numbers (Every Breath You Take)* - ***Synchronicity***
3. *Sermon (De Do Do Do De Da Da Da & Don't Stand So Close To Me)* - ***Zenyatta Mondatta***
4. *Someone To Talk To (King Of Pain & Wrapped Around Your Finger)* - ***Synchronicity***

Simple Minds
1. *Brass Band In Africa (Up On The Catwalk)* - ***Sparkle In The Rain***
2. *Theme For Great Cities (Promised You A Miracle)* - ***New Gold Dream***
3. *Theme For Great Cities 91 (See The Lights)* - ***Real Life***

U2
1. *Boomerang II (Pride (In The Name Of Love))* - ***The Unforgettable Fire***
2. *Dancing Barefoot (When Love Comes To Town)* - ***Rattle & Hum***
3. *Endless Deep (Two Hearts Beat As One)* - ***War***
4. *Hallelujah Here She Comes (Desire)* - ***Rattle & Hum***
5. *Treasure (New Years Day)* - ***War***
6. *Unchained Melody (All I Want Is You)* - ***Rattle & Hum***

THREE

BOOK LORE

Note that *Rocking The Classics, by* Edward Macan, references five other books in my list.

1. *100 Best Selling Albums of the 60s, 70s, 80s & 90s,* Amber Books, 2004
2. *100 Top Singles From 1963 - 1988,* Rolling Stone Magazine, 1988
3. *1000 Record Covers,* Michael Ochs, Taschen, 1996
4. *101 Gadgets That Changed The World,* Popular Mechanics Magazine, July 2011
5. *101 Greatest American Rock Songs,* Emily Gatlin, Bob Guccione Jr Magazine, 2016
6. *25 Albums That Rocked The World,* Chris Charlesworth, Omnibus Press, 2008
7. *30th Anniversary Of Hotel California,* Guitar World Acoustic Magazine, April 2007
8. *70s, The,* Ted Yates, Collectors Guide, 2011
9. *90125 (PVC - Piano / Vocal / Chords),* Yes, Warner, 1984
10. *90125 (Tour - Concert Tour Book),* Yes, 1984
11. *Abacab (Tour),* Genesis, 1982
12. *Agent Provocateur (Tour),* Foreigner, 1985
13. *Album Cover Album, Hipgnosis & Roger Dean, 1977*
14. *Alices Adventures In Wonderland,* Lewis Carroll, 1865
15. *All Time Top 1000 Albums,* Colin Larkin, Muze, 1999
16. *American Music (To 1955),* Gilbert Chase, McGraw-Hill
17. *Anderson, Jon,* Prog Magazine, Aug 2016
18. *Beatles 100 Greatest Songs,* Rolling Stone Magazine, 2010
19. *Beatles As Musicians, Quarrymen To Rubber Soul,* Walter Everett, Oxford University Press, 2001
    [21. *Beatles The Authorized Biography,* Hunter Davies, William Heinman, London, 1968]
20. *Beatles Illustrated Lyrics,* Alan Aldridge, Dalacorte Press, 1969
21. *Beatles The Authorized Biography,* Hunter Davies, William Heinman, London, 1968
22. *Beatles Ultimate Album Guide,* Rolling Stone Magazine, 2019
23. *Best Of OMD (Orchestral Manoeuvres In The Dark), The (PVC),* Virgin Music, 1988
24. *Best Of The Alan Parsons Project, The (PVC),* Columbia Pictures Publications, 1983
25. *Billboard Book Of Christmas In The Charts,* Joel Whitburn, Record Research, 2004
26. *Billboard Book Of Top 40 Albums,* Joel Whitburn, Watson-Guptill, 1991
27. *Billboard Book Of Top 40 Hits, 5th Edition,* Joel Whitburn, Billboard Publications, 1992
28. *Billboard Book Of Top 40 Hits, 9th Edition,* Joel Whitburn, Billboard Publications, 2010
29. *Billy Joel Live At Madison Square Garden,* Chuck Arnold, 2024
30. *Bobby Orr & The Big Bad Bruins,* Stan Fischler, Dell Publishing, 1970
31. *Breakfast In America (PVC),* Supertramp, Almo Publications, 1979
32. *Breakfast In America With Supertramp,* Martin Melhuish, The New Music, October 1978.
33. *Breakfast In Canada*, concert review, Alan Neister, Toronto Star, July 1979
34. *B-Side,* Andy Cowan, Headpress, 2023

35. *Chicago Anthology One (PVC)*, Columbia Pictures Productions, 1975

36. *Chicago Gold (PVC)*, Screen Gems Columbia, 1975

37. *CHUM Chart Book*, Stardust Productions, 1984

38. *Classic Rock,* All Music Guide, Backbeat Books, 2007

39. *Classic Rock,* Keyboard Presents, Ernie Rideout, Backbeat Books, 2010

40. *Crime Of The Century (PVC),* Supertramp, Almo Publications, 1974

41. *Crisis? What Crisis? (PVC),* Supertramp, Almo Publications, 1975

42. *Daredevil Goalie Roger Crozier*, Tom Cohen, Rutledge books, 1967

43. *Dark Side Of The Moon (PVC),* Pink Floyd, TRO, 1973

44. *Dean, Roger, 1994 Calendar*, Pomegranate Calendars & Books

45. *Desert Island Discs*, Ian Gittens, Penguin, 2022

46. *Drama,* Yes (Tour), 1980

47. *Eagles,* The Record Collector Presents, 2024,

48. *Eagles The Ultimate Guide*, Rolling Stone Magazine, January 2022

49. *Element, The,* Ken Robinson, Penguin Books, 2009

50. *Emerson, Keith,* Prog Magazine, November 2023

51. *Emerson, Lake & Palmer (PVC),* Warner Bros, 1978

52. *Emerson, Lake & Palmer Greatest Hits (PVC),* Music Sales America, 1996

53. *Emerson, Lake & Palmer,* Prog Magazine, April 2020

54. *Emerson, Lake & Palmer Live At The Royal Albert Hall* (VHS), 1993

55. *Encyclopedia Of New Wave,* Daniel Bukszpan, Sterling New York, 2012

56. *Even in the Quietist Moments (PVC),* Supertramp, Almo Publications, 1977

57. *Fragile / The Yes Album (PVC)*, Cotillion, 1972

58. *Genesis Deluxe Anthology (PVC)*, Hit & Run, 1993

59. *Genesis, The Ultimate Music Guide,* Uncut Magazine, Feb 2019

60. *Genesis, Their 40 Greatest Songs,* Prog Magazine, July 2019

61. *Give My Regards To Broad Street,* Paul McCartney, Pavilion, 1984

62. *Gordie Howe,* Stan Fischler, Grossett & Dunlap, 1967

63. *Growing Up With The Hits*, Nevin Grant, Manor House, 2015

64. *Here There & Everywhere, The 100 Best Beatles Songs*, Stephen Spignesi & Michael Lewis, Black Dog & Leventhal, New York, 2004.

65. *Hit Singles Top 20 Charts US & UK,* Dave McAleer, Carlton Books, 1994

66. *I've Got To Be Me*, Derek Sanderson & Stan Fischler, Dell Publishing, 1972

67. *Infographic Guide To Music,* Graham Betts, Cassell, 2014

68. *Is This Live? The Story Of Much Music,* Christopher Ward, Random House Canada, 2016

69. *Joshua Tree, The (PVC),* U2, Alfred Music, 1987

70. *Joshua Tree, The (Tour),* U2, 1987

71. *Led Zeppelin, Inside Their Music & Legend*, Rolling Stone Magazine, March 2022

72. *Lennon, John,* Uncut Magazine, August 2024

73. *Live Aid* - Peter Hillmore, Unicorn, 1985

74. *Magnetic Storm* - Martin Dean, Dragons World, 1984

75. *Mama (Tour)*, Genesis, 1983

76. *McCartney, 40 years,* Rolling Stone Magazine, 2013

77. *Mike Booklet I - Charts - CFGO & CFRA,* Mike, Mite, 1976

78. *Mike Booklets II - Discographies - Beatles, Genesis, Led Zeppelin, Rush,* Mike, Mite, 1976

79. *Mike Booklets III - Inventories - Records & Tapes,* Mike, Mite, 1976

80. *Mike Booklets IV - Top 100s,* Mike, Mite, 1976

81. *Mothership, (GT),* Led Zeppelin, Alfred Publishing, 2008

82. *Muntz Tape Guide,* 1974

83. *Music Is History,* Questlove, Abrams Image, New York, 2021

84. *Music That Rocked The World,* Peter Murray, Rockus, 2008

85. *New Rolling Stone Record Guide,* Dave Marsh & John Swenson, 1983

86. *Not Dead Yet,* Phil Collins, Crowne Archetype, 2016

87. *Off The Record: An Oral History Of Popular Music,* Joe Smith & Mitchell Fink, Grand Central Publishing, 1989

88. *Obsolete,* Anna Jane Grossman, Harry N Abrahms, 2009

89. *Prog 10 Years,* Prog Magazine, 2020

90. *Prog 100,* Prog Magazine, Aug 2019

91. *Record Store Days,* Gary Calamar & Phil Gallo, Sterling, New York, 2009

92. *Relayer (PVC),* Yes, Topographic Music, 1975

93. *Revolution, The History Of Turntable Design,* Gideon Schwartz, Phaidon.com, 2022

94. *Ringo, The Ultimate Music Guide,* Uncut Magazine, July 2019

95. *Rocking The Classics,* Edward Macan, Oxford University Press, 1997

    [13. *Album Cover Album,* Hipgnosis & Roger Dean, 1977]

    [41. *Dark Side Of The Moon (PVC),* Pink Floyd, TRO, 1973]

    [48. *Emerson, Lake & Palmer (PVC)*, Warner Bros, 1978]

    [119. *Yes Complete Deluxe Edition (PVC),* Warner Bros, 1981]

    [121. *Yes The Authorized Biography,* Dan Hedges, Sidgewick & Jackson, 1981]

96. *Simple Minds Walk Between Worlds & The Birth Of Synth Pop,* Classic Pop Magazine, Feb 2018

97. *Songs and Artists 2006,* Joel Whitburn, Record Research

98. *Songs From The Big Chair (PVC),* Tears For Fears, Nymph Music, 1985

99. *Squire, Chris,* Prog Magazine, Aug 2015

100. *Sting, The Stories Behind His Greatest Songs,* 360Media Magazine, 2023

101. *The Story Of Blondie,* 360Media Magazine, 2024

102. Supertramp articles about *Working Title* (*Breakfast In America*) by Ritchie Yorke, 1978.

103. *Supertramp Book,* Martin Malhuish, Omnibus Press, 1986

104. *Supertramp Returns To Loyal Fans,* Henry Mietkiewicz, Toronto Star, 1983.

105. *Surrealscapes 2011 Calendar,* Roger Dean, Sellers Publishing

106. *Tales From Beyond The Tap,* Randy Bachman, Penguin Group, 2014

107. *Talk (PVC),* Yes, Alfred Music, 1994

108. *Talk (Tour),* Yes, 1994

109. *Talking Back To The Night (PVC),* Steve Winwood, Warner Bros, 1982

110. *Tears For Fears Relive The Seeds Of Love,* Classic Pop Magazine, Nov/Dec 2020.

111. *This Is Your Brain On Music,* Daniel Levitin, First Plume, 2007

112. *To Feel The Music,* Neil Young & Phil Baker, BenBella Books, 2019

113. *Top 20 Charts,* Tony Jasper, BBC & Top Of The Pops, Blandford Press, 1984

114. *Top 40 Hits,* Nanda Lwin, Music Data Canada, 2000

115. *Tormato (Tour),* Yes, 1979

116. *U2 The Piano Collection (PVC),* Hal Leonard, 2006

117. *U2 The Stories Behind Every Song,* Niall Stokes, Carlton, 1997

118. *U2,* Record Collector Presents, 2022

119. *Unforgettable Fire,* Eamon Dunphy, Viking, 1987

120. *Union (Tour),* Yes, 1991

121. *Views,* Roger Dean, Dragons World, 1975

122. *(The) Walrus & The Carpenter, Through The Looking Glass*, Lewis Carroll, 1871.

123. *War & Peace*, Tolstoy, 1867

124. *Wings Over America (PVC)*, MPL Communications, 1977

125. *World Almanac & Book Of Facts - 73, 74, 75, 76, 77, 78 & 79*

126. *Yes Complete Deluxe Edition (PVC)*, Warner Bros, 1981

127. *Yes Complete Story,* Classic Rock Platinum Magazine, January 2022

128. *Yes The Authorized Biography,* Dan Hedges, Sidgewick & Jackson, 1981

129. *Yes The Ultimate Music Guide,* Uncut Magazine, 2018

130. *Yesyears* (Bklt), 1991

131. *Yesyears* (VHS), 1991

FOUR

BRANDS

MEDIA \ Basf \ Denon \ Fuji \ Hp \ Kodak \ Maxell \ Memorex \ RCA \ Philips \ Polaroid \ Sony \ Tdk

RECORD LABELS \ A&M \ ABC Dunhill \ Anthem \ Apple \ Aquarius \ Arista \ Asylum \ Atco \ Atlantic \ Bell \ Capital \ Casablanca \ CBS \ Chrysalis \ Cotillion \ Elektra \ Epic \ Famous Charisma \ GRT \ Island \ Jet \ Jive \ Lion \ London \ MCA \ MGM \ Mercury \ Motown \ Mushroom \ Nimbus 9 \ Polydor \ Polygram \ RAK \ Reprise \ Sire \ UA \ UNI \ Virgin \ Warner \ WEA

STEREO EQUIPMENT \ Aiwa \ Bose \ Denon \ JVC \ Mission \ Panasonic \ Pioneer \ Sanyo \ Soma \ Sony \ Teac \ Technics \ Yamaha

FIVE

CHART LORE

WEEKLY

1. \ Billboard \ US \ 83 91
2. \ CFGO \ Ottawa \ 73 74 75 76 77
3. \ CFNY \ Brampton \ Albums \ 87
4. \ CFNY \ Brampton \ Into The Eighties \ 82
5. \ CFNY \ Brampton \ Singles \ 89
6. \ CFRA \ Ottawa \ 73 74 75 77
7. \ CFTR \ Toronto \ 76 80 81 82 83 84 85 90 91
8. \ CHEZ \ Ottawa \ 91
9. \ CHFGO \ Mike \ Toronto \ 73 74 75 76
10. \ CHUM AM \ Toronto \ 72 73 74 75 \ NP 76 80 82 83 84 85 86
11. \ CHUM FM \ Toronto \ 80 82 83 84 85 86 87 88
12. \ CJBK \ London \ 83 84 85
13. \ CKLW \ Windsor \ 71
14. \ CKOC \ Hamilton \ 76 77 78 79 82 83 85
15. \ CKSL \ London \ 85 88
16. \ De Nederland Top 40 \ 83
17. \ FM 96 \ London \ Albums \ 81 82 83 85
18. \ Licorice Pizza 40 \ California \ 83
19. \ MITE \ Mike \ Toronto \ 73 74 75 76
20. \ Q107 \ Toronto \ Albums \ 79 80 82 83 84 85 86 87 88
21. \ Radio Glendon \ Toronto \ *Into The 80s* \ Albums & Singles \ 80 81 82
22. \ Radio Glendon \ Toronto \ *With A Bullet* \ Singles \ 80 81 82
23. \ (The) Record \ Canada \ Albums & Singles \ 85 86 87 88 89 90
24. \ Rock 102 \ Buffalo \ 87
25. \ Rolling Stone \ US \ 86 88
26. \ RPM \ Canada \ 82 85
27. \ Sam's \ Canada \ 88 89 92 93
28. \ WBEN FM \ Buffalo \ 82
29. \ WBLK \ Buffalo \ 83
30. \ WMGW \ Meadville \ Penn \ 76
31. \ WRKO \ Boston \ 76

ANNUAL

1. \ CFGO \ Ottawa \ 74 76 \
2. \ CFNY \ Brampton \ 82 83 84 88 90 91 \

3. \ CFRA \ Ottawa \ 73 74 \
4. \ CHUM AM \ Toronto \ (68 69 70 71 72) \ 73 79 81 82 83 84 85 \
5. \ CHUM AM \ Mike \ Toronto \ 74 75 76 \
6. \ CHUM FM \ Toronto \ 80 81 82 83 84 85 86 87 88 89 90
7. \ Q107 \ Toronto \ 84 85 86 87 97 98

ALL TIME

1. \ CFGO \ Ottawa \ 300 73
2. \ CFGO \ Ottawa \ 400 74
3. \ CFNY \ Brampton \ Top 102 Decade (80s) 90
4. \ CFNY \ Brampton \ all-time 82
5. \ CHUM AM \ Mike \ Toronto \ 300 75
6. \ CJBK \ London \ 300 84
7. \ CKDK \ Woodstock \ 1039 09
8. \ CKSL \ London \ 300 84
9. \ CKSL \ London \ 300 85
10. \ Q107 \ Toronto \ Classic 500 92
11. \ Q107 \ Toronto \ Songs Of The Century 2000
12. \ Q107 \ Toronto \ Top 107 70s 80
13. \ STEVE \ Toronto \ Top 50 70s 80
14. \ STEVE \ Toronto \ Top 50 80s 90

SIX

CONCERTS

1. April Wine \ Civic Centre \ Ottawa \ July 29, 1977
2. Bachman \ Randy \ Festival Theatre \ Stratford \ January 27, 2010
3. Bjorkquist \ Mill Stone \ Stratford \ 2015
4. Bonham (ELP) \ Kingswood Music Theatre \ Canada's Wonderland \ John \ Maple \ August 9, 1992
5. Cars *Panorama* \ CNE Grandstand \ Toronto \ August 28, 1980
6. Chapin \ Harry \ Forum \ Ontario Place \ Alex \ Toronto \ June 1978

7. Chicago \ CNE Bandshell \ Toronto \ June 14, 1983
8. Chicago \ CNE Grandstand \ Toronto \ September 6, 1987
9. Chicago *Heart & Soul* (Earth Wind & Fire) \ Molson Amphitheatre \ Toronto \ August 28, 2015
10. Chicago (& Earth, Wind & Fire) \ Budweiser Stage \ Toronto \ July 23, 2024

11. Classic Lightfoot Live \ Stratford Perth Museum \ July 09, 2023
12. De Burgh \ Chris (Supertramp) \ Civic Centre \ Ottawa \ July 3, 1977

13. Eagles *Hell Freezes Over* \ Exhibition Stadium \ John \ July 11, 1994

14. Earth Wind & Fire *Heart & Soul* (Chicago) \ Molson Amphitheatre \ Toronto \ August 28, 2015
15. Earth, Wind & Fire (& Chicago) \ Budweiser Stage \ Toronto \ July 23, 2024

16. Emerson, Lake & Palmer *Black Moon* (Bonham) \ Kingswood Music Theatre \ Canada's Wonderland \ John \ Maple \August 9, 1992
17. Emerson, Lake & Palmer (Jethro Tull) \ Kingswood Music Theatre \ Canada's Wonderland \ John \ Maple \ August 19, 1996

18. *Freedom* \ Stratford Festival \ August 27, 2021
19. Genesis *Abacab* \ CNE Grandstand \ Toronto \ August 28, 1982

20. Gentle Giant *Interview* (Starcastle) \ Civic Centre \ Ottawa \ June 26, 1976
21. Gentle Giant *Civilian* (Nash The Slash) \ Massey Hall \ Toronto \ May 10, 1980

22. Hackett \ Steve \ O'Keefe Centre \ Toronto \ September 21, 1980
23. Herman \ Woody *The Raven Speaks* \ Minkler Auditorium \ Seneca College \ North York \ Winter 1972
24. Idles \ Café De La Terrasse \ Glendon College \ York University \ Toronto \ Winter 1981
25. Jethro Tull (ELP) \ Kingswood Music Theatre \ Canada's Wonderland \ John \ Maple \ August 19, 1996

26. James \ Colin \ Lulu's \ Kitchener \ March 16, 1996

27. John \ Elton \ CNE Grandstand \ Toronto \ August 26, 1986
28. John \ Elton \ *Farewell Yellow Brick Road* \ Rogers Centre \ Toronto \ September 8, 2022

29. Kenton \ Stan \ National Arts Centre \ Ottawa \ January 1975
30. Kenton \ Stan \ *Journey To Capricorn* \ York University \ North York \ Summer 1976

31. Les Petites Tunes \ Little Trinity Church \ Toronto\ Winter 2005
32. Liverpool \ Earl Haig Collegiate \ North York \ 1978
33. Lobo \ Lansdowne Park \ Central Canadian Exhibition \ Ottawa \ August 1973
34. Luba \ Forum \ Ontario Place \ Toronto \ Summer 1984

35. Mad Pudding \ Albion Hotel \ Guelph \ Fall 1998
36. Mad Pudding \ C'est What \ Toronto \ Summer 1996

37. Mangione \ Chuck \ Forum \ Ontario Place \ Toronto \ Summer 1981
38. McBride \ Bob \ Britannia Park \ Ottawa \ Summer 1975
39. McCartney \ Paul \ *Flowers In The Dirt* \ Skydome \ Toronto \ December 7, 1989
40. Nash The Slash (Gentle Giant) \ Massey Hall \ Toronto \ May 10, 1980
41. Parsons Project \ Alan, The (Yes) \ Molson Amphitheatre \ John \ Toronto \ June 18, 1998

42. Pentatonix \ Van Andel Arena \ Grand Rapids \ Michigan \ June 2019
43. Pentatonix \ Budweiser Stage \ Toronto \ August 2023

44. Peterson \ Oscar \ York University \ North York \ Summer 1982
45. Peterson \ Oscar \ Roy Thomson Hall \ Toronto \ March 21, 1985

46. Rough Trade \ New College \ University Of Toronto \ 1981
47. Segato \ Lorraine \ The Diamond Club \ Toronto \ December 31, 1986

48. Speed Control \ Royal Canadian Legion \ Stratford \ Summer 2013
49. Speed Control \ Stratford Summer Music \ 2016

50. Starship *Knee Deep In The Hoopla* \ Kingswood Music Theatre \ Canada's Wonderland \ Maple \
      July 24, 1986
51. Starcastle (Gentle Giant) \ Civic Centre \ Ottawa \ June 26, 1976

52. Supertramp *Even In The Quietist Moments* (Chris De Burgh) \ Civic Centre \ Ottawa \ July 3, 1977
53. Supertramp *Breakfast In Canada* \ Exhibition Stadium \ Toronto \ July 21, 1979

54. Terraced Garden \ Larry's Hideaway \ Toronto \ July 26, 1984
55. Turner \ Tina *Private Dancer* \ CNE Grandstand \ Toronto \ August 14, 1985
56. White \ Ian \ Free Times Café \ Toronto
57. Wilcox \ David \ New College \ University Of Toronto \ Winter 1981

58. Yes *Tormato* \ Maple Leaf Gardens \ Toronto \ April 20, 1979

59. Yes *Drama* \ Maple Leaf Gardens \ Toronto \ August 29, 1980

60. Yes *90125* \ CNE Grandstand \ Toronto \ August 23, 1984

61. Yes *Big Generator* \ Maple Leaf Gardens \ Toronto \ December 6, 1987

62. Yes *Union* \ Skydome \ Toronto \ April 23, 1991

63. Yes *Talk* \ Kingswood Music Theatre \ John \ Maple \ August 31, 1994

64. Yes *Open Your Eyes* (Alan Parsons Project) \ Molson Amphitheatre \ John \ Toronto \ June 18, 1998

65. Yes *Ladder* \ Massey Hall \ John \ Toronto \ December 4, 1999

66. Yes *Magnification (Symphonic)* \ Molson Amphitheatre \ John \ Toronto \ August 28, 2001

67. Yes *Classic* \ Molson Amphitheatre \ John \ Toronto \ August 31, 2002

SEVEN

EARLY RAMBLE

"Whatever happened to the 45 RPM record?"

If this seems disjointed or incoherent, as you read through it, that's probably because it is. So just take it for what it is, a ramble.

A - GENERALLY SPEAKING

45 RPM records, or "singles", were considered a poor man's version of the LP record, meaning you couldn't afford the LP. Singles were what you heard on top forty AM radio, not the traditionally "less commercial" FM radio. Singles were poor versions of album tracks. Initially, the 45 was created in spite of the album, equaling the difference between 33 and 78 RPMs. Solos were shorter or non-existent. Otherwise, the singles just ended early.

Singles were inconvenient; after four minutes you had to change the record for another, rather than listen to an entire side of an album. Singles were poorly made. If they were punched off centre, you could tell, like you were listening on a boat.

Singles by themselves were inconvenient, but not when played and taped in succession. That made them sound more like albums, by more than one artist if you wished. Also, Bigger (/longer/) is not always better. Some songs have good long versions, while others just drone on way too long. Singles were sometimes the same versions as on the album, sometimes edited, or remixed. One song could have several versions. Mostly, it's nice to have more than one version (/short and long/) to listen to.

Singles were the symbol of AM radio, songs going up and down the charts. However, FM radio would not be what it is today without the DJs (/like John Majhor,[214] 1953-2007, 1050 CHUM[7] 1975-1986/) who spun the singles on AM radio.

The single sound was different as well. In fact, it may be stronger than the album sound, clearer vocals, less tinny guitar, and heavier bass. After all, the record is tracking faster through the grooves so there is less room for deviation or error. Geffen records[215] pushed the vinyl sandwich rule to the max. Their artists added more tracks to their albums and the sound suffered. It wasn't as good. Going a step further, vinyl singles may sound even better when you tape them. You can adjust the levels of the songs, just the way you like.

Use high bias chrome, not normal bias audio tapes and have Dolby noise reduction on when you record and off when you playback. The best scenario for taping is from turntable to tape deck. Belt and direct drive turntables are the best but the main thing is that you have one. When dubbing tape, use separate decks to control record levels and enhance sound. Record at normal speed or in real time. How can something

---

[214] John Mahjor, DJ, CHUM radio, Toronto, 1975-1986.
[215] Geffen Records, David Geffen, City?, Date?.

recorded at high speed sound as good? Short tapes are the strongest but 60 minute chrome tapes are no longer. For poor quality originals, commercial and homemade, take the tape out of the old shell and put it into a new one.

What better than to have two of your favourite songs on one disc, the double hit singles. Even if it is overkill, it's still nice to collect and have. Other singles start out as A and B sides and grow into double hit status, like Led Zeppelin on Atlantic Records or back to back album tracks like *Foreplay & Longtime* or *We Will Rock You & We Are the Champions*.

If Albums give you a fuller picture of what a group is about, then collecting singles from across a catalogue takes you a good part of the way there. It's when the singles are whittled down to the popular ones from the popular albums that you miss a groups' musical journey and the good, even great, music that went along with it. That is where radio stations spend most of their time.

On a side note, classic rock often means talented guitarists, bassists, or drummers but that's not all. Keyboardists are talented too, classically influenced and trained "art" and "progressive" rockers. The Eighties misunderstood classic rock. While some seventies groups reinvented themselves, others emerged for the first time. Of these, great bands like Simple Minds, Split Enz, Tears For Fears and The Fixx were passed over as "Classic".

UK singles have always been excellent in their sound quality, not to mention the convenience of small album style centres. Collecting singles into the nineties remained possible by UK and US makers, while Canadian makers were quick to phase out vinyl in favor of the CD.

While CDs and MP3s may be more convenient than vinyl, the sound has suffered. The pops and scratches are gone but the digital sound has been flattened. Highs, lows and loud sections are diminished, while midranges and soft sections are exaggerated. The warmth and contrast that is music is missing. I'll take a vinyl skip over a digital skip, any day.

Collecting singles with picture sleeve covers (mostly from the 1980s) meant collecting sometimes completely different covers from one country to another. Some picture sleeves even came in gatefold format, similar to many album jackets.

The silver linings of singles are the B-sides that did not always make their way on to an album. They are treasures, only to appear later on boxed sets, compilations, or repackaged albums.

B - PERSONALLY SPEAKING

Even my dad remarked, when this collection began in 1973, that in a few months I wouldn't be listening to the handful of singles I had collected to that point. Well, the handful now numbers almost 1800.

A Classmate commented early in high school that most of what was played on top forty radio was bubble gum. So about a year later, I started listening to FM Rock Radio, care of CKCU,[216] Ottawa's first, in November of 1975, and I also started buying albums, rather than just singles. However, the FM only idea lasted may be six months and then I went back to my AM roots. I decided then that both the FM (albums) and AM (singles) streams were important to stay in touch with popular music.

In 1972, *Roundabout* by Yes profoundly impacted my interest in popular music. After hearing it again in the summer of 1975, I began my search for the single. However, instead of finding it, I started collecting Yes albums, around the same time as my FM Radio Phase.

---

[216] CKCU FM 93.1, Carlton University, Ottawa, Ontario, 1975.

1975 marked the beginning of the end for the 45 rpm single, the final personal copies of top thirty charts for both CHUM radio in Toronto in April and CFRA[217] radio in Ottawa in July. The charts continued to appear as weekly newspaper versions but for collectors it just wasn't the same.

For singles that didn't have picture sleeves, I made my own. The best materials were covers from albums, cassettes, concert programs, piano music and postcards. These were all original items, not copies or facsimiles, and not taken from compilations of any kind.

This collection includes both what's popular and what spans across a groups catalogue and musical journey. Most of the singles are from the seventies and eighties, with only a handful from both the sixties and the nineties. Most notably absent are very many, if any (about four) songs by the Beatles. Most of those are on album, not part of this collection. Most recently, I have noted all the singles in this collection that appeared on the CKDK[218] (Woodstock, "The Hawk") *Top 1039 Of All Time*, back in January of 2008.

In all, I have created over two-hundred different possible attributes or tags for each song. Songs with the basic tags are printed in regular sentence case. Those with special tags are printed in upper case. Bold is shown for those with one of three attributes, double hit single, cover quality homemade picture sleeve, or charted on the last personal copy of the CHUM or CFRA Top 30. Those with at least two of these last three are printed in a larger font.

Long live the turntable and the audio tape deck and don't give up on your 45s.

---

[217] CFRA AM 580, Ottawa, Ontario, 1973.
[218] CKDK, FM 103.9, Woodstock, Ontario, 2007.

EIGHT

HIGHLIGHTS & IDEAS

1. 1st Homemade Picture Sleeve \ 82

2. Art \ Quilt \ 04
3. Book \ *Hit Singles* \ 10

4. Brands \ 7UP Rock Caps \ April Wine \ Crowbar \ Edward Bear,\ The Guess Who \ Lighthouse \ 73
5. Brands \ HMV London Oxford Street \ 84
6. Brands \ K-tel & Ronco \ 73

7. Charts \ *ZAP 20* \ 76

8. Equip \ 5 piece CD Platter \ 97
9. Equip \ Amplifier & Turntable \ 80
10. Equip \ CD Burner \ 08
11. Equip \ Double Tape Deck \ 92
12. Equip \ Headphones \ 75
13. Equip \ Recording Tower \ 08
14. Equip \ Soft Touch Tape Deck \ 82
15. Equip \ Stereo Tape Recorder \ 78
16. Equip \ Store 45s in clear Rubbermaid bins \ 90s
17. Equip \ Transistor Radio \ 72

18. Family & Friends \ Drew \ Singles \ 90s
19. Family & Friends \ Ian \ *Laser Rock* \ ROM Planetarium \ 78
20. Family & Friends \ Rich \ Chart Book \ Top Twenty \ 84

21. Film \ *Batman Forever* \ Soundtrack \ 19
22. Film \ *Blade Runner* \ 82
23. Film \ *Blade Runner* \ Soundtrack \ 19
24. Film \ *Fantasia* \ 71
25. Film \ *High Fidelity* \ 00

26. **Groups \ Beatles \ Beatles weekends \ CFGO & CFRA \ 74**
27. Groups \ Beatles \ *Sgt. Pepper & Rubber Soul* \ 17
28. Groups \ Buggles \ *Video Killed The Radio Star* \ 80

29. Groups \ Chicago \ Caribou TV Special \ 77

68. Groups \ Thomas Dolby \ *Blinded by Science* \ 83
69. Groups \ Thomas Dolby \ TED \ Music Director \ 06

70. Groups \ U2 \ *Achtung Baby & All That You Can't Leave Behind* \ 02
71. Groups \ U2 \ *Pride (In The Name Of Love)* \ 1st U2 pic sleeve \ 84
72. Groups \ U2 \ *Rattle & Hum* \ Album & Film \ 88
73. Groups \ U2 \ *Rattle & Hum* \ Picture Sleeve Singles \ 88
74. Groups \ U2 \ *The Joshua Tree* \ Picture Sleeve Singles \ 87
75. Groups \ U**2** \ ***The Much Videos*** \ **98**
76. Groups \ U2 \ *Unforgettable Fire Mini & Joshua Tree* Artwork \ 87

77. Groups \ Yes \ *Don't Kill The Whale* \ 1st Yes pic sleeve \ 79
78. Groups \ Yes \ *Fragile* \ Album \ 75
79. Groups \ Yes \ *Going For The One* album \ 1st current \ 2 of 3 \ 77
80. Groups \ Yes \ San Luis Obispo CA - 83 & 96 & 15 \ 83
81. Groups \ Yes \ *Soon (The Gates Of Delirium)* \ 05
82. Groups \ Yes \ Wakeman \ Stacking Keyboards \ 92
83. Groups \ Yes \ Logo *Yesyears* \ 91
84. Groups \ Yes \ Logo Classic \ 72
85. **Groups \ Yes *Tormato* tour taped \ CHUM FM \ 79**
86. Groups \ Yes \ *Yessongs* at Youth Easter Service after party \ 75

87. Label \ Crayola Colour Markers for cassettes \ 81
88. Label \ Sharpie Colour Markers for CDs \ 08
89. Label \ Sharpie Colour Pens for CDs \ 14

90. Lists \ 1 \ 1stRecord List \ 83
91. Lists \ 4 Draws' Version Of My Discography \ 90

92. Mike \ 1050 CHUM Charts \ 74
93. Mike \ CFTR Charts \ 76
94. Mike \ Group Booklets \ 77
95. Mike \ *Immigrant Song / Hey Hey What Can I Do* \ 74
96. Mike \ *Tommy* The Movie \ 75

97. Mix \ Revival Vinyl Society Playlist \ 16
98. Mix \ 4 \ *School Carnival Music* \ 09
99. Mix \ 6 \ *Sweet Soul* \ 14

100. Musicians \ Harry Chapin Concert \ 78
101. Musicians \ McCartney \ *Give My Regards To Broad Street* \ Film/Album/Book \ 84
102. **Musicians \ Meet Andy & Randy \ 10**
103. Musicians \ Randy Bachman \ Concert & Meet \ 10
104. Groups \ Wings \ *Listen To What The Man Said* \ 1st McCartney pic sleeve \ 75

105. Pairs \ *Crime Of The Century & Wind & Wuthering* \ 77
106. Pairs \ *Damned If I Do & Blinded By The Light* \ 82
107. Pairs \ *Don't Answer Me & Scratching The Surface* \ 1st Alan Parsons pic sleeve \ 84
108. Pairs \ *Dreamer & Into The Lens (I Am A Camera)* \ 1st Supertramp pic sleeve \ 82
109. Pairs \ *Dreamer & Jackie Blue* \ 76
110. Pairs \ *DSOTM & ZOSO IV* \ 76
111. Pairs \ *Forever Young & So In Love* \ 85
112. Pairs \ *Heart Of Gold & Horse With No Name* \ 73
113. Pairs \ *Hold Your Head Up & Lady* \ 83
114. Pairs \ *Last Song & You're So Vain* \ 73
115. Pairs \ *Run Thru The Light & Into The Lens (I Am A Camera)* \ 03
116. Pairs \ *Summer Breeze & Ventura Highway* \ 73
117. Pairs \ *Trick Of The Tail & Trilogy* \ 78

118. **Radio \ 1050 CHUM \ *CHUM 500* \ 73**
119. Radio \ 107.1 Juice FM \ 17
120. **Radio \ CBOT \ *Rock Concert* \ 74**
121. Radio \ CFGO & CFRA Top 30 Charts \ 73
122. Radio \ CFGO Beatles Weekend & Expos game \ 74
123. Radio \ CFNY \ British 'New Wave' Invasion Singles \ 82
124. Radio \ CFNY \ James Scott & Ted (Walker) Woloshyn - 84/85
125. Radio \ CFNY \ *Music Of The 80s* \ Notes \ 82
126. **Radio \ CFNY \ *Top 80 Of The 80s* \ 90**
127. Radio \ CFRA Beatles Weekend & Beatles 1962-1966 \ 74
128. **Radio \ CHEZ 106 \ *On Air Tonight* \ Newspaper ad \ 1st day on the air \ 77**
129. Radio \ CHEZ 106 & Q107 \ 77
130. **Radio \ CKCU \ *93.1 Year Later* \ 76**
131. Radio \ CKFH \ Maple Leafs hockey & Top 40 radio \ 72
132. Radio \ CYRK \ York University \ 79
133. **Radio \ Q107 \ *Art Rock Weekend* \ play list \ 06**
134. **Radio \ Q107 \ *Big Organ Weekend* \ 00S**
135. Radio \ Q107 \ Meeting Andy Frost \ 07
136. Radio \ Q107 \ *Psychedelic Psundays* with Andy Frost \ 90s & 00s
137. Radio \ Q107 \ Scruff Connors & Gene Valaitis \ 83/84
138. **Radio \ Q107 \ *Top 107 Of The Seventies* \ 80**
139. **Radio \ Watertown New York \ Rock Radio \ 72**

140. Singles \ *145 Chord Change* \ 15
141. Singles \ Art \ Burbank Warner 45s and Ottawa years \ 75
142. Singles \ Art \ Coloured \ 80s
143. **Singles \ Art \ Custom labels **
144. **Singles \ Art \ Different sleeves \ 80S**
145. Singles \ Art \ Elektra Butterfly Story \ 70s
146. Singles \ Art \ Famous Charisma 70s
147. **Singles \ Art \ Gatefold **

188.   Title \ *Stairway To Heaven* - The Idles \ 81

189.   TV \ CBC \ Claire Martin & Roger Waters \ *The Wall* \ 05
190.   TV \ CITY \ *City Limits* with Christopher Ward \ 83/84
191.   TV \ Grammy Awards \ Dolby, Hancock, Jones, Wonder \ 85
192.   TV \ *Heartbeat* \ 92
193.   TV \ *Much Music* \ 84
194.   TV \ *The New Music* \ JD Roberts & Jeannie Beker \ 80
195.   TV \ *WKRP In Cincinnati* \ 79

NINE

INTERNET

1. *60th Anniversary Of The LP Record*, Louis Rastelli, Globe & Mail, July 24, 2009, https://www.theglobeandmail.com/opinion/revolutionary-thinking/article4213508/

2. *A Night At The Proms With Roger Hodgeson*, Paris, 2004, https://www. youtube. com/watch?v=6aWDxuhD0FI

3. *Elton John Concert, Wembley Stadium, June 30, 1984, also featured Big Country, Kool & The Gang, Nik Kershaw & Wang Chung*, https://www.concertarchives.org/concerts/elton-john-big-country-kool-the-gang-nik-kershaw-wang-chung-067daa98-cc24-499a-82d9-ec2d1637e726

4. *From The Archive : Billy Connolly And John Bonham*, https://www.youtube.com/watch?v=PzCetFD-rrE

5. *Genesis on Genesis*, video, 1991, https://youtube. com/watch?v=snqKZ9_rATg

6. *Old & Wise - The Alan Parsons Project - David Paton*, https://www.youtube.com/watch?v=BT2U76Fbea0

7. *Roger Hodgson collaboration represents road not taken for Yes: 'One of those things that fizzled out'*, Something Else, Dec 25, 2014*45cat*, https://somethingelsereviews.com/2014/12/25/roger-hodgson-yes-trevor-rabin/

8. *Video Killed The Radio Star, The Buggles (Trevor Horn, Geoff Downes, Bruce Wooley & The Camera Club & others), The Princes Trust, 2004*, https://youtu. be/Zm0QQDMoRPU

9. *aflockofeagulls.org*

10. *albumsthattimeforgot.com*

11. *allmusic*

12. *billboard*

13. *breakfastinspain*

14. *chumtributesite*

15. *concertarchives.org*

16. *discogs*

17. *emersonlakepalmer.com*

18. *genesis-music.com*

19. *getsongbpm*

20. *jogfm*

21. *loudersound.com*

22. *omd.uk.com*

23. *rateyourmusic.com*

24. *rogerdean.com*

25. *rollingstone.com*

26. *setlist.fm*

27. *simpleminds.com*

28. *songbpm*

29. *songfacts*

30. *stevehoffman.tv*

31. *sting.com*

32. *supertramp.com*

33. *tunebat*

34. *u2.com*

35. *u2desertsky*

36. *yesworld.org*

37. *youtube*

TEN

LISTS BY CHAPTER
(lists that had origins in terms are noted as *)

1 - JUST SINGLES

1. 1.1 \ Morph I - Various \ 2009 * (origin - SS_AB)
2. 1.2 \ Morph II - Golden Treasures \ 2019
3. 1.3 \ Eric Records \ 2020 * (origin - SS_Eric_2_Artists)
4. 1.4 \ Rare \ 2017
5. 1.5 \ Cover Versions I - 60s & 70s - America \ 2009 * (origin - Ver_Cover)
6. 1.6 \ Cover Versions II - 60s & 70s - UK \ 2009 * (origin - Ver_Cover)
7. 1.7 \ Cover Versions III - 80s & 90s \ 2009 * (origin - Ver_Cover)
8. 1.8 \ *A Classical Borrow* \ 2002 & 2009 * (origin - Ear_Ork)
9. 1.9 \ Different Tune \ 2018
10. 1.10 \ Three Songs \ 2009 * (origin - ABC)

2 - SINGLES AS VISUAL ART I - LABELS

11. 2.1 \ Warner I - Burbank Trees \ 2017
12. 2.2 \ Kinney \ 2009 * (origin - Lab_Kin)
13. 2.3 \ Mercury \ 2009 * (origin - Lab_Merc)
14. 2.4 \ Elektra I - Caterpillar & Butterfly I \ 2017
15. 2.5 \ *The Dark Side Of The Label I [gem]* ABC Dunhill Decca Liberty MCA Spotlight \ 2009, 2017 & 2023
16. 2.6 \ Warner II - Colour Logo & Pinstripes I \ 2020
17. 2.7 \ Island \ 2019
18. 2.8 \ Butterfly II - Chrysalis \ 2019
19. 2.9 \ Pinstripes II - Geffen \ 2020
20. 2.10 \ EMI \ 2019
21. 2.11 \ *The Dark Side Of The Label II [gem]* - Capitol \ 2009, 2017 & 2023
22. 2.12 \ Elektra II & Asylum Late 80s \ 2017
23. 2.13 \ Custom Labels I - Domestic \ 2013
24. 2.14 \ Custom Labels II - Import \ 2013
25. 2.15 \ The Rolling Stones Own Label \ 2023

3 - SINGLES AS VISUAL ART II - PICTURE SLEEVES

26. 3.1 \ Sleeve Cover Like Album I - US Artists \ 2017
27. 3.2 \ Sleeve Cover Like Album II - UK Artists \ 2017
28. 3.3 \ Sleeve Covers Like Album III - Several From The Same Album \ 2019
29. 3.4 \ Gatefold \ 2009 * (origin - PS_GF)

30. 3.5 \ Colour Vinyl \ 2009 * (origins - CLD_B, CLD_G, CLD_R & CLD_W)
31. 3.6 \ Lyrics \ 2017

4 - SINGLES & ALBUMS

32. 4.1 \ Remix By Year \ 2009 * (origin - Ver_RMX_Year)
33. 4.2 \ *Sounds Better Than Album [gem]* \ 2009 * (origin - Ver_SBTA)
34. 4.3 \ K-TEL \ 1973
35. 4.4 \ Greatest I - Reissues \ 2013
36. 4.5 \ Greatest II - Originals \ 2013
37. 4.6 \ *Wrap* I - 70s \ 2017
38. 4.7 \ *Wrap* II - 80s \ 2017
39. 4.8 \ Not On Greatest \ 2001 & 2009 * (origin - Best_NO)
40. 4.9 \ B Side Treasures I - 70s \ 2001 & 2009 * (origin - BS)
41. 4.10 \ B Side Treasures II - 80s \ 2001 & 2009 * (origin - BS)

5 - THE GEOGRAPHY OF SINGLES

42. 5.1 \ Delay From UK, Albums Then Singles & Re-Releases \ 2012
43. 5.2 \ Same A Different B \ 2009 * (origins - B1, B2)
44. 5.3 \ Different Sleeves \ 2009 * (origins - PS1, PS2)
45. 5.4 \ Atlantic Oldies - US \ 2009 * (origin - SS_AT_O)
46. 5.5 \ Genesis We Can't Dance - US \ 2009 * (origin - Lab_Atl_Prpl)
47. 5.6 \ Parsons - US \ 2009
48. 5.7 \ Yes - US \ 2009
49. 5.8 \ Bought I - Buffalo \ 2009 * (origins - US_NY_Buff, US_NY_Buff_RT)
50. 5.9 \ Collectables Back To Back Hits - US \ 2018
51. 5.10 \ Bought II - US \ 2009 *
            (origins - US_CAL_HW, US_CAL_SLO, US_FLA_CLEAR_DVM, US_NV_RENO,
            US_NY_EHLI & US_VER)
52. 5.11 \ Bought III - UK \ 2009 *
            (origins - UK_BRIST, UK_CAMB_BEAT, UK_CAMB_JAYS, UK_CAMB_OP,
            UK_COV_HMV, UK_COV_CS, UK_LINC_RB, UK_LOND, UK_OXF_OP,
            UK_RICH_MRKT, UK_WESTM_VIRG, UK_YORK-WHS)
53. 5.12 \ Simple Minds - UK
54. 5.13 \ U2 - *Revival Of The Fittest* - US \ 2024 * (origin - SS_IGLD)
55. 5.14 \ Spun Gold - Elektra & Asylum - US \ 2024 * (origin - SS_EARG)
56. 5.15 \ Warner Back To Back Hits - US \ 2024 * (origin - SS_WBack)
57. 5.16 \ CBS Silver Back To Back Hits - US \ 2024 * (origin - SS_CBSF_G)
58. 5.17 \ Creedence Fantasy Back To Back Hits - US \ 2024

8 - THE ART OF RECORDING

59. 8.1 \ Label Halves I - Various \ 2020 * (origins - Lab_Atc_Ylw, Lab_Atl_Prpl & Lab_Fms_Chr)
60. 8.2 \ Label Halves II - Atlantic Gold & Oldies \ 2009 * (origins - SS_AT_G, SS_AT_O & SS_AT_RLZ)
61. 8.3 \ Label Almost Halves I - Motown \ 2020
62. 8.4 \ Label Almost Halves II - Arista Flashback \ 2009 * (origin - SS_ARBTB)
63. 8.5 \ Label UK No Time \ 2009 & 2020

10 - THE CANADIAN CORNER

64. 10.1 \ The 7UP Canadian Corner \ 1973
65. 10.2 \ Bryan Adams Music Videos \ 2019
66. 10.3 \ Canadiana - The Lesser Knowns I - The Seventies \ 2024
67. 10.4 \ Canadiana - The Lesser Knowns II - The Eighties \ 2024
68. 10.5 \ Canadiana - The Lesser Knowns III - The 7UP Groups \ 2024

11 - CHICAGO & THE BEATLES

69. 11.1 \ 1ˢᵗ CFRA Special Of The Month - Chicago \ 1974
70. 11.2 \ Earth, Wind & Fire & Chicago - 2024 Toronto
71. 11.3 \ McCartney - Top 40 Songs \ 2014
72. 11.4 \ (Ex) Beatles - A & B Side Non Album Singles \ 2009 * (origin - Bs)

12 - NeWavEighties

73. 12.1 \ OMD I - Commercial Picture Sleeves
74. 12.2 \ OMD II - Homemade Picture Sleeves
75. 12.3 \ Sting Greatest Songs I - The Police \ 2023
76. 12.4 \ Sting Greatest Songs II - Solo \ 2023
77. 12.5 \ Simple Minds - *Dream Rain Time [gem]* \ 1987
78. 12.6 \ Madonna Music Videos

13 - NOT NeWavEighties

79. 13.1 \ U2 Sampler \ 1986
80. 13.2 \ Joshua B Sides \ 1987 & 2001
81. 13.3 \ U2 The Much Videos \ 1998 & 2007
82. 13.4 \ Achtung Baby Cassette Singles \ 1991
83. 13.5 \ U2 Piano Collection \ 2006

14 - KING CRIMSON, MOODY BLUES, ELP & GENESIS

84. 14.1 \ ELP @ Kingswood Music Theater, Maple, 1992
85. 14.2 \ Genesis @ CNE Stadium August 1982
86. 14.3 \ *Genesis Selling A Trick Dance [gem]* \ 2013
87. 14.4 \ Genesis Top 40 Songs \ 2019

15 - LED ZEPPELIN, ALAN PARSONS & PINK FLOYD

88. 15.1 \ Zeppelin Singles I - Morphology \ 2009 & 2010 * (origin - SS_AT_RLZ)
89. 15.2 \ Zeppelin Singles II - Rolling Stone Top 40 Songs \ 2010
90. 15.3 \ Alan Parsons Singles With 3D A For Arista \ 2017
91. 15.4 \ Alan Parsons (& Yes) In Concert, 1998, Toronto
92. 15.5 \ Hipgnosis Albums \ 1986 & 2018

16 - SUPERTRAMP

93. 16.1 \ Supertramp, *Breakfast In Canada,* Exhibition Stadium, July 1979 *

128.	21.3 \ *Sa Flatt Ft* - Country \ 2001 & 2009 * (origin - Ear_Ctry)
129.	21.4 \ *Sa Flatt Ft* - Folk \ 2020
130.	21.5 \ *Sa Flatt Ft* - Funk, R&B & Soul \ 2001 & 2009 * (origin - Ear_Soul)
131.	21.6 \ *Sa Flatt Ft* - Jazz \ 2020
132.	21.7 \ *Sa Flatt Ft* - New Wave Electro Pop \ 2001 & 2009 * (origin - Ear_Tek)
133.	21.8 \ *Sa Flatt Ft* - Pop \ 2020
134.	21.9 \ *Sa Flatt Ft* - Rock \ 2020
135.	21.10 \ *Sa Flatt Ft* - Twice As Fast \ 2021
136.	21.11 \ *Sa Flatt Ft* - Orchestral \ 2009 & 2023 * (origin - Ear_Ork)
137.	21.12 \ *Sa Flatt Ft* - Chug Songs \ 2023
138.	21.13 \ *Sa Flatt Ft* - Girl Power \ 2009 & 2024 * (origin - Ear_Girl)

22 - SOUND

139.	22.1 \ Instrumental Only I \ 2001 * (origin - Ear_I)
140.	22.2 \ Instrumental Only II - B Sides & Limited Vocals \ 2001 * (origin - Ear_I)
141.	22.3 \ Sound Effects But No Voices \ 2019
142.	22.4 \ Voice I - With other sound effects \ 2019
143.	22.5 \ Voice II - Voices Only \ 2019
144.	22.6 \ Voice III - With A Countdown \ 2018
145.	22.7 \ Voice IV - Different Lead Singer \ 2018
146.	22.8 \ Voice V - Choir \ 2019
147.	22.9 \ Voice VI - Acapella \ 2019
148.	22.10 \ Voice VII - Whistling \ 2019
149.	22.11 \ Winds I - Clarinet & Flute \ 2020
150.	22.12 \ Winds II - Harmonica \ 2020
151.	22.13 \ Horns - Trombone & Trumpet (& French Horn) \ 2020
152.	22.14 \ Strings I - Violin \ 2020
153.	22.15 \ Strings II - Bits Of Guitar & Piano \ 2012
154.	22.16 \ Military Drums \ 2019
155.	22.17 \ No Drums \ 2019
156.	22.18 \ Instrumental Duos \ 2024

23 - FAMILY & FRIENDS

157.	23.1 \ Bought Spring 1973 \ 1984 * (origin - Evnt_Walk_Tor_73)
158.	23.2 \ From Michael \ 1984 & 2009 * (origin - FR_MS)
159.	23.3 \ High School Jam \ 2001 & 2009 * (origin - Evnt_Jam_79)
160.	23.4 \ Eagles Hell Freezes Over Exhibition Stadium \ 1994
161.	23.5 \ Eagles Rolling Stone Top 40 Songs \ 2021
162.	23.6 \ From Andrew 1990s \ 2009 * (origin - FR_DJ)
163.	23.7 \ From Douglas 1990s \ 2009 * (origin - FR_DB)
164.	23.8 \ Revival Vinyl Society I - The Album Cuts \ 2023
165.	23.9 \ Revival Vinyl Society II - The Singles \ 2023
166.	23.10 \ Revival Vinyl Society III - Did You Know? \ 2023
167.	23.11 \ CNE Concerts \ 2001 & 2013

ELEVEN

MUZIK LISTS I
THE SINGLES

\\ VINYL \ SINGLES \ 45S \\ 1972 \\ 10 OR MORE \\ COUNTRY SOUND \\ EDITS \\ INSTRUMENTAL \\ LIVE \\ MIA2 \ MISSING FROM GREATEST HITS ALBUMS \\ MIA3 \ BSIDES (OR ASIDES) NOT ON ALBUMS (EXCLUDES COMPILATIONS & BOXED SETS) \\ NEW WAVE & ELECTRO-POP \\ NO OVERKILL (SINGLES NOT ON ALBUMS IN MY COLLECTION) \\ PAIRS \\ PICTURES \\ PING PONG PITCH PRIZES 1986 \\ PROMOS \\ ROCK'N ROLL \\ SOUL

VINYL \ SINGLES \ 45S \ 1972 \ RKY CAMP NEAR KINGSTON ON \ ROCK RADIO FROM WATERTOWN NY \\ DEREK & THE DOMINOES \ *Layla* \\ DIAMOND, Neil \ *Song Sung Blue* \\ DOOBIE BROTHERS \ *Listen To The Music* \\ GODSPELL \ *Day By Day* \\ HOLLIES \ *Long Cool Woman* \\ LOOKING GLASS \ *Brandy (You're A Fine Girl)* \\ MILLS, Frank \ *Poor Little Fool* \\ O'SULLIVAN, Gilbert \ *Alone Again (Naturally)* \\ PROCAL HARUM \ *Conquistador* \\ VINTON, Bobby \ *Sealed With A Kiss* \\ WITHERS, Bill \ *Lean On Me* \\ YES \ *Roundabout*

VINYL \ SINGLES \ 45S \ 1978-1979-1980-1981 \\ *All Out Of Love \ Arthur's Theme \ Baker Street \ Cars \ Echo Beach \ Emotional Rescue \ Feels So Good \ Friends Of Mr. Cairo \ Hearts \ I Got You \ I'm So Straight I'm A Weirdo \ Just The Way You Are \ Let Go The Line \ Lotta Love \ Magic \ Message In A Bottle \ My Sharona \ One Way Or Another \ Ride Like The Wind \ Sailing \ Sultans Of Swing \ Time \ Turn Me Loose \ Urgent \ Video Killed The Radio Star \ Waiting For A Girl Like You*

VINYL \ SINGLES \ 45S \ CHRISTMAS \\ ADAMS, Bryan \ *Reggae Christmas* \\ BAND AID \ *Do They Know It's Christmas?* \\ BOWIE & CROSBY \ *Peace On Earth / Little Drummer Boy* \\ CALIFORNIA RAISINS \ *Rudolph The Red Nosed Reindeer* \\ COLE, Natalie \ *Christmas Song* \\ EAGLES \ *Please Come Home For Christmas* \\ EDWARD BEAR \ *Coming Home Christmas* \\ FRANKIE GOES TO HOLLYWOOD \ *Power Of Love* \\ IVES, Burl \ *Holly Jolly Christmas* \\ LAKE, Greg \ *I Believe In Father Christmas* \\ MELLENCAMP, John \ *I Saw Mommy Kissing Santa Claus* \\ SPRINGSTEEN, Bruce \ *Merry Christmas Baby \ My Home Town / Santa Claus Is Comin' To Town* \\ MCCARTNEY, Paul \ *Wonderful Christmas Time* \\ SQUIRE & WHITE \ *Run With The Fox / Return Of The Fox*

VINYL \ SINGLES \ 45S \ COUNTRY SOUND \\ DOOBIE BROTHERS \ *Slat Key Soquel Rag* \\ (GARRY) LEE \ *Rodeo Song* \\ MCCARTNEY & WINGS \ *Sally G* \\ (JIM) STAFFORD \ *Wildwood Weed* \\ (RAY) STEVENS \ *The Streak* \\ (LOUDON) WAINRIGHT III \ *Dead Skunk* \\ (ERIC) WEISBERG \ *Dueling Banjos*

VINYL \ SINGLES \ 45S \ DANCE \\ *Politics Of Dancing \ Sex Crimes \ Keep Feeling Fascination \ 12" Album Howard Jones \ Forever Live & Die* \\ *City Of Night \ Major Tom (UK) \ Major Tom (Ger) \ Nova Heart \ Situation \ Leave It \ Runaway*

VINYL \ SINGLES \ 45S \ INSTRUMENTAL \\ **DEODATA** \ *Also Sprach Zarathustra (2001)* \\ **EMERSON, LAKE & PALMER** \ *Fanfare For The Common Man* \ (Emerson) *Honky Tonk Train Blues \ Nutrocker \ Peter Gunn \ Peter Gunn* (L) \\ **(DAVID) FOSTER** \ *Love's Theme From St. Elmo's Fire* \\ **INCREDIBLE BONGO BAND** \ *Bongo Rock* \\ **KENNY G** \ *Songbird* \\ **(MIKE) OLDFIELD** \ *Tubular Bells* \\ **(ALAN) PARSONS PROJECT** \ *Lucifer* \\ **SIMPLE MINDS** \ *Alive & Kicking \ Jungleland \ Sanctify Yourself* \\ **THP ORCHESTRA** \ *Theme From S.W.A.T.* \\ **(TINA) TURNER** \ *We Don't Need Another Hero* \\ **(MASON) WILLIAMS** \ *Classical Gas* \\ **(EDGAR) WINTER** \ *Frankenstein*

VINYL \ SINGLES \ 45S \ LIVE \\ **(ALICE) COOPER** \ *I Never Cry / You & Me* \\ **DEEP PURPLE** \ *Smoke On The Water* (Made in Japan Version) \\ **EMERSON, LAKE & PALMER** \ *Peter Gunn / Knife Edge* \\ **LYNYRD SKYNYRD** \ *Free Bird* \\ **RUSH** \ *Closer To The Heart* \\ **SIMPLE MINDS** \ *Promised You A Miracle* \\ **SUPERTRAMP** \ *Breakfast In America \ Dreamer \ Take The Long Way Home* \\ **U2** \ *Gloria / Sunday Bloody Sunday* \\ **YES** \ *Roundabout / I've Seen All Good People* \\ **WINGS** \ *Maybe I'm Amazed*

VINYL \ SINGLES \ 45S \ MIA2 \ MISSING FROM GREATEST HITS ALBUMS \\ **CHICAGO** \ *Brand New Love Affair \ Free \ Gone Long Gone \ Harry Truman \ Lowdown \ You Are On My Mind* \\ **DOOBIE BROTHERS** \ *Another Park Another Sunday* \\ **EMERSON, LAKE & PALMER** \ *Nutrocker \ Stones Of Years* \\ **FOREIGNER** \ *Break It Up \ Reaction To Action* \\ **GENESIS** \ *Duchess \ Go West Young Man \ Man On The Corner \ No Reply At All \ Spot The Pigeon \ Taking It All Too Hard \ Tell Me Why* \\ **HUMAN LEAGUE** \ *Rock'n Roll* \\ **(PAUL) MCCARTNEY & WINGS** \ *Helen Wheels \ Hi Hi Hi \ Letting Go \ Maybe I'm Amazed* (L) \ *So Bad \ Venus & Mars Rock Show* \\ **ORCHESTRAL MANOEUVRES IN THE DARK** \ *Genetic Engineering \ Never Turn Away \ Telegraph* \\ **(ALAN) PARSONS PROJECT** \ *Day After Day \ Doctor Tarr \ In The Lap Of The Gods \ (The) Raven \ Sooner Or Later \ To One In Paradise \ You Lie Down With Dogs* \\ **POLICE** \ *Synchronicity II* \\ **SIMPLE MINDS** \ *Ghostdancing \ Glittering Prize \ Love Song \ Speed Your Love To Me \ This Is Your Land* \\ **STYX** \ **Why Me** \\ **U2** \ *Gloria \ In God's Country \ Two Hearts Beat As One* \\ **SUPERTRAMP** \ *Better Days \ Brother Where You Bound \ Crazy \ I'm Beggin' You* \\ **YES** \ *Does It Really Happen? \ Don't Kill The Whale \ Rhythm Of Love*

VINYL \ SINGLES \ 45S \ MIA3 \ BSIDES (OR ASIDES) \ NOT ON ALBUMS (EXCLUDES COMPILATIONS & BOXED SETS) \\ **EMERSON, LAKE & PALMER** \ *I Believe In Father Christmas \ Tiger In A Spotlight* \\ **GENESIS** \ *Evidence Of Autumn \ Go West Young Man \ Inside & Out \ It's Yourself \ Twilight Alehouse* \\ **(PAUL) MCCARTNEY & WINGS** \ *Sally G* \\ **SIMPLE MINDS** \ *Alive & Kicking (Instrumental) \ Bass Line \ Brass Band In Africa \ Glittering Prize (Theme) \ Jungleland (instrumental) \ Sanctify Yourself (instrumental) \ Saturday Girl \ Theme For Great Cities \ Theme For Great Cities 91 \ Waterfront 89* \\ **SUPERTRAMP** \ *You Started Laughing* \\ **TEARS FOR FEARS** \ *I Believe (Live) \ Pharoahs \ Sea Song \ When In Love With A Blind Man* \\ **(TINA) TURNER** \ *We Don't Need Another Hero (instrumental)* \\ **U2** \ *Alex* (C) \ *Boomerang II \ Dancing Bearfoot \ Deep In The Heart \ Endless Deep \ Everlasting Love \ Hallelujah Here She*

*Comes \ Hold On To Love \ I've Got You (Under My Skin) (C) \ Lady With The Spinning Head (C) \ Mysterious Ways (Solar Plexus Magic Hour Remix) \ (A) Room A t The Heartbreak Hotel \ Satellite Of Love (C) \ Silver & Gold \ Spanish Eyes \ Sweetest Thing \ Treasure \ Walk To The Water * **YES** \ *Abeline \ City Of Love (Live) \ It Can Happen (Live) \ Leave It (Acapella)*

VINYL \ SINGLES \ 45S \ NEW WAVE & ELECTRO-POP (excludes those by groups with many entries including human league and orchestral manoeuvres \\ **BUGGLES** \ *Video Killed The Radio Star* \\ **DEVO** \ *Whip-it* \\ **KRAFTWERK** \ *Autobahn* \\ **M** \ *Pop Muzic* \\ **(GARY) NUMAN** \ *Cars* \\ **(RICK) WAKEMAN** \ *I'm So Straight I'm A Weirdo* \\ **YAZOO** \ *Don't Go \ Only You \ Situation*

VINYL \ SINGLES \ 45S \ PAIRS \\ 73 \ Mar \ **EDWARD BEAR** \ *Last Song* \ **CARLY SIMON** \ *You're So Vain* \ North York \ Book Note \\ 73 \ May 5 \ **AMERICA** *Horse With No Name* \ **NEIL YOUNG** \ *Heart Of Gold* \ Toronto \ Sams DT \\ 76 Jul \ **OZARK MOUNTAIN DAREDEVILS** \ *Jackie Blue* \ **SUPERTRAMP** \ *Dreamer\Bloody Well Right* \ Hardwick,Vermont \\ 79 \ Mar \ **GENESIS** \ *Spot The Pigeon* \ **YES** \ *Don't Kill The Whale* \ Toronto \ Records On Wheels \\ 82 \ Feb \ **MANFRED MANN** \ *Blinded By The Light* \ **ALAN PARSONS** \ *Damned If I Do* \\ 83 \ **SUPERTRAMP** \ *Dreamer* \ **YES** \ *Into The Lens* \\ 83 \ Jul \ **POLICE** \ *Every Breath You Take* \ **FLOCK OF SEAGULLS** \ *Wishing (If I had A Photograph)* \\ **ALAN PARSONS** \ *Don't Answer Me* \ **SAGA** \ *Scratching The Surface.*

VINYL \ SINGLES \ 45S \ PICTURES \ FIRSTS \\ **ASIA** \ *Sole Survivor* \\ **COLLINS, Phil** \ *Take Me Home* \\ **ELP (LAKE)** \ *I Believe In Father Christmas* \\ **FIXX** \ *Less Cities More Moving People* \\ **FLOCK OF SEAGULLS** \ *Wishing (If I had a Photograph Of You)* \\ **FOREIGNER** \ *Urgent* \\ **GENESIS** \ *Spot The Pigeon* \\ **HUMAN LEAGUE** \ *Lebanon* \\ **LENNON, John** \ *Mind Games* \\ **ORCHESTRAL MANOEUVRES IN THE DARK** \ *Telegraph* \\ **PARSONS PROJECT, Alan** \ *Don't Answer Me* \\ **POLICE** \ *Every Breath You Take* \\ **QUEEN** \ *Killer Queen* \\ **SIMPLE MINDS** \ *Speed Your Love To Me* \\ **STARR, Ringo** \ *Photograph* \\ **SUPERTRAMP** \ *Dreamer/Bloody Well Right* \\ **TEARS FO R FEARS** \ *Shout* \\ **THOMPSON TWINS** \ *Lay Your Hands On Me* \\ **U2** \ *Pride (In The Name Of Love)* \\ **WINGS** \ *Listen To What The Man Said (75)*\\ **WINWOOD, Steve** \ *Arc Of A Diver* \\ **YES** \ *Don't Kill The Whale*

VINYL \ SINGLES \ 45S \ PING PONG PITCH PRIZES 1986 \\ **ABBA** \ *Dancing Queen* \\ **AEROSMITH** \ *Dream On & Sweet Emotion, Walk This Way* \\ **ARGENT** \ *Hold Your Head Up* \\ **BABE RUTH** \ *Theme From "For A Few Dollars More"* \\ **BUGGLES** \ *Living In The Plastic Age, On T.V. & I Am A Camera, Video Killed The Radio Star* \\ **CLAPTON** \ *I Shot The Sheriff* \\ **DR.HOOK** \ *Cover of ROLLING STONE* \\ **DOOBIE BROTHERS** \ *Listen To The Music, Long Train Running* \\ **ELECTRIC LIGHT ORCHESTRA** \ *Roll Over Beethoven,* **ELECTRIC LIGHT ORCHESTRA** \ *Telephone Line* \\ **EMERSON, LAKE & PALMER** \ *Peter Gunn* \\ **GENESIS** \ *Match Or The Day \ Pigeons* \\ **GUESS WHO** \ *These Eyes \ No Time* \\ **HEART** \ *Crazy On You \ Dreamboat Annie* \\ **HOLLIES** \ *Long Cool Woman* \\ Ping Pong Pitch Prizes \ **ELTON JOHN** \ *Goodbye Yellow Brick Road* \\ **KANSAS** \ *Carry On Wayward Son* \\ **LOVERBOY** \ *Kid Is Hot Tonight* \\ **THREE DOG NIGHT** \ *Let Me Serenade You, Old Fashioned Love Song, Shambala* \ **EDGAR WINTER** \ *Frankenstein* \\ **YES** \ *Roundabout & Long Distance Runaround, Your Move*

VINYL \ SINGLES \ 45S \ ROCK'N ROLL \\ BEATLES \ *I'm Down* \\ **(CATFISH) HODGE** \ *Boogie Man Gonna Get Ya* \\ **LED ZEPPELIN** \ *Rock & Roll* \\ **LOGGINS & MESSINA** \ *Your Mama Don't Dance* \\ **(JOHNNY) RIVERS** \ *Rockin' Pneumonia* \\ **YES** \ *I've Seen All Good People* \\ **ZZ TOP** \ *Tush*

VINYL \ SINGLES \ 45S \ SOUL \\ BLUE MAGIC \ *Sideshow* \\ **CHI-LITES** \ *Oh Girl / Have You Seen Her?* \\ **(HAROLD) MELVIN & THE BLUE NOTES** \ *If You Don't Know Me By Now* \\ **(BILLY) PAUL** \ *Me & Mrs. Jones* \\ **O'JAYS** \ *Backstabbers* \ *For The Love Of The Money* \ *Love Train* \\ **STYLISTICS** \ *Betcha By Golly Wow* \ *I'm Stoned In Love With You* \\ **(TIMMY) THOMAS** \ *Why Can't We Live Together*

TWELVE

MUZIK LISTS II
THE REST

\\ ART \ MIKE \ STEVE
\\ BOOKS \ ART \ CHARTS \ CHOIR \ CONCERT PROGRAMS \ GENERAL \ GROUPS \
  MIKE
\\ CHARTS \ TOP 100 \ ANNUAL \ ALL TIME \ FRIEND \ MIKE \ STEVE \ TOP 30
\\ CONCERTS \\ (CLUBS) \\ PLAYLISTS \ EAGLES \ 94 \\ ELP \ 92 \\ MCCARTNEY \ 89 \\ YES
  \ 87 \\ 91 \\ 94 \\ 98 \\ 99 \\ REVIEWS
\\ RECORD STORE BAGS
\\ SHEET MUSIC \ BOOKS \ SINGLE
\\ STEREO \ CURRENT \ FORMER
\\ TAPES \ AUDIO \ HOMEMADE MIXES
\\ VINYL \ TRACKS \ SUITES \\

ART \ MIKE \\ BTO \ *4 Wheel Drive* \\ CHICAGO \\ CCR \ *Live* \\ ELO \ *Ole Elo* \\ GENESIS \
Foxtrot \\ KC & THE SUNSHINE BAND \\ STEVE \\ SIMPLE MINDS \ *Live In The City Of
Light*

BOOKS \ ART \\ *1000 Record Covers \ Magnetic Storm \ Views* \\ CHARTS \\ *All Time Top 1000
Albums \ CHUM Charts \ Off The Record \ Top 40 Albums \ Top 40 Hits* Lwin \ *Top 40 Hits*
Whitburn Edition 5 \ *Top Twenty* \\ CHOIR \\ 81 \ 82 \ 84 \ 85 \ 86 \ 88 \ 89 \ 90 \\ CONCERT
PROGRAMS \\ Asia \ *Alpha* \\ Genesis \ *Mama* \\ Yes \ *90125, Going For The One, Relayer, Union,
Yesyears* \\ GENERAL \\ *A Time To Rock* \\ *American Band Stand* \\ *Heart Of Gold* \\ *Live Aid* \\
Rocking The Classics \\ GROUPS \\ BEATLES *Lyrics* \\ MCCARTNEY \ *Give My Regards To
Broadstreet* \\ SUPERTRAMP *Book* \\ U2 *Unforgettable Fire* \\ YES *Biography* \\ MIKE \\ Groups
\ Beatles \\ Genesis \\ Led Zeppelin \\ Rush \ Pt.I \\ Rush \ Pt.II

CHARTS \ TOP 100 \ ANNUAL \\ 61, 62, 63, 64, 65, 66, 67, 68, 69, 70, 71, 72, 73, 74, 75, 76, 77, 78,
79, 80, 81 82, 83, 84, 85 \ CHUM 100 \\ 73, 74 \ CFRA 100 \\ 74, 76 \ CFGO 100 \\ 80, 81, 82, 83,
84, 85, 86, 87, 88, 89, 90, 91 \ CHUM FM\\ 81, 82, 83, 84, 85, 87, 88, 90, 91 \ CFNY Best \\ 84, 85,
86, 87, 97, 98 \ Q107 107 \\ 88 \ CKSL 50, 100 \\ 90, 91 \ CFTR 68 \\ 95 \ ENERGY 108 \\ 95 \
HOT 103 \\ 72, 73 WWDJ \\ CHARTS \ TOP 100 \ ALL TIME \\ 73, 74 \ CFGO 300, 400 \\ 75 \
CHUM 300 \\ 80, 90 \ CHUM FM 100 Albums of 70s, 80s \\ 80, 90, 00 \ Q107 107 of 70s, Classic
500, Top 500 Of The Century \\ 82, 90 \ CFNY All Time, Best 102 Of Decade \\ 84 \ CJBK 500 \\
84, 85 \ CKSL 300 \\ CHARTS \ TOP 100 \ HOMESPUN \ FRIEND \\ Top 68 Albums \\ Top 77
Rock Songs Of All Time \\ Top 40 All Time Easy Listening \\ Top 100 Albums \\ MIKE \\ CHFGO
1974 Top 100 \\ 840MITE 1974 Top 250 \\ CHFGO 1975 Top 100 \\ Top 30 Groups 1968-1975 \\

Top 500 Of All Time \\ Top 49 Groups 1973, 1974, 1975 \\ **STEVE** \\ Top 50 of the 70s \\ Top 50 of the 80s \\ Top 100 Albums \ 1979 \\ Top 100 Albums \ 1980 \\ **CHARTS \ TOP 30** \\ CFGO (Ottawa) \\ CFNY \\ CFRA (Ottawa) \\ CFTR \\ CHFGO \\ CHUM \\ CJBK (London) \\ CKOC (Hamilton) \\ CKLW (Windsor) \\ Europe \\ FM 96 (London) \\ Glendon \\ MITE \\ Q107 \\ RPM \\ Sam's \\ US

CONCERTS \ 76 \ **GENTLE GIANT** 1 \\ 77 \ **SUPERTRAMP 1** \ *Even In The Quietist Moments* \ Jul.3 \\ 77 \ **APRIL WINE** \ July 29 \\ 79 \ **SUPERTRAMP** 2 \ *Breakfast In America* \ July 21 \\ 79 \ **YES 1** \ *Tormato* \ Apr.20 \\ 80 \ **GENTLE GIANT 2** \ May 10 \\ 80 \ **CARS** \ August 28 \\ 80 \ **YES** \2 **Drama** \ August 29 \\ 80 \ **STEVE HACKETT** \ Sept 21 \\ 82 \ **GENESIS** \ *Abacab* \ Aug.28 \\ 83 \ **CHICAGO 1** \ *Chicago 16* \ Jun.14 \\ 84 \ **YES 3** \ *90125* \ Aug.23 \\ 85 \ **TINA TURNER** \ *Private Dancer* \ Aug.14 \\ 86 \ **ELTON JOHN** \ Aug.26 \\ 86 \ **STARSHIP** \ Jul.24 \\ 87 \ **CHICAGO 2** \ Sept.6 \\ 87 \ **YES 4** \ *Big Generator* \ Dec.9 \\ 89 \ **MCCARTNEY** \ *Flowers In The Dirt* \ Dec.7 \\ 91 \ **YES 5** \ *Reunion* \ Apr.23 \\ 92 \ **ELP 1** \ *Black Moon* \\ 94 \ **EAGLES** \ *Hell Freezes Over* \\ 94 \ **YES 6** \ *Talk* \\ 96 \ **ELP 2 & JETHRO TULL** \\ 98 \ **YES 7** \ *Open Your Eyes* \\ 99 \ **YES 8** \ *The Ladder* \\ 01 \ **YES 9** \ *Yessymphonic*

RECORD STORE BAGS \\ **A&A** \ blue & white on yellow, orange & brown on green, orange & brown on brown (round), orange & brown on brown (square) \\ **ANDY'S RECORDS** \\ **BEGGARS BANQUET** \\ **CBS** Disques \\ **CHEAPIES** \ Hamilton, italic records & tapes, italic cds, records, & tapes, italic R & T W3 stores, 104 CHUM FM Torontos Rock, 104 CHUM FM Torontos Ultimate Rock, roman \\ **CIRCLE OF SOUND** \\ **DISCOVERY** \\ **DISCUS** \ red on grey, red hearts \\ **DR. DISK** \\ **DRIFTWOOD** \\ **FLIP CITY** \\ **FLIPSIDE** \ record Red on white \\ **GIBERT** \ Joseph \\ **HMV** \\ **HMV** \ with dog \\ **HOME OF THE HITS** \\ **INCREDIBLE RECORD & BOOKSTORE** \\ **JAYS RECORDS** \\ **KADWELL** \\ **KOPS & VORTEX** \\ **LA MUSIC** \\ **LEGEND RECORDS** \\ **LICORICE & PIZZA** \\ **LONG ISLAND SOUND** \\ **MIRABELLIS** \\ **MISTER SOUND** \\ **MUNTZ** \\ **MUSIC WORLD** \ red on white \ black on red \\ **OUR PRICE** \\ **RECORD PEDDLAR** \\ **RECORD THEATRE** \\ **RECORDS ON WHEELS** \\ **RECORDS ON WHEELS** \ entertainment has the deals bottom \ entertainment has the deals side \ entertainment has the deals \ entertainment records cassettes CDs videos \ entertainment (with wheels) \ entertainment U2 & Elton John \ entertainment U2 & Fixx \\ **RPM** \\ **SAMS** \ Barrie, Bayview, Bayview & Yorkdale, Eglinton Square, Hamilton, London, no stores, Ottawa, video man, video man French, Yonge St., Yorkdale, Yorkdale & Bayview \\ **SHAKE** \\ **WH SMITH** \\ **SUNRISE** \\ **SUPER CLEF** \\ **TREBLE CLEF** \\ **TUNES** \\ **VINYL MUSEUM** \ beach \ cat carrying records 2 locations, \ cat carrying records 3 locations \ cat flying \ CKLN \\ **VIRGIN** \\ **VORTEX**

SHEET MUSIC \ BOOKS \\ **ASIA** \\ **CHICAGO** \ *Anthology Pt.1*, *Gold* Piano& Vocal, *Gold* Sketch Scores \\ **EMERSON, LAKE & PALMER** \\ *Emerson, Lake & Palmer* \ *Greatest Hits* \\ **GENESIS** \ *Deluxe Anthology* \\ **MCCARTNEY & WINGS** \ *Wings Over America* \\ **ORCHESTRAL MANOEUVRES IN THE DARK** \ *Best Of..* \\ **(ALAN) PARSONS PROJECT** \ *Best Of..* \\ **SUPERTRAMP** \ *Breakfast In America, Crime Of The Century, Crisis What Crisis, Even In The Quietist Moments* \\ **TEARS 4 FEARS** \ *Songs From The Big Chair* \\ **U2** \ *The Joshua Tree* \\ **VARIOUS** \ *Stairway To Heaven & 51 Other Songs* \\ **WINWOOD** \ Steve \ *Talking Back To The Night* \\ **YES** \ *Complete, 90125, Fragile & Yes Album, Going For The One, Relayer, Talk*

TAPES \ AUDIO \ CASSETTE SINGLES \ GOODWILL ON NOVEMBER 28, 2002 \ COLLINS - *something happened on the way to heaven* \\ **GENESIS** \ *I Can't Dance* \\ **HAWKINS,** Sophie B \ *Damn, I Wish I was your lover* \\ **HENLEY,** Don \ *The End Of The Innocence* \\ **INXS** \ *Suicide Blonde* \\ **JOEL,** Billy \ *We Didn't Start The Fire* \ *I Go To Extremes* \\ KELLY, R \ *Gotham City* \\ **MCCARTNEY,** Paul \ *This One* \\ **SIMPLE MINDS** \ *See The Lights* \\ **STING** \ *All This Time* \ *If I Ever Lose My Faith In You* \ \ **TEARS FOR FEARS** \ *Advice For The Young At Heart* \ *Woman In Chains* \\ **U2** \\ *Discotheque* \ *Stay (Faraway, So Close!)* \ *Staring At The Sun.*

TAPES \ AUDIO \ HOMEMADE MIXES (does not include those with an extra song tacked on the back end, there need to be several extra tracks, songs to be considered in this group) \\ **BEATLES** \ *62-66 & 67-70* \ *67-70 & Rock'n Roll Music* \ *Love Songs & Rock'n Roll Music* \\ **(DAVID) BOWIE** \ *Changes One Bowie* \\ **CHICAGO** \ *Vol.1* \ *Vol.2 & 17* \\ **(BILL) COSBY** \ *Various 1* \ *2* \ *3* \ *4* (Rob) \\ **(THOMAS) DOLBY** \ *Golden Age Of Wireless* \\ **DOOBIE BROTHERS** \ *Singles* \\ **ELECTRIC LIGHT ORCHESTRA** \ *OLE & Greatest Hits* \\ **FIXX** \ *Singles* \\ **FOREIGNER** \ *Singles* \\ **GENESIS** \ *92.Live* \ *Abacab* \ *And Then There Were Three* \\ **GUESS WHO** \ *Greatest Hits* \\ **HUMAN LEAGUE** \ *Singles* \\ **MCCARTNEY** \ *Singles* \\ **MOODY BLUES** \ *Singles* \\ **ORCHESTRAL MANOEUVRES IN THE DARK** \ *Singles* \\ **POLICE** \ *Singles* \\ **QUEEN** \ *Greatest Hits* \\ **(BRIAN) SILVERSTONE** \\ **SIMPLE MINDS** \ *Sparkle In The Rain* \\ **STYX** \ *Singles* \\ **TEARS FOR FEARS** \ *Songs From The Big Chair* \\ **THREE DOG NIGHT** \ *Greatest Hits* \\ **U2** \ *Achtung Baby* \ *Joshua Tree* \ *Rattle & Hum* \\ **(IAN) WHITE BAND** \ *Studio Tapes* \\ **(STEVE) WINWOOD** \ *Singles* \\ **YES** \ *9012Live* \ *Live in LA 1979* \ *Live Talk*

VINYL \ TRACKS \ SUITES \\ **BOSTON** \ *Foreplay / Longtime* \\ **CHICAGO** \ *Ballet For A Girl From Buchanon* \\ **ELP** \ *Endless Enigma* \ *Karn Evil 9* \ *Piano Concerto 1* \ *Tarkus* \ *The Three Fates* \\ **GENESIS** \ *Domino (Glow Of The Night / The Last Domino)* \ *Firth Of Fifth* \ *Home By The Sea / Second Home By The Sea* \ *Lamb Side 1* \ *Lamb Side 2* \ *Lamb Side 3* \ *Lamb Side 4* \ *Unquiet Slumbers...In That Quiet Earth* \\ **KING CRIMSON** \ *In The Court Of The Crimson King* \\ **MOODY BLUES** \ *Tuesday Afternoon / Evening / Nights In White Satin* \\ **PARSONS** \ *I Robot Side One* \ *I Robot Side Two* \ *The Fall Of The House Of Usher* \ *Turn Of A Friendly Card* \\ **PINK FLOYD** \ *Dark Side 1* \ *Dark Side 2* \ *Shine On You Crazy Diamond* \\ **SIMPLE MINDS** \ *Love Song / Sun City / Dance To The Music* \\ **SUPERTRAMP** \ *Brother Where You Bound* \ *Crisis Side 1* \ *Crisis Side 2* \\ **TEARS FOR FEARS** \ *Broken / Head Over Heels* \\ **YES** \ *And You And I* \ *Awaken* \ *Close To The Edge* \ *Endless Dream* \ *Future Times / Rejoice* \ *Gates Of Delirium* \ *I've Seen All Good People* \ *Long Distance Runaround / The Fish* \ *Machine Messiah* \ *Starship Trooper* \ *Tales Revealing* \ *Tales Remembering* \ *Tales Ancient* \ *Tales Nous Sommes*

THIRTEEN

NAMES

INDIVIDUALS

Andrew, brother

Chris, choirmate, longtime friend & schoolmate

Colwill, Steve, radio, CKCU, CHEZ

Cottle, Jamie, radio, CJCS

Douglas, longtime friend

Durr, Jason, actor, *Heartbeat*

Elliott, Steve, radio, CFRA, CHUM

Eric, high school / university friend

Ertegun, Ahmet, founder, Atlantic Records

Hauer, Rutger, actor, *Blade Runner*

Jeff, bandmate, choirmate, longtime friend, musician & schoolmate

Kollar, John, audiophile, bandmate, longtime friend & schoolmate

Ian, audiophile, bandmate, DJ, longtime friend, schoolmate, teammate

Mahjor, John, radio, CHUM

Marsden, Dave, radio, CHUM, CFNY

Martin, Claire, TV, CBC

McGilvery, Alex, audiophile, author/editor/publisher, longtime friend & musician

Michael, audiophile, bandmate, DJ, longtime friend, musician, record store owner, schoolmate & teammate

Mista D, audiophile, DJ, The Revival Vinyl Society, The Revival House Restaurant

Neister, Alan, newspaper, Toronto Star, articles ELP, Genesis, Supertramp & Yes.

Paul, audiophile, cousin, triathlete

Radner, Gilda, *Saturday Night Live*

Rastelli, Louis, writer

Richard, brother

Sniderman, Sam, Sam The Record Man

Van Der Rohe, Mies, architect

Weller, Peter, actor, *The New Age*

White, Ian, cousin, musician (Ian White Band)

Wigan, Rob, Audiophile, DJ, Owner, The Revival House Restaurant

GROUPS

CFGO DJs \ 1973 - 1977 \ Art Stevens \ Casey Fox \ Charlie O'Brien \ Dan Ferguson \ Dean Hagopian \ Frank Sassin \ Gary Michaels \ Joe Evans \ John L'Heuri \ Mike Kooper (Cooper) \ Mike Paris \ Ric Allen \ Richard Money \ Rick Shannon \ Scottie Lomax \ Steve Derringer \ Tom Lucas.

CFNY DJs \ 1984 - 1985 \ Chris Shepherd \ Dave Marsden \ James Scott \ Ted Woloshyn

CFRA DJs \ 1973 - 1975 \ Al Dubois \ Bill Drake \ Dave Watts \ Jim Keith \ Ken "The General" Grant \ Ric Johnson \ Shelley Emmond \ Steve Emery \ Steve Young \ Stu Hillgrove \ Terry Morgan \ Tom Jeffries \ Trevor Kidd.

Chicago Bulls \ Michael Jordan \ Scottie Pippen \ Dennis Rodman

CHUM DJs \ 1973 \ Dave Charles \ Duke Roberts \ Jay Nelson \ Jim Van Horne \ Mark Edwards \ Pat St John \ Roger Ashby \ Scott Carpenter \ Terry Steele \ Tom Rivers

CHUM DJs 2 \ 1974 - 1975 \ Chuck Morgan \ Dude Walker \ Mike Cooper \ Steve Elliott

High Fidelity, movie - Jack Black, John Cusack
Hockey Biographies \ Roger Crozier \ Gordie Howe \ Derek Sanderson \ Bobby Orr
Late Night with David Letterman - Christopher Walken
Leap Year, movie - Amy Adams, Matthew Goode

MUCH MUSIC Hosts \ 1980s - 1990s \ Bill Welychka \ Diego Fuentes \ Erica Ehm \ George Strombolopoulos \ Master T \ Mike Williams \ Monica Deohl \ Natalie Richard \ Rick Campanelli \ Sook Yin Lee \ Steve Anthony \ Terry David Mulligan \ Ziggy Lorenc.

New Music, The Hosts \ JD Roberts \ Jeannie Beker \ Laurie Brown \ Denise Donlan \ Kim Clark Champniss

Q107 DJs \ 1980s - 2000s \ Al Joins \ Alex Hindmarch \ All Night Andre \ Andy Frost \ Gene Valaitus \ Jake Edwards \ Jesse Dylan \ John Derringer \ John Scholls \ Kim Mitchell \ Scruff Connors

SCTV \ Martin Short \ Andrea Martin \ Dave Thomas \ Eugene Levy

TED - Sir Ken Robinson, speaker, Daphne Zuniga, actress & film maker

SA FLATT FT
GROUP MEDLEYS

These lists are all extensions of those created in chapter 21.

1. ***Bad Side Of The Moon***, *I Wouldn't Want To Lose Your Love, Just Between You And Me, Lady Run Lady Hide, Oowatanite, You Could Have Been A Lady & You Won't Dance With Me* - **April Wine**

2. *Across The Universe, Baby You're A Rich Man, Come Together, A Day In The Life, Don't Let Me Down, Eleanor Rigby, Fool On The Hill, For No One, Hello Goodbye, Here There & Everywhere, Hey Bulldog,* ***I Am The Walrus****, In My Life, Magical Mystery Tour, Seargent Pepper's Lonely Hearts Club Band, Strawberry Fields Forever, We Can Work It Out & Yesterday* - **The Beatles**

3. *Baby I'm A Want You, Everything I Own, Guitar Man, It Don't Matter To Me, Make it With You & Sweet Surrender* - **Bread**

4. *(I've Been) Searchin' So Long, Another Rainy Day In NYC, Baby What A Big Surprise, Dialogue, Feeling Stronger Everyday, Hard Habit To Break, Harry Truman, Just You'n Me,* ***Lowdown****, No Tell Lover & Questions 67 & 68* - **Chicago**

5. *Another Park Another Sunday,* ***Black Water****, Listen to The Music, Slat Key Soquel Rag (/b), Song To See You Through (/b) & Take Me In Your Arms (Rock Me)* - **The Doobie Brothers**

6. *Best Of My Love, I Can't Tell You Why, Life In The Fast Lane,* ***The Long Run****, New Kid In Town, One Of These Nights, Tequila Sunrise, Try And Love Again, Victim Of Love (/b) & Witchy Woman* - **The Eagles**

7. *Can't Get It Out of My Head, Don't Bring Me Down & Strange Magic* - **The Electric Light Orchestra**

8. *Counting Out Time,* ***Follow You Follow Me,*** *Hold On My Heart,* ***I Know What I Like (In Your Wardrobe)****, Illegal Alien, It's Gonna Get Better, Mama, No Son Of Mine, Second Home By The Sea,* ***THAT'S ALL****, Throwing It All Away & Tonight Tonight, Tonight* - **Genesis**

9. *American Woman, Hand Me Down World, Laughing & No Sugar Tonight,* ***These Eyes*** - **The Guess Who**

10. *Black Dog, Four Sticks, Good Times Bad Times, Hey Hey What Can I Do, Stairway To Heaven &* **Whole Lotta Love** *-* **Led Zeppelin**

11. *Band On The Run, Let 'Em In, No More Lonely Nights, Once Upon A Long Ago,* **Sally G (/b)**, *So Bad, This One, Too Many People (/b), Uncle Albert/Admiral Halsey & Letting Go -* **Paul McCartney & Wings**

12. **Breakdown (/b),** *I Wouldn't Want To Be Like You, Children Of The Moon (/b), The Raven, Turn Of A Friendly Card Pt.1, Urbania (/b) & What Goes Up -* **The Alan Parsons Project**

13. *Alive & Kicking, All The Things She Said,* **Glittering Prize**, *Hypnotized, She's A River, Someone Somewhere In Summertime, This Is Your Land & Up On The Catwalk -* **Simple Minds**

14. *Bloody Well Right, Crazy, Free As A Bird,* **Give A Little Bit**, *Gone Hollywood (/b), Just Another Nervous Wreck (/b) & Sister Moonshine (/b) -* **Supertramp**

15. *(The) Big Chair (/b),* **Head Over Heels, Sowing The Seeds Of Love,** *Shout *& When In Love With A Blind Man (/b) -* **Tears For Fears**

16. *Celebrate, Liar, Never Been To Spain,* **Old Fashioned Love Song** *& Show Must Go On -* **Three Dog Night**

17. *All I Want Is You, I Still Haven't Found What I'm Looking For, Pride (In The Name Of Love), Running To Stand Still (/b),* **Stay (Faraway, So Close!)** *& Sunday Bloody Sunday, Treasure (/b) -* **U2**

18. *Does It Really Happen?, Don't Kill The Whale, Leave It, Lift Me Up,* **Long Distance Runaround (/b),** *& Release Release -* **Yes**

2020

FIFTEEN

STORES

This inventory of stores that I have purchased singles at over the years has been compiled from credit card statements, shopping mall directories & maps & store bags & receipts.

ENGLAND

1. ANDY'S RECORDS \ Cambridge
2. BEAT GOES ON \ Cambridge
3. JAYS \ Cambridge
4. OUR PRICE \ Cambridge & Oxford
5. RECORD BAR \ Lincoln
6. VIRGIN \ Westminster
7. W H SMITH \ Oxford

ONTARIO & BC

8. D & G COLLECTORS RECORDS \ Vancouver BC \ East Hastings
9. MARKET ROAD ANTIQUES \ Waterloo \ Weber St N
10. ONE OF A KINDD ANTIQUE MALL \ Woodstock \ Wilson St S
11. RAVE RECORDS \ Hamilton \ King St E
12. RECORD WORKS \ Woodstock \ Dundas St
13. SOUND FIXATION \ Stratford \ Erie St
14. ST. JACOBS ANTIQUES MARKET \ Waterloo \ King St N
15. STRATFORD ANTIQUE MARKET \Stratford \ Ontario St
16. WORLD'S COOLEST MUSIC STORE \ St Mary's \ Queen S

OTTAWA

17. GEM \ Ottawa \ Merivale Rd
18. LEGEND RECORDS \ Ottawa \ Lincoln Heights Galleria
19. MAD PLATTERS \ Ottawa \ Rideau St
20. MIRACLE MART \ Nepean \ Merivale Rd
21. SHAKE RECORDS \ Ottawa \ Laurier Ave
22. SUPER CLEF \ Nepean \ Clyde Ave

TORONTO

23. BLUE NOTE \ Toronto \ Danforth near Main
24. BOOK NOTE & RECORD \ North York \ Victoria Pk & Van Horne
25. CIRCLE OF SOUND \ Toronto \ Yonge near Gerrard
26. DISCOVERY RECORDS \ Toronto \ Queen St E
27. DISCUS \ Toronto

28. DRIFTWOOD MUSIC \ Toronto \ Queen St W
29. FLIPSIDE \ Toronto
30. HARMONY \ Toronto \ Mt Pleasant Rd, north of Eglinton
31. INCREDIBLE RECORD STORE \ Toronto \ Yonge near Bloor
32. KOPS & VINTAGE SOUNDS \ Toronto \ Queen St W
33. MISTER SOUND \ Toronto
34. OPEN CITY \ Toronto \ Danforth between Greenwood & Coxwell
35. RECORD PEDDLAR \ Toronto \ Queen St E of Yonge St
36. RECORD WORLD \ Toronto \ Yonge & Eglinton
37. SOUND CITY \ Toronto \ Queen St E
38. TOWER RECORDS \ Toronto \ Yonge & Queen
39. VORTEX RECORDS \ Toronto \ Yonge north of Eglinton

USA
40. ATLANTIC SOUNDS \ Daytona Beach \ Florida
41. BARNES & NOBLE \ Amherst \ New York
42. BOO BOO RECORDS \ San Luis Obispo \ California
43. BROKE'N RECORDS VINYL \ Port Charlotte \ Florida
44. FYE \ Buffalo \ New York
45. GALLERY OF SOUND \ Dickson City \ Pennsylvania
46. LICORICE & PIZZA RECORDS & TAPES \ California
47. MUSIC FOR A SONG \ Darien \ Georgia \ Magnolia Bluffs Factory Shops
48. MUSIC FOR LESS \ Niagara Falls \ New York
49. NICKLEODEON \ Century City \ California \ Century City Mall
50. RECORD THEATRE \ Buffalo \ Williamsville \ New York \ (closed 2017)
51. TJ'S CDs & MORE \ Port Charlotte \ Florida

CANADA (mostly)
A&A RECORDS AND TAPES
52. \ Ottawa \ Rideau Centre
53. \ Scarborough \ Bridlewood Mall \ Scarborough Town Centre
54. \ Toronto \ Yonge north of Dundas

CHEAPIES RECORDS
55. \ Hamilton \ Downtown
56. \ Toronto \ Yonge near Queen \ Yonge near Wellesley
57. \ Vaughan \ Yonge & Steeles

HMV
58. \ Coventry \ England
59. \ Edmonton \ West Edmonton Mall
60. \ Etobicoke \ Sherway Gardens
61. \ Guelph \ Stone Road Mall
62. \ Kitchener \ Fairview Park Mall
63. \ London, England \ Oxford near Hyde Park

64. \ Mississauga \ Square One
65. \ Newmarket \ Upper Canada Mall
66. \ North York \ Fairview Mall \ Yorkdale Mall
67. \ Ottawa \ Rideau Centre
68. \ Scarborough \ Scarborough Town Centre
69. \ Toronto \ Bloor west of Yonge \ Eaton Centre \ First Canadian Place \ Yonge & Eglinton \ Yonge north of Dundas
70. \ Waterloo \ Conestoga Mall

KMART
71. \ Nepean \ Merivale Rd
72. \ North York \ Bayview Village

MUSIC WORLD
73. \ East York \ Shoppers World Danforth
74. \ Guelph \ Stone Road Mall
75. \ North York \ Don Mills Centre \ Fairview Mall \ Yorkdale Mall
76. \ Ottawa \ Rideau Centre
77. \ Scarborough \ Scarborough Town Centre
78. \ Toronto \ Eaton Centre \ Yonge north of Dundas

PETER DUNN'S VINYL MUSEUM
79. \ Clearwater \ Florida
80. \ Etobicoke \ Lakeshore east of Islington \ Lakeshore east of Royal York
81. \ Toronto \ Bloor St W \ Yonge north of Dundas

RECORDS ON WHEELS
82. \ Toronto \ Yonge south of Bloor \ Yonge & Dundas

SAM THE RECORD MAN
83. \ Barrie \ Downtown
84. \ Etobicoke \ Sherway Gardens
85. \ Guelph \ Stone Road Mall
86. \ Hamilton \ Downtown
87. \ Kitchener \ Downtown
88. \ London \ White Oaks Mall
89. \ Nepean \ Bayshore Shopping Centre \ Merivale Mall
90. \ North York \ Bayview Village \ Fairview Mall \ Town & Country \ Yorkdale
91. \ Ottawa \ Carlingwood Mall \ Lincoln Fields \ Sparks St Mall
92. \ Scarborough \ Eglinton Square
93. \ Toronto \ Danforth east of Broadview \ Yonge & St. Clair \ Yonge north of Dundas \ Yonge south of Eglinton

SUNRISE
94. \ Guelph \ Stone Road Mall

95. \ Kitchener \ Fairview Park Mall
96. \ London \ Masonville Mall \ White Oaks Mall
97. \ Newmarket \ Upper Canada Mall
98. \ Toronto \ First Canadian Place \ Yonge north of Dundas
99. \ Waterloo \ Conestogo Mall

TREBLE CLEF
100.   \ Nepean \ Merivale Rd
101.   \ Ottawa \ Billings Bridge \ Rideau St \ Sparks St

WOOLCO
102.   \ North York \ Town & Country
103.   \ Scarborough \ Agincourt Mall

SIXTEEN

TERMS

*(terms that have influenced lists are noted as *)*

The format of this terms appendix was inspiration for using naming conventions in a number of other appendices. It was created as a reference for the 2009 listing of my singles collection.

1. #1 - First Copy
2. #2 - Second Copy, etc.

3. 1ST_45Z - First Single bought by a specific artist. This excludes any artists with only single song entries in this collection. Upper Case designation may show for other indicators.

4. 2CNCRTPK - Singles from two different concerts at Exhibition Stadium, 5 years apart, 1979 & 1984, & 1 seat apart
5. 2INAROW - Two different songs in a row by the same artist
6. 2LPPK - Singles from albums that were bought in pairs
7. 2PK - 2 Singles bought together, second title included *
8. 3INAROW - Three different songs in a row by the same artist
9. 3PK - 3 Singles bought together, second and third titles included

FROM...(YEARS)...
10. 60s - the 1960s [T27] *
11. 73 - 1973 - Toronto (Tor), Ottawa (Ott) 1 [T102]
12. 74 - 1974 - Ott 2 [T65]
13. 75 - 1975 - Ott 3 [T77]
14. 76 - 1976 - Ott 4 [T38]
15. 77 - 1977 - Ott 5, Tor [T47]
16. 90s - the 90s [T22] (Most from Kops & Vintage) *

17. AB - Both A & B sides noted
18. ABC - Three songs. One side, A or B, has two of the three songs *

19. B1 - Side B Song 1 *
20. B2 - Side B Song 2, etc. *
21. BS - Special B Side, usually previously unreleased at time of single, often appear later in boxed sets & compilations [T35] *
22. Best_NO - Singles do not appear on "Best of" or "Greatest Hits" collections. *

23. CDN - Canadian Artist

CHARTED - 1 of 3 - (CANADA) …[T91]
(Most of these notations are for songs that only appeared on one not several different charts.)
24. Chrt_Edge - CFNY Toronto Songs of the decade, the 1980s & Regular editions of Music of the 80's
25. Chrt_Gl - in Toronto by *Into The Eighties* at Glendon College, York University
26. Chrt_Ott - in Ottawa by CFGO &/or CFRA (1970s)
27. Chrt_Q_70S - Q 107 Top 107 Of the 70s [T73]
28. Chrt_RPM - in Canada on RPM top 50/100 singles charts
29. Chrt_Tor - in Toronto by CHUM &/or CFTR or other (1970s)

CHARTED - 2 of 3 - (CKDK, THE HAWK) … [T318]
30. Chrt_Hawk - The January 2008 listing by CKDK Woodstock of the 1039 greatest
    rock'n roll songs of all time. A & B sides noted where needed.
31. Chrt_Hawk_OK - Overkill, towards the tally of songs in this collection in the 1039.
32. Chrt_Hawk_A - The A side is in the 1039.
33. Chrt_Hawk_A_OK - The A side is overkill
34. Chrt_Hawk_B - The B side is in the 1039
35. Chrt_Hawk_B_OK - The B side is overkill

CHARTED - 3 of 3 - (OTHER)…
36. Chrt_No - out of the top 40, or originally uncharted & later released as a single [T131]
37. Chrt_UK - in the UK top 40 but not NA [T27]

COLOUR DISK…
38. CLD_B - Blue, CLD_G - Gold, CLD_R - Red, CLD_W-White *

EAR (SOUNDS LIKE…) - These tags may appear in sequence of original tags without "EAR"
39. Ear_Ctry - Country or country influence [T21] *
40. Ear_Girl - Girl Bands or predominant singing by Females *
41. Ear_I - Instrumental [T25] *
42. Ear_Mono - Not Stereo
43. Ear_Ork - Orchestral accompaniments/arrangements including strings (not just horns and winds)
    [T95] *
44. Ear_Soul - Soul, R&B, Funk [T58] *
45. Ear_Tek - Technopop, not including those artists with 5 or more singles in this collection *
46. Ear_XMAS - Christmas music [T22] *

EVENTS - 1 of 3 (1970s) CHART BASED
47. Evnt_Chrt_Last_75_Ott - in Ottawa by CFRA, Last Personal Copy of Top 30, July 1975 *
48. Evnt_Chrt_Last_75_Tor - in Toronto by CHUM, Last Personal Copy of Top 30, April 1975 *
49. Evnt_RKY_Kings_72 - At RKY Camp, Near Kingston, listening to Songs on Top 30 radio,
    Watertown New York *
50. Evnt_Walk_Ott_74 - in Ottawa, Songs on Top 30, CFGO & CFRA, Miles For Millions, May 1974
51. Evnt_Walk_Tor_72 - in Toronto, Songs on CHUM Top 30, Miles For Millions, May 1972

52. Evnt_Walk_Tor_73 - in Toronto, Songs on CHUM Top 30, Miles For Millions, May 1973

EVENTS - 2 of 3 (1970s) CONCERT BASED

53. Evnt_CBOT_74 - Songs from CBOT Rock Concert, 1974, featuring, ELO, Manfred Mann, Mike Oldfield & The Rolling Stones *
54. Evnt_CHUM_SE_76 - Songs recorded from Ottawa during overnight show by 1050 CHUM DJ Steve Elliott in the Summer of 1976 *
55. Evnt_Jam_79 - Songs played in jam sessions in June of 1979 *
56. Evnt_Laser_Tor_78 - Part of music set performed at LASEROCK, McLachlan Planetarium, Royal Ontario Museum, Toronto, March 1978 *
57. Evnt_Yes_LA_79 - Yes recorded live in Los Angeles, 1979, on the King Biscuit Flower Hour *

EVENTS - 3 of 3 (Other Decades)

58. Evnt_Fun_Strat_08 - Songs played at the Family Fun Night, June 2008
59. Evnt_Kari_Ott_99 - Karaoke at Barhaven near Ottawa
60. Evnt_Ping_Tor_86 - Awarded as prizes at Forest Grove Fun Day *Ping Pong Pitch*, 1986 * (They were eventually readded to the collection), except for Three; *Cover of Rolling Stone, Kid Is Hot Tonight & Theme From "For A Few Dollars More"*.

FROM...

61. FD_DB, FR_DJ, FR_MS, FR_RG, FR_SY, FR_TD *

62. FRA_PAR - Paris, France (1986)

HOMEMADE PICTURE SLEEVES - 1 of 3 - A & B...[T332] (no facsimiles of artwork used on any HMPS, all originals)

63. HMPS_ACA - Album Cover Art (Titles may be abbreviated for many HMPS Tags) *
64. HMPS_ACAF - Album Cover Art, Full Sleeve coverage *
65. HMPS_AP - Album Poster *
66. HMPS_BK - Book *

HOMEMADE PICTURE SLEEVES - 2 of 3 - TYPE 1 COVERS [T81]

67. HMPS_COV_CAL - Calendar Cover *
68. HMPS_COV_CPC - Concert Program Cover *
69. HMPS_COV_MAG - Magazine Cover *
70. HMPS_COV_OAC - Old Album Cover *
71. HMPS_COV_OAS - Old Album Sleeve, Cover Quality *
72. HMPS_COV_OCAC - Old Cassette Album Cover *
73. HMPS_COV_OCSC - Old Cassette Single Cover *
74. HMPS_COV_PIP - Piano Vocals Chords Interior Page *
75. HMPS_COV_POST - Postcards - Cover Quality *
76. HMPS_COV_PVCC - Piano-Vocals-Chords Cover *

HOMEMADE PICTURE SLEEVES - 3 of 3 - C TO S

77. HMPS_CP - Concert Program *

78. HMPS_DEC - Decal *
79. HMPS_MAG - Magazine *
80. HMPS_NP - Newspaper *
81. HMPS_OAS - Old Album Sleeve *
82. HMPS_PLC - Playing Cards *
83. HMPS_PVC - Piano-Vocals-Chords *
84. HMPS_SCA - Single Cover Art *

LABELS...
85. Lab_ABC - ABC Dunhill Records *
86. Lab_Apple - Apple Records *
87. Lab_Anth - Anthem Records
88. Lab_At_Prom - Atlantic Promotional *
89. Lab_Atc_Ylw - Atco Yellow & White *
90. Lab_Atl_Prpl - Atlantic Purple *
91. Lab_Cap - Capital Records *
92. Lab_Cot - Cotillion records (ELP)
93. Lab_Fms_Chr - Famous Charisma
94. Lab_Kin - Kinney - (Pre WEA) *
95. Lab_Merc - Mercury Records *

96. LINK - Notation for A side of a double hit single where this original single was the B side
97. LIST_83 - Part of Record Inventory, as of July 1983 [T199]
98. *L I V E* - Live recording [T33] *

MADE IN... - These tags may appear in sequence of original tags without "MADE"
99.   Made_Aust - Australia
100.   Made_FRA - France
101.   Made_GER - Germany
102.   Made_ITA - Italy
103.   Made_NET - Netherlands
104.   Made_UK - Great Britain [T71]
105.   Made_US - United States [T152]
106.   Made_YU - Yugoslavia

107.   O1 - Only one single by this artist in this collection
108.   OK - Overkill, Songs A & B appear in combination with other songs on other records in this collection. [T80]
109.   OK_AB - Double Hit Singles that are Overkill in this collection.

ONTARIO...
110.   ON_EY - East York, ON *
111.   ON_HAM - Hamilton, ON (Most in 1984, 1985) *
112.   ON_KIT - Kitchener, ON (1985)
113.   ON_LON - London, ON

114.   ON_NEP - Nepean, ON *
115.   ON_NY - North York, ON *
116.   ON_OTT - Ottawa, ON *
117.   ON_SCAR - Scarborough, ON [T32] (Most in 1980) *
118.   ON_TOR - Toronto, ON *
119.   ON_WOODS - Woodstock, ON

PICTURE SLEEVES
120.   PS - Picture Sleeve [T277]
121.   PS1 - Same Song, Picture Sleeve, Version One
122.   PS2 - Same Song, Picture Sleeve, Version Two
123.   PS_GF - Gate Fold Version of Picture Sleeve *
124.   PS_US - U.S. Picture Sleeve

SAM THE RECORD MAN...
125.   SAM_BAR - Barrie, ON (1985)
126.   SAM_HDT - Hamilton Downtown *
127.   SAM_NEP_BS - Nepean Bayshore (1970s)
128.   SAM_NY_BVV - North York Bayview Village *
129.   SAM_NY_YD - North York Yorkdale *
130.   SAM_Ott_CW - Ottawa Carlingwood (1970s)
131.   SAM_Scar_TC - Scarborough Town Centre *
132.   SAM_TOR_DT - Downtown Toronto *

DOUBLE HIT SINGLES -1 of 2 [T120- 1 & 2]
133.   SS - Double hit singles
134.   SS_AB - Not originally released as a double hit single but can now be considered so.
135.   SS_A&MEM - A&M Memories
136.   SS_ARBTB - Arista Back To Back (& Flashback) *
137.   SS_Cap - Capitol Starline
138.   SS_EARG - Elektra/Asylum/Reprise Gold *
139.   SS_Eric_2_Artists - Eric Oldies with A & B sides by different artists *
140.   SS_Geff - Geffen Gold
141.   SS_IGLD - Island Gold *
142.   SS_MGld - Mercury Gold
143.   SS_TSOP - The Sound Of Philadelphia

DOUBLE HIT SINGLES - 2 of 2 - (CANADA & US)...
144.   SS_AT_G - Atlantic Gold (Canada) *
145.   SS_AT_O - Atlantic Oldies (US) *
146.   SS_AT_RLZ - Atlantic Red Led Zep (Canada & US) - Original Led Zeppelin singles, later
       reissued as SS_AT_G and/or SS_AT_O *
147.   SS_CBSF_B - CBS Hall of Fame Blue (Canada From 1974)
148.   SS_CBSF_G - CBS Hall of Fame Grey (US) *
149.   SS_CBSF_R - CBS Hall of Fame Red (Canada To 1974)

150. SS_WBack - Back to back Warner (US) Hits *
151. SS_WGold - Warner Gold (WEA-Canada) Hits

STORES - 1 of 4 - GREATER OTTAWA
152. STOR_Nep_GEM - Government Employee Merchandise, Nepean (1973)
153. STOR_Nep_MM - Miracle Mart, Nepean (1973, 1974) *
154. STOR_Nep_SC - Super Clef, Nepean
155. STOR_OTT_A&A_RC - Rideau Centre (Most in 1989)
156. STOR_OTT_LEG - Legend Records, Ottawa [T115] (1990s)
157. STOR_Ott_MP - Mad Platters, Ottawa

STORES - 2 of 4 - ONTARIO & BC...
158. STOR_STJAC_Ant - St.Jacobs Antique Market (2007)
159. STOR_STRAT_Ant - Stratford Antique Market (2007)
160. STOR_VAN_D&G - D&G records in Vancouver near PNE (1999)
161. Stor_Woods_Toy - Woodstock, ON, Toy show (2007)

STORES - 3 of 4 - TORONTO 1 (TORONTO)...
162. STOR_TOR_DISC - Disc record store
163. STOR_TOR_DVM - Dunn's Vinyl Museum [T59] (1980s)
164. STOR_TOR_DVM_LS - Dunn's Vinyl Museum Lakeshore
165. STOR_TOR_HAR - Harmony Records (2007)
166. STOR_TOR_JUST4 - Just For The Record
167. STOR_TOR_KOPS - Kops & Vortex Collectibles - [T74] (2000s)
168. STOR_TOR_ROW_Nr_PT - Records On Wheels near Piccadilly Tube
169. STOR_TOR_VINT - Vintage Sounds (Kops & Vortex Collectibles) [T54] (2000s)

STORES - 4 of 4 - TORONTO 2 (SCAR, EY, NY))
170. STOR_SCAR_A&A_BM - Bridlewood Mall *
171. STOR_EY_BLN - Blue Note, East York
172. STOR_NY_ BKN - Booknote, North York [T30] (1973) *
173. STOR_NY_MW_FV - Music World, Fairview, North York (1973) *

SONG STRUCTURE...
174. Str_RNR145 - based on a 1-4-5 chord change/progression [T20] *
175. Str_Suite - Songs that have two or more distinctive sections [T48] *
176. Str_TO5 - more than 5 minutes in length *

177. [T#] - Totals # singles for groups with 5 or more

UK RECORD STORE... [T27] (1984)
178. UK_BRIST - Bristford *
179. UK_CAMB_BEAT - Beat Goes on Cambridge *
180. UK_CAMB_JAYS - Jays, Cambridge *
181. UK_CAMB_OP - Our Price, Cambridge *

182.   UK_COV_HMV - HMV, Coventry *
183.   UK_COV_CS - Card Shop, Coventry *
184.   UK_LINC_RB - Record Bar, Lincoln *
185.   UK_LOND - London *
186.   UK_OXF_OP - Our Price, Oxford *
187.   UK_RICH_MRKT - Outdoor Market, Richmond *
188.   UK_WESTM_VIRG - Virgin, West Minster *
189.   UK_YORK_WHS - W H SMITH, York *

US LOCATIONS & STORES… [T36]
190.   US_CAL_HW - Hollywood, CAL (1983) *
191.   US_CAL_SLO - San Louis Obispo, CAL (1983) *
192.   US_FLA_CLEAR_DVM - Dunn's Vinyl Museum, Clearwater, FLA (1991)*
193.   US_NV_RENO - Reno, NV (1983) *
194.   US_NY_Buff - Buffalo, NY *
195.   US_NY_Buff_RT - Record Theatre, Buffalo *
196.   US_NY_EHLI - East Hampton, Long Island, NY (1983) *
197.   US_VER - Vermont, US (1976) *

VERSIONS… - These tags May appear in sequence of original tags without "VER"
198.   Ver_Cover - Re-recorded versions of other artists songs (excludes Christmas music) *
199.   VER_E_F_1 - Tag and Tally for songs with edited and full versions in this collection *
200.   Ver_Edit - Edited versions of songs found on albums *
201.   Ver_Full - Noted only where Edited and Full versions exist in this collection.
202.   Ver_RMX - remixed version rather than just the Edited version *
203.   Ver_RMX_Year - rerecorded version recorded years after the original *
204.   VER_S_L_1 - Tag and Tally for songs with studio and live versions in this collection
205.   Ver_SBTA - single versions that sound or are better than album versions *

TITLE NOTES I
THE SINGLES

Title Notes was the first real appendix that this story ever had, from an early version…

1. *Angie,* **The Rolling Stones,** 73
2. *Another Park Another Sunday,* **The Doobie Brothers,** 74
3. *Baker Street,* **Gerry Rafferty,** 78
4. *Band On The Run,* **Paul McCartney & Wings,** 73
5. *Blinded By The Light,* **Manfred Mann's Earth Band** (76 in UK & 77 in Canada)
6. *Blue Collar Man,* **Styx,** 78
7. *Bohemian Rhapsody,* **Queen** (75 in UK and 76 in Canada)
8. *C'est La Vie,* **Greg Lake,** 77
9. *Carry On Wayward Son,* **Kansas,** 77
10. **CBOT Rock Concert, 1974,** *Father Of Night* - **Manfred Mann,** *It's Only Rock & Roll,* **Rolling Stones,** *New World Rising,* **Electric Light Orchestra,** *Tubular Bells,* **Mike Oldfield**
11. **Chicago** - **(***I've Been***) Searchin' So Long**
12. *Dancing Queen,* **Abba** (76 in UK and 77 in Canada)
13. *Does It Really Happen?,* **Yes,** 80
14. *Don't Kill The Whale,* **Yes,** 79
15. *Drift Away 73 & Drift Away 79,* **Dobie Gray**
16. *Elegantly Wasted,* **INXS,** 97
17. **Emerson, Lake & Palmer** - *Fanfare For The Common Man,* **Aaron Copeland,** 77
18. *Friends Of Mr. Cairo,* **Jon & Vangelis,** 81
19. **Genesis** - *Entangled,* 76, *Follow You Follow Me,* 78, *Abacab,* 82
20. *Glittering Prize,* **Simple Minds,** 82
21. *Goodbye Stranger,* **Supertramp,** 79
22. *Heart Of Gold,* **Neil Young,** 72
23. *Helen Wheels,* **Paul McCartney & Wings,** 73
24. *Horse With No Name,* **America,** 72
25. *I Believe In Father Christmas* (the single version with choir and orchestra), **Greg Lake,** 75
26. *I Believe In Music,* **Gallery,** 72
27. *I Robot,* **Alan Parsons,** 77
28. *I Still Haven't Found What I'm Looking For,* **U2,** 87
29. *I'm A Stranger Here,* **Les Emmerson & The Five Man Electrical Band,** 73
30. *In God's Country,* **U2,** 87
31. *Jackie Blue,* **The Ozark Mountain Daredevils,** 75
32. *Just You'n Me,* **Chicago,** 73

33. *Killer Queen,* **Queen** (74 in UK and 75 in Canada).

34. *Last Song,* **Edward Bear,** 73

35. *Listen To The Music,* **The Doobie Brothers,** 72

36. *Magic,* **Pilot** (74 in UK and 75 in Canada).

37. *Money,* **Pink Floyd,** 73

38. *Moonlight Desires,* **Gowan,** 87

39. *Nights In White Satin,* **The Moody Blues.,** 72

40. *Oh Sherrie,* **Steve Perry,** 83

41. *Photograph,* **Ringo Starr,** 73

42. *Power Of Love,* **Celine Dion,** 93, **Frankie Goes To Hollywood,** 84 and **Huey Lewis,** 85

43. *Pretty Maids All In A Row, Hotel California* **The Eagles,** 77

44. **Procal Harum -** *A Whiter Shade Of Pale,* 67

45. *Rock and Roll,* **Led Zeppelin,** 71

46. *Sister Golden Hair,* **America,** 75

47. *Space Oddity,* **David Bowie** (69 & 73)

48. *Sultans Of Swing,* **Dire Straits,** 78

49. **Supertramp -** *Dreamer, Bloody Well Right,* 74, *Breakfast In America, Working Title, The logical Song, Take The Long Way Home, Heartbreaker, Gone Hollywood,* 79, *Rudy,* 74, *Downstream,* 77, *It's Raining Again,* 82, *Goodbye Stranger, Breakfast In America Title Track,* 79.

50. *Telegraph,* **Orchestral Manoeuvres in the Dark,** 83

51. *The Last Resort,* **The Eagles,** 77

52. *The Turn Of A Friendly Card,* **The Alan Parsons Project,** 80

53. *Theme From "For A Few Dollars More",* **Babe Ruth,** 74

54. *Theme from S.W.A.T.,* **THP Orchestra, Central Forces Staff Band,** 76

55. **Thomas Dolby -** *I Scare Myself, Hyperactive,* 84

56. *Tie Your Mother Down,* **Queen,** 76

57. **U2 -** *Hold On To Love, Walk To The Water, Spanish Eyes, Silver & Gold, Deep In The Heart, The Sweetest Thing,* 87, *All I Want Is You,* 88,

58. *Waterfront,* 84 & *Waterfront 89,* 89 - **Simple Minds**

59. *We Will Rock You/We Are The Champions.* - **Queen,** 77

60. *Where The Streets Have No Name.* **U2,** 87

61. *Whole Lotta Love,* **Led Zeppelin,** 70

62. *Wildfire,* **Michael Murphy,** 75

63. *Wildwood Weed,* **Jim Stafford**

64. **Yes -** *Run Through The Light,* 80, *Roundabout,* 72, *Going For The One, Awaken,* 77, *Long Distance Runaround / The Gates Of Delirium / Soon,* 79, *White Car, Man In A White Car, Run Through The Light,* 80, *Soon,* 75, *Into The Lens / Does It Really Happen?,* 80, *Don't Kill The Whale,* 78,

65. *You're So Vain,* **Carly Simon,** 73

EIGHTEEN

TITLE NOTES II
THE REST

Title Notes was the first real appendix that this story ever had, from an early version…

1. *1962-1966, 73, Rubber Soul, 66,* **Beatles**
2. *1985 Grammy Awards Music,* **Howard Jones, Thomas Dolby, Herbie Hancock and Stevie Wonder**
3. *25 Albums That Rocked The World,* **Chris Charlesworth,** 08
4. *A Trick Of The Tail,* **Genesis,** 76
5. *ALBUM COVER ALBUM,* **Roger Dean,** 77
6. **Beatles** - *1962-1966, 1967-1970, Rock'n Roll Music, Love Songs, Hey Jude, Magical Mystery Tour*
7. **Chicago** - *Chicago II, Chicago Gold, Chicago Ork, Chicago Transit Authority, Chicago 8, Chicago 9 (Their Greatest Hits)*
8. *City Lights,* **City TV, Christopher Ward**
9. *Classic Rock All Music Guide,* 01
10. *Close To The Edge,* **Yes,** 72
11. *Crime Of The Century,* **Supertramp,** 74
12. *Dark Side Of The Moon,* **Pink Floyd.,** 73
13. *Days Of Future Passed,* **The Moody Blues,** 67
14. *Elegantly Wasted,* **INXS,** 97
15. **Emerson, Lake & Palmer** - *Hoedown,* 72, *Jerusalem,* **William Blake,** 73
16. *Encyclopedia Of New Wave,* **Daniel Bukszpan, Gerald Casale,** 12
17. *Family Man,* **Nicholas Cage,** 00
18. *Firth Of Fifth,* **Genesis,** 73
19. *Fool's Overture,* **Supertramp,** 77
20. *Furioso For Band,* **Robert W Smith,** 76
21. **Genesis** - *Wind & Wuthering,* 76, *And Then There Were Three,* 78, *Calling All Stations,* 97, *Fading Lights,* 91, *Selling England By The Pound,* 73, *Squonk,* 76
22. *Genesis LIVE, CKCU 93.Live,* **CKCU FM, School Of Journalism, Carleton University,** 75
23. *High Fidelity,* **Jack Black, John Cusack,** 00
24. *Hootenanny, (Michael Rowed The Boat Ashore, When The Saints Go Marching In* and *Camptown Races),* **Harold L. Walters, Arr.,** 76
25. *If Everyone Was Listening,* **Supertramp,** 74
26. *In A Glass House,* **Gentle Giant,** 73
27. *In The Court Of The Crimson King,* **King Crimson,** 69
28. *Isle Of Wight Festival,* 1970
29. **John Majhor,** 1953-2007, **1050 CHUM** 1975-1986,

30. *Laser Floyd*, **McLachlan Planetarium**, 1984
31. *Late Show*, **David Letterman, Christopher Walken, Fat Boy Slim**, 01
32. *Leap Year*, **Amy Adams & Matthew Goode**, 09
33. *Led Zeppelin IV, Zoso*, **Led Zeppelin,** 71
34. *Live The Way We Walk*, **Genesis**, 93
35. *Long Distance Voyageur*, **The Moody Blues**, 81
36. *Love Theme From Blade Runner* - **Vangelis**, 82
37. *Merry Christmas Rock I*, 88, *Merry Christmas Rock II*, 93
38. **Moody Blues, The** - *Days Of Future Passed* (67 & 72)
39. *New World Symphony*, **Dvorak**, 1893
40. *Obsolete*, **Anna Jane Grossman**, 09
41. *Olivet To Calvary*, **John Henry Maunder**, 81
42. *One*, **U2**, 91
43. **Paul McCartney & Wings** - *Wings Over America*, 76, *Flowers In The Dirt*, 89, *Tripping The Live Fantastic*, 00
44. *Precious Declaration*, **Collective Soul,** 97
45. **Procal Harum** - *Live With The Edmonton Symphony Orchestra*, 72, *A Whiter Shade Of Pale*, 67
46. *Psychedelic Pseventies*, **Q107, Andy Frost**,
47. *Ramble On, Led Zeppelin II*, **Led Zeppelin**, 70
48. *Rattle & Hum*, **U2, Larry Mullen Jr.,** 88
49. *Rocking The Classics*, **Edward Macan**, 97
50. *Sam The Record Man*, **Sam Sniderman**
51. *Sgt. Pepper's Lonely Hearts Club Band*, **The Beatles**, 67
52. *Shine On You Crazy Diamond Part One*, **Pink Floyd**, 75
53. **Simple Minds** - *New Gold Dream*, 82, *Sparkle In The Rain*, 84, and *Once Upon A Time*, 86
54. *Songs From The Big Chair*, **Tears For Fears**, 85
55. *Stairway To Heaven*, **The Idols**, 81
56. ***Stan Kenton Jazz Clinic*, York University**, 76
57. *Star Spangled Banner*, **Marvin Gaye**, 82
58. **Supertramp - Crisis? What Crisis?**, 75**,** *Even In The Quietist Moments*, 77, *Laser Light Show*, **Vancouver Planetarium**, 78, *Crime Of The Century*, 74, *Breakfast In America, Working Title, Breakfast In Canada*, 79, *Fool's Overture*, 77, *If Everyone Was listening*, 74, *Night At The Proms*, **Roger Hodgeson, Paris**, 04, *Famous Last Words, Don't Leave Me Now*, 82, *Crime Of The Century Title Track*, 74
59. *Tarkus*, **Emerson, Lake & Palmer**, 71
60. **Tears For Fears** - *Songs From The Big Chair*, 85 & *Sowing The Seeds Of Love*, 89
61. *TED Conferences 2006 & 2010*, **Sir Ken Robinson**
62. *The Beatles As Musicians*, **Walter Everett**, 99
63. *The Beatles Illustrated Lyrics*, **Alan Aldridge**, 69
64. *The Best Of, Live At The Royal Albert Hall*, **Emerson, Lake & Palmer**, 93
65. *The Future We Will Create, TED*, **Daphne Zuniga**, 07
66. *The Golden Age Of Wireless*, **Thomas Dolby**, 83
67. *The New Age*, **Peter Weller**, 94
68. **Thomas Dolby** - *Golden Age Of Wireless, Blinded By Science, One Of Our Submarines*, 83
69. *Top 40 Hits*, 92, *Songs and Artists*, 06, **Joel Whitburn**

70. *Top Twenty Hit Singles Charts*, **Dave McAleer**, 07

71. *Top Twenty*, **Tony Jasper**, 83

72. *Trilogy*, **Emerson, Lake & Palmer**, 72

73. **U2** - *The Joshua Tree*, 87 and *The Unforgettable Fire, Unforgettable Fire Mini Album*, 84, *The Joshua Tree*, 87, *All I Want Is You*, 88

74. *Wembley Concert 1984*, **Elton John, Paul Young, Kool & The Gang, Nik Kershaw, Wang Chung, Thompson Twins**.

75. *Wind & Wuthering*, **Genesis**., 76

76. **Yes** - *90125*, 83 & *Big Generator*, 87, *Drama*, 80, *Tormato*, 79, *9012Live*, 85, *Fragile, Close To The Edge*, 72, *Going For The One*, 77, *Yesyears*, 91, *Tormato, On The Silent Wings Of Freedom*, 78, *Whitefish*, 85, *Yes Live in LA 1979*, **King Biscuit Flower Hour, CHUM FM,** *Yes, An Authorized Biography*, **Dan Hedges, 81,** *Drama*, 80, *Keys To Ascension*, 96, *90125*, 83, *9012live*, 85, *Big Generator*, 87, *Union*, 91, *Walls, Talk*, 94, *Yes Classic Tour 2002*, **Molson Amphitheatre, Toronto,** *South Side Of The Sky*, 72, *The Yes Album*, 71, *Yesyears*, 91, *Tales From Topographic Oceans*, 73, *Fly From Here*, 11, *The Ladder*, 99,

NINETEEN

SINGLES I - THE OVERLAP

The focus of the story is my personal singles collection so the songs in this appendix and the next appendix (All The Rest) are listed in alphabetical order by title, not by artist. The list by title is inspired by the first list by title that I created back in 1984, *The Singles Inventory*. All the titles that were in that list are noted in this list and appendix Twenty as si84. This appendix is, without a doubt, the most complicated, detailed, and important.

Along with the notation for *The Singles Inventory*, I have included *mzk01* for the music file I created in 2001. For the first time in all the lists I had compiled up to that point, I grouped songs into a number of different categories, categories that would form the basis of many of the lists mentioned in *th45zz* terms in 2009 and in the eventual *45 R P aMble* story. I have also included *tnotes* for title notes, the detailed list of the first song titles ever mentioned in this story (see appendix seventeen).

I describe the Overlap appendix as follows. "If any song appears on more than one 45, then it's in this list." As a result, all the songs in this list will show both A & B sides. Going a step further, there are even singles one song on the A side and two songs on the B side that are noted as B & C. Often single letters note a particular song while AB or ABC usually refer to the record itself, often where I bought it or what the label or the sleeve looks like.

Wherever the overlap does occur, I have listed all the songs together, whether it's as few as two or as many as five. Where there are similar titles in succession, I include details about the song title, [in square brackets, ahead of the artist's name]. The seventies titles in the overlap list outnumber the eighties titles by about two to one. I have also referenced the term < see > where songs are shared between different records.

Songs are referenced either by the list they are in or by the chapter they are in, in detail [in square brackets, following the artist's name]. 23.4 means the fourth list of chapter twenty-three. It is possible that some titles in this overlap section are not even referenced in the story. The notation /w is with and ps is picture sleeve, where sleeve has not already been noted. Spacing for double hit singles is expanded.

FLAT, *ps*, *si84* & US all tally somewhere in the two to three hundreds, across appendices Nineteen & Twenty. A nod goes out to a half dozen books and the part they have played in this collection.

THE GLOSSARY

A - Side A
B - Side B
BEL - Belgium
buks - bukszpan - Encyclopedia Of New Wave, Daniel Bukszpan
C - Track C where the second side has two tracks, B & C, often recorded @ 33 & 1/3 rpm
CAN - Canada
ch - chapter
cover - cover version

DEU - Germany

FLAT - Sa Flatt Ft - It's A Flat Foot Song [394]

FLATAB - Sa Flatt Ft - A&B Sides

FRA - France

gem - a special part of the story

gtns11 - *Desert Island Discs*, Ian Gittens (the number is the chapter in the book)

instrumental - instrumental version

ITA - Italy

JAP - Japan

levitin - *This Is Your Brain On Music*, Daniel Levitin

live - live version

long - long version

mcn22 - *Rocking The Classics*, Edward Macan (the number is the page in the book)

mono - engineered in mono sound

mzk01 - *Mzk01 of 2001*

NDR - The Netherlands

original - original version

ps - picture sleeve [252]

ride11 - (Keyboard Presents) *Classic Rock*, Ernie Rideout (the number is the page in the book)

quest - *questlove* - *Music Is History* by Questlove

see - link to another record with the same song

short - short version

si84 - *Singles Inventory of 1984 [275]*

stereo - engineered in stereo sound

th45zz - *th45zz*, terms of 2009

tnotes - Title Notes, A 45 R P aMble

UK - United Kingdom

US - United States [323]

/w - with

ward - *Is This Live?* by Christopher Ward

WB - Warner Brothers

YUG - Yugoslavia

THE SONGS

1. *(I Can't Get No) Satisfaction* - **The Rolling Stones** - [#1 CAN London orange] [64, 20.7]

2. *(I Can't Get No) Satisfaction* - **The Rolling Stones** - [#2 US London green]

3. *(I've Been) Searchin' So Long* [FLAT] */ Byblos* [#1 CAN] - **Chicago**
    [74, **A** *tnotes*, 20.3, 25.5, 25.9, 29.4]

4. *(I've Been) Searchin' So Long* [FLAT] */ Byblos* [#2 US] - **Chicago**

5. *(I've Been) Searchin' So Long* [FLAT] *// Call On Me* - **Chicago**
    [CAN CBS Hall Of Fame Blue DH] [74, **A** *tnotes*, 20.3, 25.5, 25.9, 29.4, **AB** 24.2, **B** 1.9, 11.2]
    (*see - Call on Me / Prelude To Aire*)

6. *25 or 6 to 4 / Where Do We Go From Here?* - **Chicago**

[74, **A** *quest*, 11.1, 11.2, 23.3, 26.4, **AB** 30.4]

(see - Make Me Smile // 25 Or 6 To 4)

7. *Abacab / Another Record* - **Genesis** - [#1 CAN]

    [82, **A** *tnotes* 14.2, 14.4, 19.7, 20.6, 22.18, 29.6, **AB** 2.14]

    < see - No Reply At All // Abacab)

8. *Abacab / Another Record* - **Genesis** - [#2 UK /w pic sleeve]

    [82, **A** *tnotes* 14.2, 14.4, 19.7, 20.6, 22.18, 29.6, **AB** *si84*, 2.14, 3.2]

9. *Abacab // No Reply At All* - **Genesis** - [CAN Atlantic Gold Standard DH]

    [82, **A** *mzk01*, 14.2, 14.4, 19.7, 20.6, 22.18, 29.6 **AB** *tnotes*, 8.2, 30.2, **B** *ride124_126*]

10. *After The Love Has Gone // Boogie Wonderland* - **Earth, Wind & Fire**

    [CAN CBS Hall Of Fame Blue DH] [79, **AB** *ch11,* 23.6, **B** *quest*]

    (see - Boogie Wonderland (original / instrumental))

11. *Albert Flasher* - **The Guess Who** - [#1 CAN nimbus 9] [71, 20.14]

12. *Albert Flasher* - **The Guess Who** - [#2 US RCA]

13. *Alive & Kicking (original / instrumental)* [FLAT] - **Simple Minds** - [86, *ps*, **A** 26.5S **AB** 3.3, 20.5]

    (see - Don't You (Forget About Me) // Alive & Kicking)

14. *All By Myself / Last Night* - **Eric Carmen** - [76, **A** 1.8, 20.16, 25.8]

15. *All By Myself // Never Gonna Fall In Love Again* - **Eric Carmen** - [Arista Flashback DH]

    [76, **A** 1.8, 8.4, 20.16, 25.8, **AB** *si84*, 24.2, **B** 20.12, 29.5]

    (see - Never Gonna Fall In Love Again / No Hard Feelings)

16. *All I Can Do / Got A Lot on My Head* - **The Cars** - [CAN] [79, **AB**, *si84*, 2.4]

    (see - It's All I Can Do / Candy - O)

17. *All I Want Is You* [FLAT] */ Unchained Melody* - **U2** - [US] [88, *ps*, **A** 13.3, 13.5, **B** 1.7, 3.3, 5.8]

18. *All The Things She Said* [FLAT] */ Don't You Forget About Me (Live)* - **Simple Minds**

    [86, *ps*, **AB** 3.3, **B** 20.5, 25.10]

    (see - Don't You (Forget About Me) // Alive & Kicking)

19. *All The Things She Said 12* [FLAT] */Don't You Forget About Me (Live)* - **Simple Minds**

    [86, **A** 12.5, 31.1.15, **AB** 3.3, **B** 25.10]

20. *America / For Emily, Whenever I May Find Her* - **Simon & Garfunkel** - [US CBS Silver DH]

    [68, **A** 20.10, 20.16, **AB** 5.16]

21. *America (cover) / Total Mass Retain* - **Yes** - [#1 CAN mono]

    [72, **A** 19.7, 20.14, **AB** *si84*, 18.2, 30.1, **B** 18.1, 20.6, 31.1.11]

22. *America (cover) / Total Mass Retain* - **Yes** - [#2 US mono]

    [72, **A** 19.7, 20.14, **AB** *si84*, 5.7, 18.2, 30.1, **B** 18.1, 20.6, 31.1.11]

23. *America (cover) // Your Move* - **Yes** - [US Atlantic Oldies Series DH]

    [72, **A** 20.14, **AB** *si84*, 5.10, 8.2, 18.2, 19.7, 30.1, **B** *mcn37*, 17.1, 19.8, 26.2]

    (see 1 & 2 - Roundabout // Your Move & Your Move / The Clap)

24. *And You & I (part one / two)* - **Yes** - [#1 CAN mono]

    [72, **A** *mcn97_101,* 18.2, 19.7, 19.8, 20.3, 20.5, 20.16, 26.2, **AB** 30.2]

25. *And You & I (part one / two)* - **Yes** - [#2 US stereo]

    [72, **A** *mcn97_101,* 18.2, 19.7, 19.8, 20.3, 20.5, 20.16, 26.2, **AB** 5.7, 30.2]

26. *Another Day In Paradise* [FLAT] */ Heat On The Street* - **Phil Collins**

    [89, **A** 21.4, 22.15, **AB** 2.13]

27. *Another Day In Paradise // Who Said I Would?* - **Phil Collins** - [US Atlantic Oldies Series DH]

[89, **A** 21.4, 22.15, **AB** 5.4, 5.8]

28. *Another Park Another Sunday* [FLATAB] \\ *Black Water* [FLATAB] - **The Doobie Brothers**
[DH] [74, **A** *mzk01, tnotes,* 4.8, 25.3, 25.5, **AB** *si84,* 1.1, 2.1]
[**B** 21.2, 21.3, 22.9, 22.14, 22.18, 25.4, 26.2]
(see 1 - Black Water / Song To See You Through)
(see 2 - Black Water / Take Me In Your Arms (Rock Me))

29. *Arthur's Theme / Minstrel Gigolo* - **Christopher Cross** - [#1 CAN /w graphic sleeve]
[81, **A** 27.5, **AB** *mzk01, si84,* 2.6, 5.3]

30. *Arthur's Theme / Minstrel Gigolo* - **Christopher Cross** - [#2 UK /w pic sleeve]
[81, **A** 27.5, **AB** 2.6, 5.3]

31. *Arthur's Theme* // *Say You'll Be Mine* - **Christopher Cross** - [CAN WB Gold Standard DH]
[81, **A** 27.5, **AB** 2.6]
(see - Say You'll Be Mine / Spinning)

32. *As The Years Go By* - **Mashmakhan** // *Yellow River* - **Christie**
[CAN CBS Hall Of Fame Blue DH] [70, **A** 19.3]

33. *As The Years Go By / Days When We Are Free* - **Mashmakhan**

34. *Baby I'm A Want You* [FLAT] / *Truckin'* - **Bread** - [71, **AB** 2.4]

35. *Baby I'm A Want You* [FLATAB] // *Everything I Own* [FLATAB] - **Bread**
[CAN Elektra Gold Standard DH] [71/72, **AB** *si84,* 24.2]
(see - Everything I Own / I Don't Love You)

36. *Bad Moon Rising* [FLAT] // *Lodi* - **Creedence Clearwater Revival** - [US Collectables DH]
[69, **A** *buks,* 21.3, **AB** 5.9]
(see - Medley USA // Bad Moon Rising)

37. *Ballroom Blitz* [FLAT] // *Fox On The Run* - **The Sweet** - [Capitol Starline DH]
[75, **A** 21.10, **AB** *si84,* 5.1]
(see - Fox On The Run / Burn On The Flame)

38. *Ballroom Blitz* [FLAT] / *Restless* - **The Sweet** - [US] [75, **A** 5.1, 21.10]

39. *Ballroom Blitz / Rock & Roll Disgrace* - **The Sweet**

40. *Baroque - A - Nova / Wanderlove* - **Mason Williams** - [US] [68, **A** 22.2
(see - Classical Gas // Baroque - A - Nova)

41. *Behind Closed Doors* - **Charlie Rich** - [#1 CAN] [73, 20.12]

42. *Behind Closed Doors* - **Charlie Rich** - [#2 US] [73, 20.12]

43. *Bette Davis Eyes* // *Goldfinger* - **Kim Carnes** - [US Collectables DH] [81, **AB** 5.9]

44. *Bette Davis Eyes / Miss You Tonight* - **Kim Carnes** - [81, **AB** 2.10]

45. *Better Days / No In Between* - **Supertramp** - [CAN /w pic sleeve]
[85, **A** *mzk01,* 1.9, 22.5, 22.11, **AB** 5.2, 5.3]
(see - Cannonball // Better Days)

46. *Better Days / Brother Where You Bound* - **Supertramp** - [FRA /w pic sleeve]
[85, **A** 1.9, 22.5, 22.11, **AB** *mzk01,* 5.2, 5.3, **B** 20.5]

47. *Black & White / Freedom For The Stallion* - **Three Dog Night** - [72, **A** 19.6, 25.2, **AB** 2.5, **B** 1.5]

48. *Black Dog* [FLAT] \\ *Misty Mountain Hop* - **Led Zeppelin** - [#1 CAN Atlantic Gold Standard DH]
[71, **A** 22.9, 26.2, **AB** 8.2, 15.1, 15.2, 30.3]

49. *Black Dog* [FLAT] \\ *Misty Mountain Hop* - **Led Zeppelin** - [#2 JPN /w pic sleeve DH]
[71, **A** 22.9, 26.2, **AB** 1.4, 3.2, 15.2, 30.3]

50. *Black Dog* [FLAT] \\ *Misty Mountain Hop* - **Led Zeppelin** - [#3 US original DH]
    [71, **A** 22.9, 26.2, **AB** 5.8, 15.1, 15.2, 30.3]

51. *Black Water* [FLATAB] / *Song To See You Through* [FLATAB] - **The Doobie Brothers**
    [75, **A** 21.2, 21.3, 22.9, 22.14, 22.18, 25.4, 26.2, **AB** 2.1, **B** 22.2]
    (see - Another Park Another Sunday \\ Black Water)

52. *Black Water* [FLATAB] // *Take Me In Your Arms (Rock Me)* [FLATAB] - **The Doobie Brothers**
    [US WB Back To Back Hits DH]
    [75, **A** 21.2, 21.3, 22.9, 22.14, 22.18, 25.4, 26.2, **AB** 2.6, 5.15, **B** 1.5, 25.7]
    (see 1 - Another Park Another Sunday \\ Black Water)
    (see 2 - Take Me In Your Arms (Rock Me) / Slat Key Soquel Rag)

53. *Blinded By The Light (cover) / Starbird* - **Manfred Mann's Earth Band** (Bruce Springsteen)
    [77, **A** *tnotes,* 1.6, 5.1, 19.4, 22.15, **AB** 2.1]

54. *Blinded By The Light (cover)* // *Spirit In The Night*
    Manfred Mann's Earth Band (Bruce Springsteen)
    [CAN WB Gold Standard DH] [77, **A** *tnotes,* 1.6, 5.1, 19.4, 22.15, **AB** 24.7, *mzk01, si84*]

55. *Boogie Wonderland (original / instrumental)* - **Earth, Wind & Fire** - [79, *ch11,quest*]
    (see - After The Love Has Gone // Boogie Wonderland)

56. *Boogie Woogie Bugle Boy / Delta Dawn* - **Bette Midler** - [73, **A** 20.7, 22.13, 29.2]

57. *Boogie Woogie Bugle Boy* // *Do You Want To Dance?* - **Bette Midler**
    [CAN Atlantic Gold Standard DH] [73, **A** 20.7, 22.13, 29.2]

58. *Brain Salad Surgery (album excerpts / single)* - **Emerson, Lake & Palmer** - [UK]
    [74, **A** 19.8, **AB** *ps,* 1.4, 3.2, 3.4, 3.5]
    (see - Fanfare For The Common Man / Brain Salad Surgery Single)

59. *Brand New Love Affair / Hideaway* - **Chicago** - [75, **A** *mzk01,* 20.16]
    (see - Old Days // Brand New Love Affair)

60. *Break It Up / Head Games (Live)* - **Foreigner** - [81, **A** *mzk01,* **AB** *ps,* 2.13, 3.3, **B** 25.10]

61. *Breakfast In America / Gone Hollywood (Heartbreaker)* [FLAT] - **Supertramp** - [UK]
    [79, **A** 5.11, 19.9, 22.11, 26.6, **AB** *ch16, ps, si84,* 1.4, 3.3, 16.1, **B** 20.5]

62. *Breakfast In America (Live) / You Started Laughing (Live)* - **Supertramp**
    [80, **A** *mzk01,* 16.1, 19.9, 22.11, **AB** *ch16,* 25.10]
    (see - Lady / You Started laughing)

63. *C'est La Vie / Jeremy Bender* [FLAT] - **Greg Lake** (Emerson, Lake & Palmer) - [CAN]
    [77/72, **A** *tnotes,* 1.4, 20.16, 22.8, 22.17, 22.18, 26.5S, 29.4, **AB** *ch14,* **B** 21.3, 22.6, 23.9, 23.10]

64. *C'est La Vie (long / short)* [FLAT] - **Greg Lake** (Emerson, Lake & Palmer) - [US]
    [77/72, **A** *tnotes,* 1.4, 20.16, 22.8, 22.17, 22.18, 26.5L, 29.4, **AB** *ch14,* 5.1, 30.2, **B** 26.5S]

65. *California Dreamin' (cover)* - **The Beach Boys** (The Mamas & The Papas) - [86, 1.7, 2.11]

66. *California Dreamin'* - **The Mamas & The Papas** - [66, 1.7, 22.11]

67. *Call on Me / Prelude To Air*e - **Chicago** - [74, **A** 1.9, 11.2, **AB** 30.1]
    (see - (I've Been) Searchin' So Long // Call On me)

68. *Cannonball / Ever Open Door* - **Supertramp** - [85, *ps,* **AB** 2.13]

69. *Cannonball* // *Better Days* - **Supertramp** - [A&M Memories DH] [85, **B** 1.9, 22.5, 22.11]
    (see 1 & 2 - Better Days / Brother Where You Bound & Better Days / No In Between)

70. *Cat's In The Cradle / Vacancy* - **Harry Chapin** - [74, 1.7, 2.4, 29.4]

71. *Cat's In The Cradle* // *Taxi* - **Harry Chapin** - [CAN Elektra Gold Standard DH]
    [74, **A** 1.7, 29.4, **B** 20.4]

(see 1 & 2 - Taxi / Empty & Taxi // Wold)

72. *Cat's In The Cradle (cover)* - **Ugly Kid Joe** (Harry Chapin) - [US] [93, 1.7, 24.8]

73. *Chiquitita* [FLAT] / *Lovelight* - **Abba** - [80, **A** 21.13]

74. *Chiquitita // Winner Takes It All* - **Abba** - [US Atlantic Oldies Series DH]
      [80, **A** 21.13, **AB** 5.4, 8.2]

75. *Classical Gas / Long Time Blues* - **Mason Williams** - [68, **A** *mzk01,* 22.1, 29.4, **B** 20.12]

76. *Classical Gas // Baroque-A-Nova* - **Mason Williams** - [US WB Back To Back Hits DH]
      [68, **A** *mzk01,* 22.1, 29.4, **AB** 2.6, 5.15, **B** 22.2]
      (see - Baroque - A - Nova / Wanderlove]

77. *Close To You / I Kept On Loving You* - **The Carpenters** - [70, **A** 20.13]

78. *Close To You // Ticket To Ride (cover)* - **The Carpenters** (The Beatles) - [US A&M Memories DH]
      [70, **A** 20.13, **B** 1.5]

79. *Close Your Eyes / Cachet Country* - **Edward Bear** - [73, **A** 19.6]
      (see - Last Song // Close Your Eyes)

80. *Closer To The Heart (Live) / Tom Sawyer (Live)* - **Rush** - [78/81, **A** *mzk01,* **AB** 25.10, **B** 21.12]
      (see - Tom Sawyer / Witch Hunt)

81. *Cold As Ice / I Need You* - **Foreigner** - [77, **A** 19.4, 20.14, **AB** *si84,* **B** 1.9]
      (see - Feels Like The First Time // Cold As Ice // Long Long Way From Home)

82. *Cold As Ice // Feels Like the First Time* - **Foreigner** - [Atlantic Gold Standard DH]
      [77, **A** 19.4, 20.14, **AB** 8.2, **B** 26.5L]
      (see 1 - Feels Like The First Time // Cold As Ice // Long Long Way From Home)
      (see 2 Feels Like The First Time / Woman Oh Woman)

83. *Colour My World // I'm A Man* - **Chicago** - [#1 CAN CBS Hall Of Fame Red DH]
      [71, **A** 20.2, 20.10, 22.11, **AB** 11.1, 11.2, 30.2, **B** 5.1]

84. *Colour My World // I'm A Man* - **Chicago** - [#2 US CBS Silver DH]
      [71, **A** 20.2, 20.10, 22.11, **AB** 5.16, 11.1, 11.2, 30.2, **B** 5.1]

85. *Conquistador (Live) // Whiter Shade Of Pale* - **Procal Harum** - [A&M Memories DH]
      [72/67, **A** *mzk01,* 22.13, 25.1, 25.10, 29.4, **AB** *si84,* 19.7, **B** *mcn21_168, tnotes,* 1.8, 19.9, 27.6]
      (see - A Whiter Shade Of Pale / Lime Street Blues)

86. *Conquistador (Live) / A Salty Dog* - **Procal Harum**
      [72, **A** *mzk01,* 19.7, 22.13, 25.1, 25.10, 29.4, **AB** *ps,* 3.2, **B** 22.3, 22.16]

87. *Crazy* - **Supertramp** - [#1 CAN] [82, *ch16, mzk01,* 1.9, 30.1]

88. *Crazy* - **Supertramp** - [#2 NDR /w pic sleeve] [82, *ch16, mzk01,* 1.9, 3.2]

89. *Crazy On You / Dreamboat Annie* - **Heart** - [US]
      [76, **A** 20.3, 25.8, 26.5S, **AB** *mzk01, si84,* 24.6, **B** 22.3, 26.5L, 26.6]
      (see - Dreamboat Annie / Sing Child)

90. *Crazy On You // Magic Man* [FLAT] - **Heart** - [US Rock'n Mania Records DH]
      [76, **A** 20.3, 25.8, **AB** 26.5L, **B** 20.4, 21.13, 26.4]
      (see - Magic Man / How Deep It Goes)

91. *Cry* - **Godley & Crème** [FLAT] // *Cry* - **Waterfront** - [US Collectables DH]
      [85/88, **A** 19.12, 21.7, **AB** 5.9]

92. *Cry / Love Bombs* - **Godley & Creme** [85, **A** 19.12, 21.7]

93. *Cuts Like A Knife / Lonely Night* - **Bryan Adams** - [83, **A** *ward,* 10.2, 19.5, 20.4, 26.2]

94. *Cuts Like A Knife // Straight From The Heart* - **Bryan Adams** - [A&M Memories DH]
      [83, **A** *ward,* 10.2, 20.4, 26.2, **AB** 19.5]
      (see - Straight From The Heart / What's It Gonna Be?)

95. *D'Yer Ma'Ker* [FLAT] \\ *The Crunge* - **Led Zeppelin** - [#1 CAN Atlantic Gold Standard DH]
    [74, **A** 15.2, 20.8, **AB** 8.2, 15.1]

96. *D'Yer Ma'Ker* [FLAT] \\ *The Crunge* - **Led Zeppelin** - [#2 CAN original DH]
    [74, **A** 15.2, 20.8, **AB** 15.1, 23.2]

97. *D'Yer Ma'Ker* [FLAT] \\ *The Crunge* - **Led Zeppelin** - [#3 US original DH]
    [74, **A** 15.2, 20.8, **AB** 5.8]

98. *Damned If I Do / If I Could Change Your Mind* - **The Alan Parsons Project**
    [80, **AB** *mzk01*, *si84*, 15.3, 24.7]

99. *Damned If I Do* \\ *You Lie Down With Dogs* - **The Alan Parsons Project** - [DEU DH]
    [80, **AB** *ps*, 1.1, 15.3, **B** *mzk01*]
    (*see - You Lie Down With Dogs \\ Lucifer*)

100. *Dance Hall Days* [FLAT] / *Ornamental Elephant* - **Wang Chung**
    [84, **A** *buks*, 19.11, 21.7, **AB** 2.9]

101. *Dance Hall Days* [FLAT] // *Don't Let Go* - **Wang Chung** - [US Geffen Back To Back Hits DH]
    [84/87, **A** *buks*, 19.11, 21.7]
    (*see - Let's Go / The World In Which We Live*)

102. *Dancing Queen / That's Me* - **Abba**
    [77, **A** *gtns47*, *tnotes*, 5.1, 27.3, **AB** *mzk01*, *si84*, 24.3, 24.6]
    (*see - Fernando // Dancing Queen*)

103. *Dancing With Tears In My Eyes* - **Ultravox** - [#1 CAN /w pic sleeve]
    [84, *buks*, 2.8, 5.3, 19.11]

104. *Dancing With Tears In My Eyes* - **Ultravox** - [#2 UK /w gatefold **pic sleeve**]
    [84, *buks*, 1.4, 3.4, 5.3, 19.11]

105. *Danny's Song (cover) / Drown Me* - **Anne Murray** (Loggins & Messina) - [73, **A** 1.5]

106. *Danny's Song (cover) // You Needed Me* - **Anne Murray** (Loggins & Messina)
    [US Collectables DH] [73, **A** 1.5, **AB** 5.9]

107. *De Do Do Do De Da Da Da // Don't Stand So Close To Me* - **The Police**
    [A&M Memories] [80, **AB** 12.3]
    (*see - Don't Stand So Close To Me / A Sermon*)

108. *De Do Do Do De Da Da Da / A Sermon* - **The Police** - [UK] [80, **A** 12.3, **AB** *si84*, 2.14, 5.11]

109. *Dead Skunk* [FLAT] / *Needless To Say* - **Loudon Wainwright III**]
    [73, **A** *mzk01*, 21.2, 21.3, 22.14, 23.7, **AB** 23.1]

110. *Dead Skunk* [FLAT] // *Bell Bottom Pants* - **Loudon Wainwright III**
    [CAN CBS Hall Of Fame Red DH] [73, **A** *mzk01*, 21.2, 21.3, 22.14, 23.7]

111. *Dirty Laundry // I Can't Stand Still* - **Don Henley** - [CAN Asylum Gold Standard DH]
    [82, **A** 19.5, 20.5, 23.4]

112. *Dirty Laundry / Lilah* - **Don Henley**

113. *Do It Again / Fire In The Hole* - **Steely Dan** - [73, **A** 19.7, 22.15, 26.5S, **AB** *si84*]

114. *Do It Again // Rikki Don't Lose That Number* - **Steely Dan** - [UK Old Gold DH]
    [73/74, **A** 19.7, 22.15, 26.5L, **B** 29.1]
    (*see - Rikki Don't Lose That Number / Pretzel Logic*)

115. *Does Anybody Really Know What time It Is? // Free* - **Chicago**
    [CAN CBS Hall Of Fame Red DH]
    [70/71, **A** 20.14, 22.13, **AB** *si84*, 11.1, 11.2, 30.4, **B** *mzk01*]

(see - Free / Free Country)

116. *Does Anybody Really Know What time It Is? / Listen* - **Chicago**
[70, **A** 11.1, 11.2, 20.14, 22.13]

117. *Don't Answer Me \\ Don't Let It Show* - **The Alan Parsons Project** - [DH]
[84/77, **A** *ch18,* 15.4, 22.16, **AB** *mzk01, ps, si84,* 1.1, 3.2, 3.6, 24.7, **B** 19.6, 20.3]
(see - Don't Let It Show / I Robot)

118. *Don't Kill The Whale* [FLAT] */ Abeline* - **Yes**
[79, **A** 4.2, 4.8, 17.1, 18.2, 22.18, **AB** *mzk01, ps, si84, tnotes,* **B** 4.9, 22.3]
(see - Release Release \\ Don't Kill The Whale)

119. *Don't Let It Show / I Robot* - **The Alan Parsons Project**
[77, **A** 19.6, 20.3, **B** 20.5, 22.2, 22.8]
(see - Don't Answer Me \\ Don't Let It Show)

120. *Don't Stand So Close To Me / Friends* - **The Police** - [ITA /w dark pic sleeve]
[81, **A** 12.3, **AB** 2.14, 5.2, 5.3]

121. *Don't Stand So Close To Me / A Sermon* - **The Police** - [CAN /w bright pic sleeve]
[81, **A** 12.3, **AB** *si84,* 5.2, 5.3]
(see 1 - De Do Do Do De Da Da Da / A Sermon)
(see 2 - De Do Do Do De Da Da Da // Don't Stand So Close To Me)

122. *Don't Stand So Close To Me 86 / Don't Stand So Close To Me (Live)* - **The Police**
[86, **A** 4.1, **AB** *ps,* 12.3]

123. *Don't You (Forget About Me) // Alive & Kicking* [FLAT] - **Simple Minds**
[A&M Memories DH] [85, **A** *buks,* 27.5, 30.3, **B** 20.5, 26.5L]
(see - Alive & Kicking (original / instrumental))
(see - All The Things She Said / Don't You Forget About Me (Live))

124. *Don't You Know What The Night Can Do?* - **Steve Winwood** - [#1 CAN] [88, *ch13*]

125. *Don't You Know What The Night Can Do?* - **Steve Winwood** - [#2 DEU] [88, *ch13, ps*]

126. *Dream On / Somebody* - **Aerosmith** - [76, **A** 4.2, 5.1, 25.8]

127. *Dream On // Sweet Emotion* [FLAT] - **Aerosmith** - [CAN CBS Hall Of Fame Blue DH]
[76/73, **A** 4.2, 5.1, 25.8, **AB** *mzk01, si84,* 24.2, 24.6, **B** 21.12, 26.6, 27.3]
(see - Sweet Emotion / Uncle Salty)

128. *Dream Weaver / Let It Out* - **Gary Wright** - [76, **A** 25.8, 26.5S, **AB** 2.1]

129. *Dream Weaver // Love Is Alive* [FLAT] - **Gary Wright** - [CAN WB Gold Standard DH]
[76, **A** 25.8, **AB** *si84,* 2.6, 24.2, 26.5L, **B** 21.12]
(see - Love Is Alive / Much Higher)

130. *Dreamboat Annie / Sing Child* - **Heart** - [76, **A** 20.6, 22.3, 26.5S, 26.6]
(see - Crazy On You / Dreamboat Annie)

131. *Dreamer / Bloody Well Right* [FLAT] - **Supertramp** - [US]
[75, **AB** *ch16, mzk01, si84, tnotes,* 1.4, 5.2, 5.10, 16.1, 19.8, 24.7, 30.1, **B** 26.6]

132. *Dreamer / From Now On* - **Supertramp** - [CAN]
[75/77, **A** *tnotes,* 3.2, 5.2, 19.8, 24.7, **AB** *ch16, mzk01, si84,* 16.1]

133. *Dreamer (Live) / You Started laughing (Live)* - **Supertramp** - [FRA / ITA /w pic sleeve]
[80, **A** 16.1, **AB** *ch16, mzk01, ps, si84,* 3.2, 5.2, 5.3, 5.11, 25.10, **B** 20.15, 22.18]
(see - Lady / You Started Laughing)

134. *Dreamer (Live) / From Now On (Live)* - **Supertramp** - [US /w pic sleeve]
[80, **AB** *ch16, mzk01,* 5.2, 5.3, 16.1, 25.10]

135. *Drift Away (cover) / City Stars* - **Dobie Gray** (Mentor Williams & John Henry Kurtz) - [US]

[73, **A** *tnotes,* 1.5, 19.10, 22.15, **AB** *si84*]

136. *Drift Away 79 (cover) / Lovin' Arms* - **Dobie Gray** - [US]
       (Mentor Williams & John Henry Kurtz) [79, **A** *tnotes,* 1.5, 4.1, 22.15, **AB** 5.10]

137. *(The) Entertainer / The Mexican Connection* - **Billy Joel** - [US] [74, **A** 24.12]
138. *Every Breath You Take* \\ *Murder By Numbers* - **The Police** - [#1 A&M Memories DH]
       [83, **A** *buks, levitin,* 12.3, **AB** *quest,* 1.1]
       (see - *Every Breath You Take // Wrapped Around Your Finger*)
139. *Every Breath You Take / Murder By Numbers* - **The Police** - [#2 original /w pic sleeve] [DH]
       [83, **A** *buks, levitin,* 12.3, **AB** *mzk01, quest, si84,* 1.1, 3.3]
140. *Every Breath You Take* // *Wrapped Around Your Finger* - **The Police**
       [US A&M Memories DH] [83/84, **A** *buks, levitin, quest,* **AB** 12.3, **B** 20.5]
       (see - *Wrapped Around Your Finger / Someone To Talk To*)
141. *Everybody Wants To Rule The World / Pharoahs* - **Tears For Fears**
       [85, **A** *buks, quest, ward,* **AB** *ps,* 1.4, 3.3, 20.15]
       [**B** *mzk01,* 4.10, 22.2, 22.4, 22.15, 22.16, 23.9, 23.10, 29.6]
142. *Everybody Wants To Rule The World 10 / Pharoahs* - **Tears For Fears**
143. *Everything I Own* [FLAT] / *I Don't Love You* - **Bread** - [72, **A** 2.2, **AB** 2.4]
       (see - *Baby I'm A Want You // Everything I Own*)
144. *Eye In The Sky / Gemini* - **The Alan Parsons Project** - [UK]
       [82, **A** *ch18,* 15.4, **AB** *ps,* 3.2, 8.5]
145. *Eye In The Sky* // *Psychobabble* - **The Alan Parsons Project** - [Arista Flashback DH]
       [82, **A** *ch18,* 15.4 **AB** 8.4]
       (see 1 & 2 - *Psychobabble / Children Of The Moon & Psychobabble (mono) / (stereo)*)

146. *Fanfare For The Common Man (cover) / Brain Salad Surgery Single*
       Emerson, Lake & Palmer (**A** - Aaron Copeland)
       [77/74, **A** *mcn168, mzk01, ride177_181, tnotes* 1.8, 14.1, 19.7, 19.9, 20.14, 22.1, 26.2]
       [**AB** *si84,* 30.1]
       (see - *Brain Salad Surgery (album excerpts / single)*)
147. *Feel Like Making Love* [FLAT] / *When You Smile* - **Roberta Flack** - [74, **A** 19.10, 21.13]
       (see - *Killing Me Softly With His Song // Feel Like Making Love*)
148. *Feels Like The First Time / Woman Oh Woman* - **Foreigner** - [77, **A** 26.5S]
149. *Feels Like The First Time* // *Cold As Ice* // *Long Long Way From Home*
       Foreigner - [UK] [77, **A** 26.5S, **ABC** *ps,* 1.10, 3.2, **B** 19.4, 20.14]
       (*Cold As Ice // Feels Like the First Time*)
150. *Fernando* // *Dancing Queen* - **Abba** - [US Atlantic Oldies Series DH]
       [77, **A** *gtns47, tnotes,* 22.16, 27.3, **AB** 5.4, **B** 5.1]
       (see - *Dancing Queen / That's Me*)
151. *Fernando / Rock Me* - **Abba** [76, **A** 22.16]
152. *First Cut Is The Deepest (cover)* - **Keith Hampshire** (Cat Stevens) - [73, 1.5, 10.3]
153. *First Cut Is The Deepest (cover)* - **Rod Stewart** (Cat Stevens) - [77, 1.6, 2.1, 2.6]
154. *First Time Ever I Saw Your Face / Trade Winds* - **Roberta Flack** - [72, **AB** 2.2]
       (see 1 - *Killing Me Softly With His Song // Trade Winds*)

(see 2 - Where is The Love // First Time Ever I Saw Your Face)

155. *Fly Across The Sea* [FLAT] / *Four Months Out To Africa* - **Edward Bear**
  [72, **A** 10.5, 19.3, 21.8, **AB** 10.1]
  (see - You Me & Mexico // Fly Across The Sea)

156. *Follow You Follow Me* [FLAT] / *Ballad Of Big* - **Genesis** - [CAN original]
  [78, **A** *ride123, tnotes*, 14.2, 14.4, 19.7, 20.2, 21.12, 26.5S, **AB** 5.2, 30.1]

157. *Follow You Follow Me* [FLAT] // *Illegal Alien* - **Genesis** - [US Atlantic Oldies Series DH]
  [78/83, **A** *ride123, tnotes*, 14.2, 14.4, 19.7, 20.2, 21.12, 26.5S]
  [**AB** *ride124_125*, 5.4, **B** 22.3]
  (see - Illegal Alien / Turn It On Again (Live))

158. *Follow You Follow Me* [FLAT] / *Inside & Out* - **Genesis** - [US original]
  [78, **A** *ride123, tnotes*, 14.2, 14.4, 19.7, 20.2, 21.12, 26.5S]
  [**AB** 5.2, **B** *mzk01*, 4.9, 20.3, 20.5, 29.6]
  (see - Spot The Pigeon EP - Match Of The Day / Pigeons / Inside & Out)

159. *Follow You Follow Me* [FLAT] // *Misunderstanding* - **Genesis**
  [CAN Atlantic Gold Standard DH] [78/80, **A** *ride123, tnotes*, 14.4, 19.7, 20.2]
  [**AB** *si84*, 8.2, 14.2, 21.12, 24.10, 26.5L, **B** 20.15, 22.3]
  (see - Misunderstanding / Behind The Lines)

160. *Follow You Follow Me* [FLAT] // *A Trick Of The Tail* - **Genesis** - [UK Old Gold DH]
  [78/76, **A** *ride123, tnotes*, 14.2, 19.7, 20.2, 21.12, 26.5L]
  [**AB** *si84*, 1.4, 5.11, 14.4, 30.1, **B** 19.8, 20.15]

161. *Follow Your Daughter Home* - **The Guess Who** - [#1 CAN nimbus 9]
  [73, 10.1, 10.5, 22.11, 23.1]

162. *Follow Your Daughter Home* - **The Guess Who** - [#2 US RCA] [73, 22.11]

163. *Fool In The Rain* \\ *Hot Dog* - **Led Zeppelin** - [#1 CAN original Swan Song DH]
  [79, **A** 15.2, 20.5, 20.16, 29.2, **AB** 30.4, **B** 20.7, 21.2, 22.6, 22.18]

164. *Fool In The Rain* \\ *Hot Dog* - **Led Zeppelin** - [#2 CAN Atlantic Gold Standard DH]
  [79, **A** 15.2, 20.5, 20.16, 29.2, **AB** 8.2, **B** 20.7, 21.2, 22.6, 22.18]

165. *Fox On The Run* / *Burn On The Flame* - The Sweet - [75, **A** 5.1]
  (see - Ballroom Blitz // Fox On The Run)

166. *Frankenstein* / *Undercover Man* - **The Edgar Winter Group** - [CAN]
  [73, **A** *mzk01, si84*, 19.12, 20.16, 22.1, 22.18, 23.1, 24.6, 27.2]

167. *Frankenstein (mono / stereo)* - **The Edgar Winter Group** - [US]

168. *Free* / *Free Country* - **Chicago** - [71, **A** *mzk01*, 11.1, 11.2]
  (see - Does Anybody Really Know What Time It Is? // Free)

169. *Free Man In Paris* [FLAT] / *People's Parties* - **Joni Mitchell** - [74, **A** 21.13]
  (see - Help Me // Free Man In Paris)

170. *Freedom For The Stallion (cover)* / *Why Won't You Marry Me*
  Edward Bear (A - Three Dog Night) [74, **A** 1.5]

171. *From The Beginning* / *Living Sin* - **Emerson, Lake & Palmer**
  [72, **A** 14.1, 20.16, 26.5S, **AB** *ch14*, 19.8, **B** *mcn57*]
  (see - Lucky Man // From The Beginning)

172. ***Games People Play*** - **The Spinners** - [#1 CAN] [75, 1.9]
  (see - They Just Can't Stop It (Games People Play))

173. ***Games People Play*** / *Ace Of Swords* - **The Alan Parsons Project**

274

[81, **A** *ch18,* 1.9, 15.4, **AB** *si84,* 15.3, 30.1, **B** 20.2, 20.16, 22.2, 22.11, 22.16, 29.4]
(see 1 - Time // Games People Play)
(see 2 - Turn Of A Friendly Card / Snake Eyes / Games People Play)

174. *Give A Little Bit* [FLAT] */ Downstream* - **Supertramp**
    [77, **A** 16.1, **AB** *ch16, ps,* **B** 20.11, 22.17]

175. *Give A Little Bit* [FLAT] *// Dreamer* - **Supertramp** - [DH] [77/75, **AB** *ch16,* 16.1, 30.2]
    (see 1 & 2 - Dreamer / Bloody Well Right & Dreamer / From Now On)

176. *Gloria / Living A Lie* - **Laura Branigan** - [82, **A** *buks,* 1.9]

177. *Gloria // Solitaire* - **Laura Branigan** - [#1 CAN Atlantic Gold Standard DH]
    [82/83, **A** *buks,* A 1.9, **AB** 8.2]

178. *Gloria // Solitaire* - **Laura Branigan** - [#2 US Atlantic Oldies Series DH]
    [82/83, **A** *buks,* A 1.9, **AB** 5.4, 8.2]

179. *(The) Gold Bug / Snake Eyes* - **The Alan Parsons Project**
    [80, **A** *ch18,* 15.4, 20.15, 22.2, **AB** 3.3, **B** 20.2, 22.3]
    (see 1 & 2 - Prime Time / The Gold Bug & Snake Eyes / I Don't Wanna Go Home)
    (see 3 - Time / The Gold Bug)
    (see 4 - Turn Of A Friendly Card / Snake Eyes / Games People Play)

180. *Goodbye Stranger / Even In The Quietist Moments* - **Supertramp**
    [#1 ITA /w waitress pic sleeve] [79/77, **A** *ch16, tnotes,* 22.10, 27.3, **AB** 3.3, 5.3, 16.1, 20.5, **B** 22.3, 22.11]
    (see - Logical Song, The // Goodbye Stranger)

181. *Goodbye Stranger / Even In The Quietist Moments* - **Supertramp** - [#2 US /w artwork pic sleeve]
    [79/77, **A** *ch16, tnotes,* 22.10, 27.3, **AB** *si84,* 5.3, 16.1, 20.5, **B** 22.3, 22.11]

182. *Goodbye Yellow Brick Road / Young Man's Blues* - **Elton John**
    [73, **A** 24.11, **AB** *mzk01, si84,* 2.5, 24.6]

183. *Goodbye Yellow Brick Road // Bite Your Lip* - **Elton John** - [US Collectables DH]
    [73/76, **A** 24.11, **AB** 5.9]

184. *Green Eyed Lady / Tongue In Cheek* - **Sugarloaf** - [#1 Spotlight short version]
    [70, **A** 19.3, 26.5S, **AB** *si84,* 2.5]

185. *Green Eyed Lady / West Of Tomorrow* - **Sugarloaf** - [#2 Liberty long version]
    Sugarloaf [70, **A** 19.3, 26.5L, **AB** 2.5]

186. *Hard Habit To Break* [FLAT] */ Remember The Feeling* - **Chicago** - [84, A 11.2, **AB** *ps,* 2.6]

187. *Hard Habit To Break // You're The Inspiration* - **Chicago** - [CAN WB Gold Standard DH]
    [84, **AB** 11.2, 30.4]
    (see - You're The Inspiration / Once In A Lifetime)

188. *Harry Truman* [FLAT] *// Old Days* - **Chicago** - [CAN CBS Hall Of Fame Red DH]
    [75, **A** *mzk01,* 22.11, 25.3, **B** 11.2, 25.6]
    (see - Old Days // Brand New Love Affair)

189. *Harry Truman* [FLAT] */ Till We Meet Again* - **Chicago** - [75, **A** *mzk01,* 22.11, 25.3, **AB** *ps*]

190. *He Ain't Heavy He's My Brother / Cos You Like To Love Me* - **The Hollies** - [70, **A** 22.12]

191. *He Ain't Heavy He's My Brother // Carrie Ann* - **The Hollies**
    [CAN CBS Hall Of Fame Blue DH] [70/67, **A** 22.12, **AB** *si84,* 24.2]

192. *Head Games // Dirty White Boy* - **Foreigner** - [CAN Atlantic Gold Standard DH] [78, **A** 8.2]

193. *Heart Of Gold* [FLAT] *// Old Man* - **Neil Young** - [CAN Reprise Gold Standard DH]

[72, **A** *tnotes*, 21.2, 21.12, 22.12, **B** *levitin*]
(*see - Old Man / The Needle Gone & The Damage Done*)

194. *Heart Of Gold* [FLAT] \\ *Sugar Mountain* - **Neil Young** - [DH]
[72, **A** *tnotes*, 21.2, 21.12, 22.12, **AB** *mzk01, si84*, 1.1, 2.2, 23.1, 24.7, **B** 22.17, 26.2]
(*see 1 - Looking For A Love / Sugar Mountain*)
(*see 2 - Sugar Mountain / The Needle Gone & The Damage Done*)

195. *Heartache Tonight / Teenage Jail* - **The Eagles** - [79, **A** 20.17, 23.4, 23.5]
(*see - Long Run, The // Heartache Tonight*)

196. *Hearts / Freeway* - **Marty Balin** - [81, **A** *mzk01, si84*, 2.10]

197. *Hearts* - **Marty Balin** // *What's Forever For* - **Michael Murphy**
[US American Pie Back To Back Hits DH] [*81/82,* **AB** 5.10]

198. *Heat Of The Moment // Only Time Will Tell* - **Asia** - [82, **AB** *ps*, 3.3, **B** 4.10, 22.18]
(*see - Only Time Will Tell / Time Again*)

199. *Heat Of The Moment / Ride Easy* - **Asia** - [82, **AB** *ps*, 3.3, **B** 4.10]

200. *Hello I Love You / Love Street* - **The Doors** - [US] [68, **A** 19.3, **AB** 8.1]
(*see - Touch Me // Hello I Love You*)

201. *Help Me // Free Man In Paris* [FLAT] - **Joni Mitchell** - [US Asylum Spun Gold DH]
[74, **AB** 5.14, **B** 21.13]
(*see - Free Man In Paris / People's Parties*)

202. *Hey Jude / Revolution* - **The Beatles** - [68, **A** *ward,* 20.4, **AB** 11.4, **B** 1.7, 20.15]

203. *Hitchin' A Ride // Early In The Morning* - **Vanity Fare** - [DH] [70/69, **A** 19.3, 23.7]

204. *Hitchin' A Ride / Man Child* - **Vanity Fare** - [70, **A** 19.3, 23.7]

205. *Hold Your Head Up* [FLAT] / *Closer To Heaven* - **Argent** - [US]
[72, **A** 4.3, 19.7, 21.9, 26.5S, **AB** *mzk01, si84*, 5.10, 24.6, 24.7]

206. *Hold Your Head Up* [FLAT] // *God Gave Rock & Roll To You* - **Argent**
[US CBS Silver DH] [72, **A** 4.3, 19.7, 20.4, 21.9, 26.5L, **AB** 5.16]

207. *Holiday // Borderline* - **Madonna** - [CAN Sire Gold Standard DH] [84, **AB** 12.6]

208. *Holiday / Think Of Me* - **Madonna** - [DEU]

209. *Hooked On A Feeling / I've Been Down This Road Before* - **B J Thomas** - [US]
[68, **A** 1.6, **B** 20.10]

210. *Hooked On A Feeling (cover) / Gotta Have Your Love* - **Blue Suede** (B J Thomas)
[74, **A** 1.6, 22.9, 25.5]

211. *Hooked On A Feeling (cover) // Never My Love (cover)*
Blue Suede (BJ Thomas) / (The Association) - [DH] [74, **A** 22.9, 25.5, **AB** 1.6]
(*see - Never My Love / Pinewood Rally*)

212. *Hooked On A Feeling // Raindrops Keep Falling On My Head* - **B J Thomas** - [DH]
[68/69, **A** 1.6, **B** 20.12, 22.13, 27.4]
(*see - Raindrops Keep Falling On My Head / Never Had It So Good*)

213. *Hotel California / Pretty Maids All In A Row* - **The Eagles** - [#1 CAN]
[77, **A** *gtns46, levitin,* 20.5, **AB** 23.4, 23.5, **B** *tnotes* 20.10, 22.7]

214. *Hotel California / Pretty Maids All In A Row* - **The Eagles** - [#2 UK]
[77, **A** *gtns46, levitin,* 20.5, **AB** 5.10, 23.4, 23.5, 30.4, **B** *tnotes* 20.10, 22.7]

215. *Hotel California // New Kid In Town* - **The Eagles** - [CAN Asylum Gold Standard DH]
[77, **A** *gtns46, levitin,* **AB** 20.5, 23.4, 23.5, **B** 19.6]
(*see - New Kid In Town / Victim Of Love*)

216. *Hush* [FLAT] // *Kentucky Woman* - **Deep Purple** - [CAN WB Gold Standard DH]
[68, **A** 19.7, 21.9, 22.3, **AB** *si84*]

217.   *Hush* [FLAT] / *One More Rainy Day* - **Deep Purple** - [68, **A** 19.7, 21.9, 22.3]

218.   *I Believe* - **Tears For Fears** - [85, *mzk01, ps,* 1.4, 3.3, 3.4, 8.5, 20.15]
219.   *I Believe (Live)* - **Tears For Fears** - [85, *mzk01, ps,* 1.4, 3.3, 3.4, 8.5, 20.15, 25.10]
220.   *I Believe In Father Christmas / Humbug* - **Greg Lake** (Emerson, Lake & Palmer) - [CAN]
        [75, **A** *ch14, mzk01, tnotes,* 1.4, 1.8, 4.2, 22.8, 23.9, 29.3, **AB** *si84,* 30.1, **B** 22.2]
221.   *I Believe In Father Christmas (mono / stereo)* - **Greg Lake** (Emerson, Lake & Palmer) - [US]
        [75, **A** *mzk01, tnotes,* 1.4, 1.8, 4.2, 22.8, 23.9, 29.3, **AB** *ch14, ps & lyrics,* 3.6]
222.   *I Can Dance (Long Tall Glasses) (cover)* - **Shooter** (Leo Sayer)
        [75, *si84,* 1.5, 2.1, 10.3, 20.7, 22.15, 29.2]
223.   *I Got A Name* [FLAT] // *Age* - **Jim Croce** - [US DH] [73, **A** 21.4]
224.   *I Got A Name / Alabama Rain* - **Jim Croce** - [CAN]
225.   *I Got The Message / Utter Space* - **Men Without Hats** - [UK] [82, **A** 10.4, **AB** *ps, si84,* 5.11]
        (see - *The Safety Dance // I Got The Message*)
226.   *I Know What I Like (In Your Wardrobe)* [FLATAB] // *Counting Out Time* [FLATAB]
        Genesis - [UK Old Gold DH]
        [73/75, **A** 14.2, 14.4, 19.7, 20.2, 21.12, 22.3, 22.11, 23.9, 26.2, 26.5L]
        [**AB** *si84,* 1.4, 5.11, 19.8, **B** *mcn84,* 19.9]
227.   *I Know What I Like (In Your Wardrobe)* [FLAT] // *Lamb Lies Down On Broadway*
        Genesis - [US Atlantic Oldies Series DH]
        [73/75, **A** 19.7, 20.2, 21.12, 22.3, 22.11, 23.9, 26.2, 26.5L]
        [**AB** 1.4, 5.4, 8.2, 14.2, 14.4, 19.8, **B** *ride125*]
228.   *I Know What I Like (In Your Wardrobe)* [FLAT] / *Twilight Alehouse* - **Genesis** - [UK]
        [73, **A** 14.2, 14.4, 19.7, 19.8, 20.2, 21.12, 22.3, 22.11, 23.9, 26.2, 26.5S]
        [**AB** 8.1, **B** *mzk01*]
229.   *I Missed Again / I'm Not Moving* - **Phil Collins** - [US] [81, **AB** 2.14, 5.8]
        (see - *In The Air Tonight // I Missed Again*)
230.   *I Never Cry / Go To Hell* - **Alice Cooper** - [US] [77, **AB** 2.1]
231.   *I Never Cry (Live) // You & Me (Live)* - **Alice Cooper** - [DH] [77, **AB** *mzk01, si84,* 25.10]
        (see - *You & Me / It's Hot Tonight*)
232.   *I Still Haven't Found What I'm Looking For* [FLAT] / *Spanish Eyes / Deep In The Heart* - **U2**
        [CAN /w pic sleeve] [87, **A** *tnotes,* 13.5, **ABC** 1.10, 3.3, 13.2, **BC** *mzk01,* 4.10, 29.6]
233.   *I Still Haven't Found What I'm Looking For* [FLAT] / *Spanish Eyes* - **U2** - [US]
        [87, **A** *tnotes,* 13.5, **AB** 30.2, **B** *mzk01,* 4.10, 29.6]
234.   *I Still Haven't Found What I'm Looking For* [FLAT] // *Where The Streets Have*
        No Name - **U2** - [US Island Revival Of The Fittest DH]
        [87, **AB** *tnotes,* 5.13, 13.5, 30.2, **B** 20.16, 26.2]
        (see 1 - *Where The Streets Have No Name / Silver & Gold*)
        (see 2 - *Where The Streets Have No Name / Silver & Gold / Sweetest Thing*)
235.   *I Will Follow (Live) // Pride (In The Name Of Love)* [FLAT] - **U2**
        [US Island Revival Of The Fittest DH]
        [83/84, **A** *mzk01,* 25.10, **AB** 5.13, 13.3, 30.3, **B** 13.1, 13.5]
        (see - *Pride (In The Name Of Love) / Boomerang II*)
236.   *I'd Like To Teach The World To Sing* - **Coke** // **Laurie Bower Singers / Dr. Music**
        [72, **A** 20.13, 23.9, **AB** *ps,* 1.10]

237. *I'd Like To Teach The World To Sing* - **The New Seekers** - [72, 2.4, 20.13]

238. *I'm A Believer* // *Pleasant Valley Sunday* - **The Monkees** - [US DH] [66/67, **AB** 8.4]

239. *If* // *Let Your Love Go* - **Bread** - [CAN Elektra Gold Standard DH]
    [71, **A** 22.17, **AB** *si84*, 24.2, **B** 20.13]
    (see - *Let Your Love Go / Too Much Love*)

240. *If / Take Comfort* - **Bread** - [71, **A** 22.17, **AB** 2.4]

241. *If I Were A Carpenter* [FLAT] // *Dream Lover* - **Bobby Darin**
    [US Atlantic Oldies Series DH] [66, **A** 21.4, 27.6, **AB** 5.4, 8.2]

242. *If I Were A Carpenter* [FLAT] / *Rainin'* - **Bobby Darin** - [US] [66, **A** 21.4, 27.6]

243. ***If You Don't Know Me By Now*** - **Harold Melvin & The Blue Notes & Teddy Pendergrass**
    [72, *mzk01*, 1.7, 19.10, 20.10]

244. ***If You Don't Know Me By Now*** (cover) / *Move On Out* - **Simply Red** - [US]
    (A - Harold Melvin & The Blue Notes & Teddy Pendergrass)
    [89, **A** 1.7, 20.10, **AB** 2.12]

245. ***If You Don't Know Me By Now*** (cover) // *You've Got It*
    Simply Red (Harold Melvin & The Blue Notes & Teddy Pendergrass)
    [US Asylum Spun Gold DH] [89, **A** *buks*, 1.7, 20.10, **AB** 5.14]

246. *If You Leave Me Now* - **Chicago** - [#1 CAN] [76, 11.2]

247. *If You Leave Me Now* - **Chicago** - [#2 US] [76, 11.2]

248. *Illegal Alien / Turn It On Again (Live)* - **Genesis** - [UK]
    [83, **A** *ride124_125*, 22.3, **AB** *ps*, *si84*, 2.14, 3.6, 5.11, **B** *ride129*, 14.2, 25.10]
    (see 1 - *Follow You Follow Me* // *Illegal Alien*)
    (see 2 - *Turn It On Again / Behind The Lines*)

249. *Immigrant Song* \\ *Hey Hey What Can I Do* [FLAT] - **Led Zeppelin**
    [#1 CAN Atlantic Gold Standard DH] [70, **A** 15.2, **AB** 1.4, 8.2, 15.1, 30.3, **B** 4.9, 26.2]

250. *Immigrant Song* \\ *Hey Hey What Can I Do* [FLAT] - **Led Zeppelin** - [#2 US original DH]
    [70, **A** 15.2, **AB** 1.4, 30.3, **B** 4.9, 26.2]

251. *In God's Country / Bullet The Blue Sky / Running To Stand Still* [FLAT] - **U2**
    [87, **A** *tnotes*, 4.8, **ABC** *ps*, 1.10, 3.3, **C** 13.5, 22.12]
    (see - *With Or Without You* // *In God's Country*)

252. *In The Air Tonight / The Roof Is Leaking* - **Phil Collins**
    [81, **A** 20.5, 22.15, 26.5S, **AB** *ps*, 2.13, 3.4]

253. *In The Air Tonight* // *I Missed Again* - **Phil Collins** - [CAN Atlantic Gold Standard DH]
    [81, **A** 20.5, 22.15, 26.5L, **AB** 8.2]
    (see - *I Missed Again / I'm Not Moving*)

254. *In Too Deep / I'd Rather Be You* - **Genesis** - [86, **A** *ch14*]
    (see - *Mama* // *In Too Deep* >

255. *Indian Reservation* (cover) // *Birds Of A Feather* - **The Raiders** (A - Don Pardon)
    [CAN CBS Hall Of Fame Red DH] [71, **A** 1.5, 20.13]

256. *Indian Reservation* (cover) / *Terry's Tune* - **The Raiders** (A - Don Pardon) - [71, **A** 1.5, 20.13]

257. *Into The Lens / Does It Really Happen?* [FLAT] - **Yes** - [#1 UK]
    [**A** 19.6, 29.6, **AB** 1.4, 19.8, **B** 19.7, 20.3, 20.5, 26.3]

258. *Into The Lens* (***I Am A Camera***) / *Does It Really Happen?* [FLAT] - **Yes** - [#2 US]
    [**A** 19.6, 29.6, **AB** *ch18*, 1.4, 5.7, 5.10, 19.8, 30.2, **B** 19.7, 20.3, 20.5]

259. *Into The Lens* (***I Am A Camera***) (Mono / Stereo) - **Yes** - [US]
    [80, **A** *ch18*, 19.6, 29.6, **AB** *mzk01*, *si84*, *tnotes*, 1.4, 19.8, 24.7]

260. *Invisible Touch / The Last Domino* - **Genesis** - [86, **A** *ch14, mcn193, ride131,* **AB** *ps,* **B** 20.5]

261. *Invisible Touch // Throwing It All Away* [FLAT] - **Genesis** - [US Atlantic Oldies Series DH]
     [86, **A** *ch14, mcn193, ride131,* **AB** 5.4]
     (see - *Throwing It All Away / Do The Neurotic*)

262. *It Can Happen (original / Live)* - **Yes** - [#1 CAN]
     [84, **AB** *ps,* 1.4, 3.3, 18.2, **B** *mzk01,* 20.5, 25.10, 29.6]

263. *It Can Happen (original / Live)* - **Yes** - [#2 DEU]
     [84, **AB** *ps,* 1.4, 3.3, 18.2, **B** *mzk01,* 20.5, 25.10, 29.6]

264. *It Don't Matter To Me* [FLAT] / ***Call On Me*** - **Bread** - [70, **AB** 8.1, **B** 1.9]
     (see - *Make It With You // It Don't Matter To Me*)

265. *It's All I Can Do / Candy - O* - **The Cars** - [UK /w pic sleeve] [79, **AB** 1.4, 2.4]
     (see - *All I Can Do / Got A Lot On My Head*)

266. *It's Raining Again / Bonnie* - **Supertramp** - [82, **A** *ch16, tnotes,* 22.8, 29.1, **AB** *ps, si84,* **B** 20.5]
     (see 1 - *My Kind Of Lady // It's Raining Again*)
     (see 2 - *Take The Long Way Home // It's Raining Again*)

267. *Joker, The* [FLAT] / *Something To Believe In* - **The Steve Miller Band**
     [73, **A** 21.2, 21.3, **AB** *si84*]

268. *Joker, The* [FLAT] // *Rock'n Me* - **The Steve Miller Band** - [CAN Capitol Starline DH]
     [73/76, **A** 21.2, 21.3, **AB** 24.10]

269. *Joker, The* [FLAT] // *Swingtown* - **The Steve Miller Band** - [US Collectables DH]
     [73/76, **A** 21.2, 21.3, **AB** 5.9]

270. *Jump / House Of Pain* - **Van Halen** - [84, **A** *buks,* **AB** 2.6]

271. *Jump // I'll Wait* - **Van Halen** - [CAN WB Gold Standard DH] [84, **A** *buks*]

272. *Jump / Running With The Devil* [FLAT] / *House Of Pain 12* - **Van Halen**
     [84/78, **A** *buks,* **ABC** 2.6, **B** 21.9]

273. *Just The Way You Are / Get It Right The First Time* [FLAT] - **Billy Joel**
     [78, **A** *ride63_65_69,* 24.12, **B** 21.10, 22.11]

274. *Just The Way You Are // Anthony's Song (Movin' Out)* - **Billy Joel** - [US CBS Silver DH]
     [78, **A** *ride63_65_69,* **AB** 5.8, 5.16, 24.12, **B** 22.3]

275. *Just The Way You Are // She's Always A Woman To Me* - **Billy Joel**
     [CAN CBS Hall Of Fame Blue DH]
     [78, **A** *ride63_65_69,* **AB** *mzk01, si84,* 24.2, 24.12, 30.4, **B** 20.10, 22.17]
     (see - *She's Always A Woman To Me / Vienna*)

276. *Just What I Needed // Good Times Roll* [FLAT] - **The Cars** - [US Elektra Spun Gold DH]
     [78, **AB** *buks,* 5.14, **B** 21.12]
     (see - *Tonight She Comes \\ Just What I Needed*)

277. *Just You'n Me* [FLAT] - **Chicago** - [#1 CAN] [73, *tnotes,* 11.1, 11.2, 24.1]

278. *Just You'n Me* [FLAT] - **Chicago** - [#2 YUG /w pic sleeve] [73, *tnotes,* 1.4, 11.1, 11.2]

279. *Killer Queen* - **Queen** - [#1 DEU /w black & blue pic sleeve]
     [75, *si84, tnotes,* 2.4, 3.2, 5.1, 5.3, 20.15]

280. *Killer Queen* - **Queen** - [#2 NDR /w black & white pic sleeve]
     [75, *tnotes,* 2.4, 5.1, 5.3, 20.15]

281. *Killing Me Softly With His Song // Feel Like Making Love* [FLAT] - **Roberta Flack**

[CAN Atlantic Gold Standard DH] [73/74, **A** *gtns27*, 22.9, **AB** 8.2, **B** 19.10, 21.13]
(*see - Feel Like Making Love / When You Smile*)

282. *Killing Me Softly With His Song // Trade Winds* - **Roberta Flack**
[US Atlantic Oldies Series DH] [73/69, **A** *gtns27*, 22.9, **AB** 5.4]
(*see - First Time Ever I Saw Your Face / Trade Winds*)

283. *Killing Me Softly With His Song /Just Like A Woman* - **Roberta Flack**
[73, **A** *gtns27*, 22.9, **AB** *si84*]

284. *King Of Pain / Someone To Talk To* - **The Police** - [83, **A** 12.3, **AB** *si84*, 3.3, **B** 22.7]
(*see - Wrapped Around Your Finger / Someone To Talk To*)

285. *La Bamba (cover)* - **Los Lobos** (Ritchie Valens) - [87, 2.6]

286. *La Bamba // Donna* - **Ritchie Valens** - [US Eric] [59, **AB** 1.3]

287. **Lady** / *You Started Laughing* - **Supertramp**
[76, **A** 1.9, **AB** 1.4, 24.4, **B** *ch16, mzk01*, 4.9, 20.15, 22.18, 29.6]

288. *Lady In Red* [FLAT] - **Chris De Burgh** - [#1] [87, 21.7]

289. *Lady In Red* - **Chris De Burgh** - [#2 /w pic sleeve]

290. *Land Of Confusion / Feeding The Fire* - **Genesis** - [86, **A** *ch14, quest,* **AB** 30.3]

291. *Land Of Confusion // Tonight Tonight Tonight* [FLAT] - **Genesis**
[US Atlantic Oldies Series DH] [86/87, **A** *ch14, quest,* **AB** 5.4, 30.3, **B** *ride131*]
(*see - Tonight Tonight Tonight / In The Glow Of The Night*)

292. *Last Song / Best Friend* - **Edward Bear**
[73, **A** *tnotes*, 19.3, 20.15, 22.13, **AB** *mzk01, ps, si84*, 3.6, 10.1, 23.1, 24.7]

293. *Last Song // Close Your Eyes* - **Edward Bear** - [Capitol Starline DH]
[**A** *tnotes*, 19.3, 20.15, 22.13, **AB** *si84*, **B** 19.6]
(*see - Close Your Eyes / Cachet Country*)

294. *Leave It (original / acapella)* [FLAT] - **Yes**
[84, **A** *mzk01,* 26.5S, 29.2, **AB** *ps, si84*, 3.3, 18.2, 22.9]
(*see - Owner Of A Lonely Heart // Leave It*)

295. *Leaving On A Jet Plane / The House Song* - **Peter. Paul & Mary**
[#1 WB green label] [67, **A** 1.6, 20.13, 22.17]

296. *Leaving On A Jet Plane / The House Song* - **Peter, Paul & Mary** - [#2 WB orange label]

297. *Leaving On A Jet Plane // I Dig Rock'n Roll Music* - **Peter. Paul & Mary**
[CAN WB Gold Standard DH]

298. *Legs / Bad Girl* - **ZZ Top** [84, **AB** 2.6]

299. *Legs // Sharp Dressed Man* - **ZZ Top** - [US WB Back To Back Hits DH]
[84/83, **AB** 2.6, 5.15, **B** 20.7]
(*see - Sharp Dressed Man / I Got The 6*)

300. *Let It Ride* [FLAT] / *Tramp* - **Bachman - Turner Overdrive** - [74, **A** 21.9, 25.5]

301. *Let It Ride // Blue Collar* - **Bachman - Turner Overdrive** - [DH]
[74/73, **A** 21.9, 25.5, **AB** 23.2, **B** 10.3]

302. *Let My Love Open The Door* [FLAT] - **Pete Townsend** - [#1 CAN] [80, *si84*, 19.5, 21.10]

303. *Let My Love Open The Door* - **Pete Townsend** - [#2 UK] [80, *si84*, 5.11, 19.5, 21.10]

304. *Let Your Love Go / Too Much Love* - **Bread** - [71, **A** 20.13, **AB** 2.2, 2.4]
(*see - If // Let Your Love Go*)

305. *Letter, The // Sweet Cream Ladies* - **The Box Tops** - [US Collectables DH]

[67/69, **A** 1.6, 27.6, **AB** 5.9]

306. *Letter, The (Live) (cover)* - **Joe Cocker** (The Box Tops) [70, 1.6, 25.10]

307. ***Let's Go / The World In Which We Live*** - **Wang Chung** - [87, **A** 1.9]

308. *Light My Fire // Love Me Two Times* - **The Doors** - [US Elektra Spun Gold DH]
     [67, *ride24,* **A** 19.3, **AB** 5.14, **B** 20.15]

309. *Light My Fire // People Are Strange* - **The Doors** - [CAN Elektra Gold Standard DH]
     [67, *ride24,* **A** 19.3, **B** 20.15]

310. *Limelight / Urbania* [FLAT] - **The Alan Parsons Project**
     [85, **A** 1.9, **AB** *ch15, ps,* **B** 20.5, 22.3]
     (see - Stereotomy / Urbania)

311. *Listen To The Music* [FLAT] // *Long Train Running* - **The Doobie Brothers**
     [US WB Back To Back Hits DH]
     [72/73, **A** *tnotes,* 26.5L, 27.2, **AB** *ride95, si84,* 2.1, 5.15, **B** 22.12]
     (see 1 - Long Train Running // Jesus Is Just Alright)
     (see 2 - Long Train Running / Without You)

312. *Listen To The Music (short)* [FLAT] / *Toulouse Street* - **The Doobie Brothers**
     [#1 /w burbank trees] [72, **A** *ride95, tnotes,* 1.4, 26.5S, 27.2, **AB** *mzk01,* 24.6]

313. *Listen To The Music (short)* [FLAT] / *Toulouse Street* - **The Doobie Brothers**
     [#2 /w green label] [72, 1.4, **A** *ride95,* 26.5S, 27.2, **AB** *mzk01, si84,* 24.6]

314. *Live & Let Die / I Lie Around* - **Wings** - [#1 apple original]
     [73, **A** 11.3, 19.9, 20.3, 27.4, 29.4, **AB** *si84,* 11.4, 30.2, **B** 20.15]

315. *Live & Let Die / I Lie Around* - **Wings** - [#2 capital reissue UK]
     [73, **A** 11.3, 19.9, 20.3, 27.4, 29.4, **AB** *si84,* 5.11, 11.4, **B** 20.15]

316. *Logical Song, The // Goodbye Stranger* - **Supertramp** - [A&M Memories DH]
     [79, **A** *mcn86,* 19.6, 22.3, **AB** *ch16, tnotes,* 16.1, 24.10, 30.1, **B** 22.10, 27.3]
     (see - Goodbye Stranger / Even In The Quietist Moments)

317. *Logical Song, The / Just Another Nervous Wreck* [FLAT] - **Supertramp**
     [#1 ITA /w waitress pic sleeve]
     [79, **A** *ch16, mcn86, tnotes,* 16.1, 19.6, 22.3, **AB** 3.3, 5.3, **B** 19.7]

318. *Logical Song, The / Just Another Nervous Wreck* [FLAT] - **Supertramp**
     [#2 US /w artwork pic sleeve]
     [79, **A** *ch16, mcn86, tnotes,* 16.1, 19.6, 22.3, **AB** *si84,* 5.3, **B** 19.7]

319. *Long Cool Woman In A Black Dress / Look What We've Got* - **The Hollies**
     [72, **A** 4.3, 20.7, 25.1, 25.2, **AB** 24.6]

320. *Long Cool Woman In A Black Dress // Long Dark Road* - **The Hollies**
     [CAN CBS Hall Of Fame Blue DH] [72, **A** 4.3, 20.7, 25.1, 25.2, **AB** *mzk01, si84,* 24.2]

321. *Long Run, The* [FLAT] / *The Disco Strangler* - **The Eagles** - [US] [79, **A** 21.3, 27.3]

322. *Long Run, The // Heartache Tonight* - **The Eagles** - [#1 CAN Gold Standard DH]
     [79, **A** 21.3, 27.3, **B** 20.17, 23.4, 23.5]
     (see - Heartache Tonight / Teenage Jail)

323. *Long Tall Glasses* - **Leo Sayer** [75, *si84,* 1.5, 2.1, 10.3, 20.7, 22.15, 29.2]

324. *Long Run, The // Heartache Tonight* - **The Eagles** - [#2 US Elektra Spun Gold DH]
     [79, **A** 21.3, 27.3, **AB** 5.14, **B** 20.17, 23.4, 23.5]

325. *Long Train Running // Jesus Is Just Alright* - **The Doobie Brothers**
     [CAN WB Gold Standard DH] [73, **A** 22.12, **AB** *ride95*]
     (see - Listen To The Music // Long Train Running)

326. *Long Train Running / Without You* - **The Doobie Brothers**
    [73, **A** *ride95*, 22.12, **AB** *mzk01*, *si84*, 2.1, 24.6, **B** 1.9]

327. *Looking For A Love / Sugar Mountain* - **Neil Young** - [76, **B** 22.17, 26.2]
    (*see 1 - Heart Of Gold \ Sugar Mountain*)
    (*see 2 - Sugar Mountain \ The Needle Gone & The Damage Done*)

328. *Love Is Alive* [FLAT] */ Much Higher* - **Gary Wright** - [76, **A** 21.12, 26.5S, **AB** 2.1]
    < *see - Dream Weaver // Love Is Alive*)

329. *Love Song / This Earth That You Walk Upon* - **Simple Minds** - [UK]
    [81, **A** *mzk01*, **AB** 2.14, 5.12]

330. *Love Train / Who Am I?* - **The O'Jays** - [73, **A** *mzk01*, 19.10]

331. *Love Train // Time To Get Down* - **The O'Jays** - [DH] [73, **A** 19.10]

332. *Love Will Find A Way / Holy Lamb* - **Yes** - [87, **A** 18.2, 19.7, 19.9, 22.12, **AB** *ps*]

333. *Love Will Find A Way // Rhythm Of Love* - **Yes** - [CAN Atlantic Gold Standard DH]
    [87, **A** 18.2, 19.7, 19.9, 22.12, **AB** 24.10, **B** *mzk01*]
    (*see - Rhythm Of Love / City Of Love (Live)*)

334. *Lowdown* [FLAT] */ Loneliness Is Just A Word* - **Chicago** - [CAN]
    [70, **A** *mzk01*, 11.1, 19.3, 21.6, 23.9, **AB** 30.4]

335. *Lowdown (mono / stereo)* [FLAT] - **Chicago** - [US] [70, *mzk01*, 11.1, 19.3, 21.6, 23.9]

336. *Lucifer / I'd Rather Be A Man* - **The Alan Parsons Project** - [UK]
    [79, **A** *mzk01*, 22.2, **AB** *ps*, *si84*, 3.2, 5.11, 8.5, **B** 20.15]
    (*see - You Don't Believe \\ Lucifer*)

337. *Lucky Man / Knife Edge* - **Emerson, Lake & Palmer**
    [71, **A** *mcn57*, *ride183*, 20.9, 26.2, **AB** *ch14*, *si84*, 14.1, 19.8, **B** *mcn168*, 20.4]

338. *Lucky Man // From The Beginning* - **Emerson, Lake & Palmer**
    [CAN Atlantic Gold Standard DH]
    [71/72, **A** *ride183*, 20.9, 26.2, **AB** *ch14*, *si84*, 8.2, 14.1, 19.8, 30.2, **B** 20.16, 26.5L]
    (*see - From The Beginning / Living Sin*)

339. *Magic* [FLAT] */ Just Let Me Be* - **Pilot**
    [76, **A** *tnotes*, 1.9, 5.1, 21.8, 25.7, 25.9, 29.2, **AB** 19.12]

340. *Magic // Just A Smile* - **Pilot** - [Capitol Starline DH]
    [76, **A** *tnotes*, 1.9, 5.1, 21.8, 25.7, 25.9, 29.2, **AB** 19.12, **B** 4.2, 19.6]

341. *Magic Man* [FLAT] */ How Deep It Goes* - **Heart** - [US] [76, **A** 20.4, 21.13, 26.4, 26.5S]
    (*see - Crazy On You // Magic Man*)

342. *Make It With You* [FLAT] */ Why Do You Keep Me Waiting?* - **Bread** - [70, **A** 21.4]

343. *Make It With You* [FLATAB] *// It Don't Matter To Me* [FLATAB] - **Bread**
    [CAN Elektra Gold Standard DH] [70, *si84*, **A** 21.4, **AB** 24.2]
    (*see - It Don't Matter To Me / Call On Me*)

344. *Make Me Smile // 25 Or 6 To 4* - **Chicago** - [US CBS Silver DH]
    [70, **A** 20.2, 20.6, 25.9, **AB** 5.16, 11.1, 11.2, 30.4, **B** *quest*, 23.3, 26.4]
    (*see - 25 or 6 to 4 / Where Do We Go From Here?*)

345. *Mama* [FLAT] *// In Too Deep* - **Genesis** - [US Atlantic Oldies Series DH]
    [87/83, **A** *ride123_124_127_129*, 14.4, 19.7, 19.9, 20.5, **AB** 5.4, 30.2]
    (*see - In Too Deep / I'd Rather Be You*)

346. *Mama* [FLAT] */ It's Gonna Get Better* - **Genesis** - [US]
    [83, **A** *ride123_129*, 14.4, 19.7, 19.9, **AB** *ps*, *ride124_127*, 2.14, 20.5]

347. *Man On The Corner // Paperlate* - **Genesis** - [US Atlantic Oldies Series DH]
          [82, **A** *mzk01*, **AB** 5.4]

348. *Man On The Corner / Submarine* - **Genesis** - [82, **A** *mzk01*, **AB** 30.4]

349. *Maybe I'm Amazed // My Love* - **Paul McCartney** - [CAN CBS Hall Of Fame Blue DH]
          [70/73, **A** 11.3, 19.6, 19.9]
          (see - My Love / The Mess (Live))

350. *Maybe I'm Amazed (Live)* - **Wings**
          [77, *mzk01*, 2.13, 11.3, 19.6, 19.9, 20.5, 25.10, 30.2]

351. *Medley USA (Travellin' Band / The Midnight Special / Born On The Bayou / Proud Mary
          / Lookin' Out My Back Door / Green River) // Bad Moon Rising*
          Creedence Clearwater Revival - [US Fantasy Back To Back Hits DH] [69, **AB** 5.17]
          (see 1 & 2 - Bad Moon Rising / Lodi, Proud Mary / Born On The Bayou)
          (see 3 - Travellin' Band / Who'll Stop The Rain)

352. *Minute By Minute / Sweet Feelin'* - **The Doobie Brothers** - [79, **A** *ride96*, 20.13, **AB** 2.6]
          (What A Fool Believes // Minute By Minute)

353. *Misunderstanding / Behind The Lines* - **Genesis** - [CAN /w US pic sleeve]
          [80, **A** 3.3, 20.15, **AB** 14.2]
          (see 1 - Follow You Follow Me // Misunderstanding)
          (see 2 - Turn It On Again / Behind The Lines)

354. *Misunderstanding / Evidence Of Autumn* - **Genesis** - [UK /w pic sleeve]
          [80, **A** 3.3, 14.2, 20.15, AB 8.5, **B** *mzk01*]

355. *My Kind Of Lady / Know Who You Are* - **Supertramp** - [#1 ITA /w artwork on sleeve]
          [82, **A** *ch16*, 20.15, 29.2, **AB** 5.3]

356. *My Kind Of Lady / Know Who You Are* - **Supertramp** - [#2 UK /w picture on sleeve]

357. *My Kind Of Lady // It's Raining Again* - **Supertramp** - [A&M Memories DH]
          [82, **A** 20.15, 29.2, **AB** *ch16*, **B** *tnotes*, 22.8, 29.1]
          (see - It's Raining Again / Bonnie)

358. *My Love / The Mess (Live)* - **Paul McCartney**
          [73, **AB** *si84*, 2.13, 23.1, **B** 25.10]
          (see - Maybe I'm Amazed // My Love)

359. *My Sweet Lord // Isn't It A Pity* - **George Harrison** - [#1 Apple original DH]
          [70, **A** *gtns80*, **AB** *si84*, 20.4]

360. *My Sweet Lord // Isn't It A Pity* - **George Harrison** - [#2 Capitol reissue DH]
          [70, **A** *gtns80*, **AB** 2.11, 20.4]

361. *(The) Name Of The Game // Take A Chance On Me* - **Abba** - [US Atlantic Oldies Series DH]
          [78, **AB** 5.4, 8.2, **B** 22.9]
          (see - Take A Chance On Me / I'm A Marionette)

362. *Never Gonna Fall In Love Again / No Hard Feelings* - **Eric Carmen** - [76, **A** 20.12, 29.5]
          (see - All By Myself // Never Gonna Fall In Love Again >

363. *Never My Love (cover) / Pinewood Rally* - **Blue Suede** (The Association) - [74, **A** 1.6]
          (see - Windy // Never My Love)

364. *New Kid In Town / Victim Of Love* [FLAT] - **The Eagles** - [79, **A** 19.6, 20.5, 23.4, **AB** 23.5]
          (see - Hotel California // New Kid In Town)

365. *New Year's Day / Treasure* [FLAT] - **U2**
          [83, **A** 13.3, 13.5, 20.6, 22.18, 26.6, 29.6, **AB** *si84*, 2.7, 30.2]

366. *New Year's Day // Two Hearts Beat As One* - **U2** - [US Island Revival Of The Fittest DH]
  [83, **A** 13.5, 20.6, 22.18, 26.6, 29.6, **AB** 5.13, 13.3, 30.3, **B** *mzk01*, 13.1]
  (see - *Two Hearts Beat As One / Endless Deep*)

367. *(The) Night Chicago Died* [FLAT] - **Paper Lace** - [#1 CAN Polydor] [74, 21.10]

368. *(The) Night Chicago Died* - **Paper Lace** - [#2 US Mercury] [74, 2.3, 21.10]

369. *Night Moves // Mainstreet* - **Bob Segar** - [CAN Capitol Starline DH]
  [77, **A** 21.2, 27.3, **AB** *si84*, 24.2]

370. *Night Moves / Ship Of Fools* - **Bob Segar** - [US] [77, **A** 21.2, 27.3]

371. *Nights In White Satin* - **The Moody Blues** - [#1 CAN long version original]
  [72, *si84*, *tnotes*, 5.1, 8.1, 20.9, 22.11, 23.3, 26.2, 26.5L]

372. *Nights In White Satin* - **The Moody Blues** - [#2 CAN long version /w symphony]

373. *Nights In White Satin* - **The Moody Blues** - [#3 US short version]
  [72, *tnotes*, 1.4, 5.1, 8.1, 20.9, 22.11, 23.3, 23.9, 23.10, 26.2, 26.5S]

374. *No Reply At All / Dodo* - **Genesis** - [82, **A** *mzk01*, *ride124_126*, *tnotes*, **AB** 30.2, **B** 14.2, 20.5]
  (see - *Abacab // No Reply At All*)

375. *Oh Babe What Would You Say / Getting To Know You* - **Hurricane Smith** - [73, **A** 20.12]

376. *Oh Babe What Would You Say // Who Was It?* - **Hurricane Smith** - [Capitol Starline DH]

377. *Oh Sherrie* [FLAT] / *Don't Tell Me Why You're Leaving* - **Steve Perry**
  [84, **A** *tnotes*, 3.1, 21.9, 22.9, 22.15, **AB** *ps*]

378. *Oh Sherrie* [FLAT] // *Foolish Heart* - **Steve Perry** - [US CBS Silver DH]
  [84, **A** *tnotes*, 21.9, 22.9, 22.15, **AB** 5.16]

379. *Old & Wise / Children Of The Moon* - **The Alan Parsons Project**
  [#1 DEU /w blue pic sleeve] [82, **A** *ch15*, **AB** *si84*, 5.3, 5.11]

380. *Old & Wise / Children Of The Moon* - **The Alan Parsons Project**
  [#2 UK /w black pic sleeve] [82, **A** *ch15*, **AB** 5.3, 8.5]

381. *Old Days // Brand New Love Affair* - **Chicago** - [US CBS Silver DH]
  [75, **A** 11.2, 25.6, **AB** 5.16, **B** *mzk01*, 20.16]
  (see 1 & 2 - *Brand New Love Affair / Hideaway & Harry Truman // Old Days*)

382. *Old Days / Hideaway* - **Chicago** [75, **A** 11.2, 25.6, **AB** 30.4]

383. *Old Man / The Needle Gone & The Damage Done* - **Neil Young**,
  [72, **A** *levitin*, **AB** 2.2, **B** 20.12, 22.17]
  (see 1 - *Heart Of Gold // Old Man*)
  (see 2 - *Sugar Mountain / The Needle Gone & The Damage Done*)

384. *On TV* [FLAT] / *I Am A Camera* - **The Buggles** - [81, **A** 21.7, **AB** *mzk01*, *si84*, 24.6]

385. *Only Time Will Tell / Time Again* - **Asia** - [82, *ps*, **A** 22.18, **AB** 2.9, 3.3]
  (see - *Heat Of The Moment // Only Time Will Tell*)

386. *Only Women / Cold Ethyl* - **Alice Cooper** - [75, **A** 23.2, 25.7, 26.5S, 29.5, **AB** *si84*]

387. *Only Women Bleed // Welcome To My Nightmare* - **Alice Cooper**
  [CAN Atlantic Gold Standard DH] [75, **A** 20.4, 25.7, 26.4, 26.5L, 29.5, **AB** 8.2]

388. *Over The Hills & Far Away \\ Dancing Days* - **Led Zeppelin** - [#1 US original DH]
  [73, **AB** 5.8, 15.1, 15.2]

389. *Over The Hills & Far Away \\ Dancing Days* - **Led Zeppelin**
  [#2 CAN Gold Standard DH] [73, **AB** 8.2, 15.1, 15.2]

390. *Owner Of A Lonely Heart / Our Song* - **Yes**

[83, **A** *mcn193*, 18.2, 19.9, 26.5S, **AB** *ps*, *si84*, 3.3]

391.   *Owner Of A Lonely Heart // Leave It* [FLAT] - **Yes** - [CAN Atlantic Gold Standard DH]
        [83/84, **A** *mcn193*, **AB** 8.2, 18.2, 19.9, 26.5L, 30.2, **B** *mzk01*, 22.9, 29.2]
        (see - Leave It (original / acapella))

392.   *Peace Of Mind // Don't Look Back* - **Boston** - [US CBS Silver DH]
        [77/78, **A** 1.9, **AB** 5.16]

393.   *Peace Of Mind / Foreplay* - **Boston** - [US] [77, **A** 1.9, **B** 19.4, 20.14, 22.1]

394.   *Peter Gunn* [FLAT] */ Tiger In A Spotlight (Live)* - **Emerson, Lake & Palmer**
        [78/79, **A** 21.1, 22.1, **AB** *mzk01*, *si84*, 24.6, 30.2, **B** 20.17, 25.10]

395.   *Peter Gunn (Live)* [FLAT] */ Knife Edge (Live)* - **Emerson, Lake & Palmer** - [UK]
        [79, **A** 21.1, 22.1, **AB** *mzk01*, *si84*, 5.11, 25.10]

396.   *Photograph* - **Ringo Starr** - [#1 Apple original]
        [73, **A** *mzk01*, *si84*, *tnotes*, 2.13, 24.1, 25.4, 29.5]

397.   *Photograph* - **Ringo Starr** - [#2 Capitol reissue] [73, *tnotes*, 25.4, 29.5]

398.   *Piano Man // The Entertainer* - **Billy Joel** - [#1 CAN CBS Hall Of Fame Blue DH]
        [74, **A** *gtns32*, *ride61*, 20.10, 22.12, 25.5, 26.5L, **AB** 5.9, 24.12, **B** 1.9]

399.   *Piano Man // The Entertainer* - **Billy Joel** - [#2 US CBS Silver DH]
        [74, **A** *gtns32*, *ride61*, 20.10, 22.12, 25.5, 26.5L, **AB** 5.9, 24.12 **B** 1.9]

400.   *Piano Man / You're My Home* - **Billy Joel**
        [74, **A** *gtns32*, *ride61*, 20.10, 22.12, 24.12, 25.5, 26.5S]

401.   *Pinball Wizard (cover)* - **Elton John** (The Who) - [UK] [75, 1.6, 25.6, 27.4]

402.   *Pinball Wizard* - **The Who** [69, 1.6, 2.5]

403.   *Play That Funky Music* [FLAT] */ / Hot To Trot* - **Wild Cherry** - [US DH] [75, **A** 21.5]

404.   *Play That Funky Music / The Lady Wants Your Money* - **Wild Cherry** - [75, **A** 21.5]

405.   *Popcorn / At The Movies* - **Hot Butter** - [#1 original DH] [**A** 22.1]

406.   *Popcorn / At The Movies* - **Hot Butter** - [#2 Golden Treasures DH] [**A** 22.1, **AB** 1.2]

407.   *Pride (In The Name Of Love) / Boomerang II* - **U2** [84, **A** 13.1, 13.3, 13.5, **AB** *ps*, **B** *mzk01*]
        (see - I Will Follow (Live) // Pride (In The Name Of Love))

408.   *Prime Time / The Gold Bug* - **The Alan Parsons Project**
        [84/81, **AB** *ch18*, 3.6, 8.5, 15.4, **B** 20.15, 22.2]
        (see 1 & 2 - The Gold Bug / Snake Eyes & Snake Eyes / I Don't Wanna Go Home)
        (see 3 - Time / The Gold Bug)

409.   *Promised You A Miracle 12 / Theme From Great Cities* - **Simple Minds**
        [82, **A** 12.5, 31.1.15, **B** *mzk01*]

410.   *Promised You A Miracle (Live) / Book Of Brilliant Things (Live)* - **Simple Minds**
        [87, **A** *mzk01*, **AB** 3.2, 25.10]

411.   *Proud Mary // Born On The Bayou* - **Creedence Clearwater Revival**
        [#1 US Fantasy Back To Back Hits DH] [69, **AB** 5.17]

412.   *Proud Mary // Born On The Bayou* - **Creedence Clearwater Revival**
        [#2 US Collectables DH] [69, **AB** 5.9]

413.   *Psychobabble / Children Of The Moon* - **The Alan Parsons Project** - [82, **AB** 30.1]
        (see 1 - Eye In The Sky // Psychobabble)
        (see 2 - You're Gonna Get Your Fingers Burned / Psychobabble)

414.   *Psychobabble (mono / stereo)* - **The Alan Parsons Project** - [US] [82, **AB** 5.6, 15.3]

415. *Raindrops Keep Falling On My Head / Never Had It So Good* - **B J Thomas** - [US]
         [69, **A** 20.12, 22.13, 27.4]
         (see - Hooked On A Feeling // Raindrops Keep Falling On My Head)

416. *Reach Out I'll Be There (cover)* - **Gloria Gaynor** (The Four Tops) - [75, 1.5]

417. *Reach Out I'll Be There // Standing In The Shadow of Love* - **The Four Tops**
         [US Collectables DH] [66, **AB** 5.9]

418. *Release Release* [FLATAB] \\ *Don't Kill The Whale* [FLATAB] - **Yes** - [US DH]
         [78, **A** 19.7, 20.5, 22.4, **AB** 1.1, 5.7, 22.18, 30.2, **B** *tnotes*, 4.2, 4.8, 17.1, 18.2]
         (see - Don't Kill The Whale / Abeline)

419. *Revolution (cover)* - **The Thompson Twins** (The Beatles) - [UK] [85, *ps*, 1.7, 8.5]

420. *Rhythm Of Love / City Of Love (Live)* - **Yes** [87, **A** *mzk01*, **AB** 30.3, **B** 20.5, 25.10, 29.6]
         (see - Love Will Find A Way // Rhythm Of Love)

421. *Ride Like The Wind / Minstrel Gigolo* - **Christopher Cross** - [80, **AB** *mzk01*, 2.6]
         (see - Sailing // Ride Like The Wind)

422. *Rikki Don't Lose That Number / Pretzel Logic* - **Steely Dan** - [US] [74, **AB** 5.8, **B** 29.1]
         (see - Do It Again // Rikki Don't Lose That Number)

423. *Rock & Roll* \\ *Four Sticks* [FLAT] - **Led Zeppelin** - [#1 CAN Atlantic Gold Standard DH]
         [72, **A** *mzk01*, *tnotes*, 20.7, 23.3, **AB** 8.2, 15.1, 15.2, 30.3]

424. *Rock & Roll* \\ *Four Sticks* [FLAT] - **Led Zeppelin** - [#2 US original DH]
         [72, **A** *mzk01*, *tnotes*, 20.7, 23.3, **AB** 5.8, 15.2, 30.3]

425. *Rock This Town / You Can't Hurry Love* - **The Stray Cats** - [82, **A** 20.17, **AB** 2.10, **B** 1.7]
         (see - You Can't Hurry Love)

426. *Rockford Files* [FLAT] / *Dixie Lullabye* - **Mike Post** - [UK] [75, **A** 21.10, 22.1, 22.12, 25.7]
         (see - Sunny - **Bobby Bloom** // Rockford Files - **Mike Post**)

427. *Roll With It* - **Steve Winwood** - [#1 CAN /w artwork on sleeve] [88, 5.3, 19.5]

428. *Roll With It* - **Steve Winwood** - [#2 DEU /w photo on sleeve]

429. *Roundabout / Long Distance Runaround* [FLAT] - **Yes**
         [72, **A** *mcn42_81*, *mzk01*, 17.1, 19.7, 23.9, 26.2, 27.2, 31.1.35]
         [**AB** *si84*, *tnotes*, 2.2, 18.2, 19.8, 19.9, 24.6, 30.1, **B** 20.2, 21.10, 22.18]

430. *Roundabout // Your Move* - **Yes** - [CAN Atlantic Gold Standard DH]
         [72/71, **A** *mcn42_81*, *mzk01*, *tnotes*, 19.9, 23.9, 27.2, 31.1.35]
         [**AB** *si84*, 8.2, 17.1, 18.2, 19.7, 19.8, 26.2, 30.2, **B** *mcn37*, 22.9]
         (see 1 & 2 - America // Your Move & Your Move / The Clap)

431. *Roundabout (Live) // I've Seen All Good People (Live)* - **Yes** - [DH]
         [81, **A** *mcn42_81*, 19.9, **AB** *mzk01*, *si84*, 17.1, 18.2, 19.7, 20.5, 25.10]
         [**B** *mcn37*, 20.17]

432. *Roxanne / Dead End Job* - **The Police** - [US] [79, **A** *buks*, *levitin*, 12.3, 26.1]

433. *Roxanne // Synchronicity II* - **The Police** - [UK A&M Memories DH]
         [79/83, **A** *buks*, *levitin*, 26.1, **AB** *ps*, 12.3, **B** *mzk01*, 20.5]
         (see - Synchronicity II / Once Upon A Daydream)

434. *Roxanne // I Can't Stand Losing You* - **The Police** - [A&M Memories DH]
         [79/78, **A** *buks*, *levitin*, 12.3, **AB** 26.1]

435. *Ruby Tuesday* [FLAT] / *Lets Spend The Night Together* - **The Rolling Stones**
         [#1 CAN London orange] [67, **A** 21.11, 22.11]

436. *Ruby Tuesday* [FLAT] / *Lets Spend The Night Together* - **The Rolling Stones**
      [#2 US London blue]

437. *Rudolph The Red Nosed Reindeer* - **The California Raisins** - [88, *mzk01*, 29.3]

438. *Rudolph The Red Nosed Reindeer* (*Live*) - **Corey Hart** - [85, 3.5, 22.11, 25.10]

439. *Run Like Hell / Don't Leave Me Now* - **Pink Floyd** - [US] [80, **A** *ch15*, 22.3, **AB** 19.8, **B** 1.9]

440. *Run Like Hell // Comfortably Numb* - **Pink Floyd** - [US CBS Silver DH]
      [80, **A** 22.3, **AB** *ch15*, 5.8, 5.16, 19.8, **B** 26.6, 27.3, 29.5]

441. *(The) Safety Dance // I Got The Message* - **Men Without Hats** - [CAN Sire Gold Standard DH]
      [82, **B** 10.4]
      (*see - I Got The Message / Utter Space*)

442. *Sailing // Ride Like The Wind* - **Christopher Cross** - [CAN WB Gold Standard DH]
      [80, **AB** *mzk01*, *si84*, 2.6, 24.2]
      (*see - Ride Like The Wind / Minstrel Gigolo*)

443. *Sanctify Yourself / Street Hassle (Live) / Love Song (Live)* - **Simple Minds** - [UK]
      [86, **ABC** *ps*, 1.4, 2.14, 3.3, 3.4, 5.12, **BC** 25.10]

444. *Sanctify Yourself (original / instrumental)* - **Simple Minds**
      [86, **AB** *ps*, 2.14, 3.3, 3.4, 5.12]

445. *Sanctify Yourself 12 / Sanctify Yourself Dub* - **Simple Minds** - [86, **AB** 3.3, 12.5, 31.1.15]

446. *Say You'll Be Mine / Spinning* - **Christopher Cross** - [US]

447. *School's Out* / Gutter Cat - **Alice Cooper** - [72, **A** *ward*, 20.14, 22.8, **AB** 2.1]

448. *School's Out // I'm Eighteen* - **Alice Cooper** - [CAN WB Gold Standard DH]
      [72/71, **A** *ward*, 20.14, 22.8, **AB** 2.6]

449. *Sea Of Love (cover) / I Get A Thrill* - **The Honeydrippers** (Phil Phillips) - [85, **A** 1.7, 20.11]

450. *Sea Of Love / Juella* - **Phil Phillips** - [US] [59, **A** 1.7, 20.11]

451. *Seasons In The Sun* [FLAT] / *Put The Bone In* - **Terry Jacks** - [73, **A** 21.8]
      (*see - Where Evil Grows // Seasons In The Sun*)

452. *Sharp Dressed Man / I Got The 6* - **ZZ Top** - [83, **A** 20.7, **AB** 2.6]
      (*see - Legs // Sharp Dressed Man*)

453. *She Blinded Me With Science / Flying North* - **Thomas Dolby**
      [83, **A** *buks*, *quest*, 19.11, 20.4, 22.5, 22.15]
      (*see - Windpower / Flying North*)

454. *She's Always A Woman To Me / Vienna* - **Billy Joel** - [US]
      [78, **A** 20.10, 22.17, 24.12, **B** 20.15, 29.5]
      (*see - Just The Way You Are // She's Always A Woman To Me*)

455. *She's Not There / Tell Her No* - **The Zombies** - [US] [64, **A** 27.6]

456. *She's Not There / You Make Me Feel So Good* - **The Zombies** - [CAN]

457. *Shining Star* [FLAT] / *Yearnin' Learnin'* - **Earth, Wind & Fire** - [US]
      [75, **A** *ch11*, *quest*, 21.5, 22.9, 25.6, 27.2]

458. *Shining Star* [FLAT] // *That's The Way Of The World* - **Earth, Wind & Fire**
      [CAN CBS Hall Of Fame Blue DH]
      [75, **A** *quest*, 21.5, 22.9, 25.6, 27.2, **AB** *ch11*, *si84*, 24.2, **B** 19.10]

459. *Shock The Monkey / Soft Dog* - **Peter Gabriel** - [82, **A** *buks*, **AB** *si84*, 2.9]

460. *Shock The Monkey // Solisbury Hill* - **Peter Gabriel** - [US Geffen Back To Back Hits DH]
      [82/77, **AB** *buks*, **B** 22.11]

(see - Solisbury Hill / Moribund The Burgermeister)

461. *Shout* [FLAT] - **Tears For Fears** - [85, *buks, mzk01, ps, quest,* 3.3, 19.5]

462. *Shout 12* - **Tears For Fears** - [85, *buks, quest,* 3.3, 19.5]

463. *Show Must Go On, The (cover)* [FLAT] - **Three Dog Night** (Leo Sayer) - [#1 CAN brown]
      [74, 1.6, 19.6, 25.5, 29.2]

464. *Show Must Go On, The (cover)* [FLAT] - **Three Dog Night** (Leo Sayer) - [#2 US black]
      [74, 1.6, 2.5, 19.6, 25.5, 29.2]

465. *Silence Is Golden* - **The Tremeloes** - [#1 CAN] [67, 27.6]

466. *Silence Is Golden* - **The Tremeloes** - [#2 US /w pic sleeve]

467. *Sister Golden Hair / Midnight* - **America**
      [75, **A** *tnotes,* 23.9, 23.10, 25.6, 25.7, 31.1.25, **AB** 2.1]

468. *Sister Golden Hair // Ventura Highway* - **America** - [US American Pie Back To Back Hits DH]
      [75/72, **A** *tnotes,* 23.9, 23.10, 25.6, 25.7, 31.1.25]
      (see - Ventura Highway / Saturn Nights)

469. *Smoke On The Water // Woman From Tokyo* - **Deep Purple** - [CAN WB Gold Standard DH]
      [73, **A** 19.7, 26.5L, **AB** *si84,* 2.6]

470. *Smoke On The Water (short / Live)* - **Deep Purple**
      [73, **A** *buks,* 26.5S, **AB** *si84,* 2.1, 19.7, **B** *mzk01,* 25.10]

471. *Snake Eyes / I Don't Wanna Go Home* - **The Alan Parsons Project** - [US]
      [81, **A** 20.2, 22.3, **AB** *si84,* 5.6, 15.3, 30.1]
      (see 1 - The Gold Bug / Snake Eyes)
      (see 2 - The Turn Of A Friendly Card / Snake Eyes / Games People Play)

472. *Sole Survivor / Here Comes The Feeling* - **Asia** - [UK /w pic sleeve]
      [82, **A** 19.6, 22.18, 26.5S, **AB** *mzk01,* 1.4, 3.3, 5.3, 5.11]

473. *Sole Survivor (long / short)* - **Asia** - [US /w pic sleeve]
      [82, **A** 20.4, 22.18, 26.5L, **AB** 1.4, 2.9, 5.3, 19.6, **B** 26.5S]

474. *Solisbury Hill / Moribund The Burgermeister* - **Peter Gabriel** - [77, **A** *buks,* 22.11]

475. *Some Kind Of Wonderful (cover) / Wild* - **Grand Funk** (Soul Brothers Six)
      [75, **A** 1.5, 2.13, 19.4, 20.14]
      (see - We're An American Band // Some Kind Of Wonderful)

476. *Someone Saved My Life Tonight* - **Elton John** - [#1 CAN]
      [75, 2.5, 20.5, 24.11, 25.7]

477. *Someone Saved My Life Tonight* - **Elton John** - [#2 UK /w custom label]
      [75, *gtns78,* 1.4, 2.14, 20.5, 24.11, 25.7]

478. *Someone Somewhere In Summertime* [FLAT] / *King Is White & In The Crowd*
      Simple Minds - [UK] [82, *gtns78,* 1.4, 2.14, 5.12]]

479. *Someone Somewhere In Summertime (12)* [FLAT] / *King Is White & In The Crowd / Soundtrack
      For Every Heaven* - **Simple Minds** - [82, **A** 12.5, 31.1.15]

480. *Sounds Of Silence* [FLAT] // *Homeward Bound* - **Simon & Garfunkel** - [DH]
      [65/66, **A** 21.11]

481. *Space Oddity / The Man Who Sold The World* - **David Bowie** - [#1 original DH]
      [73, *buks, si84, tnotes,* 5.1, 20.4, 29.5]

482. *Space Oddity // The Man Who Sold The World* - **David Bowie** - [#2 Golden Greats DH]
      [73, *buks, tnotes,* 1.1, 5.1, 20.4, 29.5]

483. *Speed Your Love To Me* - **Simple Minds** - [84, *mzk01, ps, si84,* 26.1]

484. *Speed Your Love To Me 12* - **Simple Minds** - [84, 12.5, 26.1, 31.1.15]

485. *Spinning Wheel* [FLAT] / *More & More* - **Blood, Sweat & Tears** - [US] [69, **A** 21.6]
   (*see - You've Made Me So Very Happy // Spinning Wheel*)

486. *Spirit In The Sky // Canned Ham* - **Norman Greenbaum** - [CAN Reprise Gold Standard DH]
   [70, **A** 20.17]

487. *Spirit In The Sky / Milk Cow* - **Norman Greenbaum** - [70, **A** 20.17]

488. *Spirits In The Material World / Low Life* - **The Police** - [UK /w blue pic sleeve]
   [82, **A** *buks,* 12.3, **AB** 5.2, 5.3]

489. *Spirits In The Material World / Hungry (Flexible Strategies)* - **The Police**
   [US /w red pic sleeve] [82, **A** *buks,* 12.3, **AB** *si84,* 5.2, 5.3]

490. *Spot The Pigeon EP - Match Of The Day / Pigeons / Inside & Out* - **Genesis**
   [77, **ABC** *ch14, mzk01, si84,* 1.10, 3.6, 8.5, 24.6, **C** 4.9, 20.3, 20.5, 29.6]
   (*see - Follow You Follow Me / Inside & Out*)

491. *Stairway To Heaven* [FLATAB] \\ *Whole Lotta Love (cover)* [FLATAB]
   Led Zeppelin (**B** - *You Need Love* - Willie Dixon) - [DH]
   [71/70, **A** *gtns55, levitin, mcn37_81_138,* 20.3, 22.11, 26.6]
   [**AB** *ward,* 1.4, 15.2, 20.5, 22.9, 30.3, **B** *tnotes,* 1.6, 21.12]
   (*see - Whole Lotta Love \\ Living Loving Maid*)

492. *Stereotomy / Urbania* [FLAT] - **The Alan Parsons Project** - [#1 DEU /w green pic sleeve]
   [86, **AB** *ch15,* 3.2, 5.3, **B** 20.5, 22.3]
   (*see - Limelight / Urbania*)

493. *Stereotomy / Urbania* [FLAT] - **The Alan Parsons Project** - [#2 UK /w purple pic sleeve]
   [86, **AB** *ch15,* 3.2, 5.3, 8.5, **B** 20.5, 22.3]

494. *Straight From The Heart / What's It Gonna Be?* - **Bryan Adams** - [83, **A** 19.5]
   (*see - Cuts Like A Knife // Straight From The Heart*)

495. *Stuck In The Middle With You / Jose* - **Stealers Wheel** - [73, **A** 20.7, 21.2, 23.1, 29.2, **AB** *si84*]

496. *Stuck In The Middle With You // Star* - **Stealers Wheel** - [A&M Memories DH]
   [73, **A** 20.7, 21.2, 23.1, 29.2]

497. *Suddenly Last Summer // Only The Lonely* - **The Motels**
   [US American Pie Back To Back Hits DH] [83/82, **A** *buks,* **AB** 5.9]

498. *Suddenly Last Summer / Some Things Never Change* - **The Motels**
   [83, **A** *buks,* **AB** 2.11]

499. *Sugar Mountain / The Needle Gone & The Damage Done* - **Neil Young**
   [72, **A** 26.2, **AB** 22.17, **B** 20.12]
   (*see 1 & 2 - Heart Of Gold / Sugar Mountain & Looking For A Love / Sugar Mountain*)
   (*see 3 - Old Man / The Needle Gone & The Damage Done*)

500. *Sultans Of Swing / Eastbound Train* - **Dire Straits**
   [78, **A** *tnotes,* 20.5, 22.15, **AB** *mzk01, si84,* 2.3, 24.3, **B** 25.10]
   (*see - Twisting By The Pool / Eastbound Train (Live)*)

501. *Sunny* - **Bobby Bloom** // *Rockford Files* [FLAT] - **Mike Post**
   [US American Pie Back To Back Hits DH] [**AB** 5.9, **B** 21.10, 22.1, 22.12, 25.7]
   (*see - Rockford Files / Dixie Lullaby*)

502. *Sunshine On My Shoulder / Around & Around* - **John Denver** - [#1 original DH]
   [74, **A** 22.17, **AB** 1.1]

503. *Sunshine On My Shoulder \\ Around & Around* - **John Denver** - [#2 Golden Greats DH]

504. *Sweet Emotion* [FLAT] / *Uncle Salty* - **Aerosmith** - [73, **A** 21.12, 26.6, 27.3]
   (*see - Dream On // Sweet Emotion*)

505. *Synchronicity II / Once Upon A Daydream* - **The Police** - [UK]
      [83, **A** 12.3, 20.5, **AB** *si84*, 5.11]
      (*see - Roxanne // Synchronicity II*)

506. *Take A Chance On Me / I'm A Marionette* - **Abba** - [78, **A** 22.9]
      (*see - The Name Of The Game // Take A Chance On Me*)

507. *Take It Easy / Get You In The Mood* - **The Eagles** - [72, **A** 23.4, 23.5, 25.1, **AB** 2.2]

508. *Take It Easy // Witchy Woman* [FLAT] - **The Eagles** - [#1 CAN Asylum Gold Standard DH]
      [72, **A** 23.4, 25.1, **AB** 23.5]
      (*see - Witchy Woman / Early Bird*)

509. *Take It Easy // Witchy Woman* [FLAT] - **The Eagles** - [#2 US Asylum Spun Gold DH]
      [72, **A** 23.4, 25.1, **AB** 5.14, 23.5]

510. *Take Me Home Country Roads / Poems, Prayers & Promises* - **John Denver**
      [#1 original DH] [71, 1.1]

511. *Take Me Home Country Roads \\ Poems, Prayers & Promises* - **John Denver**
      [#2 Gold Standard DH]

512. *Take Me Home Country Roads \\ Poems, Prayers & Promises* - **John Denver**
      [#3 Golden Greats DH]

513. ***Take Me In Your Arms*** *(cover)* - **Charity Brown** (Kim Weston) - [75, 1.5]

514. ***Take Me In Your Arms (Rock Me)*** *(cover)* [FLATAB] / *Slat Key Soquel Rag* [FLATAB]
      The Doobie Brothers (Kim Weston)
      [75, **A** 1.5, 25.7, **AB** *si84*, 2.1, **B** *mzk01*, 22.1, 22.17]
      (*see - Black Water // Take Me In Your Arms (Rock Me)*)

515. *Take The Long Way Home / Rudy* - **Supertramp** - [#1 CAN pic sleeve]
      [79/75, **A** 19.6, 19.9, 20.15, 22.11, 22.12, 22.18, 26.5L]
      [**AB** *ch16, ps, si84, tnotes*, 5.3, 16.1, 20.5 **B** 20.3, 22.4]

516. *Take The Long Way Home / Rudy* - **Supertramp** - [#2 FRA pic sleeve]
      [79/75, **A** 19.6, 19.9, 20.15, 22.11, 22.12, 22.18, 26.3, 26.5S]
      [**AB** *ch16, ps, tnotes*, 3.3, 5.3, 16.1, **B** 20.3, 20.5, 22.4]

517. *Take The Long Way Home // It's Raining Again* - **Supertramp** - [US A&M Memories DH]
      [79/82, **A** 16.1, 19.6, 19.9, 20.15, 22.11, 22.12, 22.18, 26.3, 26.5S]
      [**AB** *ch16, tnotes*, 5.9, 30.2, **B** 22.8, 29.1]
      (*see - It's Raining Again / Bonnie*)

518. *Take The Long Way Home (Live) / From Now On (Live)* - **Supertramp** - [UK]
      [80, **A** 19.6, 19.9, 20.15, 22.6, 22.11, 22.12, 22.18]
      [**AB** *ch16, mzk01, ps*, 5.11, 16.1, 25.10]

519. *Takin' Care Of Business // You Ain't Seen Nothin' Yet*
      Bachman - Turner Overdrive - [DH] [74, **AB** 23.2, *si84*]
      (*see - You Ain't Seen Nothin' Yet / Free Wheeling* >

520. *Taking It All Too Hard / Silver Rainbow* - **Genesis** - [84, **A** *ch14, mzk01*, **AB** 30.1, **B** *ride129*]
      (*see - That's All \\ Taking It All Too Hard*)

521. *Taxi / Empty* - **Harry Chapin** - [72, **A** 20.4, **AB** 2.2, 2.4]
      (*see - Cat's In The Cradle // Taxi*)

522. *Taxi // Wold* - **Harry Chapin** - [US Elektra Spun Gold DH] [72, **A** 20.4, **AB** 5.14]

523. *Thank God I'm A Country Boy* [FLAT] / *My Sweet Lady* - **John Denver** - [#1 original DH]

[75, **A** 21.3, 22.17, **AB** 1.1]

524. *Thank God I'm A Country Boy* [FLAT] \\ *My Sweet Lady* - **John Denver**
[#2 Golden Greats DH]

525. *That's All* [FLATAB] / *Second Home By The Sea* [FLATAB] - **Genesis**
[84, **A** *ride129_131,* 19.6, 20.2, 31.1.34, **AB** *ps*, 21.12]
[**B** *ride123_124_125_136,* 14.3, 14.4, 20.5, 22.2, 22.18, 31.1.16]

526. *That's All* [FLAT] \\ *Taking It All Too Hard* - **Genesis** - [UK DH]
[84, **A** *ride129_131,* 19.6, 20.2, 21.12, 31.1.34, **AB** *ch14, si84,* 1.1, 2.14, 5.11, **B** *mzk01*]
(see - *Taking It All Too Hard / Silver Rainbow*)

527. *They Just Can't Stop It* **(Games People Play)** - **The Spinners** - [#2 US] [75, 1.9]
(see - *Games People Play*)

528. *Things Can Only Get Better* [FLAT] // *Life In One Day* - **Howard Jones**
[CAN WEA Gold Standard DH] [85, **A** *buks,* 21.6]

529. *Things Can Only Get Better* [FLAT] / *Why Look For The Key?* - **Howard Jones**

530. *Throwing It All Away* [FLAT] / *Do The Neurotic* - **Genesis** - [86, **A** *ch14*]
(see - *Invisible Touch // Throwing it All Away*)

531. *Tie A Yellow Ribbon Round The Ole Oak Tree* [FLAT] \\ *I Can't Believe How Much I love You*
Dawn - [# 1 US Original DH] [73. **A** 19.3, 21.10, 22.12, 23.1, 23.7, **AB** 1.2

532. *Tie A Yellow Ribbon Round The Ole Oak Tree* [FLAT] \\ *I Can't Believe How Much I love You*
Dawn - [# 2 US Golden Treasures DH]

533. *Time* // *Games People Play* - **The Alan Parsons Project** - [Arista Flashback DH]
[81, **A** 1.9, 4.2, **AB** 8.4, 24.10, **B** *ch18,* 1.9, 15.4]
(see 1 - *Games People Play / Ace Of Swords*)
(see 2 - *Turn Of A Friendly Card / Snake Eyes / Games People Play*)

534. *Time* / *The Gold Bug* - **The Alan Parsons Project** - [US]
[81, **A** 1.9, 4.2, **AB** *mzk01, si84,* 15.3, 30.1, **B** *ch18,* 15.4, 20.15, 22.2]
(see 1 & 2 - *The Gold Bug / Snake Eyes & Prime Time / The Gold Bug*)

535. *Time In A Bottle* - **Jim Croce** - [#1 CAN ABC brown] [73, 20.10, 22.17]

536. *Time In A Bottle* - **Jim Croce** - [#2 US ABC black] [73, 2.5, 20.10, 22.17]

537. *Tin Man* [FLAT] / *In The Country* - **America** - [74, **A** 21.3, **AB** 2.1]

538. *Tin Man* // *Don't Cross The River* - **America** - [US WB Back To Back Hits DH]
[74/72, **A** 21.3, **AB** 2.1, 5.15]

539. *Tom Sawyer* [FLAT] / *Witch Hunt* - **Rush** - [81, **A** 10.4, 21.12, **AB** 19.8]

540. *Tonight I Celebrate / Born To Love* - **Roberta Flack & Peabo Bryson** - [83, **A** 2.11]

541. *Tonight I Celebrate* - **Roberta Flack & Peabo Bryson** // *For Your Love* - **Ed Townsend**
[US Collectables DH] [83, **A** 2.11, **AB** 5.9]

542. *Tonight She Comes* \\ *Just What I Needed* - **The Cars** - [CAN Elektra Gold Standard DH]
[85/78, **AB** 1.1, 2.12, **B** *buks*]
(see - *Just What I Needed // Good Times Roll*)

543. *Tonight Tonight Tonight* [FLAT] / *In The Glow Of The Night* - **Genesis** - [86, **A** *ch14, ride131*]
(see - *Land Of Confusion // Tonight Tonight Tonight*)

544. *Touch Me* // *Hello I Love You* - **The Doors** - [#1 CAN Elektra Gold Standard DH]
[68/69, **AB** 19.3]
(see - *Hello I Love You / Love Street*)

545. *Touch Me* // *Hello I Love You* - **The Doors** - [#2 US Elektra Spun Gold DH]
[68/69, **AB** 5.14, 19.3]

546. *Turn It On Again / Behind The Lines* - **Genesis** - [80, **A** *ride129*, 22.6, **AB** *ps*, 8.1, 14.2]
      (see 1 & 2 - Illegal Alien / Turn It On Again (Live), Misunderstanding / Behind The Lines)

547. *Turn Me Loose / Prissy Prissy* - **Loverboy** - [80, **A** 26.5S, **AB** *mzk01*, *si84*]

548. *Turn Me Loose // The Kid Is Hot Tonight* - **Loverboy** - [CAN CBS Hall Of Fame Blue DH]
      [81/80, **A** 26.5L, **AB** *ward*, 10.4]

549. *Turn Of A Friendly Card* [FLAT] / *Snake Eyes* / *Games People Play*
    The Alan Parsons Project - [DEU]
    [81, **A** *tnotes*, **AB** 20.2, **ABC** *ps*, 1.4, 1.10, 2.14, 3.3, 3.5, 5.10, **B** 22.3, **C** *ch18*, 1.9, 15.4]
    (see 1 & 2 - Games People Play / Ace Of Swords & The Gold Bug / Snake Eyes)
    (see 3 & 4 - Snake Eyes / I Don't Wanna Go Home & Time // Games People Play)

550. *Twisting By The Pool / Eastbound Train (Live)* - **Dire Straits** - [83, **AB** 2.13, **B** 25.10]
      (see - Sultans Of Swing / Eastbound Train)

551. *Two Hearts Beat As One / Endless Deep* - **U2** - [US]
    [83, **A** *mzk01*, 13.1, 13.3, **AB** 2.7, 3.2, **B** 22.2]
    (see - New Year's Day // Two Hearts Beat As One)

552. *Unchained Melody / Hung On You* - **The Righteous Brothers** - [#1 CAN Philles Records]
    [65, **A** 1.7]

553. *Unchained Melody / Hung On You* - **The Righteous Brothers** - [#2 US Polydor]

554. *Up On The Catwalk* [FLAT] / *A Brass Band In African Chimes* - **Simple Minds** - [UK]
    [84, **A** 19.6, 26.1, **AB** *ps*, 2.14, 3.5, 5.12, **B** *mzk01*, 22.16]

555. *Up On The Catwalk 12* [FLAT] / *A Brass Band In African Chimes* - **Simple Minds**
    [84, **A** 12.5, 19.6, 26.1, 31.1.15, **B** 22.16]

556. *Urgent / Girl On The Moon* - **Foreigner** - [81, *ps*, *si84*, **AB** *mzk01*, 3.3]

557. *Urgent // Waiting For A Girl Like You* - **Foreigner** - [US Atlantic Oldies Series DH] [81, 5.4]

558. *Valerie / Slowdown Sundown* - **Steve Winwood** - [82, **AB** *si84*, 2.7, 30.2]

559. *Valerie 87 / Talking Back To The Night (Instrumental)* - **Steve Winwood** - [US] [87, **A** 3.3, 4.1]

560. *Ventura Highway / Saturn Nights* - **America** - [72, **AB** *si84*, 24.7]
      (see - Sister Golden Hair // Ventura Highway)

561. *Walking On The Moon / Bring On The Night* - **The Police** - [UK /w pic sleeve]
    [79, **A** *quest*, 20.14, 26.1, **AB** 5.2]

562. *Walking On The Moon / Visions Of The Night* - **The Police** - [CAN]

563. *Waterfront / Hunter & The Hunted* - **Simple Minds** - [UK]
    [83, **A** *tnotes*, 20.6, 20.14, 22.6, 26.1, **AB** *ps*, *si84*, 2.14, 5.12]

564. *Waterfront 12 / Hunter & The Hunted* - **Simple Minds**
    [83, **A** *tnotes*, 12.5, 20.14, 26.1, 31.1.15]

565. *Waterfront 89 / Kick It In* - **Simple Minds** - [UK] [89, **A** *mzk01*, *tnotes*, 4.1, **AB** 2.14, 5.12]

566. *We Are The Champions \\ We Will Rock You* - **Queen** - [#1 CAN DH]
    [77, **A** 20.9, **AB** *tnotes*, 1.1, 20.5, **B** *levitin*, 22.17]

567. *We Are The Champions \\ We Will Rock You* - **Queen** - [#2 UK /w pic sleeve DH]
    [77, **A** 20.9, **AB** *tnotes*, 1.1, 1.4, 2.14, 3.2, 20.5, **B** *levitin*, 22.17]

568. *We're An American Band // Some Kind Of Wonderful* - **Grand Funk**
    [US Collectables DH] [73/75, **A** 19.12, **AB** 5.9, 19.4, **B** 20.14]
    (see - Some Kind Of Wonderful / Wild)

569. *We're An American Band / Creepin'* - **Grand Funk**
    [73, **A** 19.4, **AB** *ps*, *si84*, 2.13, 3.1, 3.5, 19.12]

570. *What A Fool Believes / Don't Stop To Watch The Wheels* - **The Doobie Brothers**
    [79, **A** *buks*, *gtns60*, *ride96_103*, **AB** 2.6]

571. *What A Fool Believes // It Keeps You Running* - **The Doobie Brothers**
    [US WB Back To Back Hits DH] [79/77, **A** *buks*, *gtns60*, *ride103*, **AB** *ride96*, 2.6]

572. *What A Fool Believes // Minute By Minute* - **The Doobie Brothers**
    [CAN WB Gold Standard DH] [79, **A** *buks*, *gtns60*, *ride103*, **AB** *ride96*, *si84*, 2.6, **B** 20.13]
    (see - Minute By Minute / Sweet Feelin')

573. *When A Man Loves A Woman // Take Time To Know Her* - **Percy Sledge**
    [#1 CAN Atlantic Gold Standard DH] [66/68, **A** 19.3, 20.10, **AB** 5.4, 8.2]

574. *When A Man Loves A Woman // Take Time To Know Her* - **Percy Sledge**
    [#2 US Atlantic Oldies Series DH] [66/68, **A** 19.3, 20.10, **AB** 5.4, 8.2]

575. *When Will I See You Again / I Didn't Know* - **The Three Degrees** - [74, **A** 19.10]

576. *When Will I See You Again // Year Of Decision* - **The Three Degrees**
    [US Philly International Limited DH] [74, **A** 19.10]

577. *Where Evil Grows // Seasons In The Sun* - **Terry Jacks & The Poppy Family** - [US DH]
    [71/73, **AB** 5.8 **B** 21.8]
    (see - Seasons In The Sun / Put The Bone In)

578. *Where Is The Love // First Time Ever I Saw Your Face* - **Roberta Flack**
    [US Atlantic Oldies Series DH] [72, 8.2]
    (see - First Time Ever I Saw Your Face / Trade Winds)

579. *Where The Streets Have No Name / Silver & Gold / Sweetest Thing* - **U2** - [CAN /w pic sleeve]
    [87, **A** 20.16, 26.2, **ABC** *tnotes*, 1.10, 3.3, 13.2]
    [**AC** 13.3, 13.5, **BC** *mzk01*, 4.10, 29.6, **C** 4.2]
    (see - I Still Haven't Found What I'm Looking For
    // Where The Streets Have No Name)

580. *Where The Streets Have No Name / Silver & Gold* - **U2** - [US]
    [**A** 13.3, 13.5, 20.16, 26.2, **AB** 30.2, **B** 4.10, 29.6]

581. *While You See A Chance / Vacant Chair* - **Steve Winwood** - [81, **A** 19.5, **AB** *si84*, 2.7]

582. *While You See A Chance // Nighttrain* - **Steve Winwood** - [CAN Island Gold Standard DH]
    [81, **A** 19.5]

583. *Whiter Shade Of Pale / Lime Street Blues* - **Procal Harum**
    [67, **A** *mcn21_168*, 1.8, 19.7, 19.9, 27.6]
    (see - Conquistador (Live) // A Whiter Shade Of Pale)

584. *Whole Lotta Love (cover)* [FLAT] \\ *Living Loving Maid*
    Led Zeppelin (A - *You Need Love* - Willie Dixon) - [#1 CAN Atlantic Gold DH]
    [70, **A** *tnotes*, *ward*, 1.6, 20.5, 21.12, 22.9, **AB** 15.1, 15.2, 30.3]
    (see - Stairway To Heaven \\ Whole Lotta Love)

585. *Whole Lotta Love (cover)* [FLAT] \\ *Living Loving Maid*
    Led Zeppelin (A - *You Need Love* - Willie Dixon) - [#2 CAN Atlantic Gold Standard DH]
    [70, **A** *tnotes*, *ward*, 1.6, 20.5, 21.12, 22.9, **AB** 8.2, 15.1, 15.2, 30.3]

586. *Wild Thing (cover)* [FLAT] - **Fancy** (The Troggs) - [74, 1.6]

587. *Wild Thing* - **The Troggs** - [US] [66, 1.6, 21.12]

588. *Wildfire* [FLAT] / *Night Thunder* - **Michael Murphy** - [75, **A** *tnotes,* 21.2, 21.3, 25.7, 25.9]

589. *Wildfire* // *Mansion On The Hill* - **Michael Murphy** - [CAN CBS Hall Of Fame Blue DH]
      [75, **A** *tnotes,* 21.2, 21.3, 25.7, 25.9, **AB** *si84,* 24.2]

590. *Wildflower \ The Writing's On The Wall* - **Skylark** - [#1 CAN original DH]
      [73, **A** 10.3, **AB** 1.1]

591. *Wildflower \\ The Writing's On The Wall* - **Skylark** - [#2 US Capitol Starline DH]
      [73, **A** 10.3, **AB** 1.1]

592. *Will You Still Love Me / 25 Or 6 To 4 86* - **Chicago** - [86, **AB** 2.6, **B** 4.1]

593. *Windpower / Flying North* - **Thomas Dolby** - [UK]
      [83, **A** 20.11, 22.4, 22.11, **AB** *ps,* 3.2, 29.6]
      (see - *She Blinded Me With Science / Flying North*)

594. *Windy // Never My Love* - **The Association** - [US WB Back To Back Hits DH]
      [67, **AB** 2.1, 5.15, **B** 1.6]
      (see - *Never My Love / Pinewood Rally*)

595. *Witchy Woman* [FLAT] / *Early Bird* - **The Eagles** - [72, **A** 23.5]
      (see - *Take It Easy // Witchy Woman*)

596. *With Or Without You / Luminous Times (Hold On To Love) / Walk To The Water* - **U2**
      [87, **A** 13.3, 13.5, **ABC** *ps, tnotes,* 1.10, 3.3, 13.2, **BC** *mzk01,* 4.10, 29.6]

597. *With Or Without You // In God's Country* - **U2** - [US Island Revival Of The Fittest DH]
      [87, **A** 13.3, 13.5, **AB** *tnotes,* 5.13, 30.2, **B** *mzk01,* 4.8]
      (see - *In God's Country / Bullet The Blue Sky / Running To Stand Still*)

598. *Wonderous Stories / Awaken* - **Yes** - [#1 UK]
      [77, **A** 22.17, 29.4, **AB** *si84,* 5.11, 18.2, 19.8, 30.1, 31.1.3]
      [**B** *mcn42_188,* 18.1, 19.6, 19.9, 20.3, 20.5, 20.16, 31.1.11]

599. *Wonderous Stories / Awaken* - **Yes** - [#2 US]
      [77, **A** 22.17, 29.4, **AB** 5.7, 18.2, 19.8, 30.1, 31.1.3]
      [**B** *mcn42_188,* 18.1, 19.6, 19.9, 20.3, 20.5, 20.16, 31.1.11]

600. *World Without Love // Nobody I Know* - **Peter & Gordon** - [CAN Capitol Starline DH]
      [64, **A** 27.6]

601. *World Without Love* - **Peter & Gordon** // *Rubber Ball* - **Bobby Vee**
      [US American Pie Back To Back Hits DH] [64/60, **A** 27.6]

602. *Wrapped Around Your Finger / Someone To Talk To* - **The Police** - [UK]
      [84, **A** 12.3, 20.5, **AB** *si84,* **B** 4.10, 5.11, 22.7]
      (see 1 - *Every Breath You Take // Wrapped Around Your Finger*)
      (see 2 - *King Of Pain / Someone To Talk To*)

603. *Wreck Of The Edmund Fitzgerald / (The) House You Live In* - **Gordon Lightfoot**
      [77, **A** 20.4, 20.10, 22.15, **AB** *si84,* 24.3]

604. *Wreck Of The Edmund Fitzgerald // Race Among The Ruins* - **Gordon Lightfoot**
      [CAN Reprise Gold Standard DH] [77, **A** 20.4, 20.10, 22.15]

605. *Year Of The Cat / Broadway Hotel* - **Al Stewart** - [CAN] [77, **A** 22.14, 23.9, 29.4, **AB** 19.12]

606. *Year Of The Cat // Time Passages* - **Al Stewart** - [US Arista Flashback DH]
      [77/78, **A** 22.14, 23.9, 29.4, **AB** 19.12]

607. *You & Me / It's Hot Tonight* - **Alice Cooper** - [77, **AB** *si84,* 2.1]

(see - I Never Cry (Live) // You & Me (Live))

608.   *You Ain't Seen Nothin' Yet / Free Wheeling* - **Bachman - Turner Overdrive** - [74, 2.3]
       (see - Takin' Care Of Business // You Ain't Seen Nothin' Yet)

609.   *You Are The Sunshine Of My Life // Higher Ground* - **Stevie Wonder**
       [US Motown Yesteryears DH] [73, **A** *si84*, 23.1, **B** 20.14]

610.   *You Are The Sunshine Of My Life / Tuesday Heartbreak* - **Stevie Wonder**
       [73, **A** *si84*, 8.3, 23.1]

611.   *You Can't Hurry Love* - **The Supremes** - [US] [66, 1.7, 8.3]
       (see - Rock This Town / You Can't Hurry Love)

612.   *You Can't Hurry Love (cover) / Do You Know? Do You Care?* - **Phil Collins** (The Supremes)
       [83, *ps*, **A** 1.7]

613.   *You Don't Believe \\ Lucifer* - **The Alan Parsons Project** - [DH]
       [84/79, **AB** *si84*, 1.1, 30.2, **B** *mzk01*, 22.2]
       (see - Lucifer / I'd Rather Be A Man)

614.   *You Lie Down With Dogs \\ Lucifer* - **The Alan Parsons Project** - [DH]
       [79, **A** 15.3, **AB** *mzk01*, 1.1, **B** 22.2]
       (see - Damned If I Do / You Lie Down With Dogs)

615.   *You Me & Mexico // Fly Across The Sea* [FLAT] - **Edward Bear -** [Capitol Starline DH]
       [70/72, *si84*, **B** 19.3, 21.8]
       (see - Fly Across The Sea / Four Months Out To Africa)

616.   *You're Gonna Get Your Fingers Burned \\ Psychobabble* - **The Alan Parsons Project -** [DH]
       [82, **AB** 1.1, 15.3, 30.1]
       (see 1 & 2 - Psychobabble / Children Of The Moon & Psychobabble (mono) / (stereo))

617.   *You're So Vain* [FLAT] */ His Friends Are More Than Fond Of Robin* - **Carly Simon**
       [73, **A** *tnotes*, 21.13 **AB** *mzk01, si84*, 2.4, 23.1, 24.7]

618.   *You're So Vain* [FLAT] *// Right Thing To Do* - **Carly Simon**
       [CAN Elektra Gold Standard DH] [73, **A** *tnotes*, 21.13]

619.   *You're The Inspiration / Once In A Lifetime* - **Chicago** - [84, **A** 11.2, **AB** 2.6, **B** 1.9]
       (see - Hard Habit To Break // You're The Inspiration)

620.   *You've Lost That Loving Feeling // Unchained Melody* - **The Righteous Brothers**
       [US DH] [64/65, **AB** 5.9, **B** 1.7]

621.   *You've Made Me So Very Happy // Spinning Wheel* [FLAT] - **Blood, Sweat & Tears**
       [CAN CBS Hall Of Fame Red DH] [69, **A** 19.3, **B** 21.6]
       (see - Spinning Wheel / More & More)

622.   *Your Mama Don't Dance / Golden Ribbons* - **Loggins & Messina** - [73, **A** 20.17]

623.   *Your Mama Don't Dance // Peace Of Mind* - **Loggins & Messina**
       [US CBS Silver DH] [73, **A** 20.17, **AB** *mzk01, si84*, 5.16, 24.2, **B** 1.9]

624.   *Your Move / The Clap* - **Yes**
       [71, **A** 19.7, 22.9, **AB** *mzk01*, 17.1, 19.8, 24.6, 26.2, 30.2, **B** 22.2, 22.17]
       (see 1 & 2 - America // Your Move & Roundabout // Your Move)

625.   *Your Own Special Way / In That Quiet Earth* - **Genesis** - [CAN]
       [77, **A**, 20.16, 26.5S, **AB** 5.2, 8.1, 19.8]

626.   *Your Own Special Way / It's Yourself* - **Genesis** - [UK]
       [77, **A**, 19.8, 20.16, 26.5L, **AB** *mzk01, si84*, 1.4, 5.2, 5.11, 30.1]

627.   *Your Own Special Way // Go West Young Man* - **Genesis** - [US Atlantic Oldies Series DH]
       [77/78, **A**, 19.8, 20.16, 26.5S, **AB** *mzk01*, 5.4, 8.2]

TWENTY

SINGLES II - THE REST

THE GLOSSARY

A - Side A

B - Side B

BEL - Belgium

buks - bukszpan - Encyclopedia Of New Wave, Daniel Bukszpan

C - Track C where the second side has two tracks, B & C, often recorded @ 33 & 1/3 rpm

CAN - Canada

ch - chapter

cover - cover version

DEU - Germany

DH, *dh* - double hit

FLAT - Sa Flatt Ft - It's A Flat Foot Song

FLATAB - Sa Flatt Ft - A&B Sides

FRA - France

gem - a special part of the story

gtns11 - Desert Island Discs, Ian Gittens (the number is the chapter in the book)

instrumental - instrumental version

ITA - Italy

JAP - Japan

levitin - This Is Your Brain On Music, Daniel Levitin

live - live version

long - long version

mcn22 - Rocking The Classics, Edward Macan (the number is the page in the book)

mono - engineered in mono sound

mzk01 - Mzk01 of 2001

NDR - The Netherlands

original - original version

ps - picture sleeve

ride11 - (Keyboard Presents) *Classic Rock*, Ernie Rideout (the number is the page in the book)

quest - questlove - *Music Is History* by Questlove

see - link to another record with the same song

short - short version

si84 - Singles Inventory of 1984

stereo - engineered in stereo sound

th45zz - th45zz, terms of 2009

tnotes - Title Notes, A 45 R P aMble

UK - United Kingdom

US - United States
/w - with
ward - Is This Live? by Christopher Ward
WB - Warner Brothers
YUG - Yugoslavia

THE SONGS

1. *#9 Dream* - **John Lennon** - [75, 25.3, 29.5]
2. *50 Ways To Leave Your Lover* [FLAT] - **Paul Simon** - [75, 21.3, 22.16]
3. *(Just Like) Starting Over* - **John Lennon** - [80, 2.9, 3.3, 20.15]
4. *99 Red Balloons* [FLAT] - **Nena** - [84, 19.11, 21.13]

5. *ABC* [FLAT] [US] - **The Jackson 5** - [70, 8.3, 21.5]
6. *Adventures In Modern Recording* - **The Buggles** - [UK] [81, *ps*, 3.2, 22.4]
7. *Advice For The Young At Heart* - **Tears For Fears** - [89, 3.6, 19.5]
8. *Africa* [FLAT] - **Toto** - [83, 21.6, 29.1]
9. *After Midnight // Let It Rain* - **Eric Clapton** - [DH] [70, **B** 4.3, 20.3, 20.4]
10. *After The Goldrush* - **Prelude** - [74, 22.8, 22.9, 22.11, 25.3]
11. *Against All Odds // I Can't Believe It's True* - **Phil Collins** - [CAN Atlantic Gold Standard DH]
      [85/82, **AB** 5.4, 8.2]
12. *Against The Wind* - **Bob Segar** - [80, 3.1]
13. *Ain't No Mountain High Enough* - **Diana Ross** - [US] [70, *gtns61*, 8.3]
14. *Ain't Nobody But Me / Sister Moonshine* [FLAT] - **Supertramp**
      [76, **A** *ch16*, 19.6, 20.9, 23.9, 23.10, **AB** *si84*, 1.4, 24.4, 30.2, **B** 16.1, 19.7, 21.4, 22.11, 22.12]
15. *Air That I Breathe, The* [FLAT] // *Jennifer Eccles* - **The Hollies**
      [CAN CBS Hall Of Fame Blue DH] [74/67, **A** 21.12, 22.13, 29.4, **AB** *si84*, 24.2]
16. *All For Love* - **Adams / Stewart / Sting** - [US] [94, 10.2, 12.4, 24.8]
17. *All I Wanna Do / Run Baby Run* - **Sheryl Crow** - [US] [94, **AB** 24.8, **B** 19.6, 20.10]
18. *All Night Long* - **Lionel Ritchie** - [84, 8.3]
19. *All She Wants To Do Is Dance* - **Don Henley** - [85, 2.9, 23.4]
20. *All This Time* - **Sting** - [US] [91, 12.4, 19.5, 22.16, 24.8]
21. *All Those Years Ago* - **George Harrison** - [81, 2.13]
22. *Allentown* - **Billy Joel** - [83, 22.3, 24.12]
23. *Alone Again (Naturally)* [FLAT] - **Gilbert O'Sullivan** - [72, *mzk01*, *si84*, 21.3, 25.1, 29.5]
24. *Along Comes A Woman* - **Chicago** - [85, 2.6]
25. *Already Gone // Tequila Sunrise* [FLAT] - **The Eagles** - [US Asylum Spun Gold DH]
      [74/73, **AB** 5.14, 23.4, 23.5]
26. *Also Sprach Zarathustra (cover)* [FLAT] - **Deodato** (Richard Strauss)
      [73, *mzk01*, *si84*, 1.8, 20.4, 21.11, 22.1, 23.1, 29.4]
27. *Always Something There To Remind Me (cover)* - **The Naked Eyes** (Sandie Shaw)
      [83, *buks*, 1.7, 2.10, 19.11]
28. *American Woman* [FLATAB] \\ *No Sugar Tonight* [FLATAB] - **The Guess Who** - [DH]

[70, **AB** ch2]

29. *Angel Of Harlem* - **U2** - [88, *ps*, 3.3, 13.3, 20.7, 29.2]

30. *Angel Of The Morning* - **Juice Newton** - [81, 1.7, 2.11]

31. *Angie* - **The Rolling Stones** - [73, *si84*, *tnotes*, 2.15, 24.1, 27.3]

32. *Annie's Song* - **John Denver** - [74, 20.10, 22.17]

33. *Another Brick In The Wall Part 2* [FLAT] - **Pink Floyd**
   [80, *ch15*, *mcn80*, *ps*, *si84*, 2.13, 3.2, 19.8, 20.6, 21.9, 22.8]

34. *Another Day / Oh Woman Oh Why* - **Paul McCartney**
   [71, **A** 11.3, 11.4, 22.9, **AB** *si84*, 30.1]

35. *Another Saturday Night (cover)* - **Cat Stevens** (Sam Cooke) - [US] [74, 1.6, 19.4]

36. *Anyway You Want* - **Chicago** - [75, 20.17, 23.3]

37. *Aquarius & Let The Sunshine* - **The Fifth Dimension** - [69, 20.3]

38. *Are We Ourselves / Deeper & Deeper* - **The Fixx** - [84, **A** *buks*, **AB** *ps*, **B** 4.10, 27.5]

39. *Arias & Symphonies* [FLAT] - **The Spoons** - [82, 2.13, 10.4, 21.11, 26.1]

40. *Armageddon* - **Prism** - [79, 10.3, 23.6]

41. *At The Feet Of The Moon* - **The Parachute Club** - [84, 10.4, 22.9]

42. *Athena* - **The Who** - [82, 2.6]

43. *Atomic* - **Blondie** - [80, *ps*, *buks*, 2.8]

44. *Aubrey* - **Bread** - [72, 2.1]

45. *Autobahn* [FLAT] - **Kraftwerk** - [US] [75, *mzk01*, 21.7, 22.4, 25.6]

46. *Axel F* - **Harold Faltermeyer** - [85, 22.1]

47. *Baby I Love You* - **Andy Kim** - [US] [69, 19.3]

48. *Baby I Love Your Way (Live)* - **Peter Frampton** - [76, 25.10]

49. *Back Home Again* - **John Denver** - [74, 20.12]

50. *Back In The High Life* [FLAT] - **Steve Winwood** - [87, *ps*, 3.3, 21.8]

51. *Back Off Bugaloo / Blindman* - **Ringo Starr** - [72, **AB** 11.4]

52. *Back On The Chain Gang* - **The Pretenders** - [83, 26.1]

53. *Backstabbers* - **The O'Jays** - [US Philly International Limited] [72, *mzk01*, 4.3]

54. *Bad Bad Leroy Brown* - **Jim Croce** - [73, *si84*, 20.17]

55. *Bad Side Of The Moon (cover)* [FLAT] - **April Wine** (Elton John) - [72, 1.5, 10.1, 10.5, 21.9, 22.11]

56. *Bad Time* - **Grand Funk** - [75, 2.13]

57. *Baker Street* - **Gerry Rafferty** - [78, *tnotes*, 22.15]

58. *Ballad of John & Yoko / Old Brown Shoe* - **The Beatles** - [69, **AB** *ps*, 11.4, **B** 20.15]

59. *Band On The Run* [FLAT] / *1985* - **Paul McCartney & Wings**
   [74, **A** *tnotes*, 20.3, 20.5, 25.5, **AB** *si84*, 11.3]

60. *Barracuda // Treat Me Well* - **Heart** - [CAN CBS Hall Of Fame Blue DH] [77, **AB** *si84*, 24.2]

61. *Bat Out Of Hell // Heaven Can Wait* - **Meatloaf** - [CAN CBS Hall Of Fame Blue DH]
   [77, AB 19.12, 23.6]

62. *Batdance* - **Prince** - [89, 2.6]

63. *Beach Baby* - **First Class** - [74, 20.13]

64. *Beast Of Burden* - **The Rolling Stones** - [78, 2.15]

65. *Beautiful* - **Gordon Lightfoot** - [72, 2.2, 22.17]

66. *Beginnings // Questions 67 & 68* [FLAT] - **Chicago** - [CAN CBS Hall Of Fame Red DH]
   [71, **A** 11.2, 20.6, 22.13, **AB** 5.1, 11.1, 30.2,]

67. *Belfast Child 12* - **Simple Minds** - [89, 23.9]

68. *Bennie & The Jets* - **Elton John** - [74, 2.5, 19.6, 20.5, 22.4, 24.11, 25.10]

69. *Best Of My Love* [FLAT] - **The Eagles** - [75, 23.5, 25.4]

70. *Betcha By Golly Wow* - **The Stylistics** - [US] [72, *mzk01*, 19.10, 22.11, 22.15]

71. *Big Log* [FLAT] - **Robert Plant** - [83, ps, 2.14, 21.9]

72. *Big Love* - **Fleetwood Mac** - [87, *ps*, 2.6]

73. *Big Shot // Honesty* - **Billy Joel** - [CAN CBS Hall Of Fame Blue DH] [79, **AB** 23.6]

74. *Big Time* - **Peter Gabriel** - [86, *buks*, 30.3]

75. *Billie Jean* - **Michael Jackson** - [US 1 sided single] [83, *si84, buks, levitin, quest, ward*, 19.10, 24.4]

76. *Billy Don't Be A Hero* - **Bo Donaldson & The Heywoods** - [74, 22.16, 23.7, 25.5]

77. *Bitch Is Back, The* - **Elton John** - [74, 2.5, 24.11]

78. *Black Cars* - **Gino Vanelli** - [84, 2.13, 10.4]

79. *Black Magic Woman* - **Santana** (Fleetwood Mac) - [68, 1.5, 19.3]

80. *Black Stations, White Stations* - **M&M** - [84, *ward*, 10.4]

81. *Blue Collar Man* - **Styx** - [78, *si84, tnotes*, 19.7]

82. *Blueberry Hill* - **Fats Domino** - [57, 2.5, 20.17]

83. *Bohemian Rhapsody* - **Queen** - [76, *tnotes*, 2.4, 5.1, 20.5, 20.16, 22.9, 25.8, 26.2, 27.3, 29.5]

84. *Bongo Rock (cover)* - **The Incredible Bongo Band** (Preston Epps)
     [73, *mzk01, si84*, 1.5, 20.7, 22.1, 24.1, 25.3]

85. *Boogie Man Gonna Get Ya* - **Catfish Hodge** - [US] [73, *mzk01, si84*, 20.17, 22.6, 24.4]

86. *Boogie On Reggae Woman* - **Stevie Wonder** - [US] [75, 22.12]

87. *Born In The USA* - **Bruce Springsteen** - [84, *ps*, 3.6]

88. *Born To Be Wild // Magic Carpet Ride* [FLAT] - **Steppenwolf** - [US Goldies 45 DH]
     [68, **AB** 19.3, **B** 21.10]

89. *Born To Run* - **Bruce Springsteen** - [75, 19.4, 27.3]

90. *Born To Wander* [FLAT] // *I Just Want To Celebrate* - **Rare Earth** - [US Collectables DH]
     [71, **A** 21.5, 22.11, **AB** 5.9, B 22.6]

91. *Boy Inside The Man* [FLAT] - **Tom Cochrane & Red Rider** - [86, 2.11, 10.4, 21.8]

92. *Boys Of Summer* [FLAT] - **Don Henley** - [85, 2.9, 21.10, 23.4, 24.5]

93. *Brandy (You're A Fine Girl)* - **Looking Glass** - [72, *mzk01*, 4.3, 25.1]

94. *Broken Wings* [FLAT] - **Mr. Mister** - [85, 21.7, 22.15]

95. *Brother Louie (cover)* [FLAT] - **The Stories** (Hot Chocolate) - [73, *si84*, 1.5, 21.11]

96. *Brother Of Mine / Vultures In The City* [FLAT] - **Anderson, Bruford, Wakeman & Howe**
     [89, **AB** *ps*, **B** 20.4, 21.8]

97. *Brown Sugar* - **The Rolling Stones** - [71, 2.15]

98. *Bungle In The Jungle* [FLAT] - **Jethro Tull** - [75, 21.11, 22.3, 22.11, 22.14, 25.4, 26.2, 29.5]

99. *Burning Down The House* [FLAT] - **The Talking Heads** - [82, *buks*, 21.7]

100. *California Jam / Dr. Marvello* [FLAT] - **Klaatu**
         [77, **A** 10.3, 22.4, **AB** *si84*, 30.1, **B** 21.12, 22.13, 22.16]

101. *Call Me* - **Blondie** - [80, *buks*, 2.8, 20.14, 27.5]

102. *Calling Elvis* - **Dire Straits** - [91, 2.6, 20.5, 22.15, 24.8, 30.3]

103. *Can You Give It All To Me* [FLAT] - **Myles & Lenny** - [75, *si84*, 10.3, 21.4, 22.14, 29.1, 29.5]

104. *Can't Cry Anymore* - **Sheryl Crowe** - [US] [94, 24.8]

105. *Can't Get Enough* - **Bad Company** - [US Swan Song] [74, 20.14]

106. *Can't Get It Out Of My Head* [FLAT] - **The Electric Light Orchestra** - [US]
    [75, *ps*, 3.2, 21.12, 29.4]

107. *Candyman, The // I Want To Be Happy* - **Sammy Davis Jr.** - [Golden Treasures DH]
    [71, AB 1.2, 23.7]

108. *Carry Me* - **Stampeders** - [71, 10.3]

109. *Carry On Wayward Son / Questions Of My Childhood* - **Kansas**
    [77, *mzk01*, *si84*, *tnotes*, **A** 19.6, 22.9, **AB** 19.8, 24.6]

110. *Centerfield* - **John Fogerty** - [85, 2.6, 19.5]

111. *Centerfold* - **The J Geils Band** - [81, *si84*, 2.10, 22.10]

112. *Chameleon* [FLAT] - **Herbie Hancock** - [73, 21.6, 22.1, 25.5]

113. *Change* - **Tears For Fears** - [82, *ps*, 24.5]

114. *Chariots Of Fire* - **Vangelis** - [81, *quest*, 22.1, 27.5]

115. *Check It Out* - **John Mellencamp** - [87, *ps*, 22.14]

116. *Cherry Bomb* [FLAT] - **John Mellencamp** - [87, *ps*, 21.2]

117. *China Girl* - **David Bowie** - [83, *levitin*, 2.10]

118. *China Grove* - **The Doobie Brothers** - [73, *ride95*, *si84*, 2.1]

119. *Chipmunks Song* - **Chipmunks** - [62, 20.10]

120. *Christmas Song* - **Natalie Cole** - [88/94, *mzk01*, 29.3]

121. *Christmas Time / Reggae Christmas* [FLAT] - **Bryan Adams**
    [85, **AB** *ps*, 2.13, 3.5, 3.6, **B** *mzk01*, 10.2, 19.5, 21.5, 22.6, 23.9, 23.10]

122. *Church Of The Poison Mind* - **Culture Club** - [83, 2.13, 22.12]

123. *Cinderella Man / A Farewell To Kings* - **Rush** - [77, *si84*, **A** 10.4, **AB** 19.8, 30.3]

124. *Cisko Kid* - **War** - [73, *si84*, 19.10, 22.6]

125. *Clair* - **Gilbert O'Sullivan** - [US] [72, 20.11, 22.4, 22.11]

126. *Clap For The Wolfman* - **The Guess Who** - [74, 10.1, 20.7, 22.5, 29.2]

127. *Cocaine (cover)* - **Eric Clapton** (JJ Cale) - [77, 1.6]

128. *Come & Get It* [FLAT] - **Badfinger** - [70, 19.12, 21.12]

129. *Come & Get Your Love* [FLAT] - **Redbone** - [74, **A** 21.5]

130. *Come On Eileen* - **Dexy's Midnight Runners** - [83, *buks*, 20.16, 22.14, 29.2]

131. *Come Sail Away* - **Styx** - [US] [77, *mcn186*, *ps*, 19.9]

132. *Coming Up / Coming Up (Live) / Lunch Box Odd Sox* - **Paul McCartney**
    [80, **AB** 11.3, **B** 22.6, 25.10]

133. *Commotion // Green River* - **Creedence Clearwater Revival**
    [US Fantasy Back To Back Hits DH] [69, **AB** 5.17]

134. *Communication Breakdown \\ Good Times Bad Times* - **Led Zeppelin** - [US DH]
    [69, **AB** 5.8, 15.1, 15.2, 30.3]

135. *Control Of Me* - **Les Emmerson (The Five Man Electrical Band)** - [73, *si84*, 8.1, 10.3, 23.1]

136. *Could It Be I'm Falling In Love* [FLAT] - **The Spinners** - [73, 19.10, 21.11]

137. *Could It Be Magic // I Write The Songs* - **Barry Manilow** - [Arista Flashback DH]
    [75, **A** 1.8, **AB** 8.4]

138. *Couldn't Get It Right* [FLAT] - **The Climax Blues Band** - [77, 21.5]

139. *Cover Of A Rolling Stone* - **Dr. Hook** - [73, *mzk01*, *si84*, 1.4, 24.6]

140. *Cracklin' Rosie* - **Neil Diamond** - [US] [70, 23.7]

141. *Crazy* [FLAT] - **Seal** - [US] [91, 1.9, 21.5, 23.9, 23.10, 24.8]

142. *Crazy For You* - **Madonna** - [85, 2.9, 12.6, 27.5]

143.   *Crazy Little Thing Called Love* - **Queen** - [79, 20.17, 29.2]

144.   *Criminal Mind* [FLAT] - **Gowan** - [85, *ps*, 21.9, 29.1]

145.   *Crocodile Rock* - **Elton John** - [73, 2.5, 19.6, 20.8, 23.1, 23.10, 24.11]

146.   *Crumblin' Down* - **John Cougar Mellencamp** - [83, *ps*, 3.1]

147.   *Cry Your Eyes Out* [FLAT] - **Les Emmerson (The Five Man Electrical Band)**
         [73, *si84*, 8.1, 10.3, 21.11, 22.10, 23.9, 24.1]

148.   *Crying Over You* - **Platinum Blonde** - [85, 10.4]

149.   *Cum Hear The Band* - **April Wine** - [75, 10.1, 10.5]

150.   *Daisy Jane* - **America** - [75, 2.1]

151.   *Damn I Wish I was Your Lover* [FLAT] - **Sophie B. Hawkins** - [US]
         [92, 20.4, 21.13, 22.3, 24.8]

152.   *Dance A Little Step* - **Mashmakhan** - [73, 10.3, 19.4, 21.6, 22.11, 23.9, 25.3]

153.   *Dance To The Music* - **Sly & The Family Stone** - [68, 19.3]

154.   *Dance With Me* - **Orleans** - [US] [75, 21.4]

155.   *Dancing Fool* - **The Guess Who** - [74, 10.1]

156.   *Dancing In The Dark* - **Bruce Springsteen** - [85, *ps*, 3.6]

157.   *Dancing In The Moonlight* - **King Harvest** - [US] [73, 22.15]

158.   *Dancing In The Street* - **David Bowie & Mick Jagger** - [85, *ward*, 1.7, 2.10]

159.   *Dancing On The Ceiling* - **Lionel Ritchie** - [86, 8.3]

160.   *Daniel* - **Elton John** - [73, *si84*, 2.5, 5.1, 23.1]

161.   *Day After Day* - **Badfinger** - [71, 1.9, 27.2]

162.   *Day After Day / Breakdown* [FLAT] - **The Alan Parsons Project** - [US]
         [77, **A** *mzk01*, 1.9, 20.9, 27.2, **AB** 5.6, **B** 21.11, 22.8]

163.   *Day By Day* - **Godspell** - [72, *mzk01*, 25.1]

164.   *Daytime Nighttime* [FLAT] - **Keith Hampshire** - [72, 10.3, 21.6]

165.   *December 1963 (Oh What A Night)* [FLAT] - **Frankie Valli & The Four Seasons**
         [76, 2.1, 21.6, 25.8]

166.   *Desire* [FLAT] */ Hallelujah Here She Comes* - **U2**
         [88, **A** 13.3, 20.7, 21.2, 22.12, **AB** *ps*, 1.4, 3.3, 3.4, **B** *mzk01*]

167.   *Devil You* - **The Stampeders** - [71, 10.3, 20.7]

168.   *Dialogue* [FLAT] - **Chicago** - [72, 11.1, 11.2, 22.9]

169.   *Diamond Girl* - **Seals & Crofts** - [73, *si84*, 2.1, 20.13, 22.15]

170.   *Diamond Sun* - **Glass Tiger** - [88, *ps*, 2.11, 3.1]

171.   *Diamonds Diamonds* - **Max Webster** - [77, 10.3]

172.   *Diary* - **Bread** - [US] [72, 2.4]

173.   *Disco Duck* - **Rick Dees** - [76, 23.7]

174.   *Discotheque* - **U2** - [US] [97, *ch5*, 2.14, 13.3, 20.4, 24.8]

175.   *Dissidents* - **Thomas Dolby** - [UK] [84, *ch12, ps*]

176.   *Do I Love You \\ So Long City* - **Paul Anka** - [DH] [71, **AB** 1.2]

177.   *Do It Right* - **Bob McBride** - [74, 10.3]

178.   *Do It (Til You're Satisfied)* [FLAT] - **B T Express** - [75, **A** 21.5, 25.9]

179.   *Do They Know It's Christmas* - **Band Aid** - [84, *ps, buks, mzk01, ward*, 29.3]

180.   *Do Ya Think I'm Sexy?* - **Rod Stewart** - [78, 2.6]

181.   *Do You Feel Like I Do (Live)* - **Peter Frampton** - [76, 25.10]

182.   *Do You Really Want To Hurt Me* [FLAT] - **Culture Club** - [83, *quest*, 21.4]

183.   *Doctor Doctor* - **The Thompson Twins** - [US] [84, *ch12, ps*]

184.   *Doctor My Eyes* - **Jackson Browne** - [72, 2.2, 20.12]

185.   *Doesn't Really Matter // Standing in The Dark* - **Platinum Blonde**
         [CAN CBS Hall Of Fame Blue DH] [84, **AB** *ward*, 10.4]

186.   *Don't Bring Me Down* [FLAT] - **The Electric Light Orchestra** - [80, 20.7, 22.6]

187.   *Don't Call Us, We'll Call You* [FLAT] - **Sugarloaf** - [75, 19.4, 21.6, 22.3, 25.6]

188.   *Don't Cry* - **Asia** [83, *ps*, 2.9, 3.2]

189.   *Don't Dream It's Over* [FLAT] - **Crowded House** - [87, 2.11, 19.5, 21.8]

190.   *Don't Fear The Reaper* - **Blue Oyster Cult** - [US] [76, 19.4]

191.   *Don't Forget Me (When I'm Gone)* - **Glass Tiger** - [86, *ps, ward*, 2.11, 3.1, 20.14]

192.   *Don't Go* - **Yaz** - [UK] [82, *mzk01, ps*, 26.1]

193.   *Don't Let The Sun Catch You Crying // Girl On A Swing*
         Gerry & The Pacemakers - [US Eric DH] [64/66, **A** 27.6, **AB** 1.3]

194.   *Don't Let The Sun Go Down On Me* - **Elton John** - [74, 2.5, 24.11]

195.   *Don't Mess With Doctor Dream* - **The Thompson Twins** - [UK] [85, *ps*, 8.5]

196.   *Don't Stop / Never Going Back Again* - **Fleetwood Mac** - [77, **A** 2.1, 3.2, 20.14, **B** 21.3]

197.   *Don't Worry Be Happy* - **Bobby McFerrin** - [US] [88, 22.9]

198.   *Don't You Want Me* - **The Human League** - [82, *si84*, 3.3, 19.11]

199.   *Doo Doo Doo Doo Doo Doo Heartbreaker* - **The Rolling Stones** - [74, 2.15]

200.   *Doo Wah Diddy Diddy* - **Manfred Mann** - [64, 2.5, 19.3]

201.   *Double Vision* - **Foreigner** - [78, *ps*, 3.2]

202.   *Down Under* [FLAT] / *Crazy* - **Men At Work** - [82, **A** 21.6, 22.11, **B** 1.9, 4.10]

203.   *Dream A Little Dream Of Me (cover)* - **Mama Cass** (The Mamas & The Papas)
         (Ozzie Nelson) [68, 1.5 20.12]

204.   *Dreaming* - **Blondie** - [79, 1.9, 2.8, 27.3]

205.   *Dreaming* - **Orchestral Manoeuvres In The Dark** (OMD) - [88, *ps*, 1.9, 12.1]

206.   *Dreams* - **Fleetwood Mac** - [77, 2.1]

207.   *Drive* - **The Cars** - [84, 2.12, 22.7]

208.   *Duchess* - **Genesis** - [UK] [80, *mzk01, ps, si84*, 3.3, 5.11, 8.5, 14.4]

209.   *Dueling Banjos* - **Eric Weisberg** - [73, *mzk01*, 20.7, 22.1, 22.17, 22.18, 23.1, 27.4]

210.   *Dust In The Wind* - **Kansas** - [78, 22.14, 22.17]

211.   *Earache My Eye* [FLAT] - **Cheech & Chong** - [74, *si84*, 20.4, 21.9, 22.5, 24.4, 25.3]

212.   *Easier Said Than Done* - **Jon Anderson** - [85, 2.12, 29.3]

213.   *Easy* - **The Commodores** - [77, *quest*, 8.3, 23.6]

214.   *Ebony & Ivory* - **Paul McCartney & Stevie Wonder** - [82, *ps*, 3.6]

215.   *Echo Beach* [FLAT] - **Martha & The Muffins**
         [80, *mzk01, si84, ward*, 10.4, 19.5, 21.13, 22.11]

216.   *Edge Of A Dream* - **Joe Cocker** - [84, 2.11]

217.   *Eight Miles High* [FLAT] // *Turn Turn Turn (cover)* **The Byrds** (B - Pete Seeger)
         [CAN CBS Hall Of Fame Red **DH**] [66/65, **A** 21.4, **B** 1.5]

218.   *Electricity* - **Orchestral Manoeuvres In The Dark** (OMD) - [80, *ps*, 2.13, 12.1]

219.   *Eli's Coming* - **Three Dog Night** - [69, 2.5, 19.3]

220. *Emma* [FLAT] - **Hot Chocolate** - [UK] [75, 5.1, 19.4, 21.12, 25.6]

221. *Emotional Rescue* - **The Rolling Stones** - [80, *mzk01, si84*, 2.15]

222. *Empty Garden* - **Elton John** - [82, 2.9]

223. *End Of The Innocence* - **Don Henley** - [89, 20.5]

224. *Englishman In New York* - **Sting** - [87, *ps*, 3.6]

225. *Entertainer* - **Marvin Hamlisch** - [74, 1.9, 22.1, 27.4]

226. *Enola Gay* - **Orchestral Manoeuvres In The Dark** (OMD)
     [80, *si84*, 12.2, 19.11, 20.8, 23.9, 23.10, 30.4]

227. *Entangled / Ripples* - **Genesis**
     [76, **A** *tnotes*, 20.9, 22.17, 29.4, **AB** 1.4, 8.1, 14.3, 14.4, 19.8, 30.4, 31.1.16]
     [**B** 19.9, 29.1, 31.1.23]

228. *Europa & The Pirate Twins* - **Thomas Dolby** - [US] [83, *ps*, 2.11, 22.12, 26.1]

229. *Every Little Thing She Does Is Magic* - **The Police** - [81, *ps, si84*, 12.3]

230. *Everybody Hurts* - **REM** - [US] [93, 2.6, 19.5, 20.10, 24.8]

231. *Everybody Plays The Fool* [FLAT] // *I'm So Proud* - **The Main Ingredient**
     [US RCA Gold Standard DH] [72, **A** 19.10, 21.5]

232. *Everyday Is A Winding Road* - **Sheryl Crow** - [US] [97, 19.5, 23.9, 24.8, 29.2, 30.3]

233. *Everywhere* - **Fleetwood Mac** - [87, *ps*, 2.6]

234. *Eyes Of A Stranger* - **The Payolas** - [82, 10.4]

235. *Eyes Without A Face* [FLAT] - **Billy Idol** - [84, 2.8, 21.7]

236. *Falling In Love* \\ *So Good At Loving You* - **Hamilton, Joe Frank & Reynolds** - [DH]
     [75, **AB** 1.2]

237. *Fame* [FLAT] - **David Bowie** - [75, 21.12]

238. *Family Of Man* - **Three Dog Night** - [72, 19.3]

239. *Feeling Stronger Everyday* [FLAT] - **Chicago** - [73, 11.1, 11.2, 20.3, 30.1]

240. *Feels So Good* - **Chuck Mangione** - [78, *mzk01, si84*, 22.1]

241. *Fields Of Fire* - **Big Country** - [83, *ps*, 3.4, 26.1]

242. *(A) Fifth Of Beethoven* - **Walter Murphy** - [76, 1.8]

243. *Finally (With You)* - **The Cooper Brothers** - [74, 10.3, 19.12, 25.3]

244. *Finer Things, The* - **Steve Winwood** - [87, *ps, ch13*, 3.3]

245. *Flashdance (What A Feeling)* - **Irene Cara** - [83, 2.13]

246. *Flesh For Fantasy* - **Billy Idol** - [84, 2.8]

247. *Fly Like An Eagle* - **The Steve Miller Band** - [US] [76, 19.4]

248. *Fly Robin Fly* [FLAT] - **The Silver Convention** - [75, A 21.13]

249. *Flyer, The* - **Saga** - [83, 10.4, 26.1]

250. *For The Love Of The Money* [FLAT] - **The O'Jays** - [UK Philly International Limited]
     [74, *mzk01*, 21.5, 25.5]

251. *For Your Eyes Only* - **Sheena Easton** - [81, 2.10]

252. *Forever (Live & Die)* [FLAT] - **Orchestral Manoeuvres In The Dark** (OMD)
     [86, *mzk01, ps*, 12.1, 19.5, 21.6]

253. *Forever Young* - **Alphaville** - [85, 24.7]

254. *Fortunate Son* // *Down On The Bayou* - **Creedence Clearwater Revival**
     [US Fantasy Back To Back Hits DH] [69, **AB** 5.17]

255. *Fragile* - **Sting** - [US] [87, 5.8]

256. *Framed* - **Cheech & Chong** - [76, *si84*, 20.17, 23.3, 24.4, 25.3]

257. *Free As A Bird* - **The Beatles** - [US] [96, *ch21, ps*, 1.9, 22.3]

258. *Free As A Bird* [FLAT] - **Supertramp** - [87, *ps*, 1.9, 19.7, 29.1]

259. *Free Bird (Live)* - **Lynyrd Skynyrd** - [US] [74, *mzk01, ward*, 5.8, 25.10]

260. *Free Ride* - **The Edgar Winter Group** - [73, 26.2]

261. *Freedom* [FLAT] - **George Michael** - [90, 20.3, 20.4, 21.12, 24.8]

262. *Freeze Frame* - **The J Geils Band** - [82, *quest*, 2.10, 19.5, 22.3]

263. *Friends of Mr. Cairo* - **Jon & Vangelis** - [81, *mzk01, si84, tnotes*, 19.11, 22.4]

264. *Funny Face \\ How Close You Came To Being Gone* - **Donna Fargo** - [US DH]
     [73, **A** 20.10, **AB** 1.2]

265. *Games Without Frontiers* - **Peter Gabriel** - [80, 22.10]

266. *Garden Party* - **Rick Nelson** - [72, 2.5]

267. *Gemini Dream* - **The Moody Blues** - [81, *ch14, si84*]

268. *Genetic Engineering* - **Orchestral Manoeuvres In The Dark** (OMD) - [UK]
     [83, *mzk01, ps, si84*, 5.11, 22.3, 26.1]

269. *Get Ready* - **Rare Earth** - [70, 1.5]

270. *Get Closer* - **Seals & Crofts** - [76, 2.1]

271. *Ghostdancing* - **Simple Minds** - [86, *ps, mzk01*, 3.3]

272. *Gimmie Some Lovin' // Keep On Runnin'* - **The Spencer Davis Group**
     [US Silver Spotlight Series DH] [67/65, **A** 19.3, **AB** *ride108*, 2.5, **B** 27.6]

273. *Girls Just Wanna Have Fun (cover)* - **Cyndi Lauper** (A Robert Hazard)
     [84, 1.7, 19.5, 23.6]

274. *Girls' School \\ Mull Of Kintyre* - **Wings** - [UK DH]
     [77, **AB** *ps, si84*, 5.11, 11.4, **B** 11.3, 20.9]

275. *Glamour Boy* - **The Guess Who** - [73, 10.1, 10.5]

276. *Glittering Prize* [FLAT] - **Simple Minds** - [NDR]
     [82, *ch12, mzk01, ps, si84, tnotes*, 4.8, 21.11, 26.1]

277. *Gloria (Live) // Sunday Bloody Sunday* - **U2** - [US Revival Of The Fittest DH]
     [81/83, **A** *mzk01*, 1.9, 22.6, 25.10, **AB** 5.13, 30.3]
     [**B** 13.1, 13.5, 22.14, 22.16, 26.6]

278. *Glory Days* - **Bruce Springsteen** - [85, *ps*, 3.6, 19.5]

279. *Go All The Way* - **The Raspberries** - [72, 25.2]

280. *Go For A Soda* - **Kim Mitchell** - [84, 10.4]

281. *Going For The One / Parallels* - **Yes** - [UK]
     [77, **A** 19.9, 20.7, 22.18, **AB** *si84*, 5.11, 18.2, 19.8, 30.1, 31.1.3] [**B** *mcn40*, 19.7, 20.5]

282. *Going Up The Country* - **Canned Heat** - [68, 2.5, 20.7, 22.11]

283. *Gold* - **Spandau Ballet** - [83, *si84*, 2.8]

284. *Gone Long Gone* - **Chicago** - [79, 30.4]

285. *Good Day* - **Lighthouse** - [US] [74, 25.3]

286. *(A) Good Song* - **Valdy** - [72, 10.3, 21.4]

287. *Goodbye Superdad* - **Bill King** - [73, *si84*, 10.3, 24.4]

288. *Goodnight Tonight / Daytime Nighttime Suffering* - **Wings** - [79, **A** 11.3, **AB** 11.4]

289. *Got My Mind Set On You* - **George Harrison** - [89, 2.13, 19.12]
290. *Green Tambourine* - **Lemon Peppers** // *Yummy Yummy Yummy*
       Ohio Express [US Eric DH] [67/68, **AB** 1.3]
291. *Greensleeves* [FLAT] - **Mason Williams** - [69, 20.16, 21.11, 22.1, 23.9, 23.10]
292. *Groovy Kind Of love* - **Phil Collins** - [UK] [88, *ps*, 8.5, 29.1]
293. *Grow Some Funk Of Your Own* - **Elton John** - [76, 2.5, 25.8]
294. *Guitar Man* [FLAT] - **Bread** - [US] [72, 2.4, 25.2]
295. *Gypsies Tramps & Thieves* [FLAT] - **Cher** - [US] [71, 2.5, 21.13]

296. *Happy Together* - **The Turtles** - [US] [67, 20.13]
297. *Hats Off To The Stranger* [FLAT] - **Lighthouse** - [71, 10.1, 10.5, 21.9]
298. *Half Breed* - **Cher** - [US] [73, 2.5]
299. *Hard To Say I'm Sorry* - **Chicago** - [82, 11.2]
300. *Have You Ever Seen The Rain* // *Hey Tonight* - **Creedence Clearwater Revival**
       [US Collectables DH] [71, **AB** 5.9]
301. *Hawaii Five - O* - **The Ventures** - [68, 2.5]
302. *Head Over Heels* [FLATAB] / *When In Love With A Blind Man* [FLATAB] - **Tears For Fears**
       [85, **A** *quest*, **AB** *ps*, 1.4, 3.3, 3.4, 8.5, 21.12]
       [**B** *mzk01*, 4.10, 22.15, 22.16, 23.9, 23..10, 29.6]
303. *Heart & Soul* - **Huey Lewis** - [83, 2.8]
304. *Heart Of Glass* - **Blondie** - [79, *ward*, 2.8, 19.5, 27.3]
305. *Heart Of Rock & Roll* - **Huey Lewis** - [84, *ps*, 2.8, 20.7, 22.12]
306. *Heartbreaker* - **Pat Benatar** - [US] [80, 2.8]
307. *Heaven (original) / (Live)* - **Bryan Adams** - [84, **A** 10.2, **B** 25.10
308. *Helen Wheels* - **Paul McCartney & Wings**
       [73, *mzk01*, *si84*, *tnotes*, 4.8, 20.15, 24.1]
309. *Hello* - **Lionel Ritchie** - [84, 8.3]
310. *Hello Again* - **Neil Diamond** - [80, 2.13]
311. *Hello Goodbye* [FLATAB] / *I Am The Walrus* [FLATAB] - **The Beatles**
       [67, **B** *quest*, 20.6, 21.12, 22.5, 22.16, 23.9, 23.10, 29.4]
312. *Hello Hurray* [FLAT] - **Alice Cooper** - [73, *si84*, 21.12]
313. *Hello It's Me (cover)* [FLAT] - **Todd Rundgren** (Nazz)
       [73, *si84*, 1.5, 19.6, 21.6, 22.13, 24.1, 26.2]
314. *Here Comes The Night* - **Nick Gilder** - [78, 2.8]
315. *Hey Big Brother* - **Rare Earth** - [US] [71, 2.14]
316. *Hey You* - **Bachman - Turner Overdrive** - [75, 1.9, 2.3, 25.7]
317. *Hi Hi Hi / C Moon* - **Wings** - [73, **A** *mzk01*, 19.7, 20.3, 20.15, **AB** *si84*, 2.13, 11.3, 11.4, 30.2]
318. *Higher Love* - **Steve Winwood** - [87, *ch13*, *ps*, 3.3]
319. *Hit The Road Jack (cover)* - **The Stampeders** (Ray Charles) - [US] [75, 1.5, 20.7, 25.7]
320. *Hocus Pocus* [FLAT] - **Focus** - [73, 19.3, 21.10, 22.2, 22.10, 22.11]
321. *Hold Me Now* - **The Thompson Twins** - [UK] [84, *ps*, 8.5, 19.11]
322. *Hold On* - **The Ian Thomas Band** - [82, 1.9, 10.3]
323. *Hold On Lovers* - **Myles & Lenny** - [75, 10.3]
324. *Hold On My Heart* [FLAT] / *Way Of The World* - **Genesis** - [US]
       [92, **A** *ch14*, *ride137*, **AB** 5.5, 24.8, **B** 20.5, 20.15, 22.15]

325. *Hold The Line* - **Toto** - [79, 20.14]

326. *Holding Back The Years* [FLAT] - **Simply Red** - [86, 2.12, 21.6, 22.13]

327. *Holding On* - **Steve Winwood** - [89, *ch13, ps*]

328. *Holding On To Yesterday* // *How Much I Feel* - **Ambrosia** - [CAN WB Gold Standard DH]
     [75/78, **A** 19.4, **B** 19.5]

329. *Holly Jolly Christmas* - **Burl Ives** - [US] [65, *mzk01*, 20.12, 29.3]

330. *Homecoming* - **Hagood Hardy** - [75, 22.1]

331. *Honky Cat* [FLAT] - **Elton John** - [US] [72, 20.5, 21.6]

332. *Honky Tonk Train Blues (cover)* - **Keith Emerson** (Emerson, Lake & Palmer)
     (Meade Lux Lewis) [UK] [76, *mzk01, si84*, 1.6, 5.11, 20.7, 22.1, 30.1]

333. *Horse With No Name* - **America** - [72, *mzk01, si84, tnotes*, 2.2, 20.13, 23.1, 24.7]

334. *Hot Blooded* - **Foreigner** [78, *ch13, si84*]

335. *Hot Rod Lincoln* \\ *My Home In My Hand* - **Commander Cody & The Lost Planet Airmen**
     [DH] [72, **AB** 1.2]

336. *Hot Time in The City* - **Nick Gilder** - [78, 2.8]

337. *House Of The Rising Sun* - **Animals** - [US] [64, 20.9, 27.6]

338. *How Can You Mend A Broken Heart* - **Bee Gees** - [71, 8.1, 20.13]

339. *How Do You Do It?* - **Gerry & The Pacemakers** - [US] [64, 27.6]

340. *How Long* - **Ace** // *In A Broken Dream* - **Python Lee Jackson** - [US Eric DH]
     [75/72, **A** 5.1, 25.6, **AB** 1.3]

341. *Human* [FLAT] - **The Human League** - [86, 21.7]

342. *Hungry Heart* - **Bruce Springsteen** - [80, 3.6]

343. *Hurts So Good* - **John Cougar Mellencamp** - [82, 19.5]

344. *Hustle, The* \\ *Hey Girl, Come & Get It* - **Van Mccoy & The Soul City Symphony** - [DH]
     [75, **AB** 1.2]

345. *Hyperactive* [FLAT] - **Thomas** Dolby
     [84, *ps, quest, si84, tnotes*, 2.11, 21.10, 22.5, 22.11, 22.13, 23.9, 24.5]

346. *Hypnotized / #4* - **Simple Minds** - [UK] [95, 5.12, 20.5, 24.8]

347. *I Believe In Music* [FLAT] - **Gallery** - [72, *tnotes*, 1.5, 4.3, 21.4, 23.9, 23.10]

348. *I Can Dream About You* - **Dan Hartman** // *Rocky Top* - **Terri Gibbs**
     [US American Pie Back To Back Hits DH] [84/81, **AB** 5.10]

349. *I Can Help* - **Billy Swan** - [74, 19.4, 20.17, 21.2]

350. *I Can't Dance* - **Genesis** - [US] [92, *ch14*, 5.5, 22.3, 24.8, 29.2]

351. *I Can't Tell You Why* [FLAT] - **The Eagles** - [80, 23.4, 23.5]

352. *I Can't Wait* [FLAT] - **Nu Shooz** - [86, 21.7]

353. *I Do I Do I Do I Do I Do* - **Abba** - [76, 20.15]

354. *I Don't Like Mondays* - **The Boomtown Rats** - [79, *ward*, 2.3]

355. *I Don't Remember* - **Peter Gabriel** - [80, ch3]

356. *I Go Crazy* - **Flesh For Lulu** - [86, *ps*, 3.6, 27.5]

357. *I Got You* - **Split Enz** - [80, *mzk01, si84*, 19.5, 19.11, 30.1]

358. *I Guess That's Why They Call It The Blues* - **Elton John** - [84, 2.9, 20.11, 24.11]

359. *I Heard It Thru The Grapevine* // *You* - **Marvin Gaye** - [US Motown Yesteryears DH]
     [68, **AB** 5.9]

360. *I Just Called To Say I Love You* - **Stevie Wonder** - [84, *gtns27, quest,* 8.3, 27.5]

361. *I Just Want To Make Music* - **Tobias** - [73, 10.3, 22.11]

362. *I Know I'm Losing You (cover)* - **Rare Earth** (The Temptations) - [70, 1.5]

363. *I Know You're Out There Somewhere* - **The Moody Blues** - [88, *ch14*]

364. *I Like* - **Men Without Hats** - [82, 10.4]

365. *I Need You* - **America** - [72, 1.9, 2.2]

366. *I Ran* - **A Flock Of Seagulls** - [82, *si84,* 4.10]

367. *I Saw Mommy Kissing Santa Claus* - **John Mellencamp** - [87, *mzk01,* 22.12, 22.14, 29.3]

368. *I Scare Myself* - **Thomas Dolby** - [84, *ps, tnotes,* 2.11, 22.13, 22.15, 24.5, 26.1]

369. *I Shot The Sheriff (cover)* [FLAT] - **Eric Clapton** (Bob Marley)
     [74, *mzk01, quest,* 1.6, 19.6, 21.3, 24.6]

370. *I Started A Joke* - **The Bee Gees** - [US] [69, 8.1]

371. *I Wanna Learn A Love Song* - **Harry Chapin** - [74, 2.4]

372. *I Want To Know What Love Is* [FLAT] - **Foreigner** - [84, ps, 3.3, 21.11, 22.8]

373. *I Want A New Drug* - **Huey Lewis & The News** - [84, 2.8, 19.5, 20.7]

374. *I Will 12* - **The Fixx** - [84, **A** 26.1]

375. *I Wish* - **Stevie Wonder** - [77, *quest,* 8.3]

376. *I Wish It Would Rain Down* - **Phil Collins** - [89, 2.13, 20.5, 22.15, 29.1]

377. *I Wouldn't Want To Be Like You* [FLAT] / *Nucleus* - **The Alan Parsons Project** - [US]
     [77, **A** *ch18,* 15.4, **AB** 5.6, **B** 22.2, 27.2]

378. *I Wouldn't Want To Lose Your Love* [FLAT] - **April Wine** - [74, 10.1, 10.5]

379. *I'd Love You To Want Me* [FLAT] \\ *Am I True To Myself?* - **Lobo** - [US Golden Treasures DH]
     [72, **A** 21.4, **AB** 1.2]

380. *I'll Be Good To Ya* [FLAT] - **The Brothers Johnson** - [76, *ps,* 3.1, 21.5]

381. *I'll Be There* - **The Jackson 5** - [US] [70, 8.3]

382. *I'll Have To Say I Love You In A Song* - **Jim Croce** - [74, 2.5]

383. *I'm A Stranger Here* - **The Five Man Electrical Band** - [73, *tnotes,* 8.1, 10.3, 23.1, 23.9, 26.2]

384. *I'm Down* - **The Beatles** - [65, *mzk01,* 20.7]

385. *I'm Not In Love* - **10CC** - [US] [75, 2.3, 22.5, 22.15, 22.17, 25.7, 29.5]

386. *I'm On Fire* [FLAT] - **Bruce Springsteen** - [85, *ps,* 3.6, 21.10]

387. *I'm Running After You* - **Major Hooples Boarding House** - [75, 10.3, 20.13]

388. *I'm So Straight I'm A Weirdo* [FLAT] - **Rick Wakeman** - [80, *mzk01,* 21.11, 24.3]

389. *I'm Still Searching* - **Glass Tiger** - [88, 3.1]

390. *I'm Stoned In Love With You* [FLAT] \\ *Make It Last* [DH] - **The Stylistics**
     [72, **A** *mzk01,* 21.5, **AB** 1.2]

391. *I've Gotta Get A Message To You* - **The Bee Gees** - [68, 8.1]

392. *If I Ever Lose My Faith In You* // *Shape Of My Heart* - **Sting** - [A&M Memories]
     [US Collectables DH] [93, **A** 12.4, 19.5, 21.12, 22.12, **AB** 5.9, 24.8, 30.3]

393. *If I Was* - **Midge Ure** - [85, *ch12, ps*]

394. *If This Is It* - **Huey Lewis & The News** - [UK] [85, *ps,* 20.15]

395. *If You Could Read My Mind* - **Gordon Lightfoot** - [71, 22.17]

396. *If You Leave* - **Orchestral Manoeuvres In The Dark** (OMD) - [86, 30.2]

397. *If You Love Me Let Me Know* - **Olivia Newton - John** - [74, 2.5]

398. *If You Love Somebody, Set Them Free* - **Sting** - [85, 12.4, 30.3]

399. *If You Wanna Get To Heaven* [FLAT] - **The Ozark Mountain Daredevils**
     [74, 21.2, 22.12, 22.18]

400. *Imagine* - **John Lennon** - [71, *gtns17_25_39*, 27.3, 30.2]

401. *In Your Eyes* [FLAT] - **Peter Gabriel** - [86, 20.5, 21.12, 30.3]

402. *Indiana Wants Me* [FLAT] - **R Dean Taylor** - [70, 21.4, 22.4]

403. *Industrial Disease* - **Dire Straits** - [82, 22.5, 30.3]

404. *Invisible Sun* - **The Police** - [UK] [82, *ps*, 3.2, 22.6]

405. *Invitation To Dance* - **Kim Carnes** - [85, *ps*, 2.10]

406. *Iris* - **Split Enz** - [US] [81, 5.10]

407. *Island Girl* - **Elton John** - [75, 2.5]

408. *Isn't Life Strange* - **The Moody Blues** - [72, 20.4]

409. *It Doesn't Have To Be That Way* - **Jim Croce** - [73, 2.5]

410. *It Don't Come Easy / Early 1970* - **Ringo Starr** - [71, **AB** *si84*, 11.4]

411. *It Wouldn't Have Made Any Difference* - **Tom Middleton** - [73, 10.3]

412. *It's A Sin* - **The Pet Shop Boys** - [87, 2.10]

413. *It's Not Me Talking / I Ran So Far Away (Live)* - **A Flock Of Seagulls** - [83, **AB** *ps*, **B** 25.10]

414. *It's Only Rock & Roll* - **The Rolling Stones** - [74, 2.15, 27.1, 27.3]

415. *It's Still Rock & Roll To Me* - **Billy Joel** - [80, 20.15, 24.12, 29.1]

416. *It's Too Late* [FLAT] - **Carole King** - [71, *ps*, *si84*, 3.1, 21.13]

417. *It's My Life* - **Talk Talk** - [US] [85, *ps*, 2.10, 19.11]

418. *Jack & Diane* [FLAT] - **John Cougar Mellencamp** - [82, 19.5, 21.3]

419. *Jackie Blue* [FLAT] / ***Better Days*** - **The Ozark Mountain Daredevils** - [US]
    [75, **A** *tnotes*, 25.6, **AB** *mzk01*, *ps*, *si84*, 3.1, 5.10, 21.8, 24.7, **B** 1.9]

420. *January* - **Pilot** - [75, *ch15*, 19.12]

421. *Jazzman* - **Carole King** - [US] [74, *ps*, *si84*, 3.1, 24.4]

422. *Jerusalem (cover)* - **Emerson, Lake & Palmer** (Parry) - [UK]
    [73, *ch14*, *mcn74*, *si84*, 1.8, 5.11, 19.7, 19.8, 20.16, 29.1, 29.4, 30.1]

423. *Jet / Let Me Roll It* - **Paul McCartney & Wings** - [74, **AB** *si84*, 11.3, **B** 20.9]

424. *Joan Of Arc* - **Orchestral Manoeuvres in The Dark** (OMD) - [82, *si84*, 12.2, 30.4]

425. *Joy* - **Apollo 100** - [72, 19.3, 20.14, 22.1]

426. *Juicy Lucy* - **Klaatu** - [79, *si84*, 8.1, 10.3, 22.3]

427. *Juke Box Hero* - **Foreigner** - [81, 3.3]

428. *Junior's Farm* \\ *Sally G* [FLAT] - **Paul McCartney & Wings** - [DH]
    [74, **A** 11.3, 11.4, **AB** *si84*, **B** *mzk01*, 21.2, 21.3]

429. *Just the Two of Us* [FLAT] - **Grover Washington** - [81, 2.4, 21.5]

430. *Karma Chameleon* - **Culture Club** - [83, 22.12]

431. *King For A Day* - **The Thompson Twins** - [85, *ch12*, *ps*]

432. *Kiss From A Rose* - **Seal** - [US] [95, 19.12, 20.9, 22.9, 24.8, 27.5]

433. *Kiss You (When It's Dangerous)* [FLAT] - **Eight Seconds** - [86, 10.4, 21.7]

434. *Knee Deep In Love* - **Klaatu** - [80, 8.1, 10.3]

435. *Knowing Me Knowing You* - **Abba** - [77, *si84*, 24.3]

436. *Kokomo* - **The Beach Boys** // *Tutti Frutti* - **Little Richard**
    [US Elektra Spun Gold DH] [88/56, **AB** 5.14, **B** 20.17]

437. *Kung Fu Fighting* [FLAT] - **Karl Douglas** - [74, 21.5, 22.11]

438. *L.A. Woman // Roadhouse Blues* - **The Doors** - [US Elektra Spun Gold DH]
  [71/70, **A** 20.4, **AB** 5.14, **B** 20.15, 22.12]

439. *La Isla Bonita* [FLAT] - **Madonna** - [87, 21.13]

440. *Lady* - **The Commodores** - [81, 1.9, 8.3, 23.6]

441. *Lady* - **Styx** - [US] [75, *si84*, 1.9, 5.10, 19.6, 24.7]

442. *Lady Marmalade* - **Labelle** - [75, 25.6]

443. *Lady Run Lady Hide* [FLAT] - **April Wine** - [73, *si84*, 10.1, 10.5, 23.1]

444. *Laughing* [FLAT] / *Undun* - **The Guess Who** - [69, **B** 22.11]

445. *Lay Lady Lay // I Threw It All Away* - **Bob Dylan** - [US CBS Hall Of Fame Red DH]
  [69, **A** 27.6]

446. *Lay Your Hands On Me* - **The Thompson Twins** - [85, *buks, ch12, mzk01, ps*]

447. *Layla* - **Derek & The Dominoes** // *Montego Bay* - **Bobby Bloom** - [US Eric]
  [72, **A** *gtns35_54*, 20.3, 20.4, 25.1, **AB** 1.3]

448. *Lean On Me* - **Bill Withers** - [72, *mzk01, quest, si84*, 19.10, 25.1]

449. *Leave Me Alone* - **Helen Reddy** - [73, 20.12]

450. *Lebanon* - **The Human League** - [UK] [84, *buks, mzk01, ps*, 2.14, 3.3]

451. *Less Cities More Moving People* [FLAT] - **The Fixx** - [84, *mzk01, ps*, 3.2, 21.11, 24.5]

452. *Let 'Em In* [FLAT] - **Wings** - [76, *si84*, 2.13, 20.5, 22.3, 22.13, 22.16, 29.2]

453. *Let Go The Line* [FLAT] - **Max Webster** - [79, *mzk01, si84*, 10.3, 21.8, 22.15, 30.3]

454. *Let It Go* - **Luba** - [84, *ward*, 2.11, 10.4]

455. *Let Me Serenade You* - **Three Dog Night** - [73, *mzk01, si84*, 19.6, 20.14, 24.6]

456. *Let The River Run* - **Carly Simon** - [89, *ps*, 27.5]

457. *Let Your Love Flow* - **The Bellamy Brothers** - [76, 2.1]

458. *Let's Dance* - **David Bowie** - [83, *ps*, 2.10, 3.2]

459. *Let's Go* - **The Cars** - [79, **A** 1.9, 27.3]

460. *Let's Go Crazy* - **Prince** - [84, 2.13]

461. *Let's Talk About Me / Hawkeye* - **The Alan Parsons Project**
  [85, **A** 22.5, **AB** *ps*, 3.2, 24.5, **B** 22.2]

462. *Letting Go* [FLAT] - **Wings** - [75, *mzk01*, 2.13, 19.7, 30.1]

463. *Liar* - **Three Dog Night** - [71, 19.3]

464. *Lido Shuffle* - **Boz Scaggs** - [76, 20.12]

465. *Life In A Northern Town* - **The Dream Academy** - [86, *buks*, 2.6]

466. *Life In The Fast Lane* [FLAT] / *The Last Resort* - **The Eagles** - [US]
  [77, **A** 23.4, **AB** 5.10, 23.5, **B** *tnotes*, 19.6, 20.5]

467. *Life Is A Carnival* [FLAT] - **The Band** - [71, 21.6]

468. *Life On Your Own* - **The Human League** - [UK] [84, *ps*, 2.14, 3.3, 24.5]

469. *Life's Been Good* [FLAT] - **Joe Walsh** - [78, 19.5, 21.3, 23.4]

470. *Lift Me Up* [FLAT] - **Yes** - [91, *ch18*, 20.5, 22.16, 23.9, 24.8, 30.2]

471. *Light Of Smiles* - **Gary Wright** - [77, *si84*, 2.1, 24.4]

472. *Like A Prayer* - **Madonna** - [89, 12.6, 20.5, 22.8]

473. *Like A Rock* - **Bob Segar** - [86, *ps*, 2.11]

474. *Like A Virgin* - **Madonna** - [84, 12.6]

475. *Limelight / YYZ* - **Rush** - [81, **A** 1.9, 10.4, **AB** 19.8]

476. *Lion Sleeps Tonight, The* - **The Tokens** - [61, 23.7]

477. *Listen To The Radio* [FLAT] - **The Pukkah Orchestra** - [84, 10.4, 21.11]

478. *Listen To What The Man Said* - **Wings**
[75, *mzk01, ps, si84,* 2.13, 11.3, 20.3, 22.11, 25.7, 29.1]

479. *Little Lies* - **Fleetwood Mac** - [87, *ps,* 2.6]

480. *Live To Tell* - **Madonna** - [84, 12.6]

481. *Livin' Thing* - **The Electric Light Orchestra** - [77, 22.14]

482. *Living In The Past* - **Jethro Tull** - [73, *mcn48,* 22.11]

483. *Living Years, The* [FLAT] - **Mike & The Mechanics** - [88, 21.11, 22.8, 29.1]

484. *Locomotion (cover)* - **Grand Funk** (Little Eva) - [74, *ps,* 1.5, 1.9, 3.1, 19.12, 25.5]

485. *Locomotion* - **Orchestral Manoeuvres In The Dark** (OMD) - [84, *ps, si84,* 1.9, 12.1]

486. *Lonely People* - **America** - [75, 2.1]

487. *Long Long Way* - **Ian Thomas** - [74, 10.3, 29.5]

488. *Long Time* - **Boston** - [77, *mcn214,* 19.4, 20.2]

489. *Looking Out For #1* - **Bachman - Turner Overdrive** - [76, 2.3, 20.16]

490. *Lords' Prayer* - **Sister Janet Mead** - [74, *si84,* ch24]

491. *Lorelei* - **Styx** - [76, 25.8]

492. *Losing My Religion* - **REM** - [US] [91, 2.6, 24.8]

493. *Lost Without Your Love* - **Bread** - [77, 2.4]

494. *Lotta Love* - **Nicolette Larson** - [79, *mzk01, si84,* 2.6, 22.11, 24.3]

495. *Louie Louie* - **The Kingsmen** // *Twist & Shout* - **The Isley Brothers** (Bert Russell)
[US Eric DH] [63/62, **AB** 1.3, **B** 1.5]

496. *Love Grows* - **Edison Lighthouse** - [70, 23.7]

497. *Love Her Madly* - **The Doors** - [71, 2.4, 19.6]

498. *Love Hurts (cover)* [FLAT] - **Nazareth** (Roy Orbison) - [76, *si84, ward,* 1.6, 21.9, 25.8]

499. *Love Is A Battlefield* [FLAT] - **Pat Benatar** - [83, *buks,* 2.8, 21.13, 22.5, 22.10]

500. *Love Is Blue* - **Paul Mauriat** - [68, 23.7]

501. *Love Is The Drug* - **Roxy Music** - [76, 8.1, 25.8]

502. *Love Me Love Me Love* - **Frank Mills** - [71, 23.7]

503. *Love The One You're With* [FLAT] - **Stephen Stills** - [71, 19.3, 21.5]

504. *Love Theme From St Elmos Fire* - **David Foster** - [85, 22.1, 27.5, 29.1]

505. *Love Will Keep Us Together* - **The Captain & Tenille** - [76, 25.7]

506. *Lovers In A Dangerous Time* - **Bruce Cockburn** - [84, 10.4]

507. *Loves Me Like A Rock* - **Paul Simon** - [73, 20.12]

508. *Lucy In The Sky With Diamonds (cover)* - **Elton John** (The Beatles)
[75, 1.6, 2.5, 20.5, 20.16, 29.5]

509. *Lyin' Eyes* - **The Eagles** - [75, 23.4, 23.5]

510. *Ma* - **Rare Earth** - [US] [71, 2.14]

511. *MacArthur's Park* - **Richard Harris** - [US] [68, 5.8]

512. *Mad World* - **Tears For Fears** - [UK] [83, *buks, ps,* **A** 8.5, 26.1]

513. *Madame Butterfly* [FLAT] - **Malcolm McLaren** - [84, *gtns63,* 21.11]

514. *Mademoiselle / Light Up* - **Styx** - [76, **A** 19.7, **AB** 20.15]

515. *Magic* [FLAT] - **Olivia Newton - John** - [80, *mzk01, si84,* 1.9, 2.13, 21.13, 27.5]

516. *Major Tom* [FLAT] - **Peter Schilling** - [83, *buks, mzk01,* 19.11, 21.11]

517. *Make Me Do (Anything You Want)* - **A Foot In Cold Water** - [72, *si84*, 5.1, 10.3, 20.4]

518. *Mama Told Me (Not To Come) (cover)* - **Three Dog Night** (Randy Newman) - [70, 1.5, 2.5]

519. *Mandy (cover)* // *It's A Miracle*) - **Barry Manilow** - [Arista Flashback DH]
     (*Brandy* - Scott English - **[** 75, **A** 1.5, **AB** 8.4, 24.2, **B** 25.6]

520. *Masquerade* - **Edward Bear** - [72, 10.1, 105, 19.3]

521. *Material Girl* - **Madonna** - [84, 12.6]

522. *May The Cube Be With* - **Thomas Dolby's Cube** - [85, *ps*, 2.11]

523. *Me & Mrs. Jones* - **Billy Paul** - [72, *mzk01, si84*, 19.10, 20.10]

524. *Merry Christmas Baby* - **Bruce Springsteen** - [US] [87, 19.5, 25.10, 29.3]

525. *Message In A Bottle* - **The Police** - [79, *buks, mzk01, si84*, 26.2]

526. *Messages* - **Orchestral Manoeuvres In The Dark** (OMD) - [UK] [80, *ps*, 12.1, 26.1]

527. *Middle Of The Road* [FLAT] - **The Pretenders** - [84, 21.13]

528. *Midnight At The Oasis* [FLAT] - **Maria Muldaur** - [74, *si84*, 21.13, 22.15, 25.5]

529. *Million Vacations* - **Max Webster** - [79, 10.3]

530. *Mind Games* - **John Lennon** - [73, *mzk01, ps, si84*, 24.1]

531. *Minstrel Gypsy* [FLAT] - **The Stampeders** - [73, 10.3, 21.12]

532. *Miracles* - **Jefferson Starship** - [75, *si84*, 24.3]

533. *Mirror Man* - **The Human League** - [83, *buks, ps, si84*, 3.2]

534. *Miss You* - **The Rolling Stones** - [78, 2.15, 22.12]

535. *Missing You* [FLAT] - **John Waite** - [84, 2.10, 21.8]

536. *Mixed Emotions* - **The Rolling Stones** - [US] [89, 2.15, 2.13]

537. *Modern Love* - **David Bowie** - [83, *ps*, 2.10]

538. *Molly* - **Bearfoot** - [74, 10.3]

539. *Money / Any Colour You Like* - **Pink Floyd** - [US]
     [73, **A** *ch15, levitin, tnotes*, 22.4, 22.15, 26.2, 26.6]
     [**AB** 5.8, 19.8, 19.12, 30.2, **B** *mcn72_141*, 22.2, 22.18]

540. *Money's Too Tight To Mention* - **Simply Red** - [86, *buks*, 2.12]

541. *Monster Mash* - **Bobby Boris Pickett** - [US] [62/73, 5.1, 20.8, 22.3]

542. *Moondance* // *Domino* - **Van Morrison** - [US WB Back To Back Hits DH]
     [70, **A** 20.11, **AB** 2.6, 5.15]

543. *Moonlight Desires* - **Gowan** - [87, *ps, tnotes, ward*, 3.6, 22.15]

544. *Moonlight Feels Right* - **Starbuck** - [US] [76, *si84*, 1.2]

545. *More More More* [FLAT] - **The Andrea True Connection** - [76, *si84*, 1.2, 21.13, 25.9]

546. *More You Live The More You Love, The* - **A Flock Of Seagulls** - [84, *ps*, 24.5, 26.1]

547. *Morning After, The* - **Maureen McGovern** - [73, *si84*, 24.1, 27.4]

548. *Morning Has Broken* - **Cat Stevens** - [72, 20.9, 22.17, 23.6]

549. *Morning Train* - **Sheena Easton** - [81, 2.10, 20.11]

550. *Mothers Talk / Sea Song* - **Tears For Fears** - [85, *ps*, **A** 4.2]

551. *Mr. Roboto* - **Styx** - [US] [83, *ps*, 5.8, 19.7]

552. *Mr. Tambourine Man* // *All I Really Want* - **The Byrds** - [US CBS Silver DH]
     [65, **A** 27.6, **AB** 5.16]

553. *Mrs. Robinson* // *Old Friends & Book Ends* - **Simon & Garfunkel**
     [US CBS Silver DH] [68, **A** 27.4, **AB** 5.16]

554. *My Best Friend's Girl / Moving in Stereo* - **The Cars** - [UK]
     [78, **AB** 1.4, 2.4, **B** 20.2, 22.7, 23.9]

555. *My Brave Face / Flying To My Home* - **Paul McCartney** - [89, *ch11*]

556. *My Cherie Amour // Don't Know Why I Love You* - **Stevie Wonder**
[US Motown Yesteryears DH] [69, **A** 19.10, **AB** *si84*, 24.2]

557. *My Ding A Ling // Johnny B Goode* - **Chuck Berry** - [DH] [72/58, **AB** 20.7, **B** *levitin*]

558. *My Hometown / Santa Claus Is Coming To Town* - **Bruce Springsteen**
[85, **AB** *ps*, 3.6, **B** *mzk01*, 25.10, 29.3]

559. *My Life* - **Billy Joel** - [79, 22.15, 24.12]

560. *My Music* - **Loggins & Messina** - [73, 25.3]

561. *My Sharona* - **The Knack** - [79, *buks*, *mzk01*, *ps*, *si84*, 2.11, 24.3]

562. *Need You Tonight* [FLAT] - **INXS** - [88, 21.8]

563. *Never Again The Dancer* - **A Flock Of Seagulls** - [84, *ps*, 24.5, 26.1]

564. *Never Been To Spain* [FLAT] - **Three Dog Night** - [72, 19.6]

565. *Never Surrender* [FLAT] - **Corey Hart** - [85, 3.4, 21.8]

566. *Never Tear Us Apart* - **INXS** - [88, *buks*, 20.9]

567. *Never Turn Away* - **Orchestral Manoeuvres In The Dark** (OMD) - [UK] [84, 2.14]

568. *New Moon On Monday* - **Duran Duran** - [83, 2.11]

569. *New Song* - **Howard Jones** - [84, *buks*, 19.5, 19.11]

570. *New World Man* - **Rush** - [82, 2.3]

571. *Night To Remember* [FLAT] - **Prism** - [78, 10.3, 21.11]

572. *Nightshift* - **The Commodores** - [85, 8.3]

573. *Nikita // Take Me To The Pilot* - **Elton John** - [US Collectables DH] [86/70, **AB** 5.9]

574. *No More Lonely Nights* [FLAT] - **Paul McCartney** - [84, *ps*, 22.9]

575. *No No Song* - **Ringo Starr** - [75, 2.13, 25.6]

576. *No Son Of Mine* [FLAT] / *Living Forever* - **Genesis** - [US]
[91, **A** *ch14*, *ride130*, 19.7, 20.5, 22.3, 29.1, **AB** 5.5, 5.8, 24.8, 30.2, **B** *ride134_136*]

577. *No Time* - **The Guess Who** - [70, *mzk01*, 24.6]

578. *Nobody Does It Better* - **Carly Simon** - [77, 2.4, 27.4]

579. *Nobody Told Me* - **John Lennon** - [83, *ps*, 20.15, 22.6, 29.1]

580. *Nothing In Common* - **The Thompson Twins** - [87, *ps*, 27.5]

581. *Nutrocker (cover) / Great Gates Of Kiev (cover)* - **Emerson, Lake & Palmer**
(**A**-B Bumble & The Stingers, Mussorgsky) (**B** Mussorgsky)
[71, **A** *ch14*, *mzk01*, 22.1, 23.9, **AB** 1.8, **B** *levitin*, 14.1]

582. *Oh Father* - **Madonna** - [US] [84, 12.6]

583. *Oh Girl // Have You Seen Her?* - **The Chi-Lites** - [DH] [72/71, **A** 19.10, 22.12, **AB** *mzk01*]

584. *Oh My Lady* - **The Stampeders** - [73, 10.3, 22.12]

585. *Oh No* - **The Commodores** - [81, 8.3, 23.6]

586. *Oh Very Young* - **Cat Stevens** - [US] [74, 25.5]

587. *Oh What A Feeling* - **Crowbar** - [71, 10.1]

588. *OK Blue Jays* - **Lenz, Kosinec & Hampshire** - [83, 20.12]

589. *Old Fashioned Love Song, An* [FLAT] - **Three Dog Night** - [US]
[71, *mzk01*, *si84*, 19.6, 21.4, 24.6]

590. *Old Time Rock & Roll* - **Bob Segar** - [79, 2.11, 20.7, 27.3]

591. *On The Border* - **Al Stewart** - [77, 19.12, 21.4]

592. *On The One For Fun* - **The Dazz Band** - [83, 8.3, 23.6]

593. *Once In A Lifetime / This Must Be The Place* - **The Talking Heads** - [80, **A** *gtns54*, 1.9]

594. *Once Upon A Long Ago* [FLAT] - **Paul McCartney** - [87, *ps*, 3.2]

595. *One I Love, The* - **REM** - [87, 24.8]

596. *One Man Band* - **Three Dog Night** - [70, 19.3]

597. *One More Night* - **Phil Collins** - [85, 3.3]

598. *One Night In Bangkok* - **Murray Head** - [85, *ps*, 19.11, 20.3, 22.11, 24.5]

599. *One Night Lovers* - **Tom Middleton** - [75, 10.3]

600. *One Of These Nights* [FLAT] - **The Eagles** - [75, *levitin*, 23.4, 23.5, 25.7]

601. *One Small Day* - **Midge Ure** - [84, *ps*, 2.8, 24.5, 26.1]

602. *One Step Ahead* [FLAT] - **Split Enz** - [US] [81, *si84*, 5.10 19.5, 21.12]

603. *One Thing Leads To Another* - **The Fixx** - [83, *buks, ps*, 19.11]

604. *One Tin Soldier* - **The Original Cast** - [69, 22.16, 26.2]

605. *One Way Or Another* - **Blondie** - [79, *buks, mzk01, si84*, 2.8, 19.5, 24.3]

606. *Only Love Can Break Your Heart // Cinnamon Girl* - **Neil Young**
     [CAN Reprise Gold Standard DH] [70/69, **A** 20.10]

607. *Only Sixteen (cover)* - **Dr. Hook** (Sam Cooke) - [76, 1.5, 20.13, 25.8]

608. *Only You (cover)* [FLAT] - **Ringo Starr** (The Platters)
     [75, *ps*, 1.6, 1.9, 2.13, 3.2, 21.3, 22.5, 22.15]

609. *Only You 12* [FLAT] - **Yaz** - [82, *buks, mzk01, si84*, 1.9, 21.7]

610. *Only You Can Rock Me* - **UFO** - [78, *ps, si84*, 2.8, 3.2, 3.5]

611. *Oowatanite* [FLAT] - **April Wine** - [US] [75, 22.7]

612. *Open Your Heart* - **The Human League** - [81, *ps, si84*, 3.3, 26.1]

613. *Opportunities* - **The Pet Shop Boys** - [86, *buks*, 2.11]

614. *Orly* - **The Guess Who** - [73, 10.1, 10.5, 22.14]

615. *Our House* - **Madness** - [83, *buks*, 2.9]

616. *Out In The Country* - **Three Dog Night** - [70, 19.3]

617. *Outa Space* - **Billy Preston** - [73, 25.1]

618. *Overkill* - **Men At Work** - [83, *ps*, 22.15]

619. *Painted Ladies* - **Ian Thomas** - [73, *si84*, 24.1, 25.4]

620. *Pale Shelter* - **Tears For Fears** - [83, *buks, ps,* 2.13, 19.11]

621. *Paloma Blanca* - **The George Baker Selection** - [76, 2.1, 5.1, 22.1]

622. *Panama* - **Van Halen** - [84, 2.6]

623. *Papa Don't Preach* - **Madonna** - [84, 12.6]

624. *Paper In Fire* - **John Cougar Mellencamp** - [US] [87, *ps*, 3.1]

625. *Patio Lanterns* - **Kim Mitchell** - [86, 10.4]

626. *Patricia The Stripper // Don't Pay The Ferryman* - **Chris De Burgh**
     [A&M Memories DH] [75/82, **A** 20.11]

627. *Peace On Earth & Little Drummer Boy* - **David Bowie & Bing Crosby** - [US]
     [78, *mzk01*, 29.3]

628. *Philadelphia Freedom* - **Elton John** - [75, 2.5, 20.5, 24.11, 25.6]

629. *Pick Up The Pieces* [FLAT] - **The Average White Band** - [75, *si84*, 21.5, 22.2]

630. *Pioneer & Six Months In A Leaky Boat* - **Split Enz**
    [82, **AB**, *si84*, 19.6, 20.3, 20.4, 23.9, 29.2, 29.4, 30.1]

631. *Pipes Of Peace* - **Paul McCartney** - [83, 20.3, 22.16]

632. *Please Come Home For Christmas* - **The Eagles** - [78, 2.12, 20.10, 23.5, 29.3]

633. *Poor Little Fool* - **Frank Mills** - [72, *mzk01*, 23.7]

634. *Power Of Love* - **Celine Dion** - [US] [93, *tnotes*, 1.9, 24.8]

635. *Power Of Love* - **Frankie Goes To Hollywood** - [84, *mzk01*, *tnotes*, 1.9, 2.13, 20.4, 29.3]

636. *Power Of Love* - **Huey Lewis** - [85, *tnotes*, 1.9, 2.8, 27.5, 29.1, 29.2]

637. *Precious & Few* [FLAT] - **Climax** - [US Arista Flashback DH] [72, 8.4, 21.11]

638. *Pretty City Lady* - **Bob McBride** - [72, 10.3]

639. *Pretty Lady* - **Lighthouse** - [73, *si84*, 10.1, 10.5, 24.1, 25.4]

640. *Promises Promises* - **The Naked Eyes** - [83, *buks*, 2.10]

641. *Purple Rain* - **Prince** - [84, *ps*, 2.13, 3.5, 23.6, 27.5]

642. *Put A Little Love In Your Heart* - **Annie Lennox & Al Green** - [88, 29.3]

643. *Puttin On The Ritz (cover)* [FLAT] - **Taco** (Harry Richman / Irving Berlin)
    [82, *buks*, 1.7, 21.6, 29.2]

644. *Question* - **The Moody Blues** - [US] [70, 20.3]

645. *Radar Love* [FLAT] - **Golden Earring** - [74, *si84*, 5.1, 20.4, 21.10]

646. *Radio Ga Ga* - **Queen** - [84, *ps*, 2.11]

647. *Rainbow Song* - **America** - [73, 2.1]

648. *Rain Dance* - **The Guess Who** - [71, 20.14]

649. *Raise A Little Hell* - **Trooper** - [78, 2.5, 10.3, 19.12, 23.7]

650. *Ramblin' Man* [FLAT] - **The Allman Brothers Band** - [73, 19.6, 20.7, 21.2, 21.3, 26.2]

651. *Rapture* - Blondie - [81, *buks*, 2.8]

652. *Raven, The* [FLAT] - **The Alan Parsons Project** - [US] [76, *mzk01*, 5.6]

653. *Reaction To Action* - **Foreigner** - [84, *ch13*, *mzk01*, *ps*]

654. *Red Rain* - **Peter Gabriel** - [86, 20.5, 30.3]

655. *Red Skies* - **The Fixx** - [82, *buks*, *si84*, 26.1]

656. *Reeling In The Years* - **Steely Dan** - [73, *si84*, 20.14]

657. *Reflex, The* - **Duran Duran** - [84, 2.11]

658. *Reminiscing* [FLAT] - **The Little River Band** - [78, *si84*, 21.6]

659. *Riddle, The* [FLAT] - **Nik Kershaw** - [84, *ps*, 3.2, 21.7, 22.10, 22.16]

660. *Riders On The Storm* [FLAT] - **The Doors** - [71, 2.2, 2.4, 21.6]

661. *Right Place Wrong Time* [FLAT] // *Such A Night* - **Dr. John**
    [CAN Atlantic Gold Standard DH] [73, **A** *quest*, 19.3, 21.9, **AB** *si84*]

662. *Right Thing, The* - **Simply Red** - [87, 2.12]

663. *Ring Out Solstice Bells / A Christmas Song / Another Christmas Song / Magic Bells*
    (Ring Out Solstice Bells) - **Jethro Tull** - [UK] [77, *ps*, **ABC** 1.10]

664. *Rise Up* - **Parachute Club** - [83, *ward*, 10.4]

665. *Rock & Roll Hoochie Koo* [FLAT] - **Rick Derringer** // *Time Of The Season*
    The Zombies - [US Eric DH] [74/68, **A** 21.9, **AB** 1.3, **B** 19.3]

666. *Rock & Roll Part 1 \\ Rock & Roll Part 2* - **Gary Glitter** - [DH] [72, **AB** 1.2, **B** 20.11, 25.2]
667. *Rock Lobster* [FLAT] - **B 52s** [78, *buks*, *ward*, 2.6, 19.5, 21.10]
668. *Rock Me Amadeus* [FLAT] - **Falco** - [85, *buks*, 21.7]
669. *Rock On* - **David Essex** - [74, 5.1, 25.9]
670. *Rock The USA / Under The Boardwalk (cover)* - **John Mellencamp** (B - The Drifters)
    [85, **AB** *ps*, **B** 1.7]
671. *Rock Your Baby* [FLAT] - **George McRae** - [74, **A** 21.5]
672. *Rocket Man* - **Elton John** - [72, 2.5, 24.11, 25.1]
673. *Rockin' At Midnight* - **The Honeydrippers** - [84, 20.7, 20.13]
674. *Rockin' Pneumonia (cover)* - **Johnny Rivers** (Huey Piano Smith) - [73, *mzk01*, 1.5, 20.7, 29.2]
675. *Rocky Mountain Way // Hold On* - **Triumph** - [CAN CBS Hall Of Fame Blue DH]
    [77, **A** 1.5, 20.14, **B** 1.9]
676. *Rodeo Song* - **Garry Lee** - [US] [81, *mzk01*, 20.7, 23.9]
677. *Roll On Down The Highway* - **Bachman - Turner Overdrive** - [75, 2.3, 22.7]
678. *Roll Over Beethoven* - **The Electric Light Orchestra** - [US]
    [73, *levitin*, *mzk01*, *si84*, 20.7, 22.14, 24.6]
679. *Romantic Traffic* - **The Spoons** - [83, 2.13, 10.4]
680. *Roxy Roller* - **Sweeney Todd** - [76, 20.14]
681. *Runaway (With My Love) 12* - **Tapps** - [84, 10.4]
682. *Run Through The Light / Man In A White Car* [FLAT] - **Yes** - [US]
    [80, **A** 4.2, 20.6, 23.9, 29.6, **AB** *ch18*, 1.4, 5.7, 19.8, 30.2, **B** 22.16, 29.4]
683. *Run To You / This Time* - **Bryan Adams** - [85, **AB** *ps*, *ward*, 3.1, 10.2]
684. *Run With The Fox* - **Chris Squire & Alan White (Yes)**
    [81, *mzk01*, *si84*, 20.16, 22.8, 23.9, 29.3]
685. *Running Back To Saskatoon* - **The Guess Who** - [72, 10.1, 10.5, 25.10, 26.2]
686. *Russians* - **Sting** - [86, *ps*, 1.8, 3.6, 12.4, 22.4, 22.17, 29.5]

687. *Sad Songs* - **Elton John** - [84, 24.11]
688. *Sadeness* [FLAT] - **Enigma** - [91, 21.11, 22.8, 22.9, 24.8]
689. *Sail On* - **The Commodores** - [79, 8.3, 23.6]
690. *Sandy* - **The Hollies** - [75, 24.6]
691. *Sara* [FLAT] - **Starship** - [86, 21.8, 22.12]
692. *Saturday In The Park* - **Chicago** - [72, *quest*, 11.1, 11.2, 20.16, 25.2]
693. *Saturday Night's Alright For Fighting* - **Elton John** - [73, *ride89*, 2.5, 24.11, 25.3]
694. *Save A Prayer* - **Duran Duran** - [85, 2.11]
695. *Save Me* - **Atomic Rooster** - [72, 2.4]
696. *Save The Last Dance For Me // When My Little Girl Is Smiling*
    The Drifters - [US Atlantic Oldies Series DH] [60/62, **AB** 8.2]
697. *Saved By Zero* - **The Fixx** - [US] [83, *buks*, *ps*, 3.2]
698. *Say Has Anybody Seen My Sweet Gypsy Rose* - **Dawn** - [US] [73, 23.7]
699. *Say Say Say* - **Paul McCartney & Michael Jackson** - [83, *ps*, 11.3]
700. *Say You Say Me* - **Lionel Ritchie** - [85, 8.3]
701. *Scarborough Fair // I Am A Rock* - **Simon & Garfunkel** - [US CBS Hall Of Fame Red DH]
    [68/66, **A** 20.10, 27.6]

702. *Scorpio* - **Dennis Coffey** - [72, 22.1]
703. *Scratching The Surface* [FLAT] - **Saga** - [83, *mzk01, si84*, 10.4, 21.8, 24.7]
704. *Secret* - **Orchestral Manoeuvres In The Dark** (OMD) - [85, 12.2, 30.4]
705. *See Me Feel Me / Overture From Tommy* - **The Who** - [69 **B**, 22.2, 22.13]
706. *See The Lights / Theme For Great Cities 91* - **Simple Minds** - [UK]
          [91, *ps*, **A** 4.2, 5.12, 8.5, 23.9, 24.8]
707. *September* - **Earth, Wind & Fire** - [78, *ch11*]
708. *Sexual Healing* [FLAT] - **Marvin Gaye** - [82, 21.5, 23.6]
709. *Shambala* - **Three Dog Night** - [73, *mzk01, si84*, 19.3, 24.6]
710. *Shattered* - **Pat Benatar** - [85, 2.8]
711. *She Drives Me Crazy* [FLAT] - **The Fine Young Cannibals** - [89, 21.8]
712. *She's A River* [FLAT] - **Simple Minds** - [UK] [95, 3.5, 5.12, 24.8]
713. *She's Got A Way* - **Billy Joel** - [71, 24.12]
714. *She's So Cold* - **The Rolling Stones** - [80, 2.15]
715. *Shine* - **Collective Soul** - [US] [94, 5.5, 24.8]
716. *Shout It Out Loud / Nothing To Lose* - **Kiss** - [76, *si84*, **A** 23.2, 25.8]
717. *Show Me The Way (Live)* - **Peter Frampton** - [76, *gtns78*, 3.2, 25.8, 25.10]
718. *Showdown At Big Sky* - **Robbie Robertson** - [87, 10.4]
719. *Sideshow* - **Blue Magic** - [74, *mzk01*, 8.1, 19.10]
720. *Sign Of Fire* - **The Fixx** - [83, *buks, ps, ch12*]
721. *Signs // Absolutely Right* [FLAT] - **The Five Man Electrical Band** - [Golden Treasures DH]
          [71, **AB** *si84*, **B** 21.10]
722. *Silent Running* - **Mike & The Mechanics** - [86, *ch14*]
723. *Silent Night Holy Night* - **Bing Crosby** - [US] [45, 2.5]
724. *Silly Love Songs* - **Wings** - [76, *si84*, 2.13, 11.3, 20.5]
725. *Sing* - **The Carpenters** - [US] [73, 22.8]
726. *Sitting At The Wheel* - **The Moody Blues** - [83, *ps*, 2.13]
727. *Sitting On A Poor Man's Throne* [FLAT] - **Copper Penny**
          [73, *si84*, 10.3, 21.6, 22.15, 24.4]
728. *Sitting On The Dock Of The Bay* [FLAT] // *My Lover's Prayer* - **Otis Redding**
          [US Atlantic Oldies Series DH] [68/66, **A** 21.3, 22.3, 22.10, 27.6, AB 5.4]
729. *Situation* - **Yaz (featuring Alison Moyet)** - [82, *mzk01, si84*, 26.1]
730. *Sledgehammer* - **Peter Gabriel** - [86, *buks, quest, ward*, 19.9, 30.3]
731. *Small Town* - **John Mellencamp** - [85, 3.1]
732. *Smile Has Left Your Eyes, The* - **Asia** - [83, *ps*, 2.9]
733. *Smiling In Winter* - **The Spoons** - [82, 2.13, 10.4, 26.1]
734. *So In Love* - **Orchestral Manoeuvres In The Dark** (OMD) - [85, *buks, ps*, 12.1, 24.7]
735. *So You Are A Star \\ Ma Ma Ma Baby* - **The Hudson Brothers** - [Golden Treasures DH]
          [75, **A** 25.3, **AB** 1.2]
736. *Somebody* - **Bryan Adams** - [85, 10.2]
737. *Somebody To Love* - **Queen** - [76, 20.9, 22.8, 22.9]
738. *Someday* [FLAT] - **Glass Tiger** - [86, *ward*, 2.11, 21.8, 29.1]
739. *Something About You* [FLAT] - **Level 42** - [86, *buks, ps*, 21.7]
740. *Something Happened On The Way To Heaven // Hang In There Long Enough* - **Phil Collins**
          [US Atlantic Oldies Series DH] [90, **AB** 5.4]

741. *Somewhere Down The Lazy River* - **Robbie Robertson** - [87, 10.4]
742. *Song Sung Blue* - **Neil Diamond** - [72, *buks, mzk01, si84,* 20.12, 24.3, 29.5]
743. *Songbird* - **Kenny G** - [87, *mzk01,* 22.1]
744. *Soon (edit from The Gates Of Delirium) / Sound Chaser* - **Yes** - [US]
    [75, **A** 1.4, 18.1, 20.2, 20.3, 20.16, 29.6, 31.1.11]
    [**AB** 5.7, 18.2, 19.8, 30.3, **B** 23.9, 23.10]
745. *SOS // Ring Ring* - **Abba** - [US Atlantic Oldies Series DH] [75/73, **AB** 5.4]
746. *Soul Man (cover)* - **The Blues Brothers** (Sam & Dave) - [US] [78, *ps,* 1.5, 3.1]
747. *Southern Nights* [FLAT] - **Glen Campbell** - [77, 21.3]
748. *Souvenir* - **Orchestral Manoeuvres In The Dark** (OMD)
    [81, *buks, si84,* 12.2, 26.1, 30.4]
749. *Sowing The Seeds Of Love* [FLAT] - **Tears For Fears**
    [89, *buks, ps, quest,* 3.6, 19.6, 20.3, 20.5, 21.12, 22.3]
750. *Spies Like Us / My Carnival* - **Paul McCartney** - [85, *ps,* **AB** 2.11, 11.4]
751. *Spill The Wine* - **Eric Burden** - [70, 22.5, 22.10, 22.11]
752. *Spirit Of Radio / Circumstances* - **Rush** - [80, **A** 10.4, **AB** 2.3, 19.8]
753. *Squeezebox* - **The Who** - [76, 2.5]
754. *Stand By Me // Yakety Yak* - **Ben E. King** - [US Atlantic Oldies Series DH]
    [62, **A** 20.8, **AB** 1.1]
755. *Stand By Me (cover)* [FLAT] - **John Lennon** (Ben E King) - [75, 1.6, 20.8, 21.8, 25.3]
756. *Stand Or Fall* - **The Fixx** - [82, *buks, ch12*]
757. *Standing On Higher Ground* - **The Alan Parsons Project** - [87, *ch18,* 15.4]
758. *Star Baby* - **The Guess Who** - [74, 10.1]
759. *Star Wars Theme / Cantina Band* - **Meco** - [US] [77, **AB** 22.1]
760. *Staring At The Sun* - **U2** - [US] [97, *ch5,* 2.14, 24.8]
761. *Start Me Up* - **The Rolling Stones** - [US] [81, *gtns37, ps,* 2.15]
762. *Stay (Faraway, So Close!)* [FLAT] */ I've Got You Under My Skin* - **U2 / & Frank Sinatra**
    [93, **A** 13.3, 13.5, 21.9, 24.8, **AB** *ch5,* **B** 20.13]
763. *Stay In The Light* [FLAT] - **Honeymoon Suite** - [84, 10.4, 21.10]
764. *Stayin' Alive* [FLAT] - **The Bee Gees** - [77, *levitin,* 21.5]
765. *Steppin Out* [FLAT] - **Joe Jackson** - [82, 21.10]
766. *Still* - **Commodores** - [79, 8.3, 23.6]
767. *Still In The Game* - **Steve Winwood** - [82, *si84,* 2.7, 30.2]
768. *Still The One* - **Orleans** - [76, 20.13]
769. *Stones Of Years / A Time And A Place* - **Emerson, Lake & Palmer**
    [71, **A** *ch14, mcn88_89_94, mzk01,* 14.1 **AB** 19.7, 19.8]
770. *Straight Shootin' Woman* - **Steppenwolf** - [74, 20.7, 20.14]
771. *Strange Magic* [FLAT] - **Electric Light Orchestra** - [76, 21.12]
772. *Streak, The* - **Ray Stevens** - [US] [74, *mzk01,* 20.7, 22.5, 23.7, 25.5]
773. *Strong Enough / Leaving Las Vegas* - **Sheryl Crow** - [US]
    [94, **A** 20.10, 21.2, **AB** 24.8, **B** 20.4, 21.3]
774. *Strut* - **Sheena Easton** - [84, 2.10]
775. *Stuck With You* - **Huey Lewis & The News** - [86, 2.8, 20.15]
776. *Subdivisions* - **Rush** - [83, *ward,* 10.4]
777. *Suicide Blonde* - **INXS** - [90, *ps,* 22.12]

778.   *Summer (The First Time)* [FLAT] - **Bobby Goldsboro** - [US] [73, *si84*, 21.11, 22.3, 24.3]

779.   *Summer Breez* [FLAT] - **Seals & Crofts** - [72, *si84*, 21.4, 24.7]

780.   *Summer In The City* [FLAT] / *Nashville Cats* - **The Lovin' Spoonful** - [66, **A** 21.8, **AB** 1.2]

781.   *Summer Of '69* - **Bryan Adams** - [85, 10.2]

782.   *Sun Goes By* - **Dr. Music** - [72, *si84*, 22.13, 24.3]

783.   *Sunny Days* - **Lighthouse** - [73, 4.3, 10.1]

784.   *Sunshine In The Shade* - **The Fixx** - [84, *ch12, ps*]

785.   *Sunshine of Your Love / SWLABR* - **Cream** - [US] [68, **A** 8.1]

786.   *Superstition* [FLAT] - **Stevie Wonder** - [72, *levitin*, 21.6]

787.   *Sussudio* - **Phil Collins** - [85, *ps, ride135*, 3.3]

788.   *Sweet Caroline* - **Neil Diamond** - [69, 2.5]

789.   *Sweet City Woman \\ Gator Road* - **The Stampeders** - [Golden Treasures DH] [71, **AB** 1.2]

790.   *Sweet Freedom* - **Michael McDonald** - [86, 27.5]

791.   *Sweet Home Alabama* [FLAT] - **Lynyrd Skynyrd** - [US]
         [74, **A** 5.8, 20.4, 21.2, 21.3, 22.6, 26.2]

792.   *Sweet Surrender* [FLAT] - **Bread** - [72, *si84*, 2.4]

793.   *System Of Dr Tarr & Professor Feather, The* - **The Alan Parsons Project** - [US]
         [76, *ch18*, 5.6, 15.4]

794.   *Tainted Love (cover)* - **Soft Cell** (Gloria Jones) - [82, *buks*, 1.7, 19.5]

795.   *Take It To The Limit* - **The Eagles** - [76, 20.10, 22.7, 23.5, 29.5]

796.   *Take Me Home* - **Phil Collins** - [85, *ch14, ride130*]

797.   *Take My Breath Away* - **Berlin** - [86, 27.5]

798.   *Take On Me* [FLAT] - **A-Ha** - [85, *buks, ward*, 2.6, 19.5, 19.11, 21.11]

799.   *Takin' It To The Streets* - **The Doobie Brothers** - [76, *rideout96*, 2.1, 25.9]

800.   *Talking out Of Turn* - **The Moody Blues** - [81, *ch14, si84*]

801.   *Teach Your Children* [FLAT] // *Woodstock* - **Crosby Stills Nash & Young**
         [US Atlantic Oldies Series DH] [70, **A** 21.3, **AB** 5.4, 8.2]

802.   *Telegraph* - **Orchestral Manoeuvres In The Dark** (OMD) - [83, *mzk01, ps, si84, tnotes*, 4.8]

803.   *Telephone Line* - **The Electric Light Orchestra** - [77, *mzk01, si84*, 22.3, 24.6]

804.   *Tell Me Something Good* [FLAT] - **Rufus** - [74, 21.5]

805.   *Tell Me Why / Dreaming While You Sleep (Live)* - **Genesis**
         [91, **A** *ch14, mzk01*, **AB** 8.5, 24.8, **B** *ride137_138*, 25.10]

806.   *Tesla Girl* - **Orchestral Manoeuvres In The Dark** (OMD) - [84, 12.2, 24.5, 30.4]

807.   *Thank You* [FLAT] - **Sly & The Family Stone** - [70, *quest*, 21.5]

808.   *Thank You For Being A Friend* // *Lonely Boy* - **Andrew Gold**
         [US Asylum Spun Gold DH] [78/77, **AB** 5.14]

809.   *That Was Yesterday* - **Foreigner** - [85, *ps*, 3.3]

810.   *That's The Way (I Like It)* - **KC & The Sunshine Band** - [75, 23.7]

811.   *Theme From A Summer Place* // *Song From Moulin Rouge* -
         Percy Faith - [CAN CBS Hall Of Fame Red DH] [68, **A** 20.10, 22.1]

812.   *Theme From New York New York* // ***You & Me*** - **Frank Sinatra**
         [CAN Reprise Gold Standard DH] [**A** 20.12]

813.   *Theme From Shaft* - **Isaac Hayes** - [US] [71, *mzk01, quest*, 27.4]

814. *Theme From SWAT* - **THP Orchestra** - [76, *si84*, *tnotes*, 22.1, 25.8]

815. *There's A Kind Of Hush (cover)* - **The Carpenters** (Hermans Hermits) - [US] [76, 1.5]

816. *These Dreams* - **Heart** - [86, 2.11]

817. *These Eyes* [FLAT] - **The Guess Who** - [69, *mzk01*, *si84*, *ward*, 21.11, 22.13, 24.6, 30.3]

818. *Things We Do For Love* - **10CC** - [77, 19.6, 20.14]

819. *This Flight Tonight* - **Nazareth** - [74, 20.7]

820. *This Guys In Love With You* - **Herp Albert** - [68, 20.12, 22.13]

821. *This Is Love* - **George Harrison** - [87, 2.13, 19.12]

822. *This Is Not America* - **David Bowie & Pat Metheny** - [85, 2.10, 27.5]

823. *This Is Your Land* - **Simple Minds** - [UK] [89, 5.12, 8.5, 20.5]

824. *This One* [FLAT] - **Paul McCartney** - [89, *ch11*]

825. *Three Times A Lady* - **The Commodores** - [78, 8.3]

826. *Tide Is High, The* [FLAT] - **Blondie** - [80, *buks*, 2.8, 21.13]

827. *Tie Your Mother Down* - **Queen** - [77, *tnotes*, 2.4, 20.15, 23.3]

828. *Time (Clock Of The Heart)* - **Culture Club** - [83, 2.13]

829. *Time After Time* - **Cyndi Lauper** - [84, *buks*, ch5]

830. *Time Warp* [FLAT] / *Sweet Transvestite* - **Rocky Horror Picture Show**
[75, **A** 21.10, **AB** *si84*, B 20.7]

831. *Today's The Day* - **America** - [76, 2.1]

832. *Top Of The World* [FLAT] - **Carpenters** - [73, 21.13]

833. *Total Eclipse Of The Heart* - **Bonnie Tyler** - [83, *quest*, 19.6]

834. *Touch & Go* - **The Cars** - [80, 1.9]

835. *Touch & Go* - **Emerson, Lake & Powell** - [86, *ps*, 1.9, 3.2]

836. *Touch Of Magic* [FLAT] - **James Leroy** - [73, 10.3, 21.3, 22.13]

837. *Train (cover)* - **Shooter** (Leo Sayer) - [75, 1.5, 10.3]

838. *Travellin' Band // Who'll Stop The Rain* - **Creedence Clearwater Revival**
[US Fantasy Back To Back Hits DH] [70, **AB** 5.17]

839. *True* [FLAT] - **Spandau Ballet** - [82, *si84*, 2.8, 21.6]

840. *True Blue* - **Madonna** - [86, 20.8, 20.12]

841. *Truly* - **Lionel Ritchie** - [82, 8.3]

842. *TSOP* - **MFSB** - [74, 22.2, 25.5]

843. *Tubthumping* [FLAT] - **Chumbawumba** - [US] [97, 21.10, 22.13]

844. *Tubular Bells* - **Mike Oldfield** - [US]
[74, *buks*, *mcn140*, *mzk01*, 5.8, 19.8, 19.9, 22.1, 22.17, 25.5, 27.1]

845. *Tuesday Afternoon* - **The Moody Blues** - [US] [67, *ch14*, 8.1, 20.16, 22.11, 29.4]

846. *Turn To Stone* - **The Electric Light Orchestra** - [77, 20.14]

847. *Tush* - **ZZ Top** - [75, *mzk01*, 20.17]

848. *Tusk* - **Fleetwood Mac** - [79, 2.6, 22.16]

849. *TV Dinners* [FLAT] - **ZZ Top** - [83, *ps*, 2.6, 21.9, 23.6]

850. *Twelfth Of Never* - **Donny Osmond** - [73, 20.12]

851. *Twilight Zone* - **Golden Earring** - [82, *si84*, 22.5]

852. *Two For The Show* - **Trooper** - [77, 10.3, 19.12]

853. *Two Out Of Three Ain't Bad* - **Meatloaf** - [77, 19.12, 23.6]

854. *Two Tribes* - **Frankie Goes To Hollywood** - [84, *ps*, 2.13]

855. *Uncle Albert & Admiral Halsey / Too Many People* [FLAT] - **Paul McCartney**
    [71, **A** 20.3, 22.5, 22.9, 22.13, **AB** *si84*, 11.3, 30.1]
856. *Under My Thumb* - **Streetheart** - [83, 1.7, 10.4]
857. *Under The Boardwalk // Ruby Baby* - **The Drifters** - [US Atlantic Oldies Series DH]
    [64/58, **A** 1.7, **AB** 8.2]
858. *Union Of The Snake* - **Duran Duran** - [83, *buks*, 2.13, 3.3]
859. *Up On Cripple Creek // The Weight* - **The Band** - [US Collectables DH]
    [69/68, **A** 19.3, **AB** 5.9]
860. *Up Where We Belong* - **Joe Cocker & Jennifer Warnes** - [82, 27.5]
861. *Uprock* - **The Rock Steady Crew** - [UK] [84, *ps*, 23.6]
862. *Uptown Girl* - **Billy Joel** - [83, 24.12]

863. *Venus (cover)* - **Bananarama** (Shocking Blue) - [86, 1.7]
864. *Venus & Mars Rock Show* - **Wings** - [75, *mzk01*, 2.13, 11.3, 20.3, 29.1, 30.1]
865. *Video Killed The Radio Star* - **The Buggles** - [79, *buks, mzk01, si84*, 2.7, 24.3, 24.6, 27.3]
866. *View To A Kill* - **Duran Duran** - [85, 2.13, 27.5]
867. *Voice, The* - **The Moody Blues** - [81, *ch14, si84*, 1.9]
868. *Vogue* - **Madonna** - [US] [90, *gtns59*, 12.6, 20.5, 24.8]

869. *Waiting For A Girl Like You* - **Foreigner** - [81, *mzk01, si84*, 2.13, 3.3]
870. *Wake Me Up Before You Go* - **Wham** - [84, *gtns33*, 19.5]
871. *Wake Up & Live* - **Bob Marley** - [79, 23.6]
872. *Walk Like An Egyptian* [FLAT] - **The Bangles** - [86, 21.13, 22.10]
873. *Walk Of Life* [FLAT] - **Dire Straits** - [85, 19.5, 21.10]
874. *Walk On* - **Neil Young** - [74, 1.9, 25.3]
875. *Walk This Way* - **Aerosmith** - [77, *si84, mzk01*, 24.6]
876. *Walking In Rhythm* - **The Blackbyrds** - [US] [75, *si84*, 19.10, 22.11, 24.4, 25.6]
877. *Walking On Back* - **Edward Bear** - [73, *ps, si84*, 3.6, 10.1, 10.5, 19.4, 20.15, 25.3]
878. *Watching Over You / Hallowed Be Thy Name* - **Greg Lake** (Emerson, Lake & Palmer)
    [77, **A** *ch14*, 22.17, **B** 20.11]
879. *Watching The Wheels* - **John Lennon** - [BEL] [81, *ps*, 1.4, 2.9, 3.3]
880. *Watching The World Go By* - **Les Emmerson** - [75, 10.3]
881. *Waterloo* - **Abba** - [74, 20.15]
882. *We Belong* - **Pat Benatar** - [84, 2.8]
883. *We Didn't Start The Fire* - **Billy Joel** - [89, 24.12]
884. *We Don't Need Another Hero* [FLAT] - **Tina Turner** - [85, *ps*, 3.1, 21.13, 22.15, 27.5]
885. *We Live For Love* - **Pat Benatar** - [80, 2.8]
886. *We'll Be Together* - **Sting** - [87, *ps*, 3.6, 12.4]
887. *We're Here For A Good Time* - **Trooper** - [79, 2.5, 10.3, 19.12]
888. *We're Off Ya Know* - **Klaatu** - [78, *si84*, 2.13, 10.3, 30.1]
889. *Welcome Back* - **John Sebastien** - [75, 20.12]
890. *Wells Fargo / Theme from "For A Few Dollars More" (The Mexican)* [FLAT] - **Babe Ruth**

[UK] [74, **AB** *mzk01*, *si84*, 1.4, 24.6, **B** *tnotes*, 4.9, 5.1, 21.6, 22.2, 22.18, 25.3]

891. *Werewolf* - **The Five Man Electrical Band** - [74, 10.3, 25.5]
892. *West End Girls* - **The Pet Shop Boys** - [84/86, *buks*, 2.10, 5.1, 19.11, 22.4, 26.1, 29.1]
893. *What A Feeling* - **Irene Cara** - [83, 27.5]
894. *What Do I Know* - **Saga** - [85, 10.4, 26.1]
895. *What Goes Up* [FLAT] - **The Alan Parsons Project** - [US] [78, 5.6]
896. *What The Hell I Got* - **Pagliaro** - [75, 10.3]
897. *What's Love Got To Do With It?* - **Tina Turner** - [83, 3.1]
898. *When I Need You* - **Leo Sayer** - [77, 2.1, 20.9]
899. *When Doves Cry* - **Prince** - [84, *quest*, 2.13, 27.5]
900. *When Love Comes To Town / Dancing Barefoot* - **U2 & B.B King**
        [88, **A** 20.7, **AB** 3.3, *ps*, **B** *mzk01*]
901. *When We Was Fab* [FLAT] - **George Harrison** - [87, *ward*, 2.13, 19.12, 21.12, 22.6]
902. *Wherever I Lay My Hat (That's My Home)* - **Paul Young** - [83, 23.6]
903. *White Hot* - **Red Rider** - [80, 20.14]
904. *White Room* - **Cream** - [US] [68, 8.1]
905. *White Wedding* - **Billy Idol** - [83, 2.8]
906. *Who Are You* [FLAT] - **The Who** - [UK] [78, *ps*, 20.4, 21.10]
907. *Who's That Girl* - **Madonna** - [85, 27.5]
908. *Why Can't We Be Friends?* [FLAT] - **War** - [75, *ps*, 21.6]
909. *Why Can't We Live Together* [FLAT] - **Timmy Thomas** - [US] [73, *mzk01*, 19.3, 21.5]
910. *Why Me?* [FLAT] - **Styx** - [79, *mzk01*, 21.6, 22.18]
911. *Wild Boys* - **Duran Duran** - [84, *buks*, 2.11, 3.3]
912. *Wild Eyes* - **Stampeders** - [71, 10.3, 20.7]
913. *Wildwood Weed* - **Jim Stafford** // *Daisy A Day* - **Jud Strunk** - [DH] [74, **A** *tnotes*, 21.2, 23.9]
914. *Will It Go Round In Circles* [FLAT] - **Billy Preston** - [73, *si84*, 19.6, 21.6, 22.12, 29.2]
915. *Wipeout* // *Surfer Joe* - **Surfaris** - [US] [63, 1.2, 20.7]
916. *Wishing (If I Had A Photograph Of You)* - **A Flock Of Seagulls** - [83, *mzk01*, *ps*, *si84*, 19.11]
917. *Wishing You Were Here* - **Chicago** - [74, 22.3, 30.4]
918. *With A Little Luck* - **Wings** - [UK] [78, *si84*, 2.13, 5.11, 11.3, 20.5]
919. *Without You* - **Harry Nilsson** - [72, 1.9]
920. *Woman* - **John Lennon** - [US] [81, *ps*, 2.9]
921. *Woman In Chains* - **Tears For Fears** - [89, *buks*, *ps*, 3.6, 20.5]
922. *Wonderful Christmas Time* - **Paul McCartney** - [85, *mzk01*, 29.3]
923. *Working For The Weekend* - **Loverboy** - [82, 10.4]
924. *World I Know, The* - **Collective Soul** - [US] [95, 5.5, 24.8]

925. *Yah Mo B There* - **James Ingram** - [83, 23.6]
926. *Yesterday* [FLAT] - **The Beatles** - [65, *gtns13*, *levitin*, 20.2, 22.17]
927. *You Are So Beautiful* // *High Time We Went* - Joe Cocker - [A&M Memories DH]
        [74/72, **A** 22.17]
928. *You Are The One* - **Lionel Ritchie** - [83, 8.3]
929. *You Are What I Am* [FLAT] - **Gordon Lightfoot** - [72, 21.3]
930. *You Belong To The City* - **Glenn Frey** - [85, 23.4]

931. *You Better Run* - **Pat Benatar** - [80, *si84*, 2.8, 20.14]
932. *You Can Call Me Al* - **Paul Simon** - [US] [86, 2.6]
933. *You Can't Dance* [FLAT] - **Jackson Hawke** - [76, 10.3, 21.10]
934. *You Could Have Been A Lady* [FLAT] - **April Wine** - [US] [72, 26.2]
935. *You Don't Mess Around With Jim* - **Jim Croce** - [72, 20.12]
936. *You Girl* - **Lighthouse** - [72, 10.1, 10.5, 20.14]
937. *You Light Up My Life* - **Debbie Boone** - [78, 2.1, 20.10]
938. *You Little Trustmaker* // *Miss Grace* - **The Tymes** - [US Collectables DH]
         [74/75, **AB** 5.9]
939. *You Make Loving Fun* - **Fleetwood Mac** - [77, 2.1]
940. *You Make Me Feel Like Dancing* - **Leo Sayer** - [76, 2.1]
941. *You May Be Right* - **Billy Joel** - [80, 24.12]
942. *You Really Got Me* - **The Kinks** - [US] [64, *levitin*, 8.1, 27.6]
943. *You Sexy Thing* - **Hot Chocolate** - [76, 8.5]
944. *You Take Me Up* [FLAT] - **The Thompson Twins** - [84, 21.7, 22.12]
945. *You Won't Be There* - **The Alan Parsons Project** - [80, *si84*, 15.3]
946. *You're In My Heart* - **Rod Stewart** - [77, 2.1, 20.11]
947. *You're My Best Friend / '39* [FLAT] - **Queen** - [76, **A** 20.15, 25.9, **AB** 2.4, **B** 21.3]
948. *You're No Good (cover)* [FLAT] - **Linda Ronstadt** (Betty Everett / Dee Dee Warwick) - [US]
         [75, *si84*, 1.5, 21.13, 24.4]
949. *You're Sixteen* - **Ringo Starr** - [74, *si84*, 1.6, 2.13, 20.17]
950. *You're Still The One* - **Copper Penny** - [73, *si84*, 10.3, 19.3, 24.4]
951. *You've Got A Friend* [FLAT] // *Steamroller* - **James Taylor**
         [US WB Back To Back Hits DH] [71, **A** *gtns48*, 21.4, **AB** 5.15]
952. *Young & Restless* - **Prism** - [80, 10.4]
953. *Your Song* - **Elton John** - [US] [71, *ride81*, 24.11]

TWENTY - ONE

SINGLES III - B [A]

B [A] is listed as a way of referencing a B side song back to it's A side.

1. *#4 [Hypnotized]* - **Simple Minds**
2. *'39 [You're My Best Friend]* - **Queen**
3. *1985 [Band On The Run]* - **Paul McCartney & Wings**
4. *25 Or 6 To 4 86 [Will You Still Love Me?]* - **Chicago**
5. *Abeline [Don't Kill The Whale]* - **Yes**
6. *Absolutely Right [Signs]* - **The Five Man Electrical Band**
7. *Ace Of Swords [Games People Play]* - **The Alan Parsons Project**
8. *All I Really Want [Mr. Tambourine Man]* - **The Byrds**
9. *Am I True To Myself [I'd Love You To Want Me]* - **Lobo**
10. *Anothony's Song (Movin' Out) [Just The Way You Are]* - **Billy Joel**
11. *Any Colour You Like [Money]* - **Pink Floyd**
12. *Awaken [Wonderous Stories]* - **Yes**
13. *Baroque-A-Nova [Classical Gas]* - **Mason Williams**
14. *Better Days [Jackie Blue]* - **The Ozark Mountain Daredevils**
15. *Blindman [Back Off Bugaloo]* - **Ringo Starr**
16. *Bloody Well Right [Dreamer]* - **Supertramp**
17. *Blue Collar [Let It Ride]* - **Bachman - Turner Overdrive**
18. *Bonnie [It's Raining Again]* - **Supertramp**
19. *Boogie Wonderland [After The Love Has Gone]* - **Earth, Wind & Fire**
20. *Book Of Brilliant Things (Live) [Promised You A Miracle (Live)]* - **Simple Minds**
21. *Boomerang II [Pride (In The Name Of Love)]* - **U2**
22. *Borderline [Holiday]* - **Madonna**
23. *Born On The Bayou [Proud Mary]* - **Creedence Clearwater Revival**
24. *Brass Band In African Chimes [Up On The Catwalk]* - **Simple Minds**
25. *Breakdown [Day After Day]* - **The Alan Parsons Project**
26. *Bring On The Night [Walking On The Moon]* -**The Police**
27. *Brother Where You Bound [Better Days]* - **Supertramp**
28. *Bullet The Blue Sky [In God's Country]* - **U2**
29. *C Moon [Hi Hi Hi]* - **Wings**
30. *Call On Me [It Don't Matter To Me]* - **Bread**
31. *Candyman, The [I Want To Be Happy]* - **Sammy Davis Jr.**
32. *Cantina Band [Star Wars Theme]* - **Meco**
33. *Children Of The Moon [Old & Wise & Psychobabble]* - **The Alan Parsons Project**

34. *Cinnamon Girl [Only Love Can Break Your Heart]* - **Neil Young**

35. *Circumstances [Spirit Of Radio]* - **Rush**

36. *City Of Love (Live) [Rhythm Of Love]* - **Yes**

37. *Clap, The [Your Move]* - **Yes**

38. *Cold As Ice [Feels Like The First Time]* - **Foreigner**

39. *Comfortably Numb [Run Like Hell]* - **Pink Floyd**

40. *Counting Out Time [I Know What I Like (In Your Wardrobe)]* - **Genesis**

41. *Crazy [Down Under]* - **Men At Work**

42. *Creepin' [We're An American Band]* - **Grand Funk**

43. *Daisy A Day* - Jud Strunk [*Wildwood Weed* - **Jim Stafford**]

44. *Dancing Barefoot [When Love Comes To Town]* - **U2**

45. *Daytime Nighttime Suffering [Goodnight Tonight]* - **Wings**

46. *Deep In The Heart [I Still Haven't Found What I'm Looking For]* - **U2**

47. *Deeper & Deeper [Are We Ourselves?]* - **The Fixx**

48. *Do I Have To? [Always On My Mind]* - **The Pet Shop Boys**

49. *Dodo [No Rely At All]* - **Genesis**

50. *Does It Really Happen? [Into The Lens]* - **Yes**

51. *Domino [Moondance]* - **Van Morrison**

52. *Don't Kill The Whale [Release Release]* - **Yes**

53. *Don't Know Why I Love You [My Cherie Amour]* - **Stevie Wonder**

54. *Don't You Forget About Me (Live) [All The Things She Said]* - **Simple Minds**

55. *Down On The Bayou [Fortunate Son]* - **Creedence Clearwater Revival**

56. *Downstream [Give A Little Bit]* - **Supertramp**

57. *Dr. Marvello [California Jam]* - **Klaatu**

58. *Dreaming While You Sleep (Live) [Tell Me Why]* - **Genesis**

59. *Early 1970 [It Don't Come Easy]* - **Ringo Starr**

60. *Eastbound Train [Sultans Of Swing]* - **Dire Straits**

61. *Eastbound Train (Live) [Twisting By The Pool]* - **Dire Straits**

62. *Endless Deep [Two Hearts Beat As One]* - **U2**

63. *Entertainer, The [Piano Man]* - **Billy Joel**

64. *Even In The Quietist Moments [Goodbye Stranger]* - **Supertramp**

65. *Evidence Of Autumn [Misunderstanding]* - **Genesis**

66. *Farewell To Kings, A [Cinderella Man]* - **Rush**

67. *Flying To My Home [My Brave Face]* - **Boston**

68. *Foreplay [Peace Of Mind]* - **Boston**

69. *Freedom For The Stallion [Black & White]* - **Three Dog Night**

70. *From Now On (Live)[Take The Long Way Home (Live)]* - **Supertramp**

71. *From Now On [Dreamer]* - **Supertramp**

72. *Games People Play [Turn Of A Friendly Card]* - **The Alan Parsons Project**

73. *Gator Road [Sweet City Woman]* - **The Stampeders**

74. *Get It Right The First Time [Just The Way You Are]* - **Billy Joel**

75. *Girl On A Swing [Don't Let The Sun Catch You Crying]* - **Gerry & The Pacemakers**

76. *Gold Bug, The [Prime Time] & [Time]* - **The Alan Parsons Project**

77. *Gone Hollywood [Breakfast In America]* - **Supertramp**

78. *Good Times Bad Times [Communication Breakdown]* - **Led Zeppelin**

79. *Good Times Roll [Just What I Needed]* - **The Cars**

80. *Great Gates Of Kiev, The [The Nutrocker]* - **Emerson, Lake & Palmer**

81. *Green River [Commotion]* - **Creedence Clearwater Revival**

82. *Hallelujah Here She Comes [Desire]* - **U2**

83. *Hallowed Be Thy Name [Watching Over You]* - **Greg Lake** (Emerson, Lake & Palmer)

84. *Hang In There Long Enough [Something Happened On The Way To Heaven]* - **Phil Collins**

85. *Have You Seen Her? [Oh Girl]* - **The Chi - lites**

86. *Hawkeye [Let's Talk About Me]* - **The Alan Parsons Project**

87. *Head Games (Live) [Break It Up]* - **Foreigner**

88. *Heaven (Live) [Heaven (original)]* - **Bryan Adams**

89. *Heaven Can Wait [Bat Out Of Hell]* - **Meatloaf**

90. *Hey Girl Come & Get In [The Hustle]* - **Van McCoy & The Soul City Symphony**

91. *Hey Hey What Can I Do [Immigrant Song]* - **Led Zeppelin**

92. *Hey Tonight [Have You Ever Seen The Rain]* - **Creedence Clearwater Revival**

93. *High Time We Went [You Are So Beautiful]* - **Joe Cocker**

94. *Hold On [Rocky Mountain Way]* - **Triumph**

95. *Honesty [Big Shot]* - **Billy Joel**

96. *Hot Dog [Fool In The Rain]* - **Led Zeppelin**

97. *How Close You Came To Being Gone [Funny Face]* - **Donna Fargo**

98. *How Much I Feel [Holding On To Yesterday]* - **Ambrosia**

99. *Human Body [Play The Game]* - **Queen**

100.   *Humbug [I Believe In Father Christmas]* - **Greg Lake** (Emerson, Lake & Palmer)

101.   *Hungry For You [Spirits In The Material World]* - **The Police**

102.   *I Am A Camera [On TV]* - **The Buggles**

103.   *I Am A Rock [Scarborough Fair]* - **Simon & Garfunkel**

104.   *I Am The Walrus [Hello Goodbye]* - **The Beatles**

105.   *I Can't Believe How Much I Love You [Tie A Yellow Ribbon Round The Ole Oak Tree]*
        Dawn

106.   *I Just Want To Celebrate [Born To Wander]* - **Rare Earth**

107.   *I Lie Around [Live & Let Die]* - **Wings**

108.   *I Need You [Cold As Ice]* - **Foreigner**

109.   *I Ran So Far Away (Live) [It's Not Me Talking]* - **A Flock Of Seagulls**

110.   *I Robot [Don't Let It Show]* - **The Alan Parsons Project**

111.   *I Threw It All Away [Lay Lady Lay]* - **Bob Dylan**

112.   *I Want To Be Happy [The Candyman]* - **Sammy Davis Jr.**

113.   *I Write The Songs [Could It Be Magic?]* - **Barry Manilow**

114.   *I'd Rather Be A Man [Lucifer]* - **The Alan Parsons Project**

115.   *I'm A Man [Colour My World]* - **Chicago**

116.   *I'm So Proud [Everybody Plays The Fool]* - **The Main Ingredient**

117. *I've Been Down This Road Before [Hooked On A Feeling]* - **B.J. Thomas**

118. *I've Got You (Under My Skin)* - **Frank Sinatra & Bono** *[Stay (Faraway So Close]* - **U2**

119. *I've Seen All Good People (Live) [Roundabout (Live)]* - **Yes**

120. *In A Broken Dream* - **Python Lee Jackson** - *[How Long* - **Ace]**

121. *Inside & Out [Spot The Pigeon & Follow You Follow Me]* - **Genesis**

122. *It Can Happen (Live) [It Can Happen (original)]* - **Yes**

123. *It's A Miracle [Mandy]* - **Barry Manilow**

124. *It's Gonna Get Better [Mama]* - **Genesis**

125. *Jennifer Eccles [The Air That I Breathe]* - **The Hollies**

126. *Jeremy Bender [C'est La Vie]* - **Emerson, Lake & Palmer**

127. *Johnny B Goode [My Ding Ling]* - **Chuck Berry**

128. *Just A Smile [Magic]* - **Pilot**

129. *Just Another Nervous Wreck [The Logical Song]* - **Supertramp**

130. *Keep On Runnin' [Gimmie Some Lovin']* - **The Spencer Davis Group**

131. *Kid Is Hot Tonight [Turn Me Loose]* - Loverboy

132. *Knife Edge [Lucky Man]* - **Emerson, Lake & Palmer**

133. *Lamb Lies Down On Broadway [I Know What I Like (In Your Wardrobe)]* - **Genesis**

134. *Last Domino, The [Invisible Touch]* - **Genesis**

135. *Last Resort, The [Life In The Fast Lane]* - **The Eagles**

136. *Leaving Las Vegas [Strong Enough]* - **Sheryl Crow**

137. *Let It Rain [After Midnight]* - **Eric Clapton**

138. *Let Me Roll It [Jet]* - **Paul McCartney & Wings**

139. *Let Your Love Go [If]* - **Bread**

140. *Light Up [Mademoiselle]* - **Styx**

141. *Living Forever [No Son Of Mine]* - **Genesis**

142. *Living Sin [From The Beginning]* - **Emerson, Lake & Palmer**

143. *Lodi [Bad Moon Rising]* - **Creedence Clearwater Revival**

144. *Lonely Boy [Thank You For Being A Friend]* - **Andrew Gold**

145. *Long Distance Runaround [Roundabout]* - **Yes**

146. *Long Long Way From Home [Feels Like The First Time]* - **Foreigner**

147. *Long Time Blues [Classical Gas]* - **Mason Williams**

148. *Love Me Two Times [Light My Fire]* - **The Doors**

149. *Love Song (Live) [Sanctify Yourself]* - **Simple Minds**

150. *Low Life [Spirits In The Material World]* - **The Police**

151. *Luminous Times (Hold On To Love) [With Or Without You]* - **U2**

152. *Lunch Bunch Odd Sox [Coming Up]* - **Paul McCartney**

153. *Ma Ma Ma Baby [So You Are A Star]* - **The Hudson Brothers**

154. *Magic Carpet Ride [Born To Be Wild]* - **Steppenwolf**

155. *Mainstreet [Night Moves]* - **Bob Seger**

156. *Make It Last [I'm Stoned In Love With You]* - **The Stylistics**

157. *Man In A White Car [Run Through The Light]* - **Yes**

158. *Mess, The (Live) [My Love]* - **Paul McCartney**

159. *Miss Grace [You Little Trustmaker]* - **The Tymes**
160. *Montego Bay* - **Bobby Bloom** - *[Layla* - **Derek & The Dominos**]
161. *Moving In Stereo [My Best Friend's Girl]* - **The Cars**
162. *Mull Of Kintyre [Girl's School]* - **Wings**
163. *My Carnival [Spies Like Us]* - **Paul McCartney**
164. *My Home In My Hand [Hot Rod Lincoln]*
           Commander Cody & His Lost Planet Airmen
165. *Nashville Cats [Summer In The City]* - **The Lovin' Spoonful**
166. *Needle Gone & The Damage Done, The [Old Man & Sugar Mountain]* - **Neil Young**
167. *Never Going Back Again [Don't Stop]* - **Fleetwood Mac**
168. *No Sugar Tonight [American Woman]* - **The Guess Who**
169. *Nobody I Know [World Without Love]* - **Peter & Gordon**
170. *Nucleus [I Wouldn't Want To Be Like You]* - **The Alan Parsons Project**
171. *Oh Woman Oh Why [Another Day]* - **Paul McCartney**
172. *Old Brown Shoe [The Ballad Of John & Yoko]* - **The Beatles**
173. *Old Friends & Book Ends [Mrs. Robinson]* - **Simon & Garfunkel**
174. *On The Rolls [Devil Inside]* - **INXS**
175. *Once In A Lifetime [You're The Inspiration]* - **Chicago**
176. *Once Upon A Daydream [Synchronicity II]* - **The Police**
177. *Overture From Tommy [See Me Feel Me]* - **The Who**
178. *Parallels [Going For The One]* - **Yes**
179. *People Are Strange [Light My Fire]* - **The Doors**
180. *Pharoahs [Everybody Wants To Rule The World]* - **Tears For Fears**
181. *Pretty Maids All In A Row [Hotel California]* - **The Eagles**
182. *Questions 67 & 68 [Beginnings]* - **Chicago**
183. *Questions Of My Childhood [Carry On Wayward Son]* - **Kansas**
184. *Reggae Christmas [Christmas Time]* - **Bryan Adams**
185. *Restless [Ballroom Blitz]* - **The Sweet**
186. *Revolution [Hey Jude]* - **The Beatles**
187. *Ride Easy [Heat Of The Moment]* - **Asia**
188. *Ripples [Entangled]* - **Genesis**
189. *Roadhouse Blues [L.A. Woman]* - **The Doors**
190. *Rocky Top* - **Terri Gibbs** - *[I Can Dream About You* - **Dan Hartman**]
191. *Ruby Baby [Under The Boardwalk]* - **The Drifters**
192. *Rudy [Take The Long Way Home]* - **Supertramp**
193. *Run Baby Run [All I Wanna Do]* - **Sheryl Crow**
194. *Running To Stand Still [In God's Country]* - **U2**
195. *Running With The Devil [Jump]* - **Van Halen**
196. *Sally G [Junior's Farm]* - **Paul McCartney & Wings**
197. *Salty Dog, A [Conquistador (Live)]* - **Procal Harum**
198. *Santa Claus Is Coming To Town (Live) [My Home Town]* - **Bruce Springsteen**
199. *Sea Song [Mothers Talk]* - **Tears For Fears**

200. *Second Home By The Sea [That's All]* - **Genesis**
201. *Sermon, A [De Do Do Do De Da Da Da] & [Don't Stand So Close To Me]* - **The Police**
202. *Shape Of My Heart [If I Ever Lose My Faith In You]* - **Sting**
203. *Silver & Gold [Where The Streets Have No Name]* - **U2**
204. *Silver Rainbow [Taking It All Too Hard]* - **Genesis**
205. *Sister Moonshine [Ain't Nobody But Me]* - **Supertramp**
206. *Slat Key Soquel Rag [Take Me In Your Arms (Rock Me)]* - **The Doobie Brothers**
207. *Smoke On The Water (Live) [Smoke On The Water]* - **Deep Purple**
208. *Snake Eyes [Turn Of A Friendly Card]* - **The Alan Parsons Project**
209. *So Good At Loving You [Falling In love]* - **Hamilton, Joe Frank & Reynolds**
210. *So Long City [Do I Love You]* - **Paul Anka**
211. *Someone To Talk To [King Of Pain] & [Wrapped Around Your Finger]* - **The Police**
212. *Song From Moulin Rouge [Theme From A Summer Place]* - **Percy Faith**
213. *Song To See You Through [Black Water]* - **The Doobie Brothers**
214. *Sound Chaser [Soon]* - **Yes**
215. *Spanish Eyes [I Still Haven't Found What I'm Looking For]* - **U2**
216. *Standing In The Dark [Doesn't Really Matter]* - **Platinum Blonde**
217. *Standing In The Shadow of Love [Reach Out I'll Be There]* - **The Four Tops**
218. *Steamroller [You've Got A Friend]* - **James Taylor**
219. *Such A Night [Right Place Wrong Time]* - **Dr. John**
220. *Sunday Bloody Sunday [Gloria (Live)]* - **U2**
221. *Surfer Joe [Wipeout]* - **Surfaris**
222. *Sweet Cream Ladies [The Letter]* - **The Box Tops**
223. *Sweet Transvestite [Time Warp]* - **Rocky Horror Show**
224. *Sweetest Thing [Where The Streets Have No Name]* - **U2**
225. *SWLABR [Sunshine Of Your Love]* - **Cream**
226. *Take Me To The Pilot [Nikita]* - **Elton John**
227. *Tequilla Sunrise [Already Gone]* - **The Eagles**
228. *That's The Way (Of The World) [Shining Star]* - **Earth Wind & Fire**
229. *Theme For Great Cities '91 [See The Lights]* - **Simple Minds**
230. *Theme From "For A Few Dollars More" (The Mexican) [Wells Fargo]* - **Babe Ruth**
231. *Theme From Great Cities [Promised You A Miracle]* - **Simple Minds**
232. *This Must Be The Place [Once In A Lifetime]* - **The Talking Heads**
233. *This Time [Run To You]* - **Bryan Adams**
234. *Tiger In A Spotlight (Live) [Peter Gunn]* - **Emerson, Lake & Palmer**
235. *Time & A Place, A [Stones Of Years]* - **Emerson, Lake & Palmer**
236. *Time Of The Season* - **The Zombies** - *[Rock & Roll Hoochie Koo* - **Rick Derringer**]
237. *Tom Sawyer (Live) [Closer To The Heart (Live)]* - **Rush**
238. *Too Many People [Uncle Albert & Admiral Halsey]* - **Paul McCartney**
239. *Total Mass Retain [America]* - **Yes**
240. *Treat Me Well [Barracuda]* - **Heart**
241. *Trick Of The Tail, A [Follow You Follow Me]* - **Genesis**

242. *Turn It On Again (Live) [Illegal Alien]* - **Genesis**
243. *Turn Turn Turn [Eight Miles High]* - **The Byrds**
244. *Tutti Frutti* - **Little Richard** *[Kokomo* - **The Beach Boys**]
245. *Twilight Alehouse [I Know What I Like (In Your Wardrobe)]* - **Genesis**
246. *Twist & Shout* - **The Isley Brothers** - *[Louie Louie* - **The Kingsmen**]
247. *Unchained Melody [All I Want Is You]* - **U2**
248. *Unchained Melody [You've Lost That Lovin' Feeling]* - **The Righteous Brothers**
249. *Under The Boardwalk [Rock The USA]* - **John Cougar Mellencamp**
250. *Undun [Laughing]* - **The Guess Who**
251. *Urbania [Limelight & Stereotomy]* - **The Alan Parsons Project**
252. *Vienna [She's Always A Woman To Me]* - **Billy Joel**
253. *Visions Of The Night [Walking On The Moon]* -**The Police**
254. *Vultures In The City [Brother Of Mine]* - **Anderson, Bruford, Wakeman & Howe**
255. *Walk To The Water [With Or Without You]* - **U2**
256. *Way Of The World [Hold On My Heart]* - **Genesis**
257. *We Will Rock You [We Are The Champions]* - **Queen**
258. *Weight, The [Up On Cripple Creek]* - **The Band**
259. *When In Love With A Blind Man [Head Over Heels]* - **Tears For Fears**
260. *When My Little Girl Is Smiling [Save The Last Dance For Me]* - **The Drifters**
261. *Whiter Shade Of Pale, A [Conquistador]* - **Procol Harum**
262. *Who'll Stop The Rain [Travellin' Band]* - **Creedence Clearwater Revival**
263. *Witch Hunt [Tom Sawyer]* - **Rush**
264. *Woodstock [Teach Your Children]* - **Crosby, Stills, Nash & Young**
265. *Yakety Yak [Stand By Me]* - **Ben E. King**
266. *You [I Heard It Through The Grapevine]* - **Marvin Gaye**
267. *You & Me [Theme From New York New York]* - **Frank Sinatra**
268. *You Can't Hurry Love [Rock This Town]* - **The Stray Cats**
269. *You Started laughing (Live) [Dreamer (Live)]* - **Supertramp**
270. *You Started Laughing [Lady]* - **Supertramp**
271. *Yummy Yummy Yummy* - **The Ohio Players** - *[Green Tambourine*
       The Lemon Peppers]
272. *YYZ [Limelight]* - **Rush**

SINGLES IV - BY ARTIST

10 CC - *I'm Not In Love & Things We Do For Love*

A Flock Of Seagulls - *I Ran, It's Not Me Talking, Never Again The Dancer, The More You Live The More You Love & Wishing (If I Had A Photograph Of You)*

Abba - *(The) Name Of The Game, Chiquitita, Dancing Queen, Fernando, I Do I Do I Do I Do I Do, I'm A Marionette, Knowing Me Knowing You, Lovelight, Ring Ring, Rock Me, SOS, Take A Chance On Me, That's Me, Waterloo & Winner Takes It All*

Ace - *How Long*

Adams / Stewart / Sting - *All For Love*

Adams, Bryan - *Christmas Time, Cuts Like A Knife, Heaven, Lonely Night, Reggae Christmas, Run To You, Somebody, Straight From The Heart, Summer Of '69, This Time & What's It Gonna Be?*

Aerosmith - *Dream On, Somebody, Sweet Emotion, Uncle Salty & Walk This Way*

A-Ha - *Take On Me*

Albert, Herp - *This Guys In Love With You*

Allman Brothers Band, The - *Ramblin' Man*

Alphaville - *Forever Young*

Ambrosia - *Holding On To Yesterday & How Much I Feel*

America - *Daisy Jane, Don't Cross The River, Horse With No Name, I Need You, In The Country, Lonely People, Midnight, Rainbow Song, Saturn Nights, Sister Golden Hair, Tin Man, Today's The Day & Ventura Highway*

Anderson, Bruford, Wakeman & Howe - *Brother Of Mine & Vultures In The City*

Anderson, Jon - *Easier Said Than Done*

Andrea True Connection, The - *More More More*

Animals - *House Of The Rising Sun*

Anka, Paul - *Do I Love You & So Long City*

Apollo 100 - *Joy*

April Wine - *Bad Side Of The Moon, Cum Hear The Band, I Wouldn't Want To Lose Your Love, Lady Run Lady Hide, Oowatanite & You Could Have Been A Lady*

Argent - *Closer To Heaven, God Gave Rock & Roll To You & Hold Your Head Up*

Asia - *Don't Cry, Heat Of The Moment, Here Comes The Feeling, Only Time Will Tell, Ride Easy, Sole Survivor, The Smile Has Left Your Eyes & Time Again*

Association, The - *Never My Love & Windy*

Atomic Rooster - *Save Me*

Average White Band, The - *Pick Up The Pieces*

B 52s - *Rock Lobster*

B T Express - *Do It (Til You're Satisfied)*

Babe Ruth - *Theme from "For A Few Dollars More" (The Mexican) & Wells Fargo*

Bachman - Turner Overdrive - *Blue Collar, Free Wheeling, Hey You, Let It Ride, Looking Out For # 1, Roll On Down The Highway, Takin' Care Of Business, Tramp & You Ain't Seen Nothin' Yet*

Bad Company - *Can't Get Enough*

Badfinger - *Come & Get It & Day After Day*

Balin, Marty - *Freeway & Hearts*

Bananarama - *Venus*

Band Aid - *Do They Know It's Christmas*

Band, The - *Life Is A Carnival, Up On Cripple Creek & The Weight*

Bangles, The - *Walk Like An Egyptian*

Beach Boys, The - *California Dreamin' & Kokomo*

Bearfoot - *Molly*

Beatles, The - *Ballad of John & Yoko, Free As A Bird, Hello Goodbye, Hey Jude, I Am The Walrus, I'm Down, Old Brown Shoe, Revolution & Yesterday*

Bee Gees, The - *How Can You Mend A Broken Heart, I Started A Joke, I've Gotta Get A Message To You & Stayin' Alive*

Bellamy Brothers, The - *Let Your Love Flow*

Benatar, Pat - *Heartbreaker, Love Is A Battlefield, Shattered, We Belong, We Live For Love & You Better Run*

Berlin - *Take My Breath Away*

Berry, Chuck - *Johnny B Goode & My Ding A Ling*

Big Country - *Fields Of Fire & In A Big Country*

Blackbyrds, The - *Walking In Rhythm*

Blondie - *Atomic, Call Me, Dreaming, Heart Of Glass, One Way Or Another, Rapture & Tide Is High*

Blood, Sweat & Tears - *More & More, Spinning Wheel & You've Made Me So Very Happy*

Bloom, Bobby - *Montego Bay & Sunny*

Blue Magic - *Sideshow*

Blue Oyster Cult - *Don't Fear The Reaper*

Blue Suede - *Gotta Have Your Love, Hooked On A Feeling & Never My Love & Pinewood Rally*

Blues Brothers, The - *Soul Man*

Bobby Goldsboro - *Summer (The First Time)*

Boomtown Rats, The - *I Don't Like Mondays*

Boone, Debbie - *You Light Up My Life*

Boston - *Don't Look Back , Foreplay, Long Time, Peace Of Mind*

Bowie, David - *China Girl, Fame, Let's Dance, Modern Love, Space Oddity & The Man Who Sold The World*

Bowie, David & Bing Crosby - *Peace On Earth & Little Drummer Boy*

Bowie, David & Mick Jagger - *Dancing In The Street*

Bowie, David & Pat Metheny - *This Is Not America*

Box Tops, The - *The Letter, & Sweet Cream Ladies*

Branigan, Laura - *Gloria, Living A lie & Solitaire*

Bread - *Aubrey, Baby I'm A Want You,* **Call On Me,** *Diary, Everything I Own, Guitar Man, I Don't Love You, If, It Don't Matter To Me, Let Your Love Go, Lost Without Your Love, Make It With You, Sweet Surrender, Take Comfort, Too Much Love, Truckin' & Why Do You Keep Me Waiting?*

Brothers Johnson, The - *I'll Be Good To Ya*

Brown, Charity - *Take Me In Your Arms*

Browne, Jackson - *Doctor My Eyes*

Buggles, The - *Adventures In Modern Recording, I Am A Camera, On TV & Video Killed The Radio Star*

Burden, Eric - *Spill The Wine*

Byrds, The - *All I Really Want, Eight Miles High, Mr. Tambourine Man & Turn Turn Turn*

California Raisins, The - *Rudolph The Red Nosed Reindeer*

Campbell, Glen - *Southern Nights*

Canned Heat - *Going Up The Country .*

Captain & Tenille, The - *Love Will Keep Us Together*

Cara, Irene - *Flashdance (What A Feeling)*

Carmen, Eric - *All By Myself, Last Night, Never Gonna Fall In Love Again & No Hard Feelings*

Carnes, Kim - *Bette Davis Eyes, Goldfinger, Invitation To Dance & Miss You Tonight*

Carpenters, The - *Close To You, I Kept On Loving You, Sing, There's A Kind Of Hush, Top Of The World & Ticket To Ride*

Cars, The - *All I Can Do, Candy - O, Drive, Good Times Roll, Got A Lot on My Head, It's All I Can Do, Just What I Needed, Let's Go, Moving in Stereo, My Best Friend's Girl, Tonight She Comes & Touch & Go*

Catfish Hodge - *Boogie Man Gonna Get Ya*

Chapin, Harry - *Cat's In The Cradle, Empty, I Wanna Learn A Love Song, Taxi, Vacancy & Wold*

Cheech & Chong - *Earache My Eye & Framed*

Cher - *Gypsies Tramps & Thieves & Half Breed*

Chicago - *(I've Been) Searchin' So Long, 25 Or 6 To 4, 25 Or 6 To 4 '86, Along Comes A Woman, Anyway You Want, Beginnings, Brand New Love Affair, Byblos, Call On Me, Colour My World, Dialogue, Does Anybody Really Know What time It Is?, Feeling Stronger Everyday, Free, Free Country, Gone Long Gone, Hard Habit To Break, Hard To Say I'm Sorry, Harry Truman, Hideaway, I'm A Man, If You Leave Me Now, Just You'n Me, Listen, Loneliness Is Just A Word, Lowdown, Make Me Smile, Old Days, Once In A Lifetime, Prelude To Aire, Questions 67 & 68, Remember The Feeling, Saturday In The Park, Till We Meet Again, Where Do We Go From Here?, Will You Still Love Me, Wishing You Were Here & You're The Inspiration*

Chi-Lites, The - *Have You Seen Her?& Oh Girl*

Chipmunks - *Chipmunks Song*

Christie - *Yellow River -*

Chumbawumba - *Tub Thumping*

Clapton, Eric - *After Midnight, Cocaine, I Shot The Sheriff & Let It Rain*

Climax - *Precious & Few*

Climax Blues Band, The - *Couldn't Get It Right*

Cochrane, Tom & Red Rider - *Boy Inside The Man*

Cockburn, Bruce - *Lovers In A Dangerous Time*

Cocker, Joe & Jennifer Warnes - *Up Where We Belong*

Cocker, Joe - *Edge Of A Dream, High Time We Went, The Letter & You Are So Beautiful*

Coffey, Dennis - *Scorpio*

Coke // Laurie Bower Singers / Dr. Music - *I'd Like To Teach The World To Sing -*

Cole, Natalie - *Christmas Song*

Collective Soul - *Shine & The World I Know*

Collins, Phil - *Against All Odds, Another Day In Paradise, Do You Know? Do You Care?, Groovy Kind Of love, Hang In There Long Enough, Heat On The Street, I Can't Believe It's True , I Missed Again, I Wish It Would Rain Down, I'm Not Moving, In The Air Tonight, One More Night, Something Happened On The Way To Heaven, Sussudio, Take Me Home, The Roof Is Leaking, Who Said I Would? & You Can't Hurry Love*

Commander Cody & The Lost Planet Airmen - *Hot Rod Lincoln & My Home In My Hand*

Commodores, The - *Easy, Lady, Nightshift, Oh No, Sail On, Still & Three Times A Lady*

Cooper Brothers, The - *Finally (With You)*

Cooper, Alice - *Cold Ethyl, Go To Hell,* Gutter Cat, *Hello Hurray, I Never Cry, I'm Eighteen, It's Hot Tonight, Only Women Bleed, School's Out, Welcome To My Nightmare & You & Me*

Copper Penny - *Sitting On A Poor Man's Throne & You're Still The One*

Cream - *Sunshine of Your Love, SWLABR & White Room*

Creedence Clearwater Revival - *Bad Moon Rising, Born On The Bayou, Commotion, Down On The Bayou, Fortunate Son, Green River, Have You Ever Seen The Rain, Hey Tonight, Lodi, Proud Mary, Travellin' Band & Who'll Stop The Rain*

Croce, Jim - *Age, Alabama Rain, Bad Bad Leroy Brown, I Got A Name, I'll Have To Say I Love You In A Song, It Doesn't Have To Be That Way Time In A Bottle & You Don't Mess Around With Jim*

Crosby Stills Nash & Young - *Teach Your Children & Woodstock*

Crosby, Bing - *Silent Night Holy Night*

Cross, Christopher - *Arthur's Theme, Minstrel Gigolo, Ride Like The Wind, Sailing, Say You'll Be Mine & Spinning*

Crow, Sheryl - *All I Wanna Do, Can't Cry Anymore, Everyday Is A Winding Road, Leaving Las Vegas, Run Baby Run & Strong Enough*

Crowbar - *Oh What A Feeling*

Crowded House - *Don't Dream It's Over*

Culture Club - *Church Of The Poison Mind, Do You Really Want To Hurt Me, Karma Chameleon & Time (Clock Of The Heart)*

Darin, Bobby - *Dream Lover, If I Were A Carpenter & Rainin'*

Davis Jr., Sammy - *The Candyman, & I Want To Be Happy*

Dawn - *I Can't Believe How Much I love You, Say Has Anybody Seen My Sweet Gypsy Rose & Tie A Yellow Ribbon Round The Ole Oak Tree*

Dazz Band, The - *On The One For Fun*

De Burgh, Chris - *All The Love I Have Inside, Don't Pay The Ferryman, Lady In Red & Patricia The Stripper*

Deep Purple - *Hush, Kentucky Woman, One More Rainy Day, Smoke On The Water & Woman From Tokyo*

Dees, Rick - *Disco Duck*

Denver, John - *Annie's Song, Around & Around, Back Home Again, My Sweet Lady, Poems, Prayers & Promises, Sunshine On My Shoulder, Take Me Home Country Roads & Thank God I'm A Country Boy*

Deodato - *Also Sprach Zarathustra*

Derek & The Dominoes - *Layla*

Derringer, Rick - *Rock & Roll Hoochie Koo*

Dexy's Midnight Runners - *Come On Eileen*

Diamond, Neil - *Cracklin' Rosie, Hello Again, Song Sung Blue & Sweet Caroline*

Dion, Celine - *Power Of Love*

Dire Straits - *Calling Elvis, Eastbound Train, Industrial Disease, Sultans Of Swing, Twisting By The Pool & Walk Of Life*

Dolby, Thomas - *Dissidents, Europa & The Pirate Twins, Flying North, Hyperactive, I Scare Myself, She Blinded Me With Science & Windpower*

Dolby's Cube (Thomas) - *May The Cube Be With*

Donaldson, Bo & The Heywoods - *Billy Don't Be A Hero*

Doobie Brothers, The - *Another Park Another Sunday, Black Water, China Grove, Don't Stop To Watch The Wheels, It Keeps You Running, Jesus Is Just Alright, Listen To The Music, Long Train Running, Minute By Minute, Slat Key Soquel Rag, Song To See You Through, Sweet Feelin', Take Me In Your Arms (Rock Me), Takin' It To The Streets, Toulouse Street, What A Fool Believes & Without You*

Doors, The - *Hello I Love You, L.A. Woman, Light My Fire, Love Her Madly, Love Me Two Times, Love Street, People Are Strange, Riders On The Storm, Roadhouse Blues & Touch Me*

Douglas, Karl - *Kung Fu Fighting*

Dr. Hook - *Cover Of A Rolling Stone & Only Sixteen*

Dr. John - *Right Place Wrong Time & Such A Night*

Dr. Music - *Sun Goes By*

Dream Academy, The - *Life In A Northern Town*

Drifters, The - *Ruby Baby, Save The Last Dance For Me, Under The Boardwalk & When My Little Girl Is Smiling*

Duran Duran - *New Moon On Monday, Reflex, Save A Prayer, Union Of The Snake, View To A Kill & Wild Boys*

Dylan, Bob - *I Threw It All Away & Lay Lady Lay*

Eagles, The - *Already Gone, Best Of My Love, Early Bird, Get You In The Mood, Heartache Tonight, Hotel California, I Can't Tell You Why, Life In The Fast Lane, Lyin' Eyes, New Kid In Town, One Of These Nights, Please Come Home For Christmas, Pretty Maids All In A Row, Take It Easy, Take It To The Limit, Teenage Jail, Tequila Sunrise, The Disco Strangler, The Last Resort, The Long Run, Victim Of Love & Witchy Woman*

Earth, Wind & Fire - *After The Love Has Gone, Boogie Wonderland, September, Shining Star, That's The Way Of The World & Yearnin' Learnin'*

Easton, Sheena - *For Your Eyes Only Morning Train & Strut*

Edgar Winter Group, The - *Frankenstein, Free Ride & Undercover Man*

Edison Lighthouse - *Love Grows*

Edward Bear - *Best Friend, Cachet Country, Close Your Eyes, Fly Across The Sea, Four Months Out To Africa, Freedom For The Stallion, Last Song, Masquerade, Walking On Back Why Won't You Marry Me & You Me & Mexico*

Eight Seconds - *Kiss You (When It's Dangerous)*

Electric Light Orchestra, The - *Can't Get It Out Of My Head, Don't Bring Me Down, Livin' Thing, Roll Over Beethoven, Strange Magic, Telephone Line & Turn To Stone*

Emerson, Lake & Palmer - *A Time And A Place, Brain Salad Surgery, C'est La Vie, Fanfare For The Common Man, From The Beginning, Great Gates Of Kiev, Hallowed Be Thy Name, Honky Tonk Train Blues, Humbug, I Believe In Father Christmas, Jeremy Bender, Jerusalem,*

Knife Edge, Living Sin, Lucky Man, Nutrocker, Peter Gunn, Stones Of Years, Tiger In A Spotlight & Watching Over You

Emerson, Lake & Powell - *Touch & Go*

Emmerson, Les (Five Man Electrical Band) - *Control Of Me, Cry Your Eyes Out & Watching The World Go By*

Enigma - *Sadeness*

Essex, David - *Rock On*

Faith, Percy - *Song From Moulin Rouge & Theme From A Summer Place*

Falco - *Rock Me Amadeus*

Faltermeyer, Harold - *Axel F*

Fancy - *Wild Thing*

Fargo, Donna - *Funny Face \\ How Close You Came To Being Gone*

Fats Domino - *Blueberry Hill*

Fifth Dimension. The - *Aquarius & Let The Sunshine*

Fine Young Cannibals, The - *She Drives Me Crazy*

First Class - *Beach Baby*

Five Man Electrical Band, The - *Absolutely Right, I'm A Stranger Here, Signs & Werewolf*

Fixx, The - *Are We Ourselves, Deeper & Deeper, I Will, Less Cities More Moving People, One Thing Leads To Another, Red Skies, Saved By Zero, Sign Of Fire, Stand Or Fall & Sunshine In The Shade*

Flack, Roberta - *Feel Like Making Love, First Time Ever I Saw Your Face, Just Like A Woman, Killing Me Softly With His Song, Trade Winds, When You Smile & Where Is The Love*

Flack, Roberta & Peabo Bryson - *Tonight I Celebrate*

Fleetwood Mac - *Big Love, Don't Stop, Dreams, Everywhere & Little Lies, Tusk & You Make Loving Fun*

Flesh For Lulu - *I Go Crazy*

Focus - *Hocus Pocus*

Fogerty, John - *Centerfield*

Foot In Cold Water, A - *Make Me Do (Anything You Want)*

Foreigner - *Break It Up, Cold As Ice, Dirty White Boy, Double Vision, Feels Like The First Time, Girl On The Moon, Head Games, Hot Blooded, I Need You, I Want To Know What Love Is, Juke Box Hero, Long Long Way From Home, Reaction To Action, That Was Yesterday, Urgent, Waiting For A Girl Like You & Woman Oh Woman*

Foster, David - *Love Theme From St Elmos Fire*

Four Tops, The - *Reach Out I'll Be There & Standing In The Shadow of Love*

Frampton, Peter - *Baby I Love Your Way, Do You Feel Like I Do & Show Me The Way*

Frankie Goes To Hollywood - *Power Of Love & Two Tribes*

Gabriel, Peter - *Big Time, Games Without Frontiers, I Don't Remember, In Your Eyes, Moribund The Burgermeister, Red Rain, Shock The Monkey, Sledgehammer, Soft Dog & Solisbury Hill*

Gallery - *I Believe In Music*

Gaye, Marvin - *I Heard It Thru The Grapevine, Sexual Healing & You*

Gaynor, Gloria - *Reach Out I'll Be There*

Genesis - *A Trick Of The Tail, Abacab, Another Record, Ballad Of Big, Behind The Lines, Counting Out Time, Do The Neurotic, Dodo, Dreaming While You Sleep, Duchess, Entangled, Evidence Of Autumn, Feeding The Fire, Follow You Follow Me, Go West Young Man, Hold On My*

Heart, I Can't Dance, I Know What I Like (In Your Wardrobe), I'd Rather Be You, Illegal Alien, In That Quiet Earth, In The Glow Of The Night, In Too Deep, Inside & Out, Invisible Touch, It's Gonna Get Better, It's Yourself, Lamb Lies Down On Broadway, Land Of Confusion, Living Forever, Mama, Man On The Corner, Misunderstanding, No Reply At All, No Son Of Mine, Paperlate, Ripples, Second Home By The Sea, Silver Rainbow, Spot The Pigeon EP (Match Of The Day & Pigeons), Submarine, Taking It All Too Hard, Tell Me Why, That's All, The Last Domino, Throwing It All Away, Tonight Tonight Tonight, Turn It On Again, Twilight Alehouse, Way Of The World & Your Own Special Way

George Baker Selection, The - *Paloma Blanca*

Gerry & The Pacemakers - *Don't Let The Sun Catch You Crying, Girl On A Swing & How Do You Do It?*

Gibbs, Terri - *Rocky Top*

Gilder, Nick - *Here Comes The Night & Hot Time in The City*

Glass Tiger - *Diamond Sun, Don't Forget Me (When I'm Gone), I'm Still Searching & Someday*

Glenn Frey - *You Belong To The City*

Glitter, Gary - *Rock & Roll Part \\ Rock & Roll Part*

Godley & Creme - *Cry & Love Bombs*

Godspell - *Day By Day*

Gold, Andrew - *Lonely Boy & Thank You For Being A Friend*

Golden Earring - *Radar Love & Twilight Zone*

Gowan - *Criminal Mind & Moonlight Desires*

Grand Funk - *Bad Time, Creepin', Locomotion, Some Kind Of Wonderful, We're An American Band & Wild*

Gray, Dobie - *City Stars, Drift Away, Drift Away 79 & Lovin' Arms*

Greenbaum, Norman - *Canned Ham, Milk Cow & Spirit In The Sky*

Guess Who, The - *Albert Flasher, American Woman, Clap For The Wolfman, Dancing Fool, Follow Your Daughter Home, Glamour Boy, Laughing, No Sugar Tonight, No Time, Orly, Raindance, Running Back To Saskatoon, Star Baby, These Eyes & Undun*

Hamilton, Joe Frank & Reynolds - *Falling In Love \\ So Good At Loving You*

Hamlisch, Marvin - *Entertainer*

Hampshire, Keith - *Daytime Nighttime & First Cut Is The Deepest*

Hancock, Herbie - *Chameleon*

Hardy, Hagood - *Homecoming*

Harris, Richard - *MacArthur's Park*

Harrison, George - *All Those Years Ago, Got My Mind Set On You, Isn't it A Pity, My Sweet Lord, This Is Love & When We Was Fab*

Hart, Corey - *Never Surrender & Rudolph The Red Nosed Reindeer*

Hartman, Dan - *I Can Dream About You*

Hawkins , Sophie B. - *Damn I Wish I was Your Lover*

Hayes, Isaac - *Theme From Shaft*

Head, Murray - *One Night In Bangkok .*

Heart - *Barracuda, Crazy On You, Dreamboat Annie, How Deep It Goes, Magic Man, Sing Child, These Dreams & Treat Me Well*

Henley, Don - *All She Wants To Do Is Dance, Boys Of Summer, Dirty Laundry, End Of The Innocence, I Can't Stand Still & Lilah*

Hollies, The - *The Air That I Breathe, Carrie Ann, Cos You Like To Love Me , He Ain't Heavy He's My Brother, Jennifer Eccles, Long Cool Woman In A Black Dress, Long Dark Road, Look What We've Got, Sandy*

Honeydrippers, The - *I Get A Thrill, Rockin' At Midnight & Sea Of Love*

Honeymoon Suite - *Stay In The Light*

Hot Butter - *At The Movies & Popcorn*

Hot Chocolate - *Emma & You Sexy Thing*

Hudson Brothers, The - *So You Are A Star \\ Ma Ma Ma Baby*

Human League, The - *Don't You Want Me, Human, Lebanon, Life On Your Own, Mirror Man & Open Your Heart*

Idol, Billy - *Eyes Without A Face, Flesh For Fantasy & White Wedding*

Incredible Bongo Band, The - *Bongo Rock*

Ingram, James - *Yah Mo B There*

INXS - *Devil Inside, Need You Tonight, Never Tear Us Apart, On The Rolls & Suicide Blonde*

Isley Brothers, The - *Twist & Shout*

Ives, Burl - *Holly Jolly Christmas*

J Geils Band, The - *Centerfold & Freeze Frame*

Jacks & The Poppy Family, Terry - *Put The Bone In, Seasons In The Sun & Where Evil Grows*

Jackson Five, The - *ABC & I'll Be There*

Jackson Hawke - *You Can't Dance*

Jackson, Joe - *Steppin Out*

Jackson, Michael - *Billie Jean -*

James Leroy - *Touch Of Magic*

Jefferson Starship - *Miracles*

Jethro Tull - *Bungle In The Jungle, Living In The Past , Ring Out Solstice Bells / A Christmas Song / Another Christmas Song / Magic Bells*

Joel, Billy - *(The) Entertainer, Allentown, Anthony's Song (Movin' Out), Big Shot, Get It Right The First Time, Honesty, It's Still Rock & Roll To Me, Just The Way You Are, My Life, Piano Man, She's Always A Woman To Me, She's Got A Way, The Mexican Connection, Uptown Girl, Vienna, We Didn't Start The Fire, You May Be Right & You're My Home*

John, Elton - *Bennie & The Jets, Bite Your Lip, Bitch Is Back, Crocodile Rock, Daniel, Don't Let The Sun Go Down On Me, Empty Garden, Goodbye Yellow Brick Road, Grow Some Funk Of Your Own, Honky Cat, I Guess That's Why They Call It The Blues, Island Girl, Lucy In The Sky With Diamonds, Nikita, Philadelphia Freedom, Pinball Wizard, Rocket Man, Sad Songs, Saturday Night's Alright For Fighting, Someone Saved My Life Tonight, Take Me To The Pilot, Young Man's Blues & Your Song*

Jon & Vangelis - *Friends of Mr. Cairo*

Jones, Howard - *Life In One Day, New Things, Things Can Only Get Better & Why Look For The Key?*

Kansas - *Carry On Way Son, Dust In The Wind & Questions Of My Childhood*

KC & The Sunshine Band - *That's The Way (I Like It)*

Kenny G -*Songbird*

Kershaw, Nik - *The Riddle,*

Kim, Andy - *Baby I Love You*

King Harvest - *Dancing In The Moonlight*

King, Ben E. - *Stand By Me & Yakety Yak*

King, Bill - *Goodbye Superdad*

King, Carole - *It's Too Late & Jazzman*

Kingsmen, The - *Louie Louie*

Kinks, The - *You Really Got Me*

Kiss - *Nothing To Lose & Shout It Out Loud*

Klaatu - *California Jam, Dr. Marvello, Juicy Lucy, Knee Deep In Love & We're Off Ya Know*

Knack, The - *My Sharona*

Kraftwerk - *Autobahn*

Labelle - *Lady Marmalade*

Lauper, Cyndi - *Girls Just Wanna Have Fun & Time After Time*

Led Zeppelin - *Black Dog, Communication Breakdown, D'Yer Ma'Ker, Dancing Days, Fool In The Rain, Four Sticks, Good Times Bad Times, Hey Hey What Can I Do, Hot Dog, Immigrant Song, Living Loving Maid, Misty Mountain Hop, Over The Hills & Far Away, Rock & Roll, Stairway To Heaven, The Crunge & Whole Lotta Love*

Lee, Garry - *Rodeo Song*

Lemon Peppers - *Green Tambourine*

Lennon, John - *# Dream, (Just Like) Starting Over, Imagine, Mind Games, Nobody Told Me, Stand By Me, Watching The Wheels & Woman*

Lennox, Annie & Al Green - *Put A Little Love In Your Heart*

Lenz, Kosinec & Hampshire - *OK Blue Jays*

Leo Sayer - *You Make Me Feel Like Dancing*

Level 42 - *Something About You*

Lewis, Huey & The News - *Heart & Soul, Heart Of Rock & Roll, I Want A New Drug, If This Is It, Power Of Love & Stuck With You*

Lightfoot, Gordon - *(The) House You Live In, Beautiful, If You Could Read My Mind, Race Among The Ruins, Wreck Of The Edmund Fitzgerald & You Are What I Am*

Lighthouse - *Good Day, Hats Off To The Stranger, Pretty Lady, Sunny Days, You Girl*

Little Richard - *Tutti Frutti*

Little River Band, The - *Reminiscing*

Lobo - *Am I True To Myself? & I'd Love You To Want Me*

Loggins & Messina - *Golden Ribbons, My Music, Peace Of Mind & Your Mama Don't Dance*

Looking Glass - *Brandy (You're A Fine Girl)*

Los Lobos - *La Bamba*

Loverboy - *Prissy Prissy, The Kid Is Hot Tonight, Turn Me Loose, Working For The Weekend*

Lovin' Spoonful, The - *Nashville Cats & Summer In The City*

Luba - *Let It Go*

Lynyrd Skynyrd - *Free Bird & Sweet Home Alabama*

M&M - *Black Stations, White Stations*

Madness - *Our House*

Madonna - *Borderline, Crazy For You, Holiday, La Isla Bonita, Like A Prayer, Like A Virgin, Live To Tell, Material Girl, Oh Father, Papa Don't Preach, Think Of Me, True Blue, Vogue & Who's That Girl*

Main Ingredient, The - *Everybody Plays The Fool & I'm So Proud*

Major Hooples Boarding House - *I'm Running After You*

Mama Cass - *Dream A Little Dream Of Me*

Mamas & The Papas, The - *California Dreamin'*

Manfred Mann - *Doo Wah Diddy Diddy*

Manfred Mann's Earth Band - *Blinded By The Light, Spirit In The Night & Starbird*

Mangione, Chuck - *Feels So Good*

Manilow, Barry - *Could It Be Magic, I Write The Songs, It's A Miracle & Mandy*

Marley Bob - *Wake Up & Live*

Martha & The Muffins - *Echo Beach*

Mashmakhan - *As The Years Go By, Dance A Little Step & Days When We Are Free*

Mauriat, Paul - *Love Is Blue*

Max Webster - *Diamonds Diamonds, Let Go The Line & Million Vacations*

McBride, Bob - *Do It Right & Pretty City Lady*

McCartney, Paul - *Another Day, Coming Up, Flying To My Home, Lunch Box Odd Sox, Maybe I'm Amazed, My Brave Face, My Carnival, My Love, No More Lonely Nights, Oh Woman Oh Why, Once Upon A Long Ago, Pipes Of Peace, Spies Like Us, The Mess, This One, Too Many People, Uncle Albert & Admiral Halsey & Wonderful Christmas Time*

McCartney, Paul & Michael Jackson - *Say Say Say*

McCartney, Paul & Stevie Wonder - *Ebony & Ivory*

McCartney, Paul & Wings - *Band On The Run, Helen Wheels, Jet, Junior's Farm, Let Me Roll It & Sally G*

Mccoy, Van & The Soul City Symphony - *Hey Girl, Come & Get It & The Hustle*

McFerrin, Bobby - *Don't Worry Be Happy*

McGovern, Maureen - *Morning After, The*

McLaren, Malcolm - *Madame Butterfly*

McRae, George - *Rock Your Baby*

Meatloaf - *Bat Out Of Hell, Heaven Can Wait & Two Out Of Three Ain't Bad*

Meco - *Cantina Band & Star Wars Theme*

Mellencamp, John - *Check It Out, Cherry Bomb, Crumblin' Down, Hurts So Good, I Saw Mommy Kissing Santa Claus, Jack & Diane, Paper In Fire, Rock The USA, Small Town & Under The Boardwalk*

Melvin, Harold & The Blue Notes Featuring Teddy Pendergrass - *If You Don't Know Me By Now*

Men At Work - ***Crazy*** & *Down Under*

Men Without Hats - *(The) Safety Dance, I Got The Message, I Like & Utter Space*

MFSB - *TSOP*

Michael McDonald - *Sweet Freedom*

Michael, George - *Freedom*

Middleton, Tom - *It Wouldn't Have Made Any Difference & One Night Lovers*

Midler, Bette - *Boogie Woogie Bugle Boy, Delta Dawn & Do You Want To Dance?*

Mike & The Mechanics - *The Living Years & Silent Running*

Miller Band, The Steve - *Fly Like An Eagle, The Joker,* Rock'n Me, Something To Believe In & Swingtown

Mills, Frank - *Love Me Love Me Love & Poor Little Fool*

Mitchell, Joni - *Free Man In Paris, Help Me & People's Parties*

Mitchell, Kim - *Go For A Soda & Patio Lanterns*

Monkees, The - *I'm A Believer & Pleasant Valley Sunday*

Moody Blues, The - *Cities, Gemini Dream, I Know You're Out There Somewhere, Isn't Life Strange, Nights In White Satin, Question, Sitting At The Wheel, Talking out Of Turn, Tuesday Afternoon & The Voice*

Morrison, Van - *Domino & Moondance*

Motels, The - *Only The Lonely , Some Things Never Change & Suddenly Last Summer*

Mr. Mister - *Broken Wings*

Muldaur, Maria - *Midnight At The Oasis*

Murphy, Michael - *Wildfire, Mansion On The Hill, Night Thunder & What's Forever For*

Murphy, Walter - *(A) Fifth Of Beethoven*

Murray, Anne - *Danny's Song, Drown Me & You Needed Me*

Myles & Lenny - *Can You Give It All To Me & Hold On Lovers*

Naked Eyes, The - *Always Something There To Remind Me & Promises Promises*

Nazareth - *Love Hurts & This Flight Tonight*

Nelson, Rick - *Garden Party*

Nena - *99 Red Balloons*

New Seekers, The - *I'd Like To Teach The World To Sing*

Newton - John, Olivia - *If You Love Me Let Me Know & Magic*

Newton, Juice - *Angel Of The Morning*

Nicolette Larson - *Lotta Love*

Nilsson, Harry - *Without You*

Nu Shooz - *I Can't Wait*

O'Jays, The - *Backstabbers, For The Love Of The Money, Love Train, Time To Get Down & Who Am I?*

O'Sullivan, Gilbert - *Alone Again (Naturally) & Clair*

Ohio Express - *Yummy Yummy Yummy*

Oldfield, Mike - *Tubular Bells*

Orchestral Manoeuvres In The Dark - *Dreaming, Electricity, Enola Gay, Forever (Live & Die), Genetic Engineering, If You Leave, Joan Of Arc, Locomotion, Messages, Never Turn Away, Secret, So In Love, Souvenir, Telegraph & Tesla Girl*

Original Cast, The - *One Tin Soldier*

Orleans - *Dance With Me & Still The One*

Osmond, Donny - *Twelfth Of Never*

Ozark Mountain Daredevils -***Better Days,*** *If You Wanna Get To Heaven & Jackie Blue*

Pagliaro - *What The Hell I Got*

Paper Lace - *(The) Night Chicago Died*

Parachute Club, The - *At The Feet Of The Moon & Rise Up*

Parsons Project, The Alan - *(The) Gold Bug, Ace Of Swords, Breakdown, Children Of The Moon, Damned If I Do, Day After Day, Don't Answer Me, Don't Let It Show, Eye In The Sky, Games People Play, Gemini, Hawkeye, I Don't Wanna Go Home, I Robot, I Wouldn't Want To Be Like You, I'd Rather Be A Man, If I Could Change Your Mind, Let's Talk About Me, Limelight, Lucifer, Nucleus, Old & Wise, Prime Time, Psychobabble, Snake Eyes, Standing On Higher Ground, Stereotomy, The Gold Bug, The Raven, The System Of Dr Tarr & Professor Feather, Time, Turn Of A Friendly Card, Urbania, What Goes Up, You Don't Believe, You Lie Down With Dogs, You Won't Be There & You're Gonna Get Your Fingers Burned*

Paul, Billy - *Me & Mrs. Jones*

Payolas, The - *Eyes Of A Stranger*

Perry, Steve - *Don't Tell Me Why You're Leaving, Foolish Heart & Oh Sherrie*

Pet Shop Boys, The - *Always On My Mind, Do I Have To?, It's A Sin, Opportunities & West End Girls*

Peter & Gordon - *Nobody I Know & World Without Love*

Peter, Paul & Mary - *I Dig Rock'n Roll Music, Leaving On A Jet Plane & The House Song*

Phillips, Phil - *Juella & Sea Of Love*

Pickett, Bobby Boris - *Monster Mash*

Pilot - *January, Just A Smile, Just Let Me Be & Magic*

Pink Floyd - *Another Brick In The Wall Part, Any Colour You Like, Comfortably Numb, Don't Leave Me Now, Money & Run Like Hell*

Plant, Robert - *Big Log*

Platinum Blonde - *Crying Over You, Doesn't Really Matter & Standing in The Dark*

Police, The - *Bring On The Night, De Do Do Do De Da Da Da, Dead End Job, Don't Stand So Close To Me, Every Breath You Take, Every Little Thing She Does Is Magic, Friends, Hungry (Flexible Strategies), I Can't Stand Losing You, Invisible Sun, King Of Pain, Low Life, Message In A Bottle, Murder By Numbers, Once Upon A Daydream, Roxanne, A Sermon, Someone To Talk To, Spirits In The Material World, Synchronicity II, Visions Of The Night, Walking On The Moon & Wrapped Around Your Finger*

Post, Mike - *Dixie Lullabye & Rockford Files*

Prelude - *After The Goldrush*

Preston, Billy - *Outa Space & Will It Go Round In Circles*

Pretenders, The - *Back On The Chain Gang & Middle Of The Road*

Prince - *Batdance, Let's Go Crazy, Purple Rain & When Doves Cry*

Prism - *Armageddon, Night To Remember & Young & Restless*

Procal Harum - *Conquistador, Lime Street Blues, A Salty Dog & Whiter Shade Of Pale*

Pukkah Orchestra, The - *Listen To The Radio*

Python Lee Jackson - *In A Broken Dream*

Queen - *Bohemian Rhapsody, '39, Crazy Little Thing Called Love, Human Body, Killer Queen, Play The Game, Radio Ga Ga, Somebody To Love, Tie Your Mother Down, We Are The Champions, We Will Rock You & You're My Best Friend*

Rafferty, Gerry - *Baker Street*

Raiders, The - *Birds Of A Feather, Indian Reservation & Terry's Tune*

Rare Earth - *Born To Wander, Get Ready, Hey Big Brother, I Just Want To Celebrate, I Know I'm Losing You & Ma*

Raspberries, The - *Go All The Way*

Red Rider - *White Hot*

Redbone - *Come & Get Your Love*

Redding, Otis - *My Lover's Prayer & Sitting On The Dock Of The Bay*

Reddy, Helen - *Leave Me Alone*

REM - *Everybody Hurts, Losing My Religion & The One I Love*

Rich, Charlie - *Behind Closed Doors*

Righteous Brothers, The - *Hung On You & You've Lost That Loving Feeling*

Ringo Starr - *Back Off Bugaloo, Blindman, Early, It Don't Come Easy, No No Song, Only You, Photograph & You're Sixteen*

Ritchie, Lionel - *All Night Long, Dancing On The Ceiling, Hello, Say You Say Me, Truly, You Are The One*

Rivers, Johnny - *Rockin' Pneumonia*

Roberta Flack & Peabo Bryson - *Born To Love & Tonight I Celebrate*

Robertson, Robbie - *Showdown At Big Sky & Somewhere Down The Lazy River*

Rock Steady Crew, The - *Uprock*

Rocky Horror Picture Show - *Sweet Transvestite & Time Warp*

Rolling Stones, The - *(I Can't Get No) Satisfaction, Angie, Beast Of Burden, Brown Sugar, Doo Doo Doo Doo Doo Doo Heartbreaker, Emotional Rescue, It's Only Rock & Roll, Let's Spend The Night Together, Miss You, Mixed Emotions, Ruby Tuesday, She's So Cold & Start Me Up*

Ronstadt, Linda - *You're No Good*

Ross, Diana - *Ain't No Mountain High Enough*

Roxy Music - *Love Is The Drug*

Rufus - *Tell Me Something Good*

Rundgren, Todd - *Hello It's Me*

Rush - *Cinderella Man, Circumstances, Closer To The Heart, Farewell To Kings, Limelight, New World Man, Spirit Of Radio, Subdivisions, Tom Sawyer, Witch Hunt & YYZ*

Saga - *The Flyer, Scratching The Surface & What Do I Know*

Santana - *Black Magic Woman*

Sayer, Leo - *Long Tall Glasses & When I Need You*

Scaggs, Boz - *Lido Shuffle*

Schilling, Peter - *Major Tom*

Seal - *Crazy & Kiss From A Rose*

Seals & Crofts - *Diamond Girl, Get Closer & Summer Breez*

Sebastien, John - *Welcome Back*

Segar, Bob - *Against The Wind, Like A Rock, Mainstreet, Night Moves, Old Time Rock & Roll & Ship Of Fools*

Shooter - *I Can Dance (Long Tall Glasses) & Train*

Silver Convention, The - *Fly Robin Fly*

Simon & Garfunkel - *America, For Emily, Whenever I May Find Her, Homeward Bound, I Am A Rock, Mrs. Robinson, Old Friends / Book Ends, Scarborough Fair, Sounds Of Silence*

Simon, Carly - *His Friends Are More Than Fond Of Robin Let The River Run, Nobody Does It Better, Right Thing To Do & You're So Vain*

Simon, Paul - *50 Ways To Leave Your Lover, Loves Me Like A Rock & You Can Call Me Al*

Simple Minds - *#4, A Brass Band In African Chimes, Alive & Kicking, All The Things She Said, Belfast Child, Book Of Brilliant Things, Don't You Forget About Me, Ghostdancing, Glittering Prize, Hunter & The Hunted, Hypnotized, Kick It In, King Is White & In The Crowd, Love Song, Promised You A Miracle, Sanctify Yourself, See The Lights, She's A River, Someone Somewhere In Summertime, Speed Your Love To Me, Street Hassle, Theme For Great Cities, This Earth That You Walk Upon, This Is Your Land, Up On The Catwalk, Waterfront & Waterfront 89*

Simply Red - *Holding Back The Years, **If You Don't Know Me By Now,** Money's Too Tight To Mention, Move On Out, The Right Thing & You've Got It*

Sinatra, Frank - *Theme From New York New York & **You & Me***

Sister Janet Mead - *Lords' Prayer*

Skylark - *Wildflower \ The Writing's On The Wall*

Sledge, Percy - *Take Time To Know Her & When A Man Loves A Woman*

Sly & The Family Stone - *Dance To The Music & Thank You*

Smith, Hurricane - *Getting To Know You, Oh Babe What Would You Say & Who Was It?*

Soft Cell - *Tainted Love*

Spandau Ballet - *Gold & True*

Spencer Davis Group, The - *Gimmie Some Lovin' & Keep On Runnin'*

Spinners, The - *Could It Be I'm Falling In Love & They Just Can't Stop It **(Games People Play)***

Split Enz - *I Got You, Iris, One Step Ahead, Pioneer & Six Months In A Leaky Boat*

Spoons, The - *Arias & Symphonies, Romantic Traffic & Smiling In Winter*

Springsteen, Bruce - *Born In The USA, Born To Run, Dancing In The Dark, Glory Days, Hungry Heart, I'm On Fire, Merry Christmas Baby, My Hometown & Santa Claus Is Coming To Town*

Squire & Alan White (Yes) ,Chris - *Run With The Fox*

Stafford, Jim - *Wildwood Weed*

Stampeders, The - *Carry Me, Devil You, Gator Road, Hit The Road Jack, Minstrel Gypsy, Oh My Lady, Sweet City Woman & Wild Eyes*

Starbuck - *Moonlight Feels Right*

Starship - *Sara*

Stealers Wheel - *Jose , Star & Stuck In The Middle With You*

Steely Dan - *Do It Again, Fire In The Hole, Pretzel Logic Reeling In The Years & Rikki Don't Lose That Number*

Steppenwolf - *Born To Be Wild, Magic Carpet Ride & Straight Shootin' Woman*

Stevens, Cat - *Another Saturday Night, Morning Has Broken & Oh Very Young*

Stevens, Ray - *The Streak, The*

Stewart, Al - *Broadway Hotel , On The Border, Time Passages & Year Of The Cat*

Stewart, Rod - *Do Ya Think I'm Sexy?, First Cut Is The Deepest & You're In My Heart -*

Stills, Stephen - *Love The One You're With*

Sting - *All This Time, Englishman In New York, Fragile, If I Ever Lose My Faith In You, If You Love Somebody, Set Them Free, Russians, Shape Of My Heart & We'll Be Together*

Stories, The - *Brother Louie*

Stray Cats, The - *Rock This Town & You Can't Hurry Love*

Streetheart - *Under My Thumb*

Strunk, Jud - *Daisy A Day*

Stylistics, The - *Betcha By Golly Wow, I'm Stoned In Love With You & Make It Last*

Styx - *Blue Collar Man, Come Sail Away, Lady, Light Up, Lorelei, Mademoiselle, Mr. Roboto & Why Me?*

Sugarloaf - *Don't Call Us, We'll Call You, Green Eyed Lady, Tongue In Cheek & West Of Tomorrow*

Supertramp - *Ain't Nobody But Me, Better Days, Bloody Well Right, Bonnie, Breakfast In America, Brother Where You Bound, Cannonball, Crazy, Downstream, Dreamer, Even In The Quietist Moments, Ever Open Door, Free As A Bird, From Now On, Give A Little Bit, Gone Hollywood (Heartbreaker), Goodbye Stranger, It's Raining Again, Just Another Nervous Wreck, Know Who You Are, **Lady,** Logical Song, My Kind Of Lady, No In Between, Rudy, Sister Moonshine, Take The Long Way Home & You Started Laughing*

Supremes, The - *You Can't Hurry Love*

Surfaris - *Surfer Joe & Wipeout*

Swan, Billy - *I Can Help*

Sweeney Todd - *Roxy Roller*

Sweet, The - *Ballroom Blitz, Burn On The Flame, Fox On The Run, Restless & Rock & Roll Disgrace*

Taco - *Puttin On The Ritz*

Talk Talk - *It's My Life*

Talking Heads The - *Burning Down The House, Once In A Lifetime & This Must Be The Place*

Tapps - *Runaway (With My Love)*

Taylor, James - *Steamroller & You've Got A Friend*

Taylor, R Dean - *Indiana Wants Me*

Tears For Fears - *Advice For The Young At Heart, Change, Everybody Wants To Rule The World, Head Over Heels, I Believe, Mad World, Mothers Talk, Pale Shelter, Pharoahs, Sea Song, Shout, Sowing The Seeds Of Love, When In Love With A Blind Man & Woman In Chains*

Thomas Band, The Ian - *Hold On , Long Long Way & Painted Ladies*

Thomas, B J - *Hooked On A Feeling, I've Been Down This Road Before, Never Had It So Good & Raindrops Keep Falling On My Head*

Thomas, Timmy *Why Can't We Live Together*

Thompson Twins, The - *Doctor Doctor, Don't Mess With Doctor Dream, Hold Me Now, King For A Day, Lay Your Hands On Me, Nothing In Common, Revolution & You Take Me Up*

THP Orchestra - *Theme From SWAT*

Three Degrees, The - *I Didn't Know, When Will I See You Again & Year Of Decision*

Three Dog Night - *Black & White, Eli's Coming, Family Of Man, Freedom For The Stallion, Let Me Serenade You, Liar, Mama Told Me (Not To Come), Never Been To Spain An Old Fashioned Love Song, One Man Band, Out In The Country, Shambala & The Show Must Go On*

Tobias - *I Just Want To Make Music*

Tokens, The - *The Lion Sleeps Tonight*

Toto - *Africa & Hold The Line*

Townsend, Ed - *For Your Love*

Townsend, Pete - *Let My Love Open The Door*

Tremeloes, The - *Silence Is Golden*

Triumph - *Hold On & Rocky Mountain Way*

Troggs, The - *Wild Thing*

Trooper - *Raise A Little Hell, Two For The Show & We're Here For A Good Time*

Turner, Tina - *We Don't Need Another Hero & What's Love Got To Do With It?*

Turtles, The - *Happy Together*

Tyler, Bonnie - *Total Eclipse Of The Heart*

Tymes, The - *Miss Grace & You Little Trustmaker*

U2 - *All I Want Is You, Angel Of Harlem, Boomerang II, Bullet The Blue Sky, Deep In The Heart, Desire, Discotheque, Endless Deep, Gloria, Hallelujah Here She Comes, I Still Haven't Found What I'm Looking For, I Will Follow, In God's Country, Luminous Times (Hold On To Love), New Year's Day, Pride (In The Name Of Love), Running To Stand Still, Silver & Gold, Spanish Eyes, Staring At The Sun, Sunday Bloody Sunday, Sweetest Thing, Treasure, Two Hearts Beat As One, Unchained Melody, Walk To The Water, Where The Streets Have No Name & With Or Without You*

U2 & B.B King - *Dancing Bearfoot & When Love Comes To Town*

U2 & Frank Sinatra - *I've Got You Under My Skin & Stay (Faraway, So Close!)*

UFO - *Only You Can Rock Me*

Ugly Kid Joe - *Cat's In The Cradle*

Ultravox - *Dancing With Tears In My Eyes*

Ure, Midge - *If I Was & One Small Day*

Valdy - *(A) Good Song*

Valens, Ritchie - *Donna & La Bamba*

Valli & The Four Seasons, Frankie - *December (Oh What A Night)*

Van Halen - *House Of Pain, I'll Wait, Jump, Panama & Running With The Devil*

Vanelli, Gino - *Black Cars*

Vangelis - *Chariots Of Fire*

Vanity Fare - *Early In The Morning, Hitchin' A Ride &* Man Child

Vee, Bobby - *Rubber Ball*

Ventures, The - *Hawaii Five -* O

Wainwright III, Loudon - *Bell Bottom Pants, Dead Skunk & Needless To Say*

Waite, John - *Missing You*

Wakeman, Rick - *I'm So Straight I'm A Weirdo*

Walsh, Joe - *Life's Been Good .*

Wang Chung - *Dance Hall Days, Don't Let Go,* **Let's Go,** *Ornamental Elephant & The World In Which We Live*

War - *Cisko Kid & Why Can't We Be Friends?*

Washington, Grover - *Just the Two of Us*

Waterfront - *Cry*

Weisberg, Eric - *Dueling Banjos*

Wham - *Wake Me Up Before You Go*

Who, The - *Athena, Overture From Tommy, Pinball Wizard, See Me Feel Me, Squeezebox & Who Are You*

Wild Cherry - *Hot To Trot, The Lady Wants Your Money & Play That Funky Music*

Williams, Mason - *Baroque - A - Nova, Classical Gas, Greensleeves, Long Time Blues & Wanderlove*

Wings - *C Moon, Daytime Nighttime Suffering, Girls' School, Goodnight Tonight, Hi Hi Hi, I Lie Around, Let 'Em In, Letting Go, Listen To What The Man Said, Live & Let Die, Maybe I'm Amazed, Mull Of Kintyre, Silly Love Songs, Venus & Mars Rock Show & With A Little Luck*

Winwood, Steve - *Back In The High Life, Don't You Know What The Night Can Do?, Finer Things, Higher Love, Holding On, Nighttrain, Roll With It, Slowdown Sundown, Still In The Game, Talking Back To The Night, Vacant Chair, Valerie, Valerie* 87 *& While You See A Chance*

Withers, Bill - *Lean On Me*

Wonder, Stevie - *Boogie On Reggae Woman, Don't Know Why I Love You, Higher Ground, I Just Called To Say I Love You, I Wish, My Cherie Amour, Superstition, Tuesday Heartbreak & You Are The Sunshine Of My Life*

Wright, Gary - *Dream Weaver, Let It Out, Light Of Smiles, Love Is Alive & Much Higher*

Yaz (featuring Alison Moyet) - *Don't Go, Only You & Situation*

Yes - *Abeline, America, And You & I, Awaken, City Of Love, The Clap, Does It Really Happen?, Don't Kill The Whale, Going For The One, Holy Lamb, I've Seen All Good People Into The Lens (**I Am A Camera**), It Can Happen, Leave It, Lift Me Up, Long Distance Runaround, Love Will Find A Way, Man In A White Car, Our Song, Owner Of A Lonely Heart, Parallels,*

Release Release, Rhythm Of Love, Roundabout, Run Through The Light, Soon, Sound Chaser, Total Mass Retain, Wonderous Stories & Your Move

Young, Neil - *Cinnamon Girl, Heart Of Gold, Looking For A Love, Old Man, Only Love Can Break Your Heart, Sugar Mountain, The Needle Gone & The Damage Done & Walk On*

Young, Paul - *Wherever I Lay My Hat (That's My Home)*

Zombies, The - *She's Not There, Tell Her No, Time Of The Season & You Make Me Feel So Good*

ZZ Top - *Bad Girl, I Got The 6, Legs, Sharp Dressed Man, Tush & TV Dinners*

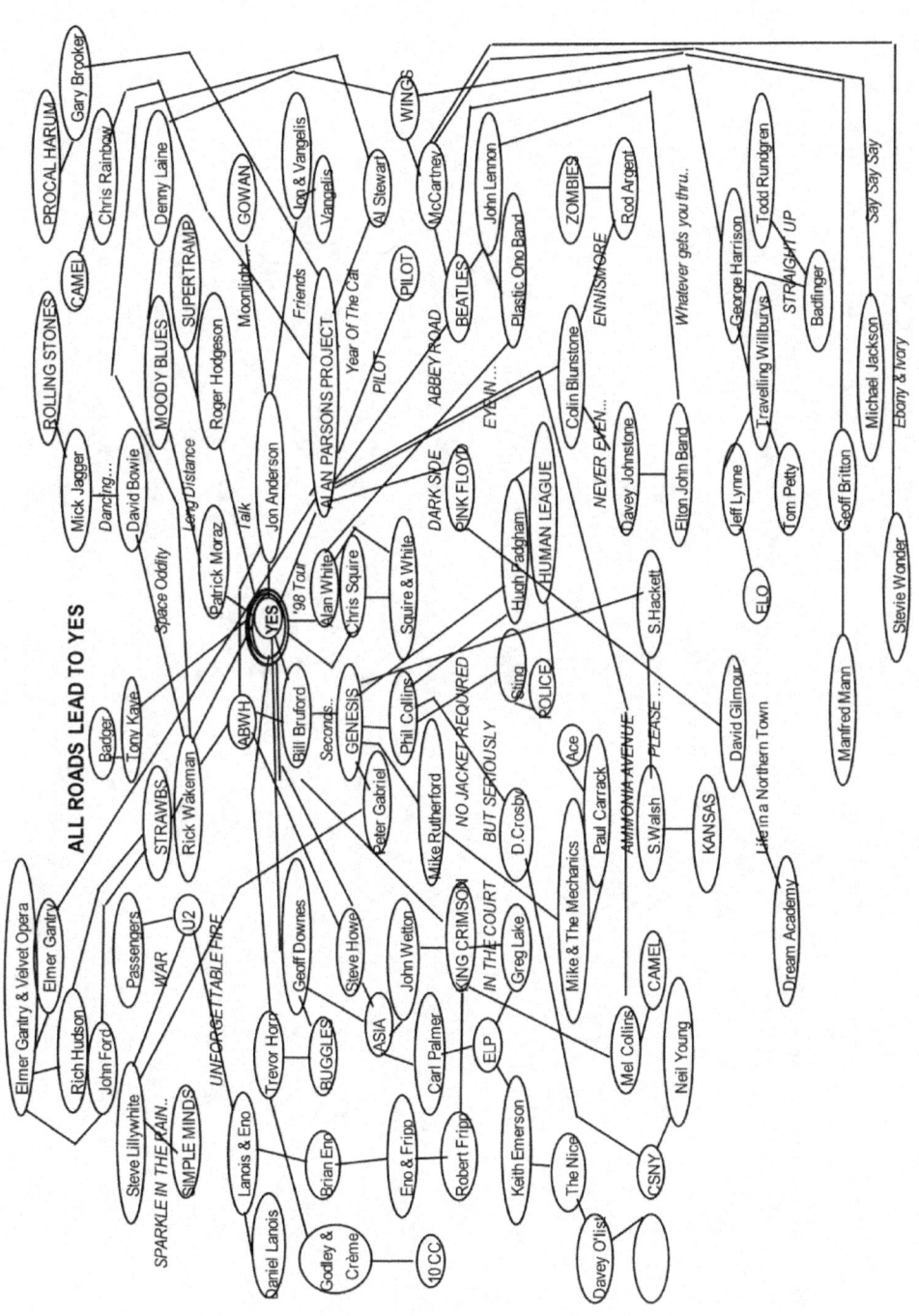